311302

Contents

To Jasmine and Cassie, my vision of the future.

Introduction to ExpressExec

ExpressExec is 3 million words of the latest management thinking compiled into 10 modules. Each module contains 10 individual titles forming a comprehensive resource of current business practice written by leading practitioners in their field. From brand management to balanced scorecard, ExpressExec enables you to grasp the key concepts behind each subject and implement the theory immediately. Each of the 100 titles is available in print and electronic formats.

Through the ExpressExec.com Website you will discover that you can access the complete resource in a number of ways:

» printed books or e-books;
» e-content – PDF or XML (for licensed syndication) adding value to an intranet or Internet site;
» a corporate e-learning/knowledge management solution providing a cost-effective platform for developing skills and sharing knowledge within an organization;
» bespoke delivery – tailored solutions to solve your need.

Why not visit www.expressexec.com and register for free key management briefings, a monthly newsletter and interactive skills checklists. Share your ideas about ExpressExec and your thoughts about business today.

Please contact elound@wiley-capstone.co.uk for more information.

Introduction to

Expression?

Introduction

This chapter introduces the concept of vision and compares it to a corporate statement of intent. It explains how a company without a vision is likely to flounder, and discusses briefly some of the benefits of having a strong vision.

Former US president George Bush famously coined the phrase "the vision thing" in a derisory tone when he was criticized for lacking Ronald Reagan's sense of purpose for America. He had evidently not read the words of statesman Henry Kissinger, who claimed: "Leaders must invoke an alchemy of great vision. Those leaders who do not are ultimately judged failures, even though they may be popular at the moment."[1] Nor had he considered the performance of John F. Kennedy, whose vision of putting a man on the moon by the end of the 1960s had so energized the US space program.

Most companies are begun with at least some idea of where their founders want to go. After all, if you don't know where you're going, how do you decide on the way to get there, and how do you know when you're lost? A vision is like a corporate constitution, a declaration of intent. And in some cases visions have created or transformed whole industries: think of Henry Ford's idea of a car for every worker, or Steve Jobs' concept of a personal, desktop computer rather than a giant shared machine.

A company without a vision is likely to flounder, particularly in a time of rapid change, a fact even some die-hard skeptics have been forced to acknowledge. Take Lou Gerstner, who declared not long after taking over as CEO of IBM in 1993: "The last thing IBM needs is a vision."[2] By the 1995 annual report, after announcing new operating principles and a major cultural change, he was ready to admit: "What IBM needs most right now is a vision."[3] By 1997, he was trumpeting his vision of IBM as the company best equipped to take businesses into the new networked world in eight-page advertising inserts in a dozen major newspapers.[4]

One of the most important benefits of having a vision is that it is a powerful way of uniting people towards a common goal. Especially during times of organizational change or when a company is in difficulties, it is important for everyone to be pulling together to achieve a shared vision.

MORE THAN A MISSION STATEMENT

Mission and vision statements (76%) were second only to strategic planning as a whole (80%) in the most widely used tools used by senior managers in Bain & Company's 8th Annual "Management Tools

Survey," published in 2001.[5] And mission and vision statements were cited as one of the tools most likely to bolster integration efforts across a company.

A compelling vision is far more powerful and all-inclusive than a mission statement alone, however, particularly one that – as so many are – is little more than a collection of business buzzwords. A vivid example of the latter was given by Dilbert creator Scott Adams, whose Website features a mission statement generator that results in wonderful corporate gobbledegook.[6] He was asked by Logitech's co-founder and vice-chairman Pierluigi Zappacosta to pose as Ray Mebert, a management consultant who was going to help executives draft a new mission statement for the company's New Ventures Group.

Adams disguised himself with a wig and a false moustache, before deriding the existing statement – "to provide Logitech with profitable growth and related new business areas" – and leading an exercise in which managers brainstormed words and ideas for a new one. The result? "The New Ventures Mission is to scout profitable growth opportunities in relationships, both internally and externally, in emerging, mission inclusive markets, and explore new paradigms and then filter and communicate and evangelize the findings." Drawing a last diagram, a picture of Dilbert, Adams took off his wig and the Logitech managers realized they'd been duped, although they apparently enjoyed the joke.[7]

Without a vision, a mission and the strategies based on it may merely reflect the status quo or react to recent events. With a vision, the organization is able to create its own opportunities and be proactive and innovative.[8]

WHAT THIS BOOK IS ABOUT

This book explores how the idea of corporate vision has developed and what the experts have to say about it. It considers all the different components of a vision and how visions have had to adapt to take account of globalization and technological developments such as the Internet. Most importantly, it looks at how the best organizations are using the power of a vision to move forward and make the best of their business and their workforce.

NOTES

1 Sidey, H. (1980) "The task of the leader." *Time*, October 20, p. 39.
2 *Wall Street Journal*, July 29, 1993.
3 Lipton, M. (1996) "Demystifying the development of an organizational vision." *Sloan Management Review*, **37** (June), 83–92.
4 Morris, B. (1997) "IBM really wants your e-business: Big Blue goes great gray." *Fortune*, November 10.
5 Business Wire (2001) "'Tried and true' beats out 'new economy' tools by 2:1 in Bain and Company's 8th Annual Management Tools Survey." *Business Wire*, June 13.
6 www.dilbert.com/comics/dilbert/career/bin/ms2.cgi.
7 Associated Press (1997) "See you in the funny papers: 'Dilbert' creator pulls a corporate fast one on California executives." *Dallas Morning News*, November 16, p. 7.
8 Nanus, B. (1996) "Leading the vision team." *The Futurist*, **30**, May 1.

Definition of Terms

Various definitions of "vision" are offered in this chapter. It can be described as:

» a guiding philosophy and a tangible image;
» a realistic, attractive, credible future for an organization;
» what the organization will do in the face of ambiguity; and
» a picture of a destination, the larger goal.

The benefits of vision and visionary leadership are also outlined.

Somewhat confusingly, there are almost as many definitions of "vision" as there are theorists writing about it. James Collins and Jerry Porras, authors of *Built to Last,* quote one executive as saying: "I've come to believe that we need a vision to guide us, but I can't seem to get my hands on what 'vision' is. I've heard lots of terms like mission, purpose, values, and strategic intent, but no one has given me a satisfactory way of looking at vision that will help me sort out this morass of words. It's really frustrating!"

Indeed, in *Built to Last*, Collins and Porras view the function of a leader as "to catalyze a clear and shared vision of the organization and to secure commitment to and vigorous pursuit of that vision."[1] Collins and Porras's own conceptualization of vision is that it has two main components, a guiding philosophy and a tangible image. The guiding philosophy is "a system of fundamental motivating assumptions, principles, values, and tenets" that stems from the organization's core beliefs, values, and purpose. Making up the tangible image are a mission and a vivid description. The mission is "a clear and compelling goal that serves to unify an organization's effort. An effective mission must stretch and challenge the organization, yet be achievable."

Burt Nanus, author of *Visionary Leadership*, defines vision as "a realistic, credible, attractive future for an organization." He continues:

"It is a carefully formulated statement of intentions that defines a destination or future state of affairs that an individual or group finds particularly desirable. The right vision is an idea so powerful that it literally jump-starts the future by calling forth the energies, talents, and resources to make things happen. A visionary leader is one who has the ability to formulate a compelling vision for the future of his or her organization, gain commitment to it, and translate that vision into reality by making the necessary organizational changes."[2]

According to Nanus,[3] the right vision can lead to a number of benefits for an organization.

» It attracts commitment and energizes people.
» It creates meaning in workers' lives, by making them feel they are part of a greater whole.
» It establishes a standard of excellence and stimulates improvement.

» It bridges the present and the future by focusing the organization on its desired future state.

In contrast to Collins and Porras, who view "mission" as a component of "vision", Nanus differentiates between the two. He comments: "A vision is not a mission. To state that an organization has a mission is to state its purpose, not its direction."

Another perspective is offered by Mark Lipton, director of The Leadership Center, Milano Graduate School of Management and Urban Policy, New School for Social Research:

> "Unlike goals and objectives, a vision does not fluctuate from year to year but serves as an enduring promise. A successful vision paints a vivid picture for the organization and, though future-based, is in the present tense, as if it were being realized now. It illustrates what the organization will do in the face of ambiguity and surprises."[4]

And from Harvard professor Rosabeth Moss Kanter we have:

> "A vision (romantic term that it is) is a picture of a destination, an end state that will be achieved via the change. It reflects the larger goal not to be lost sight of while concentrating on the concrete activities mounted in pursuit of the goal. A vision is not necessarily a detailed and full-blown strategy; sometimes it is a general statement of purpose."[5]

Danny Miller, research professor at Columbia Business School in New York, stresses the benefits to be gained from a strong vision, describing "the core vision and its orchestration that gives a company character and direction, harmonizes strategy and processes, and motivates people to work toward a common objective."[6]

Peter Senge *et al.*[7] emphasize that a shared vision is a vehicle for building shared meaning in an organization, particularly if it is built in a participative way. They see vision as representing the organization's guiding aspirations, comprising:

» *Vision*: an image of our desired future;
» *Values*: how we expect to travel to where we want to go;

» *Purpose or mission*: what the organization is here to do; and
» *Goals*: milestones we expect to reach before too long.

They stress:

> "Not all visions are equal. Visions which tap into an organization's deeper sense of purpose, and articulate specific goals that represent making that purpose real, have unique power to engender aspiration and commitment. . . . The content of a true shared vision cannot be dictated; it can only emerge from a coherent process of reflection and conversation."[8]

Dan Ciampa and Michael Watkins, authors of *Right from the Start*, give some helpful questions to illustrate what a vision should contain: "Vision has no deadline – no 'by when.' It can be as precise as the response to the question 'Where are we heading this year?' or as lofty as 'If we could develop exactly the kind of company we wanted, what would it be like?' An effective vision . . . should answer the question 'Given what this place has to do, its priorities, and how it expects to move forward, what will it look like and how will people act when it has arrived?'[9]

To summarize, a vision can be described as:

» a description of the organization's guiding philosophy or aspirations;
» a statement of purpose;
» a picture of where and how the organization wants to be in the future; and
» a promise or a goal.

A vision can be used in the following ways:

» to create shared meaning in an organization;
» to generate commitment and meaning in people's work;
» to stimulate improvement; and
» to guide decision making.

A visionary leader is someone who is able to:

» put into words a compelling vision for the organization;
» persuade people to commit to the vision; and
» empower people and the organization to achieve the vision.

Perhaps the last word should go to Sal Marino, columnist for *Industry Week*:

> "Dreaming things that never were is not a science. It's an art practiced by visionaries who manage by faith instead of by formula. They are driven by an unquestioning belief that the lessons of the past will inevitably invent the successes of the future. They see visions where others see vacuums. They say 'We can' when others say 'We can't.' "[10]

NOTES

1 Collins, J.C. and Porras, J.I. (1996) *Built to Last: Successful Habits of Visionary Companies*. HarperBusiness, London.

2 Nanus, B. (1996) "Leading the vision team." *The Futurist*, **30**, May 1.

3 Nanus, B. (1992) *Visionary Leadership*. Jossey-Bass, San Francisco.

4 Lipton, M. (1996) "Demystifying the development of an organizational vision." *Sloan Management Review*, **37** (June), 83–92.

5 Kanter, R.M. (1987) "Moving ideas into action: mastering the art of change." Harvard Business School case study 9-388-002.

6 Miller, D. and O'Whitney, J. (1999) "Beyond strategy: configuration as a pillar of competitive advantage." *Business Horizons*, May–June.

7 Senge, P., Roberts, C., Ross, R.B., Smith, B.J. and Kleiner, A. (1994) *The Fifth Discipline Fieldbook: Strategies and Tools for Building a Learning Organization*. Nicholas Brealey Publishing, London.

8 Senge, P., Roberts, C., Ross, R.B., Smith, B.J. and Kleiner, A. (1994) *The Fifth Discipline Fieldbook: Strategies and Tools for Building a Learning Organization*. Nicholas Brealey Publishing, London.

9 Ciampa, D. and Watkins, M. (1999) *Right From the Start*. Harvard Business School Press, Boston, MA, p. 168.

10 Marino, S.F. (1999) "Where there is no visionary, companies falter." *Industry Week*, March 15.

Evolution

This chapter uses the achievements of twentieth-century business visionaries to provide some context for the visions of today's companies. Those discussed are Henry Ford, Konosuke Matsushita, Alfred P. Sloan, Walt Disney, Leo Burnett, Akio Morita, Ray Kroc, Thomas Watson, Jr., Sam Walton, Bill Gates, Steve Jobs, Ted Turner, Jack Welch, Tim Berners-Lee, and Jeff Bezos.

There have always been visions and visionaries. The ten commandments given to Moses on tablets of stone can be seen as a vision statement, and most religions have their equivalents. Visions are necessary for people and organizations to make progress, to give them something to aim towards.

The power of vision is possibly best illustrated by considering some examples of people who have proved to be less than visionary. Of course, hindsight is a wonderful capability, but think about the following statements:

» "Everything that can be invented has been invented" (Charles H. Duell, Commissioner, US Office of Patents, 1899).

» "This 'telephone' has too many shortcomings to be seriously considered as a means of communication" (Western Union internal memo, 1876).

» "Heavier-than-air flying machines are impossible" (Lord Kelvin, President, Royal Society, 1895).

» "Who the hell wants to hear actors talk?" (H.M. Warner, founder of Warner Brothers, 1927).

» "I think there is a world market for maybe five computers" (Thomas Watson, Chairman of IBM, 1943).

» "There is no reason anyone would want a computer in their home" (Ken Olson, founder of Digital Equipment Corp., 1977).

Visionaries also represent both the good and bad sides of human nature. Martin Luther King may have had a dream, but so did Adolf Hitler, and his vision of a racially pure society led to the deaths of millions of people. Hitler's dictatorship was initially very popular in Germany because it led to economic recovery and a fast reduction in unemployment, and the Führer had a loyal following among both politicians and industrialists. This goes to show that the real power and implications of a strong vision may only be truly evident after the event.

BUSINESS VISIONARIES

Let's consider the background to the visions of today's companies by examining the achievements of some of the twentieth century's great business visionaries. Many of the following are controversial characters and they were not all right all of the time, but it is undeniable that they left their mark on the corporate world.

Henry Ford: a car for everyone

Henry Ford (1863–47) founded the Ford Motor Co. in 1903, at a time when the only cars being produced were luxury models for the rich. His vision was different: "I will build a car for the great multitude . . . so low in price that no man will be unable to own one."[1] The Model T Ford, first produced in 1908, was an enormous success and created a mass market for cars. Ford also introduced assembly-line production and a $5 minimum daily wage (at a time when the average wage in the auto industry was $2.34 for nine hours) as well as inventing the dealer franchise system for selling and servicing cars.

Konosuke Matsushita: entrepreneurial philanthropy

Konosuke Matsushita (1894–1989) founded the Matsushita Electric Industrial Co., now one of the largest manufacturers of consumer electric appliances worldwide. As well as generating growth using innovative marketing practices, such as advertising in newspapers, which was then unusual, Matsushita formulated a business philosophy founded on the slogan "harmony between corporate profit and social justice." He wanted the company to produce essential consumer goods at the lowest possible prices, thereby enhancing the general quality of life. He also took an unusually egalitarian approach to his employees for the time, encouraging entrepreneurship in the company's divisions and introducing a five-day working week in 1960.

Alfred P. Sloan: the divisionalized corporation

Alfred P. Sloan (1875–1966) ran General Motors (GM) for more than 25 years and created the first divisionalized corporate structure. He reorganized the company into five divisions, each making cars that fell within a different price band. Production was decentralized to allow operating units freedom to compete, while administration was centralized in order to co-ordinate company policy and strategy. Sloan avoided going head to head with Ford in the mass market, but instead created specific ranges, such as the Chevrolet and the Cadillac, catering to particular sectors, which today would be called market segmentation. Under his guidance GM began to dominate the market, and its cars soon accounted for more than half of all US automobile sales.

Walt Disney: the business of happiness

Walt Disney (1901–66) founded Disney Brothers Studio in 1923 with his brother Roy, to produce animated cartoons. Over the next few years he created the world-famous cartoon character Mickey Mouse and made the first full-length animated film, *Snow White*, as well as later coming up with the concept of the entertainment theme park, opening Disneyland in 1955. His vision was "to bring happiness to millions"[2] and in trying to do so he created the world's largest multimedia company.

Leo Burnett: the power of pictures

Leo Burnett (1891–1971), who founded the Leo Burnett Agency with De Witt O'Kieffe in 1935, was a major figure in the creative revolution in advertising in the 1950s. Previously images had been little more than decoration alongside words, which were the most important part of advertising. Burnett saw that visual elements appealed more to people's emotions than did verbal logic, a concept that was to become increasingly important with the advent of television. His agency was responsible for creating such global icons as Tony the Tiger for breakfast cereal and the Jolly Green Giant for vegetables.

Akio Morita: creating a worldwide brand

Akio Morita (1921–99) co-founded Sony (originally called Tokyo Telecommunications Engineering) with Masaru Ibuka in 1946. He created one of the first global corporations, now a worldwide leader in technology development and responsible for such innovations as the pocket-sized transistor radio, the Walkman portable cassette player, and the 3.5" floppy disk. Morita studied both Western and Eastern cultures and tried to combine the best of both, and foresaw before many of his contemporaries the power of a brand name that suggested high quality wherever it was applied.

Ray Kroc: efficient fast food

Ray Kroc (1902–84) did not invent the hamburger assembly line and minimal menu that characterize McDonald's – he took the idea from Maurice and Richard McDonald, whose business he eventually bought out – but he did see their potential: "Visions of McDonald's restaurants dotting crossroads all over the country paraded through my brain."[3] Starting in 1955 with his first franchised outlet, Kroc applied industrial mass production techniques to fast food, as well as supplying franchises with detailed specifications for exactly how the food should be prepared and served. The company is now ubiquitous in almost every country in the world.

Thomas Watson, Jr.: flexible corporate computing

Thomas Watson, Jr. (1914–93) became president of International Business Machines (IBM) in 1952 and took over as CEO on his father's death in 1956. Once described by *Fortune* as "the greatest capitalist who ever lived,"[4] he transformed the company from a supplier of mechanical tabulators and typewriters into a giant in corporate computing, whose name is synonymous with IT worldwide. One enormous gamble that shows his prescience was the $5bn he invested in developing System/360 computers, introduced in 1964, which made the company's existing products obsolete but which revolutionized the industry, allowing customers to begin with a small machine and move up to a larger one as their needs for computing grew, taking their existing software with them.

Sam Walton: "Every Day Low Prices"

Sam Walton (1918–92) had a passion for customer service and what he called "Every Day Low Prices." His ambition was "to lower the cost of living for everyone."[5] Wal-Mart, today the US's biggest retailer, led a crusade for discount retailing, slashing prices and relying on volume to lead to profits. Walton also foresaw as early as 1966 the need for computerization of logistics and inventory control, and the capacity of the company's database is now second only to that of the Pentagon.[6]

Bill Gates: exploiting ideas

Bill Gates (1955–) is one of the world's richest men and founder (with friend Paul Allen) in 1975 of Microsoft, a company with such global influence that between 1999 and 2001 the US Justice Department tried unsuccessfully to have it broken up as a monopoly. Some commentators claim that he is a copier rather than a visionary, but it is undeniable that he has a genius for seeing the potential in others' ideas. For example, he acquired MS-DOS, now the basic PC operating system, as Q-DOS from Seattle Computer Products for $50,000 and then licensed it to IBM. The concept behind Microsoft's Windows operating system, first introduced in 1990, had been invented by Xerox PARC and used commercially by Apple six years before. And even though Gates failed initially to see the potential of the Internet, the company's Web browser, Internet Explorer, is now one of two industry leaders.

Steve Jobs: making computing fun

Steve Jobs (1955–) co-founded Apple in 1976 with friend Stephen Wozniak, beginning the personal computer revolution with the Apple II and continuing to reinvent the PC in the 1980s with the Macintosh. Jobs made computers relevant for ordinary people rather than just companies, and pioneered the easy-to-use graphical user interface and mouse technology. He left Apple in 1985 to pursue other ventures, such as software developer NeXT and movie company Pixar. Jobs returned to Apple in 1997 as interim CEO, a role made permanent in 2000, and revitalized what had become a flagging company with key innovations such as the multi-colored iMac. Jobs has always tried to stay ahead of the pack, commenting: "Innovation distinguishes between a leader and a follower."[7]

Ted Turner: the future of news

Ted Turner (1938–) is one of today's most influential television executives. He is head of one of the largest media companies in the world, Time Warner, now part of America Online (AOL). He accelerated the spread of cable television throughout the US with "superstation" WTBS, which supplied cable stations with low-cost sports and entertainment programs by satellite. Perhaps his most visionary creation is Cable News Network (CNN), the first 24-hour television news station, which is now broadcast worldwide. CNN's news-led approach, determination to minimize production costs and its desire always to be first on the scene led to a style that has had a lasting influence on news broadcasting throughout the world.

Jack Welch: be number one or two

Jack Welch (1936–) was voted *Industry Week's* CEO of the decade in 1999 and was chairman and CEO of General Electric (GE) from 1981–2001. *Fortune* ranked him the toughest boss in America and he was given the nickname "Neutron Jack" after he slashed GE's payroll by a quarter, but over his 20-year tenure he transformed a disparate group of businesses into a hugely successful and well-respected conglomerate. His basic philosophy was that if the company was not number one or two in its global market, it should exit. His management style was informal and he paid close attention to the "people" side of the business, combining that with an almost fanatical attention to detail and monthly strategy sessions with his top executives. Professor Noel Tichy of the University of Michigan Business School compares him to GM's Alfred P. Sloan in influence, saying "Welch would be the greater of the two because he set a new, contemporary paradigm for the corporation that is the model for the twenty-first century."[8]

Tim Berners-Lee: global information sharing

Tim Berners-Lee (1955–) invented the World Wide Web in 1989 and as such was responsible for facilitating the subsequent transformation of global information sharing and communication. He described his vision as: "The dream behind the Web is of a common information space in which we communicate by sharing information . . . There was a second part of the dream, too, dependent on the Web being so generally used that it became a realistic mirror . . . of the ways in which we work and play and socialize."[9] In 1994 he founded W3C, the World Wide Web Consortium, intended to lead the technical evolution of the Web, produce standards for Web technologies, and campaign for universal Web access.[10]

Jeff Bezos: have fun and make history

Jeff Bezos (1964–), *Time*'s Man of the Year in 1999, is founder and CEO of Amazon.com, the world's largest electronic retailer. His stated ambition is: "Work hard, have fun, make history."[11] He had a successful career on Wall Street but after seeing Internet usage statistics in 1994 claiming that the Internet was growing at 2300% a year, he saw the potential to create a new kind of bookstore that would have an almost limitless catalog. He realized that to be successful in e-tailing it would be necessary "to do something that simply cannot be done any other way."[12] Immensely successful despite barely turning a profit, Amazon.com is now the best-known brand in electronic retailing, and boasts "Earth's Biggest Selection™,"[13] having expanded into music, video games and DVDs, toys, electronics, software, home improvement products, auctions and zShops, independent retailers who have virtual store fronts on Amazon's site.

Timeline

» 1903 Henry Ford forms the Ford Motor Co.
» 1917 Konosuke Matsushita founds Matsushita Electric.
» 1923 Alfred P. Sloan becomes president and CEO of General Motors.
» 1923 Walt Disney opens cartoon studio in Hollywood.
» 1935 Leo Burnett founds advertising agency in Chicago.
» 1946 Akio Morita and Masaru Ibuka form Tokyo Telecommunications Engineering, later to become Sony.
» 1955 Ray Kroc opens the first McDonald's outlet.
» 1956 Thomas Watson, Jr. becomes CEO of IBM on his father's death.
» 1962 Sam Walton opens first Wal-Mart store.
» 1975 Bill Gates co-founds Microsoft with Paul Allen.
» 1976 Steve Jobs co-founds Apple with Stephen Wozniak.
» 1980 Ted Turner launches Cable News Network.
» 1981 Jack Welch becomes chairman and CEO of General Electric.
» 1989 Tim Berners-Lee proposes global hypertext project, later to become the World Wide Web.
» 1995 Jeff Bezos opens Amazon.com.

NOTES

1 Iacocca, L. (2000) "Driving force: Henry Ford." *Time*; see www.time.com/time/time100/builder/profile/ford.html.
2 Shickel, R. (2000) Ruler of the Magic Kingdom: Walt Disney." *Time*; see www.time.com/time/time100/builder/profile/disney.html.
3 Gross, D. (1996) *Forbes Greatest Business Stories of All Time*. John Wiley & Sons, New York.

4 IBM press release; see www.ibm.com/press/bios_twatsonjr.html.

5 Wal-Mart press release; see www.walmartstores.com.

6 Huey, J. (2000) "Discounting dynamo: Sam Walton." *Time*; see www.time.com/time/time100/builder/profile/walton.html.

7 www.askmen.com/men/apr00/21_steve_jobs.html.

8 Byrne, J.A. (1998) "How Jack Welch runs GE: a close-up look at how America's #1 manager runs GE." *Business Week*, June 8.

9 Berners-Lee, T. "The World Wide Web: A very short personal history." See: www.w3.org/People/Berners-Lee/ShortHistory.

10 More information on W3C can be found on its Website, www.w3.org.

11 www.askmen.com/men/may00/26c_jeff_bezos.html.

12 Quittner, Joshua (1999) "Jeffrey P. Bezos: Biography." *Time*, December 27.

13 www.amazon.com.

The E-Dimension

A chapter on the Internet and how dotcoms without a vision have failed. The chapter also outlines the need for a vision in e-business and discusses how the Internet changes companies' relationships with their customers. Contents include:

» the four stages of developing an e-business;
» how Cheap Tickets has exploited the power of the Internet;
» how the Internet is revolutionizing operations at Nestlé; and
» personalization and a sense of community at the US Mint.

The development of the Internet has enabled significant changes to take place in the ways that companies do business and communicate with their customers. It has also intensified the speed of development. Jay Walker, founder of Priceline.com, comments, "It is now possible for a business to go from a concept to a company with five million customers very quickly – literally in less than a year." However, these very possibilities have led to a great deal of hype and unrealistic expectations.

Harvard strategy professor Michael Porter views the Internet pragmatically as an enabling technology that affects companies' sources of competitive advantage, both in terms of operational effectiveness and strategic positioning: "It makes it harder for companies to sustain operational advantages, but it opens new opportunities for achieving or strengthening a distinctive strategic positioning."[1]

Porter points out that it is nevertheless not enough to focus on improving operational effectiveness, particularly because Internet applications are easily and quickly copied. A company must have a sustainable advantage based on a distinctive strategic direction. One way in which this strategic direction can be expressed is, of course, in a strong and compelling vision.

DOTBOMBS

A lack of vision has been behind the failure of many apparently successful dotcoms. These companies focused on maximizing revenue and market share rather than on being profitable; their revenue came from such sources as advertising rather than from offering real added value for which customers would be willing to pay. Competition between Internet companies has primarily concentrated on price, as Porter explains: "Instead of emphasizing the Internet's ability to support convenience, service, specialization, customization, and other forms of value that justify attractive prices, companies have turned competition into a race to the bottom."[2]

High-profile failed companies such as Pets.com, natural health site Clickmango.com and consumer goods price comparison site Brandwise.com either overestimated the market for their niche products or failed to make themselves sufficiently distinctive from other offerings. A company wishing to exploit the Internet to its advantage has to identify a real market need where it will be able to deliver value to the customer, and build a vision of how it can deliver that market need better than anyone else. Internet guru Patricia Seybold, author of *Customers.com*, comments: "A lot of dotcoms aren't delivering a really good end-to-end customer experience. They think of the customer as just another part of the business. They don't understand that the customer is at the core of the business."[3]

Marketing guru Seth Godin, author of *Permission Marketing*, has an interesting perspective on the failure of many dotcoms. He claims that when the future was the realm of science fiction writers – the communications satellite was imagined by Arthur C. Clarke, the robot by Isaac Asimov – we had big dreams. After so many of their predictions became reality, "a lot of the poetry and guts went out of our vision." Godin claims that "our dreams, alas, have been handed over to the MBAs," many of whom worked at the dotcoms. The result? "The MBAs made the Internet trivial. They dreamed small dreams – and most of those weren't realized. . . . Without a big, hairy, audacious goal, it's too easy to be distracted by momentary setbacks."[4]

AN E-BUSINESS VISION

It is not just the dotcoms that need big goals. Many traditional "bricks-and-mortar" businesses are approaching the Internet and e-business in a piecemeal fashion, focusing on incremental changes in information technology or marketing. That is no longer enough if the possibilities offered by the Internet are to make a real difference to an organization. Cathy Neuman, deputy global e-business practice leader at Pricewater-houseCoopers, explains: "You have to be willing to start with a clean sheet of paper in terms of your strategy and your organization and your business model, and that is sometimes hard to understand and even more difficult to implement."[5]

In creating an e-business vision, Neuman recommends that CEOs ask themselves three questions:

» *How deep do we want to go with e-business?* E-business concepts should be applicable throughout the organization: intranets for streamlining internal processes and improving knowledge management; links with suppliers; more information from customers; greater collaboration across the value chain.

» *How different is our focus to any of our competitors?* Think of new business models rather than copying what others are doing.
» *How dedicated are we to changing the organization?* "This has to do with putting the vision on the wall, making that vision stick, and getting the leadership and the company behind it," says Neuman.[6]

To provide some context for answering these questions, Pricewater-houseCoopers outlines four stages through which organizations pass when developing e-business:

1 *Presence* – the organization has a Website and links such as electronic data interchange with suppliers. The goals are cost-effectiveness and greater reach.
2 *Integration* – e-business plays a major role in the organization's strategy. More features are provided for customers, real business transactions take place, and there is an exchange of critical information with suppliers and partners. Transaction costs are lowered, which brings competitive advantages, and organizations begin to think about new ways of doing business.
3 *Transformation* – the organization looks further afield than its immediate group of suppliers and customers. Business processes are moved to an electronic model and operations may be unbundled, retaining only those that are core to market position. Knowledge is shared more than ever before with customers and partners.
4 *Convergence* – the organization uses its knowledge to focus on creating the greatest value for the customer. It integrates with other organizations inside and outside its industry, creating cross-industry supply chains and networked organizations.[7]

Cheap Tickets is one company that has been able to reinforce its existing business by effective use of its Website. "We are the typical, traditional business who leveraged themselves onto the Web, as opposed to trying to start out as a Website," says CEO Sam Galeotos.[8] CheapTickets.com, which unusually for an dotcom has been profitable for 10 consecutive quarters (as at August 2001), was added to the company's original travel stores and call centers, and the call centers and Website combined now account for 98% of the company's sales.

The 24-hour nature of the Internet allows Cheap Tickets to reinforce its desire to offer good customer service and the site offers air fares, car rental, cruises and hotel accommodation, as well as e-ticketing capabilities. The company's vision is to be the leading provider of discount leisure travel in the US[9] and it is one of the most-visited travel Websites, with over 10 million registered users,[10] holding out against stiff competition from companies such as Travelocity, Expedia, and Priceline.

Best practice: Nestlé

At Swiss multinational food giant Nestlé, the Internet is being used to help transform the whole way the company operates, towards its vision of "providing the best foods to people throughout their day, throughout their lives, throughout the world."[11] The organization is investing nearly $2bn over three years in what CEO Peter Brabeck-Letmathe calls "an e-revolution."[12]

The first step has been to improve two-way communication between retailers and Nestlé. Store owners in the US are able to order products online, eliminating most phone and fax orders and cutting processing costs, and this initiative will soon be extended to most countries in which Nestlé operates. NestleEZOrder was the first direct-to-retailer e-commerce Website to be developed by a major food company. Daily sales reports and demand forecasts from large retailers also help reduce inventory.

Sharing information within the company has also led to savings, particularly in procurement, where costs have been cut by up to 20%. This has been partly due to pooling orders for higher discounts, but also through intelligence. For example, one buyer in Switzerland was having difficulty obtaining kosher meat. He posted an online message and a colleague told him of a supplier in Uruguay.[13]

The Web initiative is being led by Nestlé's US subsidiary, the largest in the group. It has adopted the catchphrase "Make e-business the way we do business."[14] No separate e-business division has been created; rather, each existing operating division has an "e-business catalyst," whose responsibility it is to work with managers to create a Web-based strategy.

Nestlé does not use the Internet as a retail channel, since this might upset its traditional partners. Instead, more than 20% of its annual advertising spend will be on the Web. The company experimented with advertising-related Websites in the late 1990s, such as www.buitoni.co.uk, with Italian recipes, wine information, and regional information, and www.wonka.com, about a range of products based on Willy Wonka's chocolate factory (created by Roald Dahl). These still exist but Nestlé was unsure how to take the concept further, so talked to experts from inside and outside the company who it thought might have some of the answers. E-commerce marketing manager Todd Manion explains: "We put a lot of questions to these folks – especially people from the portal sites. We asked, 'What's really happening in the marketplace? What are customers telling you? What have you discovered that can help us drive our business?' "[15]

As a result of this research, the company realized that in addition to its brand-centered sites, it should treat the brand as a resource and put the consumer first. Therefore it is now creating sites to give consumers information and assistance, such as VeryBestBaking.com and VeryBestBaby.com. The intention is to build a better relationship with consumers and enhance trust. "The first stage was just making Websites," says Brabeck-Letmathe. "The second stage was adding interactivity, so we could communicate with our customers. And the third stage, where we will be in five years, will see consumers help us develop the business idea and products we want to make."[16]

"If our initiative is successful," says Nick Riso, leader of Nestlé US's e-business program, "e-business will permeate the company's DNA and all of our thoughts. We won't need e-catalysts. In the end, the term 'e-business' has to disappear. I have to work myself out of a job."[17]

TALKING TO CUSTOMERS

One of the main benefits of the Internet, as illustrated in the Nestlé best practice study, is the possibility of two-way communication between company and customers. For organizations that stress excellence in customer service as part of their vision, this holds tremendous potential.

Many consumers like the personalization that can be part of exploring the Web, even though the ability of, for example, Amazon.com to greet returning customers by name or suggest what they might like to buy based on previous purchases is enabled by "cookies" that allow companies to collect and track information on a surfer's Web activities.

In return, Websites whose customers register for service obtain valuable data on sales patterns, preferences, and even on what catches people's attention to make them click on a particular area of the site.

It is not just commercial organizations that can use the Internet to gain information and opinions from customers. The US Mint has been using the Web to help in its proposed change from being a lumbering bureaucracy to an efficient and exciting organization whose staff have a sense of purpose in their work. As part of its drive to change its customers' expectations, the Mint has been getting feedback on coin designs over the Internet. A group of 13 designs posted on its Website in December 1998 generated 11.7 million hits in one day, as well as 130,000 e-mails and thousands of letters over the next few weeks.

In another initiative, the HIP (History In your Pocket) Pocket Change site is an educational resource for teachers and a "digital sandbox" where children can play with coins and learn about American history. It also has the goal of developing into an online community for those interested in coins and coin collecting.[18]

In August 2001 the US Mint was ranked as one of the top 50 US organizations using the Internet to expand and enhance their business by Ziff Davis *Smart Business* magazine. This list considers the Internet's contribution in such areas as sales growth and profitability, cost savings, expansion into new business areas, faster delivery of products, improved market share and brand recognition, and boosting customer and employee satisfaction.[19]

NOTES

1 Porter, M.E. (2001) "Strategy and the Internet." *Harvard Business Review*, March.

2 Porter, M.E. (2001) "Strategy and the Internet." *Harvard Business Review*, March.

3 Maruca, R.F. (2000) "State of the new economy." *Fast Company*, September, p. 105.

4 Godin, S. (2001) "Change agent." *Fast Company*, **50** (September), p. 96.

5 Chief Executive (2000) "Creating the vision." *Chief Executive*, January.

6 Chief Executive (2000) "Creating the vision." *Chief Executive*, January.

7 PricewaterhouseCoopers and The Conference Board (2000) *Electronic Business Outlook for the New Millennium*. PricewaterhouseCoopers.

8 Schwalb, S.H. (2001) "Staying a steady course." *Internet World*, January 15.

9 Cheap Tickets press release, February 1, 2001.

10 Cheap Tickets press release, March 6, 2001.

11 www.nestle.com.

12 Echikson, W. (2000) "Nestlé: an elephant dances." *Business Week*, December 11.

13 Echikson, W. (2000) "Nestlé: an elephant dances", *Business Week*, December 11.

14 Breen, B. (2001) "Change is sweet." *Fast Company*, June.

15 Breen, B. (2001)"Change is sweet." *Fast Company*, June.

16 Business Week (2000) "A food giant forges an e-revolution." *Business Week* online original, December 11.

17 Breen, B. (2001) "Change is sweet." *Fast Company*, June.

18 Muoio, A. (1999) "Mint Condition." *Fast Company*, December.

19 US Mint press release, August 30, 2001.

The Global Dimension

The globalization of business brings extra responsibilities, particularly in the area of ethics and social responsibility. This chapter describes how the best companies, such as The Body Shop, are responding. It also considers:

» the benefits of diversity;
» keeping communication of the vision consistent throughout the company; and
» benefiting from local expertise.

Many companies of all sizes and in all sectors operate on a global level – if they don't have a physical presence in several countries they may purchase or supply internationally, particularly if they retail via the Internet. Globalization expands a company's potential to compete, but also leads to other problems in terms of ethics, cultural differences, and the difficulties of communicating with a dispersed workforce. These issues can be particularly acute when an organization is trying to build or maintain cohesion and a common purpose through a shared vision.

SOCIAL RESPONSIBILITY

Globalization has recently been receiving a very bad press in some quarters. Demonstrations against global capitalism have been increasing, most recently at the G-8 summit in Genoa, Italy. In response to the activists, companies are having to reconsider some of their business practices. Nike has been criticized over the working conditions in its Asian factories, for example, Home Depot for its use of tropical hardwoods and Starbucks for its treatment of workers on coffee plantations.[1]

All of this means that companies' visions and codes of ethics need to address the issue of corporate social responsibility. How socially responsible a company aspires to be is of interest not only to investors, but also to customers and employees. Richard Edelman, CEO of Edelman Public Relations Worldwide in New York, claims that potential graduate recruits are asking tough questions about a company's social practices, and that European firms' more developed commitment to social responsibility is leading to a "halo effect" among consumers worldwide.

To prevent a vision being more rhetoric than reality, a corporate (or social) responsibility audit measures a company's performance against its core values, ethics policy, operating practices, management systems, and the expectations of key stakeholders, such as owners, employees, suppliers, customers, and the local community.[2] In one test of a responsibility audit process, eight companies with award-winning operations still discovered significant gaps in four areas: employee relations, quality systems, community relations, and environmental practices. They also discovered discrepancies between corporate and employee values.[3]

Best practice: The Body Shop

One of the organizations best known for conducting social audits is natural cosmetics company The Body Shop. It is a global business, operating through international franchises covering 47 countries, 23 languages and 12 time zones, and describes itself as "multi-local."

Founder Anita Roddick calls the company's approach "putting our money where our heart is." The Body Shop's mission statement is as follows:

» "To dedicate our business to the pursuit of social and environ-mental change.
» To creatively balance the financial and human needs of our stakeholders: employees, franchisees, customers, suppliers and shareholders.
» To courageously ensure that our business is ecologically sustain-able: meeting the needs of the present without compromising the future.
» To meaningfully contribute to local, national, and international communities in which we trade, by adopting a code of conduct which ensures care, honesty, fairness, and respect.
» To passionately campaign for the protection of the environment, human and civil rights, and against animal testing within the cosmetics and toiletries industry.
» To tirelessly work to narrow the gap between principle and practice, whilst making fun, passion, and care part of our daily lives." [4]

Since 1994 The Body Shop has conducted regular social and ethical audits, a process that it has now outsourced to accountants KPMG.[5] Out of the 100 international reports evaluated for the United Nations Environmental Program, The Body Shop's Values Report 1997 (the latest available) scored the highest rating.

The Values Report contains information on the company's perfor-mance in relation to social, environmental, and animal protection issues. Feedback from stakeholders allows the company to report on areas that were praised, those with which people were dissatisfied, and on improvements to which it has committed itself.

One example of The Body Shop's commitment to responsible global trading is its Community Trade program. This is a purchasing program whose goal is "to support sustainable development by sourcing ingredients and accessories directly from socially and economically marginalized producer communities." The company buys products at a fair price, covering production and wages as well as an investment in the community. The communities themselves benefit through increasing employment, income, skills development, and additional social initiatives, such as an organization in Nepal that promotes AIDS awareness and offers scholarships to enable girls to attend school.

The Body Shop is also refreshingly honest when it comes across shortcomings in its approach. In relation to the Community Trade program, it comments: "This has been a grand experiment, a new venture for a global retailer – there were no textbooks telling us how to ethically source ingredients for our products. But where there have been difficulties, we have persevered and worked with communities to find solutions."

In addition, The Body Shop Foundation donates financial and other support to grass-roots organizations worldwide working in the areas of human and civil rights, and environmental and animal protection. It supports organizations such as the Brazilian Healthcare Project in the Amazon region, First Peoples Worldwide, an advocate for indigenous peoples, and Environmental Justice, a campaign to address the extensive use of highly toxic pesticides in Cambodia.

The public's attitude to the company certainly seems to be positive. A Millennium Poll on corporate social responsibility conducted among 23,000 people in 23 countries rated The Body Shop the most socially responsible company in the UK, 10th in the US and 14th in the world.

ONE CORPORATE CULTURE, DIFFERENT NATIONAL CULTURES

G. Pascal Zachary, management writer and author of *Show-Stopper!*, draws a vivid picture of the character of today's multinational companies:

"The best corporations set the pace in diversity. Their mission is to match people and needs, regardless of nationality, race, or ethnicity. And the best managers want employees to retain their differences in order to make the most of their uniqueness and the most of the creative tension spawned by those differences. Employers don't want hollow harmony. They want a cosmopolitan corporation."[6]

Nevertheless, there is a dilemma here – this diverse corporation still wants to present a consistent message to customers and other stakeholders wherever they are in the world. It needs to develop a vision of a corporate culture that transcends and makes the most of the different national cultures represented within it.

One company that seems to have achieved this balancing act is global consultancy McKinsey & Co. In the 1970s the majority of its consultants were American; by 1999 only 40% of its 4800 consultants were from the US, the rest representing more than 80 nationalities, and its managing director, Rajat Gupta, comes from India.[7] The company takes the best people from wherever they are in the world, in furtherance of part of its mission "to attract, develop, excite, and retain exceptional people."[8]

McKinsey's overall corporate culture is strong and unique: as *Fortune* magazine described it, "It is that culture, unique to McKinsey and eccentric, which sets the firm apart from virtually any other business organization."[9] There is a set of values and aspirations to which all consultants are expected to adhere. Within this framework, there is freedom to do whatever consultants think is right for the company. Performance evaluation is based on the impact consultants have on their clients, how they develop other people, and how they contribute to the firm's knowledge.[10] Each office is also evaluated annually by a consultant from somewhere else in the world. "There's an obligation to see things from other points of view," comments a McKinsey partner. "That's hardwired into this place."[11]

CONSISTENT COMMUNICATION

Organizations operating in several countries face problems in ensuring that any corporate communication is consistent and accurate, which is particularly important when it relates to the corporate vision. It is of course possible to use company newsletters or e-mail to broadcast a message, but the best companies are employing more interesting methods.

For example, delivery company Federal Express has an internal private business television network called FXTV that incorporates more than 1000 satellite connections in the US, Canada, and Europe.[12] A five-minute videotape message is broadcast daily to all work sites and repeated throughout the day so that all employees can watch it. This concentrates on how the individual efforts of employees contribute to the company's overall vision. On a monthly basis there are "town hall meetings" or phone-in shows where employees can talk directly to senior managers. Transcripts of these broadcasts are also made available to employees.[13]

Immediately after General Electric's annual meeting of its top 500 executives, a video of the CEO's speech is circulated to attendees together with a guide to how to use it with their teams. A week later more than 750 videos in 8 languages are distributed to all GE locations worldwide. This ensures that people at all levels are able to take on board the company's latest direction.[14] As *The Financial Times* commented, the skill of former CEO Jack Welch was "identifying important themes and spreading them through the organization."[15]

Welch did this through what he called the GE "Operating System," "a year-round series of intense learning sessions where Business CEOs, role models, and initiative champions from GE as well as outside companies, meet and share intellectual capital."[16] New CEO Jeff Immelt, who took over from Jack Welch in 2001, traveled all over the world to meet employees, customers, suppliers, and investors, to signal the transfer of power in a very direct way.[17]

A MULTI-LOCAL MULTINATIONAL

Dutch consumer products conglomerate Unilever is one example of a company that is using a single worldwide IT infrastructure both to communicate with its employees and to ensure that information from all parts of the organization can be shared company-wide. The group's overall vision is "meeting the everyday needs of people everywhere" and it relies on local expertise in each community to guide its development, a concept it calls being "a truly multi-local multinational."[18] The company stresses, "the free exchange of knowledge and experience among people of different ages and nationalities is key to our success."[19]

For instance, in relation to brands, anyone involved in marketing or developing a brand can gain information relating to it from around the world via a central server. Someone might want to discover why certain brands are more successful in some markets than in others, which may be useful in planning packaging changes or changing advertising strategy.[20] In addition, practices and processes perfected in one country can be shared with other countries with the same problems, such as limited infrastructure or political instability. Ideas formulated at Hindustan Lever in India have been transferred to the Philippines, the Congo, and Indonesia, for example.[21] This kind of innovation is particularly important for companies operating in developing countries. Keki Dadiseth of Hindustan Lever explains: ''There are a lot more poor people in the world than rich people. To be a global business and to have a global market share, you have to participate in all segments.''[22]

If Unilever truly is to fulfill its vision of meeting the needs of people everywhere, it needs to exploit the full potential of its local managers. In addition to the information sharing enabled by its common IT infrastructure, the company operates international assignment programs to allow managers to experience work and life in other countries.[23] These promote knowledge and cultural understanding, as well as enhancing networking and subsequent collaboration among managers worldwide.

NOTES

1 Elliott, M. (2001) ''How to talk to protesters.'' *Time*, August 13.
2 More information on social responsibility audits is available from The New Economics Foundation (www.neweconomics.org); the Institute of Social and Ethical Accountability (www.accountability. org.uk), which publishes a framework for accountability management, AA1000; www.socialaudit.org; and the Council on Economic Priorities (www.cepnyc.org), which developed an international standard for social auditing, SA 8000.
3 Waddock, S. and Smith, N. (2000) ''Corporate responsibility audits: doing well by doing good.'' *Sloan Management Review*, Winter.
4 Source: www.bodyshop.co.uk; The Body Shop annual report 2000; ''The Road Ahead: A summary of The Body Shop Values Report 1997.'' Mission statement © The Body Shop, reproduced by permission.

5 The Body Shop annual report 2000.

6 Zachary, G.P. (2000) "Mighty is the mongrel." *Fast Company*, July.

7 Zachary, G.P. (2000) "Mighty is the mongrel." *Fast Company*, July.

8 www.mckinsey.com/firm/values/.

9 Huey, J. (1993) "How McKinsey does it." *Fortune*, November 1.

10 www.mckinsey.com/firm/values/.

11 Zachary, G.P. (2000) "Mighty is the mongrel." *Fast Company*, July.

12 Grensing-Pophal, L. (2000) "Follow me." *HR Magazine*, February.

13 Government Accounting Office (2000) *Human Capital: Key Principles from Nine Private Sector Organizations*. United States General Accounting Office, Washington, DC.

14 Byrne, J.A. (1998) "How Jack Welch runs GE." *Business Week*, June 8.

15 London, S. (2001) "Maintaining growth of Welch years will be a tough challenge." *The Financial Times*, September 4.

16 www.ge.com/operating_system/intro?bottom.htm.

17 Eisenberg, D. (2001) "Jack who?" *Time*, September 10.

18 www.unilever.com/co/oc.html.

19 www.unilever.com/ca/wu_di.html.

20 Fisher, A. (2001) "How IT underpins group's global business strategy." *The Financial Times*, August 8.

21 Balu, R. (2001) "Act local, think global." *Fast Company*, May.

22 Balu, R. (2001) "Strategic innovation: Hindustan Lever." *Fast Company*, June.

23 www.unilever.com/ca/wu_di.html.

The State of the Art

A chapter on the various ways that visions are being developed and used today. It covers:

» current research on vision;
» why an organization needs a vision;
» the possible pitfalls of a strong vision;
» how a vision can be used to communicate outside the organization; and
» the need for a vision in mergers and acquisitions.

VISION RESEARCH

Various research programs in the last few years have investigated and provided insight into the importance of vision for today's organizations. Perhaps the best known is that conducted by James C. Collins and Jerry I. Porras for their book *Built to Last: Successful Habits of Visionary Companies.*[1]

During a six-year study at the Stanford University Graduate School of Business, Collins and Porras compared 18 successful and long-lived companies with 18 of their top competitors. The question they asked was: What makes the visionary, truly exceptional companies different from the others? The companies studied included Hewlett-Packard, 3M, Johnson & Johnson, Procter & Gamble, Merck, Sony, Motorola, and Nordstrom. They had all outperformed the stock market by a factor of 12 between 1925 and 1975.

As a result of the research, Collins and Porras were able to conceptualize a framework for a well-conceived vision, which consists of two main components: a core ideology, made up of core values and a core purpose; and an envisioned future, a 10–30-year Big, Hairy, Audacious Goal (BHAG) and a vivid description.[2]

John Kotter studied over 100 companies that were attempting to transform themselves, through programs such as total quality management, re-engineering, right sizing, restructuring, and cultural change. Based on the research he recommended eight steps to transforming an organization.

1 Establishing a sense of urgency.
2 Forming a powerful guiding coalition.
3 Creating a vision.
4 Communicating the vision.
5 Empowering others to act on the vision.
6 Planning for and creating short-term wins.
7 Consolidating improvements and producing still more change.
8 Institutionalizing new approaches.[3]

In another project, researchers at the University of Nevada and the State University of New York asked chief executives about the structure, content, and formulation of their vision for their companies.[4] All but one of the 331 CEOs who replied were able to provide a written vision statement. They were asked to evaluate their visions against a list of items, such as action-oriented, inspirational, risk-taking.

The research revealed seven factors that were important in vision statements: formulation, implementation, innovative realism, generality, degree of detail, risk propensity, and profit orientation. Researchers also found that executives who believed that their vision needed to be accepted throughout the organization and emphasized long-term strategy and operational realism were more likely to be successful in achieving change in their organizations.

Commenting on this research, Maria Nathan concludes:

> "Not all executives describe vision in the same manner. Vision is an intriguing phenomenon that touches upon issues of leadership, motivation, empowerment, cognitive complexity, and self-transforming organizations. It may define a pathway to success for the future of the firm or it may describe the goals a firm has set. Bottom-line, vision may be what those in charge think it is."[5]

Mark Lipton analyzed over 30 international studies that had organizational vision as a central variable, and concluded: "Managers who develop and communicate a vision skillfully can make a profound organizational impact."[6] He claims that managing with a vision has five benefits for an organization.

1 It improves performance against measures such as profit, return on shareholder equity, employee turnover, and rate of new product development.
2 It promotes change, serving as a road map for a company undergoing transformation.
3 It provides the foundation for a strategic plan.
4 It motivates employees and assists in the recruitment of talented people.
5 It keeps decision making in context, providing focus and direction.

Lipton conducted further research into the vision statements of companies in a list of the "100 Best companies to work for in America" (Levering, R. and Moskowitz, M. (1993) *The 100 Best Companies to Work for in America*, Currency/Doubleday, New York). He found that there were three common themes: the organization's mission or purpose, the strategy for achieving that purpose, and elements of culture that were required to achieve the mission and support the strategy.[7]

Why does an organization need a vision?

A vision provides the context against which the organization will act to propel itself into the future. It delineates and clarifies the direction in which those within the organization wish to go, allowing goals to be set to help them reach their destination. Particularly if the vision is stretching and challenging, it helps the organization to focus on its future and generates excitement, passion, and a sense of purpose.

Dan Ciampa and Michael Watkins, authors of *Right from the Start*, distinguish between *pull* and *push* in relation to vision:

> "By making the future attractive, the vision gives employees reasons for wanting the organization to work in ways consistent with it. It provides a rationale for abandoning the status quo and thus 'pulls' employees toward it, in contrast to other motivational tools that 'push' people to act in particular ways. A vision that is commonly held can also alleviate employees' anxiety about change if they can see how change is linked to the strategy and how it leads down a path that is clear rather than cloudy and uncertain."[8]

It is not vital to have a written statement of the vision; it is far more important that those at the top of the organization are able to explain the vision in a compelling way in five minutes or less. If it is complicated or cannot be clearly expressed, it is not an effective vision.

For the vision to be of benefit, the leaders of the organization must also be able to embody it in their behavior as well as their words. Continental Airlines' CEO Gordon Bethune is one who does, named one of the 50 best CEOs in the US for the third consecutive year by *Worth* magazine.[9]

The company's vision is expressed in its "Go Forward Plan," which has four elements: fly to win, fund the future, make reliability a reality, and working together. Explicit in the notion of working together is improving communication, something at which Bethune excels. "It's the most common thing in the world to see Gordon out at a break-room in an airport talking about what's going on," says Michelle Meissner, director of human resource development. "I've run into them both [Bethune and Greg Brenneman, former president and chief operating officer] at the airport on a Friday night where they're just stopping by to talk to employees."[10]

In addition, Bethune has a policy of full disclosure, sharing bad news as well as good, again demonstrating his commitment to communication. Meissner again: "Our CEO and President have told us that they will tell us everything – short of what they could be thrown in jail for telling us. If it affects our company, or our lives, and the work we do, they're going to tell us."[11]

Managers at all levels at Continental are also expected to live out the company vision. Employees are surveyed every year with questions such as "Has your leader informed you about the Go Forward Plan?" and "Has your leader set measurable, specific goals based on the Go Forward Plan?" Leaders who receive good scores in these surveys are given bonuses; those who don't will not have much of a future with the company.[12]

The approach certainly seems to work. In 2001 Continental received the following awards or plaudits: Best Transatlantic Airline; Airline of the Year; No. 18 in *Fortune*'s 100 Best Companies to Work For; No. 2 in *Fortune*'s Most Admired US Airlines; No. 1 Best Managed US-based Global Airline; No. 1 in Customer Service; and Best Frequent Flyer Program.[13]

The pitfalls of vision

Andrzej Gorecki and Steven Power, director and general manager of consultancy Retail Directions Group, point out that a vision may not necessarily be beneficial:

"A vision is only a tool and, like all tools, it can be instrumental in either creation or destruction. A positive outcome can only be expected if the tool is suitable for the purpose, and if it is used with skill. Also, the more powerful the tool, the more potential good or harm it can produce. This is why a strong vision can generate a massive success or can destroy your business."[14]

They identify the following potential pitfalls.

» You may be heading towards the wrong destination.
» You may run out of resources before you reach your destination.
» You may change your mind.
» You may burn your bridges, only to find out later that you need to go back.

It must be within the organization's ability to achieve the vision it sets itself. That doesn't mean that the vision has to be easy – it should still stretch and challenge those within the organization – but it should not be so overambitious that it can never be achieved.

MicroStrategy Inc. is a development company of decision support software that over 10 years grew from a two-man partnership to a global organization with over 2000 employees. Its vision was "to make intelligence accessible everywhere."[15] CEO Michael Saylor boasted in 2000: "I want to make sure that everyone gets real-time intelligence every hour, every day, every week, to make better-informed decisions. We live in an ignorant world. Our mission is to purge that ignorance."[16]

A little under one year later, the company's stock plummeted from $226.75 a share to $86.75 following a restatement of earnings and a Securities and Exchange Commission investigation into pricing. The company had grown too big too fast, and hadn't paid sufficient attention to its own information systems. It was forced to toughen its accounting practices, broaden its customer base, and lay off one-third of its staff. Saylor was also forced to take a hard look at the organization's vision and strategy, and identify areas where it had no competitive advantage and therefore should not try to compete. "It's not that we don't have a grandiose vision anymore," he said. "We still do. But it's a vision over the next 10 years, not the next 12 months."[17]

Another danger is that the successor to a strong, visionary leader may experience problems in establishing their own identity within the organization. It is too early to tell what kind of CEO Jeffrey Immelt will be at General Electric, but it is undeniable that Jack Welch will be a hard act to follow. Welch has been called "the businessman's favorite businessman,"[18] a "legendary chairman" and a "corporate icon."[19] He is also closely identified with the company; as Immelt himself said at the annual managers' meeting in January 2001: "Everybody at GE thinks they work for Jack; every customer of GE thinks they buy from Jack; every political person thinks they deal with Jack."[20]

Nevertheless, Welch is sanguine about his successor's likely effect. When asked what GE would look like in 2021, he replied: "The portfolio will look different. I don't know how exactly. But he's got the courage and the brains to figure out where to go. And he's got a board – I think this is critical – he's got a board that knows that what I did wraps yesterday's fish."[21] Time will tell how GE's vision changes.

The view from outside the organization

Visions are, of course, not only used within the organization but frequently to communicate to external stakeholders. These stakeholders may be mentioned in a vision statement as being vital to the firm's success. However, unless this concept is backed up by actions it invites distrust and is a hostage to fortune. For example, the chief executive of UK-based Barclays Bank, Matthew Barrett, claimed in February 2000 that his bank's vision included the objective of "superiority in the range of products, services, and value propositions available to customers."[22] This was not received well by customers of small village branches, some 171 of which were due to be closed in April 2000.

At one village in Northumberland, Belford, customers had signed petitions, organized sit-ins and set up road-blocks with farm machinery to try to get the bank to alter its decision, but the closure went ahead. The leader of the campaign commented: "This closure is going to cause a substantial amount of hardship for people in the village, especially the elderly, infirm, and people with small children. Our nearest bank will be in Seahouses, 10 miles away."[23]

There is also a need to be careful when changing a vision, particularly as regards communication, as the following quote makes clear: "[Rentokil] was long famed in the City at least until recently for its mission statement that it aimed to increase profits by 20% every year. But this week it will announce pre-tax profits of around £540mn, up from £490mn the previous year. This, of course, is an increase of only 10%. Rentokil, however, has recently jettisoned the 20% goal and has argued instead that its mission statement only applied 'so long as it's not at the expense of long-term growth.' However, the City does not seem to be too happy with this change in ambition, and the company's share price graph over recent months makes sorry viewing."[24]

And some visions that actually might be quite successful invite skepticism from the wider community. Philip Morris, which owns food company Kraft and brewer Miller as well as its tobacco business, lists as part of its vision, "To conduct our businesses as a responsible manufacturer and marketer of consumer products, including those intended for adults."[25] Chief executive of Philip Morris, Geoffrey C. Bible, commented that only responsible manufacturers would have a role in shaping the industry's future. The company's latest advertising campaign in the US concentrates on the public work and projects that it funds; in the past year it has been the best performer on the Dow Jones index.

Nevertheless Clive Bates, director of anti-smoking campaign group ASH, commented: "Philip Morris want to say 'we've changed' and draw a line under all the flak they've been getting. But they haven't actually adjusted. ... If one tobacco company started acting ethically, the others would simply wipe it out of the market."[26] Fine words have to be backed up by visible action if they are to be believed.

Visions in mergers and acquisitions

Integrating previously separate organizations often requires a new vision to be formed for the merged company. This may reflect mainly elements of the dominant partner, if there is one, or the opportunity may be exploited to take the best of both entities and create something new, particularly if additional change is required.

Drug giant Novartis was created in 1996 by the merger of Ciba and Sandoz. In this case the decision was taken to develop a new vision to try to overcome "turf wars" between employees of the two companies. CEO Daniel Vassela commented: "Creating a merged company is like having a child: each parent looks for resemblances in the eyes and face. But it has its own identity. Both sides will need to step back a bit and not impose their own culture on it."[27] He went on to explain: "Alignment is extremely important. If you get an organization aligned toward common objectives, you don't have the centrifugal forces or in-fighting that can tear it apart. From the beginning we focused on what we wanted to be – something different from the past of Ciba and Sandoz."[28]

In its first year, the merged company achieved a 38% increase in operating profit, 43% increase in net profit and 19% sales growth. Its vision is "to develop innovative medicines and so improve lives."[29]

When a company is about to be taken over, particularly if it has experienced financial difficulties or job losses, there is a pressing requirement to communicate to staff about the need for change and a new vision for the company. In 2001 Dresdner Bank had been through two failed mergers, with Deutsche Bank and Commerz Bank, and was being taken over by German insurer Allianz. The board of managing directors had outlined a vision to transform Dresdner into a European advisory bank focused on capital markets and concentrating on its core business. However, this would lead to job cuts and branch closures.

Andreas Georgi, responsible for the retail banking division, was keen to generate understanding among his staff for the changes that had to be made. He felt it was not possible to rely on line management, and wanted to reach everyone in one hit. Georgi therefore contacted change management consultancy Root Learning. At the center of its method for communicating complex issues are what it calls "Root Maps," comic-book-style graphics and metaphors.

Three maps were prepared after weeks of discussion, illustrating through the use of cars, roads, bridges, rivers, and icebergs the competitive German banking market, how Dresdner's retail business was structured, and what its future was likely to be as part of the Allianz group.

Some 16,000 Dresdner staff arrived at nine conference centers across Germany one afternoon in June to attend three hours of presentation and discussion of these posters, in groups of ten and with the help of facilitators. "Socratic dialog" was used, so that rather than being offered conclusions staff had to ask questions and explore the issues to further their understanding.

More than 80% of employees reported that they found the process valuable, and Georgi believes that they are now convinced of the need to embrace the new corporate vision.[30]

Trends in vision development

Organizations are experimenting with different ways of developing their visions and giving them more power. For example, Linda Armantrout, an illustrator and facilitator in Louisville, Colorado, helps organizations to visualize their goals in a pictorial vision statement. This translates what is an abstract verbal statement into a colorful image designed to communicate both the intellectual and emotional aspects of the vision.

The process involves three steps.

1 The CEO and a designated liaison identify small groups of three to six people to take part. Each group represents a business function and its members are personally invited by the CEO to be involved.
2 Each group meets for a one-hour session with the liaison and Linda Armantrout. The artist uses markers and flip-chart sheets to draw out the group's vision of the organization, how they see the business today and tomorrow, and their role within it. This more creative approach means that participants feel freer to express their views.
3 A few days later, Linda Armantrout produces illustrations that identify patterns and issues from each group. These are given to the CEO and senior managers. A two-hour session takes the same brainstorming approach as used with the groups to develop a single illustration for the organization as a whole.

The result is a hand-drawn watercolor picture that vividly captures the essence of the vision. Organizations not only hang this on their wall but can also use it in internal communications, on posters, T-shirts, videos, training material, and computer screensavers.

The pictorial vision statement for Banc One Leading Corp., for example, is a globe surrounded by images representing its clients and services, such as the airplanes and coaches that it leases. Linda Armantrout comments: "Instead of a written statement in bloodless business language, the illustration appeals to the emotions. I'm giving the vision statement a new twist."[31]

Another approach is storytelling. Michael Lissack and Johan Roos,? authors of *The Next Common Sense,* explain why this can be so valuable: "Storytelling is how we make sense ... The power of a story is that it allows the listener to recreate an experience in their mind ... The power of storytelling helps us consolidate our experiences to make them available in the future, either to ourselves or to others."[32]

Joel ben Izzy works as a travelling storyteller with corporate clients, helping them use stories to communicate their vision and values. Steve Hoffmann is vice-president of the imaging electronics division of

Agilent Technologies, a diversified technology company that used to be part of Hewlett-Packard. He works with ben Izzy to improve his communication skills. "My issue is how to get the business vision out in front of people so they connect with it," he said.

After his division diversified, he had to convince employees that it was good to work in both the old and new parts of the business. Ben Izzy used an old Chinese proverb that parents can give children two things: roots and wings. Hoffman explained how he used this: "I tell people if you're working in the 'Roots' area, your career can get ahead because it's critical to our business. For those working on 'Wings,' it's also important because it's allowing us to do something new."[33]

Hoffmann explains that he finds stories useful because they help to frame and simplify messages. They are also more memorable than more conventional slide presentations or speeches. As his organization has grown, it is more difficult for him to talk to people face to face, so in a public speech it is all the more important to convey information in a way that people can remember. "You have to put your own self out there, make yourself vulnerable," he says. "You have to say, 'Here is the vision and this is why it's important to me.' "

Another very personal story illustrates what he means. Hoffmann and his wife adopted a child from China two years ago. When they went to the orphanage, which was in a very poor area of the country, to collect their daughter he was obviously emotional, but found that the real emotions didn't flow until later. They returned to their hotel, and at two o'clock in the morning he was sending a photograph of the child to everyone on his e-mail address list. It was then that he cried. Sharing his experience with all his friends and family made him connect his business – producing chips for digital cameras – with his life almost for the first time. Previously his engineering-related mindset had seen the chips as nothing but data and had not really related them to the product they ended up in.

Hoffmann explains that after he has told a story several times, he knows it has worked when he hears the same story back, told by other people in a slightly different version. In that way it spreads throughout the organization.[34]

NOTES

1 Collins, J.C. and Porras, J.I. (1996) *Built to Last: Successful Habits of Visionary Companies*. HarperBusiness, London.

2 Collins, J.C. and Porras, J.I. (1996) "Building your company's vision." *Harvard Business Review*, September–October.

3 Kotter, J.P. (1995) "Leading change: why transformation efforts fail." *Harvard Business Review*, March–April.

4 Larwood, L., Falbe, C.M., Kriger, M.P. and Miesing, P. (1995) "Structure and meaning of organizational vision." *Academy of Management Journal*, **39**(3), 740–69.

5 Nathan, M.L. (1996) "What is organizational vision? Ask chief executives." *Academy of Management Executive*, **10** (February 1), 82–3.

6 Lipton, M. (1996) "Demystifying the development of an organizational vision." *Sloan Management Review*, **37** (June), 83–92.

7 Lipton, M. (1996) "Demystifying the development of an organizational vision." *Sloan Management Review*, **37** (June), 83–92.

8 Ciampa, D. and Watkins, M. (1999) *Right from the Start*. Harvard Business School Press, Boston, MA, p. 188.

9 www.continental.com/corporate/corporate_07_03_08.asp.

10 Grensing-Pophal, L. (2000) "Follow me." *HR Magazine*, February.

11 Grensing-Pophal, L. (2000) "Follow me." *HR Magazine*, February.

12 Grensing-Pophal, L. (2000) "Follow me." *HR Magazine*, February.

13 www.continental.com.

14 Gorecki, A. and Power, S.R. (1995) "Could a corporate vision destroy your business?" *The Quality Magazine*, October.

15 Salter, C. (2000) "People and technology – MicroStrategy Inc." *Fast Company*, April.

16 Salter, C. (2000) "People and technology – MicroStrategy Inc." *Fast Company*, April.

17 Salter, C. (2001) "The re-education of an Internet CEO." *Fast Company*, May.

18 The Economist (1999) "The revolutionary spirit." *The Economist*, September 18.

19 Byrne, J.A. (1998) "How Jack Welch runs GE." *Business Week*, June 8.

20 Eisenberg, D. (2001) "Jack Who?" *Time*, September 10.

21 Kirkland, R. and Colvin, G. (2001) "Jack: the exit interview." *Fortune*, September 17.

22 Barclays news release, August 9, 2000.

23 Independent (2000) "Customers who lose services not impressed by bank statements." *Independent*, April 8.

24 Guardian (2000) "Briefcase: Watch out for: Rentokil Initial." *Guardian*, May 17.

25 Philip Morris annual report 2000.

26 Rogers, D. (2001) "Killing them softly." *The Financial Times Creative Business*, July 24, p. 14.

27 Smith, K.W. (2000) "A brand-new culture for the merged firm." *Mergers & Acquisitions*, June.

28 Koberstein, W. (1998) "Evolution of value." *Pharmaceutical Executive*, July 1.

29 Novartis annual report 2001.

30 Major, T. (2001) "Hearts and minds set for recovery." *The Financial Times*, July 23; Fairlamb, D. (2001) "All that glitters. . ." *Business Week*, August 13.

31 www.artfax.com/artfax and author's interview with Linda Armantrout.

32 Lissack, M. and Roos, J. (2000) *The Next Common Sense*. Nicholas Brealey Publishing, London, pp. 143–53.

33 O'Brien, T. (2001) "A storyteller for our time." SiliconValley.com, February 4.

34 Author's interview with Steve Hoffmann.

In Practice

This chapter outlines case studies of companies that are using their vision in compelling ways to make progress and achieve success. The companies are Boehringer Ingelheim, a German pharmaceutical multinational; Woodward Communications, a US multimedia company; Innocent, a UK producer of fresh, natural drinks; SK Group, a Korean conglomerate and Enron, a US energy company.

This chapter describes some detailed case studies of organizations that are exploiting the power of vision to its full advantage.

BOEHRINGER INGELHEIM: VALUE THROUGH INNOVATION

Boehringer Ingelheim GmbH is a German pharmaceutical multinational with some 27,000 employees in more than 60 countries, and sales in 2000 of more than €6bn in 2000.

In 1993 the board decided that there was a need to formulate a vision for the worldwide organization. This was the culmination of a period of rapid change following the death of the principal shareholder in 1991. The company had restructured, but had not paid sufficient attention to the "soft" factors of gaining employee acceptance of the reorganization and its goals.

Formulating the vision

Consultancy Wolff Olins was engaged to help in the vision process and worked with a steering group from Boehringer Ingelheim, made up of the corporate director of public relations, the corporate director of human resources, the head of the pharmaceutical strategic business unit, and the country manager for Italy.

The process began with a careful analysis of the existing situation at the company and in its environment, as well as a review of what was known of competitors' corporate philosophies. Attention then turned to the content of the vision itself.

Boehringer Ingelheim wants to retain its independence, to continue to grow, and to rank among the best in the world in its sector. This demands continual innovation. This innovation is a means of creating added value for the customer in products and services. These two insights led to the basis of the vision, Value through Innovation ("Werte schaffen durch Innovation"). The other five vision principles outlined below followed from the extensive research that had been undertaken, and weeks of discussion went into deciding how they should be expressed.

The principles were then tested against the existing corporate culture to try to establish the potential consequences if staff did act in line with the vision. Questions were asked, such as, "Does our new service for pharmacies really give the customer added value?" or "Is our new packaging technology really innovative?" Once everyone was sure that the new vision would help in decision making, the board was able to confirm its acceptance.

The eventual vision statement is as follows:

"Boehringer Ingelheim's corporate vision is founded on five key principles, statements which together form a shared ambition and worldwide commitment.

Change is our opportunity: Without change there can be no progress.

Value will be our competitive advantage: In a competitive world, we expect our customers constantly to demand more for less.

Innovation in everything will be our challenge: We will only deliver outstanding value to our customers if we are innovative in everything we do.

Waste is our enemy: We need to have one of the lowest cost bases in the industry, if we are to deliver outstanding value to our customers.

Our distinctive character is our strength: We are worldwide and measure ourselves against world class standards. Yet we are also a corporation with family traditions in which people are valued as individuals.

"Collectively, the principles add up to Value through Innovation, the vision which strengthens Boehringer Ingelheim's business worldwide and keeps it competitive.

"The vision statement recognizes that, in a competitive and fast changing world, the values of products, services, and companies are constantly changing. In order for things to have real value to the customer, they have to be superior to any other offering – and therefore be better than they were before.

"In today's global markets, real customer value can only be created by the Boehringer Ingelheim corporation constantly finding ways of doing new things well, or doing the same things better. Thus the only way for the company to create Value is through Innovation."

Communicating the vision

The vision was presented at the group's annual top management conference at the beginning of 1994. The chairman of the shareholders' committee, Erich von Baumbach, and three board members explained the vision in detail, illustrating the discussion with examples and video clips. One key moment occurred when the board member responsible for the pharmaceutical division drove on to the stage in a Sinclair C5, a one-person electric car that never went into full-scale production, and spoke about the problems of introducing innovation simply for the sake of it. The most significant symbol of the event was the baton that von Baumbach handed to each participant, asking them to invest all their energy in implementing the vision and passing the message on to every employee.

This event concluded with participants being split into groups and asked to produce articles for a glossy magazine called *Fortune 2004*, with a cover story reporting on Boehringer Ingelheim and the changes that had occurred since the establishment of the vision. The articles were professionally bound and given to participants as a reminder.

The concept behind this top management event was so successful that it was adopted as the model for regional conferences for operating managers on three continents, and then for 40 national vision conferences and over 100 individual companies.

During 1994 and 1995, every Boehringer Ingelheim employee attended one of hundreds of Value through Innovation (VTI) workshops focusing on areas such as research, production, personnel, patents, and public relations. These workshops proved particularly fruitful. For example, in the pharmaceutical manufacturing division in Ingelheim, they resulted in more than 400 suggestions for improvements to processes, equipment- and management of resources. In Bangkok, awards were presented to the "Innovators of the Month" as a reward for the high number of ideas generated, and in Belgium databases were established to hold staff suggestions so that these could be readily shared with colleagues.

The company also established a magazine, *Vision*, in 1994, written in English and distributed to all employees four times a year. The editorial team comprises journalists from both inside and outside the company and articles concern the group and its subsidiaries, the pharmaceutical sector, and other subjects not directly related to the work environment.

Vision and leadership

Boehringer Ingelheim realized that the vision would be useless unless it was implemented through good management. It therefore developed a set of accompanying leadership principles, again through extensive discussion. These are as follows:

"Realizing our vision is our objective
Improvement is our ambition
Teamwork is our task
Persistence is our character
Communication is our key
Delegation is our duty
Delivering results is our goal."

These principles were announced at the 1995 top management conference. Furthermore, the Institute for Management Development (IMD) in Lausanne, Switzerland, and partner organizations in Germany, France, the UK, the US, South Africa, and Brazil ran five-day seminars over the following two years that were attended by 2300 managers. These specially tailored programs focused on the importance of teamwork, communication, delegation, and a results orientation.

Maintaining the momentum

Boehringer Ingelheim introduced an annual VTI Day to maintain enthusiasm for the vision. During these, staff across the world are able to gain insights into the company's progress, exchange experiences with other departments and national subsidiaries, and develop new goals for their own performance. The first VTI Day was held in 1995. A series of video conferences were held over 24 hours to allow the board of managing directors to communicate with all their subsidiaries either by video or, where this was not technically possible, by telephone. Employees were able to ask questions of board members and there was a link to an artist in the foyer of the administration building at corporate headquarters, who was creating a huge wall collage symbolizing a world map made up of cartons used for the company's products. In many cases there was a standing ovation when employees saw their own country being created on the map.

Since 1995 the annual events have included in-house exhibitions, lectures, and workshops as well as multimedia events. The headquarters at Ingelheim contributes videos, brochures, newsletters, and exhibition stands on the most important topics for that particular year so that subsidiaries worldwide can discuss the same subjects in the spirit of Vision and Leadership.

Conclusion

Surveys among managers and employees in 1995 and 1996 confirmed that all staff were familiar with the vision and understood its implications. These surveys also led to some deficiencies in implementation being identified and followed up.

As a result of the changes introduced and inspired by the vision, interdepartmental and international collaboration has improved, the company has enhanced its attractiveness to new recruits, job satisfaction in production has been improved by the introduced of self-directed work teams, processes have speeded up, and waste in purchasing has been considerably reduced. Since the start of the process sales have tripled, from DM4bn in 1993 to DM12bn in 2000.

KEY LESSONS

» Time needs to be taken to find the right words for the vision.
» The vision must be practical so that it will be possible to implement it.
» Regular communication with all employees is essential and will lead to further innovations.

Source: www.boehringer-ingelheim.com; additional information provided by company. Vision statement and leadership principles © Boehringer Ingelheim GmbH, reproduced by permission.

WOODWARD COMMUNICATIONS: BUILDING OUR TOMORROW, TODAY

Woodward Communications, Inc. (WCI) is a multimedia communications company with nearly 700 employees at 16 locations in the US. It is owned by the Woodward family and its employees through an employee stock ownership plan (ESOP), which was instituted in 1992 when the trust purchased 30% of the company stock. In 2001, employee ownership was increased to 61% with the purchase of additional stock from the Woodward family. WCI's flagship publication, the *Telegraph Herald*, is a general-interest daily newspaper that began life as the *Dubuque Visitor* in 1836. The company publishes other weekly newspapers and also has divisions covering trade publications, radio stations, commercial printing, and Internet services.

As operator of an ESOP, the company feels very strongly about the benefits of participatory management. It decided it needed a vision of how it wanted the organization to be in the future so that it could plan effectively. It also took the view that the vision needed to be shared, encompassing personal values and needs as well as corporate ones, and reflecting an all-encompassing sense of collective identity.

WCI embarked on an 18-month process of consultation with eight employee focus groups and interviews with the Woodward family members and corporate managers. Letters were sent to all employee owners explaining the vision process and asking for their input to the content of the statement. Volunteers were recruited for the focus groups, and in addition a survey was sent to all employee owners asking them to comment on management practices relating to employee participation and teamwork.

The vision was finalized by a group consisting of representatives from the focus groups, the executive committee, and the corporate operating group. It incorporates the company's slogan, "Building our tomorrow, today," and is as follows:

Vision statement

"We commit to being the dominant creator and provider of communication and information products and services in every market we enter.

We will achieve our vision honestly and ethically.

We are 'Building our tomorrow, today' by equal commitment to:

-People-

Each of us has the capability to be self-directed and self-motivated. We encourage and respect each other as we strive to realize our potential by balancing our professional and personal lives.

-Customers-

Our customers are our first priority. By listening to our customers, we will provide innovative, quality, and timely solutions which exceed our customers' expectations.

-Leadership-

We embrace leadership which encourages input and values participation from all employees through teamwork, training, and continual dedication to self-development.

-Community Service-

Through our products, resources, and personal involvement, we support efforts to enhance our communities' culture, economy, and environment.

-Growth-

We will grow by aggressively pursuing new products, new services, and new markets.

-Performance-

We enhance our long-term profitability through sustained investment in evolving technology, and through encouragement of innovation and risk-taking.

As an ESOP company, we share the risks and rewards of innovation as we realize our vision and achieve our strategic plans."

Mission statement

After creating its vision statement, WCI decided that it would be worthwhile to revise its mission statement, which had been developed in 1981. This was also prepared with input from employee focus groups and the result was as follows:

"Woodward Communications, Inc. is committed, fully and equally to the following:

...remaining a family/employee-owned corporation, concentrating on the information/communications field, primarily in the Midwest;

...increasing our sales and profitability through customer service, internal growth, expansion, and acquisitions;

...improving the quality of products and expanding services to the public;

...sustaining investment in evolving technologies;

...developing our human resources through self-development, training, and teamwork."

Strategic planning

After creating the vision and revising the mission statement, WCI began a process leading to a three- to five-year strategic plan to help it realize its vision. Again, this involved employee owners in the spirit of participatory management, and began by identifying gaps between the vision and the company's current performance.

The vision is outlined in the employee owner handbook as well as on small plastic cards given out at the time of orientation. Employee owners often refer to the statement as a helpful guide that shows the values that are important to the company and its owners.

From 1997 to 1999, the company developed "A Snapshot in Time," business and marketing plans to help each division, unit, and the overall corporation focus on areas for growth and expansion.

Since the implementation of the vision statement, the company has added acquisitions in newspaper, weekly, speciality publications, commercial printing, and broadcast divisions. WCI has experienced annual revenue growth of 6–9%. During the nine years of the employee stock ownership plan, WCI's stock value has grown by 120%.

KEY LESSONS

» Involving employees in creating the vision is a powerful signal of the company's commitment to participatory management.
» The vision needs to be translated into action.

> » Other elements of the company's strategic planning process should be revised in line with the vision.

Source: www.wcinet.com; additional information supplied by company. Vision and mission statements © Woodward Communications, Inc., reproduced by permission.

INNOCENT: DRINKS THAT TASTE GOOD AND DO YOU GOOD

Innocent, based in West London, produces fresh, natural drinks, currently consisting of fruit smoothies and yoghurt "thickies." The company was founded by three friends in 1998, with the vision of making drinks that tasted good and are good for you. Innocent drinks contain no concentrates, sugar, or preservatives – the smoothies are made from crushed fruit and the thickies from yoghurt, fruit, and honey – and one smoothie, containing three-quarters of a pound of fruit, provides the recommended daily intake of fruit.

Innocent's founders, Richard Reed, Adam Balon, and Jon Wright, had no experience in the soft drinks industry, but believed that the concept of healthy drinks to combat today's hectic lifestyle was a strong one. They conducted taste tests among their friends before buying £500 worth of fruit, turning it into smoothies and selling them from a stall at Jazz on the Green, a London music festival. They put up a sign saying, "Do you think we should give up our jobs to make these smoothies?" and put out a bin saying "YES" and another saying "NO." At the end of the weekend the "YES" bin was so full that they felt confident enough to resign and begin the company in earnest.

Making it real

It took nine months of searching, however, to find the right juice manufacturing partner. Most of the companies they approached said that totally natural juices were a good idea but impractical, and that it would be better to use concentrates or add preservatives. "Our business is only about this one thing," says Richard Reed. "It's about being totally unadulterated. This has informed everything, from the name of the company through to the integrity of the product that goes into the bottles. If you take that away from us, we're suddenly the same as everyone else.''

Finally they found a family-run company that had been making freshly squeezed orange juice for 15 years and respected Innocent's ethos. ''They're fantastic people to work with,'' comments Reed. ''They share the same ideals, the same passions. We work together on recipe development and coming up with ideas, and each has areas of expertise that the other doesn't, so together we make a strong team.''

Press comment has certainly been favorable. Innocent's smoothies have been variously described as ''the most gorgeous on the planet,'' ''luxurious and healthy too'' and ''undoubtedly the best.'' They were voted the best smoothie in the UK by BBC2 television program *Food and Drink*. And consumers seem equally impressed, writing in to the company with comments such as ''I honestly couldn't believe that it was possible to create such a beautiful concoction,'' ''never has a product been so good for me and made me smile in equal measure'' and ''I've always been a big fan of fried potato slices, but I can't help think that your drinks are better than chips.''

Nevertheless, Reed says wryly that the company feels guilty taking this praise. ''We don't do anything apart from take what nature gives and put it into bottles. You should really go and thank your local tree or something. We're absolutely nailed down to our one core passion, so we don't mess around with nature, we don't adulterate.'' Or, as the label on Innocent's cranberry and raspberry smoothie says, ''The game's up. We've been rumbled. It isn't us that makes these drinks. It's a much larger operation, with a global business portfolio encompassing forestry, agriculture, mining, the weather, and chickens ... And the name of this shadowy figure? Nature – four billion years and still going strong.''

Innocent now supplies drinks to outlets throughout the UK and the Republic of Ireland, in stores including Harrods, Harvey Nichols and Waitrose, independent retailers, and coffee chains such as Caffe Nero and Coffee Republic. In the medium term it anticipates supplying to European cities, but distribution globally is not practical because the fresh product has a short shelf-life and needs to be kept chilled.

The company's next product will be veggies: vegetable and fruit juices such as carrot with mango or carrot, apple and ginger. These are combinations designed to counter the public's traditionally poor perception of vegetable juices, as well as having additional health benefits. Reed admits that Innocent is not good at getting new products to market on time. "We've got very high standards in terms of how good it's got to taste and how consistent we can make it, and it just takes time. Our attitude is it may be late but it's going to be great. If it doesn't taste good enough then we're not going to launch it."

Living the vision

In its continual quest to make drinks that taste good, Innocent is very particular about the fruit it uses. Because the smoothies contain nothing else, their taste is totally dependent on obtaining the best-quality fruit, and can in fact change slightly from week to week depending on the precise varieties. The company "follows the sun" around the world, from the northern to the southern hemisphere, and literally takes the fruit from the areas where the sun is shining. For example, in the spring its oranges come from countries such as Jamaica, Egypt, and Morocco, whereas in the summer they are from Brazil, South Africa, and Argentina. Not only does Innocent insist on specific varieties, such as Smooth Cayenne pineapples or Alphonso mangoes, it tries to deal direct with the plantations to allow it to choose the best crops, harvested at the optimum time.

Innocent also considers that every company should take responsibility for its impact on the local community and the wider environment. So as well as giving all unsold smoothies each week to the homeless through the charity Crisis, using electricity from sustainable sources and recycling everything possible, the company is working with an non-governmental organization called Women for Sustainable Development to fund the planting of mango trees in Bombay for people who have land but are too poor to plant anything. Instead of selling their labor to plantations, these people are then able to tend their own crops and thus treble their income. There is a second scheme providing cows for families so they can sell the milk to the local milk co-operative, and Women for Sustainable Development also organizes additional elements such as irrigation and life insurance for workers.

In addition, Innocent hopes that in future it will be able to advise on setting up a food business so that the people involved can add more value to their fruit.

Reed explains:

> "We're not here to save the world, but if we can run our business responsibly towards the environment, if we can help out in the place where our good comes from, the question is why wouldn't we? I guess that's just part of our commitment to deserving the name Innocent. We passionately believe that if you take responsibility from the beginning and make it part of your business system, as you get bigger you just do more of it. If you take lots of little steps you'll find you've actually gone quite a long way."

A natural approach to business

The company's commitment to making people feel good is also reflected in its approach to business, which is overwhelmingly angled towards having fun. Its bottle labels incorporate jokes and brain-teasers, which are regularly changed; the company logo is a cartoon face with nothing but eyes and a halo, and part of its Website is a virtual gym (www.innocentgym.co.uk). The "company rule book," which is freely available to customers at the point of sale, is quirky and humorous. For example, one page says:

> "Try to keep your work and emotional life separate
> It's a good rule, but we're sorry, we can't. You see, the thing is we're really quite emotional. We love making drinks, we love drinking them, and we especially love everyone who buys them. In fact, you're unlikely to find a more passionate set of people than those who work at Fruit Towers [the company's headquarters]. Jon's up early to check that the juice is flowing, Adam's in the van getting the bottles to you as fast as his little wheels will carry him, and Richard's sat in the corner stroking his mangoes. If you're ever in the area, pop by. We'd really love to see you."

Reed reports that they do regularly have visitors and will always welcome them, however large the company gets.

"I think the challenge as you get bigger is to think increasingly small. We get letters and e-mails from all sorts of people, which is great. It's all part of wanting to keep things human and natural, because it's not just about the product, although that's the most important thing, but about being natural in the way you do business, natural in the way you talk to people. We think it is essential that our image and our reality is the same thing; we don't hide behind a marketing facade. We basically make it clear to people who we are, what we do and why we do it, and we hope in return that people like it."

KEY LESSONS

» The vision should cover all areas of the way the company does business.
» Customers respond to the vision if it resonates with their own views.
» A well-founded vision can expand with the company as it grows.

Source: www.innocentdrinks.co.uk; Innocent company rule book; author's interview with Richard Reed.

SK GROUP: A GLOBAL LEADER OF THE INFORMATION AGE

The SK Group is the third largest conglomerate in Korea, a vertically integrated organization encompassing companies in a number of areas including energy production and distribution, fibers, petrochemicals, engineering and construction, telecommunications, films and international trade, and finance. It has 40 group companies on six continents and 25,000 employees.

SK was founded as Sunkyong Textiles Limited in 1953 producing woven textiles. Its founder, Jong-Kun Choe, had a vision of making it into an international corporation. This vision had been achieved by 1998 when the group changed its name to SK as part of a new corporate identity. In 2000 chairman Kil-Seung Son refined the original vision, restating it as "To become one of the global leaders of the information age."

In order to achieve this vision, SK acknowledges that it depends strongly on knowledge management. Therefore it needs to build and exploit the knowledge of its employees. It is taking a number of strategic initiatives in this regard, such as joint ventures or strategic alliances with high-potential start-ups, and business-to-business Websites such as ChemRound.com and TeleMerc.com.

The management system

In addition SK is leveraging its existing management principles and corporate values to foster its vision. These are embodied in the SK Management System (SKMS) and the Super Excellence program (SUPEX). These will help it develop "the smartest knowledge work-force possible, employees who will bring a keen competitive edge to the workplace."

SKMS is a management development strategy that is based on respecting each employee's creativity and dignity. The system has five objectives: to instill in employees the group's vision, values, and goals; to encourage the highest performance; to foster collaboration between diverse groups of people; to establish, develop, and reward individuals' unique talents; and to promote understanding and acceptance of the group's business principles.

The responsibilities of managers under the system are to understand their employees' capabilities and aspirations, explain lines of authority and responsibility, and value everyone's view when making decisions. In this way employees will be encouraged to do their best and thrive in a supportive environment.

SUPEX is a proprietary management tool underpinning SKMS, with the underlying concept of "aiming beyond," setting targets above what appears to be satisfactory. This challenges all staff to work towards the highest level of excellence.

SK considers that it is well prepared for the knowledge management era by focusing on its vision and building on its SKMS and SUPEX models. This has also sustained the group through recent difficulties in the wider economy: "Our people continued to perform at peak, and achieved superior results. Indeed, even in the turbulence of a fast-changing economic and social climate, we have leveraged our knowledge and experience, turning any setbacks into value-creating opportunities for the future.''

KEY LESSONS

» A vision will change as the company grows and expands.
» The vision needs to be bolstered by a compatible management system.
» A strong vision will sustain the company through difficult times.

Source: www.sk.com

ENRON: CREATING VALUE AND OPPORTUNITY FOR YOUR BUSINESS

Fortune has named Enron Corp. the most innovative company in the US six years in a row. It is now one of the world's largest traders of energy products such as oil, electricity, and natural gas, having transformed itself over the last 20 or so years from a far more straightforward gas pipeline company.

Enron describes its business as "to create value and opportunity for your business." This is an interesting vision, since it is defined in terms of the outcome and benefit for the customer, not for the organization itself, and it also allows the company to be tremendously flexible. It is also a development of the previous vision, to become "the world's leading energy company," an aspiration that had been achieved. Underpinning the revised vision have been some radical strategies that have not only made Enron successful but have also created new kinds of trading operation.

The most basic description of Enron's activity is that it buys and sells gas and electricity. However, as *Fortune* comments, "Saying that Enron trades electricity and gas is like saying that Thomas Edison made records. In most cases, Enron executives didn't just start dabbling in the natural gas and power trading business; they invented the entire concept. Never before had gas and power been traded like commodities."

The company has been able to create new markets in the way that it does mainly because of deregulation. It pushed for deregulation when other companies were trying to hold on to regulatory protection and, because it had invested in infrastructure and brand building, it was able to claim first-mover advantages. For example in gas Enron created new markets outside the US by building pipelines and power plants in those countries whose energy needs were unmet.

In its bid to create value for customers' businesses, Enron has also expanded into areas outside energy. It has launched trading operations in paper, plastics, and even Internet bandwidth. The company explains: "We make commodity markets so that we can deliver physical commodities to our customers at a predictable price . . . Many of the things we do have never been done before . . . Every day we strive to make markets in other industries that need a more efficient way to deliver commodities and manage risk, such as metals, forest products, bandwidth capacity, and steel."

Ken Rice, in charge of bandwidth training at Enron, describes the company's approach: "We try to look at markets that don't exist and dream about them existing. In every case Enron was one of perhaps two companies that thought a market could exist. And every time we'd start, all the established players would say, 'It can't be done. It's not fungible. It can't be stored. What expertise do you bring? The system isn't broken.'"

Enron has even created a new division, Enron Net Works, to create internal start-up companies and test the viability of its business model in non-energy-related markets. ClickPaper traded one million tons of paper, pulp, and wood in the first six months of its existence, in contrast to independent B2B (business-to-business) marketplace PaperExchange, which traded only 50,000 tons in 18 months. Deal-Bench provides Web-based project management software, Commodity Logic offers Web-based back-office system software, and EnronCredit trades bankruptcy swaps, allowing companies to sell off their credit risk and transfer it to someone else.

The approach has certainly been successful. In second quarter 2001, Enron achieved a 40% increase in net income, to $404mn, a 58% increase in energy volumes delivered, and a 32% increase in earnings per share.

Source: www.enron.com; Aspesi, C. and Vardhan, D. (1999) "Brilliant strategy, but can you execute?" *McKinsey Quarterly*, **1**; O'Reilly, B. (2000) "The power merchant." *Fortune*, April; Schonfeld, E. (2001) "The power brokers." *Business 2.0*, January; Bartlett, C.A. and Glinska, M. (2001) "Enron's transformation: from gas pipelines to new economy powerhouse." Harvard Business School case study 9-301-064, March 16.

Key Concepts and Thinkers

A chapter on the key concepts of vision and the most influential thinkers in the field. The advice of various management writers is outlined, including Warren Bennis, Rosabeth Moss Kanter, Henry Mintzberg, and Peter Senge. The concepts described are those such as:

» vision engineering;
» goals;
» mission statements;
» vision retreats;
» scenario planning; and
» values statements.

Agincourt – Richard Olivier, the son of great actor Sir Lawrence Olivier, conducts leadership training at Cranfield School of Management in the UK. He uses the example of Henry V and the Battle of Agincourt to illustrate communication of a vision. "Henry does not concentrate on the problem but on the solution," he says. "He ignores the problem. He includes himself with the men. And he gives them an image of how they must be in order to succeed. . . . It's not a selfish vision but if it succeeds it will also do him a lot of good. He will own the victory but it is not just for him. He allows people to share ownership of his vision." Olivier believes this style of management training is valuable, because it helps people to look at leadership and vision in a different way.[1]

Bennis, Warren – Warren Bennis is distinguished professor of business administration, and founding chairman of the Leadership Institute at the University of Southern California's Marshall School of Business. He has written or co-written more than 20 books on leadership and management, including *The Future of Leadership* and *Organizing Genius*. Warren Bennis on vision:

"At the heart of every Great Group is a shared dream. All Great Groups believe that they are on a mission from God, that they could change the world, make a dent in the universe."[2]

"How do you make people feel that what they're doing is somewhat equivalent to a search for the Holy Grail? . . . The vision must have meaning, a deep meaning."[3]

"To choose a direction, a leader must first have developed a mental image of a possible and desirable future state of the organization. This image, which we call a vision, may be as vague as a dream or as precise as a goal or mission statement. The critical point is that a vision articulates a view of a realistic, credible, attractive future for the organization, a condition that is better in some important ways than what now exists."[4]

Campbell, Andrew – Andrew Campbell is a director of the Ashridge Strategic Management Centre in London, whose research focuses on multi-business companies, corporate-level strategy, and the role of the corporate centre. He is also a consultant and academic. He has written nine books on strategy, including *A Sense of Mission* and *Corporate-Level Strategy*. Andrew Campbell on vision:

"A vision and a mission can be one and the same ... but vision and mission are not fully overlapping concepts ... When a vision is achieved, a new vision needs to be developed ... A vision is, therefore, more associated with a goal whereas a mission is more associated with a way of behaving."[5]

"Both vision and strategic intent are flawed concepts because they have an unbalanced view of organizations. Vision is too much focused on goals and on the future."[6]

Collins, James P. - Jim Collins describes himself as "a student and teacher of enduring great companies–how they grow, how they attain superior performance, and how good companies can become great companies."[7] He founded a management research laboratory in Boulder, Colorado, where he conducts research projects and works with managers from private, public, and social sectors. He has co-written four books, including *Good to Great* and *Built to Last*. Jim Collins on vision:

"A well-conceived vision consists of two major components: core ideology and envisioned future. Core ideology ... defines what we stand for and why we exist ... The envisioned future is what we aspire to become, to achieve, to create."[8]

"There is a big difference between being an organization with a vision statement and becoming a truly visionary organization. The difference lies in creating alignment - alignment to preserve an organization's core values, to reinforce its purpose, and to stimulate continued progress towards its aspirations."[9]

"Visionary leaders die. Visionary products become obsolete. Visionary companies go on forever."[10]

Engineering, vision - In the mid-1990s Robert Frisch, then vice-president of Gemini Consulting, pioneered an approach that he called "vision engineering." A group of managers from the company that is trying to establish a vision begins by studying cards containing facts or trends relating to their industry. This helps them to identify drivers of change, which Frisch describes as follows: "They are waves coming toward the shore. Some are bigger than others, but they are all headed toward us. We can either build a surfboard to ride them, or let them crash over us." Second, managers identify how each driver affects each link of the value chain; third, they assess the capabilities and assets the company must have to avoid the threats and make the most of its opportunities. This provides a shared view of the world, against which it is possible to make practical decisions on developing a vision, rather than merely having theoretical discussions.[11]

Goals – Goals (or objectives) are statements of what the organization wants to achieve in the next few years, for example in relation to sales, profitability, return on investment, market share, customer satisfaction, and quality improvement. They give a specific answer to the question: What do we want to accomplish? Goals have been described as "dreams with a deadline." They follow the direction set by the vision, and need to be detailed enough to allow resources to be allocated and priorities set.

Kanter, Rosabeth Moss – Rosabeth Moss Kanter is Ernest L. Arbuckle Professor of Business Administration at the Harvard Business School. She is an internationally renowned expert and specializes in business strategy, innovation, and the management of strategic and organizational change. She has written 15 books, including *Evolve!*, *The Change Masters* and *When Giants Learn to Dance*. Rosabeth Moss Kanter on vision:

"People need imagination. They need to be able to see and grasp new possibilities before they become concrete."[12]

"Too often executives announce a plan, launch a task force, and then simply hope that people find the answers – instead of offering a dream, stretching their horizons, and encouraging people to do the same."[13]

"Leaders talk about communicating a vision as an instrument of change, but I prefer the notion of communicating an aspiration. It's not just a picture of what could be; it is an appeal to our better selves, a call to become something more. It reminds us that the future does not just descend like a stage set; we construct the future from our own history, desires, and decisions."[14]

Kotter, John P. – John Kotter is the Konosuke Matsushita Professor of Leadership at the Harvard Business School. He is one of the world's foremost authorities on leadership and change. He is the author of eight books, including *Leading Change*, *The New Rules: How to Succeed in Today's Post Corporate World*, and *Matsushita Leadership*. John Kotter on vision:

"Most discussions of vision have a tendency to degenerate into the mystical. The implication is that a vision is something mysterious that mere mortals, even talented ones, could never hope to have. But developing good business direction isn't magic. It is a tough, sometimes exhausting process of gathering and analyzing information. People who articulate such visions aren't magicians but broad-based strategic thinkers who are willing to take risks."[15]

"I think the more that you get in touch with your own hopes and dreams and ideals, the more that you see the difference or the gap between your dreams and the current reality, the more you're propelled, regardless of fear, to do something."[16]

"Without a sensible vision, a transformation effort can easily dissolve into a list of confusing and incompatible projects that can take the organization in the wrong direction or nowhere at all."[17]

Mintzberg, Henry – Henry Mintzberg is John Cleghorn Professor of Management Studies at McGill University, Montreal. He is one of today's most distinguished management authors, specializing in strategy and organization. He is the author of 10 books, including *The Nature of Managerial Work*, *The Strategy Process*, and *The Rise and Fall of Strategic Planning*. Henry Mintzberg on vision:

"The most successful strategies are visions, not plans. Strategic planning, as it has been practiced, has really been strategic programming, the articulation and elaboration of strategies, or visions, that already exist. When companies understand the difference between planning and strategic thinking, they can get back to what the strategy-making process should be: capturing what the manager learns from all sources . . . and then synthesizing that learning into a vision of the direction that the business should pursue."[18]

"The problem is that planning represents a calculating style of management, not a committing style. Managers with a committing style engage people in a journey. They lead in such a way that everyone on the journey helps shape its course. As a result, enthusiasm inevitably builds along the way."[19]

"Vision is unavailable to those who cannot 'see' with their own eyes. Real strategists get their hands dirty digging for ideas, and real strategies are built from the occasional nuggets they uncover

... The big picture is painted with little strokes."[20]

Mission statements – Mission statements seem to have become ubiquitous in recent years: most companies seem to produce one, as do not-for-profit organizations such as charities, schools, hospitals, and churches. Even formally state-owned companies in socialist Cuba are being taught how to write a mission statement as part of the country's reform process or "perfeccionamiento."[21] Writers such as Stephen Covey advocate writing personal and family mission statements.[22] The concept was even immortalized on film in 1996 in *Jerry Maguire*, where the sports agent played by Tom Cruise writes a 25-page statement entitled "The things we think and do not say: the future of our business," and is unceremoniously fired a week later.[23] A vision and a mission (or purpose) may be one and the same thing, but often an organization will have both. In general in such circumstances, the vision tends to be a broadbrush statement of the organization's aspirations or desired future direction; a mission statement is more prosaic and practical, including some or all of the following elements:

» A definition of the business: Who are we?
» The markets served: What do we do?
» The organization's principles or beliefs: Why do we exist?

As with a vision, it is important for the content of a mission statement to be consistent with the reality in the organization, or it will be dismissed as irrelevant. Overblown or otherwise meaningless mission statements are often called "motherhood and apple pie."

Some mission statements seem to be used more as a communication device with external stakeholders, reprinted in the company's annual report and other literature but not used to any great effect within the organization. As Lucy Kellaway writes in *The Financial Times*: "The main thing wrong with most mission statements is ... that they are flim-flam, and badly written flim-flam at that. ... They are better viewed as a kind of corporate advertising ... Mission statements reflect what companies think the rest of the world wants from them."[24]

Nanus, Burt – Burt Nanus is an emeritus professor at the Gordon S. Marshall School of Business at the University of Southern California. He has written or co-written four books on leadership, including

Leaders: The Strategies for Taking Charge and *Visionary Leadership*. Burt Nanus on vision:

"A vision is a target that beckons ... Note also that a vision always refers to a future state, a condition that does not presently exist and never existed before. With a vision, the leader provides the all-important bridge from the present to the future of the organization."[25]

"The right vision is an idea so powerful that it literally jumpstarts the future by calling forth the energies, talents, and resources to make things happen."[26]

"Nothing could be more common in organizations than a vision that has overstayed its welcome ... The vision may in fact have been the right one at the time it was formulated, but rarely is it right for all time. The world changes, and so must the vision."[27]

Porras, Jerry – Jerry Porras is Lane Emeritus Professor of Organizational Behavior and Change at Stanford University. He has written or co-written two books, *Built to Last* and *Stream Analysis: A Powerful Way to Diagnose and Manage Organizational Change*. His research interests are organizational vision and leadership. Jerry Porras on vision:

"Vision provides guidance about what core to preserve and what future to stimulate progress toward."[28]

"Vision setting should take place at all levels of an organization and each group should set its own vision – consistent, of course, with the overall vision of the corporation."[29]

"Visionary companies display a remarkable resiliency, an ability to bounce back from adversity."[30]

Retreat – Burt Nanus recommends a vision retreat, which he defines as "a meeting of a carefully chosen group of individuals engaged in a structured series of exercises designed to identify and assess vision alternatives for an organization."[31] This includes the group's leader, managers, professionals, and possibly outsiders, as well as a facilitator, who may be an external consultant. The discussion during the retreat focuses on the organization's characteristics and future possibilities, and the break with the normal work environment allows thinking to be freer and more creative. Nanus recommends the following five-phase approach to running a vision retreat:

1 Preparation. Establish the purpose for the retreat and its goals, arrange the site, invite participants.
2 Initial meeting. Two days of discussion on the vision audit (the character of the organization and its current mission and strategy), the vision scope (stakeholders, opportunities, and threats, what is wanted from the new vision) and the vision context (the organization's future economic, technological, social, and other environments).
3 Analysis and report cycle. Three scenarios of the future are prepared by the facilitator and participants have a few weeks to develop potential vision statements.
4 Final meeting. A day for discussion of alternative visions, selection of one, and exploration of the strategic implications.
5 Post-retreat activities. Communicate the results of the retreat to the wider organization, develop strategies for implementing the vision. There is also a need for later monitoring and evaluation of the implementation process.

Scenario planning – The technique of scenario planning was pioneered at oil company Royal Dutch/Shell in the 1970s. Companies develop scenarios or stories to depict major changes that could happen in the world that could have an impact on the way they operate. Once various scenarios have been created, the company can then investigate how it could react if the scenario happened in reality. Peter Schwartz, co-founder and chairman of the Global Business Network (GBN), a leading consultancy in strategic planning, comments: "It's not about predictions. Scenarios are about trying to avoid getting the future wrong in fundamental ways. It's a different way of thinking."[32]

GBN claims that scenario planning can be used in the following ways:

» to shed light on the short- and long-term risks and opportunities associated with particular decisions and investment;
» to explore emerging opportunities for products, services, technology, and new markets;
» to identify how the new economy will affect a business;
» to inspire key stakeholders to make changes necessary to transform an organization;

» to catalyze innovation or new kinds of value creation; and

» to create alignment and commitment to an organization's vision.[33]

Senge, Peter M. – Peter Senge is a senior lecturer at the Massachusetts Institute of Technology and chairperson of the Society for Organizational Learning, a global community of organizations, researchers, and consultants. He is one of the world's foremost experts on learning organizations. He has written or co-written four books, including *The Fifth Discipline: The Art and Practice of the Learning Organization* and *The Dance of Change: The Challenges of Sustaining Momentum in Learning Organizations*. Peter Senge on vision:

"The practice of shared vision involves the skills of unearthing shared 'pictures of the future' that foster genuine commitment and enrollment rather than compliance."[34]

"Vision – an image of the future we seek to create – is synonymous with intended results. As such, vision is a practical tool, not an abstract concept."[35]

"How do individual visions become shared visions? A useful metaphor is the hologram, the three-dimensional image created by interacting light sources . . . If you divide a hologram, each part, no matter how small, shows the whole image intact. Likewise, when a group of people come to share a vision for an organization, each person sees an individual picture of the organization at its best . . . But the component pieces of the holograms are not identical. Each represents the whole image from a different point of view."[36]

Slogans or strategic principles – Many organizations have a slogan or strategic principle that encapsulates their vision and corporate strategy. Famous examples are Avis's "We try harder," Hewlett-Packard's "Invent" or British Airways' "The world's favourite airline." These can be used to communicate the vision memorably inside the company, in advertising, or on business cards. They can also be utilized as a quick reminder to managers and employees of the organization's strategic direction, which can inform their decision making. However, slogans can come back to haunt a company. There were more than a few wry smiles over the UK's Independent Insurance's slogan "reinventing insurance" when the company collapsed spectacularly in June 2000 amid allegations of unrealistically low premiums and over-reliance on reinsurance.

Values statements – Values statements are intended to help managers with complex decision making. Having a clear statement of values can be used to guide employees in the behavior expected of them, and also in recruitment, to aim towards a match between the values of new employees and those of the organization. Perhaps the best-known example of a values statement is healthcare group Johnson & Johnson's "Credo:"

> "Our Credo
>
> We believe our first responsibility is to the doctors, nurses, and patients, to mothers and fathers and all others who use our products and services.
>
> In meeting their needs everything we do must be of high quality.
>
> We must constantly strive to reduce our costs in order to maintain reasonable prices.
>
> Customers' orders must be serviced promptly and accurately. Our suppliers and distributors must have an opportunity to make a fair profit.
>
> We are responsible to our employees, the men and women who work with us throughout the world.
>
> Everyone must be considered as an individual.
>
> We must respect their dignity and recognize their merit.
>
> They must have a sense of security in their jobs.
>
> Compensation must be fair and adequate, and working conditions clean, orderly, and safe.
>
> We must be mindful of ways to help our employees fulfill their family responsibilities.
>
> Employees must feel free to make suggestions and complaints.
>
> There must be equal opportunity for employment, development, and advancement for those qualified.
>
> We must provide competent management, and their actions must be just and ethical.
>
> We are responsible to the communities in which we live and work and to the world community as well.

We must be good citizens – support good works and charities and bear our fair share of taxes.

We must encourage civic improvements and better health and education.

We must maintain in good order the property we are privileged to use, protecting the environment and natural resources.

Our final responsibility is to our stockholders.

Business must make a sound profit.

We must experiment with new ideas.

Research must be carried on, innovative programs developed, and mistakes paid for.

New equipment must be purchased, new facilities provided, and new products launched.

Reserves must be created to provide for adverse times.

When we operate according to these principles, the stockholders should realize a fair return."[37]

This was developed by the company's founder, General Robert Wood Johnson, in 1943, and emphasized that the first responsibility of managers and employees was to customers, rather than shareholders. The Credo has been updated periodically over the years after consultation with employees, although its principles have remained the same. It is now available in 36 languages throughout the group's 195 operating companies. The worth of the Credo was demonstrated in the 1980s when Johnson & Johnson's drug Tylenol® was adulterated with cyanide and used as a murder weapon. During the crisis numerous decisions were made based on the values statement, and the company's good reputation was maintained.[38]

In fact, Ralph S. Larsen, Johnson & Johnson's CEO, is quoted as saying:[39] "The core values embodied in our credo might be a competitive advantage, but that is not why we have them. We have them because they define for us what we stand for, and we would hold them even if they became a competitive disadvantage in certain situations."

Visioning – A visioning workshop or series of workshops is one way to create or revise a vision for an organization. As part of the process, managers and employees should examine why the company is in business, what its core philosophy is, how people relate to colleagues and customers, what markets, products and services the company addresses, and how it wants to be seen by others. Sufficient time must be allowed for the visioning process to encompass people at all levels of the organization, not just senior managers. This helps to ensure that as many people as possible "own" the eventual vision because they helped to create it. At the highest level discussion should focus on articulating the vision itself, what has been called "writing the jingle."[40] With middle managers, the focus is on implementing the vision, and lower down the organization the emphasis is on the organizational practices and processes to ensure that the vision is able to be made operational.

Vision statement - Many organizations that develop a vision write it down and communicate it through a vision statement. This is a written description of the vision, a word picture of what the organization wants to become. It is not absolutely necessary to do this, but it does serve two purposes: it becomes a public document and therefore helps the organization remember and stick to its vision. Finding the right words for the vision statement may also help to clarify the visioning process itself and make sure that everyone understands the vision.

Zealots - Paul Branstad and Chuck Lucier from consultancy Booz-Allen & Hamilton call practical visionaries "zealots." These people are "visibly passionate about achieving results today, creating a superior business for tomorrow, and continuously forging development opportunities for their people."[41] They are prepared to make themselves and other people uncomfortable if it will lead to transformation or growth. A zealot need not be a CEO; in large companies they are normally line managers with profit responsibility. Branstad and Lucier further describe them as "choreographers of implementation," emphasizing that they don't only come up with great new ideas but also make sure these are put into practice. Booz-Allen & Hamilton takes the view that a "shift to a zealot-driven organization is the only reliable path to sustained 15–20% returns."[42] One example Branstad and Lucier give is John Barth of Johnson Controls Inc., who revolutionized the company's automotive components business and masterminded the successful acquisition of auto interior design company Prince. Barth is now the president and chief operating officer of the company, which has become a global group with the largest North American presence in the Japanese automobile industry.

NOTES

1 Beckett, F. (1999) "Give us a plan, Henry." *Guardian*, October 19.

2 Bennis, W. (1997) "The secrets of great groups." *Leader to Leader*, **3** (Winter).

3 Kurtzman, J. (1997) "An interview with Warren Bennis." *Strategy & Business*, third quarter.

4 Bennis, W. and Nanus, B. (1985) *Leaders: The Strategies for Taking Charge*. Harper and Row, New York.

5 Campbell, A., Devine, M. and Young, D. (1990) *A Sense of Mission*. Economist Books, London.

6 Campbell, A., Devine, M. and Young, D. (1990) *A Sense of Mission*. Economist Books, London.

7 www.jimcollins.com/pageload.asp?pagename=mai_abou.html.

8 Collins, J.C. and Porras, J.I. (1996) "Building your company's vision." *Harvard Business Review*, September–October.

9 Collins, J. (1996) "Aligning action and values." *Leader to Leader*, **1** (Summer).

10 Collins, J. and Porras, J. (1995) "The ultimate vision." *Across the Board*, January.

11 Stewart, T.A. (1996) "A refreshing change: vision statements that make sense." *Fortune*, September **30**, p. 195.

12 Kurtzman, J. (1999) "An interview with Rosabeth Moss Kanter." *Strategy & Business*, third quarter.

13 Kanter, R.M. (1999) "The enduring skills of change leaders." *Leader to Leader*, **13** (Summer).

14 Kanter, R.M. (1999) "The enduring skills of change leaders." *Leader to Leader*, **13** (Summer).

15 Kotter, J.P. (1990) "What leaders really do." *Harvard Business Review*, May–June.

16 Link & Learn (2001) "Leadership: Facing your fears... and the Internet." *Link & Learn*; see http://64.69.116.148/archives/leadership/leadership_q_and_a_john_kotter.htm.

17 Kotter, J.P. (1995) "Leading change: why transformation efforts fail." *Harvard Business Review*, March – April.

18 Mintzberg, H. (1993) "The fall and rise of strategic planning." *Harvard Business Review*, January–February.

19 Mintzberg, H. (1993) "The fall and rise of strategic planning." *Harvard Business Review*, January–February.

20 Mintzberg, H. (1993) "The fall and rise of strategic planning." *Harvard Business Review*, January–February.

21 Goering, L. (2001) "Cuban businesses in midst of revolution." *Chicago Tribune*, August 13.

22 Covey, S.R. (1999) *The Seven Habits of Highly Effective Families*, Simon & Schuster, New York.

23 www.spe.sony.com/movies/jerrymaguire/nonshock/moviestuff/exclusive/mission.html.

24 Kellaway, L. (2000) "Statements that sum up mission impossible." *The Financial Times*, March 20.

25 Bennis, W. and Nanus, B. (1985) *Leaders: The Strategies for Taking Charge*. Harper and Row, New York.

26 Nanus, B. (1996) "Leading the vision team." *The Futurist*, May.

27 Nanus, B. (1992) "Visionary leadership: how to re-vision the future." *The Futurist*, September/October.

28 Collins, J.C. and Porras, J.I. (1996) "Building your company's vision." *Harvard Business Review*, September – October.

29 Collins, J.C. and Porras, J.I. (1991) "Organizational vision and visionary organizations." *California Management Review*, 34(1).

30 Collins, J. and Porras, J.I. (1995) "The ultimate vision." *Across the Board*, January.

31 Nanus, B. (1996) "Leading the vision team." *The Futurist*, May.

32 Fost, D. (1998) "How to think about the future." *American Demographics*, February.

33 www.gbn.org/public/gbnstory/scenarios/index.htm. More information on scenario planning is available in Ringland, G. (1998) *Scenario Planning: Managing for the Future*. John Wiley & Sons, Chichester, UK; Schwartz, P. (1996) *The Art of the Long View: Paths to Strategic Insight for Yourself*. Doubleday Currency, New York; van der Heijden, K. (1996) *Scenarios: The Art of Strategic Conversation*. John Wiley & Sons, Chichester, UK.

34 Senge, P. (1990) *The Fifth Discipline: The Art and Practice of the Learning Organization*. Doubleday Currency, New York.

35 Senge, P.M. (1998) "The practice of innovation." *Leader to Leader*, **9** (Summer).
36 Senge, P.M. "The leader's new work", www.sol-ne.org/res/kr/new work.html.
37 © Johnson & Johnson, reproduced by permission.
38 www.jnj.com/who_is_jnj/cr_index.html.
39 Yearout, S. (2001) "Multi-level visioning." *Training & Development*, March.
40 Yearout, S. (2001) "Multi-level visioning." *Training & Development*, March.
41 Branstad, P. and Lucier, C. (2001) "Zealots rising: the case for practical visionaries." *Strategy & Business*, 1st quarter.
42 Salz, P. (2001) "The 21st century enterprise." *Fortune*, July 23, p. S7.

Resources

This chapter outlines the arguments and suggestions presented by the best authors on vision: James Collins and Jerry Porras, Burt Nanus, and Peter Senge. There is also a list of useful Websites.

USEFUL BOOKS AND ARTICLES

Collins, J.C. and Porras, J.I. (1996) *Built to Last*. HarperBusiness, London

Collins and Porras conducted a long-term study of 18 enduringly successful companies to identify what underlay their success. The research established the following myths about great companies:

» **Myth 1**: It takes a great idea to start a great company – in fact, few of the visionary companies began life with a great idea.

» **Myth 2**: Visionary companies require great and charismatic visionary leaders – a charismatic leader can be detrimental to a company's long-term prospects.

» **Myth 3**: The most successful companies exist first and foremost to maximize profits – visionary companies pursue a cluster of objectives, of which making money is not necessarily the primary one.

» **Myth 4**: Visionary companies share a common subset of "correct" core values – there is in reality no "right" set of core values for a visionary company.

» **Myth 5**: The only constant is change – a visionary company rarely changes its core ideology.

» **Myth 6**: Blue-chip companies play it safe – instead, they are not afraid to make bold commitments.

» **Myth 7**: Visionary companies are great places to work, for everyone – only those who fit well with the core ideology will find a visionary company a great place to work.

» **Myth 8**: Highly successful companies make their best moves by brilliant and complex strategic planning – rather, they make some of their best moves by experimentation, trial and error, and opportunism.

» **Myth 9**: Companies should hire outside CEOs to stimulate fundamental change – the research found only two companies that had looked outside for a CEO.

» **Myth 10**: The most successful companies focus primarily on beating the competition – visionary companies focus primarily on beating themselves.

» **Myth 11**: You can't have your cake and eat it too – visionary companies are able to hold and exploit two opposing ideas at the same time.

» **Myth 12**: Companies become visionary primarily through "vision statements" – creating a statement can be a helpful step, but it is only one of thousands of steps in a never-ending process to becoming a visionary company.

Rather than the myths, truly great companies are able to manage continuity and change and to develop a vision. The vision consists of a core ideology and an envisioned future. Core ideology "defines the enduring character of an organization – a consistent identity that transcends product or market life cycles, technological breakthroughs, management fads, and individual leaders." It has two parts, core values and core purpose. The core values are the organization's essential and enduring tenets. There is no universally right set of core values; an organization decides for itself which values it wants to hold, and these normally number between three and five. The book gives guidance on how to identify core values. The core purpose is the organization's reason for being, "it captures the soul of the organization." It should not be confused with goals or business strategies. Again, the book gives examples of effective statements of purpose and suggestions for the questions to ask to ascertain it. Collins and Porras comment: "You do not create or set core ideology. You *discover* core ideology. You do not deduce it by looking at the external environment. Ideology has to be authentic. You cannot fake it."

The second component of the vision is the envisioned future. This is an audacious goal plus vivid descriptions of what it would be like to achieve the goal. Passion, emotion, and conviction are essential parts of the description. In addition to having a vision, you need to have alignment with it within the organization. "Building a visionary company requires 1% vision and 99% alignment. When you have superb alignment, a visitor could drop in from outer space and infer your vision from the operations and activities of the company without ever reading it on paper or meeting a single senior executive."

Nanus, B. (1992) *Visionary Leadership: Creating a Compelling Sense of Direction for Your Organization*. Jossey Bass, San Fransisco

Nanus explains why vision is the most important attribute of leadership and outlines a step-by-step process for creating and implementing a new sense of direction for the organization. He defines a vision as "a realistic, credible, attractive future for the organization." The right vision can accomplish a number of things for a company.

» It attracts commitment and energizes people.
» It creates meaning for employees.
» It establishes a standard of excellence against which people can measure themselves.
» It bridges the present and the future and focuses the organization on where it is heading.

A good vision can be described as follows.

» It is a mental model of a future state.
» It is realistic enough so that people believe it can be achieved, but idealistic enough that there is a degree of stretch in getting there.
» It is appropriate for the organization and the environment.
» It reflects high aspirations.
» It clarifies purpose and direction.
» It inspires enthusiasm and encourages commitment.
» It is well articulated and easily understood.
» It reflects the uniqueness of the organization, its distinctive competence, what it stands for, and what it is able to achieve.
» It is ambitious.

When developing a vision it is important to involve the organization's main constituencies; don't try to do it alone. There is also a need to keep an open mind and not be constrained in your thinking. The process of developing the vision involves learning everything you can about the organization so that you understand it and conducting a vision audit, assessing the organization's current direction and momentum. Key questions to be asked here include:

» Does the organization already have a clearly stated vision?
» Do the key leaders know where it is heading, and agree on the direction?
» Do its structures, processes, personnel, incentives, and information systems support the current direction?

Targeting the vision then involves starting to narrow in on questions such as:

» What are the boundaries or constraints to the vision?
» What must the vision accomplish?
» What critical issues must be addressed?

Setting the context of the vision concerns looking to a desirable future, making informed estimates of what the future environment might look like. First, categorize future developments in the environment that might affect the vision; second, list the expectations for the future in each category; third, determine which of these expectations is most likely to occur; fourth, assign a probability of occurrence to each expectation. Developing future scenarios follows from the previous step. The expectations determined then need to be combined into a few brief scenarios so that they produce a range of possible alternative futures and alternative visions. The final step is choosing the best possible vision for your organization. Determine which vision meets the criteria of a good vision, is compatible with the organization's culture and values, and can be applied to a broad range of possible scenarios. Once the organization has decided on a vision it needs to be translated into reality and made to happen. That is not the end of the process, however – Nanus describes it as "running a race with no end," since there is a need to for re-visioning to make sure the organization stays on the right track. There is an appendix to the book on visionary leadership in the public sector.

Senge, P.M., Roberts, C., Ross, R.B., Smith, B.J. and Kleiner, A. (1994) *The Fifth Discipline Fieldbook: Strategies and Tools for Building a Learning Organization.* Nicholas Brealey Publishing, London

Shared vision is one of Senge's five disciplines of the learning organization,[1] the others being systems thinking, personal mastery, mental models, and team learning. It is defined as "building a sense of commitment in a group, by developing shared images of the future we seek to create, and the principles and guiding practices by which we hope to get there." *The Fifth Discipline Fieldbook* describes experimentation and research into the learning organization, and offers exercises, theories and methods, toolkits and resources for people and organizations that wish to put the disciplines into practice. According to Senge *et al.*, the discipline of building shared vision consists of people within the organization articulating "their common stories – around vision, purpose, values, why their work matters, and how it fits in the larger world." A strategy for building shared vision is built around the following precepts.

» Every organization has a destiny, a deep purpose that expresses its reason for existence.

» Clues to understanding that destiny can be discovered in the founder's aspirations and the reasons for the industry coming into existence.

» Not all visions are equal – visions that tap into an organization's deep sense of purpose are more powerful.

» Many members of the organization have a collective sense of its underlying purpose.

» At the heart of building shared vision is designing and evolving processes in which people at every level can talk about what matters to them.

» Creative tension emerges when we hold clear pictures of our vision juxtaposed with reality.

The sense of shared purpose and destiny that the organization is trying to draw out is based on four components.

» Vision: an image of our desired future.
» Values: how we expect to travel where we want to go.
» Purpose or mission: what the organization is here to do.
» Goals: milestones we expect to reach before too long.

The Fifth Discipline Fieldbook outlines what a leader can expect as they build a shared vision; how to design an organization's governing ideas; a detailed strategy for building shared vision – telling, selling, testing, consulting, and co-creating; the role of the CEO; various exercises for developing a vision; and strategic priorities. The section on personal mastery also includes a self-examination exercise on defining your personal vision, what you want to create of yourself and the world around you, and one on linking your personal vision to that of the organization.

RELATED PUBLICATIONS

Bennis, W. and Nanus, B. (1985) *Leaders: The Strategies for Taking Charge*. Harper and Row, New York.

Collins, J.C. and Porras, J.I. (1991) "Organizational vision and visionary organizations." *California Management Review*, **34**(1).

Collins, J.C. and Porras, J.I. (1996) "Building your company's vision." *Harvard Business Review*, September–October.

Nanus, B. (1996) "Leading the vision team." *The Futurist*, **30** (1 May).

Senge, P.M. (1990) *The Fifth Discipline: The Art and Practice of the Learning Organization*. Currency Doubleday, New York.

Senge, P.M. (1990) "The leader's new work: building learning organizations." *Sloan Management Review*, Fall.

Senge, P.M., Kleiner, A., Roberts, C., Ross, R., Roth, G. and Smith, B. (1999) *The Dance of Change: The Challenges of Sustaining Momentum in Learning Organizations*. Nicholas Brealey, London.

OTHER ARTICLES WORTH CONSULTING

Kotter, J.P. (1990) "What leaders really do." *Harvard Business Review*, May–June.

Kotter, J.P. (1995) "Leading change: why transformation efforts fail." *Harvard Business Review*, March–April.

Lipton, M. (1996) "Demystifying the development of an organizational vision." *Sloan Management Review,* **37** (June).

Mintzberg, H. (1994) "The fall and rise of strategic planning." *Harvard Business Review*, January–February.

WEBSITES

The following websites may be useful to organizations wishing to explore individual aspects of their vision:

» *AccountAbility - www.accountability.org.uk* - An international membership organization aiming to improve the accountability and performance of organizations worldwide. AccountAbility is committed to strengthening the social responsibility and ethical behavior of the business community and non-profit organizations, by promoting best practice social and ethical accounting, auditing, and reporting and developing standards and certification for professionals. The Website offers information on membership and standards.

» *Global Business Network (GBN) - www.gbn.org* - A worldwide organization that engages in a collaborative exploration of the future, discovering the frontiers of knowledge and creating innovative tools for strategic action. GBN explores the future through scenario thinking and planning, rich experiential meetings, learning journeys, online conversation, and connections with experts. The Website provides publications, news, and information about training seminars.

» *New Economics Foundation (NEF) - www.neweconomics.org* - A think-tank that combines research, advocacy, training, and practical action. NEF's priority areas are participative democracy, local economic renewal, and reshaping the global economy, including corporate accountability. The Website offers news, publications, and information about tools available.

» *Society for Organizational Learning (SoL) - www.solonline.org* - A global learning community dedicated to building knowledge about fundamental institutional change. SoL discovers, integrates, and implements theories and practices for the interdependent development of people and their institutions. The Website gives details of events, courses and workshops, learning communities, and other resources.

» *World Future Society - www.wfs.org* - A non-profit education and scientific organization for people interested in how social and technological developments are shaping the future. It has a membership of over 30,000 in more than 80 countries, including sociologists, scientists, corporate planners, educators, and students. The Website offers paid access to various publications, including *The Futurist* magazine.

» *World Wide Web Consortium (W3C) - www.w3.org* - An organization created in 1994 to lead the World Wide Web to its full potential by developing common protocols that promote its evolution and ensure its operability. W3C has more than 500 member organizations worldwide. The Website offers information and news on World Wide Web history, developments and standards, as well as an A-Z glossary.

The following business and news publications are useful to consult for company information and articles:

» *Business Week* – www.businessweek.com
» *Fast Company* – www.fastcompany.com
» *Financial Times* – www.ft.com
» *Fortune* – www.fortune.com
» *Harvard Business Review* – www.hbsp.harvard.edu/products/hbr/
» *Time* – www.time.com

NOTE

1 Senge, P.M. (1990) *The Fifth Discipline: The Art and Practice of the Learning Organization*, Currency Doubleday, New York.

Ten Steps to Making it all Work

Ten steps for developing and communicating a vision in your organization.

1 Decide who to involve in developing the vision.
2 Establish where you are now.
3 Establish possible directions for the organization.
4 Choose the vision.
5 Decide on a communication strategy.
6 Ensure that management behavior is consistent.
7 Establish feedback mechanisms.
8 Allocate the necessary resources to make the vision happen.
9 Reward behavior consistent with the vision.
10 Check periodically that the vision still holds true.

DEVELOPING THE VISION

1. Decide who to involve in developing the vision

Developing a vision for an organization is something that is sometimes done by the chief executive or founder alone, but that makes it a very lonely and occasionally unproductive exercise. A vision solely based on one person's ideas may also not be the best that could be imagined. Hiring consultants to develop a vision for you is also not always a good idea. A better and more powerful way to energize everyone in the organization around the vision is to involve people from all levels in its formulation.

Involving a cross-section of the organization in developing a new vision results in the following benefits.

» The vision will incorporate a wide range of viewpoints and expertise.
» A brainstorming or other kind of participatory approach allows people's ideas to be tested and refined by the opinions of others. Therefore the resulting vision is likely to be broader and of better quality.
» People who are involved in developing the vision are more likely to be committed to it. They also gain a deeper understanding of the organization and the challenges and opportunities it faces.
» The process is beneficial for team-building.

Choose who you would like on your team, ask them if they want to be involved, and then outline their responsibilities and what you expect of them during the process. Most vision teams will include the CEO.

2. Establish where you are now

Once the vision team has been assembled, you need to set to work finding out as much as possible about the organization's context and current situation. Only when you know where you are can you start to move forward. Begin with the company's history, so that you understand how it reached where it is today. It may also be worth considering the experience of other similar organizations, particularly if there is a direction that has already been followed that has not proved successful.

Then make sure you have a thorough grounding in the present. Carry out strategic analyses such as SWOT (strengths, weaknesses, opportunities, threats) and PESTLE (political, economic, social, technological, legal, and environmental factors). Also establish what would happen if the organization carried on as it is now.

Finish establishing the context of the vision by focusing on possible futures for the organization. This can be done through studying forecasts from various sources, or by constructing scenarios.

3. Establish possible directions for the organization

In this step you start pulling together potential visions that will address the factors, opportunities, and threats identified in the previous stage. The vision team needs to ask and answers questions such as the following.

» What is the purpose of the organization? What are we in business for?
» Who are we in business for?
» Why does our work matter to us?
» Why does our work matter to other people?
» What ensures success in our business?
» Who benefits from what we do?
» What direction do we want the organization to take?
» What do we want the organization to look like?
» What resources do we have available to help us to move forward?

Considering these questions will give you a set of possible futures for the organization.

4. Choose the vision

To make a choice between visions, you need to assess the alternatives against the challenges and opportunities you have identified as facing the organization. Which vision will help you to address these most effectively?

Great care obviously has to be taken when deciding which direction to take, since focusing on the wrong destination could be damaging. The vision should not be too vague, or it will be meaningless, but it also should not be too tightly defined since that could unnecessarily constrain the organization.

The vision must be both desirable and achievable. The organization as a whole should be comfortable with the direction it is to take, and should be sufficiently motivated and energized by the possibilities it presents.

A successful vision should be challenging but not so ambitious or grandiose that it overstretches the organization's resources. It should also not involve taking risks that could result in severe detriment or long-term harm to the organization.

Once the vision team has chosen their desired vision, this may need to be taken to the board for final approval before it is communicated to the rest of the organization.

COMMUNICATING THE VISION

5. Decide on a communication strategy

The way the vision is communicated may have a significant impact on how easily it is accepted by the wider organization. The members of the vision team will have been living with their ideas and concepts for quite some time, so they may not be capable of distancing themselves from it so that they can see it through other people's eyes.

Employees will primarily want to know how a new vision for the organization will change the way in which they work. In addition, will there be any implications for the organization's relationships with its customers? Only after they have absorbed the impact on their day-to-day activities will staff be able to take on board any more cerebral messages wrapped up in the vision, about broader purpose or aspirations. It is therefore vital that front-line managers are involved in dissecting and disseminating the vision.

When choosing how and in what ways to communicate the vision, consider the following.

» Keep it simple – don't use jargon. Anything that is too complicated will be quickly forgotten.
» Use metaphors, analogies, and examples to describe the vision, rather than dry prose. Draw a vivid word picture of what the organization will look like when it achieves its vision.
» Remind people of what the organization has achieved in the past, to tap into their sense of pride.
» Contrast the vision of where you want to take the organization with its current position and context. If the organization is in difficulties,

remind employees of the problems that might arise if nothing is changed.

» Don't choose only one form of communication – the more you reinforce the message, the more it will be understood and remembered. You could hold mass meetings or focus on smaller groups, and you may want to employ video or other visual forms of communication in addition to memos and newsletters.

» Make sure that all forms of communication are consistent, otherwise the credibility of the message will be undermined.

» Remember that communication of a vision is not a once-and-for-all event; it should be continuous and it should proceed at a pace that ensures that people understand and accept where the organization is headed.

Communication of a vision is not just to staff but also to investors, customers, suppliers, and possibly the wider community. Similar principles apply as for communicating with staff, except that information conveyed to stakeholders is of necessity somewhat more formal.

6. Ensure that management behavior is consistent

It is all very well communicating the vision in words and pictures, in formal speeches and informal communications, but even the best-constructed communication strategy will be defeated if those at the top of the organization don't lead by example. Senior managers must be seen to behave in ways that are consistent with the vision.

Coherence among the board is necessary for a vision to be implemented successfully. It is up to the CEO to ensure that all board members are committed to the vision and determined to make progress towards it. It is also for the CEO to decide and make plain what sanctions will be levied against any senior manager who steps out of line.

7. Establish feedback mechanisms

Two-way communication is always more powerful than one-way messages, so it is important to establish opportunities for employees to give their feedback on the content and performance of the vision.

Set up mechanisms to allow employees to exchange ideas among themselves and with managers. To obtain the maximum amount of information, these should not involve too much effort on the part of employees, and there should be no suspicion of monitoring or coercion.

Possibilities for feedback can be low- or high-tech. They include suggestion boxes, employee surveys, online bulletin boards or in-house communities, noticeboards or graffiti walls, staff meetings, and letters to the company newsletter.

In addition, consider whether it would be valuable to obtain feedback from your customers, suppliers, or other stakeholders on the content of the vision and the organization's progress towards it.

IMPLEMENTING THE VISION

8. Allocate the necessary resources to make the vision happen

A vision is not mere words but must be translated into action. However, don't move more quickly than the organization can cope with. At times you may need to create momentum for the vision by making some changes quickly, but at others you may want to proceed very slowly and ensure that at each stage you have the greatest possible buy-in from managers and staff.

As part of their commitment to the vision, members of the board should be prepared to provide sufficient resources for it to be implemented effectively. Any skimping or holding back in this area will undermine all other efforts.

Resources obviously do not only include financial resources but also sufficient staff and physical resources, such as equipment and facilities. As part of vision planning, these need to be factored in to the organization's budgeting process and made available as and when necessary.

9. Reward behavior consistent with the vision

In the same way that managers are expected to behave in ways that are consistent with the vision, employees should be clear about what their role is and any changes that they need to make in their day-to-day behavior. One way of ensuring that this happens is to make the vision the yardstick against which everything else is measured.

Behavior that is consistent with the vision should be publicly rewarded. This could be as part of a performance management or bonus system, if applicable, or more informally with incentives such as departmental celebrations, vouchers, away-days, or whatever fits with the company culture.

The possibility of sanctions for behavior that runs counter to the vision must also be considered and a decision made that applies throughout the organization. Again, managers must be seen to live out the vision in the same way as staff are expected to do.

MAINTAINING THE VISION

10. Check periodically that the vision still holds true

The vision should be flexible enough in the first place that it can encompass minor changes in direction or fields of business. Therefore it should rarely require revisiting. Continual changes of direction are a danger signal for the organization.

Nevertheless, while a vision is intended to be for the long term, it is not set in stone and does need to be reviewed occasionally, at intervals that are suitable for the organization, its activities, and its environment. The purpose of the review is to check how much progress has been made towards the vision, and that it is still applicable to the organization's current situation.

Think about the areas of business in which the organization is involved. Are they all consistent with the vision? Have there been any developments in the environment or in technology, for example, that present opportunities that are just too good to miss?

Because vision also involves an element of passion and commitment, it is also worth asking whether the organization is still doing what it wants to do. If people no longer feel good about the organization and the direction it is taking, it may be time for a reassessment of the vision.

Frequently Asked Questions (FAQs)

Q1: What is a vision?

A: See Chapter 2.

Q2: Is a vision the same as a mission statement?

A: See Chapter 2.

Q3: How has the Internet affected a company's need for a vision?

A: See Chapter 4.

Q4: What kind of vision do you need for e-business?

A: See Chapter 4.

Q5: What additional issues do global companies need to take into account?

A: See Chapter 5.

Q6: How can you transform an organization with a vision?

A: See Chapter 6.

Q7: Are there any pitfalls inherent in having a vision?

A: See Chapter 6.

Q8: Does a vision have to be in writing?

A: See Chapter 6.

Q9: How does a company visualize alternative futures?

A: See Chapter 8.

Q10: What do I do to develop a vision for my company?

A: See Chapter 10.

Acknowledgments

I would like to thank all those who have talked to me and given me information about their companies and their experiences. In particular, thanks are due to Linda Armantrout, Judith von Gordon-Weichelt of Boehringer Ingelheim GmbH, Steve Hoffmann of Agilent Technologies, Inc., Richard Reed of Innocent Ltd and Sid Scott of Woodward Communications, Inc.

Personal thanks go to Jon Lansdell, Kate Santon, and Sue Hunter for continual encouragement and acting as sounding boards; to my parents and their partners, Janet and Jim, Frank and Alison, for always being there; to my daughters, Jasmine and Cassie, for understanding closed doors and late dinners, and for believing that their mum's the best; and to Jack, for the kind of support that only he can give.

About the Author

Sally Lansdell is a writer and editor specializing in business and management. She had extensive experience in industry and also spent five years as a researcher for the Ashridge Strategic Management Centre, where she co-wrote Economist Intelligence Unit report "Do You Need a Mission Statement?" with Andrew Campbell.

Index

blues singer. In 1921, Teagarden joined the Houston band called Peck Kelley's Bad Boys, named after its pianist-leader, a man Teagarden compared to Art Tatum. (Kelley wasn't recorded until 1957, and those tapes, first issued in 1983, reveal him to be, not another Tatum, but a skillful stride and swing player with an original style.) In 1927 Teagarden went with a band led by Doc Ross to New York, where he stayed, often sitting in with Fletcher Henderson or other black bands: "You couldn't keep Jack out of Harlem," said Coleman Hawkins. It was in Harlem that Teagarden befriended the equally forward-looking trombonist Jimmy Harrison.

A good example of Teagarden's style—it seemed to emerge full-blown and remained intact throughout his career—is his opening blues solo on Louis Armstrong's "Knockin' a Jug" (1929). Guitarist Eddie Lang contributes another of his remarkable accompaniments. (See music example.)

Teagarden's warm, burry tone and easy fluency are immediately attractive, and one should note the way he builds this two-chorus solo. The crux here is the beginning of the second chorus. Teagarden slides upward in a gesture that creates a surprising momentum, sustained by drummer Kaiser Marshall, who chooses this moment to switch to brushes. Teagarden doesn't slide between notes as much as many of his contemporary trombonists, but when he does, as going into the ninth measure of the second solo chorus, he rips upward in a distinctive manner. He uses a terminal vibrato, one which starts to shake or vibrate only after it's been held for a bit, as did Armstrong. The result is a naturally voice-like sound.

A typically charming example of his singing is the 1929 "Basin St. Blues" mentioned above. Two years later he would remake this number with Nichols in a larger group called the Charleston Chasers. It included clarinetist Benny Goodman, drummer Gene Krupa and Glenn Miller. He would introduce the number with the words, "Won't you come along with me?," which became identified with the song.

Goodman's main impact would come, of course, later, but he wasn't a novice in 1931. Like the Dorsey brothers and Glenn Miller, Goodman was in the late twenties playing in studios and working out his own kind of jazz. His apprenticeship was served in his native Chicago, where white musicians were developing a post-New Orleans manner. Playing in the shadow of King Oliver, young players such as cornetists Muggsy Spanier and Jimmy McPartland, tenor saxophonist Bud Freeman, and guitarist Eddie Condon, all of whom would become prominent in the thirties, were trying a gutsier approach to the music. We can hear something of this playing in "Nobody's Sweetheart," recorded by McKenzie's and Condon's Chicagoans in 1927. Over the strong bass of Jim Lannigan, clarinetist Frank Teschemacher takes a solo, wild in conception and tone, and the group, over the drumming of Gene Krupa, gradually works up to a climax full of what Mezz Mezzrow called "jumping joy." A year later, in 1928, the 19-year-old Benny Goodman recorded a brash "That's A Plenty" that underscored the influences of Teschemacher and Jimmie Noone.

In 1928, one could hear in Chicago an almost bewildering array of music,

Example 7-6.
Jack Teagarden's solo on "Knockin' a Jug." This record has been issued in the unusual key of A major. The guitar staff includes highlights only.

from the Dodds brothers to "spasm" bands—whose soloists were often playing kazoos and washboards—from Earl Hines's elegant piano in Jimmy Noone's group to the beginnings of a blues style called boogie-woogie: Clarence "Pinetop" Smith recorded his "Pinetop's Boogie Woogie" there in 1928. Chicago was jumping, and yet the music was moving inexorably eastward to New York, and moving just as inexorably in style towards the swing that dominated the thirties. It was in New York that Bessie Smith was singing of her changing her "lock and key," that Paul Whiteman was recording his hot numbers and popular tunes, that the young Duke Ellington was beginning his career, competing with now forgotten bands led by Charlie Johnson, Fess Williams, or Lloyd Scott.

By the end of the decade, the various styles of small group jazz were jostling side by side with big bands playing early swing. Guitarist Eddie Lang and violinist Joe Venuti, who, like Nichols, made their livings in radio studios and dance bands, joined together in the studios to record an early kind of chamber jazz, including some duets. With a larger group that featured Benny Goodman and Jack Teagarden, they played in 1931 a hot, aggressive style on one of their most admired recordings. The number was "Farewell Blues," and it was the old New Orleans Rhythm Kings piece from 1922. After the ensemble comes a series of infectious solos. Goodman still plays with the woody, even gritty tone he learned from New Orleans clarinetists. Venuti, who would continue to play in his hard-driving, yet perfectly controlled style into the seventies, enters with a series of double-stops, plays a see-sawing phrase, and ends, in a sudden hush, on a harmonic note, a high F barely stated. After fine solos by Teagarden and his brother, trumpeter Charlie Teagarden, the piece ends with riffs by the band which foretell the swing arrangements soon to be nationally known.

HARLEM STRIDE PIANO

Extensions of New Orleans jazz, then, were being played by a wide variety of New York-based musicians. But New York's black community in Harlem had its own jazz tradition as well. It too developed out of ragtime, and its standard-bearers were pianists, "ticklers" such as James P. Johnson, Willie "the Lion" Smith, Luckey Roberts, unknowns such as a man called Abba Labba and world-famous figures such as Fats Waller. Their piano-playing style was called stride, and it was the first, and main, influence on the piano playing of Art Tatum and Duke Ellington.

Stride developed seamlessly out of an earlier generation of flashy ragtime players all along the East coast. One of the best known was Eubie Blake (1883-1983), who was born in Baltimore. "In my time," he said, "it was all very competitive. You always looked to compose things to be built on tricks that nobody else but you could do. That's why so many things that I composed didn't even have names until much later . . . I was up against *real* piano players, so I had to depend on my tricks if I was gonna cut *them*. Those *tricks* became my rags" (Al Rose, *Eubie Blake*, p. 43). As heard beginning in 1917 on piano rolls—paper rolls cut for player pianos—and on recordings, Blake's tricks are impressive. Significantly, Blake's performances leave room for improvisation, which may be heard by comparing Blake's piano roll of his "Charleston Rag" with his other recordings of the same piece. No two performances are exactly alike.

Blake, later the composer of hit songs such as "I'm Just Wild About Harry" and "Memories of You," began his professional career playing ragtime and popular tunes at rent parties and in sporting houses (brothels). A rent party was originally, as the name implies, a means for some urban apartment dwellers to find the money to pay their rent. They would cook up some food, make up or buy some liquor, hire a piano player and have a party for which they would charge admission. Later, some of these parties became a regular occurrence. Some hosts and hostesses even printed up cards advertising their parties. Sometimes more than one pianist would show up, and a job would turn into a jam session, even a "cutting" session. Piano playing was, as Blake said, an informal but also a highly competitive business, where a pianist would sit down to play, only to be challenged and sometimes driven off by the other pianists in the house.

Such players were the aristocrats of jazz, their clothes as elegant as their playing, their very entrances into the clubs in which they played practiced. Duke Ellington once hired a man to precede him exclaiming to everyone concerned, "Did you hear? Duke Ellington's coming!" It was no wonder that East Coast pianists developed unusual skills. Born in New Brunswick, New Jersey, in 1894 and nicknamed the "father of stride," James P. Johnson explained the relative virtuosity of his style and that of other Harlem pianists: "New York developed the orchestral piano—full, round, big, widespread chords and tenths—a heavy bass moving against the right hand. The other boys from the South and West at that time played in smaller dimensions—like thirds played in unison. We wouldn't dare do that because the public was used to better playing" (Tom Davin, "Conversations with James P. Johnson," *Jazz Review* 1959). As early as the second decade of the century, a Harlem tickler would be called upon to play a vast repertoire in all the keys with virtuosic grace (Willie "the Lion" Smith, a Johnson contemporary, said he knew over 500 songs.). And many of the best of these pianists became important composers, producing jazz and ragtime tunes, classical-oriented longer works and even Broadway shows.

The style called "stride" was named for its left-hand figures, with their characteristic "oom-pah" sound, made by striking a single note low in the bass on the first and third beats of a measure—the "oom"—and filling in with a chord in midrange on beats two and four. This effect is similar to the left hand in ragtime, but there are important differences: Greater virtuosity was expected of stride players, and the beat of stride was subtly swinging. Pianist Dick Wellstood has written, "It is possible to play an otherwise impeccable stride bass and ruin it by playing inappropriate right hand patterns. By pulling and tugging at the rhythms of the left, the right hand provides the swing" (Dick Wellstood,

James P. Johnson around 1940. (Courtesy Rutgers
Institute of Jazz Studies)

notes to *Donald Lambert: Harlem Stride Classics*, Pumpkin 104). The pianists would
sometimes vary the "oom-pah" with walking figures, or strummed chords as
James P. Johnson does on "Jingles," and return to the characteristic stride on
shouting out-choruses. Their right hands played looser, often more vocal figures
and melodies than older ragtime players, who tended to depend on broken
(arpeggiated) chords in strict rhythm. Stride pianists worked out, especially on
fast pieces, certain set patterns, but they also were known for improvising, for
being able to wring almost endless variations on popular tunes, blues or their
own compositions. In cutting contests stride pianists were famous for being able
to play all night and into the next day. Still, the most influential of their recorded
compositions, like Johnson's "Carolina Shout," were carefully constructed for
variety and an effective climax. They are unified, but also exuberant, outgoing,
full of humor and zest.

James P. Johnson recorded "Carolina Shout" on October 18, 1921, after
having recorded it as a piano roll in 1918. (The piano roll of "Carolina Shout"
was a definitive influence on the young Duke Ellington, who learned to play the
piece by copying the fingerings on his player piano.) The 1921 performance
(SCCJ) contains eight 16-bar sections, the first five in the key of G and the last

three in C. The final phrases of all eight choruses are similar: They serve to "wrap up" each individual chorus, but also help to unify the whole, as we come to expect the rhythms and bass lines that complete the chorus. The left-hand part is very tricky, in some places sustaining an "oom-pah" pattern – in which the "oom" is a low note, and the "pah" a chord played above it – and at others varying the figure to something like: "oom-pah, oom-oom-pah, oom-pah-oom." (See music example.)

Example 7–7.
James P. Johnson, "Carolina Shout" (1918), first eight measures of second section as performed on a recording of August 15, 1944. The left hand is the same as the 1921 version described in the text; the right hand improvises.

"Carolina Shout" is not a ragtime piece: It is rather a set of variations on one chord progression, and doesn't contain a contrasting theme, or interludes, as do rags. The name "Carolina Shout" refers to the ring shout, an African-derived dance and music, originally religious, that Johnson observed his mother perform when he was a child. Originally a circle dance in which the dancers make short shuffling steps, the shouts that James P. Johnson would have observed, were, it is likely, dances accompanied by "short repeated refrains which revolve around equally short melodic statements" (Scott Brown, *James P. Johnson*, p. 21). Johnson used this call and response pattern in the seventh chorus. He also had the experience of playing for dancers from the deep South who still remembered the traditions. As Willie "the Lion" Smith put it, "Shouts are stride piano – when James P., Fats [Waller], and I would get a romp-down shout going, that was playing rocky, just like the Baptist people sing. You don't just play a chord to that – you got to move it and the piano." (*Music on My Mind*, p. 83).

In 1927, Johnson recorded "Snowy Morning Blues" (JP), like "Carolina Shout" a set of variations on a chord progression. It is not technically a blues, but rather a 16-bar form divided into 8 and 8. It has a kind of noble sadness that was one of Johnson's characteristic moods. Johnson's flexibility is heard in his series of accompaniments to singers such as Ethel Waters and Bessie Smith. One hears his cheerful striding in Smith's vaudeville-like "Lock and Key," and in the Waters number, "Guess Who's in Town," but he sounds appropriately ominous on Smith's classic "Backwater Blues," with his stormy rolled chords and tremolos.

By the mid-twenties, Johnson was well known as a composer of songs such as the flapper's favorite, "The Charleston," and also of love songs such as "If I Could Be With You (One Hour Tonight)." Following the lead of Eubie Blake, whose all-black show "Shuffle Along" was the Broadway hit of 1921, Johnson wrote the revue "Runnin' Wild" in 1923. By the end of the decade, he seemed more interested in composing classical-oriented works based on folk themes, such as "Yamekraw" (a "Negro Rhapsody"), than in playing in jazz bands. "Yamekraw" was premiered auspiciously at Carnegie Hall in 1928 with W.C. Handy conducting and Fats Waller at the piano, and was dramatized in a short film. But Johnson lived in relative obscurity in the thirties, when he more or less retired to Queens in New York City.

He reemerged in 1939, and, despite a series of strokes, made some notable recordings throughout the forties that proved he could adapt his basically orchestral style to the demands of swing music. One of his best recordings from 1939 is the "Liza" he recorded for Columbia. Again he creates a series of variations, some highly technical, on the chord progression. By varying his techniques, he makes each chorus virtually a separate little piece, creating a structure that resembles the classical idea of variation more than does most jazz. In 1943, Johnson recorded the solo number "Carolina Balmoral," improvising 17 inventive choruses on a 16-bar folk dance. The next year he led a date for Blue Note, making in the company of swing tenor Ben Webster and drummer Sid Catlett at least one masterpiece, "After You've Gone." Catlett accompanies Johnson's solo chorus with a snug, pushing rhythm: Johnson sounds serenely imperturbable. He suffered a severe stroke in 1951 and remained an invalid until his death four years later. Johnson had written scores of tunes and shows, an opera, symphony and rhapsodies. On February 21, 1992, some of his orchestral works were performed again, at Lincoln Center. But he remains known, quite rightly, as "the Father of Stride Piano."

His musical children were many and various. One actual protégé was Fats Waller, a brilliant stride pianist and born entertainer whose singing and inspired clowning made him more famous than his mentor. Waller didn't merely sing popular tunes. He seemed to explode them with witty asides and sarcastic phrasing. His very voice seemed to mug on tunes such as the hilarious "Your Feet's Too Big," which he paraphrases, singing "Your pedal extremities are colossal!" He was the composer of "Ain't Misbehavin'," "Honeysuckle Rose," "Jitterbug Waltz" and scores of other tunes, often with lyricist Andy Razaf, and many place Waller in the company of Irving Berlin and other top songwriters. Around 1918, when Waller was 14, he was presented to James P. Johnson as a promising pianist. He played for Johnson the composer's "Carolina Shout," which Waller had learned from the piano roll. Johnson tutored and encouraged him, and eventually introduced him to other pianists and to the nightclub scene. Willie the Lion remembered first seeing Waller as an ungainly boy, badly dressed, following Johnson around: Smith nicknamed him "Filthy." Before he met Johnson, Waller was largely self-taught. After an apprenticeship playing organ in silent movie theaters, and after several years of playing under the tutelage of James P., Waller made his first recordings in 1922. He would record frequently until his death on a westbound train in December of 1943. Not as form conscious as James P. Johnson, but technically impressive and with an even prettier touch, Waller favored lusher chords, and played with a rhythmic exuberance that seemed perfectly to match his ebullient personality. He was a brilliant parodist even as a pianist. His solo version of "Honeysuckle Rose" includes passages of whimsical daintiness: He sounds like an elephant dancing on tiptoes.

Several of his best solo recordings were made in 1929. These include his own "Handful of Keys," recorded on March 1. An aggressive stride showpiece played at a fast tempo, it has two themes, each 32 bars long. After a functional introduction, it enters the basic theme, with its AABA format. The second chorus is quite similar to the first, except that it is played an octave higher. The third begins with a brief transition to a new key—a fourth higher, as in

Fats Waller at home with his Steinway, Harlem, 1924. (Courtesy Rutgers Institute of Jazz Studies)

rags—and a new theme, a 32-bar ABAC, played once rather freely. Then immediately Waller returns to the first theme for two final choruses, the last including the most wide-ranging improvisation.

The title of "Numb Fumblin'," recorded the same day, is an obvious joke based on a well known fact: Waller was an astonishingly heavy drinker, but never sounded as if he were fumbling. Certainly there's no sign of intoxication in the gorgeous, delicate playing of this slow 12-bar blues which, as we have noted of other blues, does not have a theme per se but rather is freely improvised from the opening lick in the right hand. There's remarkable variety in Waller's approach to the piano here. The first two choruses contrast delicate right-hand runs with a lusher right hand balanced dynamically with unusual care. The third chorus is more percussive, while the fourth is stride, with mostly chords being played in both hands. The fifth introduces a rocking boogie-woogie figure, while the sixth is more virtuosically florid, showing off not only Waller's speed but his pearly tone. Then there is a gentle coda, an unusual end to this unusually romantic blues.

EARL HINES

James P. Johnson, Fats Waller, Willie "the Lion" Smith, were part of a tight nucleus of pianists. The other most important jazz pianist to emerge in the twenties, also an Easterner—he was born around Pittsburgh in 1903—was more of a maverick. We have already mentioned Earl Hines's work with Louis Armstrong. Hines got his start with the Pittsburgh band of male singer Lois Deppe, with whom he recorded in 1923. One of Hines's trademarks, his use of right hand octaves to play the melody, was his answer to the problem of making himself heard over the Deppe band: "My style was recognized as unusual, but the band was so large that I had to figure out a way to be heard, because they were constantly drowning me out. So I started to use the octaves, and with octaves I could cut through the sound of the band" (Stanley Dance, *The World of Earl Hines*, p. 26). Later Hines's playing would be called "trumpet style," not just because he used octaves—a commonplace in piano music—but because his improvised lines sounded less orchestral than horn-like in their direction, accenting, and brightness. Hines explained: "Now when people talk of my 'trumpet style,' I think they usually mean when I play phrases . . . like a trumpet player would play, but I used tremolo to give an effect like his vibrato, too. I'd reduce the weight of the note and use the sustaining pedal as the sound of the note thinned out" (*The World of Earl Hines*, p. 52).

Hines's first recording, "Congaine," from November 3, 1923, is his own 32-bar ABAC piece played by a group called Deppe's Serenaders. It includes some muddily recorded ensemble choruses, and a 32-bar solo by Hines played with a flashy showiness that probably owed something to James P. Johnson. His mid-chorus break employs a standard ragtime lick that Lil Hardin, Mary Lou

Williams and others used. But it is followed by several moments where Hines breaks up the left-hand bass in ways that nobody else did at that time. The last four measures are especially exciting, suggesting almost a half time effect.

Here and in his introduction and brief solo on "Dear Old Southland," also recorded with Deppe, Hines is already playing octaves in his right hand to better project the melody, and he has a brassy sound all his own. On the "Southland" solo, he uses a James P. Johnson left-hand pattern, similar to the example given earlier, that breaks up the "oom-pah" pattern.

But it is Hines's work with Armstrong in 1928, and his solo recordings from the same year, that displayed fully his distinctive style. That style was marked by his generally percussive touch, and by a rough quality, which was emphasized by his use of highly dissonant chords. His dazzling runs were unique in that they were not composed of simple repeated patterns, and he had an extremely active left hand that would interact intriguingly with his right. The result was a startling original sound, full of surprises, played with an almost jolting aggressiveness. He was also adventurous: Other pianists loved to watch him play a series of flamboyant runs that seemed to leave him stranded. At the last second, he would vault all his self-created obstacles and end up just where he wanted to be.

Hines recorded some extraordinary piano solos in December 1928 for OKeh and for QRS. Hines is in full flower here. He introduces and breaks stride rhythms at will, and introduces turbulent runs and unexpected dissonances in performances that are notable nonetheless for their constant swing. These

Earl Hines, Boston, early 1970's. (Photo by Michael Ullman)

performances include his well-known composition, "A Monday Date," a 32-bar AABA piece which he begins in the OKeh version in a stride style modified in the first chorus by some slides and fills in the left hand. The second chorus of the OKeh recording is actually an interlude, an example, like that in Armstrong's "Potato Head Blues," of a musician playing the introduction after the first chorus, that is designed to give variety to a string of choruses. The third chorus mixes a stride bass with "walking" tenths (tenths moved up and down by steps), a technique that Waller also used. The fourth, even more unpredictable chorus, begins with something like an oom-oom-pah routine, and includes a bridge with one of his distinctive, out-of-left-field runs, and it leads to an A section in which the left hand stops the rhythm. At least it seems to: Hines sounds as if he has lost the beat, but he is absolutely accurate. The rest of the performance is just as notable. In the exuberant fifth chorus (in the second A), the left hand has a chromatic run that one would have expected the right hand to play. In the sixth chorus, Hines accompanies his right hand with stabbing offbeat chords in a manner that would during the forties be called "comping."

He was 20 years ahead of his time with this technique. But he got even better with age. From December 1928 through 1947, he led a successful big band in Chicago which recorded such delightful Hines features as "Piano Man." Then he joined the Louis Armstrong All Stars from 1948 through 1951. In the fifties he performed some obscure Dixieland jobs and was more or less ignored. Then Hines returned in the sixties and seventies, making dozens of solo recordings of blues and ballads and originals. Taking advantage of the long-playing record, he would create wildly dissonant introductions, and slowly work into masterful free improvisations, sometimes without even stating the theme. One such example, and there were many, is the eleven minute "Deep Forest" from 1974 (on Halcyon 120): Near the end Hines plays a passage over a pedal point that might have come from McCoy Tyner or other pianists who matured in the sixties. (There is more on Hines in Chapter 9.)

By the end of the twenties there was, then, a covey of accomplished Eastern pianists connected with the stride school, pianists whose effect on jazz and show business was profound. In the South and Midwest, blues and boogie-woogie pianists were heard regularly, but virtuoso stride was centered in Harlem. It was a style that had to be modified when pianists were placed, as they were more and more often in the thirties, in the position of supporting a band. But it is notable that the two exemplary band leaders, Duke Ellington and Count Basie, came out of stride. Ellington memorized "Carolina Shout" as a youngster and later followed James P. Johnson around Harlem. When still a beginning pianist, Basie pressed Fats Waller for lessons and advice. And the outstanding virtuoso in jazz piano, Art Tatum, was an extension, still astonishing, of the school of which James P. Johnson was the father.

8 Duke Ellington

Edward Kennedy Ellington was born in Washington on April 29, 1899 and died, world-renowned, 75 years later. His achievements are astonishing, in their richness and importance to American music, in their influence and in their sheer bulk. He is said to have composed, wholly or in part, as many as 1000 pieces. He composed dozens of popular songs, including "Sophisticated Lady" and "In a Sentimental Mood," and he had his hand in the composition of others, such as "Mood Indigo" and "I'm Beginning to See the Light." But the fact remains that Ellington would be the major jazz composer if he had never written a popular song. Because with Ellington, it is not merely a single line of melody here or a pretty turn of phrase there that counts, but a constant and consistent flow of distinctive ideas, perfectly realized and carefully thought out.

He played piano effectively, even brilliantly, but his main instrument, as has often been said, was his band. He was a masterful orchestrator. The sounds of his band were unique: full-bodied, sumptuous, mysterious, varied in texture and effect. He broke all the rules—perhaps he was merely unconcerned with them—introducing dissonance to an unparalleled degree in jazz. Ellington called his individual musicians his "sound identities," and he kept in mind their strengths and limitations. He explained his technique in his autobiography, the aptly titled *Music Is My Mistress*: "You take a guy using a thing like [trombonist] Charlie Irvis did: you had limitations on how far he could go with it before it became ugly or uninteresting. The same applied with Tricky [trombonist Tricky Sam Nanton] at the top of the horn. You take the limitations on how many notes you can make effectively, and you have a little problem with your writing. In other words, you have to write to fit the limitations. But any time you have a problem you have an opportunity" (p. 108).

He liked to place those sound identities in unusual relations with one another. As Barney Bigard wrote, "He had a distinctive touch to everything. He would take my clarinet part and make the trombone play it. He had the whole front section in different keys for some measures. Anything you like to name" (*With Louis and the Duke*, p. 62). Ellington might take the reed section and assign the top note to a tenor saxophone rather than to the usual alto and place Harry Carney's baritone saxophone somewhere in the middle rather than on the bottom. His greatest effects sometimes came from the simplest means.

Yet his music was challenging. On his first night with the band, in the Cotton Club in 1928, Bigard was perplexed: "I remember the weird chords that would come in behind us. I wasn't used to that kind of chording at all, but the more I played with them, the more accustomed my ear got to it all. I used to go to Duke in the intermission and say, 'Those chords behind me on such-and-such a number: they just don't sound right to me.' He would sit right down and show me what he was doing" (p. 47). In 1943 Dizzy Gillespie played with the Ellington band for a few weeks, and even so astute a musician as he said: "To play with Duke you have to forget everything you know" (Dizzy Gillespie, *To Be or Not to Bop*, p. 184).

Ellington virtually invented the instrumental jazz ballad, or what Gunther Schuller has called "mood pieces," such as the sublime "Creole Love Call" and "Mood Indigo." He is responsible for less obvious innovations as well, such as the three trombone choir which he began to use in the thirties. Ellington wrote the perfect piece for this section, the virtuosic "Slippery Horn." He loved

Duke Ellington, early 1940's, with (from left) Ray Nance, Rex Stewart, "Tricky" Sam Nanton, Harry Carney, Johnny Hodges, and drummer Sonny Greer. (Courtesy Rutgers Institute of Jazz Studies)

musical color, and he kept certain textures in his arrangements, the clarinet trio, for instance, long after the fashion for them had died out. He seemed to pay particular attention to the bass, hiring throughout his career a series of forward-looking bassists—from New Orleans bassist Wellman Braud to modernists Jimmy Blanton, Oscar Pettiford and Charles Mingus (for the beginning of 1953)—who would allow him to use the bass as one of the versatile voices of the orchestra. In 1935 Ellington hired bassist Billy Taylor (not the pianist), without letting go of Braud, and the band performed and recorded with two bassists for several months! Nor should we neglect Ellington's sense of humor, the humor that prompted him to write in 1959 the delightful "Malletoba Spank" for his band and nine percussionists, that was responsible for his eccentric titles or that prompted his occasional parodies of earlier styles or other bands, such as the first half of "Controversial Suite." (Its subtitle was "Before My Time," another joke: Ellington pretended he was younger than he was.)

He was nonetheless a serious musician who knew the importance of his music. He also knew where his inspiration came from. In 1931 Ellington wrote, perhaps to counter critics who compared him to classical impressionists Delius and Ravel: "My men and my race are the inspiration of my work. I try to catch the character and mood and feeling of my people. The music of my race is something more than the American idiom. It is the result of our transplantation to American soil and was our reaction, in plantation days, to the life we lived. What we could not say openly we expressed in music. The characteristic, melancholic music of my race has been forged from the very white heat of our sorrows and from our gropings. I think the music of my race is something that is going to live, something which posterity will honor in a higher sense than merely that of the music of the ballroom." Implicit in this statement are political attitudes normally associated with the modern generations of jazz artists. Ellington's belief that jazz should be, or could be, a concert music is evident in his 1935 film, "Symphony in Black," in which he appears composing at the piano and conducting his band. His titles, from "Black Beauty" to "Black, Brown and Beige" anticipate by many years the "black is beautiful" message of the sixties.

Ellington liked to describe himself as launched at birth into the lap of luxury before an adoring audience, his family. His father was a butler for a wealthy Washington family and is said to have sometimes catered at the White House. His mother stayed home and babied Edward. When he was four, Ellington would write, he once slipped and cut his finger, which turned into an emergency for the family. When he got pneumonia, his mother called two doctors, and could hardly be restrained from bringing in more. Brought up in a middle class family, Ellington took piano lessons from a woman prophetically named Mrs. Clinkscales. He preferred painting. He didn't become seriously interested in music until his early teens, when he heard a pianist named Harvey Brooks and learned James P. Johnson's "Carolina Shout" from the piano roll. Later he would play "Carolina Shout" for its composer.

During an illness, Ellington wrote two pieces: "Soda Fountain Rag" and "What You Gonna Do When the Bed Breaks Down?" He began his music career by playing these pieces at parties. Soon Ellington, though still toying with the idea of becoming a professional artist—he was offered a scholarship at an art school—had a small band. He had met some of the musicians who would be with him in the years to come, including saxophonist Otto Hardwick, and, more importantly, drummer Sonny Greer. Greer was born in New Jersey in 1895, but found himself in Washington in 1919, where he played with the Marie Lucas Orchestra at the Howard Theater. An experienced musician, he met Ellington that year and played a first job with him on March 20, 1919. He would stay with Ellington until 1951. Greer is primarily known as a colorist. In the thirties he would sit enthroned behind his drums, surrounded by gongs, tubular bells, blocks and even tympani. He was indeed full of ideas, and percolating effects, and he swung in his own way—Ellington called him "the world's best percussionist reactor." His energy kept things afloat.

In 1922, Ellington and Hardwick and trumpeter Arthur Whetsol followed Sonny Greer to New York City. Unable to make a living, they returned to Washington. A year later, they were back to stay, playing as a band under the leadership of banjo player Elmer Snowden. By February 1924, a coup of sorts took place and Snowden left the band. It has been suggested that Snowden was taking more than his share of the band's income. In *Music is My Mistress*, Ellington commented wryly: "Elmer Snowden was the businessman of the group, and eventually he got so good at business that he went his way" (p. 70). The leadership of the band may first have been offered to Greer. Reluctantly, Ellington took over. It now seems inevitable that he would: He was the only member of that early band who had an artistic vision, an idea of how the music should sound or could sound.

They made some test recordings for Victor in 1923 that were never issued. The first surviving recordings of the band, billed as "The Washingtonians," were made in November of 1924, when they were playing a long engagement at a small place called the Kentucky Club. (Later its name would be changed to the Hollywood Club.) The key pieces they made that day, "Choo Choo" and "Rainy Nights," reflect Ellington's background in ragtime and stride. They feature a Charleston beat and are built around several themes. They are also too cute to be of lasting interest.

Ellington's personality, and the personality of his band, was emerging. As a composer and arranger, he was largely self-taught, and at the very first, it seems, he was relatively conventional. Several musicians helped change that by bringing in the influence of New Orleans. In mid-1927 Ellington hired bassist Wellman Braud, who had grown up in the Crescent City. Before that, in 1926, he hired Sidney Bechet, whom he had first heard in Washington in 1923. "My first encounter with the New Orleans idiom came when I heard Sidney Bechet in my home town," Ellington wrote in *Music is My Mistress*. "I have never forgotten the power and imagination with which he played" (p. 417). And before that, back in

1923, he had replaced the sweet-toned trumpeter Arthur Whetsol with Bubber Miley, a native New Yorker who got his New Orleans sound from King Oliver. (Whetsol returned to the band in 1928 after it had expanded.) For a time Bechet and Miley were in the band together, and every night they would be featured in a cutting contest. Ellington said he learned from them that music should, or could, speak, that it should be sharply characterized and openly emotional: "*Call* was very important in that kind of music. Today, the music has grown up and become quite scholastic, but this was *au naturel,* close to the primitive, where people send messages in what they play, calling somebody, or making facts and emotions known" (p. 47). After Bechet's departure Ellington would hire another New Orleans clarinetist, Barney Bigard. Bechet had another crucial role in the Ellington band: He was alto saxophonist Johnny Hodges's idol and mentor. The influence of Bechet's playing, with its sweeping legato effects and grand glissandos and unabashed lyricism, transformed Hodges into Ellington's most famous soloist.

Miley's role was even more important. Born in South Carolina in 1903 and raised in New York, Miley was hired to replace trumpeter Johnny Dunn in Mamie Smith's band. He is said to be the trumpeter on some Mamie Smith recordings of 1921 and 1922. Reedman Garvin Bushell told Nat Hentoff about a week he and Miley spent listening to King Oliver in Chicago, presumably in 1921 when they were on tour with Mamie Smith. Touched by the band's blues-playing and expressive overall sound, "Bubber and I sat there with our mouths open" (Hentoff, "Garvin Bushell and New York Jazz in the 1920's," *Jazz Review,* February 1959).

Miley worked with the Washingtonians in September 1923, and he brought his gutsy trumpet style to the Ellington band, where he stayed, with occasional sabbaticals, until 1929. He installed the growl in the Ellington band. As Ellington recognized his importance immediately, Miley helped transform the group, known first for its sweet melodies, into an intriguing jazz band, with elegant arrangements designed to feature "primitive" sounds. As Duke's son Mercer Ellington opined, "The band was motivated around him and everything depended upon his being in it, not only because of his solo role, but because of the phrases he knew and because of what his knowledge contributed in the backgrounds" (Mercer Ellington, *Duke Ellington in Person,* p. 24).

The growling trumpet sound, and later, with the addition of Tricky Sam Nanton as trombonist, the growling trombone, became an identifying characteristic of the band's sound. When Miley left in 1929, eventually to die of tuberculosis, and was replaced by Cootie Williams, Williams gradually figured out that he should learn the growl as well, that that was what he was expected to do. Mercer, a trumpeter himself, has described the technique of the growl: "There are three basic elements in the growl: the sound of the horn, a guttural gargling in the throat, and the actual note that is hummed. The mouth has to be shaped to make the different vowel sounds, and above the singing from the throat, manipulation of the plunger adds the *wa-wa* accents that give the horn a language. I should add that in the Ellington tradition a straight mute is used *in* the horn besides the plunger outside, and this results in more pressure. Some players use only the plunger, and then the sound is usually coarser, less piercing, and not as well articulated" (*Duke Ellington in Person*, p. 25).

Miley provided the sound, and Ellington the context that made it significant. But even here Miley had something to add. Miley originated the key melodic phrases in the band's first distinctive recordings, "East St. Louis Toodle-Oo" (SCCJ) and "Black and Tan Fantasy." Both titles were recorded repeatedly in 1926 and 1927, as was another early masterpiece, "Creole Love Call." Ellington said that "Toodle-Oo" (or "Toodle-O" as it was sometimes spelt) referred to a broken, uneven walk—perhaps, he suggested, of an old man returning from work in the fields. (Mark Tucker's book on Ellington's early years has much to say on this and other matters.) The piece begins with a series of moaning saxophone chords, over which Miley enters with a speech-like first theme with wah-wah mute. (See music example.)

Example 8-1.
Duke Ellington and Bubber Miley, beginning of "East St. Louis Toodle-Oo" (Vocalion version, November 29, 1926). Banjo not shown, drums and piano inaudible. The accompaniment is played alone as an introduction, then Miley plays over it the second and third time for the first two A sections of the AABA theme. This is the second time, Miley's first entrance.

In the 1926 recording, this 32-bar theme is followed by a B section of 18 bars, dominated by Tricky Sam Nanton, and then by a return to the A section. Following this, two more versions of the B theme occurs, this time played by brass and then ensemble, and then a final return to the original theme. There is nothing startling about the scheme of the piece, but its dusky mood, its tense but understated main theme, the hard blues nature of the sound, are strikingly original. Ellington relocated or cut the ragtimey B section in later performances (two are on SCCJ), which points out another typically Ellingtonian practice: He never stopped tinkering with his arrangements, adjusting pieces to changes in personnel, situation or fashion, drastically reworking pieces that were sometimes 30 years old.

Miley solos ecstatically on "Black and Tan Fantasy," another jungle number. This one is a blues which Ellington ends with a reference to the most famous theme of Chopin's "Funeral March" sonata. The most startling aspect of the wonderful "Creole Love Call" is the result of its opening, which features the wordless vocal of Adelaide Hall floating above the band. She later improvises a solo, growling like another Tricky Sam Nanton. There is no other vocal like it.

At the end of 1927, Ellington got his big break. He only needed one. A violinist named Andy Preer had been leading a band at Harlem's Cotton Club. When he died, the club's managers offered King Oliver the job. It is difficult to imagine Oliver playing the shows, accompanying singers, tap dancers and chorus lines the way the Cotton Club demanded. Perhaps for that reason he held out for more money. The management held auditions, and Ellington auditioned and was hired. He always said that it was because the man who did the hiring was late and heard only Ellington's band. But Ellington was also the recommendation of Jimmy McHugh, a songwriter who was putting together the Cotton Club shows. Ellington opened on December 4, 1927 and thanks to the radio broadcasts that went out from the club, his band became famous nationwide. He would stay for most of the next five years. This is one of many instances in which radio exposure changed the career of a jazz artist.

Jim Haskins has described the shows: "Ellington's band usually led off with a show piece and played two or three numbers during the revue, almost always including their 'Harlem River Quiver' which they had recorded on the Victor label. The bulk of the show was written by Jimmy McHugh, although for part of it he had a partner, [lyricist] Dorothy Fields" (*The Cotton Club*, p. 47). Haskins also calls the Cotton Club a "peculiar institution." Peculiar it was. Situated in Harlem and featuring many of Harlem's greatest talents, it was a segregated club that catered to a white clientele and occasional privileged blacks. By the late twenties, Harlem was a fad, and many wealthy folk, entertainers and tourists would go to the Cotton Club to see what they considered primitive entertainment: The club was decorated like a plantation, and some of the skits involved sexually provocative dances performed in "African" attire. Owned by gangster Owney Madden, who took the place over from heavyweight champion Jack Johnson, the Cotton Club had a seating capacity of 700. It had had a grand opening in 1923. The club put on a two-hour show several times a night, and they would change that show twice a year. Haskins notes that at the Cotton Club, "Production was also important, and under [Dan] Healy's direction the Cotton Club became probably the first night club to feature actual miniature stage sets and elaborate lighting as well as spectacular costumes" (*The Cotton Club*, pp. 40–41).

Ellington's jungle music was perfect for this setting, but he had an immediate problem when he joined the club. He had been using six pieces at the Kentucky Club and suddenly needed at least 11. He had made some additions since the Kentucky Club: Baritone saxophonist Harry Carney had joined the band, offering his inimitable, broadly reedy sound—like that of Coleman Hawkins played on a larger horn. Ellington went after, and got, Barney Bigard from the King Oliver band who could play tenor, and soloed on clarinet in long, gracefully twisting lines, almost weightless, that Ellington exploited perfectly. In 1928, alto saxophonist Johnny Hodges joined the band. Then a fast, bold player, he had a big, buttery tone, and perfect control over pitch and volume. In later years, he could play a rocking blues or lush ballad with peerless grace. Hodges developed a readily identifiable technique and style and stance. A sleepy-eyed, cagey-looking man, he would stand, rocking backwards on his heels while with his perfect timing and sense of the dramatic, he would, in a technique perhaps learned from Sidney Bechet, slide upwards towards an accented note in an extended glissando. When he arrived, it was an event.

By February 1932, Ellington had a distinguished big band, with Hodges, Carney and Bigard on reeds; Tricky Sam Nanton, Juan Tizol and Lawrence Brown on trombones; Arthur Whetsol, Freddie Jenkins, and Cootie Williams on trumpets; and a rhythm section consisting of himself, guitarist Freddie Guy, bassist Wellman Braud, and Sonny Greer. Several of the newcomers deserve mention: Each one brought a special quality and new possibilities to the band, and Ellington would write to evoke those qualities. Juan Tizol from Puerto Rico played a valve trombone, an instrument with keys like a trumpet rather than a slide. He rarely improvised, but wrote hits such as "Caravan" and "Perdido." Lawrence Brown did solo: He had a large, languorous tone, and liked to play pretty tunes. He found his tone, he said, by trying to imitate a cello. He also showed off his speed and technique on such features as "The Sheik of Araby" (May 1932).

Cootie Williams, Bubber Miley's replacement, became as celebrated for his work with mutes as Miley himself. He would stay with Ellington until November 1940, when he left to join Benny Goodman. Then he led his own bands, big and small, and toured as a single, rejoining Ellington in 1962. He would stay with the band until 1975, a year after Duke's death.

The band not only grew in size, as did most bands in the late twenties, but in experience. At the Cotton Club, they played their own swing numbers, played the music of Jimmy McHugh, and did many of the accompaniments. Ellington was forced to learn to write show tunes of various types, and to push the latest dances. Ellington got to observe the best of his peoples' artistes, as he would call them, and no doubt he found their company stimulating. Gunther Schuller thinks the years at the Cotton Club were decisive musically: "There, by writing and experimenting with all manner of descriptive production and dance numbers, Ellington's inherent talent and imagination could develop properly." (It's interesting to note that modern classical composers were also liberated and inspired by working with choreography. They included Igor Stravinsky, Debussy, Ravel, and Aaron Copland).

By 1930 Ellington had begun a string of distinguished recordings, including the mysteriously haunting "Mood Indigo." Using different names for his group, Ellington recorded "Mood Indigo" several times for several labels within a matter of weeks. The famous theme is stated by trumpeter Arthur Whetsol, muted, accompanied by Barney Bigard's clarinet and the muted trombone of Tricky Sam Nanton. They sounded like one instrument. The scoring that proved so effective is shown in the example. (See music example.)

*At the very start of the record, the trombone misses this note.

Example 8-2.
"Mood Indigo" (1930, Okeh version), by Ellington, Irving Mills and "Barney" Albany Bigard. Wind parts, measures 1-4.

The band could also play fast numbers, such as the spirited "Ring Dem Bells," by Ellington and Irving Mills, also from 1930. This is a punchy, rushing swing number with a jaunty theme through which the band moves towards a group of wildly dissonant chords. It's notable for the use of the chimes that gives it its name—played by a man soon to be a band leader, Charlie Barnet—and for Hodges' luxurious solo.

By 1930, the band was a success, having been broadcast virtually nightly from the Cotton Club for three years. Ellington was already being considered a major composer: The comparisons with classical composers began in the early thirties. Sparked and promoted by a brilliant manager, Irving Mills, he played with a Ziegfield show in 1929, a show that was written by Gershwin. He appeared in two movies in this period: the all-black short film of 1929, "Black and Tan Fantasy" and in the blackface duo Amos and Andy's "Check and Double Check" (1930). In 1931, Ellington was famous enough to be invited for his first visit to the White House (James Lincoln Collier, *Duke Ellington*, p. 101).

The next year he introduced singer Ivie Anderson with a recording whose title became a watchword of the big band movement: "It Don't Mean a Thing (If It Ain't Got That Swing)." The full band accompanies Anderson, a lively, original singer, with an exemplary lightness: Even Harry Carney's baritone sax, filling in behind the singer, seems to sparkle. By the mid-thirties, Ellington had written for his band a distinctive book in every area of big band jazz, and the band was the unparalleled master of moody blues and ballads. Ellington's piano playing was becoming more and more distinctive: His unusual introductions, often percussive downward runs, were as identifiable as the incredibly rich reed section, colored by the blend of Harry Carney's baritone, Hodges's alto, and Bigard's clarinet. Ellington's arrangements were full of variety and lively insights, and yet they never sounded restless or feverish. He used the brass subtly, remembering throughout the swing era that trumpets could play softly.

The band made its first European tour in the summer of 1933: It was rapturously received. The band was also an economic success: An anonymous, but respectful, article in the magazine *Fortune* in August 1933 begins with the headline that the Ellington band was bringing in 250,000 dollars a year. No wonder it caught *Fortune's* attention. *Fortune* mentions that Ellington was at work at a five-part suite entitled "Africa," "The Slave Ship," "The Plantation," "Harlem," and that the last would be "a climactic restatement of the themes." Clearly Ellington was preparing, even in 1933, to break new ground, and he already knew that he would be trying to capture the history of black people in America in his music.

Ellington's beloved mother died in 1934. The next year he wrote the four-part "Reminiscing in Tempo," the first of his suites to be recorded. This piece extended over two 78 records, and its themes are developed and interrelated. But many critics found the very idea of a suite by a jazz band pretentious, and the response was disappointing. The two-part 1937 "Diminuendo in Blue and Crescendo in Blue" (SCCJ) was more successful. This is a blues based, one might say, on simple riffs. But Ellington takes the blues through four keys, allowing striking passages of dissonance along the way, and his riffs are more complex than those of any other band in the thirties. The number takes its title from its falling (diminuendo) and then rising (crescendo) volume. It begins with the full band, works its way down to just the rhythm section and then builds back up, an artificial structure that does not prevent the piece from swinging mightily.

Ellington's significant recordings of the thirties are too numerous to name, but we should mention "Sophisticated Lady," introduced in February 1933, "In a Sentimental Mood" from 1935, up-tempo swingers such as his versions of "Bugle Call Rag" from 1932 and 1933 and the impressionistic "Daybreak Express" (1933), with its robust evocation of a train at full throttle. Challenged by financial pressures and the competition from numerous other swing bands, Ellington made pop records, vocals and pieces celebrating the latest dances as well: "Skrontch" is one depressing example. But even the commercial Ellington was distinctive.

STRAYHORN, BLANTON AND WEBSTER JOIN THE BAND

The best was still to come. By the late thirties Ellington's band had swelled to what had become the standard sixteen people. He made two critical additions, which helped define a particularly productive period, from 1939 to 1941. In

Ben Webster at the 1964 World's Fair in Queens, New York City. (Courtesy Rutgers Institute of Jazz Studies)

autumn of 1939, he picked up a young bassist, Jimmy Blanton, and the next January, he hired tenor saxophonist Ben Webster. Webster, a veteran of groups led by Bennie Moten and Cab Calloway, came directly from the Teddy Wilson band.

Jimmy Blanton seemed to come out of nowhere. He was born in Tennessee in 1918 and by 1937 was playing a three-string bass with a band in St. Louis. Ellington found him at the Coronado Hotel Ballroom there. As Ellington said, "We didn't care about his experience. All we wanted was that sound, that beat, and those precision notes in the right places, so that we could float out on the great and adventurous sea of expectancy with his pulse and foundation behind us . . . He was a sensation" (*Music is My Mistress*, p. 164). Almost immediately Ellington began writing for Blanton, who had a precise, buoyant beat, a rich tone and who could play melodies with impressive speed and lyricism. Ellington would record a series of duets with this young phenomenon, but just as striking are the parts he opened up for Blanton in his band arrangements of 1940: Blanton helps state the theme of "Jack the Bear," shares the melody of a chorus of "Chloe" with Cootie Williams and is given a long stretch of melody in "Sepia Panorama."

In that number, a sensual mid-tempo piece, Blanton shares the first chorus, a 12-bar blues, with the wind sections. The innovative form of the piece alternates 8-bar sections with 12-bar blues choruses, as follows:

I.   Blues (band and bass solo)

II. 16-bar theme (two 8-bar phrases)

III. 8-bar passage (band and Harry Carney)

IV. Blues (piano and bass duet)

V.   Blues (Ben Webster solo)

Then a repeat of:

III. 8-bar passage (band and Harry Carney)

II. First half of 16-bar theme (8 bars)

I.   Blues (band and bass solo), plus 2 bars.

Like many of Ellington's pieces ("Koko," "Jack the Bear"), "Sepia Panorama" has an arch form, with a beginning that works up to various events, and then a return to a varied (in this case reversed) form of the beginning. Its highlights include a passage in which Blanton plays essentially a duet with Ellington, skipping skillfully around the delightfully spare piano part. What happens after that duet is the startling, breathy entrance, all coyness and innuendo but suggesting great power, of Ben Webster.

Less celebrated than Coleman Hawkins and Lester Young, Ben Webster seems their equal. He had a huge tone, which he sometimes brought down to a sensuous whisper. But he could also put a rasp and a growl into his sound, and he provided brief explosions in pieces like the small band "Linger Awhile," designed mainly to feature Rex Stewart's cornet. (Greer's drumming is marvelous on "Linger Awhile," when he accompanies Stewart's bouncy line with swishing brushes, then switches to sticks behind the tumultuous Webster.) Ellington wrote the up-tempo, angular, even boppish "Cotton Tail" (SCCJ) for Webster in 1940: Webster's thrilling solo, probably prepared in advance, became one of his most famous. Also in 1940, Webster was the main soloist on "All Too Soon," broke up the Latin feel of "Conga Brava," and, at dances, would be let loose to improvise ballads such as "Star Dust": The live, informal "Star Dust," recorded at a ballroom in Fargo, North Dakota on November 7, 1940, finds Webster building an exquisite solo over three choruses.

In 1939, Ellington hired, first as lyricist, and then as arranger and co-composer, Billy Strayhorn, a little man with a sweet disposition and a taste for romantic music who seemed content for the rest of his life to stay in Duke's shadow. Ellington called Strayhorn his alter ego: No wonder, for Strayhorn studied the Ellington book so carefully he could reproduce all of the master's effects. Whereas other composers struggle to be original, Strayhorn and

Ellington were delighted when listeners couldn't tell their works apart. Throughout their relationship, which lasted until Strayhorn's death in 1967, "Sweet Pea," as Ellington nicknamed Strayhorn, became increasingly important as a co-composer to Ellington.

Nevertheless, Strayhorn had his own musical identity, which we can hear in pieces such as his exquisite "Chelsea Bridge." Smooth, elegant in its movement, "Chelsea Bridge" is harmonically sophisticated, characterized by its unexpected connections between chords and changing key centers. The studio recordings—there were two in 1941—are also graced by haunting Ben Webster solos. Strayhorn's writing is subtle, elusive, debonair, his piano playing graceful, suggesting the influence of Art Tatum, where Ellington's is percussive. As a composer, Ellington adds dissonance by enriching simple chord progressions; Strayhorn designed more complex sequences of chords and made them seem inevitable. When he felt he needed to, he could write straightforward swingers such as the ever popular "Take the A Train," which Strayhorn said he penned in imitation of Fletcher Henderson. "Take the A Train" became the band's theme song.

Even this conscious exercise in simplicity is more complex than it first appears, as can be heard in the active saxophone parts which accompany the first trumpet solo by newcomer Ray Nance. Its arrangement has its subtleties as well, as in the interlude just after that chorus, when the volume shifts from soft to loudly brassy. During this interlude there are heavy accents every three beats,

Billy Strayhorn in the late 1950s with Harry Carney (seated). Notice the coiled neck of the baritone saxophone, which keeps it to a manageable length. (Courtesy Rutgers Institute of Jazz Studies)

creating the momentary illusion that the meter has changed from four beats to three a measure.

Gerry Mulligan would create in 1949 a similar effect in his composition "Jeru" for Miles Davis. But in the thirties, Ellington's and Strayhorn's most advanced ideas, though widely admired, were only emulated by a few. Charlie Barnet, who frankly modelled his band on Ellington's, recorded many of Ellington's pieces, but in simpler arrangements. Chick Webb tried to come as close as possible to the original when he recorded Ellington's "Azure." Sy Oliver, Willie Smith, and others created delightful versions of Ellington items for the Lunceford band, in their very different styles. But in the late 1940s the Ellington influence was everywhere. It permeated the works of Gil Evans, Charles Mingus and Mulligan, and one can hear his influence in the more recent writing of Thad Jones and Toshiko Akiyoshi.

By the end of the thirties, the Ellington band was playing with polish and power and Ellington was manipulating the sounds of his players with ever greater skill. An Ellington arrangement might sound almost improvised, but was usually the result of Ellington's incessant, and thought-provoking, calculations, and would often include the thoughts and second thoughts of band members. Every arrangement was subject to endless revision. One of the things Dizzy Gillespie noticed when he joined Ellington was that his score, with its indistinct directions to go from letter to letter, was incomprehensible to a newcomer. The many changes the arrangement had gone through rendered his part unreadable.

One of the Ellington masterpieces of the period is the Victor "Ko-Ko," which survives in two takes. As recorded on March 6, 1940, "Ko-Ko" (SCCJ) is a mid-tempo work with a menacing atmosphere. Intended as a number for a never completed opera, "Boola," with an African theme, "Ko-Ko" is almost entirely written. It begins with an 8-bar introduction during which Greer plays an insistent pattern on tom-toms and Blanton is held to a repetitive patter of alternating quarter notes. Over this static background, Carney enters with a long held E^b which he was instructed to play in even eighth notes while the trombones repeat a riff over him. From there on each section is a 12-bar blues in E^b minor. The theme is a riff-like conversation between Juan Tizol and the reed section, which goes on for the first chorus. Then Nanton enters and solos using his wa-wa mute, this time over the brass, for two choruses. At the beginning of chorus four, Ellington, in the originally issued take, plays a strikingly dissonant chord, followed by a rising and falling run in a foreign key: The brittle sound breaks the Nanton mood. After Ellington plays three such phrases, completing his chorus, the entire band flares up to a fortissimo chord, and then we hear Blanton taking a solo break, walking down from a high E^b. He gets two more such breaks, but curiously they are played in different order on the two takes. Ellington also revamped his solo contributions. In the first take Ellington sounds decorative: In the second he is more assertive. These are minor details, but the instant revisions by Ellington and Blanton show two (at least two) great musical minds at work, improving an already startling conception. For "Ko-Ko" is startling: it is an instrumental work, at times dissonant to an extreme, a piece without a singable melody that is powerfully, unforgettably evocative.

Equally unforgettable is Ellington's solo piece for Cootie Williams, "Concerto for Cootie" (SCCJ). In three minutes, it showcases virtually all his talents and sounds, beginning with the tightly muted sound with its fast, fluttering vibrato with which Williams plays the opening theme. The AABA piece begins in F major with an 8-bar introduction in which Blanton plays harmony along with the band, followed by a 10-bar A section which keeps Williams in mid-range with a mute. That A section with its unusual length is repeated and then we have an 8-bar B section which Williams plays more harshly, using his plunger (wa-wa) mute. The sound is controlled, dark, but after the A section returns, a modulation occurs upwards into D^b major, and Williams breaks out into a shiningly cheerful open-horned passage, a second theme, that transforms the atmosphere. Another modulation brings us back to the original key and themes. No short exposition can suggest the many beauties of this piece—not even the influential extended discussion of French composer Andre Hodeir does so. (It was published in English in 1955 in Hodeir's *Jazz: Its Evolution and Essence*.) One barely remembers that the second time Williams plays the A theme, he lessens the vibrato that distinguishes his first statement. And yet that detail, and others like it, make this work the endlessly rewarding performance that it is. This piece was later given lyrics and transformed into a popular vocal hit with the title "Do Nothin' Till You Hear From Me." Several other Ellington songs began life as instrumentals.

Like other bands, Ellington's was affected by the war, with its restrictions on travel, the changing audience it produced, and its pressures on a largely draftable personnel. Among other losses, Cootie Williams left to join the Benny Goodman band. (Ray Nance, who replaced him, also played violin, so Ellington would introduce him as the "string section.") Many felt that his band would never be as consistently brilliant again, but he continued to challenge himself as a composer. In 1943, Ellington was able to arrange a Carnegie Hall concert for the band, and he responded to the opportunity with a new suite, "Black, Brown and Beige." It was a big, and some thought, bloated, attempt to reproduce musically the history of the black race in America.

Ellington took the project seriously: When it was issued by Victor, he offered interpretative notes, as told to Inez Cavanaugh, that described his inspiration. The piece begins with a work song, "the voice of a fighting man working . . . like a diamond put to work." The day of rest is celebrated in "Come Sunday," when the workers are said to exclaim: "We have no organ, no lovely white church with its steeple shining in the sun, but we are singing, and we do believe." A section about the blues is sung by Joya Sherrill. Three dances follow. A West Indian dance is dedicated to the free Haitians who helped the Americans during the Revolutionary War. The "Emancipation Celebration" is, Ellington said, the most complex dance: "This composition describes the admixture of joyfulness on the part of the young people and the bewilderment of the old on that 'great gettin' up mornin'.' " "Sugar Hill Penthouse" is of course dedicated to the elegant section of Harlem in which Ellington lived: "If you ever sat on a beautiful magenta cloud overlooking New York City, you were on Sugar Hill."

The piece was not a critical success. One can understand why. It was disconcerting to those who went to Carnegie Hall expecting to hear dance music and perhaps to those who did not want to be disturbed by a frank celebration of African-American life. Some of the effects, such as the thunderous chords by the band at the beginning, seemed grandiose. But there were many poetic moments as well. "Black Brown and Beige" was the forerunner of the longer pieces and suites that would take up much of Ellington's time for the rest of his life.

He was able to hold a band together despite personnel changes and the general decline of the big bands that came with World War II, but it's unclear that his band ever made a profit after the war. Ellington survived and supported the band with the substantial revenues from his popular compositions. He kept those "expensive gentlemen," as he called his band members, in order to be able to hear his compositions played immediately after he wrote them—compositions such as the innovative piano feature, "Clothed Woman" (1947), with its nearly atonal but blues-based solos framing a middle section of stride piano.

He added some extraordinary musicians. The remarkably agile bassist Oscar Pettiford (with the band from 1945-1948), the round-toned trumpet player Clark Terry (1951-1959), the powerful drummer Louis Bellson (1951-1953) were among them. After being featured on "The Hawk Talks" and elsewhere, Bellson left the band and was replaced eventually by another dynamic drummer, Sam Woodyard (1955-1966). To the nucleus of his reed section—Hodges and Carney—Ellington added clarinetist and tenor saxophonist Jimmy Hamilton, who replaced Barney Bigard in 1943; Russell Procope, an alto saxophonist who joined in 1946; and tenor saxophonist Paul Gonsalves in 1950. This celebrated reed section remained intact until 1968.

That would have been hard to predict in the mid-fifties: Then the band was in trouble. Some thought Ellington was nearing the end. He had been getting bad reviews and was playing before smaller audiences. A bit of inspired improvisation changed all that. At the Newport Jazz Festival of 1956, Ellington pulled out a number the band had rarely played in recent years, "Diminuendo in Blue and Crescendo in Blue." As he usually did in live performances of this piece, he opened it up for a tenor saxophone solo between the two sections. He called on Paul Gonsalves, whose breathy tenor saxophone sound was based on that of Ben Webster, to improvise a few choruses of blues. Inspired, Gonsalves played over two dozen choruses. The crowd rose from its seats and danced in the aisles, and the Ellington band was big news again.

Ellington never had to look back. His success prompted a burst of activity. In 1959, he and Billy Strayhorn composed "The Queen's Suite" for the Queen of England. An evocative series of movements that includes the remarkable piano solo, "A Single Petal of a Rose," this suite is mostly written, yet there is no doubt about the jazz nature of the work. As is the case with many of Ellington's suites, there are no common musical motives among the movements. Some critics complained that the Ellington-Strayhorn suites were merely sequences of loosely assembled pieces. Yet this criticism seems unfair, since the same is true of many classical suites. Such works are held together by dramatic planning and effective use of contrast.

Besides, Ellington and Strayhorn did find new ways of organizing and unifying some of their suites. In the four movements of "Suite Thursday"—played with slight pauses between them—Ellington and Strayhorn used unifying devices such as recurrent motives. The first movement of this suite written in the fall of 1960 for the Monterey Jazz Festival is a blues for most of its length, and the last is a straight 12-bar blues. This last movement makes explicit the blues feeling and allusions of the earlier sections. At the 1986 conference of the International Duke Ellington Study Group (held at Rutgers University) Andrew Homzy of Concordia College in Montreal analyzed the structure of the suite, and showed that much of it is based on a motive of two notes given at the very beginning of the suite. This interval, technically a descending minor sixth, is shown in the example. (See music example.)

minor 6th

Example 8–3.
Opening motive of Ellington's "Suite Thursday."

The last movement, "Lay-By," sums up the material of "Suite Thursday" with its explicit return to the earlier motive. In the 1963 performance, recorded live in Paris and issued on *The Great Paris Concert*, Ray Nance solos on violin, repeating the two note motive over and over.

Ellington's late work is notable for its sheer breadth. The projects that dominated the last years of his life were his Sacred Concerts. Three were completed, of which the second is the larger and more important work. (He was evidently still searching for ways of improving the third when he died on May 24, 1974: It was recorded live for RCA on October 24, 1973.) The First Sacred Concert included a reprise of "Come Sunday," some lovely songs, and some passages that could not be called songs, for example, a section in which the chorus reads the names of the books of the New Testament. Between each name, the band plays in unison one note of a melody. As the chorus continues, the notes of the band's melody get higher and higher, as the "edifice" of the New Testament is erected by the chorus. The melody is completed when the name of the last book is read. Ellington said he tied the music of this sacred concert together in an unusual, verbal way: He used six-note phrases in the instrumental sections to represent the six syllables of "In the beginning God," the opening of the Bible in the King James version.

The Second Sacred Concert was first performed at St. John the Divine's in New York City on January 19, 1968. Ellington called it a public display of his

Duke Ellington, Ann Arbor, Michigan, early 1970's.
(Photo by Michael Ullman)

gratitude to God and "the most important thing I have ever done." (*Music is My Mistress*, p. 269) Critic John S. Wilson wrote in *The New York Times* that the "new work glowed with Mr. Ellington's artistry as a direct, highly communicative melodist," and that it was "a succession of fresh, warm Ellington tunes."

The Second Sacred Concert begins with a feature for baritone saxophonist Harry Carney, "Praise God." The second part, "Supreme Being," begins with, as Ellington's program notes read, "a section of cacophony" that "represents the scene before the Supreme Being created order." One hears a slowly building, polytonal band part of great rhythmic complexity (parts suggest 5/4 and other meters) that ends in a huge, dissonant climax, which is followed by the voices of the chorus rising up to the words "Supreme Being." "Praise God" returns at the end of the concert in a different guise, as a vocal section of the last part, "Praise God and Dance," helping to unify the piece.

Ellington's lyrics are problematic. Bach wrote his cantatas to celebrate a specific church event. Ellington wants to celebrate the universe, and he is in turn serious and hip, naive, and flip. Still, whatever one thinks of the sometimes crashing brass in the piece or of Ellington's occasional whimsicality of phrase, the range of styles in the Second Sacred Concert is impressive in itself. The overall theme is freedom. Its longest section, "It's Freedom," divided into eight parts, includes a recitation in which Ellington gives us his "four major moral freedoms," which he says he learned from the recently deceased Billy Strayhorn: "Freedom from hate unconditionally; freedom from self-pity; free-

Example 8–4.
Duke Ellington, "T.G.T.T." (1968), duet for electric piano and voice.

dom from fear of doing something that would help someone more than it does me; and freedom from pride that makes me feel I am better than my brother."

The Swedish singer Alice Babs produces two of the concert's exquisite moments. In a section called "Heaven," she follows the four-bar introduction by Ellington with a 16-measure vocal, sung freely, which, after another four bars by Ellington, leads to a Johnny Hodges solo. Hodges's control over volume and tone is astonishing: He soars and dances ethereally in a solo that expresses the theme of "Heaven" as well as music can. Ellington contrasts Babs's out-of-tempo opening with the swinging four of Hodges's solo: The rhythm changes again in the end, when the band plays an uptempo samba behind Babs. Later, Babs sings the wordless "T.G.T.T.," meaning, Ellington says, "too good to title." And indeed it is. (See music example.)

Ellington set great store by these Sacred Concerts, but we shouldn't neglect other late masterpieces. From the "Far East Suite" he wrote with Strayhorn and recorded in 1966, "Bluebird of Delhi (Mynah)" builds up from a little clarinet lick to hair-raising chords for the whole band. Ellington's fascinating suite "The Afro-Eurasian Eclipse" was recorded in 1971. He featured his own pianism more and more, notably on his 1962 trio recording, *Money Jungle*, featuring modern jazz leaders drummer Max Roach and bassist Charles Mingus. Ellington's piano style, often brusque, playful and percussive, was widely admired by other pianists. Modern jazz pianists such as Thelonious Monk, Mal Waldron, and Randy Weston have testified to his influence on their playing. Even pianists who chose not to play like Ellington admired his innovative style of spare comping, the strange effects he poked out behind soloists, which he shared with his otherwise musical opposite Count Basie. And many learned dissonant voicings by studying his records.

In 1967, Ellington honored the lately deceased Billy Strayhorn with an album entitled *And His Mother Called Him Bill*. It included the subtly swinging "The Intimacy of the Blues," and a solo piano feature, virtually an afterthought: Strayhorn's "Lotus Blossom." Recorded after the band's session had ended—the noise of the departing band is heard behind the piano—the solo piano version of "Lotus Blossom" turns out to be one of Ellington's most personal statements. This casual setting for a deeply felt statement was typical of the man. Ellington was a romantic who didn't like to wear his heart on his sleeve. He owed a lot to Strayhorn, whom he loved, and to his other co-workers, Bubber Miley, Harry Carney, Johnny Hodges. No band ever sounded better, in more different ways, than his. Ellington depended on his musicians, his sound identities, to create the unique textures that make up what some have called "the Ellington effect." But "Lotus Blossom" finds him creating that effect—one might almost call it a spell—by himself, and his uniquely personal playing of the Strayhorn piece reminds us that the ultimate source of Ellington's music was Ellington himself. No big band writer since the forties has safely ignored Ellington, but no one has been able to reproduce the quality of his sounds or the spirit of his music. He was not only inexhaustible, but irreplaceable.

9 Ridin' in Rhythm: The Thirties and Swing

The thirties began amid a world-wide depression that devastated the record industry, dispersed its musicians, and kept listeners at home where they, in a nice irony, helped to sow the seeds of the great swing explosion of a few years later by listening to radio, with its many broadcasts of live bands: hot, sweet and indifferent. In 1932, Benny Goodman was an accomplished studio musician, and a well known sideman, but hampered by a recording industry in a serious decline, he made only three sessions. He hung on, and by 1934, he had formed his own band, which played from June to October at Billy Rose's Music Hall in New York City. Goodman was a promising leader: but he wasn't a star. Then in December, he was picked as the "hot" attraction on the National Biscuit Company's "Let's Dance" radio show, broadcast late at night in New York and at a more reasonable hour in California.

What happened next has been made into a Hollywood movie, *The Benny Goodman Story* (1955). The band went on a coast-to-coast tour in July 1935. Moving slowly west, Goodman played in ballroom after ballroom and bombed. Despite the fact that he had a band of young jazz musicians, Goodman tried to keep the repertoire sweet and danceable. Then, when he reached the Palomar Ballroom in Los Angeles on August 21, with nothing to lose, he let loose with the swing arrangements he had been aching to play all along. The crowd, which knew these charts from his "hot" broadcasts, erupted. The Goodman band, and the swing era, which would last into World War II, was launched.

Soon, swing music was being played all over the country in hotel rooms, in large ballrooms, in nightclubs, colleges, and movie theaters. For a young fan, this was what writer Bill Gottlieb has called with forgivable partisanship, "The Golden Age of Jazz." The audiences, which were still segregated, included larger numbers of white youths than ever before. The new listeners were knowledgeable, and sometimes even fanatical. The fans would line up around a bandstand, calling for their favorite songs or singers or musicians. They knew who was playing what in which band, and they followed their favorites just the way sports fans did. In the larger theaters of the day, movies and newsreels alternated with live bands on stage. When a band would come to town to play a theater, followers would often line up hours before opening time, and then sit through a movie several times just so they could see their band on successive stage shows. On occasion, big bands also played behind variety shows as they had in the twenties. But, by the mid-thirties, many bands were coming out of the pits and onto the stage for good. Playing to audiences which pressed up against the bandstand or to crowds of jitterbugs, the bands were the stars.

Their leaders were superstars. The swing era made national celebrities, and wealthy men, out of some leaders: Goodman, rival clarinetist Artie Shaw, Glenn Miller, the Dorseys. The situation was not completely rosy. The black groups of Ellington, Cab Calloway, Count Basie and Jimmy Lunceford profited from the swing era, but the biggest beneficiaries were white and played sweetly. The mass white audience identified more easily with such groups. Some of the best black bands, such as those of Teddy Wilson and Benny Carter, struggled or, as did Fletcher Henderson's, disappeared during the swing era.

Nor did every brilliant instrumentalist have the temperament to be a big band leader, who must be part entertainer, part businessman, and part social worker, have an iron constitution and an indefatigable tolerance for travel. Jack Teagarden and trumpeter Bunny Berigan led two of the many bands built, on the Louis Armstrong model, around a star soloist. Despite some wonderful records, these bands didn't survive. They were not distinctive enough, and their leaders were haphazard businessmen who didn't receive the necessary support from managers and patrons. Celebrated though many swing jazz bands were, the commercial bands, some called "sweet" and others derogatorily nicknamed "Mickey Mouse" bands, were more popular than the jazzier groups.

As the thirties progressed, many bands were playing arrangements based on the work of Fletcher Henderson. In *The Kingdom of Swing*, which he wrote with Irving Kolodin in 1939, Benny Goodman laid out the ground rules for such a swing arrangement: "The whole idea is that the ensemble passages . . . have to be written in more or less the same style that a soloist would use if he were improvising. That is, what Fletcher [Henderson] really could do so wonderfully was to take a tune like 'Sometimes I'm Happy' [BBJ] and really improvise on it himself, with the exception of certain parts of the various choruses which would be marked solo trumpet or solo tenor or solo clarinet [where the soloist would be expected to improvise]. Even here the background for the rest of the band would be in the same consistent vein, so that the whole thing really hung together and sounded unified. Then, too, the arranger's choice of the different key changes is very important, and the order in which the solos are placed, so that the arrangement works up to a climax." (p. 162) By the height of the big band era, the size and instrumentation of the groups had become more or less regularized. There were three or four trumpets, two or three trombones, two alto saxophones, a tenor, and a baritone, which played above a rhythm section of piano, guitar,

string bass and drums. Each wind section—trumpets, trombones and saxophones—had a first chair player, a leader who set the phrasing, breathing and
articulations for the section. (In the reed section, it was the first alto saxophone.)

There's one crucial aspect of big band playing that Goodman takes for
granted: the rhythm. As Joe Garland put it in one of his 1933 titles, six years
before he wrote the hit "In the Mood," swing music was "Ridin' in Rhythm." By
the early thirties, rhythm sections had changed. Bands had permanently substi-
tuted the string bass for the huffing tuba, where in the 1920s either had been
acceptable. What they played changed too. Whereas twenties bassists usually
used an oom-pah style, playing every other beat, thirties bass players began to
play walking lines, one note to a beat. The result was a lighter, more buoyant
rhythm.

Gradually drummers learned to lighten their beat as well, eventually
keeping the rhythm on the recently invented high-hat or "sock" cymbals. The
high-hat is essentially a stand, usually placed at the drummer's left, that holds
two cymbals close together face to face horizontally. On the floor is a foot pedal
which, when depressed, brings the cymbals together with a "chick" sound.
During the mid-twenties, the stand was only about a foot high and it was called
the "low-sock" or "floor cymbal," but by the end of the decade it was high
enough so that the cymbals could be struck by a drummer's sticks as well.
Previously drummers such as Zutty Singleton or Vic Berton used two hands on
one cymbal to get similar effects. Using one hand to hold the stick, they would
control the ringing of the cymbal by gripping it with the other. Now, using only

Chauncey Morehouse, a creative drummer of the late 1920s, with his elaborate
percussion collection (but no high-hat). (Courtesy of Rutgers Institute of Jazz Studies)

a foot, a drummer could produce a variety of sounds, ranging from muffled to openly ringing, depending on how much he or she opened or closed the high-hat.

Thirties drummers drew on the innovations of their predecessors. Warren "Baby" Dodds, who played with the King Oliver and Louis Armstrong groups of the twenties, popularized the use of a type of repetitive pattern in the final choruses—they would be called "ride" patterns—so that a consistent forward momentum could be created when the music called for it. (Most of his contemporaries prided themselves in essentially playing along with the melody, producing lines as busy as a trumpet's.) One that Dodds used consisted of drum rolls called "press" rolls after the manner in which they were produced on the snare drum. The illustration shows what it sounded like. (See example.)

ONE — TWO —THREE —FOUR
(roll)   (roll)

Example 9–1.
Press roll pattern

While the ride pattern filled in beats two and four, the bass drum was hit on one and three or on all four beats. Characteristic of New Orleans drummers, the press-roll pattern was also used well into the thirties by such drummers as Dave Tough and Sid Catlett.

But for most drummers, the high-hat became the focus of the new "swing" drum style. Young drummers like Walter Johnson of Henderson's band learned to accent beats two and four with the high-hat rather than with a press roll. Typically in the swing style, the high-hat would be closed on beats two and four, which makes the subtle accent. (See example.)

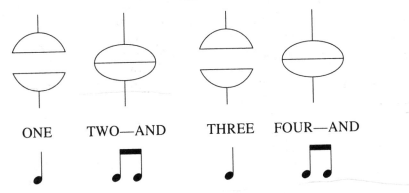

ONE   TWO—AND   THREE   FOUR—AND

Example 9–2.
Swing style high-hat playing.

The result was a clearly focused, steady and powerful beat that could drive a big band without overwhelming it. As Jimmy Crawford, drummer for the Jimmy Lunceford band in the thirties, exclaimed: "I switched over to the upstairs pedal because the new beat was takin' things by storm. It's the greatest thing ever invented . . . you can hold everything together with that snap." ("The Zildjian Story," a booklet by the cymbal manufacturer Avedis Zildjian, no date or author, p. 8).

The rest of the rhythm section changed as well. As they did in the twenties, guitarists were still strumming a chord on every beat, but were working on smoothing out their style: connecting chords by changing as few fingers as possible while giving a slight accent on the second and fourth beats, thus reinforcing the drummer's accents on two and four. Most band pianists pared their left hands down and were playing fewer notes with an airier touch. The dashing Earl Hines may be the quintessential late twenties jazz pianist: Teddy Wilson, with his elegant runs and swift-fingered authority, is the best representative of the newer, and smoother, style that dominated the thirties.

At the end of the twenties, relatively few big bands were "swinging." One of the remarkable features of the music of the mid-thirties is the sudden profusion of hard-driving swing bands playing in the new style. Perhaps the suddenness is only apparent. The slump in the recording industry during the early thirties meant that those years were relatively poorly documented. When the big bands were recorded again in profusion, the new rhythmic approach that powered the swing era had spread widely. By the mid-thirties, more big bands were swinging harder than ever before, and many were playing with unprecedented precision as well. No band had been more important to these developments than Fletcher Henderson's, with its key arrangers, Don Redman, Benny Carter, Henderson himself and his brother Horace.

FLETCHER HENDERSON

Henderson was an unlikely innovator. A gentle, unassertive man in a hardnosed business, Henderson has been described by Gunther Schuller as being merely the right man in the right place, a superior talent scout able to exploit the creativity of others. He was more than that. Henderson assembled the best Eastern jazz band in the twenties, hiring first Coleman Hawkins and Louis Armstrong and then trombonist Jimmy Harrison, and at various times trumpeters Joe Smith, Red Allen and Roy Eldridge, all key soloists. He had the musical sense to allow Redman to develop his skills as an arranger for his band, and when Redman left, he began to arrange himself. Henderson's writing, simpler than that of Redman or Benny Carter, more dependent on riffs and solos, had a subtle power that fit the mood of the swing era. One can observe Henderson's touch as an arranger by comparing the 1926 "Stampede," arranged for the Henderson band by Don Redman, with the leaner 1937 arrangement by Henderson himself. Henderson's arrangements helped spark Benny Goodman's success, as Goodman readily acknowledged. In *The Kingdom of Swing,* Goodman noted that it was Henderson's pieces, "with their wonderful easy style and great background figures, that really set the style of the band" (p. 161).

Fletcher Henderson was born in Georgia in 1897. He was well educated, receiving a degree in chemistry at Atlanta University College in 1920. Hoping to do research, he moved to New York City. Instead, he found himself working as a song plugger and pianist for the Pace and Handy Music Company (Handy being W.C. Handy), playing the sheet music for customers to hear. He organized his first band to tour with singer Ethel Waters, who made him study James P. Johnson piano rolls so that he would be able to play the blues. Early in 1924, according to Walter Allen's definitive *Hendersonia: The Music of Fletcher Henderson and His Musicians,* he was elected the leader of a new band that would play at the Club Alabam in Manhattan. The band included tenor saxophonist Coleman Hawkins, and Don Redman playing alto, clarinet and arranging. That group was hired to play at the Roseland, where they were described by *Variety* as "one of the best in the field, colored or white."

Coleman Hawkins (1904–1969) would eventually be recognized as the first great tenor saxophonist—the "father of the tenor saxophone"—but he was described in these early years as "a slap-tongue artist of considerable rank" (*Variety,* October 1925, quoted in *Hendersonia,* p. 139). At the beginning of his career, he was playing in the conventional style of the early twenties, when the saxophone was still thought to be a novelty instrument, and saxophonists liked to make a percussive sound by clucking with their tongues. While with Henderson, Hawkins would develop an extraordinarily influential, propulsive, legato style. Big-toned, alternately aggressive and romantic, fluently legato, Hawkins's tenor solos eventually developed a restless, almost relentless inevitability. But at the beginning he was playing in the older, heavily tongued, staccato manner: In later years, when confronted with one of these early recordings in which he clucks censoriously in slap-tongued outbursts, Hawkins would say that the saxophonist was his father, not himself.

Born in West Virginia in 1900, and thus four years older than Hawkins, Don Redman was a child prodigy, who played trumpet at age three, and picked up a proficiency in all the wind instruments by the time he was 12. He studied instrumental technique at the Boston Conservatory, which was, with the nearby New England Conservatory, the first American music school to admit blacks. By his own admission, he was not a great improviser, and his high-pitched, half-spoken singing has dated, but it would be difficult to overestimate Redman's importance as a composer and arranger. In his works for Henderson, many of the principles of big band arranging were established. These include the rewriting of the given theme rhythmically and melodically to make it fit a jazz style, and the use of alternating brass and reed choirs.

The Henderson band began recording immediately and frequently, and through the recordings, we can see its rapid progression from a slapdash six piece group to a commanding dance band able to play all sorts of music. (Band members were proud of their ability to play waltzes in difficult keys.) That development was important to their survival. There was some pressure, even in the twenties, and even from a black newspaper such as the *Chicago Defender*, to develop a sophisticated, gentle sound. "Soft, sweet and perfect in dance rhythm . . . and his boys get 'hot', too—not the sloppy New Orleans hokum, but real peppy blue syncopation," was the praise of the *Defender's* music columnist when Henderson appeared in Chicago in 1926 (*Hendersonia*, p. 168).

Henderson's earliest recordings don't sound sweet or soft. On the two takes from August 9, 1923 of "Dicty Blues," a piece written by Henderson and arranged by Redman, a four-bar introduction is followed by a figure played by chimes—"dicty" meant high-class, and nothing was classier than chimes. This break is followed by the ensemble playing in Dixieland style, the trumpet carrying the lead, and Don Redman playing shrill obbligato figures on clarinet. Coleman Hawkins solos in his strongly stomping style. Slap-tongued in places, this solo also includes some delicate ornaments which suggest what is to come.

In 1924, the band recorded "Teapot Dome Blues," with its many written breaks, a written coda, and, behind the trombone solo of Teddy Nixon, the sax section playing chords. (The title refers to the so-called "Teapot Dome" scandal of the early twenties, in which high officials of the Harding administration were accused of misusing funds associated with the nation's oil reserves. Teapot Dome was an oil reserve.) That year also saw "Go 'Long, Mule," with its trio of clarinets—a favorite Don Redman device. During the initial statement of the theme, the "head," Redman wrote short phrases for the saxes that fill in behind the brass. In this detail, we can hear beginnings of the conversation between the brass and reeds that lasted throughout the swing era. "Shanghai Shuffle" from October 10, 1924 has more separate parts for brass and reeds, and Redman writes in crescendos during the final chorus to bring in much needed variation in volume. Redman's oboe playing on this piece was the first use of that instrument in jazz.

In "Copenhagen" (BBJ) Redman uses a constantly shifting scheme, alternating in the first 16 bars, for instance, trumpet and then clarinet trios with ensemble improvisations. Later in the arrangement short written passages for the ensemble give way to improvisations, as well as a 16-bar chorus for brass and clarinet obbligato by the fluid Buster Bailey that is interrupted by a clever break—one bar of banjo and one bar of tenor sax.

Fancy though this sounds, "Copenhagen" still has forward motion. The Henderson band, with its superior musicianship, is able to take the complicated Redman arrangements and make them work. Redman was in fact in line with the taste of the twenties dance bands: Paul Whiteman's band used arrangements that were equally elaborate, even fussy. In fact, one of Redman's last arrangements for Henderson was an amusing 1927 tribute to, and parody of, the Whiteman style, "Whiteman Stomp," composed by Fats Waller. This piece outdoes Whiteman himself in its humorously complicated changes of mood and rhythm. Later Whiteman himself recorded this parody of his work!

Soon, most of the basics of big band writing were already in place in Fletcher Henderson's group. The band was swinging more, as we hear in the

1926 recording of "The Stampede" (SCCJ) with a group that included Rex Stewart in Louis Armstrong's chair. The structure of this hard-driving arrangement goes like this:

Intro: Two four-bar sections with breaks by Stewart.

Chorus One: First theme—ABAC, eight bars each.

Chorus Two: Hawkins solo based on the chords of the first theme, including a couple of dramatic honks during the second A.

Four-bar interlude

Chorus Three: Second theme, Joe Smith solo and rhythm only—also ABAC, with slightly different chords than in choruses one and two.

Four-bar interlude

Chorus Four: Written "soli" (group solo) on second theme, featuring a clarinet trio and fancy banjo strumming.

Chorus Five: Hot solo by Rex Stewart based on the A and B of the *first* theme, then whole band, partly written and partly improvised, for AC. Band has melody of second theme added here since the chords are similar and the second theme fits over the first theme's chords. This creates a kind of summary and conclusion.

Two-bar tag ending.

Stewart solos vigorously, and the ensemble passages that follow have a comparable dash. The piece swings mightily, the rhythm being defined by Bob Escudero's two-beat tuba playing. That would change. In March 1929, John Kirby was hired to play the bass part, and he alternated tuba and string bass. By 1933, in line with the national trend, he was playing only string bass.

In 1927, Don Redman left Henderson to join a Detroit-based band, the McKinney's Cotton Pickers, a band he transformed into a tight, swinging group that shone in Redman pieces such as "Rocky Road." For new arrangements, Henderson looked to his younger brother Horace, whose "Hot and Anxious" of 1931 was one source of the riff later known as "In the Mood," and to the brilliant Benny Carter, one of the most elegant swing alto saxophonists and a fine trumpeter, whose virtuosic writing, smooth and rich, for saxophone choir, became his trademark. Born in New York in 1907, Carter taught himself arranging by studying, among other sources, stock arrangements. He would go well beyond his sources, writing charts that echoed the elegance, economy and tonal opulence of his own playing. Henderson recorded Carter's arrangement of "Somebody Loves Me," on October 3, 1930.

The performance demonstrates admirably the flowing 4/4 beat that was crucial to the swing era. With the rhythm section firmly and smoothly chugging away behind him, Benny Carter solos, suggesting the smooth legato statements that seem to skate above the beat that he would record in later years. Schuller

Benny Carter on his seventy-fifth birthday, August 8, 1982, Sweet Basil nightclub, Manhattan. (Photo by Michael Ullman)

has also praised the deft syncopated lines Carter wrote in an arrangement recorded by Henderson later in 1930, "Keep a Song in Your Soul."

Henderson himself seems to have quietly observed and learned from his arrangers, Redman and Carter, and from others. He did little writing for his band until 1930, but the very first things he wrote were superb crystallizations of the big band style. His "Honeysuckle Rose" of December 9, 1932 culminates as the band plays a series of riffs that remind one of "Tea for Two," and that are, like so much of Henderson's writing, simple, swinging, and effective.

That same day in December, Henderson recorded one of his arrangements of Jelly Roll Morton's "King Porter Stomp," a piece Henderson recorded repeatedly before Goodman made it famous. Every swing band would later play it, usually in a Henderson-derived arrangement. "New King Porter Stomp" (BBJ; a Goodman version is there too) features a rollicking solo by Hawkins who is captured here and on "Honeysuckle Rose" at an interesting point in his career, in which he was experimenting with a floating, off-the-beat approach to rhythm. Before this, and after 1935, he was known for his hard, chugging swing. His work here is harmonically sophisticated, ornate, and driving despite its rubato feel and repeated glissandi. Hawkins's solo depends on the vital effect of his broad vibrato, or the soaring, almost suspended feeling he gets by suddenly lightening his tone, as in the eighth bar of his solo. The riffing of the band at the end of this piece, and the accumulated tension it created, would be noticed by virtually every swing band leader.

In 1934, the Henderson band suffered an irremediable blow when Hawkins left for England: He would stay in Europe until chased home by the impending war in 1939. (Hawkins returns in Chapter 11.) Henderson briefly tried Lester Young as a replacement for Hawkins, then settled on Ben Webster. Despite the personnel changes and despite the fact that the band was in financial trouble, Henderson continued to record. One of the most memorably melodic of his compositions, "Down South Camp Meeting," featuring trumpeter Red Allen, was recorded by his own band on September 12, 1934 (BBJ). This has all the melodicism and clarity of Henderson's other work. Only one section of the piece contains room for improvisation: "Down South Camp Meeting" demonstrates how written jazz can work with a minimum of soloing. Over the now suave sounding rhythm section, the reeds state the first theme quietly. The second theme is played first by the reeds while the brass comment, and then with the roles reversed. A short transitional passage leads to a clarinet trio down low, which is then repeated an octave higher with the band behind it in a hair-raising effect. The piece, which was later recorded by Benny Goodman, ends abruptly with a two-measure coda.

Many of Henderson's other pieces were recorded by Goodman, especially the writing he was doing after 1934 on numbers such as "Christopher Columbus," "Blue Lou," and "Stealing Apples." Urbane, swinging lightly, yet perfectly adapted to the intrusion of long solos, or choruses of extended riffing, Henderson's charts were one foundation of the swing era. But his own band was never the success it should have been. The last of a depressing series of setbacks came in November 1934. Henderson's group, after playing a week in Detroit, resigned when their leader was unable to pay them. He would regroup in 1935, but was soon mainly writing arrangements for others, finally joining Goodman as a staff arranger and sometime pianist in 1939. He would lead a band again in the forties, but Henderson's real work was over in the middle of the previous decade, when the swing era passed by one of its creators. Henderson expressed little bitterness. Externally serene until his death in 1952, Henderson did not live to see the reissues of his ground-breaking work: Referring to his truncated career as a band leader, one such collection was called *A Study in Frustration* (Columbia C4L 19). The frustration is ours, not Henderson's.

BLACK BANDS AND SOLOISTS

Henderson did his work well. By 1934, there was a host of fine big bands, many stocked with ex-Henderson writers and players. Even earlier, in 1933, Benny Carter was leading a band that recorded numbers such as his "Lonesome Nights," with its startlingly precise, flowing choruses for the saxophone section. Based on a simple, descending theme, "Lonesome Nights" features a short solo by pianist Teddy Wilson whose light touch and firm accents would charm audiences throughout the swing era. In some ways a less surprising pianist than Earl Hines, Wilson had a way, comparable to Carter's own, of making elegance swing. He lightened his left hand, and played lengthy lines with his right that pushed the beat subtly.

It is instructive to compare the recordings of "Rosetta" by Earl Hines and Teddy Wilson, as Henry Martin suggested in his book *Enjoying Jazz* (pp.165-169). (We will discuss the originally issued takes. An alternate take of each was first issued in 1981.) Hines coauthored this composition, which he recorded with his big band in 1933, and as a piano solo for Victor in 1939. The originally issued take of the Hines piano solo begins with a dissonant eight-bar introduction. During the first chorus, his lightly striding left hand is fairly regular. Then he begins to surprise. He inserts a four-bar interlude with left hand chords that rise chromatically. Then, during the second chorus he launches into a contrapuntal examination of the chords that is difficult for even experienced listeners to keep up with. Sometimes his left hand drops out. Elsewhere it sticks on a trill, or glides upward in a run. Generally it punctuates what the right hand is doing. (See music example.)

Example 9-3.
Earl Hines, interlude and beginning of second chorus on "Rosetta" (1939).

In the bridge of the second chorus, he begins with a characteristic rising figure, which he continues in complicated rhythms. He then descends calmly in even eighth notes—but here Hines uses the whole tone scale rather than the expected chords. (See music example.)

The third chorus begins with a return to a more traditional stride style in the left hand, but that is interrupted by a left hand trill at the bridge, and a strange interlude, during which he modulates down a whole step (from F major to the key of Eb). Hines returns to more conventional stride patterns for the final chorus.

Wilson recorded "Rosetta" as a piano solo in 1935, in the key of Eb throughout. Taken at a slower tempo, his performance begins with an introduction,

Example 9-4.
Earl Hines, whole tone passage at the end of the bridge on
the second chorus of "Rosetta" (1939).

similar to Hines's but less dissonant. The playing that follows is strikingly
graceful, with florid right-hand runs and sophisticated harmonies that contrast
with the often raw dissonance of what Hines does. Wilson's left hand pauses in
places, as did Hines's, to suggest a dialogue with the right, but the Wilson left
hand is in general more steady, and fuller than Hines's, less startling, but
buoyantly effective in a more elegant style. Most pianists of the thirties and early
forties would follow the path set out by Wilson.

Wilson would go on to lead his own band, and would record some of the
most important small group sides of the decade, but in 1933 he was soloing in
Carter arrangements such as "Symphony in Riffs" which, as recorded on October 16, unfolds over the sweetly chugging beat of drummer Sid Catlett, who
uses brushes throughout. This 32-bar AABA piece is based, as its title suggests,
on a simple, short repeated theme—a riff. The arrangement neatly balances
ensemble sections, such as the written sax solo of the A parts, with solos such as
the wonderfully flamboyant J.C. Higginbotham trombone statement on the
bridge. The piece ends with a neatly organized final chorus that pits the brass
against the reeds.

Meanwhile, in 1931 and then again the next year, Don Redman, now
leading his own orchestra, had recorded his most striking composition, the
"Chant of the Weed." This number, with its reference to marijuana, then the
musicians' favorite drug, became the Redman band's theme song. This was one
of many references to marijuana in jazz songs: Among others, Louis Armstrong
made "Muggles"—a muggle was a marijuana cigarette. Armstrong once dedicated a part of a radio broadcast to "viper" Mezz Mezzrow—a viper was what
students of the sixties would call "a pothead", and Mezz Mezzrow, besides
being a jazz clarinetist, was such a notorious marijuana dealer that "mezz"
became another nickname for the drug. In 1934, Armstrong recorded "Song of
the Vipers." Cab Calloway had a hit with his "Reefer Man," and also with
"Kickin' the Gong Around," with its coded references to opium.

"Chant of the Weed" begins with four bars of a mysterious, unresolved
theme stated by the reeds and muted brass, which alternates with four bars of
the almost blandly close harmony of the reeds, who play a dreamy melody over
the clomping woodblocks of drummer Manzie Johnson. The contrast between

those two moods creates much of the effect of "Chant of the Weed." The piece is in the standard 32-bar AABA form, but the first four bars of each A section and the entire bridge use the whole tone scale. The 1932 recording has a chirpy alto solo by Don Redman, who also sang such numbers as "Miss Hannah" in a high, light voice that stressed the novelty aspect of his repertoire. Redman kept his band together until the end of the swing era: At its best, it featured fine soloists such as trumpeter Red Allen, trombonist Benny Morton and the powerfully adept drummer Sid Catlett, whose breaks and flamboyant background patterns swing such numbers as the 1936 "Bugle Call Rag." Redman re-recorded "Chant of the Weed" in 1940.

In 1934, the year Benny Goodman put together his first big band, the swing group of black drummer Chick Webb recorded a number that Goodman, and most other swing bands, would play for years, "Stompin' at the Savoy." Despite a crippling deformity that left him hunch-backed and undersized, Webb was one of the most powerful drummers of the thirties. Born in 1909 in Baltimore, he moved to New York in 1925. By the next year Webb was leading his own band, which began playing long engagements at the Savoy Ballroom late in 1931. Soon, the band was identified with its venue. To another band, playing at the Savoy meant battling Chick Webb's group—alternating sets to see who the audience liked best—and Webb only admitted defeat once, when Ellington reputedly wiped him out. In a profile by Whitney Balliett, Buddy Rich described Webb behind his drums: "Chick Webb was startling. He was a tiny man with

Chick Webb around 1940. (Courtesy Rutgers Institute of Jazz Studies)

this big face and big, stiff shoulders. He sat way up on a kind of throne and used a 28-inch bass drum which had special pedals for his feet and he had those old goose-neck cymbal holders. Every beat was like a bell" (Balliett, *American Musicians*, p. 229).

Unfortunately, he can barely be heard in most of his recorded legacy. However, that steady, quiet but pushing beat, that powerful crisp style can be heard throughout "Stompin' at the Savoy" (1934, BBJ), written by saxophonist Edgar Sampson. Avoiding the busy playing of earlier drummers, Webb used accents sparingly, but effectively: His brush accents are audible at the end of the last chorus of "Stompin.'" On "Don't Be That Way" (1934, BBJ), also by Sampson, he hits the cymbals in time with the entrances of the brass, adds fills on snare drum and cymbals, and takes a brush solo on the last bridge. On "That Naughty Waltz" (BBJ) his sticks on the high-hat come through loud and clear — for once he is prominently recorded. He is most evident, of course, on the few occasions when he solos, and he takes thrilling solos in the middle of "Undecided" (1939) and on "Harlem Congo" (1937, BBJ). These solos tend to be perpetual motion affairs in eighth notes, made dramatic by Webb's powerful, varied sound and his unexpected accents. Webb was also reportedly a master of the slow, but inevitable sounding crescendo that powered the final choruses of many swing arrangements.

"Stompin' at the Savoy" and "Don't Be That Way" were bigger hits for other orchestras than for Webb, but he had an ace-in-the-hole when he discovered a 16-year-old singer, Ella Fitzgerald. On June 12, 1935 she recorded with Webb "I'll Chase the Blues Away" and "Love and Kisses," two forgettable tunes that are saved by the pure, blithe sound and buoyant swing of Fitzgerald's early voice. Webb knew what he had in her: A record date the following April consisted only of Fitzgerald's vocals, and her vocals were heavily featured in the remaining Webb recordings. After Webb died prematurely, in 1939, Fitzgerald led the band herself until 1942, when she went out on her own. Fitzgerald is discussed further in Chapter 23.

JIMMY LUNCEFORD

One of the most admired bands, famous for its showmanship and precise style, was Jimmy Lunceford's, which featured the writing of Sy Oliver. Born in 1902, the son of a choirmaster, Lunceford was educated in the Denver school system where the musical director was Wilberforce Whiteman, Paul Whiteman's father, before attending Fisk University in Tennessee. After receiving a music degree and teaching for a while, he assembled a band that included students and associates from Fisk.

Lunceford started slowly, recording two tunes in 1930 and two in 1933, but in 1934, his band began recording steadily. His first hit was "White Heat" from January 1934, a Will Hudson composition that had the band swinging powerfully and with technical skill. Hudson was one of the most prolific white arrangers of the day. Henderson had recorded several Will Hudson pieces. Hudson emulated Gene Gifford of the Casa Loma Orchestra, an influential white swing band. (Their "Casa Loma Stomp" is on BBJ.)

The Lunceford group had arrived in New York in 1933. They brought Sy Oliver with them. Oliver had presented some arrangements to Lunceford, and though he was then evidently a weak trumpet player, he was asked to join the band for their engagement at New York City's Lafayette Theater. He went along, and in the six years he spent with Lunceford, was responsible for much of the band's most distinctive music. Other arrangers were used as well: Alto player Willie Smith wrote a chart of Ellington's "Mood Indigo" (BBJ) which, with its twittering saxophone lines, is startlingly unlike the composer's own performances. Pianist Ed Wilcox and trombonist Eddie Durham, who was also an early pioneer of the electric guitar, contributed many innovative works. The Lunceford band's writing was as imaginative as its execution was skilled. "Sleepy Time Gal" (1935), arranged by Wilcox, includes difficult double-time passages for the saxophone section performed with admirable precision. After Wilcox's solo, the band enters with a surprising key change that still startles. Lunceford himself wrote the striking "Stratosphere" (BBJ), a virtuoso arrangement which, as Gunther Schuller has written, includes "four-tone clusters and bitonal harmonies [that] threaten several times to suspend altogether the tonal center of D minor." (A cluster is a dissonant group of notes played simultaneously, such as happens when you put your arm down on the piano; bitonal harmonies suggest two different keys at once.)

Even the Lunceford charts that were not similarly advanced were frequently difficult to play, as revivalists have discovered when they have attempted to perform them. Common wisdom has it that Lunceford never had great soloists, but alto saxophonist Willie Smith was a sensational and unique stylist who was widely considered the equal of Johnny Hodges and Benny Carter. Joe Thomas played a rugged swing tenor, and Paul Webster soloed impressively on trumpet, as did Ed Wilcox on piano. In 1937 Trummy Young was added on trombone, and he made a hit out of "Margie," singing in a high, soft tenor voice, and playing a smooth, elegant solo. The band also had a powerful drummer in Jimmy Crawford, who learned, somewhat against his will, to play with the two-beat feel that arranger Sy Oliver, going against the times, often demanded.

In general, Lunceford mixed a commercial repertoire with unexpected numbers played in innovative ways. Sometimes the unexpected proved commercial. In a surprising interpretation, Willie Smith's arrangement of the popular chestnut "Put on Your Old Grey Bonnet" (1937) is a vibrant uptempo swinger, with some dazzling runs for two saxophones and a trumpet. Lunceford recorded "Down by the Old Mill Stream" and "My Melancholy Baby" in 1938 and the ever-popular "Easter Parade" and "Ain't She Sweet" in 1939. The following year he made a piece based on a theme from Beethoven's "Pathetique Sonata" (1940).

Jimmy Lunceford and his Orchestra in a still from their 1936 short. Note Jimmy Crawford's elaborate percussion setup. (Courtesy Rutgers Institute of Jazz Studies)

Lunceford realized that a swing band was not just a music-making machine, but a show. The Lunceford band was as showy as they came, as captured in a few filmed numbers. As George Simon has written: "The trumpets would throw their horns in the air together; the saxes would almost charge off the stage, so enthusiastically did they blow their horns; the trombones would slip their slides toward the skies; and throughout the evening the musicians would be kidding and shouting at one another, projecting an aura of irresistible exuberance" (*The Big Bands,* p. 329).

Among the recordings of the Lunceford band are two superb numbers built, one might say, on opposite principles: "Organ Grinder's Swing" (SCCJ and BBJ) is an example of ingenious arranging, while "Uptown Blues" (BBJ) is a lightly scored series of solos. For his "Organ Grinder's Swing," recorded on August 31, 1936, Sy Oliver had a clarinet and muted trombone play for eight bars the innocent melody of a nursery rhyme over Crawford's clomping woodblocks. Then Oliver growls a bluesy trumpet refrain while what sounds like two baritone saxophones lay down a kind of boogie-woogie line. These sections are repeated, but with a difference. This time the melody is stated in a varied form by Ed Wilcox on a tinkling celeste, and the next eight bars, instead of Oliver's rough trumpet, we hear the guitarist Al Norris soloing lightly over the smooth-as-silk reeds—his entrance is magical. The whole arrangement, with its many exquisitely unexpected details, swings lightly, gracefully, and the soloing is stellar.

"Uptown Blues" is equally relaxed. It is what musicians called a "head" arrangement—a riff arrangement that can be devised by the musicians on the spot and that can be memorized, kept in one's head. It opens with a descending phrase by the band, with trills, which leads almost directly into an expansive solo, over simple, but beautifully played riffs, by alto saxophonist Willie Smith, showing off his remarkable high register in a penetrating climactic note. Then come two brilliantly shouting choruses by trumpeter Snooky Young, who builds his solo over the ingratiating riffs behind him towards a screaming conclusion. The piece ends in a decrescendo.

"Uptown Blues" was recorded in 1939. In 1942, after a considerable turn-over in personnel, the Lunceford sound became less subtle. The arrangements, such as "Yard Dog Mazurka" by newcomer Gerald Wilson, were more obviously spectacular and brassy. Some thought the band exceeded the bounds of good taste, but it was still distinctive and not without influence. The white California band of Stan Kenton, which had always emulated Lunceford, followed Lunceford in this direction during the 1940s. Like many of the best big bands, the Lunceford group would fade during the war. Lunceford himself collapsed while signing autographs, and died in Oregon on July 12, 1947.

CAB CALLOWAY

The Lunceford group was not at all unusual in its commercial ventures: Benny Goodman's first recording for Victor as a leader was something called "Hunkadola." Every big band had to have singers, boy singers or girl singers, as they were called, or both—and sometimes, as we have seen with Ella Fitzgerald and the Webb band, those singers came to dominate the band's recorded output. Because of changing tastes, reissues of swing band recordings have often under-represented the vocal numbers made in the thirties, but listeners should keep in mind that band vocalists, more typically sweet or humorous than bluesy, were an important part of the era. Certainly they were a part of the Lunceford repertoire. Early on Lunceford added a vocal trio to such numbers as "My Blue Heaven," and many of his recordings featured the pleasant, but glib sounding voice of Dan Grissom on cleverly arranged numbers such as "I'll See You in My Dreams" (1937).

The extraordinary popularity of another black band—that of singer Cab Calloway—was founded on its leader's personality and vocals. Calloway is a phenomenon. Born in 1907, he began his career in Chicago as a singer and dancer. By 1930, he was in New York, fronting a hard-swinging, rough-and-ready band called the Missourians, whose recorded output features several uptempo re-workings of the scheme of "Tiger Rag" (such as "Market Street Stomp" on BBJ) and a few atmospheric numbers such as the growling "Prohibition Blues." Under Calloway's leadership, this group was gradually transformed into a smooth, eloquent, flexible big band that became a mainstay of the Cotton Club.

It was a remarkable achievement for a singer, not an instrumentalist, who has become best known for jivey vocals and for his clever songs celebrating invented characters such as the immortal "Minnie the Moocher." Calloway's charisma was almost unparalleled. A big man, he would dance frenetically in front of his band, his long hair flapping (in his generation, many black people straightened their hair), chanting "Hi-de-ho" to ecstatic audiences. He was famous for his hip talk—in the thirties it was called hep talk. He published a short glossary of such slang in 1938 which he celebrated in his recording "Jive (Page One of the Hepster's Dictionary)." He had a flexible voice with a remarkable wide range. He sang ballads, but not tear-jerkers, pulling at certain phrases or exaggerating an accent to suggest the barest hint of a parody. (In this approach he resembled Fats Waller.) His novelty numbers are still pleasing. After the success of the 1931 "Minnie the Moocher," he kept the key phrase of its chorus ("hi-de-ho" or "hi-de-hi") alive in a series of popular songs such as "You Gotta Ho-De-Ho (To Get Along With Me)," "Keep that Hi-De-Hi In Your Soul," and "The Hi-De-Ho Miracle Man."

Calloway's vocals, and his energetic personality, were at the heart of any Calloway performance, but those vocals and that personality were displayed in front of a series of remarkable big bands. In 1936 this band featured tenor saxophonists Ben Webster and Foots Thomas, the wonderful bass player Milt Hinton, and sterling trumpet and trombone sections. When Webster left, Calloway hired another star tenor saxophonist, the big-toned Leon "Chu" Berry, whose expressive playing was featured in "Ghost of a Chance" (1940). Berry was one of the leading lights of his generation, even praised by Hawkins, until he died tragically in a car crash in 1941. In 1939, Calloway helped prod jazz history along again when he hired the young, and then almost unknown, Dizzy Gillespie.

As a result of its coast-to-coast broadcasts from the Cotton Club, and because of its records in the mid to late thirties, Calloway's band was one of the nation's most popular, and its players were among the best paid in the business. Calloway worked half of each year playing shows in the Cotton Club. Then he took his own show on the road. In his book, *Bass Line,* Milt Hinton describes the routine: "After six months [at the Cotton Club] the repetition of the show started getting to you. By the fourth or fifth month most of the guys began feeling restless and stale on the job and even at home. But knowing it was only a matter of time before they'd be able to get some fresh air made anything seem alright. When we'd go back on the road it was the Cab Calloway Show again. We'd have a girl singer like June Richmond or Mary Louise, a featured tap dancer, a comedian, and the Cotton Club Boys. We'd start by playing theaters. The show would be about an hour and a half long and we'd do three or four a day. The tour usually began in a New York theater where the audience was different from the Cotton Club, then moved to Newark, Philadelphia, Atlantic City, Baltimore, Washington, Pittsburgh, and so forth . . . Finally at the end of three months we'd have worked our way out to California. By this time things were so monotonous it was a relief to go into the Million Dollar Ballroom in L.A. and play dance music for a couple of weeks. When we finished the Coast, we'd start back. Only this time we'd do one-night dances in much smaller and more rural places" (p. 80).

Even for this relatively pampered band, the routine was trying. Hinton talks of racial incidents, and of the difficulty of finding housing and food in some of the small towns where the band played dances. The band members were stars of a sort, but not immune to racial insult. Neither were they immune, as Hinton suggests, to the boredom of playing similar music night after night. They got around this by finding interesting arrangements that were sometimes played when Calloway was offstage.

The recorded legacy of the Calloway band is rich, and in it the singer shows some sensitivity to his band's desire to play hot jazz and challenging arrangements. Virtually every Calloway song features an instrumental solo or two, and he promoted numbers showcasing individual members, such as "Pluckin' the Bass" for Milt Hinton, where he showed off his rapid slap bass solo style. That style, which involves making a percussive sound by slapping the strings, was mostly used by bassists in featured spots, rather than for accompaniment. The smoothly swinging 1937 "Bugle Blues" opens up to feature Chu Berry and others, and Calloway's hot scat vocal proves that the singer could improvise with the best in his band.

KANSAS CITY BANDS

We have been concentrating on black bands based in the East, but it should be noted that some of the most exciting big bands of the thirties came from the Midwest and Southwest, particularly from the Kansas City area. The region was dotted with what have been called the territory bands, so called because they were not, as far as union rules were concerned, centered in a single city or union. They were also called travelling bands: In his autobiography *Twenty Years on Wheels*, band leader Andy Kirk talks about having to switch from travelling band status to being a Kansas City band when finally he settled in that city. The territory bands include groups led by the likes of George E. Lee, Zack Whyte and Alphonse Trent, all of whom played dance music and blues in the ballrooms of Kansas City and environs. Several of these bands recorded: In 1929, Zach Whyte, whose home base was Cincinnati, made a version of "West End Blues" in which his trumpets played a written-out Armstrong-style solo in unison. Alphonse Trent did in 1930 an uptempo "St. James Infirmary" in an arrangement that shows the influence of Don Redman. It features the astonishingly fleet trombone playing of Snub Mosley and exciting bits by two musicians who later became well known: violinist Stuff Smith, and trumpeter Peanuts Holland. Significantly, Sy Oliver wrote for both of these bands before joining Lunceford.

Kansas City was a Mecca for musicians from the Southwest. It was a wide-open, one might say vice-ridden, town that was a central marketplace for the region's trade. From 1928 to 1939, the town was dominated by its flamboyant crime boss, Tom Pendergast, a gangster-politician whose interest in night life helped make Kansas City the region's entertainment capital. In *Bird Lives!*, Ross Russell describes the surprise of talent scouts John Hammond and Joe Glaser in

1934 at what they found: "To their astonishment they found Kansas City a honeycomb of nightclubs that had been operating without interruption all through Prohibition, as if the Volstead Act [which prohibited liquor] did not exist, and all through the hard years of the early 1930's, as if there were no Depression either. They discovered cabarets, show bars, refurbished speak-easies, music lounges, taverns, bars, honky-tonks, dance halls, saloons, and just plain nightclubs . . . All of these clubs had live music" (p. 30).

Music permeated the entertainment district. There were blues singers, boogie-woogie pianists, small groups and big bands, and the music went from dusk to dawn as musicians went from one small dive to another to jam in competitive sessions with their rivals and peers. No wonder some of the most innovative improvisers of the period, from Lester Young and Ben Webster to Charlie Christian and Charlie Parker, came out of or through Kansas City. Charlie Parker served his musical apprenticeship in the cabarets of Kansas City: Count Basie found his musical identity there. Kansas City bands became known, quite rightly, for their easy way with the blues. Perhaps because they were close to the Southern sources of country blues, and perhaps because of the informal nature of the jam sessions, Kansas City jazz was often a riff-driven blues music.

The best known bands nationally were led by Andy Kirk, Bennie Moten, Count Basie and Jay McShann. In 1929, Andy Kirk became the leader of a Texas band that would soon move to Kansas City. Called originally Terrence T. Holder's Dark Clouds of Joy Orchestra, it became well known as Andy Kirk and His Twelve Clouds of Joy. Kirk was born in Kentucky in 1898, moved to Denver while still a child, and like Lunceford was educated under Wilberforce White-man, Paul Whiteman's father. Kirk grew up in an integrated environment where he heard relatively little black music. He didn't immediately become a musician. After a stint as a postman, he joined the Denver band of violinist George Morrison as a tuba player and bass saxophonist. Later, while in Dallas, he switched to Terrence Holder. When Holder's group ran into difficulties, Kirk assumed the leadership of the band.

In 1929, they first performed with the person who helped create the group's lasting appeal, pianist and arranger Mary Lou Williams. A strong, eclectic instrumentalist who would in her long career record everything from boogie-woogie to modern jazz, Mary Lou Williams was originally brought into the band as a substitute during an audition for Jack Kapp, a record executive and later the founder of Decca Records, who was in 1929 combing Kansas City to find a new band. Kapp liked the band, and the pianist, for in the ensuing record date he insisted that Williams, then the wife of the band's alto saxophonist John Williams, be the pianist.

Soon she was not only the group's most celebrated soloist, but the arranger and composer of many of their recordings. Her charts have a light, bouncing swing and are marked by characteristic details such as her occasional use of a tenor saxophone lead instead of the usual alto. (Tenor saxophonist Dexter Gordon has said that Kirk's tenor, the now underrated Dick Wilson, influenced him, and that he particularly liked Williams's arrangements because of the

Mary Lou Williams at the piano, late 1940's. (Courtesy Rutgers Institute of Jazz Studies)

prominent tenor parts.) Like Ellington, Williams would mix up the sections, creating an unusual sound by placing a trumpet among the reeds, for example.

Williams' "Walkin' and Swingin' " (March 2, 1936) is mostly written: It's a succession of riffs and smooth reed parts, played over the gentle swing of a polished rhythm section. A phrase played by a trumpet and saxophones at the end of the second chorus would be the basis of a bebop tune: Thelonious Monk's "Rhythm-a-ning." During the last bridge, part of the popular "Peanut Vendor" is interpolated. At the same session, Kirk recorded the impressive "Lotta Sax Appeal" featuring the boldly pushing sax solo of Dick Wilson, and the next day the ensemble proved its power on the opening choruses of "Git." In April 1936, this band made their biggest commercial hit, the ballad "Until the Real Thing Comes Along," featuring the soaring, mellifluous vocal of Pha Terrell—its climax is sung in high falsetto. (They had recorded the song in March with drummer Ben Thigpen singing.) This recording would improve the Kirk band's fortunes markedly. Between April 1936, and the end of 1937, the band recorded twenty-eight sides, of which nineteen were Terrell vocals. Kirk later regretted that he was unable to make as many swinging jazz recordings as he wanted to.

Still, the 1939 "Floyd's Guitar Blues," is notable because in it guitarist Floyd Smith plays a recent invention, the electric guitar. His solo begins with woozily bent chords: He then continues by emphasizing the sustaining power of his new instrument with held high notes, played with a tight fast vibrato. The record suggests the future, but later guitarists refined the sound.

The character of Kirk's Clouds of Joy would change in the forties, when Mary Lou Williams left, followed by the departure of Pha Terrell. Terrell went on to become, as did many of the big band singers, a single attraction. In 1943 the band recorded "McGhee Special," trumpeter Howard McGhee's essay in the modern style that was developing. Kirk disbanded in 1948, and has worked in business since, sometimes getting a band together for a specific event.

The most powerful figure in Kansas City jazz from 1923 when he made his first recordings until his premature death in 1935 was Bennie Moten, who was born in the city in 1894. A pianist originally influenced by ragtime, Moten began with a six-piece band which he first took into a recording session in September 1923 behind two blues singers. On the instrumental "Crawdad Blues" the soloists are capable, even the banjo player, and there is a bit of double time near the end, a trick found on only a few recordings of that time. It was a sign of his success that Moten expanded his group, recording his own raggy "South" in 1924 with eight pieces, including two cornets. The sound resembles King Oliver's, and perhaps demonstrates a direct influence from Oliver's records. The sound soon changed: It became a more propulsive, lighter ensemble already by the 1925 "South Street Blues." The 1926 "Muscle Shoals Blues," by a 10-piece group, is an easy-swinging, almost casual blues performance pushed along amiably by Vernon Page's tuba. One can hear the band's development in the second "South," recorded in 1928: As if acknowledging the dated quality of the composition, the band plays with a kind of ricky-ticky rhythm in the first chorus. They seem to be looking backward with some amusement on an earlier music.

Eddie Durham, who we mentioned as an arranger for Lunceford in the mid-thirties, had joined Moten in 1929, and his writing was crucial to the development of the band's sound. The best of Moten came at his last session in December 1932, when the band with pianist Bill Basie and soloists such as tenor saxophonist Ben Webster, trumpeter "Hot Lips" Page and bassist Walter Page played numbers like "Lafayette" and "Prince of Wails" and "New Orleans." The last featured Jimmy Rushing, a husky-voiced blues singer who managed to sound sophisticated as well as joyful while shouting the blues in the best Kansas City manner.

"Lafayette," written by Durham with some help from Basie, showcases several of the band's strongest players. After some piano chords by Basie, Walter Page plays in the slap bass style. As soon as Ben Webster enters with a characteristically aggressive, ingratiating solo, Page goes into a hard-driving walking bass. This style of bass accompaniment was first made by "doubling up" the oom-pah of earlier times. Where a bassist of 1923 might play c, pause, g, pause, in 1932 the same individual might play c, c, g, g, filling in the pauses. (The next step in walking bass came when bassists decided to avoid those repetitions and play scale passages. Finally, around 1940, Jimmy Blanton with the Duke Ellington band and others of his generation introduced added chromatic notes which ushered in the modern approach to bass playing.) Oran "Hot

Lips" Page, unrelated to the bassist, follows in a solo that displays his brilliant growling style with mutes. "Lafayette" includes a clearly recorded solo for drummer Willie McWashington, a rarity in this era. Other Moten recordings are discussed in Chapter 10.

BENNY GOODMAN

Moten died just as the swing era proper hit. He never benefited from Goodman's popular success. That success, and the fact that publicists dubbed Goodman "the King of Swing," has caused a kind of backlash against the Benny Goodman band and its recordings. Goodman's was a tightly disciplined, joyless band, the story goes, thwarted by Goodman's chary disposition and perfectionist leadership and dependent on the arrangements of earlier, more talented bands and band leaders. The recordings, and the testimony of musicians and fans, prove otherwise. Goodman's groups never achieved the ineffable swing, the rapturous cumulative power, of Basie, and he sometimes didn't appreciate his soloists sufficiently—the uniquely spirited pianist Jess Stacy was always underused. Nevertheless the Goodman bands, as we hear on live recordings, had a special buoyancy, and Goodman's fluent, accurate clarinet playing was a great asset. Goodman not only floated brilliantly over the band during its last choruses: His lyrical blues solos—the one on "One O'Clock Jump" from the 1938 Carnegie Hall concert, for example—were vigorous and heartfelt. In the thirties, he used a bright—one might almost say, optimistic—tone, with a fast, eloquent terminal vibrato. He sometimes growled, and sometimes began a phrase with a bark. Goodman was at home in the company of the great black stars, as we hear in his bouncing introductory solo on Billie Holiday's "What a Little Moonlight Can Do" (1935).

As time went on, Goodman inflected his sound less, probably one result of the lessons he took with the pure-toned classical clarinetist, Reginald Kell. Despite the change in style, until the end of his life he could swing a tune mightily, as he did on the spectacular "The World is Waiting for the Sunrise" at the 1958 Brussels World Fair. By that time he was using longer, more flowing phrases than earlier in his career, as can be heard by comparing the trio version of "After You've Gone" from 1935 with a small band version made in 1960. In the early "After You've Gone," Goodman frequently alternates quarter notes with two eighths, in a kind of "dum-dada-dum-dada" figure. In the second half of several measures (4, 6, 9, 13, 15), he introduces a figure of four eighth notes. (See music example.)

The later solo is different, but equally valid. In 1960, the tone seems softer. His phrases are certainly longer, and he builds them up out of motives. The first phrase takes up 10 measures, and is built out of a triplet turn that finally breaks out into a rising arpeggio in measure six. The next phrase, measures 12 through 17, explores a rising arpeggio, taking its four notes and playing them at different points of each measure. (See music example.)

Example 9–5.
Benny Goodman, beginning of his solo on "After You've Gone" (1935).

Example 9–6.
Benny Goodman, beginning of his solo on "After You've Gone" (1960).

His initial success at first surprised even Goodman, who when he was putting together his first band, seemed unsure how commercial he should make it. John Hammond urged him to swing, and helped find the musicians who would prove to be the band's stars: the exciting and interactive drummer Gene Krupa, trumpeter Harry James, trumpeter Ziggy Elman (who brought in some Jewish dance music—klezmer—to the band), Stacy and saxophonist Vido Musso.

After the West Coast tour that made the band's name, Goodman returned to New York. Beginning in 1935, the band recorded almost monthly. Some of those records, even those which sold well at the time, seem mildly disappointing now. Some of the uptempo swing numbers—Goodman called them "killer-dillers"—such as the 1936 "Christopher Columbus" sound flat today. Goodman's band was as precise as any ensemble before or since—he admired classical groups such as the Budapest String Quartet. Occasionally that virtuosity seems misused. The changes in volume on "Don't Be That Way," when in the penultimate chorus the band whispers, demonstrates their skill, but the surging opening choruses of "Swingtime at the Rockies," played with equal control, are more exciting.

In July of 1935, Goodman recorded for the first time with his trio, featuring his flamboyant drummer, Gene Krupa, and black pianist Teddy Wilson. (The absence of a bass was not unusual at the time.) Daringly for the time, Goodman, at John Hammond's behest, began to appear live with this interracial group. It was a notable step in segregated America. There were no regular black members of the Goodman band, or of other bands. Later of course there were exceptions to this rule. Artie Shaw hired black vocalist Billie Holiday in 1938, but she left because of the mistreatment she received from hotel managers and others. In 1940, Goodman would hire trumpeter Cootie Williams to join his band, and Roy Eldridge was the featured trumpeter of the Gene Krupa band from 1941 to 1943. In 1939, an integrated band of women, the International Sweethearts of Rhythm, began its distinguished career. These examples prove that Goodman's 1935 hirings of first Teddy Wilson and then vibraphonist Lionel Hampton, actions taken when he was leading the country's most popular swing band, were influential.

Benny Goodman plays for dancers, 1938. The dancer with the moustache is saxophonist Adrian Rollini. (Courtesy Rutgers Institute of Jazz Studies)

The first trio performances captured some of Goodman's most free-wheeling playing on record, on the "After You've Gone" mentioned above, and on the restrained, elegant "Body and Soul" (SCCJ), where he allows Wilson to steal the honors with his dazzling elaborations of the first bridge and the beginning of the second chorus. The addition of vibraphonist Lionel Hampton created one of the most exciting groups of the mid-thirties. If Goodman and Wilson were, comparatively, cool, elegant players, Hampton was a heavy hitting swinger, a perfect foil to the oblique Wilson. In the last choruses, Hampton would thump his mallets down hard, then beat out what sounded like trumpet riffs while emitting a high cackling sound with his voice. Bouncing behind the vibes or sometimes on top of a snare drum—he is also a fine drummer—he seemed to represent the wild excitement that was one part of the legacy of swing. Hampton could also play a fine ballad, as he proved on the quartet's "Moonglow."

On January 16, 1938, Goodman broke another barrier, when he triumphantly presented his band, joined by stars of the Basie and Ellington groups, to a rapturous audience in sold-out Carnegie Hall. Black musicians had appeared there playing various types of music, but this was the first full evening of jazz at Carnegie Hall, and with an integrated cast. Goodman approached the date with some trepidation, and even thought of adding a comedian to warm up the crowd. It was a triumph from the beginning, and fortunately it was recorded. It is a sign of how far jazz had come that Goodman included a series of tunes with pedagogical intent. He meant to show the history of jazz from the seemingly antiquated "Sensation Rag" of the ODJB to an example of the hip present, Harry James's "Life Goes to a Party." The retrospective included short tributes to Bix Beiderbecke and Louis Armstrong, and a laughing evocation of the vaudeville clarinet of Ted Lewis.

The medley is most important because it suggests that the idea of jazz history and of a distinctive jazz repertoire was becoming prevalent. That December (1938), John Hammond produced his first "From Spirituals to Swing" concert, which presented at Carnegie Hall the Basie band and Goodman's sextet, but also folk blues, gospel, and the boogie-woogie pianist Pete Johnson. In 1939, the publication of Frederick Ramsey's and Charles Edward Smith's book *Jazzmen* would send researchers scurrying to New Orleans, where they would unearth, among other players, trumpeter Bunk Johnson. The prestige of Hammond's concerts (he produced another in 1939), which built on Goodman's Carnegie Hall debut, and the nostalgia about earlier music and musicians indicated by *Jazzmen* and those researchers, helped lead to a re-awakened interest in small group jazz, old and new (including a Dixieland revival which we discuss in Chapter 12).

Goodman's concert also included many of his current hits, but its highlight was the 12-twelve minute version of "Sing Sing Sing." The piece is an oddity, a remaking of a number by trumpeter Louis Prima which was combined with the riffs of Fletcher Henderson's "Christopher Columbus." At Carnegie Hall, it became a series of dazzling solos, including the eerie extended solo by Goodman which he plays over the light tomtoms of Gene Krupa. He begins, as on the studio version which is on BBJ, with a reference to a phrase the band had just played, and he builds sensitively, aided both by the dynamics of Krupa and by the melodic echoes of pianist Jess Stacy. Goodman ends in a dramatic hush, as he plays first a high A and then, miraculously, in perfect pitch, the C above that. After a burst of applause, Stacy enters, at first tentatively. Soon he gathers his forces to play a luminous solo which builds on the eerily floating mood established by Goodman, without ceasing to swing. He sounds like Fats Waller improvising on a piece by Debussy. Finally there's a rush as the band wails to a finish over Krupa's exuberant clatter.

While Goodman continued to perform throughout 1939, and broadcast regularly as part of the "Camel Caravan," a weekly show out of New York sponsored by Camel Cigarettes, the Goodman band was soon dispersed, as Gene Krupa and Harry James went out to form their own groups, to be followed by Hampton and Wilson. Krupa created an outstanding ensemble that in 1941 featured Roy Eldridge on pieces such as "Rockin' Chair" and "After You've Gone" and Anita O'Day's creative vocals, and then, in the late forties, Krupa led an up-to-date group with young modernists like trumpeter Red Rodney. James, an admirable hot soloist, proved enamored of his broad vibrato and bravura technique: When he wasn't imitating Basie charts in his band, he was playing—to great acclaim—bathetic ballads or technical display pieces such as "The Flight of the Bumblebee."

Goodman countered the loss of James by hiring Cootie Williams from the Ellington band. An even more important addition to the band was hired, again on the urgent recommendation of John Hammond, in August of 1939. This was Charlie Christian, a young black electric guitarist, who would be the premier force on his instrument for decades to come. Christian was born in Texas in 1916, and played in a family band around Oklahoma City where his guitar-playing father took the family in 1921. In the thirties he played in his brother's band, "The Jolly Jugglers," and with Alphonse Trent. He would debut with Goodman's small group, now a sextet. Although it included Cootie Williams, Christian was its star. His light, loping style, darkish sound, and rhythmic bounce were at the service, it seemed, of a musical mind as fluent and adventurous as his fingers were fleet. With the help of arranger Jimmy Mundy, Christian and Goodman put together a feature for the guitarist called "Solo Flight." Before he died in 1942 of tuberculosis, Christian would take part in the crucial jam sessions at Minton's in New York City that helped consolidate the so-called bebop revolution, which we will discuss in Chapter 12.

We can hear Christian's value as an improviser in a casual setting—the musicians didn't know they were already being recorded—on a number that has been released as "Ad Lib Blues." It is from a session, one of the marvels of the Goodman discography, that featured Goodman with Count Basie and members of his band, including trumpeter Buck Clayton and tenor saxophonist Lester Young, bassist Walter Page and Jo Jones on drums. Christian begins with an intriguing series of blues phrases—when Jones enters the piece takes off. As the piece develops, the first four bars of each chorus are played by each soloist alone, an old blues routine used, for example, in "Bugle Call Blues" and Ellington's "Sepia Panorama." Christian demonstrates his uncanny ability to make simple phrases rhythmically surprising and to maintain a relaxed swing. (See music example. Also, see photograph on next page.)

Example 9–7.
Charlie Christian's solo on "Ad-Lib Blues" (1940) with the Benny Goodman Septet.

Young's breaks are twisting, climbing constructions. As can also be heard on the "Good Morning Blues" from the Spirituals to Swing Concert of 1939, Young and Christian were especially compatible improvisers: on that number, which after the introduction becomes a slow blues, both of them build their solos from short opening phrases.

A back injury forced Goodman to disband in July 1940, and when the clarinetist regrouped in October, he seemed to have a new agenda. His band now featured many new arrangements less attuned to dancing, by Eddie Sauter and Mel Powell, pieces such as Sauter's "Benny Rides Again" and "Concerto a la King," little concertos for Benny, and Mel Powell's "Mission to Moscow." "The Earl," recorded without a drummer, is pianist Powell's tribute to Earl Hines, and his piano playing here reflects his mentor's. Powell worked on and off with Goodman through 1955, then went on to become a professor of composition at Yale University, winning a Pulitzer Prize in 1990. Goodman had heard Eddie Sauter's highly original work for the band of xylophonist Red Norvo. The arrangements he did for Goodman were equally original. He uses a simulation of baroque trills and counterpoint in the opening of "Clarinet a la King," and on

A recording session of October 28, 1940. From left: Lester Young, Jo Jones (drums), Buck Clayton, Freddie Green (rhythm guitar), Benny Goodman, Walter Page (bass), Charlie Christian, Count Basie. (Courtesy Harry Swisher)

"Benny Rides Again" he maintains an almost constant, nervous interplay between clarinet and orchestra before ending with some dramatic dissonance.

Clearly Goodman's ambitions had changed. In 1940, the clarinetist had been on top of the dance band business for half a decade. On May 1, 1940 Goodman played the Mozart Concerto for Clarinet with conductor Leopold Stokowski. 1940 was also the year he recorded Bela Bartok's "Contrasts," a piece commissioned by Goodman, with the composer on piano and violinist Joseph Szigeti. Goodman may have wanted to move in different directions in jazz as well. After the war, Goodman flirted with, but eventually rejected, the new style called Bebop. In 1948, he was playing not only "Bugle Call Rag" and "Stompin' at the Savoy," but "Chico's Bop." His new septet had young black tenor saxophonist Wardell Gray. Goodman seemed to be trying to adapt his own playing to the latest thing.

He never quite succeeded, but somewhere along the line, he must have realized that he didn't need to find a new style. For the rest of his life, Goodman would play basically the music he developed in the late thirties, although that style was informed by traces of the developments of modern jazz, and he continued to essay occasional modernist arrangements. He was a revered figure until his death in 1986, but never as important a musician as he was in the late thirties. Goodman's playing never went into a decline, but swing bands did. In a public television tribute to Goodman broadcast shortly before the clarinetist's death, Frank Sinatra told a story about Goodman. In 1942, Sinatra had just left the Tommy Dorsey band, and was beginning, rather nervously, a solo career. He was playing a theater with Benny Goodman, who introduced the skinny young singer casually—then there was a startling roar from the audience, startling evidently to Sinatra as well as to Goodman, who said, "What the hell is that?" That was the future—in which singers, once appealing appendages to big bands, meant to look enticing and sing blandly, would become more popular than the bands that spawned them.

If Benny Goodman had a real rival during the swing era, it was another clarinetist, equally accomplished, the debonair Artie Shaw. Shaw had his first big hit when he recorded in July 1938 an instrumental version, arranged by himself and by Jerry Gray, of Cole Porter's "Begin the Beguine" (BBJ). In his autobiography, *The Trouble with Cinderella*, Shaw sounds virtually burdened by success ever after. His cool, liquid clarinet, inventively played, appealed surprisingly to a mass market, but Shaw was essentially a serious musician, troubled by fame and by the fact that he was unable, as he thought, to play the most challenging music he had in him. He was caught in a bind—he wanted to be a popular artist and he wanted to perform music that intrigued him. He ended up quitting his band, suddenly in 1939, only to reform it the next year. He performed sporadically in the forties, experimenting with different approaches, then stopped playing by the mid-fifties. Beginning in 1983, he sanctioned, and rehearsed, a new Artie Shaw band, which recreated Shaw's hit recording "Star Dust" (the original is on BBJ) and other such pieces with clarinetist Dick Johnson playing Shaw's parts.

Shaw and Benny Goodman weren't the only band leaders trying new things in the forties, which saw Harry James and Tommy Dorsey and even Earl Hines adding string sections to their bands. With or without strings, the Dorsey band, though not always a jazz band, was special: for its elegant arrangements of pieces as far afield as "Song of India" (1937, BBJ), for its ensemble work, for the blithely romantic, technically perfect solos of its leader, and for Sinatra's vocals on "Street of Dreams," "Violets for Your Furs" and "Polka Dots and Moonbeams." Sinatra's slyly phrased vocals, then sung in a light baritone—his voice would deepen later—may not have reminded many listeners of Billie Holiday or Louis Armstrong, whom he admired. But their unaffected lyricism, their ability to tell a story, influenced many later jazz musicians and most singers.

Bands like Shaw's, Goodman's, Dorsey's and Glenn Miller's did not always play challenging jazz. As we have seen, many of the leaders felt by 1940 that they needed something new, and they were searching, with string sections, untried arrangers and esoteric material, to find a different formula than that worked out by Fletcher Henderson and others at the beginning of the decade. Because of World War II, with its entertainment taxes and restrictions on travel, and because of changing tastes, the swing era had reached an appropriate end by the mid-forties. Despite the efforts of the stars and of younger musicians, jazz would never be quite so popular again. But the swing bands were more than just popular: Together they raised the art of ensemble playing to a level that has never been surpassed in jazz or popular music.

One of the last swing bands to achieve prominence in the thirties turned out to be the most enduring of all. Count Basie emerged from the Midwest in 1936 with the most stunning soloists and the most propulsive rhythm section of them all. One of the greatest jazz musicians, Basie deserves a chapter of his own.

10 Count Basie

By the time he died on April 26, 1984, Count Basie had led a jazz band for about 50 years. He was absolutely central to jazz. A determined man with a shy, evasive smile, he epitomized swing, and every time he played he seemed to reiterate the importance of the blues. One of the music's great editors, as a player and as a band leader, Basie played fewer notes in an evening than some pianists played in a chorus, but he rocked the rafters when he wanted to. His solos were terse, understated, impeccably timed. He liked to play a few ringing notes and then let them air out over the steady chug of his rhythm section. Sometimes he would hold a single note, listen to the harmony rearrange itself underneath, and then at the last second descend in a clump of chords to the tonic: His timing reminded one of a supremely confident batter who waits until a pitch is almost by him before poking it out to right field.

Basie conducted unobtrusively from the piano, with an occasional enigmatic nod, a bemused glance or a seemingly noncommittal phrase on the piano. At the end of a piece, he might wave his arms, but that gesture was for the benefit of the audience, not the orchestra. At times oddly passive about his career, he might never have had a national reputation if producer John Hammond hadn't heard a broadcast from Kansas City of an early Basie band, playing at the Reno Club in the spring of 1936. But he was resolute when it mattered. In 1929, he talked his way into the Bennie Moten band, the top band in the Southwest. Moten was a piano player, and the hardest thing he ever did, Basie concluded later, was to become the pianist for a band led by another piano player. Somehow, Basie, who called himself a "conniver," convinced Moten to spend more time managing and fronting his band.

The Count Basie band, though a late-comer to the swing era—it didn't hit New York until the end of 1936—was inimitable, second in historical impact only to that of Duke Ellington. Its rhythm section—Basie, guitarist Freddie Green, bassist Walter Page and drummer Jo Jones—produced a smooth, subtle 4/4 beat that sounded like a whisper but had the power of a train. When it was going right, Page's big-toned bass, the tasteful ching of Jones's high-hat cymbal, Green's steady, contained strumming, and Basie's occasional chords seemed to merge into a single instrument. One of the most exciting effects in jazz can still be heard in recordings in which Basie's brass wails through a chorus, then suddenly drops out, leaving the rhythm section to sweep along after it. Behind the ensemble, the rhythm floats, pushes and prods: Alone it carries on sublimely, producing a subdued tension and excitement most jazz groups can only dream of. "You don't have to kill yourself to swing," Basie once said, and his band proved it every time they played.

Basie's thirties band was what Albert Murray, collaborator on Basie's autobiography *Good Morning Blues* (1985), calls his Old Testament band. It began to change its character as its personnel changed during the war, and by 1950, after the bottom dropped out of the big band era, Basie ended up fronting a small group. Then, in 1952, prodded by Billy Eckstine, Basie began what Murray calls his New Testament band. There was no duplicating the old group, which depended heavily on its brilliant soloists and on informal arrangements thrown together by musicians with long experience with one another. So Basie transformed his sound, featuring accomplished, tightly executed ensemble work and the carefully crafted arrangements of band members such as trumpeter Thad Jones, saxophonists Frank Foster and Ernie Wilkins, and of outsiders such as

Count Basie in the mid-1940's. (Courtesy Rutgers Institute of Jazz Studies)

Neal Hefti, Benny Carter (formerly of the Fletcher Henderson band), Quincy Jones and organist Wild Bill Davis, who contributed the band's biggest hit, "April in Paris."

Basie found a new style and he made it work. In the late fifties and sixties, the New Testament band set a standard for ensemble playing. Unlike the earlier band, the new band often sounded best when playing slowly and softly. One of its enduring hits, "Lil' Darlin'," is played at such a slow tempo that the band sounds like it's floating.

But in the seventies the band seemed to ossify, imitating with lessening conviction the effects that band members had created in the fifties. Eventually only Basie seemed to keep alive the spirit that he took with him out of Kansas City in the mid-thirties. That the last decade of Basie's life did not prove unproductive musically was due to the work of record producer Norman Granz, who coaxed Basie into making small group records, including two trio dates that featured his piano, a session in which he accompanied Kansas City blues shouter Joe Turner, and three albums that paired him with the flamboyant pianist Oscar Peterson, a compatible opposite. These albums represented the final flowering of a remarkable talent, and establish Basie forever as one of the great jazz pianists.

Basie wouldn't agree. His autobiography is filled with the names of pianists he wouldn't dare play after. Early on he decided, probably wrongly, that he could not compete with the most agile pianists, and he changed his style accordingly, willingly sacrificing a virtuosity that must have cost him a considerable struggle to achieve. Instead, he became the consummate ensemble pianist. He knew precisely what he wanted from his band as well. The last pages of his autobiography admonish a young unnamed drummer then with his band to "keep his eye on the sparrow," Basie's nickname for himself: "You can't have four leaders. . . . That's why I tell them in my band, 'Keep your eyes on the fellow at the piano. The sparrow. He don't know nothing, but just keep your eyes on him and we'll all be together on what's going down' " (pp. 381–82). Of course the sparrow knew a lot. One of the things he knew was that less is often more. Given the parsimony of his own playing, it is no wonder that he abhorred overblown soloing from others. In rehearsal, Basie would edit every arrangement that came to him until it was lean and swinging.

At a symposium in Boston in March 1986, saxophonist Billy Mitchell told a story about Basie that suggests that his timing in speech was as perfect as it was in music. During a concert, Basie made a mistake in a solo, and Mitchell leaned over to him and asked teasingly, "What was that note?" Basie kept playing for a bit and then replied, "It don't matter none." He continued to play for about half a minute and then added, "But if you play one like it you're fired."

Basie was born in 1904 in Red Bank, New Jersey. His father was a caretaker for a wealthy local family—Red Bank was then a fashionable resort town. His mother played some piano, and took in laundry. The first thing Basie really wanted to do in his life, he says in *Good Morning Blues*, was to make it possible for her to stop working. Basie heard music at the carnivals that came to Red

Bank, and he did chores for the manager of the Palace movie theater, where he could hear vaudeville performers. He discovered early that he could pick out on the piano any tune he heard, but he wanted to play drums until he met drummer Sonny Greer, who later became Duke Ellington's drummer. After hearing Greer a few times, "I had sense enough to know that I'd never be able to do what he did up there" (p. 33).

As a child, Basie listened to ragtime, but the dominant piano music in his area was stride. Basie heard such distinguished stride pianists as the legendary New Jersey-ite Don Lambert, and he received a few lessons from Fats Waller. He still thought of himself as a vaudeville pianist, not a jazzman, until one morning in Oklahoma City in the mid-twenties. Traveling with a vaudeville show led by a woman named Gonzelle White, Basie awoke in his hotel room to the sound of a big band. He rushed outside and found the Kansas City band of bassist Walter Page, his Blue Devils. Despite his many other musical experiences, he had never heard a big jazz band live. He talks about it in *Good Morning Blues:*

"Everything about them really got to me, and as things worked out, hearing them that day was probably the most important turning point in my musical career so far as my notions about what kind of music I really wanted to try to play was concerned. Not to get ahead of the story, I'll just say when I look back at just about every step I've taken since I ran into those guys that morning, I can see quite a lot to bear out the old saying, 'Once a Blue Devil, always a Blue Devil' " (p. 5).

Basie, who was to become one of the best blues players in the music, "hadn't ever played the blues" before this. But he was immediately captivated by the Blue Devils' blues feeling. As he discovered when he went to hear the band the following evening, everything the Blue Devils played had it: "They were not really playing all that much blues that night. But they were still bluesy. . . . Sometimes you hear new things and it scares you. But this time I just wanted to play with them" (p. 8). Within a year, in 1928, he was playing with them, and when later he "connived" his way into the Bennie Moten band, he tried to bring some Blue Devils with him. For the rest of his life, the genial swing, the snappy showmanship, the deep blues feeling of the Blue Devils remained his standard. (Unfortunately the Blue Devils only recorded two titles, in 1929, and without Basie. But they are fine records.)

Basie recorded for the first time with the Moten band, in October 1929, but his most celebrated work with the band came in December 1932. He added a touch of Eastern stride to their riffing recordings. Basie was influenced by Earl Hines and by his mentor Fats Waller, as one can hear in the light dancing passages of "Moten Swing" (SCCJ and BBJ), a recording that alternates his piano phrases with short, shouting responses by the saxophones. The drive of the rhythm, which Basie described as a "steady rump rump rump rump in that medium tempo," though often spoken of as a general feature of Kansas City jazz, seems rather a product of Walter Page's bass, and it would be refined in Basie's own groups with Page.

The Bennie Moten band around 1929. The three people in the center are, from left, Bill "Count" Basie, singer Jimmy Rushing, and Moten. Just to the right of Rushing is trombonist, guitarist, and composer Eddie Durham. Trumpeter Hot Lips Page is at far left. (Courtesy Rutgers Institute of Jazz Studies)

Basie became a band leader briefly in 1934, then rejoined Moten. After Moten died unexpectedly on April 2, 1935 during a botched tonsillectomy, his band was led by his relative Buster Moten but it soon disintegrated. Basie left, and by the end of 1935 was invited to put a band together for a steady job at the Reno Club in Kansas City. With the help of the respected Blue Devils alumnus, saxophonist Buster Smith, a nine-piece group was assembled which Basie would later say was meant to be as close as possible to the Blue Devils style. He called it his "Three, Three and Three" band, after its three trumpets, three reeds and three rhythm men. In it Blue Devils and Moten alumni Walter Page and Hot Lips Page and baritone saxophonist Jack Washington were joined by a variety of others, including in 1936 Jo Jones and Lester Young.

Jones helped revolutionize jazz drumming. He frequently kept a light 4/4 beat on his cymbals and sometimes used his bass drum for punctuation or emphasis rather than to beat every quarter note. His playing was crucial to the development of the band. Born in 1911 in Illinois, Jones began his career working in travelling carnival shows, then worked with territory bands. He is probably the drummer on two titles recorded by Lloyd Hunter's Serenaders in 1931. In 1933 he moved to Kansas City, and soon was playing with Basie. He was an innovator whose elegantly graceful solos and rhythm work could be heard into the seventies. His high-hat work was exemplary: Behind the piano solo on Basie's "Time Out" (1937), his high-hat can be heard opening and closing with a "whoosh" in unexpected places. Jones was also unusual in that he used the high-hat at slow tempos—where most drummers used brushes or press roll ride patterns—as in Basie's "I Left My Baby" (1939).

Jones sometimes played the bass drum softly on all four beats, as was standard at the time. Elsewhere, to achieve a lighter sound, he didn't use the bass drum at all, or used it for accents, usually in conjunction with figures played on other parts of the drum set. We can hear such figures and accents behind Lester Young's solo early in the 1937 live radio broadcast performance of "John's Idea." At the end of a 1938 broadcast of "Nagasaki," he plays, just before Young's four-bar solo, a figure that includes bass drum "kicks" to the rhythm of the horn riffs. Jones liked to back Lester Young with his suspended cymbal, giving a cushion of support that became standard among the next generation.

Lester Young was the band's most influential soloist. Light, supple and airy, his tone on tenor was derived, according to Young, from his early years imitating Frankie Trumbauer's C-melody saxophone. Though Young's tone was what struck his contemporaries—most tenor players at the time were emulating the gruff, sonorous tone of Coleman Hawkins—Young's solos seem fresh today because he created wistful, elusive melodies and was able on fast tunes to roll off bright, well-structured choruses as intelligent as they were exciting. He was a mystery, a great spontaneous composer whose inventions sound as natural as breathing. As will be shown in the next chapter, one can analyze his solos; one can also sing them. Other additions to the band also made a difference. Basie's band had the lyrical trumpeter Buck Clayton. Clayton brought with him Herschel Evans, a tenor saxophonist in the Hawkins mold, and Basie soon learned to juxtapose the sounds of Evans and Young, and even to encourage some friendly competition between the two.

Basie knew the sound he wanted, and arranger, trombonist, and guitarist Eddie Durham was a key person in achieving that sound. Even before Basie was with the Moten band he had collaborated with Durham on a couple of arrangements as part of his campaign to talk himself into the Moten band. Durham tells of Basie's working habits: When they were asked to work out a piece for Moten, Basie would come up with a phrase, give it to Durham and then go out for a drink. By the time Basie returned, Durham would have most of the piece finished, and Basie might provide a final phrase. "Moten Swing," usually credited to Bennie and Buster Moten, was written in this way, according to Durham (see *The World of Count Basie*, p. 64). Durham eventually became frustrated with this informality in Basie's own band and with the need to keep the writing simple, and he went out on his own as an arranger in the summer of 1938.

Other Basie arrangers, and the players themselves, had to produce the sound Basie wanted to hear. As Basie tells it:

"By the time we first started getting that band together at the Reno, I already had some pretty clear ideas about how I wanted a band to sound like. I knew how I wanted each section to sound. So I also knew what each one of the guys should sound like. I knew what I wanted them there for . . . I have my own little ideas about how to get certain guys into certain numbers and how to get them out. I had my own way of opening the door for them to let them come in and sit around [take a solo] awhile. Then I would exit them. And that has really been the formula of the band all down through the years" (*Good Morning Blues,* p. 170).

These "little ideas" were embodied in the rather simple structure of many early Basie pieces, which were based on riffs, short, repeated phrases played by one section of the band, and often answered by another. (Often the saxes state the riff and the brass respond.) These riffs, as in "One O'Clock Jump" (BBJ), could be used to support a soloist, or in the last choruses, to build toward a rousing conclusion. (See music example.)

Example 10-1.
Some riffs used at the end of "One O'Clock Jump" (1937).

Often the riff would originate with one musician who would play it behind a soloist, and then would be joined by the other members of his section or by the whole band. This was common practice in the jam sessions of the period, and this is how "head" arrangements could be devised. In the right hands, the repetition was thrilling.

It was the nine-piece band broadcasting from the Reno Club that John Hammond heard and brought to the attention of *Down Beat* readers and record companies. One unexpected result was disastrous. While Hammond was working out a potentially lucrative record contract for Basie with Columbia, an executive of Decca falsely presented himself to Basie as an emissary from Hammond and got Basie to sign with his company. This contract, which bound him until early in 1939, offered no royalties, and paid less than union scale for recording each side. Hammond was horrified when he heard of it: "Back in New York I called Local 802 to protest these outrageous terms, and did manage to raise the per-side payment to scale, but there was nothing the union would do to break the contract" (*John Hammond on Record,* 171). As it turned out, the Decca sides included such big hits as "One O'Clock Jump" and "Jumpin' at the Woodside" (BBJ).

The Count Basie Orchestra, San Francisco, October 1939. From left to right: Buddy Tate (with Freddie Green's guitar behind his head), Benny Morton, Earle Warren, Harry "Sweets" Edison (playing trumpet with sunglasses), Dickie Wells, Jack Washington (holding alto saxophone, baritone beside him), Dan Minor, Lester Young (standing for his solo). Notice Young's eccentric posture. Also note the hat mutes for the brass. (Courtesy Harry Swisher)

Hammond and booking agent Willard Alexander brought the band, now expanded to the standard 16 men, on tour, beginning at the Grand Terrace in Chicago on November 7, 1936. They were not an instant success. They were expected to play behind the stage show, and Basie was expected to introduce some of the acts. But half of the band didn't read music well, and couldn't play such numbers as the classical "Poet and Peasant Overture" with any conviction. As for announcing, Basie said, "I never did have a lot of words." Fletcher Henderson was asked to contribute some arrangements to help the band out, but they still failed to catch on. Of his first New York engagement, at the Roseland Ballroom at Christmas, Basie said: "We didn't raise any hell in there either."

The problem was that the band, in order that it could be heard in large dance halls, had been enlarged suddenly, and the bigger group could not recreate immediately the loose swing that first captured Hammond's attention, especially when they were reading unfamiliar arrangements. Hammond managed to document the style he admired by recording four tunes (and one extra take) with a Basie quintet using a minimum of arrangements in Chicago on November 9, 1936 for Columbia's Vocalion division. (The date was formerly thought to be October 9.) The small group sides, issued under the names of drummer Jones and trumpeter Carl Smith to evade Basie's Decca contract, are rightly among the most famous swing recordings. Basie introduces the first number "Shoe Shine Boy" with a swinging chorus, his first on record since 1932. And his style has changed, become spare and delicate. Then Basie turns the piece over to Lester Young, "comping" behind him with well placed chords.

(Young's work is discussed in Chapter 11.) Jo Jones varies his accompaniment brilliantly on the Jimmy Rushing feature "Evenin'." Behind Basie's initial chorus, he keeps the pulse with a tightly controlled swish on his cymbals; when Young begins to solo, he opens up a little, and then when Rushing sings, Jones lets the cymbals ring joyously: It's as if he threw open a curtain to the sun. On the climax of Young's solo on Gershwin's "Oh, Lady Be Good," Jones drums more brightly and Basie begins to play chords on every beat in guitar style.

The big band sides are not as uniformly successful at first, but Basie's piano is always worth hearing. He begins his first big band side, "Honeysuckle Rose" (January 21, 1937), striding in the first bars in tribute to the song's composer Fats Waller, but then he suddenly settles into his new spare style. This arrangement uses Henderson's riffs and it is striking to compare the ornate Coleman Hawkins solo on the Henderson recording of 1932 (discussed in Chapter 9) with the boldly lyrical Lester Young solo on Basie's version. The "Pennies from Heaven" that was recorded next continues the Wallerish theme of this date, as Basie engages in some characteristic fooling, compressing the little "Pennies from Heaven" phrase comically, making the pennies sound like spare change indeed. But the rest of the arrangement is pedestrian.

The band continued to struggle for some months, as several live broadcasts from the "Chatterbox" of the William Penn Hotel in February 1937, proved. The band sounds terrific at times, routine at others. The rhythm section was coming together, but was due for a new guitarist. At the beginning of a piece issued as "Oh, Lady Be Good No. 2," Basie, who shows he can still play fast runs when he wants to, is working smoothly with Jones and Page. Guitarist Claude Williams duets with Basie a bit, but when he strums chords they sometimes ring out a bit awkwardly. (Williams, who also soloed on violin with Basie, went on to master that instrument.)

Once again, John Hammond provided an answer when he took Basie to hear rhythm guitarist Freddie Green. Basie found in Green someone content with sustaining the disciplined 4/4 rhythm that the band needed. The smoothest rhythm guitarist in the business, Green would soon free Basie's own playing: There was no need for him to keep the beat any longer. The rhythm section, now assembled, was not immediately a finished product. Far from being part of a heritage common to Kansas City jazz groups, as some writers have carelessly suggested, the sound of the Old Testament band rhythm section was a hard won achievement of Basie, Green, Page, and Jones. The other bands from the area, those of Alphonse Trent, George Lee, and Moten, did not have rhythm sections that resembled Basie's, and neither did later groups such as the one led by pianist Jay McShann. McShann's bassist Gene Ramey remembered Walter Page telling the others in his rhythm team, "Now listen, we gotta get the balance! You gotta stay out of the way, or we'll have to get rid of either the piano or the guitar." Page was an innovative player who did more than walk a bass line: He often added accents that broke up the walk, as behind Billie Holiday singing "He's Funny That Way" in 1937 (SCCJ). More rarely, he even double-timed, as behind Basie's organ solo on "Live and Love Tonight" (1939). Basie rehearsed repeatedly with the rhythm alone, and soon he had the balance that he, and Page, wanted.

The change can be heard in the Decca recordings made in March and especially on a June 30, 1937 broadcast from the Savoy Ballroom. Here the band sounds fully at ease with the arrangements. The trumpets don't merely spit out their chorus of "Moten Swing," they phrase it; Jones's splashes on cymbals and his snare and tomtom thumps are used for color and to boot along an already swinging band; and there are few irrelevant sound effects. The new spirit can be heard on the rhythm section's chorus of the uptempo "Shout and Feel It," in which bassist Page creatively breaks up the walking beat. They were ready for their upcoming recording sessions, the July 7 date on which they played their theme "One O'Clock Jump," soon to be imitated by every swing band in the country, and the August 9 date in which they recorded Eddie Durham's "Time Out" and "Topsy." Basie's opening solo on "One O'Clock Jump" (BBJ) became part of the tune to many musicians who admired his witty play with dissonance.

In the next years, the Basie band would record almost monthly, building a reputation for their ineffable swing: The "kid from Red Bank," as Basie called himself in sentimental moments, was leading the definitive Kansas City band. He learned to use the resources of his band carefully, alternating the light tone of Lester Young with the big-bottomed tenor of Herschel Evans, letting Buck Clayton introduce melodies and Harry "Sweets" Edison swing through final choruses. Though not known for its ballads, the band recorded several classics, including the 1938 "Blue and Sentimental," introduced grandly by the lush, cavernous tenor of Herschel Evans, but also offering an exquisite, delightfully pointed clarinet solo by Lester Young. Lester Young opens the master take of the 1939 "Taxi War Dance" with a startling solo—he begins humorously by quoting "Old Man River," and then continues with bluesy elegance. On numbers like "One O'Clock Jump" the band learned to build excitement by gradually crescendoing riffs, but Basie knew the value of surprise as well. Occasionally, as on "Easy Does It" from 1940, he would have Lester Young build to a pitch of excitement and then, just where another band leader would bring the brass crashing in, Basie would enter pianissimo over the rhythm. Another 1940 number, "Broadway," features the bigger, more showy sound the band was then developing and would continue to develop in the war years.

World War II brought inevitable changes in personnel to the band. Even before, Basie's band was shocked by the death in 1939 of Herschel Evans, who was replaced by the Texas tenor Buddy Tate. Lester Young left in December 1940. (He would return to the band at the end of 1943 for almost a year.) The famous Basie rhythm section was broken up when first Walter Page left in 1942 and then Jo Jones was drafted in the fall of 1944. As shown by the number of recordings, and their variety, the band remained popular during the forties. That is not surprising, as Basie continued to feature stars such as Jimmy Rushing, and at various times saxophonists Don Byas and Illinois Jacquet, and trombonist J.J. Johnson. After the war, with a new rhythm section—drummers

Basie and Lester Young, 1944. (Photo by Gjon Mili, courtesy Harry Swisher)

included Shadow Wilson, Gus Johnson, and, briefly, the famously flamboyant Buddy Rich—Basie frequently performed more intricate arrangements alongside his characteristic blues and riff numbers.

After Basie regrouped in the fifties, as described above, his band never received the critical acclaim of the first one, but it became equally popular with audiences, partly as a result of the brilliant vocalist Joe Williams's success with "Goin' to Chicago" and "Every Day I Have the Blues" and partly because the artful, though sometimes brash, writing of Neal Hefti and others was appropriate to a time when big bands were playing for concerts rather than for dances. This band continued to play former Basie hits such as "Jumpin' at the Woodside," but its character was defined in such recordings as *Basie* of 1957, the Neal Hefti date in which they made "Lil' Darlin' " and, perhaps in a throwback to Herschel Evans, featured the aggressive tenor of Eddie "Lockjaw" Davis on "Flight of the Foo Birds" and on other numbers. *Basie*, a.k.a. *The Atomic Mr. Basie*, remains one of that band's most revered albums.

"Shiny Stockings," a piece by tenor player Frank Foster recorded by Basie in 1956, illustrates the virtues of the fifties band. The unpretentious theme is stated by the brass precisely, every waver, smear, and glissando made in perfect synchronization. Yet the piece has the light, tiptoeing quality typical of Basie. Just as typical, and just as admirable, are the easy-going, informal-sounding tunes found on *Chairmen of the Board*: the naive, countryish "Blues in Hoss' Flat" by Foster, with its near raucous conversation between brass and saxes; the sweet, jumpy "Kansas City Shout" by Ernie Wilkins; and the gospel-influenced "The Deacon" by Thad Jones. Jones also contributes the carefully modulated "Speaking of Sounds" whose theme is carried in unison by Jones's cornet and Eddie Jones's bass (a pairing he later used when writing for his own band). The intricate sax passages of "Mutt and Jeff" would never have been possible in earlier bands. Nor would one have expected the sophisticated wit of the opening fanfare of "H.R.H." And this album, it should be noted, is composed solely of pieces by band members.

Basie maintained the style of this band for the rest of his career, if not always the level of writing and playing: His best men often started bands of their own, usually in Basie's image. (The Thad Jones-Mel Lewis band is the best example.) In his seventies, Basie was unable to find a new style: His composers, such as the popular Sammy Nestico, seemed to be echoing earlier Basie pieces.

That makes the small-group records that Basie made for Pablo Records seem even more miraculous. One can hear Basie, with bassist Ray Brown and drummer Louis Bellson, sketch the melody of "I'll Always Be in Love With You," or play a variety of brilliantly subdued blues on *For the First Time*. On *Kansas City Shout* Basie accompanies Kansas City blues singers Joe Turner and Eddie Cleanhead Vinson. He appears with the Lester Young-influenced tenor saxophonist Zoot Sims on *Basie and Zoot*, playing among other numbers a new version of "Honeysuckle Rose," the Fats Waller composition Basie first recorded in 1937 with Young. On the 1975 version, Basie sounds exuberant, agile, free, swinging easily, as easily as if he were cutting butter, to use one of his own expressions. "I haven't ever heard but a few guys who could really do that," he

The Basie band in the late 1960's at the Monterey, California festival. Eddie "Lockjaw" Davis is soloing. (Courtesy Rutgers Institute of Jazz Studies)

said, "and I never did tell them what they were doing, because I didn't want them to know what I was stealing from them." By the time he died, there were few musicians of his generation left to steal from. If there's someone around today who can swing as if he were cutting butter, he probably learned how from Basie.

11 The Small Bands and Virtuoso Soloists of the Thirties

The jam sessions in Kansas City during the thirties are legendary. In small clubs like the Subway, players tested themselves and each other in informal, but sometimes deadly serious, bouts that pushed soloists to make it new. Musicians talked about the time in December 1933 when Lester Young, Ben Webster, Herschel Evans and Dick Wilson—all tenor saxophonists—took on the visiting Coleman Hawkins. Lester Young was supposed to have emerged victorious, but Hawkins may have had his revenge in 1939, when after returning from six years in Europe, he showed up at a New York night club and reestablished himself, for the time being, as the boss of the tenor saxophone in front of an audience that included Lester Young's greatest fan, Billie Holiday. (When *Down Beat* reported Hawkins the winner, Holiday wrote to the editors and proclaimed that everyone knew Young had triumphed: "Les Young Wasn't Carved" was the caption the editor put to her letter, published in the October 15, 1939 issue.) Jam sessions were used to establish and reestablish reputations, but they were also used to exchange ideas and to experiment. They were the seedbeds of the next wave of jazz, and they were rites of passage: When a teenaged Charlie Parker first showed up at a Kansas City jam session, he was driven off the stage because he wasn't ready.

The thirties may have been the big band era, but much important music was made in small clubs by small groups. By mid-decade New York's 52nd Street, "Swing Street" as it was called, or "the street that never slept," was lined between Fifth and Sixth Avenues with basement jazz clubs like the Onyx, the Famous Door, and Kelly's Stable, where Coleman Hawkins used to sit and listen late at night, and where "after a couple quarts of scotch," he would play "about ten choruses on 'Body and Soul.'" That experience led to his most famous recording, the 1939 "Body and Soul" for Victor.

160

Six years earlier Hawkins had teamed with trumpeter Red Allen to make a series of small group records like "I Wish I Could Shimmy Like My Sister Kate." Much of the recording group was made up of members of the Fletcher Henderson band. Like many prominent soloists, Hawkins and Allen looked to recording sessions and club dates for the solo space that the big bands denied them. Soon big band leaders themselves were presenting smaller groups within their bands, groups such as Benny Goodman's trio and quartet, Artie Shaw's Gramercy Five, Bob Crosby's Bobcats. Small band jazz flourished during the thirties wherever musicians gathered together in afterhours clubs, recording studios, or in places on 52nd Street or in Kansas City's club district to play the best music they could in informal settings. Along with the competition created by that activity, and along with the increasingly demanding big band arrangements that many musicians were confronting, there was an increase in the technical virtuosity, harmonic knowledge and musical skills of jazz players that is one of the key legacies of the thirties. During the thirties as well, jazz singing came to an early maturity, when in 1933, the 18-year-old Billie Holiday, one of the music's most influential vocalists and an important musician by any standard, stepped into the studio for the first time.

Many of the best small group sessions of the decade were almost casually organized by producers like John Hammond or by the owners of budding record companies, like Commodore's Milt Gabler, who began in 1938. There was a flurry of small band recording towards the beginning of the decade, and again towards the end. Throughout the period, bands of like-minded musicians were given names like The Rhythmakers, or The Chocolate Dandies, which wasn't a set group at all: At least five different aggregations recorded as the Chocolate Dandies between 1928 and 1933. Some of these informal recording groups were integrated: The Chocolate Dandies that recorded "Cherry" in 1928 had Don Redman and Jimmy Dorsey on alto saxophones. As noted in Chapter 9, publicly mixed groups came later.

A particularly successful Chocolate Dandies session occurred on December 3, 1930, when Benny Carter, Coleman Hawkins, Jimmy Harrison and trumpeter Bobby Stark recorded five tunes, including two classics, "Bugle Call Rag" and Carter's "Dee Blues." "Bugle Call Rag" begins with an agitated chorus by Stark, whose pinched tone and sharp pitch suggest some insecurity. Then follows a series of short solos by Carter on alto saxophone, Hawkins, Carter again on clarinet, and by trombonist Jimmy Harrison, whose career would be cut short in 1931 when he died at the age of 30 of a stomach ailment.

With Jack Teagarden, Harrison was influential in the development of the jazz trombone into a flowing, flexible instrument free from the smears of the tailgate style or the staccato leaps of the Miff Mole approach: as cornetist Rex Stewart wrote, "Jimmy's concept was to swing it as a trumpet" (*Jazz Masters of the Thirties*, p. 52). His second chorus on "Bugle Call Rag" is a good example, with its punchy Armstrong-like attack. Like Armstrong, he also builds intensity by developing his ideas. He begins with a series of C's, and follows that by a series of high A♭'s, a variation of the same idea. Then he plays a three-note idea, A♭, G, F, A♭, which he develops for the next few bars. (See music example.)

Example 11-1.
Jimmy Harrison, beginning of his second solo on "Bugle Call Rag" (1930).

Harrison's 12-bar statement on "Dee Blues" is in a more fluid style, and shows off his delicate and unusually rapid vibrato.

Harrison and Teagarden became fast friends, according to Stewart, who remembers a cutting session in which "Harrison gave new life to that old broad 'Dinah,' while Teagarden had the cats screaming their approval when he swung—and I mean swung—in waltz time, 'The World is Waiting for the Sunrise!'" (*Jazz Masters of the Thirties*, p. 148). The two should share the title Stewart assigns to Harrison: Father of the Swing Trombone.

In 1932 a series of three recording sessions took place in which an all-star interracial band called the Rhythmakers was assembled to accompany the mediocre piping of singer Billy Banks. Banjoist and rhythm guitar player Eddie Condon did the assembling. Condon was a native of Indiana, born in 1905, a scrappy and a witty man, who came to New York in May of 1928, and decided, as he put it, that this "would be a great place to raise a band." His band, with Gene Krupa and Frank Teschmacher, didn't find work, so Condon began selling himself as a record producer. Like Teagarden, he spent his after hours hanging around Harlem. When Irving Mills, manager of Ellington and others, wanted to promote singer Billy Banks, he turned to Condon, who called friends such as trumpeter Red Allen and pianist Fats Waller. One highlight is W. C. Handy's "Yellow Dog Blues" (July 26, 1932), where on two takes the interaction among Allen, Waller, clarinetist Jimmy Lord and fellow clarinetist Pee Wee Russell, here on saxophone, is incandescent. Waller's accompaniment is extraordinary, as is his stomping solo on the last take, on which he is creatively backed by Zutty Singleton's dancing drums.

The musical relationship between Condon and Fats Waller continued, and it is perhaps to Condon's credit that one of Waller's most wonderful performances, the "Pretty Doll" of 1940, came on a Condon-led date. Waller's delicate, lacey introduction is like golden sunlit filigree, and his selfless accompaniment to Pee Wee Russell's fetching, introverted clarinet solo is equally satisfying.

By 1940 Waller was a star, whose bulk, bulging eyeballs, and campy singing were known all over the world. (Australian recording engineer Robert

Parker has noted that Waller had an especially fervent following in his country.) This disciple of James P. Johnson was a larger-than-life symbol of jazz to many: He is, for example, the model for the piano-playing hero of Eudora Welty's story "Powerhouse." Waller's wider fame began in 1934, when he began recording under his own name for Victor. He sang and played hundreds of songs with his small band, songs such as "Two Sleepy People" (1938), whose seductive message he renders with a kind of mock unctuousness, as if he were much too hip to seduce anyone. He introduces "It's a Sin to Tell a Lie" (1936) with a chorus of sublime uptempo stride, which he follows with a vocal that he does in tones that seem to imitate everything from a shower-stall bass—all false resonance—to a baby-talking girl. When he comes back on piano he lightens his touch and manages to swing even harder. (Some of Waller's solo piano works are discussed in Chapter 7).

ART TATUM, ROY ELDRIDGE, DJANGO REINHARDT

Waller was the most popular stride pianist; the younger Art Tatum (1909-56) was his idol. Tatum was an unprecedented figure, a virtuoso whose improvisations seemed to be literally stunning. Musicians remember the first time they heard Art Tatum the way people are supposed to remember their first kiss. When Oscar Peterson first heard him, he temporarily gave up the piano. Fellow Toledoan Francis Williams gave it up permanently, becoming a trumpeter to avoid competing with Tatum. Tatum determined the career of other musicians as well: Classically trained at the Krakow Conservatory, Polish-born pianist Adam Makowicz decided in 1960 to become a jazz pianist when he heard a Tatum record on the Voice of America's radio show "Jazz Hour."

Much earlier, in 1926 or 1927, Rex Stewart was touring with Fletcher Henderson's band when he heard the teenaged Tatum: "The experience was almost traumatic for me, and, for a brief spell afterward, I toyed with the idea of giving up my horn and returning to school . . . Coleman Hawkins was so taken by Tatum's playing that he immediately started creating another style for himself, based on what he'd heard Tatum play that night—and forever after dropped his slap-tongue style" (*Jazz Masters*, pp. 181-182). Tatum was not only Fats Waller's favorite pianist—"God is in the house," he once announced in a club when he noticed the blind pianist Tatum in the audience—he became the idol of younger men, Nat Cole and bebop pianists such as Bud Powell, Hank Jones and Tommy Flanagan.

Hank Jones said of Tatum: "Nobody plays like him—we just play around the fringes of Art. You'd listen to the ideas that he expressed with that phenomenal technique, and that technique was only a means of expressing ideas, just as an artist uses brushes and colors to paint a picture . . . If you listen to him long enough and hard enough, gradually you begin to understand some of the things he's doing." Jones sums up, "He should be everybody's favorite pianist" (Ullman, "Hank Jones: A Profile," in *Alternative Review*).

He wasn't. Some listeners are put off by Tatum's florid runs, by what seems like the very excesses of his style. Critic André Hodeir complained in *Toward Jazz* that Tatum worked out some of his pieces in advance. Hodeir ignored the fact that this practice, and the practice of playing versions of light classics, which Hodeir found equally offensive, was familiar among pianists such as James P. Johnson and Fats Waller.

Tatum's was a rich, exotic style. He liked rubato introductions, and, like one of his influences, Earl Hines, he frequently threatened to abandon the beat by introducing careening runs. While he does overuse certain devices, such as his cleanly played downward runs, Tatum did not merely decorate tunes: He recomposed their harmonies and produced endlessly fascinating variations on their melodies. Other pianists remember times when Tatum would play chorus after chorus of a song, changing the harmonies and voicings in each repetition. It's no wonder he inspired the next generation of beboppers, given their well known interest in expanded harmonies and subtle voicings.

In concert he played variations of prearranged pieces, but in a club, or after-hours party, he was a more whimsical and adventurous pianist. Performances taped during a private party in Beverly Hills in 1955 (and issued on Emarcy) find him in an informal mood, playing requests and fooling around. After claiming that he has forgotten "Without a Song," he produces an unaffected, flowing rendition that's a marvel of relative simplicity. He introduces "Danny Boy" with sentimentally strummed chords, then builds to some disturbing dissonance—a case study in reharmonization. Tatum interjects a few bars of

Art Tatum in the late 1940's. (Courtesy Rutgers Institute of Jazz Studies)

"Nobody Knows the Trouble I've Seen" into his "Body and Soul," approaches "September Song" with intimations of melodrama that he dispels in a swirl, and produces an astoundingly complex counterpoint with his left hand during the last chorus of "Someone to Watch Over Me," while playing the melody chastely with his right. He not only reharmonizes "Too Marvelous for Words" (SCCJ), he briefly changes the key during the last bridge.

At his most dazzling, Tatum could produce what musicologist Felicity Howlett has called "the impression of an impenetrable brilliance." That brilliance is an extension of the Harlem stride pianist's emphasis on technical virtuosity, but it's difficult to trace its development in Tatum, since Tatum, even as a teenager, was a prodigy. Clearly he studied classical piano, and he listened to and imitated piano rolls. Even before he lost most of his eyesight, he played compulsively: Many of the stories that abound about Tatum revolve around the long hours during which he would perform, usually in some after-hours club to an audience of devotees. Tatum's technique, and harmonic brilliance, is the result of hours of intelligent experimentation and practice.

By the time he made his first issued solo recordings, on March 21, 1933—he had previously recorded behind singer Adelaide Hall and cut a version of "Tiger Rag" unissued until after his death—Tatum already had a major reputation among musicians. His performance that day of "Tiger Rag" proved the point of his fans. "Tiger Rag" is of course the old New Orleans number, composed of three themes, that the Original Dixieland Jazz Band first recorded in 1918. Perhaps influenced, suggests Howlett, by the Ellington recording of 1929, Tatum in his "Tiger Rag" seems to turn his piano into an orchestra, and something of a three-ring circus! He begins in Hines-like fashion, with some strangely evocative chords. Then he takes off in a rush, playing at approximately 350 beats a minute, using a slew of ideas that include a whole tone passage, an extraordinary passage in thirds at the end, and other extravagant displays. "Tiger Rag" was one of his great display pieces, and he played it in a similar fashion through at least much of his career, as can be heard by comparing this early recording with the 1940 version for Decca Records.

During most of the thirties, Tatum worked as a soloist. In 1943, he formed a trio with bassist Slam Stewart and guitarist Tiny Grimes, who on recordings sometimes sounds as if he were holding on grimly for dear life. No wonder: In the 1944 trio version of "Body and Soul," Tatum quotes, according to pianist Dick Hyman, 11 other compositions, ranging from Gershwin's "I Got Plenty of Nothin' " to Leoncavallo's "Vesti La Giubba," and including both Fritz Kreisler's "Humoresque" and the pop ditty "How Much Is That Doggie in the Window" (*Contemporary Keyboard*, October 1981).

Although it's often said that his elaborate style was unsuited to the blues, Tatum proved in his recordings for Decca with singer Joe Turner, and in the "Trio Blues" made in 1956 with Red Callendar and Jo Jones, that he could play gorgeous, expressive blues. In fact, one of Tatum's most admired recordings is the version of W. C. Handy's "Aunt Hagar's Blues" (JP; also called "Aunt Hagar's Children") that he recorded for Capitol Records in 1949. During the first few measures of the second chorus he totally reharmonizes the piece, at the same time producing a deeply soulful blues feeling. (See music example.)

Example 11–2.
Art Tatum, beginning of the second chorus of "Aunt Hagar's Blues" (1949).

His astonishing runs are here too, such as the one early in the fourth chorus. He was often this experimental on the blues. In the 1941 blues "Lonesome Graveyard," he opens eerily, accompanies singer Joe Turner simply, then takes a solo chorus whose strange initial chords virtually paralyze guitarist Oscar Moore, who must find a way to harmonize with him (Schuller, *The Swing Era*, pp. 486–487).

In the fifties Tatum was extensively recorded by Norman Granz for his Clef and Verve labels: Tatum made almost 200 songs as a soloist. He also recorded with small groups. Tatum loved to accompany both instrumentalists and singers. "I don't know why—he played all through them," Tommy Flanagan has said (*Jazz Lives*, p. 115). His active style of accompanying created problems for some soloists, who were virtually overrun by Tatum's figures, or made to sound comparatively frilly and weightless. Ben Webster, who by the time he recorded with Tatum in September 1956 had developed a huge, breathily nuanced tone, proved imperturbable. After a relatively chaste introduction by Tatum on "Gone With the Wind," Webster enters with a rushing sound, up high, that seems both passionate and subtle. And he continues with a masterful paraphrase of the melody that seems timeless. For many, this collaboration with Webster will be an appealing introduction to Art Tatum, who died at the age of 46 of uremic poisoning on November 5, 1956, a little over a month after these recordings were made.

Tatum's trio of piano, bass and guitar had its precedents, most notably in the trio of Nat "King" Cole which was formed in 1937. Cole's fresh, light piano runs, recalling his idol Earl Hines, and his sophisticated Tatum voicings made him the envy of many younger players. Such diverse pianists as Oscar Peterson, Ahmad Jamal and Bill Evans studied Cole's work. During the forties, Cole became better known as a singer than as a pianist.

One of Tatum's earliest jobs, in the late twenties, was around Toledo with the band of drummer Speed Webb, best known today for the quality of his sidemen. In 1928, these included trumpeter Roy Eldridge, lovingly nicknamed "Little Jazz," who would go on to become one of the most celebrated trumpet players of the swing era. Born in Pittsburgh in 1911 to a musical family—his older brother Joe was a professional saxophonist—he was touring by the time he was 16, but would wait until the mid-thirties, when he was with Fletcher Henderson, to achieve fame. As a young jazz trumpeter, he was at first more impressed by the brashness of Rex Stewart and the clean articulation of Red Nichols than by the majesty of Louis Armstrong. Even more important to him were what musician and scholar John Chilton has called "the fast-running intricacies of Coleman Hawkins": Eldridge told Chilton that he learned Hawkins's solo on the Fletcher Henderson record "Stampede" note for note, and that his early style, especially his long, legato phrases, was an attempt to play Hawkins on the trumpet. Hawkins and Eldridge eventually became best friends. Other probable influences include trumpeters Jabbo Smith and Red Allen, the former for his speed and the latter for his harmonic daring.

Eldridge moved to New York in November 1930, and immediately started jamming in after-hours clubs. Some musicians—and they were the audience that counted—were critical: "The rule seemed to be that you told newcomers the

Roy Eldridge at Jimmy Ryan's nightclub in Manhattan, early 1970's.
(Photo by Michael Ullman)

things you didn't like about their playing, and not the things you liked. So, Hot Lips Page heard me, and said, 'Why are you playing like an ofay [a white person]?' Well, he knew his stuff, so I took note of that, and Chick Webb, who was guaranteed to speak his mind, said, 'Yeah, you're fast, but you're not telling me any story,' and those words sunk right into me. At that time I had this thing about playing as fast as I could all the time, I double-timed every ballad I did, and never held a long note. I was able to run the changes on any song, and do nice turn-arounds at the end of each eight bars, but I wasn't developing my solos." The revelation came when he heard Louis Armstrong in person: "Every phrase led somewhere, linking up with the next one, in the way a storyteller leads you on to the next idea. Louis was developing his musical thoughts, moving in one direction. It was like a plot that finished with a climax" (from John Chilton's notes to *Roy Eldridge: The Early Years,* Columbia Records).

Eldridge didn't imitate Armstrong, but he learned to tell his own kind of story, playing fast-moving solos that virtually crackle. His phrases were varied and thoughtfully linked, often climaxing in a bleating high note, to be followed by an abrupt drop of an octave or more. The effect of an Armstrong solo is of majestic control: Eldridge specializes in a rushed intensity. Eldridge, who studied piano, knew his harmony as well: When it came to the bridges of tunes, he didn't coast. Like bebop musicans to come, he attacked the changes with an aggressiveness that showed his complete confidence. That speed, intensity, orderliness, and confidence can be heard in his choruses with his own band on the 1937 "After You've Gone," a song that Armstrong had recorded in 1929. One notices at first the sheer drive of Eldridge's choruses, and his startling unaccompanied breaks, with their crawling, winding chromatic lines. (See music example.)

Example 11–3.
Roy Eldridge's first break, measures 12–17 of the first chorus after the vocal in "After You've Gone" (1937).

That chromaticism, alleviated by occasional octave jumps, is one of his trademarks. One can easily hear why Dizzy Gillespie and other modernists idolized Eldridge for his speed, harmonic inventiveness, and his own ability to tell a story.

Eldridge had a more lyrical side, as heard on his opening solo on Teddy Wilson's 1939 recording of "What Shall I Say?," which also features Billie Holiday. His ballads could also be intense, as heard on the solos from a session with Hawkins—the 1940 Chocolate Dandies session for Commodore. Eldridge's solos on "I Surrender Dear"—there were three takes—have a wild pathos created partially by his wailing effects.

In the late thirties, Eldridge toured with his own band, but his greatest fame came after April 1941 when he joined, as featured soloist, Gene Krupa. Among his celebrated features with Krupa was a remake of his feature on "After You've Gone," and a new version of Hoagy Carmichael's "Rockin' Chair" (SCCJ), which was first recorded by Louis Armstrong in 1929 with the composer as a second vocalist. Arranged by Benny Carter, the Krupa "Rockin' Chair" was recorded in two takes on July 2, 1941. (SCCJ contains the original master. An alternate take appeared by error on some early copies of SCCJ, and was available regularly on *Roy Eldridge—The Early Years*.) The lyrics picture an old man who can't get out of his chair, even to get a drink. Armstrong treated it both majestically—in his trumpet solo—and with light humor, in the vocal. Eldridge introduces an unexpected, biting, growling intensity into "Rockin' Chair." The arrangement begins with Eldridge playing freely over sustained chords by the band. On both takes, Eldridge begins in his solo to suggest double time, a technique he may have picked up from Hawkins, who double times as early as the 1929 "One Hour." A comparison of the two takes and of broadcast versions of the arrangement shows that Eldridge was improvising freely. There are some recurrent phrases, but he nonetheless managed in every version to create a new, spellbinding solo. The ending, which has the trumpeter trading phrases with a clarinet, is an amusing parody of nineteenth-century operatic arias in which a soprano singer alternates phrases with a flute—two examples out of many are the ending of the "mad scene" in Donizetti's *Lucia di Lammermoor* and "Ombra Leggiera" from Meyerbeer's opera *Dinorah*.

After leaving Krupa's band in 1943, Eldridge led his own big band again, taking time out for stints with Artie Shaw (1944-1945), Krupa again (1949) and Benny Goodman (1950). From the fifties on, Eldridge, like most jazz musicians, specialized in small groups, appearing for a time with Coleman Hawkins. His style changed, as he extended his high range and lost some speed, and sometimes indulged in chromatic noodling: Many of his solos would typically climax with a shrieking, pinched high note. Sometimes, as in the hair-raising ending to his two choruses of blues on Billie Holiday's "Fine and Mellow," recorded for the 1957 television show "The Sound of Jazz," those high notes are gripping. (Eldridge never approached the mechanical excesses of Ellington's trumpeter Cat Anderson or of band leader Maynard Ferguson in his use of his upper range.) In the seventies, he could be found as part of the house band in Jimmy Ryan's in New York, playing Dixieland. At the end of his playing career, he found himself participating in a style that he had helped supplant.

In some ways, Eldridge did for the trumpet what Tatum did for the piano: With his speed and intensity he extended its possibilities. The man who did the same for the jazz guitar—and this is an indication of how firmly established jazz had become abroad—was a Belgian-born gypsy named Django Reinhardt. The first European to be treated by American jazz stars as an equal – Django recorded with Coleman Hawkins, Rex Stewart, and Benny Carter and toured America with Duke Ellington in 1946 – Reinhardt was unique. Born in 1910, he grew up in a gypsy caravan, and never learned to read. He signed his name with an X. He played violin first and then guitar during his peripatetic years, presumably in the flamboyant style of the gypsies he travelled with. Throughout his life, he alternated steely single note runs with swirling chordal passages in gypsy style, something like flamenco style. In 1928, his caravan caught fire and his burned left hand was permanently crippled, the fifth finger more or less welded to the two fingers next to it. Reinhardt compensated by using the paralyzed fingers to play chords, holding the strings down with them the way blues players use a bottleneck. With the other fingers he fretted the strings and fingered fast runs. In the end he played faster than any jazz guitarist before him.

His recording career began in March 1928 when he accompanied, on the banjo, an accordionist and slide whistle player in four popular tunes. For the next five years he recorded, infrequently, with popular musicians such as singer Jean Sablon, who made the probably forgettable "Je Suis Sex-Appeal" in April 1933. It's unclear how Reinhardt learned jazz, but he must have heard it in Paris. Around 1932, Django approached violinist Stephane Grappelli, as Grappelli told author Whitney Balliett: "One night when I finish work, this big, dark funny-looking man come in and say, 'Hey! I'm looking for a violinist to play hot.' It was Django" (Balliett, *American Musicians*, p. 212).

Nothing happened until two years later, when Reinhardt wandered into a hotel on the Champs-Élysées where Grappelli was playing for customers taking tea. According to Grappelli, Django started to accompany him and they were joined by Django's brother Joseph, who played rhythm guitar. This was the kernel of the group that would be named, after a club of jazz devotees started by French critic Hugues Panassié, the Quintet of the Hot Club of France. This all-string band – it included two more guitars just to strum the chords and a bass, but no piano or drums – made its first recordings in December of 1934. Reinhardt introduces "Dinah" (SCCJ) from that session with a few strummed chords, then begins the first chorus with an improvised solo over the two rhythm guitars and bass. He never plays the theme exactly, though the second A comes closest to what was written. Even here, he ornaments with numerous subtle trills and slides. With a flair comparable to Armstrong's, Reinhardt leads into the second chorus with an arpeggio that ends in a delicate trill, followed by bouncy lines whose energy distinguishes them from the less pronounced lines of the first chorus. Then he launches into a long downward sequence of triplets ending on a repeated low note and then high note. This wild phrase extends from the last two measures of the first A through the entire second A. (See music example.) The bridge is played in octaves, including a subtle touch in which he slides downward at the end of the first phrase, while gently strumming the strings with his right hand. (Playing guitar in octaves became all the rage around 1960, when Wes Montgomery popularized it.) The final A brings a repeated triplet figure again, in which Reinhardt repeats the same notes over and over. He ends

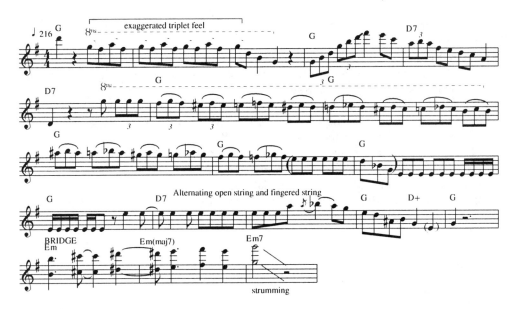

Example 11–4.
Django Reinhardt, beginning of second chorus on "Dinah" (1934).

this brisk, flowing solo, full of beautifully spun out phrases and subtle twists, with some simple closing chords.

Then Reinhardt becomes an accompanist. He is innovative even here, transforming the sound of the rhythm section behind Grappelli's solo with devices such as a high tremolo, followed by riffing, and then syncopated chords. Eddie Lang had proved in the twenties that a guitarist could create varied textures with chords and single lines behind a soloist. Lang played in a delicate, classical manner. Reinhardt uses comparable techniques, but he plays with fierce intensity.

On the next number, "Tiger Rag," Grappelli shows the elegant drive that made him a serious rival to the most recorded jazz violinist of the time, Joe Venuti. (Others included two African-Americans, the rough-and-ready Stuff Smith and the sweeter-sounding Eddie South, nicknamed "the dark angel of the violin.") Grappelli plays clipped phrases with the sure pitch of a trained musician.

The Quintet of the Hot Club of France with Stephane Grappelli did not survive into the forties. Grappelli, a precise natty man, was frustrated by Reinhardt's irresponsibility. The guitarist would disappear for days at a time, missing engagements and record dates. He told time by the sun, Grappelli would say. The two did not see each other from 1940 until 1946, because Grappelli insisted on staying in London during World War II and Reinhardt insisted on Paris. Reinhardt was a prolific composer, and wrote many new pieces for the group he led without Grappelli, replacing him with a clarinet. His "Swing de Paris" of December 1940 is a blues with a bridge, that is, an AABA form where each A section is a 12-bar blues. This was a highly unusual structure at the time. Elsewhere, he favored the minor mode, perhaps because of his gypsy heritage.

Grappelli was influenced, he said, by Bix Beiderbecke's impressionist piano compositions. Perhaps Reinhardt was also, or perhaps he got the soft sounding harmonies and gently vague melodies of pieces such as "Nuages" more directly from hearing the likes of Debussy and Ravel. "Nuages" (Clouds), which he recorded repeatedly starting in 1940, became a hit as "The Bluest Kind of Blues." It has a languorous melody that descends chromatically over slower moving chords. The basic chord progression of the A sections would be simply ii-V-I except that Reinhardt uses the flat sixth chord to substitute for the ii. Since the flat sixth is a diminished fifth away from the ii, this is called a diminished fifth substitution: It was a favorite device of the bebop players in the forties and later. (See music example.)

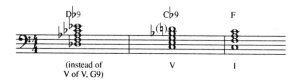

Example 11-5.
Example of diminished fifth ("flat five") substitution. (Compare the end of Goodman's 1935 "After You've Gone" excerpt in Chapter 9.)

Reinhardt would continue to record, often reunited with Grappelli, until his premature death in 1953. He recorded an unaccompanied, poignant, free-sounding "Nuages" in 1951. He remains one of the most important guitarists in jazz, whose direct influence is still heard in guitarists such as Philip Catherine and Birelli Lagrene. He should also be remembered for his experiments in harmony, and for lovely compositions such as "Manoir de Mes Reves." His poise, cool tone and inventiveness at fast tempos were suggestive of innovations to come. It is certain that the beboppers were aware of Reinhardt. Reinhardt, and Grappelli for that matter, used double time in a way the boppers echoed, and he used some of the chord substitutions they liked. He experimented with the whole tone scale in pieces such as the strange-sounding, oddly titled "Diminushing" (1947; on a 1945 broadcast it was called "Diminushing Blackness"). Perhaps the boppers even borrowed the idea of "-ology" titles—"Anthropology," "Ornithology," "Crazeology"—from Reinhardt's 1935 "Djangology," a straightforward piece until one gets to the 4-bar bridge.

COLEMAN HAWKINS

In the mid-thirties, Reinhardt recorded regularly with visiting American jazzmen. In 1934, he recorded four tracks accompanying the then expatriate saxophonists Coleman Hawkins and Benny Carter, both of whom found Europe

Coleman Hawkins.
(Courtesy Rutgers Institute
of Jazz Studies)

more congenial racially than Manhattan. Hawkins and Carter would develop their styles abroad, while Carter also arranged for fine British musicians in London. Both missed the best years of the swing era at home, but European jazz musicians benefitted from their presence. Django had no trouble adapting to these stars on the four numbers recorded on April 28, 1937, although he gets no solo space. "Crazy Rhythm" is the most exciting number, since each of the saxophonists gets a chorus before Hawkins takes two, and everyone has brilliant things to say. First are two French players, and one can't help but admire the stunning fast run at the end of André Ekyan's alto solo, and the brilliant motivic play in the bridge of Alix Combelle's very Hawkinsish solo. Clearly, Europe was producing first-rate jazz musicians by this time. Benny Carter's solo has a relaxed floating swing and impressive development of motives. Finally there's Hawkins, who is incredibly complex in harmony and yet rhythmically straight-forward and driving. (He left his rubato phase mentioned in Chapter 9 by 1935.)

Benny Carter recorded again with Django in Paris on March 7, 1938. Two months later he was back home after close to three years abroad. Chased by the hostilities that would result in the Second World War, Coleman Hawkins soon followed. Hawkins returned to Manhattan in July of the following year to begin one of the most productive periods of his career. On October 11, 1939, he recorded his most famous performance, a restless solo on "Body and Soul" that captures perfectly his percolating energy and harmonic mastery. Played with a warm, confiding tone, his "Body and Soul" demonstrates his harmonic inge-nuity, his use of double time, and intricate development of rhythmic motifs. (See music example.)

It struck contemporary listeners as daring melodically—Hawkins never explicitly runs through the written melody, but rather improvises, beginning quietly in the lower ranges of the tenor, and building his solo relentlessly while

Example 11–6.
Coleman Hawkins, first chorus of his solo on "Body and Soul" (1939). Note that Hawkins suggests many chords other than those shown, which are played by the rhythm section.

rising in pitch. The solo was celebrated immediately—*Down Beat* ran a transcription of the first chorus as early as September 15, 1940, noting that many musicians already considered it "the greatest record Coleman Hawkins ever made." At the end of the forties, bebop singer Eddie Jefferson put words to Hawkins's improvisation, and when Jefferson died in 1979, the vocal group

Manhattan Transfer recorded a version with the words modified to pay tribute to both Jefferson and Hawkins.

Hawkins would in the next years record frequently as a soloist, often for newer small labels such as Keynote. He had no trouble getting involved with the new trends in jazz, and in the mid-1940s became the first person to record unaccompanied saxophone improvisations.

LESTER YOUNG AND BILLIE HOLIDAY

But, though Hawkins was still the boss of the tenor to many, he would not be the most influential tenor player on the generation to come. That honor goes to Count Basie's star, Lester Young. Talking about Lester Young to writer Ross Russell in 1949, bop tenor star Dexter Gordon said: "Hawk was the master of the horn, a musician who did everything possible with it, the right way. But when Pres [Young] appeared, we all started listening to him alone. Pres had an entirely new sound, one that we seemed to be waiting for" (reprinted in *The Art of Jazz*, p. 212).

Born in 1909 and raised in the vicinity of New Orleans, Lester Young, who would be dubbed "Pres" by Billie Holiday, got his early musical experiences in the family band led by his father Willis Handy Young. Lester studied violin, trumpet, and – more seriously – drums before settling on an alto saxophone by the age of 13. We know that the band played, among other things, marches. Young spoke about having his sight reading tested by his overbearing father. When he flunked the test – he had been playing by ear – he was temporarily kicked out of the band: "Now you know my heart was broke, you dig. I went and cried and gave up my little teardrops." Then he taught himself to read.

After leaving the family band in 1927 due to one of many disputes with his father, who like many of his generation did not seem to appreciate the peculiar inventiveness and originality of his son, Lester freelanced with various bands, including the famous Blue Devils in 1930, and did several tours with King Oliver in 1932 and 1933. He spent some time in Minneapolis, and in 1933 Young settled in Kansas City, the city with which he would be identified by jazz historians. In 1934 he joined Count Basie, but left the band to try out with Fletcher Henderson's organization. He was meant to replace Coleman Hawkins, who had departed for Europe. It didn't work out. Henderson admired Young's original tone and flowing solos: His band members did not. Soon, Young was being coached by Henderson's wife, who made him listen to Coleman Hawkins records in the hope that he would pick up Hawkins's robust approach and sound. He refused, and made his way back to Kansas City where eventually he rejoined Basie.

His first recordings were made with Basie, as mentioned in Chapter 10, on November 9, 1936. Young players eagerly memorized his solos on "Shoe Shine Boy" and "Oh, Lady Be Good." On the latter, Young begins with a little three-note idea, then uses that to start a longer idea (measure 2). He takes the last two notes of that idea (end of measure 3) and plays with them for a while. This piece is a master class on how to expand short ideas, and how to pace a solo. (See music example.)

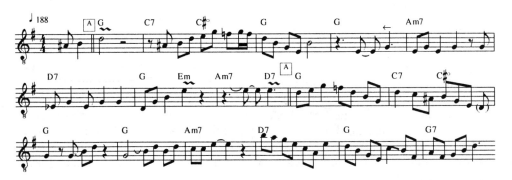

Example 11–7.
Lester Young, beginning of his solo on "Lady Be Good."

"Shoe Shine Boy," also known as "Shoe Shine Swing," was mentioned in Chapter 10. On take one (the originally issued take) of this 32-bar number, Young takes two choruses, which begin with an attention-getting phrase that has been quoted by hundreds of players since. Young alternates between two notes, a higher and a lower, and with each repetition, drops the lower one in pitch: here from E to E♭ to D. Young's sense of form was so vivid that he couldn't resist tying together the first half of the chorus by ending with a short version of the same phrase, just before the bridge (measures 15 and 16). (See music example.)

A similar routine appears at the last A of the first chorus, and it appears in its wildest and fastest form in the second A of the second chorus. (See music example.)

The group had worked out some accents to be played on beat four of every two bars of the bridge. On the first take, Jones at first emphasizes beat one of the bridge. Nonetheless, it was the first take that was originally issued, probably because producer John Hammond, or Basie himself, preferred the solos on this imperfect, though stirring, performance.

Perfection was hard to come by in those days before tape and splicing, when producers and artists had to choose among complete takes. Young's most famous composition, the catchy riff tune "Lester Leaps In," was recorded in two takes in September 1939 with Young and six other members of the Basie band.

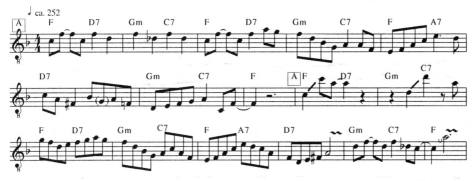

Example 11–8.
Lester Young, first 16 bars of his solo on "Shoe Shine Boy" (master take).

Example 11–9.
Lester Young, bars 9–16 of his second chorus on "Shoe Shine Boy" (master take).

Both takes of this number based on the chord changes of "I Got Rhythm" had serious, though hardly fatal, errors. On the originally issued take, the master (SCCJ), Basie begins to solo in the middle of Young's second chorus (the third chorus of the overall performance), then realizes his error and joins the stop time pattern being played by the rest of the rhythm section. On the alternate take, Young solos beautifully, and Basie plunges right into the stop time pattern for Young's second chorus, as planned. But later on the brass players make mistakes in their background riffs. The result was two flawed takes of otherwise marvelous music. Young's playing on "Lester Leaps In" became another favorite of the new generation of saxophone players.

After leaving Basie, Young had a brief, unsensational fling at leading his own band. Then he decided to join the more successful group of his brother Lee, who was working in Hollywood and Los Angeles. They came to New York in September 1942, but in February 1943 Lester Young's father and stepmother died, and the Young brothers dissolved their band. Lester played at Minton's Playhouse and elsewhere in New York City before rejoining Basie by December. The next year he traveled with Basie, appeared in the award-winning short jazz film "Jammin' the Blues" and won the *Down Beat* poll as top tenor player.

In the thirties Young had been known for his fresh tone—bright but with an underlying wistfulness—and for his clean articulation and precise rhythms. A few years later, as we can hear in the 1944 "After Theatre Jump," he was playing with a heavier tone, and a lazier, almost dragging approach to rhythm. Few of his recordings from this period have the tight economy of his solo on "Oh, Lady Be Good": Their appeal comes from their more frequent melodic surprises and emotional depth. He continued to emphasize the melodic line: This emphasis has caused composer George Russell to describe him usefully as a "horizontal" player, meaning that he thinks in terms of the melodic line (which is written horizontally on music paper), and while developing his patterns and sequences, was willing to allow those lines to clash momentarily with the underlying chords (which are written vertically). Russell contrasts this with Coleman Hawkins's "vertical" approach: Hawkins articulated each chord in a given progression—Russell says he "checks in" with each chord. In a Hawkins solo, we pay attention to the chord progression and to his cleverness in dealing with the progression, often by implying passing chords and upper chordal extensions. With a Lester Young solo, we focus on the succession of melodies and on his use of motives.

"After Theatre Jump" begins with a little motive, which is used in each of the first four measures, and then is expanded into the phrase beginning in measure 5. The second eight bars begin with a melodic idea centering around E♭ and C. Measure 12 is a surprise, with its change in register and raspy tone. (See music example.)

Example 11–10
Lester Young, beginning of his solo on "After Theatre Jump."

Young makes no attempt, as he would have earlier in his career and did on "Lady Be Good," to connect the bridge with the preceding section. From 1943 on, Young seems to be using the bridge of an AABA tune to introduce contrast. His treatment of the bridge in the various choruses here illustrates another tendency that appears after 1943: He structures his bridges similarly. The bridge on the second chorus of "After Theatre Jump" begins with two variants of the motive heard in the first bridge. (See music example.)

Example 11-11.
Lester Young, bridge (first seven measures) of his second chorus on "After Theatre Jump" (1944).

Then Young ascends with the wide leaps also heard in the first bridge. (There is an alternate take of this piece that was issued in the 1980s.) Young was still growing musically, but, tragically, he was inducted into the army to be stationed at Fort McClellan in Alabama on December 1.

The army couldn't have found a less promising recruit. Young was 35, a drinker and habitual smoker of marijuana. He was besides a sensitive, private and somewhat eccentric man, little fitted to the disciplines of military life. Nor was he reconciled to the endemic racism he encountered. He wasn't allowed to join a military band. Then on February 1, 1945, he was arrested for possession of marijuana and barbiturates. He barely defended himself at the court martial, where it was admitted that Young had never hidden his use of drugs. Young was sentenced to a year in the military barracks of Fort Gordon, Georgia, but was dishonorably discharged on December 1, 1945.

He resumed his career at a time when he was more popular than ever, commanding high fees and winning magazine polls. The month of his release he played exquisitely plaintive, and then fiery, choruses on a blues with a bridge—"D.B. Blues," sardonically dedicated to the detention barracks of the army. At the same session, he masterfully transformed "These Foolish Things" into a heartrending lament, on which he improvises throughout and ends unaccompanied.

Habitually wearing a porkpie hat—its flat shape looked like a pie—he remained eccentric, approaching the bandstand with mincing steps, speaking in a slang-filled language that expressed a tremendous wit. In a light high voice with a touch of a Southern accent, he called everyone "Pres," identified white people as "grey boys" and noted the presence of a bigot by suggesting he "felt a draft." Whitney Balliett has noted some other Young-isms: "Bing and Bob" were the police; an attractive girl, a "poundcake." When he liked something, he had eyes for it—Stan Getz proudly recalled that Young told him he had eyes for his playing.

Perhaps Young is still misunderstood. Those who knew him well, such as Horace Silver, who played piano for Young in 1953, found him a poignant, if often brilliantly hilarious, figure: "If you were a member of his band and he opened up to you, he was beautiful. He'd keep you laughing all the time . . . But he'd come off the bandstand and go right in the dressing room. He wouldn't go out till it was time to go on the bandstand again . . . I was riding home from a gig one night in the car and . . . somehow I felt he felt dejected or something and he told me—he called everybody 'Prez'—he said, 'Well, Prez, I really don't think nobody really likes old Prez' . . . That's the way he felt" (*Jazz Lives*, pp. 84–85).

Young experienced a long physical decline, produced by his alcoholism, and perhaps, a recent study speculates, by syphilis contracted in the thirties and never cured, which was to end in 1959 with his death in New York City. (His last engagement, in Paris, was dramatized in the 1986 movie *Round Midnight*, starring Dexter Gordon as the Young-like figure.) Though uneven from 1953 on, his later recordings include some gems in a new style. On the 1956 "Pres Returns," a rocking blues where he is accompanied, as on so many of his best recordings, by Teddy Wilson and drummer Jo Jones (see the photograph), Young enters his second solo with a casual-sounding phrase quoted from his 1936 solo on "Boogie-Woogie." This relaxed statement is made unforgettable by the evocative shades of Young's still-delicate tone, now made even more suggestive by the hints of breathiness and by a bit of a growl. Each of the ensuing choruses begins with an equally strong idea: The solo as a whole builds in intensity until the final choruses of simple riffs. Young is no virtuoso here: The power of his late playing, when it worked, came from his exquisite choice of notes.

Teddy Wilson (left), Lester Young (center), and Jo Jones (right) listening back to their recording in January 1956. (Courtesy Harry Swisher)

He had a lyrical conception that was virtually unique among instrumentalists. Whatever his doubts about his acceptance, Pres had legions of admirers and imitators, among them such important saxophonists as Stan Getz, Zoot Sims, Warne Marsh, Dexter Gordon, and even Charlie Parker. Young might be said to have only one peer, however, and that was the singer Billie Holiday. Holiday's awful life has been repeatedly documented — and sensationalized in the 1972 movie *Lady Sings the Blues,* starring Diana Ross — until her personal woes, including the drug addiction which seemed to dominate the last years of her life, are as well known as her artistry. Tragic though that life was, and expressive though her voice was in her later years of that tragedy — Amiri Baraka has spoken of her as expressing "a black landscape of need" — Billie Holiday should be remembered more for her perfect taste and vital musical intelligence, for the joy as well as poignancy in her singing, for the way she transformed even the most forgettable melodies and jejune lyrics, and with a slight catch in her voice and a subtle reworking of a tune's rhythm, turns banal sentimentality into adult drama.

The woman who transformed jazz singing, adapting what she heard in Louis Armstrong, Bessie Smith and Ethel Waters to create a lighter, more flexible style, was born in 1915 in Baltimore. She would die 44 years later in a New York City hospital while guarded by policemen sent to arrest her for drug abuse. Her father was Clarence Holiday, a jazz guitarist who performed with Fletcher Henderson but who did not live with the family. Holiday moved with her mother to Manhattan in 1928. There, driven by poverty, she evidently tried prostitution, for which she was briefly imprisoned, and then began singing.

John Hammond heard her in a club in 1933. He later wrote that he "decided that night that she was the greatest jazz singer I had ever heard" (*John Hammond on Record*, p. 92). Later that year, Hammond recorded her with another one of Holiday's early fans, Benny Goodman. Even on this first, probably nerve-wracking, session one hears her winsome charm and the youthful bounce and balance of her rhythmic conception. She sounds a little like Mildred Bailey, a favorite among many jazz musicians.

Holiday would be featured in a seminal series of small group recordings led by Teddy Wilson between 1935 and 1939. (The series ended after she declared with characteristic and perfectly justified self-assertiveness that she would be nobody's "girl singer" and thenceforth led her own recording groups.) These include the 1935 "What a Little Moonlight Can Do," with its good-humored seductiveness, and "Miss Brown to You," which has her lazy-sounding initial statement in which she floats over the accompaniment with an easy grace all her own. Her first "hit," according to record producer Michael Brooks, was the 1936 "I Cried for You," which sold 15,000 copies.

"I Cried for You" was made on June 30, 1936. A few weeks later, on July 10, and evidently because there was a problem with the scheduled fourth number during a recording session, Holiday sang one of her rare, but incomparable, blues. (The title of her autobiography, *Lady Sings the Blues*, was meant to suggest her hard life, not her repertoire.) It's a remarkable accomplishment. On "Billie's Blues" Holiday sings the blues with a lightness of execution, a sophistication, that does not trivialize, as so many subsequent singers did, the emotional quality of the traditional form.

Her sides featuring Lester Young in 1938 include "Back in Your Own Backyard" with Young's hard-swinging chorus, and "I Can't Get Started" with Holiday's somewhat sardonic vocal and Young's deceptively relaxed, rhythmically complex half chorus, in two very different takes. Their musical relationship—there was also a fitful personal one—is best seen in memorable passages where Holiday sings while Young plays caressingly around her. Young was loathe to single out his own recordings, but when pressed by Leonard Feather to pick out a favorite, he chose, besides "Taxi War Dance" with Basie, two collaborations with Holiday, "A Sailboat in the Moonlight" and "Back in Your Own Backyard." He might have chosen their marvelous rendition of "He's Funny That Way" (SCCJ) from 1937, in which her vocal devices—her use of a downward slide at the end of phrases and her subtle vibrato—are so entrancing that they almost distract us from her rhythmic ingenuity. (A music example of Holiday appears in Appendix 1.)

These recordings sold modestly at the time. Holiday received more notoriety for later recordings such as that dark song of protest from 1939, "Strange Fruit," about lynchings in the South. Holiday wrote the music to "Strange Fruit" to accompany a poem written by Lewis Allen. (She did not improvise this song after witnessing a lynching, as the movie *Lady Sings the Blues* would have it.) A powerful performance sung with a poised bitterness that is both sincere and artful, "Strange Fruit" is a sobering masterpiece that took jazz singing into a new realm.

She expresses a different, more lively kind of bitterness in another composition, her well known "God Bless the Child," which Holiday wrote and re-

Billie Holiday in the late 1940's. (Courtesy Rutgers Institute of Jazz Studies)

corded in 1941, evidently to taunt her mother, who refused to lend her money. "God bless the child," the lyric goes, "that's got his own." (Eric Dolphy's innovative version of this song is discussed in Chapter 15, with a music example.) She made a successful recording of "Gloomy Sunday" in 1941 and in 1944 she helped write the hit "Don't Explain," in which the singer urges a wayward husband not to lie about, among other things, the lipstick on his collar.

Not all of her repertoire was this gloomy, although many of her hits seem to mirror the disruptions of her life, her unhappy marriage, her bouts with liquor and heroin which led to incarceration in 1947, and eventually to her premature death in 1959. Through it all, at least in public, Holiday maintained her dignity. Even her later recordings, in which the range of her cracking voice is severely limited, suggest power as well as pathos. She never depended on vocal virtuosity. With her elegant rhythmic sense, her poignant vibrato and indescribable tonal quality, she illuminates songs from within. One of her most famous performances came on her blues "Fine and Mellow," performed live on television on December 8, 1957. Singing her trenchant lyrics — "Love is just like a faucet, it turns off and on" — in the company of Lester Young, Coleman Hawkins and Roy Eldridge, Holiday stood entranced and entrancing, her head to one side and arms moving in slow circles. No blues is more affecting. Holiday virtually invented modern jazz singing, and her lyricism has affected instrumentalists such as Miles Davis as well as singers such as Carmen McRae, Betty Carter, and Abbey Lincoln, whose harshly voiced songs of protest come out of "Strange Fruit."

Jazz became popular in the thirties, which was also a decade of real accomplishment for jazz musicians. In the twenties, groups such as those of Red Nichols experimented with whole tone scales and other "modern" harmonic ideas, but they used them in obvious, self-conscious ways. In the experimental music of the thirties, one hears a greater tolerance of dissonance, and one observes musicians discovering new ways to voice dissonant chords, either on the piano or among the instruments of the band, so that dissonance enriches the whole sound, rather than standing out freakishly. These harmonic ideas became the obsession of the next generation, the beboppers.

The smoothly chugging rhythmic style of the thirties had its advantages. The oom-pah rhythms of many 1920s groups limited soloists to developing short rhythmic phrases over this constantly shifting background. Even the stomp style of playing, while clearly laying down four beats to the bar, often laid them down so heavily that subtle improvising styles were made impossible. This may be one reason why Bix Beiderbecke made some of his best recordings supported lightly by Eddie Lang's guitar and by unobtrusive drums and piano, with no bass instrument at all. A competent thirties rhythm section laid down a more predictable, even-flowing foundation. This "groove" allowed the improviser more freedom to generate long phrases without interrruption, to play short phrases if desired, to play as lightly or heavily as the situation demanded.

Probably no one who heard, say, Goodman's 1938 Carnegie Hall concert, or who observed the astonishing popularity of Cab Calloway, to say nothing of

Glenn Miller or the Dorseys or Artie Shaw later, would have predicted that the swing era, buffeted by wartime restrictions on entertainment, tested by changes in taste, and challenged by a new generation of jazz musicians, would be essentially over by the mid-forties. But those who listened to Charlie Christian bursting out of Goodman's groups, who observed the popularity of the "cool" ensemble led by bassist John Kirby, who heard Roy Eldridge with Krupa, Dizzy Gillespie with Calloway or Charlie Parker with Jay McShann, would know that, musically at least, the scene was changing again.

12 The Scene Changes: The Forties and Bebop

"My music emerged from the war years . . . and it reflected those times in the music. Fast and furious, with the chord changes going this way and that way, it might've looked and sounded like bedlam, but it really wasn't."

Gillespie (*To Be or Not . . . to Bop*, p. 201)

While the World War was devastating much of Europe, it was also unsettling the music industry in America. The problems ranged from a shortage of shellac, which was then used to make records, to a shortage of dancers, particularly male, to fill the ballrooms. The transportation system that used to bring bands to dance halls all over the country was strained.

Neither were musicians exempt from the draft. Because of their tight-knit nature and dependence on individual expression, jazz bands particularly suffered from rapid turnovers in personnel. Although Count Basie found replacements for Lester Young and Jo Jones when they were simultaneously served induction papers in September 1944, the sound of his band was irretrievably altered by the loss of those stars.

The bands that survived during the war had to scuffle. Transportation was a constant worry, as the movement of most buses and trains were overseen by the military. The Ellington band continued to travel, retaining its buses by playing, virtually daily, free concerts at army bases before going on to the dances that were its bread and butter.

Those dances were more expensive to attend. A stiff entertainment tax of 20 percent made stepping out to the big bands costlier. This is not to say that the big bands were destroyed precipitously by the war, any more than they were replaced immediately by new music. Ellington's series of Carnegie Hall concerts which began in 1943 were a personal triumph as well as a major step for jazz. Stan Kenton's phenomenal popularity began after the war, when he seemed to flaunt the public with his progressive jazz concerts and found that some fans loved him anyway. Woody Herman's Second Herd, which also absorbed some of the new music, had a similar success in the postwar years. The more traditional Glenn Miller band, which made the sweetly swinging "In the Mood" in 1939, disbanded in 1942 so Miller could form and direct an armed forces band.

Miller's music became even more popular between his enlistment and his mysterious disappearance in a small plane in December 1944. (Neither Miller nor the plane were found.)

Still, there is evidence that the jazz and swing audience was splintering. A swing band, with its sometimes elaborate showiness, made a complicated appeal to audiences, and it satisfied a variety of people, from the hotblooded jazz fans who pressed against the bandstand to observe their favorite soloists, to the others, equally hotblooded in another way, who were moving sinuously with their partners to a shuffling beat. Jazz would never again find a way of satisfying so many interests simultaneously.

When jazz changed, only a few of the swing fans came along. Perhaps the segment of the swing audience that used to go to hear the bands primarily for the vocalists found it more satisfying to hear the singers when they became single attractions. Popular singing—pioneered by veteran Bing Crosby and practiced by younger singers such as Jo Stafford, Frank Sinatra, and Peggy Lee—was entering a kind of golden age. But the fans of these singers sometimes abandoned jazz.

REVIVALISM IN JAZZ

Soon there would be factions in the jazz world itself, between progressives and "moldy figs," lovers of traditional jazz exclusively. By the end of the thirties, the music was ready for a revolution, and for a counterrevolution: For the new music, which was called first rebop and then bebop, and for the New Orleans or Dixieland revival. (Black musicians, who tended to be less sentimental about the old South and more sensitive about the implications of "Dixieland," with its reference to the old Mason-Dixon line separating North and South, preferred to call it "New Orleans" music.) Perhaps tired of the formulas and clichés of the lesser big bands, some jazz fans took a fond look backwards. Perhaps the cataclysm of the war fed a desire for an older, simpler music, made in a stable, relaxed community. At any rate, the 1939 publication of *Jazzmen* by Frederick Ramsey and Charles Edward Smith helped spark the New Orleans revival. There were signs of a new kind of interest in jazz history even earlier. When Paul Whiteman played "Livery Stable Blues" at his Aeolian Hall concert in 1924, it was to demonstrate how far jazz had come from that crude beginning. When Benny Goodman included historical items in his 1938 Carnegie Hall concert, it was with more affection. By the end of the thirties, groups such as the Hot Jazz Club of America and the United Hot Club Association offered reissues of twenties jazz 78s to their subscribers.

The book *Jazzmen* had discussed a legendary New Orleans trumpeter named Bunk Johnson (1879-1949), long out of the music business. Soon, Johnson was found, fitted with false teeth which he needed in order to play, and praised intemperately, not only as the tutor of Louis Armstrong, in itself a false claim, but as his superior. Johnson's modest trumpet style represented to his fans an older, purer style, made before jazz became commercial. In 1942, Johnson made his first recordings ever: They have a somewhat fragile effervescence and a wistfulness often marred by the unrefined playing of his mates. When Johnson came to perform in New York, some fans made his seemingly miraculous resurrection into virtually a religious experience. Johnson's sweetly affecting statements were hailed as the true jazz at last.

The attempt to make time stand still was naive. For one thing, Johnson may have represented to some an earlier era, but his recordings do not in fact sound like the New Orleans jazz of the twenties. Nor was Johnson as much of a purist as his fans. When in 1947 he was given the opportunity to lead his own band at the Stuyvesant Casino in New York City, Johnson shocked some fans by playing and recording a repertoire that included not only New Orleans classics, but popular songs such as "You're Driving Me Crazy" and "Out of Nowhere." He insisted that his was a dance band and should play current popular songs.

During the early forties numerous Dixieland revival bands sprung up, composed of young white musicians attempting to recreate the sounds of Oliver and Morton. One of the best was the Yerba Buena Jazz Band of San Francisco led by trumpeter Lu Watters. Listeners delighted in the music, which they imagined to be a window on a simpler past. Politics as well were involved in this yearning for a "purer," and presumably more instinctive, music, which was seen as coming straight out of the hearts and souls of black folk. Not surprisingly, the New Orleans jazz revival coincided with the beginning of the folk music revival which immortalized the black singer and songwriter Leadbelly and white political songster Woody Guthrie.

The traditionalist movement led to some fine recordings by older musicians such as the Bechet recordings we have mentioned, made for Blue Note, a new label started in 1939. Other "conservatives" benefitted as well. Blue Note recorded boogie-woogie pianists such as Albert Ammons and Meade Lux Lewis. Numbers such as Lewis's "Honky Tonk Train Blues," which he had recorded in 1928 (his 1937 version is in SCCJ), prompted a fad for boogie-woogie, a hard driving type of 12-bar blues playing. Every dance band had in the late thirties a boogie-woogie number. Goodman played Mary Lou Williams's "Roll 'Em" and Will Bradley had a hit with "Beat Me Daddy, Eight to the Bar." At the same time, guitarist Eddie Condon became more active as a recording artist, and figures such as the clarinetist Pee Wee Russell, whose odd, searching style never fit into the swing era, made some of his best recordings for the Commodore label. (A music example of Russell appears in Appendix 1.) These include the 1944 recording with pianist Jess Stacy, "Take Me to The Land of Jazz."

But while a portion of the jazz audience was entranced by the sounds of these early styles, the land of jazz was shifting inexorably underneath their feet. Race relations in the United States were changing. There was little fond looking back in black communities during and after the war. The war brought about, Lerone Bennett argued in *Before the Mayflower*, "a new set of relationships" between blacks and whites. It coincided with and helped precipitate an increasingly impatient activism among black political figures. The signs of that impatience were historically important. Even before America had entered the war, black leader A. Philip Randolph had voiced a demand for equal treatment in defense industries, and had threatened a march on Washington if his demands were not met. They were met, with an Executive Order, on June 25, 1941.

African-American life was celebrated in a group of new magazines: *Jet* and *Ebony*, among others, were founded in the war years. The Congress of Racial Equality was founded—and staged its first sit-in—in 1943. At a time when it had more money to spend, and more power to wield, black America, unintimidated by wartime race riots, was asserting itself in a great variety of ways. The new generation of musicians reflected, and contributed, to the times. Bebop involved a reinterpretation of the elements of music. This new strikingly modern-sounding music, hip and upbeat, also reflected one kind of response to the problems of the war years, as suggested above by Gillespie.

THE NEW GENERATION

The new wave of jazz musicians, the bop musicians, by and large eschewed the role of entertainer that came quite naturally to someone like Louis Armstrong. While trumpeter Dizzy Gillespie might dance, clown, and sing hip novelty vocals, Charlie Parker would merely announce his numbers and then stand up and play. Miles Davis, as was frequently noted during the 1950s, might stand up and play with his back turned to the audience. The black musicians who came to the fore in the postwar era tended to have more formal education, were more skilled as instrumentalists, and, it would seem, more obviously socially conscious than any generation of jazz musicians before them. They learned from the virtuosity of Art Tatum, of Lester Young and Roy Eldridge, and they built a style that required advanced skills from every player. Startlingly to some, these younger musicians presented themselves first and foremost as expressive musicians.

One can see that by examining their repertoire. Every swing band recorded popular material for commercial reasons. But what may have seemed clever or cute in the thirties can sometimes seem embarrassingly trite today. It's difficult to enjoy the more commercial sides of even a good band like Andy Kirk's. Perhaps because they were never big business in the first place, the new generation of musicians made fewer obviously commercial recordings. They recorded blues, originals, and, often, new versions of standards whose chord changes intrigued them. There were hundreds of new melodies written over the "I Got Rhythm" changes, and quite a few based on the Lionel Hampton band's 1942 hit "Flying Home" (BBJ). Among the themes based on the chords of "How High the Moon" are "Ornithology," credited to Charlie Parker and trumpeter Benny Harris, Coleman Hawkins's "Bean at the Met" and Lennie Tristano's "Lennie-Bird." The chords of "What Is This Thing Called Love?" spawned Tadd Dameron's "Hot House" and Lee Konitz's wittily named "Subconscious Lee" (SCCJ), among others.

The practice was not new. In the twenties and in the swing era, dozens of fast tunes were written over the changes of "Tiger Rag." Nor did it show a poverty of invention on the part of the boppers. The melodies of many of their compositions are ideally adapted to the particular rhythmic life of their music and stand apart from their models. The best lines of the boppers, like "Ornithology" and Parker's "Anthropology" (based on "I Got Rhythm") have unforgettable melodies. So do many of the original tunes not based on standard changes, including Parker's "Confirmation," Thelonious Monk's " 'Round Midnight" and Gillespie's "A Night in Tunisia."

The progressive jazz musicians focussed on small band jazz, reemphasizing the importance of improvisation after a swing era which often stressed ensemble work. (In this stress on small groups they were like the New Orleans revivalists.) "Rebop" or "bebop" was possibly named after the snare drum accents of someone like Kenny Clarke or, others have suggested, after the syllables Dizzy Gillespie used to sing when teaching his musicians a new song. The sounds "bebop" and "rebop" had both been used in scat singing since the twenties. The 1928 McKinney's Cotton Pickers' "Four or Five Times" includes the vocal line "Bebop one, bebop two, bebop three." The band chants "bebop" after Ella Fitzgerald's scat chorus on Chick Webb's " 'Tain't What You Do" (1939) and in 1939 as well, Glenn Miller recorded an Eddie Durham piece called "Wham (Re-Bop-Boom-Bam)." The rhythmic energy of the music probably made the attribution of the term bebop to what Parker and Gillespie were doing seem appropriate. When in 1945, Gillespie entitled a piece "Be-Bop," he helped fix the term in the public consciousness. (But not immediately, as Peter Tamony pointed out: *Down Beat* preferred *rebop* through 1946. See Tamony, "Bop: The Word," in *Jazz: A Quarterly*, Spring 1959.)

To many the music seemed to spring up full-blown in the unlikely gardens of the small, uptown clubs of Manhattan. Partially that is because its beginnings were poorly documented: In August 1942 a strike against recording companies was called by the musician's union. As the union recognized, live music was threatened by the recently expanded practice of playing recordings on radio. The union wanted compensation in the form of a royalty payment to be paid to the union by record companies. Until the union negotiated a new contract, no new instrumental recordings, with the exception of certain sides made expressly for the armed forces, were supposed to have been made. (The armed services recordings were called V-Discs, and they went all over the world.) The ban went into effect on August 1, 1942. It was settled piecemeal: Decca came to terms in September 1943, Blue Note settled in November 1943, and Columbia and Victor held out until November 1944. Singers were unaffected by the ban, so the strike had the unexpected effect of thrusting Frank Sinatra and a few others into greater fame. Although they could still make broadcasts, the big bands, with their big expenses, suffered grievously. Listeners were of course denied the privilege of hearing the new developments in jazz as they were occurring.

One can only speculate if the new music would have been recorded during those years anyway. Established companies would probably not have been interested. In fact it's been argued that the strike opened business opportunities for the small labels that began shortly afterwards, companies such as Savoy, Dial and Keynote which recorded the younger players. (Scott DeVeaux, "Bebop and the Recording Industry: the 1942 AFM Recording Ban Reconsidered," *J.A.M.S.*) By 1942, according to Dizzy Gillespie, much of the new music was in place, and the only question was, "Could we all survive as modernists, without any further ties to the mother dance bands?" Bop never achieved the widespread popularity of swing, but it got plenty of attention from the press and public. A year after the recording ban ended, Gillespie was sufficiently popular to organize his own big band.

The new music that confronted those who, returned from the war, strolled by 52nd Street or who heard the early recordings of Charlie Parker was indeed different. Even musicians were surprised by it. Pianist Hank Jones, who would later record with Charlie Parker, grew up on Fats Waller, Teddy Wilson, Tatum, and perhaps was most influenced by Nat "King" Cole's early piano solos. Jones came to New York City from Michigan in 1944. "When I came to New York I wasn't playing anything remotely like bebop. People were here like [pianists] Bud Powell, Al Haig, Duke Jordan, and Parker and Gillespie. I came down to a place called the Spotlite—the first club I went into. They worked at the Three Deuces as well. I heard the music and liked it immediately. The work that was facing me was to try to assimilate and not lose what I already had, to absorb some of this brand new style of playing. I didn't always succeed, but I had to do it."

John Lewis, who would play with the Dizzy Gillespie big band and then form the Modern Jazz Quartet, first heard Charlie Parker when he was in the army. He found the experience overwhelming: "I heard Charlie Parker on the radio with the Jay McShann band in 1942 in July, just before I went overseas. Nobody knew him. It was coming over the camp radio—it was a broadcast from the Savoy. We heard him and it was literally astounding to everyone who heard him. He played perfectly. There was no fumbling, no notes you could do without or that weren't good. All complete ideas. He kept on inventing complete, wonderful ideas."

The music that Parker was playing was new, but bebop didn't come out of nowhere. Virtually all of the leaders of the new music were trained in the big bands. To find the beginnings of bop, one looks to the big bands of the late thirties and early forties, to the small band recording sessions of soloists such as Lester Young and Charlie Christian, and to clubs where musicians jammed and experimented, places like Monroe's and Minton's in Harlem.

Minton's was originally a dining room in the Hotel Cecil on West 118th Street. A retired saxophonist, Henry Minton turned the place into a club, which he hired saxophonist and ex-bandleader Teddy Hill to manage. Hill in turn hired a rhythm section—it often included Thelonious Monk on piano and Kenny Clarke on drums—and set up almost nightly jam sessions. There Charlie Christian—who was from 1939 to 1941 a featured member of Benny Goodman's ensembles—played his most experimental music. Christian's flowing phrases, with their effortless swing, fit into the swing era seamlessly.

In front of Minton's Playhouse, Harlem, 1948. Left to right: Thelonious Monk, Howard McGhee, Roy Eldridge, Teddy Hill. (Courtesy Rutgers Institute of Jazz Studies)

They also looked forward to the new music. Miles Davis, when moved to discuss the beginnings of bop, talked about Charlie Christian's influence, particularly in the Midwest: "I think bop branched off from Charlie Christian" (Ian Carr, *Miles Davis*, p. 10). Bassist Red Callender points out that Christian was, as were so many of the new generation, a scholar of music: "Charlie Christian, Lester Young, and Bird. I think they all influenced each other . . . Prior to that when a guy would take a chorus on a song and get to the release, or the bridge, they never did really analyze those things, they'd skate through; but starting with Charlie Christian, he really dug the interrelated chords leading in and out of a bridge [of an AABA form]—turnbacks. Charlie Parker, Charlie Christian, Lester Young, and Dizzy Gillespie, they really had a steady flow through there" (Ira Gitler, *Swing to Bop*, pp. 40–41).

One can hear this steady flow during Christian's solo choruses in "Stompin' at the Savoy," recorded at Minton's in May 1941 by a fan with a private recording machine. He was playing with a band that included Nick Fenton on bass, the young Thelonious Monk on piano, a fiery Roy Eldridge protégé named Joe Guy on trumpet and Kenny Clarke on drums. Monk had not yet developed his characteristic style—he was playing in the tradition of Teddy Wilson, and sounded a bit like Jess Stacy. Christian plays brilliantly, using driving riffs and short phrases during the A sections of this AABA tune, and flows through the more complicated bridge changes with long, intricate lines.

Behind him, Kenny Clarke plays in the style that would become typical of bop drummers. He provides a shimmering, bell-like background by emphasizing the cymbals and using the actual drums for punctuations instead of timekeeping. Clarke made the ride cymbal the focus of the beat, and in doing so, according to Dizzy Gillespie, "set the stage for the rhythmic content of our music" (*To Be or Not . . . to Bop,* p. 137). "Kenny's style of drumming, with 'bombs' and 'klook-mops' in the bass drum and regular rhythm in the cymbals was ideal for me," Gillespie added (p. 98). Budd Johnson concurred, saying "this transition all came through, I would say, the drums."

Like Gillespie, Kenny Clarke knew what he was looking for. "My brother [a bass player] liked Jimmy Blanton a lot," he said, "and he thought that this style should be kept up by a light drummer who let the bass line be heard. That's how I started experimenting with the continuous cymbal line" (*Swing to Bop,* p. 53). Simultaneously, bass players started to play more chromatic, flowing, walking lines. Then "the beat had a better flow. It was lighter and tastier. That left me free to use the bass drum, the tom-toms and snare for accents. I was trying to lay new rhythmic patterns over the regular beat. Solo lines were getting longer. Soloists needed more help from the drummer—kicks, accents, cues, all kinds of little things like that" (Ross Russell, *Bird Lives,* p. 133). Clarke's decision to keep a light beat on the cymbals is the foundation of the bebop style: His accents—especially the bass drum bombs—identified the new style.

DIZZY GILLESPIE

Dizzy Gillespie said that meeting Clarke in 1938 was "the most important thing that happened to me musically during this period." A lot had been happening in those years to Gillespie, who would become, with Charlie Parker, virtually a symbol of bebop. Born in Cheraw, South Carolina in 1917, John Birks Gillespie took up several instruments as a child, settling on trumpet in time to win a scholarship to a private school, Laurinburg Technical Institute, in 1932. He also studied, mostly informally, the piano and became a master of chord changes. By 1935, Gillespie was in Philadelphia, where he worked professionally with the Frankie Fairfax band, and sat around, as organist Bill Doggett attested, talking about chord changes. Considering Dizzy's reputation for clowning, it's useful to remember that musicians considered him the scholar of the bebop movement: "He was completely into studying," said Billy Eckstine.

He was modelling his style on Roy Eldridge's fiery playing, and largely because of the similarity in their styles, Gillespie was hired by Teddy Hill after Eldridge left. He toured Europe with the Hill Band and recorded his first solo with them in 1937, the Eldridge-influenced chorus on "King Porter Stomp." In 1939, he joined the prestigious Cab Calloway big band. (In a famous incident Dizzy Gillespie was thrown out of the band in 1941 when Calloway accused him of throwing a spitball at the leader during a performance: It turned out years later that another band member had thrown the spitball, but Gillespie's hijinks

Dizzy Gillespie around 1980. (Photo by Michael Ullman)

were so well known that Calloway assumed he was the culprit.) Calloway recorded Gillespie's Latin-flavored "Pickin' the Cabbage" in 1940: It contains a Gillespie solo in the tradition of Eldridge. In the months to come he would develop his own voice. Not as majestic as Armstrong, nor crackling with intensity as Eldridge, Gillespie's style is full of fast runs, unexpected pauses, and places where he holds a dissonant note, hovering like a hummingbird until he alights on the resolving tone. Whereas half of the excitement of an Eldridge solo comes from the sense of strain in the way he reaches for notes, Gillespie always sounds wryly assured. His style is made dramatic by the way he moves from simple melodic statements to rapid strings of triplets, by his radical shifts in dynamics, and by his unexpected leaps in pitch. His tone is more nasal than that of most swing trumpeters, which initially bothered some listeners: He makes up for it with his harmonic and rhythmic imagination. Here again, his scholarly habits helped him. He describes working with the Edgar Hayes band, and coming across an arrangement by reedman Rudy Powell: "Rudy wrote this arrangement for Edgar Hayes that had this wierd change, an E-flat chord built on an A [in the bass], the flatted fifth. When I ran across that in the music, it really hit—boom! . . . I played that thing over and over, and over again, and started using it in my solos." (See music example.)

He started to emphasize the flatted fifth, hitting one in a ballad arrangement and holding it: "From doing this I found out that there were a lot of pretty notes on a chord that were well to hold, instead of running over them . . . There are a lot of pretty notes on a chord, and if you hold them for an extended time, it adds a hue" (*To Be*, p. 92).

flatted fifth

Example 12–1.
An E♭ chord with A in the bass.

Like other swing and bop innovators, Gillespie was finding new "pretty notes" in the chords that he was working with. These include "higher" intervals. Let's take, for example, in the C major scale, the first, third and fifth notes (C, E, G)—a major triad. Musicians like to make this basic triad more interesting by adding notes to it. On a piano, one can try adding a B♭, a D, and even an F♯ above that. From the point of view of a C major scale, these notes would be called the flatted seventh, the ninth, and the raised eleventh. Those higher notes, usually called higher intervals because one counts upward from the tonic, create intriguing tensions when they are played over the C-E-G chord. Adapting them to a musical phrase, a soloist might play them with some connecting notes. A soloist might also want to change the basic intervals, in particular by flatting the fifth note of the C scale, the G, making it a G♭. This flatted fifth, which Gillespie talks about above, was a favorite of the boppers, and became by the end of the forties a cliché.

Gillespie typically gives Charlie Parker credit for developing modern solo ideas first. If so, Dizzy still deserves credit for his writing, which made available some of the new harmonic ideas to other musicians. They picked up on his innovative pieces early. Woody Herman recorded his "Down Under" in July 1942 (BBJ). His ideas for compositions came either from chords he discovered at the piano or from a rhythmic kernel. The A section of his "Salt Peanuts" was just a riff, he said—a riff whose jagged leaps one can hear the trumpets play towards the end of Lucky Millinder's "Little John Special," also from July 1942. Gillespie was a member of the trumpet section for that recording, and he says he authored that riff. The riff is preceded by a Gillespie solo that's a microcosm of the budding bop style. Gillespie's best known piece, "A Night in Tunisia," was first recorded by Sarah Vaughan in December 1944, under its original title, "Interlude." The Boyd Raeburn Orchestra recorded it in its more usual instrumental guise in January 1945 (BBJ).

Gillespie wrote the exotic "A Night in Tunisia" while with the Benny Carter band during the winter of 1941-1942: "During the break I sat down at the piano to improvise some chord changes. Actually they were thirteenth chords—A-thirteenth, resolving to D minor. I looked at the notes of the chords as I played the progression and noticed that they formed a melody. All I had to do was write a bridge, put some rhythm to it . . . The melody had a very Latin, even Oriental feeling, the rhythm came out of the bebop style—the way we played with rhythmic accents—and that mixture introduced a special kind of syncopation in the bass line . . . The heavily syncopated rhythm in the bass line probably gave a whole lotta cats ideas. From that point in jazz, the bass didn't have to go boom,

boom, boom, boom. Instead it went boom-be, boom-be" (*To Be*, pp. 171-172). (See music example.)

Example 12-2.
Dizzy Gillespie, "A Night in Tunisia," beginning of theme. Gillespie takes advantage of the diminished fifth relationship between E♭ and the V chord, which is A.

There is a dramatic buildup to a break after the theme chorus, which generations of players have since used to display their technique.

Kenny Clarke has said that Dizzy has the "gift of rhythm," that he's a natural. He's not merely a natural. He has also been a student of rhythm. When fellow Calloway trumpeter, also his roommate, Mario Bauza took him to hear some of his native Afro-Cuban music, Gillespie immediately decided he wanted to bring the authentic rhythms of the congas into jazz. Bauza was later the music director of the progressive Latin band led by Machito. Gillespie remained fascinated with Latin rhythms, and no one had a larger influence in bringing those rhythms into jazz: In the forties he would hire the conga player Chano Pozo, presenting him at a famous Carnegie Hall concert on September 29, 1947. Without suggesting that the two musics were totally compatible, he wanted what he called the "outside influence" of Afro-Cuban drumming to enrich jazz rhythmically. Jazz and Afro-Cuban music could sleep in the same bed—or at least the same room, he surmised.

Later, he made it happen. Gillespie's biggest hit with his big band was "Manteca," which he wrote with Chano Pozo. Pozo presented Gillespie one night with the sketch of a piece—a bass line, and then riffs for the saxophones, trombones and trumpets. "But Chano wasn't too hip about American music. If I'd let it go like he wanted it, it would've been strictly Afro-Cuban, all the way. There wouldn't have been a bridge . . . So I started writing a bridge. I was sitting down at the piano writing the bridge, and thought I was writing an eight-bar bridge. But after eight bars, I hadn't resolved back to B-flat, so I had to keep on going and ended up writing a 16-bar bridge" (*To Be*, p. 321). The success of this piece, and of Gillespie's other efforts for Latin jazz, brought to the attention of other jazz players the remarkable rhythmic resources in Cuban music, with its characteristic beat or "clave." Latin-influenced jazz, and jazz-influenced Latin music, became an important part of the scene from this time onwards.

Rhythmically, Gillespie felt that he was influenced by Parker as well as by Kenny Clarke: "Charlie Parker heard rhythms and rhythmic patterns differently, and after we started playing together, I began to play, rhythmically, more like him" (*To Be*, p. 177). That may have been in the period from December 1942 to the fall of 1943, when both Gillespie and Parker were in Earl Hines's band, or in May 1944, when both played briefly with what started off as a splinter group from the Hines organization and turned into one of the key cradles of bop, Billy Eckstine's big band.

Perhaps Earl Hines didn't quite know what he was getting into when late in 1942 he hired Dizzy Gillespie, already accoutred with the goatee and beret that would soon symbolize the bopster in the public eye, and other budding bop musicians such as trumpeter Benny Harris—who would write the bop anthems "Little Benny" (also known as "Crazeology" on SCCJ) and "Ornithology" (partly credited to Parker)—drummer Shadow Wilson and the inimitable Parker, playing tenor saxophone. Hines was reputedly dismayed at some of what they played, though impressed by their musicianship. Of Dizzy he said, "He was very serious about music and he and Charlie Parker were always working on the exercise books they had accumulated" (*The World of Earl Hines*, p. 91).

The Hines band provided Parker and Gillespie the chance to refine their techniques and exchange ideas. The press and the public often had the idea that the bopsters were either sullen or snobbish, but Gillespie remembers most the "camaraderie" he experienced at the time, when young musicians were eagerly exchanging ideas and discoveries. Travelling across the country with Hines, after opening at the Apollo Theater on January 15, 1943, Parker and Gillespie spread the word in numerous after-hours jams. (A few were recorded and eventually issued.) Bassist Oscar Pettiford, soon to be the most celebrated bop bassist, walked his bass three miles to join them. "Wherever they went," Ross Russell adds, "Charlie and Dizzy were hailed as visiting celebrities" (*Bird Lives*, p. 149).

In February 1944, Gillespie participated in what has been widely called the first true bop recording session. Perhaps that's a misnomer: The date was led by tenor saxophonist Coleman Hawkins, always one of the first musicians to investigate the latest trends. (In October 1944, he would record with Thelonious Monk, when Monk was little thought of by older musicians.) They recorded two boppish numbers, Hawkins's "Disorder at the Border" and Gillespie's intriguing "Woody 'n' You," named for Woody Herman. Again, Gillespie started with intriguing combinations of chords. When it came to the melody, he wrote: "I didn't try to express anything in particular, just music, just what the chords inspired" (*To Be*, p. 186). In other words, he wrote the chords first, and then developed a melodic line that is easily suggested by the chord sequence. The chords for the A sections of this AABA piece do not begin in the home key of D♭ major. Instead they begin in the key of F, then descend to E♭, and finally to D♭. The melodic line is a fairly simple riff which Gillespie states once in each key.

By April 1944, Gillespie was with the big band of singer Billy Eckstine.

Eckstine had been the biggest celebrity in the Hines band, besides the leader himself. Born in 1914 in Pittsburgh, and hence a little older than Parker or Gillespie, Eckstine was a fine singer, with a smooth, vibrato-laden baritone voice and perfect diction. He liked ballads but his biggest hits with Hines, with whom he sang from 1939 to 1943, were blues, especially "Stormy Monday" and the provocatively titled "Jelly, Jelly" of December 1940. Eckstine played some trumpet and valve trombone, and he had eyes, as Lester Young would say, for the new music. In 1943, he left Hines to work as a single. Then in the spring of 1944 he started his own big band dedicated to playing the new music of Dizzy Gillespie, Tadd Dameron, and others: He immediately hired Dizzy Gillespie as music director and Charlie Parker to head the reed section.

By April 1944, Gillespie was recording with the Eckstine band: He solos on Eckstine's "I Stay in the Mood for You" and can be heard on one of the Eckstine's bands most celebrated numbers, "Blowing the Blues Away" from the following December. It is mostly a tenor saxophone battle, between Gene Ammons and Dexter Gordon, who were among the first bebop tenor saxophonists. Gordon's hard, tight tone gives his playing a kind of monumental quality, but his agile phrasing comes out of what Young, Parker and Gillespie were doing.

Eckstine saw his band as primarily a concert band, but there were few concerts to play. For most of its existence—it survived until 1947, when Eckstine went out as a single—the group played dances and made vocal recordings. It had an impact nonetheless. Gil Fuller, who would later become the musical director for Dizzy's big band and play a crucial role in adapting bop to big band jazz, was previously one of Eckstine's arrangers. He notes that the band was so overwhelming that it even eclipsed the Lunceford band at a joint concert in Brooklyn.

Gillespie himself dates the beginning of the bebop era from late in 1944, when he had left Eckstine and co-led a small group with Oscar Pettiford: "The opening of the Onyx Club on 52nd Street represented the birth of the bebop era . . . The initial group consisted of Max Roach (drums), Oscar Pettiford (bass), George Wallington (piano), and me. We really wanted Charlie Parker, and we sent him a telegram, but he didn't get it" (*To Be*, p. 202). Instead they got the remarkable Don Byas (1912-1977), a big-toned tenor saxophonist who was able to make the transition from swing to bop, and who was admired for his command of difficult and intricate patterns. He was highly influential until he moved to Europe in 1946.

MARY LOU WILLIAMS, BUD POWELL, AND THELONIOUS MONK

The presence of the white pianist George Wallington suggests that the techniques of bop were rapidly spreading beyond the black community. Wallington played in bebop jam sessions in the early forties, and his work resembled that of his contemporary Earl "Bud" Powell, although he reportedly did not know Powell until 1943. Gillespie called Powell "the definitive pianist of the bebop era," praising "the fluidity of his phrasing." Perhaps Wallington was also influenced by the early style of the other most innovative pianist of the new music, Thelonious Monk. On their part, both Powell and Monk came under the informal tutelage of Mary Lou Williams. It was an interesting relationship. Williams, pianist and arranger for Andy Kirk's band, blossomed in the forties, partially because of her relationship with the young boppers. Her apartment became one of several meeting places for these people, and both Bud Powell and Thelonious Monk worked on voicings and compositions in her company. Her influence and support were more than useful to these, the most celebrated pianists to emerge from the bop movement.

Williams's works started to take on modern characteristics, such as the comping left hand and dense harmonies of her protégés. She had her own agenda, however: In 1945, she created a unique and unheralded work, her *Zodiac Suite*. The trio recording has been available for some time. Each of the 12 sections has one or two themes, often with tempo changes and interludes. Ostinato bass parts appear in at least half the pieces. The first theme of "Taurus" suggests Debussy, while its second theme, with the bass and drums, recalls Ellington. "Pisces" is a jazz waltz, and the memorable "Libra" begins with major sevenths descending by half steps. The fifth part, "Leo," has a march theme that moves freely between the chords of D major, F major, and A. Since these chords are separated by thirds rather than fifths, a weakened sense of tonality results. Williams also superimposes different keys over the A major bass line in measures 11 through 14, creating bitonality. These techniques of modern classical composers had rarely been used in jazz. (See music example.)

The recorded premiere of the *Zodiac Suite*, performed by a chamber orchestra at New York's Town Hall on December 31, 1945, was finally issued in 1991. For her inventiveness in adapting the new ideas, Mary Lou Williams might be called an honorary member of the new generation.

Her protégés were among its brightest stars. The quintessential bop pianist, Bud Powell was born in New York in 1924, and received early training, as did most pianists, in classical music: He retained his love of Bach to the end, recording "Bud on Bach" for Blue Note in 1957. Even more important to him was the playing of Teddy Wilson and of Billy Kyle in the John Kirby band, both originally disciples of Earl Hines; he also came under what might be called the spell of Art Tatum. Tatum was a family acquaintance, and Powell heard him early. He was challenged rather than overwhelmed by Tatum's virtuosity, his finger dexterity and by his playful mastery of harmonies. The speed of Tatum's right-hand runs, his exotic chord substitutions, and even his delightful manner of quoting fragments of related tunes in an improvisation were absorbed by the boppers.

By 1940, Bud Powell was hanging around, and sometimes playing at, Minton's, where he rubbed up against Thelonious Monk, the house pianist. Powell was never as radical as Monk. He stayed within the virtuoso tradition of Art Tatum, but his right hand took on some of the rattling force he heard in Monk. With his left hand he played jabbing chords. His left hand was not

Example 12–3.
Mary Lou Williams, bars 8–21 of "Leo" from the *Zodiac Suite* condensed score.

deficient: When prodded at a nightclub by an Art Tatum jibe—no one else could have so provoked him—Powell demonstrated his ambidexterity by playing a whole piece with his left hand. Nonetheless, Powell realized, as did Basie before him, that a busy left hand would only interfere with the active lines of the walking bass. Like a bebop drummer, he added accents to fill up holes and played aggressive chords to suggest harmonies to other soloists and to provide a springboard for his own horn-like runs.

Powell's first recordings were made with the sextet and big band of trumpeter Cootie Williams, whose groups from 1942 to 1944 performed an eclectic repertoire. They recorded blues sung and played by Eddie "Cleanhead" Vinson, standards, Ellingtonia, and an occasional Monk tune, including in 1942 "Epistrophy," which Monk wrote with Kenny Clarke. In 1944, Cootie Williams made the first recording of the ballad " 'Round Midnight," Monk's most famous composition. (Later Dizzy Gillespie added an introduction that became a standard part of most performances.) Bud Powell was one of several progressive musicians in the band. Rarely the featured soloist, he nonetheless demonstrated an already distinctive style in such snatches as his loping, percussive introduction and solo on "Floogie Boo" (January 1944). His brief solos elsewhere on record, and in live performances, were enough to inspire other pianists: In Detroit, Tommy

Bud Powell around 1950.
(Courtesy Rutgers Institute
of Jazz Studies)

Flanagan "heard Bud by accident when I saw a Cootie Williams band. I never heard his style of piano playing before—that forceful" (*Jazz Lives*, p. 116).

Bud Powell impressed virtually everyone; he scared quite a few as well. Singer-pianist Carmen McRae talked perceptively of Powell's playing: "His piano playing to me was always a little frantic, never relaxed. He never relaxed, as though he was trying to do so much and get it all out because he did not have enough time to fool around" (Art Taylor, *Notes and Tones*, p. 140). He didn't have as much time as he should have. By all accounts a shy, sensitive man, Powell was arrested during the period he was performing with Cootie Williams, and reportedly beaten around the head by policemen. Although it is not certain that the beating was the sole cause, for the rest of his life he suffered repeated mental breakdowns. Heedless of his special talent, doctors tried shock therapy on him. (According to his lawyer, Max Cohen, Powell once told his doctors that he had composed 600 pieces, which they put down as one of his delusions of grandeur. He was simply telling the truth.) By the sixties—Powell would die in 1966—he was competent to take care of himself, but silent and withdrawn. (When asked about his conversations with Bud Powell at the 1963 record date that resulted in *Our Man in Paris*, Dexter Gordon, not a fast talker himself, looked wide-eyed and commented, "Well—there were long pauses.")

Powell made his first records as a leader in 1947, with bassist Curley Russell and drummer Max Roach. Born in 1924, Roach was already one of the most powerful bebop drummers. Later he would become one of its most significant leaders. For Roost Records, Powell updated the Dixieland warhorse "Indiana," introduced Monk's "Off Minor" and performed one of his own compositions, "Bud's Bubble."

Two years later, Powell went back into the studios, beginning a series of records for what is now the Verve label and for Blue Note Records. A magnificent trio session for Verve, with bassist Ray Brown and Max Roach, took place in 1949. Among the six titles were four Powell originals, including "Celia," a lyrical medium tempo line expressed with refreshing sensitivity by all three musicians. The standard "Cherokee" is Powell's tour de force. At a breakneck tempo, he expounds the theme in a counterpoint arrangement that exploits both hands to the fullest. Then he takes off on one of the most incandescent piano improvisations ever recorded. Powell's solo demonstrates his ease at fast tempos and a variety of ideas: shimmering bell-like effects on the bridge, tongue-in-cheek classical quotations, and bluesy runs. (See music example.)

A few months later, in August 1949, he brought a quintet of young stars to the studio—Sonny Rollins on tenor, Fats Navarro on trumpet, Tommy Potter on bass, and Roy Haynes on drums—and made classic recordings of "Bouncing with Bud" and "Wail" (these two had previously been recorded under different names) and "52nd St. Theme," then created a vibrant trio performance of "Ornithology." In 1951, he returned to the studios and created a thrilling version of "A Night in Tunisia" (SCCJ) that proved Powell virtually the equal of Parker and Gillespie. Powell's break near the beginning of "A Night in Tunisia" is as dramatic as any by the two wind players. The same day he recorded another piece with a Latin beat, his own "Un Poco Loco" (JP), with its brilliant Latin-jazz drumming by Max Roach. "Un Poco Loco" seems to have been inspired by a Latin "montuno," a vamp over a few chords that may be repeated for as long as one wants to improvise. Powell's piece is a preview of the "modal" jazz movement to come.

In later years Powell's playing was erratic, the result of his poor health. At times he was brilliant, at other times technically insecure. Part of the story of his last years—his friendship with a young Frenchman named Francis Paudras—was dramatized in the French film *'Round Midnight* (1986), along with some of Lester Young's story. His forties and fifties recordings were his most influential. Although it's commonly said that Bud Powell simply adapted Charlie Parker to the piano, his achievement was greater than that. His melodic lines have their own distinctively angular shape, and his improvisations are more relentlessly dominated by eighth notes than were Parker's. His spare use of the left hand, rumbling in the lower register, has influenced many pianists since. He was a gifted composer as well.

It took audiences longer to appreciate Powell's mentor, Thelonious Monk. Though as a result of his playing at Minton's, Monk was readily acknowledged as one of the originators of bop, he developed a style that seemed to threaten, as well as excite, other progressive musicians. Fierce though they were, Bud Powell's lines flowed. He was essentially a bop musician. Monk's music seemed more tangential to the mainstream of bop. (Gillespie said that Monk's contributions were spiritual and harmonic.) With his thumping chords, long pauses, his home-grown technique, Monk seemed to cultivate a deliberate awkwardness. Yet he swung passionately and imposed his own radically unique sense of timing on the structures of popular songs and the blues. Unlike many of his peers, Monk still admired stride piano and respected—in his own way—written

Example 12–4.
Bud Powell, beginning of his solo on "Cherokee" (right hand only).

Thelonious Monk in the mid-1960's. (Courtesy Rutgers Institute of Jazz Studies)

melodies. Listening to a Monk improvisation, one hears his repeated references to the written theme.

While looking backwards to James P. Johnson, Monk was in fact reinventing the sound of the piano, listening to its resonances and exploring its overtones. He even held his hands differently. Most pianists are taught to hold their hands, fingers rounded, above the keys. Monk played with his hands and fingers flat and virtually level with the piano. Then he would dart at single notes and clusters from above like an airhammer. Initially, his playing sounded so odd that many listeners, musicians among them, were put off. His compositions— " 'Round Midnight," "Ruby, My Dear," "Well, You Needn't," "Blue Monk"— were accepted earlier than was his playing.

He was born in Rocky Mount, North Carolina on October 10, 1917. When he was four his family moved to New York, where he would remain for the rest of his life. His early musical experiences include playing gospel piano in church and playing as part of a travelling show organized by a "doctor" who sold patent medicines. By the early forties, as we have seen, he was working as a sideman and appearing as the house pianist at Minton's, where he was recorded by a fan. One can hear his still-emerging style on the session he did with Coleman Hawkins in 1944. But there is nothing on record between that session and 1947, when Monk was signed by Alfred Lion of Blue Note Records: Monk would become one of this intrepid producer's passions. On October 24, 1947, Monk recorded for Blue Note one of his most enduring ballads, "Ruby, My Dear," and one of his most characteristic tunes, "Well, You Needn't." "Well, You Needn't" is an AABA tune based entirely on two motives, labelled 1 and 2 in the musical example. The first motive is defined by its first three notes and an ascending direction. The second motive is easy to identify: Its rhythm sounds like the title "Well, You Needn't." In context the second motive seems like an answer to the first. At the end of each A section, a version of motive 1 is heard. And the bridge is based completely on this motive, heard at a variety of pitches. This clever, some might say nearly obsessive, use of motives is typical of one kind of Monk composition, which sounds playful, whimsical, and strikingly coherent. (See music example.)

Example 12-5.
Thelonious Monk, "Well You Needn't."

The early Monk masterpieces for Blue Note also include "Misterioso" (1948) and "Criss Cross" (1951). (Both are in SCCJ.) The former is a blues with a leanly repetitive quarter note rhythm whose very regularity begins to sound whimsical. Its "mystery" comes from the pitches, which outline intervals of sixths and suggest the whole tone scale. Some of the fun of the usual performances of the piece comes when the band moves from this awkward sounding theme into relaxed improvisations on the blues. Monk must have counted on that contrast. "Criss Cross," like "Well, You Needn't" and other AABA Monk pieces, has two main motives. It begins with a little downward turn. Monk places this motive in various unexpected places, and answers it with a leaping motive. That second motive becomes the basis for the bridge.

Sometimes, Monk would embellish the AABA form with interludes, codas and other appendages, to create forms that were more complicated than they appeared. For example, "Thelonious" took this form:

A, a simple riff theme with a half-step motive, eight bars.

A again, eight bars.

B, an involved development of the rhythm of A, 10 bars.

A', eight bars plus a two-bar tag to make 10 bars.

Perhaps this tricky outline explains why it was rarely performed, even by Monk, since its appearance on his first record as a leader (for Blue Note, October 1947). One of its resurrections occurred on the 1967 album *Underground*. This underappreciated album also contains several little known Monk tunes, such as "Boo Boo's Birthday," with its surprising form: an eight-bar A, which is repeated; then a five-bar bridge—and that is all! This 21-bar form is followed scrupulously in the solos. He wrote beautifully unsentimental ballads as well: "Ruby, My Dear," "Ask Me Now," "Crepuscule with Nellie," and his most famous piece, "Round Midnight" (JP). The latter, recorded first for Blue Note in 1947, has been recorded by hundreds of jazz musicians and has had lyrics put to it. (See example in Chapter 16.)

Monk's recordings in the fifties revealed an increased refinement and elaboration of his totally original technique. He took extraordinary chances as a soloist. On the first take of "The Man I Love," recorded with Miles Davis in 1954, Monk plays the A parts of his choruses in what might be called half-time. He leaves out notes, stretching his theme statement over a steadily chugging rhythm section, creating a dislocation that is still startling. At the bridge he pauses, then plays in regular time. On the second take, he plays the first two A's in a similar manner, then pauses so long at the bridge that Davis plays a few notes to fill the void. Another striking conception is his solo on the master take (take one) of "Bag's Groove" (SCCJ) from the same session. In several places during this blues in F, he sets up a pattern, then defeats our expectations by changing it. He begins with a simple riff that he creates by alternating the notes F and C—eventually he alters this riff, bringing in F# as well. (See musical example.)

At the end of his second chorus he introduces a fragment of his blues theme "Misterioso," which also involves alternating notes. With admirable persistence, he stays with this alternating note idea in his third chorus, which he makes exciting by changing the notes and intervals each time, building towards thicker chords and tenser rhythms. The fourth chorus is all chords. Next he starts a little riff that he explores for choruses five and six, changing the last note each time. Next Monk explores the simple half step E to F. By not "comping" with his left hand, Monk creates a spare sound through which the bass line of Percy Heath shines. Heath should be given some credit for the success of this solo: Strongly supportive throughout, he even plays double stops (chords) behind Monk's eighth chorus, a technique that was rarely used by jazz bassists at the time.

When Ellington talked about musicians as "sound identities," he might have had Monk in mind. No pianist got as distinctive a sound as Thelonious Monk, and no jazz composer besides Ellington himself has written such strongly characterized pieces. His influence on some instrumentalists, including pianists from Randy Weston to Ran Blake to Chick Corea, has been decisive. In subtle

Example 12-6.
Thelonious Monk, first chorus of his piano solo on "Bag's Groove" (1954).

ways, his audacity and percussiveness has influenced most adventurous jazz piano since the fifties. His insistence on melody, his humorously blunt treatment of standards, has influenced scores of pianists. The little-known figure Herbie Nichols absorbed some of Monk's compositional daring, though Nichols' skittering piano style seems far from Monk's model. Another fascinating pianist and composer of the fifties, Elmo Hope, seemed equally influenced by Bud Powell and Monk.

Monk's eccentricity was famous. We now know about his illnesses as well—he was hospitalized repeatedly in the sixties for depression. He withdrew from performing in the seventies. His last performances were at the 1975 and 1976 Newport Jazz Festivals in New York. He died in 1982.

THE MIXED ACCEPTANCE OF BEBOP

Looking back, it is remarkable how much was accomplished in the first postwar years by a loosely allied group of young musicians who were often scorned by older players, misunderstood by the press, and considered by a curious public as—alternately—harmless eccentrics or hard-living rebels. In 1938, the hippest jazz recording would be something like the Kansas City Six's "I Want a Little Girl," featuring the lazy, yearningly melodic clarinet of Lester Young. Seven years later, a listener would confront Gillespie's "Shaw 'Nuff," or Parker's version of "Cherokee"—"Koko"—with its pellmell introduction and virtuoso solos by Gillespie, Parker and drummer Max Roach. The change, a shift in emphasis or a mini-revolution in taste, happened extraordinarily quickly.

Bop may not have been appreciated as its creators desired, but it received plenty of attention, even early on. Cab Calloway may have been the first bop critic, when he dubbed what he heard "Chinese music." Columnist Jimmy Cannon said, more amusingly, that it sounded like "a hardware store in an earthquake." In the early twenties, jazz was considered bad for one's health. The worst thing the critics said in 1945 was that bop wasn't jazz. A media campaign pitted the "moldy figs" against the bopsters, pictured as oddball eccentrics who, dressed in goatees and berets, talked a new hip language barely comprehensible to the general public. (This preconception, harmless enough, persisted surprisingly long: The late fifties television series, "The Many Loves of Dobie Gillis," included the goateed character Maynard G. Krebs, a lovable, perpetually unemployed slob in a beret and sweatshirt who talked "hip" and whose most prized possessions were his Thelonious Monk records.)

The elaborate competition between musics reached a kind of apogee in 1947, when on the radio in New York jazz historian Rudi Blesh pitted a group of traditionalists featuring Red Allen against an assemblage of bop players featuring Parker and Gillespie and collected by Barry Ulanov, a critic who promoted the new music. They staged a battle of bands, first with each group playing its own repertoire and then by having them play compositions in common. The radio listeners were supposed to write to declare which band they preferred. The modernists won. But the music shouldn't have been submitted to this kind of competition.

It should also have gotten more respect from the media and the academic world. An article on bop that appeared in *Collier's* on March 20, 1948 began: "You can't sing it. You can't dance it. Maybe you can't even stand it. It's bebop." That's at least amusing. The 1950 edition of the *Grove Dictionary of Music* did not include a separate article on Charlie Parker. It did have this telling description of what it called "be bop":

"The rhythm section of a 'be bop' band plays in a chaotic manner and constantly employs South American rhythmic figures which are incompatible with those of true jazz. (It is not unusual to see bongos in a 'be bop' band.) This rhythmic background of irregular jumps fails to make a support either for the improvisations of jazz soloists or for the instinctive dance of North American Negroes."

In 1950, the *Grove Dictionary* still preferred its vision of "instinctive" Negroes to the reality of what Charlie Parker and Dizzy Gillespie had to offer. And it preferred that jazz be a dance music rather than an art music. Even more cruelly, the new music was associated in the media with drugs—heroin in particular—and identified with the sleazy clubs that most jazz musicians were forced to work in. Charlie Parker was a heroin addict, and admitted publicly that his addiction hurt his playing. But many young musicians of the forties, among them some of the most famous names in jazz, became hooked themselves, presumably hoping that acquiring Parker's habit would help them play like the master. One would think that the devastation wreaked by drugs on this generation of musicians could hardly have been exaggerated—and yet it was, by an unsympathetic, sensationalist media and by thrill-seeking fans.

Bop musicians had little choice but to play in clubs, which some have called "upholstered sewers." Today 52nd Street sounds romantic, a street lined with jazz clubs with the greatest musicians alive inside. But the clubs themselves were dingy and uncomfortable. By 1947, many of them had been replaced by strip joints, and the music moved to Broadway, to places like "Birdland." Some bop musicians, Parker among them, developed a deep-seated antagonism to the club owners on whom they depended. In Jack Chambers's *Milestones: The Music and Times of Miles Davis*, Frank Sanderford describes a scene in Chicago's Argyle Club, where he watched a club owner plead "querulously" to a resentful Parker quintet that they return to the stand. In 1972, Max Roach wrote, "What 'jazz' means to me is the worst kind of working conditions, the worst in cultural prejudice. I could go down a list of club names throughout the country which are a disgrace to somebody who has been in the business as long as I have . . . Jazz to me has meant small dingy places, the worst kinds of salaries and conditions that one can imagine" ("What 'Jazz' Means to Me," *The Black Scholar*, Summer 1972, pp. 3-6).

BIG BANDS

In 1945, the year that saw the real emergence of bebop, these musicians must have been more hopeful. Gillespie and Parker recorded some definitive bop statements that year. In February 1945, Parker took a lyrical solo on Gillespie's "Groovin' High" that made many young saxophonists take notice. On May 11, among other things, they recorded Dizzy's "Shaw 'Nuff." This theme, and two others recorded the same day—Gillespie's "Salt Peanuts" and Tadd Dameron's "Hot House"—began with the dazzling unison lines that would become standard in bop and much modern jazz. Precision and speed of execution seemed to replace, at least in written sections, the emphasis on texture and harmony heard in swing arrangements. On "Shaw 'Nuff" (SCCJ), despite a tempo of about 264 beats per minute, Gillespie is at ease and dazzling. He shows off his high notes on the bridge, and begins the last A section with a triplet figure that has long been one of his favorites. (See music example.)

Example 12–7.
Dizzy Gillespie's solo on "Shaw 'Nuff" (1945). The bass of Curley Russell is of course playing throughout, but is shown here only during Gillespie's pauses.

In 1945, Gillespie and Parker appeared together twice at Town Hall. Separately each would be a headliner at Carnegie Hall over the next few years. Gillespie was sufficiently popular to put together a big band in 1946. (His first attempt, in 1945, failed after a disastrous Southern tour. For decades afterwards, Gillespie would start "Manteca" by chanting, "I'll never go back to Georgia.") In the next four years, he would lead this group, whose charts included "Two Bass Hit" and "Cool Breeze," "Our Delight" (BBJ) and one of the band's most exciting showpieces, the incredibly fast "Things to Come" (BBJ). Composer ~~George Russell contributed what~~ might be the most innovative piece to the band's book. "Cubano Be, Cubano Bop" paid tribute to the merging of the two musics, jazz and Afro-Cuban. Recorded in December 1947, this six-minute piece gave conga drummer Chano Pozo a prominent role throughout, and as an interlude between the two parts, he chanted and soloed. Others, including Stan Kenton, were experimenting with Latin elements around the same time, but with "Cubano Be, Cubano Bop," Gillespie, Russell, and Pozo arrived at an earthy authenticity that nobody else had yet achieved.

The charts by Gil Fuller and by Gillespie himself were brassy and rhythmically exciting—his trumpet section was bright-toned and loud. Gillespie's band was never precise, but it had a wild spirit. The sheer volume and the dominance of his trumpet section influenced other bands, and Gillespie's genial scatting in numbers such as "Oop-Pop-A-Da" and "In the Land of Oo-Bla-Dee"—the latter by Mary Lou Williams—helped popularize bop, while starting a mild fad among jazz singers.

Woody Herman's orchestra in Chicago, 1970's. (Photo by Michael Ullman)

Clarinetist Woody Herman imitated that lighter side of bop with a George Wallington composition, "Lemon Drop," a 1948 recording featuring a band vocal. (In 1951, the band presented it on a radio broadcast with Charlie Parker sitting in.) Born in Milwaukee in 1913, Herman had been a member of the dance band of Isham Jones in the mid-thirties. When that disbanded in 1936, Herman started his own band, modelling his sound on Count Basie. By the mid-forties, Herman was leading what was known as Herman's Herd, a wildly swinging group with some young modernists in it and innovative scores by composer Ralph Burns. He disbanded after the war, and regrouped in 1947 with the Second Herd, a bopping ensemble that featured an unusual group of saxophonists, three tenors and a baritone, plus a lead alto—instead of the usual two altos, two tenors and baritone.

That band would be known as the Second Herd and the tenor and baritone saxophonists would become known, after a Jimmy Giuffre composition, as the Four Brothers, so called because they all shared a musical "family resemblance" to Lester Young. The original Brothers were soon-to-be stars Stan Getz, Zoot Sims, the lesser known tenor saxophonist Herbie Steward, and ...ent baritone saxophonist Serge Chaloff. Recorded in 1947, "Four Brothers" (bbJ) has the reeds playing an immediately attractive, flowing line, whose relaxed movement is the result of Giuffre's skillful writing rather than any simplicity in the basic ideas. Giuffre's piece seemed to unite the graceful forward motion of a Lester Young solo with elements—heard in the long melodic lines and the rhythmic punctuations of the brass, for instance—of the newer music.

Herman's "Four Brothers" band, as it came to be known, was somewhat successful, but the real big band phenomenon of the time was Stan Kenton. His music was dubbed "progressive jazz," after a 20-piece band he introduced in 1949 at Carnegie Hall. The size of the orchestra, and the verbal ingenuity with which he described it and later manifestations of the band, were typical of Kenton.

Kenton was born in Kansas in 1911, and began rehearsing his own band in 1940. In 1941 he organized his Artistry in Rhythm Orchestra. A charming, charismatic, persuasive man, a masterful organizer and publicist—if he had gone into religion, Art Pepper once said, he would have been a Billy Graham—Kenton managed to make progressive, bop-influenced music that pleased the public. He made it seem important, and he made audiences pleased with themselves for understanding the latest thing. Critics were leery of him, but fans loved the vigor and bombast of the Kenton bands, which grew larger and louder over time, and took on more and more pompous names: "Innovations in Modern Music" (early 1950s) and "The Neophonic Orchestra" (mid-1960s). "We didn't care what the critics said," wrote unabashed Kenton fan Joe Goldberg, "because Stan spoke to us, and because we knew that what he was doing was important. One of the reasons we knew that was that Stan kept telling us so. Bill Holman, an arranger who succeeded for a while in making the band swing, once said, 'I did one thing called "Boop-Boop-De-Doop." Stan could never bring himself to

Stan Kenton and his band in the late 1950's. The saxophonist with glasses is Lennie Niehaus. (Courtesy Rutgers Institute of Jazz Studies)

introduce it. He always wanted titles like 'Artistry in Cosmic Radiation' " (Notes to *The Comprehensive Stan Kenton,* Capitol Records STB 12016).

Kenton was a popularizer, but he was more than that. He had hits as early as 1941, when he made "Artistry in Rhythm," and 1945, when he made "Tampico" featuring singer June Christy. In 1947, his "Peanut Vendor" with an authentic Latin rhythm section was one of the best selling jazz records. In the last years of the forties, he hired arrangers such as Pete Rugolo, Bill Holman, and Bill Russo, to make intriguing arrangements and compositions, and he hired some of the best, predominantly white, soloists of the time: alto saxophonists Lee Konitz and Art Pepper, drummer Shelly Manne, trombonist Kai Winding, singers Anita O'Day, Chris Connor and June Christy. By the beginning of the fifties, Kenton's was the poll-winning big band, and his soloists garnered many of the votes on their instruments.

Too many of Kenton's arrangements begin expressively and feature fine solos, only to end in screeching brass. But some pieces are still satisfying. In a "blindfold test" for *Down Beat,* Leonard Feather's famous column in which musicians listened to unidentified records, Charlie Parker singled out Rugolo's "Elegy for Alto," recorded by Kenton in 1947. The "Progressive" band also recorded Rugolo's interesting "Monotony" as well as made a couple of embarrassing experiments, such as the unintentionally comic "This is My Theme." This number has June Christy reciting a poem which, with its lurid descriptions of bleak emotional states, sounds like it was meant to be a footnote to T.S. Eliot's

"Waste Land." To today's listener, it's closer to "The Little Shop of Horrors." Rugolo's varied pieces were one aspect of the band's book, notable for its great range. What other band would include everything from obvious arrangements of "Malaguena" and "Dark Eyes" to Bob Graettinger's 1951 "City of Glass," an extended score which owes more to modern classical music than to jazz? To Kenton's credit, he encouraged many innovative composers. He was also a pioneer in the college jazz band movement from 1959 on.

By the end of the decade, the new music was sufficiently intriguing, or threatening, that other band leaders, Charlie Barnet among them, hired bop musicians and commissioned bop numbers. As noted in Chapter 9, Benny Goodman also made a stab at the new music.

MORE BOP SOLOISTS

Wardell Gray and Theodore "Fats" Navarro, whose high voice prompted people to call him, among other unfortunate nicknames, "Fat Girl," should have been among the stars of the fifties. Both died tragically young because of heroin, but not before they made a lasting impact. Gray was born in Oklahoma City in 1921. He was with the revolutionary Earl Hines band in 1943, and moved to Los Angeles in 1945, becoming part of the active jazz scene on L.A.'s Central Avenue.

His lithe, flexible tone was in the tradition of Lester Young, and Gray also learned firsthand from Parker, with whom he recorded "Relaxin' at Camarillo" in 1947. That was the year Gray went into the studios for Ross Russell's Dial Records, and played the two-tenor battle, "The Chase," an exciting recording that pitted Dexter Gordon's hard tone against Gray's more genial smoothness. They incidentally whetted the public's taste for tenor battles. Russell would record Gordon in tandem with Teddy Edwards later that year, and in the next decade the teams of Eddie "Lockjaw" Davis-Johnny Griffin and Zoot Sims-Al Cohn would build on what Gray and Gordon accomplished. When asked why Gray and Gordon, two handsome young men with budding talents, couldn't capitalize on the interest their recording aroused by going on tour together, Gordon responded, "Well, we weren't exactly reliable." Both had heroin habits.

If, as many say, the ability to play a ballad is the sign of a mature jazz musician, Wardell Gray was mature in 1949, when, with a rhythm section, he made the three-minute masterpiece of lyrical tenor playing, "Easy Living," a coherent, gracefully relaxed solo the ends of whose phrases seem to float away effortlessly, like a leaf on a gentle breeze. At the same date, he made his famous blues "Twisted," which has boppish accents without the angularity we expect from bop lines. Gray's solo on this 12-bar blues is full of Parkerisms, and echoes some of Lester Young's ideas as well. His solo begins with a reference to Parker's solo on "Billie's Bounce" (1945). Later, Gray begins a chorus by quoting from "Swinging On a Star" Singer Annie Ross would take this solo, which is made appealing by its melodic logic and easy-going lyricism, and write words to it in 1952. Some of her lyrics are shown under the music in the example. (See music example.)

Example 12-8.
Wardell Gray, "Twisted" (1949), theme chorus and first improvised chorus.
Underneath are some of the words added in 1952 by Annie Ross.

Her hit record, remade 20 years later by pop artist Joni Mitchell, proves that some bop was accessible to the general public. Singers such as Eddie Jefferson and King Pleasure, who specialized in this practice of setting recorded improvisations to words, also found that bebop could appeal to large audiences—as long as it was sung. Wardell Gray never benefitted from this appeal, even though he worked with Goodman and Basie. His addiction persisted, and in 1955, his body was found in the desert outside Las Vegas. He was widely presumed to have died of an overdose or injured himself in a fall, and then been transported to the desert by panicked acquaintances.

Navarro's story is hardly prettier. He was born in Florida in 1923: Twenty years later, he was working in Andy Kirk's swing band beside trumpeter Howard McGhee, a Roy Eldridge protégé who would participate in the bop revolution, recording with Parker and others. At the beginning of 1945, Navarro replaced Dizzy Gillespie in the cradle of bop, Billy Eckstine's band. Navarro was a Gillespie disciple with a sweeter tone and, when he was healthy, more power. Superbly fluent, he had such a talent for melodies that he rarely had to rely on speed for effect. He was most heavily featured between 1947 and 1949 when he was with Dameron's band which, thanks to Navarro's brilliance and Dameron's distinctive writing, rivalled the small groups of Gillespie and Parker.

One of Navarro's most impressive solos occurs on the Dameron blues, recorded in two takes in 1947, "The Squirrel." The theme is a little riff, reminiscent of "Mop Mop," a riff that swing players enjoyed (see example in Chapter 16). But the simplicity is deceptive, because here the riff is underpinned by a succession of sophisticated chords. Navarro's solo exhibits his power and range—his second chorus on each take begins with a shouting high phrase—but just as important as his skill is his inherent musicality, the lyrical tone with which he begins, the graceful, and suspenseful, way—with a long bluesy note—that he connects his two choruses, like Parker on "Billie's Bounce."

Although he had an attractive piano style, Dameron never wanted to be a soloist, and probably never wanted to be a bandleader. Like composer George Russell, he had to become both to survive: Only at the height of the swing era—or in the studios, doing television or movie work—was it possible to make a living as an arranger-composer. By all accounts a gentle and rather shy man, born early enough—like Gillespie and Monk in 1917—to be influenced by swing, Dameron began his career writing for the Kansas City big band of Harlan Leonard, for whom he created "Dameron Stomp" in 1940. He composed the ballad, still a standard, "If You Could See Me Now" for Sarah Vaughan, and wrote pieces for Dizzy Gillespie, including "Our Delight" (BBJ) and "Good Bait," which Gillespie recorded and which became staples of Dameron's own repertoire as a band leader. Perhaps Dameron's most challenging bop theme is "Hot House." Written to fit the chords of "What Is This Thing Called Love?," "Hot House" is a difficult, complex line that uses all the harmonic elevenths and thirteenths that the boppers liked. Dameron also wrote impressionistic band pieces, such as the gorgeous "Fontainebleau" and "Dial B for Beauty," which came in the fifties.

Dameron's brilliant little group was doomed. Navarro, weakened by heroin and tuberculosis, was too ill to accompany the band to Paris in 1949: Miles Davis filled in for him. By 1950, his condition was even more serious. Navarro's last recordings came from a club date in June 1950. Later issued on Columbia, the session found the once cherubic Navarro, now cadaverously thin, playing beautifully, although with a small sound, alongside Charlie Parker and Bud Powell. On July 7, 1950, he died at the age of 26. An addict himself, Dameron seemed to fade away in the middle fifties until his well-publicized conviction in 1958 for substance abuse. In 1962, after some more treatment, he made a comeback with *The Magic Touch*, an all-star big band session recorded for Riverside. He died in 1965 in New York.

Still experimental at the beginning of the forties, by the middle of the decade modern jazz could not be denied. Nor could its innovations. The role of every instrument was rethought to fit the early bebop bands. Most horn players affected the high, fast style of Gillespie and Parker, and they struggled to achieve some of the masters' harmonic sophistication. But while some clarinetists, such as the estimable Buddy DeFranco, adapted to bop, the clarinet, virtually a symbol of the swing era, by and large disappeared from bop ensembles. One might have expected that inherently awkward instrument, the slide trombone, to suffer a similar fate. It could have, had it not been for the extraordinary virtuosity of J. J. Johnson. Born in Indianapolis in 1924, Johnson began his career in the bands of Clarence Love and "Snookum" Russell, whose trumpeter, Fats Navarro, had a strong impact on Johnson's playing. (Johnson has said that he was also influenced by Lester Young, Roy Eldridge, Jack Teagarden and Harlan Leonard's trombonist, Fred Beckett.) From 1942 to 1945, he worked with Benny Carter's big band, making his earliest recording, "Love for Sale," in 1943.

By 1945, he was playing with Count Basie, mostly in New York, where he relocated in 1946, playing for the next few years in small groups around the city with, among others, Bud Powell, Max Roach, Miles Davis, Parker and Gillespie. He transformed his instrument: Imitating the fast, clean lines of Gillespie and Parker, he played, imperturbably, sparkling phrases with trumpet-like speed. By 1947 he had also lightened his tone, occasionally using a felt mute to achieve a dryly attractive sound something like a French horn.

His virtuosity and boppish articulations impressed his peers: Today one can see that some of his early solos suffer from an emphasis on speed and from his reliance on memorized formulas that incorporated such bop trademarks as the flatted fifth. Johnson's solos on takes 3 and 4 of "Crazeology" (1947; take 4 is on SCCJ) with Parker begin with the same phrase and contain other whole phrases in common. The same is true of the two renditions of Johnson's "Blue Mode" from 1949. Later he would rely less on formulas; eventually his solos, often based brilliantly on motives, were spontaneous and wholly satisfying.

His impact was immediate. Johnson proved that the trombone could be a bop instrument, and his darkish tone made it inevitable that the lower brass instruments would be used in the "cool" jazz to come. Johnson would go on to co-lead, with Danish trombonist Kai Winding, one of the most popular groups of the fifties. His many impressive achievements include his solo on a 1961 recording of "Moritat" (also known as "Mack the Knife"), which begins with a rhythmically enlivened version of Kurt Weill's theme and continues as he builds in the modal manner from a single scale, connecting without a break to the next chorus. (See music example.)

Example 12-9.
J.J. Johnson, beginning of his trombone solo on "Mack the Knife (Moritat)" (1961).

Johnson is equally accomplished as a composer of works for jazz band, for orchestra, and for film and television soundtracks.

Depending on one's ears and predilections, bop can be seen as either a logical extension of thirties jazz or as revolutionary, as a music based on a new look at the chords, or as a reflection of the war years and of new attitudes on life, race, and competition: One common explanation for the difficulty of many bop tunes has been that these problems were invented at jam sessions at Minton's, and were designed to keep incompetents off the stage and to teach oldsters a lesson or two. But obviously there was more to it than that. Bop built on the achievements of the thirties and yet seemed completely fresh. It had many contributors, several stars, and at least one undoubted genius, Charlie Parker.

13 Charlie Parker

"Bird was kind of like the sun, giving off the energy we drew from him. We're still drawing on it. His glass was overflowing. In any musical situation, his ideas just bounded out, and this inspired anyone who was around . . . Bird contributed more and received less than anybody."
—Max Roach

"I treated [Charlie Parker] as some kind of musical god. As far as the music being difficult, I never thought about it. It just seemed like sounds I never heard before and I knew I'd never hear again."
—Sheila Jordan

Charlie Parker is one of the great legends of jazz, and, as many commentators have noted, it is difficult to think of his music without considering his larger-than-life image. Parker was, as musicians, friends and unrelated gossips tell us, sensitive, aggressive, fascinating, generous, irresponsible and finally self-destructive, a potent creative genius who liked to shop for toys for his adopted child, a man with a talent for making himself loved but with whom no one could afford to be friends. He died in 1955 when he was 34 looking 20 years older; his face, captured in photographs, can be boyishly attractive, or, towards the end, puffy, sick-looking and repellent. As an improviser, he was fluent, soulful, witty, gutbucket and sophisticated. He used a biting tone that changed the way people heard the alto saxophone. His phrasing changed the way people heard jazz. It wasn't merely his speed, but his timing, the way he introduced a slow bluesy phrase, sometimes traditional, and then pealed away from it with a rush of twisting 16th notes. The variety and subtlety of his phrasing, at any tempo, makes his solos difficult to transcribe. Like Charlie Christian, he seemed to eat up the chord changes—he made complicated chord progressions like that of "Cherokee" his specialty.

A bird in flight who influenced the playing of every alert jazz musician since, he was a demigod to many, including one Dean Benedetti, who followed Parker from club to club recording his solos, interested only in Bird's song. A professional saxophonist, Benedetti heard and collected all of Parker's early recordings, transcribed many of them, and in 1947 took a portable record-cutting machine to the Hi-De-Ho Club in Los Angeles, and for almost two weeks recorded Parker's solos on acetates—homemade 78's. Later, he was able to switch to the new tape technology, as an early reel-to-reel tape—at first paper-based—became available. (These recordings were eventually found, and issued by Mosaic Records in 1990.) Benedetti's devotion was exemplary, but there were others as entranced by Parker, as the plethora of taped Parker performances attests.

Amateur psychologists among jazz critics, citing his longstanding heroin addiction and his subsequent irresponsibility with money—including that of other people—remembering his wives and many love affairs, have summed Parker up as a "psychopath" (Ross Russell), or a "sociopath" (James Lincoln Collier). The psychiatrist who examined him at Bellevue Hospital, where he went to get help in 1954, suggested that he had a "hostile evasive personality," which may mean that he was hostile and evasive to a doctor of another race who didn't recognize his particular talents or sympathize particularly with his situation.

Although for a few months after his release from Bellevue he tried living with Chan Richardson, the mother of two of his children, in New Hope, Pennsylvania, Parker was obviously no middle class suburbanite. He was not necessarily a sociopath, either, if we consider a sociopath as one whose behavior is consistently, belligerently, antisocial. It depends on what society we are talking about. Absorbed in music, he kept late hours, indulged in liquor and drugs, and married at the age of 16. He was doing what many musicians were doing then, and what many have done since. Using standards that may not apply, we can call him a social deviant, but he was adapting to the subculture he

The Metronome All Stars recording session of January 3, 1949, featuring many of the leading young modernists. Parker's head is blocking the last name of drummer Shelly Manne. The conductor next to him is Pete Rugolo. (Courtesy Rutgers Institute of Jazz Studies)

found himself in—later many imitated him. In the last five years of his short life, when his health and behavior were deteriorating, Parker was making recordings with strings, with big bands, bongo players, and choruses. He was accused by hardcore bop fans, even on the air by announcer "Symphony Sid" Torin, of becoming commercial. His answer was that it was all music, and that labels didn't mean much to him. It seems inconsistent to call him a sociopath in one breath, and denigrate him for reaching out to a wider public in another.

Dizzy Gillespie, who called him "the other half of my heartbeat," saw Parker as "a very sensitive person, in the way that many creative people are. Everything made a profound impression on him. He was also very loyal, and he had a terrific sense of humor." There are scores of musicians younger than Parker who remember his patronage and encouragement. Singer Sheila Jordan is one: "I loved Bird. He was so good to me. He turned me on to Stravinsky, to Bartok, to the dance, to painters. People think that all Bird did was play and shoot up dope. He was a brilliant man. He had an extensive vocabulary; he rarely used slang. He painted for a while . . . He encouraged me."

His personality will always be controversial, but there should be little doubt about Parker's music. Parker's technique, speed and flexibility were as astounding to listeners as was his tart tone, so unlike the sounds of Benny Carter or Johnny Hodges, to name two of the top altos before him. His phenomenal technique was not applied coldly. Innovative as he was, Parker played soulfully, as his great blues recordings attest. Summing up Parker's contribution, Gillespie is typically perceptive: "Charlie Parker played very syncopated and sanctified. There was nobody playing like it in our style . . . Charlie Parker's contribution to our music was mostly melody, accents, and bluesy interpretation. And the notes! 'Bird' has some notes in his melodies, the lines that he wrote that are deep, deep notes, as deep as anything Beethoven ever wrote. And he had little things that he used to play inside. He'd play other tunes inside the chords of the original melody [by quoting these other tunes], and they were always right" (*To Be*, p. 151).

Imitating Parker, generations of lesser musicians have taken to quoting unrelated tunes in their solos. But no one has done this with the wit and almost fierce appropriateness of Charlie Parker. At a 1949 Carnegie Hall concert, Parker begins a solo on "Cheryl" with several typically melodic choruses followed by a stop-time routine with drummer Roy Haynes. Parker then, in an extraordinary feat that suggests a scholarly commentary on jazz history, quotes the entire introduction to Louis Armstrong's "West End Blues." Armstrong's solo was unaccompanied and in free time: Parker fits it to a chord sequence and plays it in a loose time in contrast to the regular pulse of the rhythm section.

This routine appears in several other Parker blues solos of that year. It was characteristic of him to have favorite licks as well as quotations that he used for months at a time before moving on to new favorites. Some seemed to fulfill a structural need for Parker: He tended to quote from the beginning of the clarinet solo of "High Society" at the beginning of an eight-bar phrase, and after either a held note or a pause. Elsewhere he quotes, sarcastically as it were, from sources as wide-ranging as the English tune "Country Gardens," the Toreador song from the opera *Carmen*, and even the trumpet tune from Stravinsky's *Petrushka* (Third Tableau). Parker's wide listening habits revealed themselves in his quotations, as well as his unique ability to comment on music even while it was being created. Drummer Roy Haynes has described Parker's ability to make suggestive musical statements about what was happening in the club: Parker might note the entrance of an attractive woman with a phrase of "A Pretty Girl," for instance.

With some justification, Parker felt that his talents were unappreciated by the world at large. He was for most of his career condemned to play in unventilated clubs filled with noisy customers, and he never received the respect that at least some classical musicians do. His death went unreported by *The New York Times*, which nonetheless ran articles during the period on Woody Herman, Count Basie, and other jazz artists.

But he was not without honors. By his twenty-ninth year he had been presented as a leader in Carnegie Hall and in Town Hall repeatedly, and from 1946 on he was a consistent poll winner. Ellington expressed his admiration for Parker, and in *Down Beat* in 1948, Stan Kenton called him "the best improviser in jazz today." On December 15, 1949, Birdland, the club named after Parker, opened with a gala evening in which Lester Young and others performed. Ten days later, on Christmas Day, Parker's quintet was again presented at Carnegie Hall, where he played the "Cheryl" described above. He was not yet 30.

EARLY YEARS

Parker was born in Kansas City, Kansas on August 29, 1920 to Addie and Charles Parker, Sr. His father abandoned the family when, in 1927, Addie took her family to Kansas City, Missouri. In 1931, Parker graduated from public school, and two years later he was playing baritone and alto horns—smaller relatives of the tuba—in the school band of Lincoln High. He also fooled with the tuba and took up the clarinet. In 1933, his mother bought him an alto saxophone. In an interview, Parker said that at first the purchase meant little to him. Nonetheless, by 1934 he was playing alto with the dance band of pianist Lawrence "88" Keyes. In 1935 Parker left high school to officially become a musician. His first professional engagement, on November 28, earned him one dollar and 25 cents. (Throughout this chapter we are indebted to the Parker chronology by Gordon Davies, published in installments in *Discographical Forum*, 1970–1971.)

He was largely self-taught, and audacious as well as determined. It must have been in 1935 that Parker, with other members of the Lawrence Keyes band, sat in with members of the Basie band. In an incident that was made so much of in the 1988 movie *Bird*, directed by Clint Eastwood, Jo Jones is supposed to have reacted to Parker's fumbling solo efforts by taking his cymbal and crashing it to the floor at the feet of the struggling saxophonist. Parker himself talked about another humiliation. When he was a rank beginner, knowing only a little of "Lazy River" and "Honeysuckle Rose," and only one key signature, he sat in at the High Hat on 22nd and Vine: "I was doing all right until I tried doing double tempo on 'Body and Soul.' Everybody fell out laughing. I went home and cried and didn't play again for three months." He didn't give up. Later he talked about his early practice regime: "I took the scales a half a step at a time [C major, C#, D, etc.] . . . After I learned the scales, I taught myself to play the blues in all the 12 keys. Then I learned 'I Got Rhythm' and 'Cherokee' in all the 12 keys. Then I was ready." This would make a perfectly good syllabus for a college jazz improvisation course today. Clearly he was not the average undisciplined teenager.

In 1936, Parker, then 16, married Rebecca Ruffin, whom he met when her family boarded with the Parkers. On Thanksgiving day, Parker and the band he was with had a car accident that killed a friend and broke three of the alto saxophonist's ribs. It is possible he first used heroin as a painkiller after the accident. In any case, not long afterward, he without comment demonstrated to Rebecca the act of shooting heroin into his veins. He was an addict.

He was also developing a style. Like all young jazz players, he had his models: Later he would mention an early influence, the fast, mellifluous playing of Jimmy Dorsey. More important was a figure closer to home, Buster Smith—nicknamed "Prof" or "Professor"—who had been with Bennie Moten and first recorded with Walter Page's Blue Devils in 1929. Parker was probably influenced by, as Gunther Schuller has noted, Smith's "tone and attack, certain turns of phrase, and his basically linear conception." During much of 1937, Parker played with Smith and occasionally sat in with the Jay McShann band, the group with which he would make his first recordings. That summer, he travelled to perform at a resort in the Ozark Mountains with George E. Lee, a trip most notable because of the lessons in chord changes he received there from the group's guitarist, Efferge Ware. (Later, in 1942, the two privately recorded with a drummer; four titles were first issued in 1991.)

By fall, 1937, he was with McShann and Smith again, settling with McShann when Smith left for New York City. Somewhere along the line, he got his nickname, Yardbird or Bird: According to McShann, the band's car ran over a chicken one night, and Parker insisted on going back to pick up that "yardbird." Buster Smith was obviously a draw for him: After a short stint early in 1939 with another top Kansas City band, that of Harlan Leonard, Parker followed the older alto player to New York City, appearing, ragged and broke, at Smith's apartment. Parker purposely got a job washing dishes at Jimmy's Chicken Shack in Harlem so he could study the restaurant's featured pianist, Art Tatum. During this time he spent some of his afterhours at places like Monroe's Uptown House, where the jamming started at four a.m. At the end of 1939, he fell under the influence of another little known guitarist, Biddy Fleet, who worked over with him the chords of what would become one of his featured numbers: "Cherokee." With Fleet at Dan Wall's Chili House, Parker had what he later asserted was a revelation: that he could get the sounds he had been hearing and imagining by playing the "higher intervals" (ninths, elevenths, thirteenths) of the appropriate chords of a tune.

With these new ideas, Parker returned to Kansas City in February 1940 to join the new Jay McShann big band. McShann, a blues and boogie-woogie pianist, knew a good thing when he heard it. McShann hired Parker as the musical director of his band's book, which consisted largely of Basie-influenced riff arrangements and blues. The style was congenial to Parker: When the Basie recordings from the 1936 Jones-Smith session were issued, Parker had memorized Lester Young's solos.

In the fall of 1940, McShann took his crew on a tour. On November 30, they were in Wichita, where eight McShann musicians were invited to make some informal recordings in a radio studio that day. It was thought that these recordings, usually called the Wichita transcriptions, were made for radio broadcasts, and that there were two dates. But Bob Davis reported in *Down Beat* (12/90) that there was only the single session and that the recordings were made just for fun.

These informal recordings were among Parker's first. (In August the same fans had recorded—poorly—two tunes by the band in a club. These have not been issued, but the other Wichita transcriptions were issued in 1974. In addition, an undated solo saxophone performance issued on both the Stash and Philology labels may predate the McShann numbers by a few months.) The November sides show the young saxophonist's eclecticism and versatility: He plays a mellifluous "Coquette," and a Coleman Hawkins-influenced "Body and Soul"—he actually quotes from the famous 1939 Hawkins recording in his second eight bars. The arrangement of this piece, with its double-time trumpet choruses, echoes the "Body and Soul" Roy Eldridge made with Chu Berry, the tenor saxophonist after whom Parker named his first son. Parker enters the bridge with the same lick Eldridge used on this 1938 recording.

Parker takes a solo on "Oh, Lady Be Good" that, with its long lines and light rhythmic flow, hearkens back to Lester Young's groundbreaking 1936 recording. Parker begins with a reference to "Lester Leaps In" and, on the bridge, he develops a descending idea that Young used on his "Oh, Lady Be Good." Then Parker begins his solo on "Honeysuckle Rose" with a quotation from Young's solo on the same tune with Basie (January 1937).

These private recordings are enlightening now, but were then unknown to the public. It was a short solo he played on one of the McShann band's Decca 78's a few months later that shook up musicians across the country. Recorded on April 30, 1941, "Hootie Blues" was an informal blues designed to feature the vocal of Walter Brown. For musicians, Parker stole the show. (See music example.)

Parker's melodic, lyrical approach to the blues—he never stomped the blues—is something like that of Lester Young. Rhythmically, Parker has gone beyond Young, who was still tied to an eighth note flow. Parker's solo has more of a narrative, speech-like looseness. His fast solo chorus on another influential McShann recording for Decca, "The Jumping Blues" from 1942, began with a

Example 13–1.
Charlie Parker's solo on "Hootie Blues" with Jay McShann's band (1941).

simple phrase which was later to turn up in the bop anthem "Ornithology." (See music example.)

Example 13–2.
Charlie Parker, beginning of his solo on "The Jumpin' Blues" with Jay McShann's band (1941).

It was inevitable that Parker would leave Jay McShann's band, especially after the McShann band opened, as it did on January 2, 1942, at the Savoy Ballroom in Manhattan. Parker was always fascinated with New York City—he told Rebecca Ruffin Parker that he would become a great musician if he went there to stay. (Their marriage was over by this time.) In Manhattan with McShann, Parker again spent much of his time at after-hours places. Unwilling to leave New York, he broke with McShann in July.

He was progressing rapidly, as we hear in the version of his specialty, "Cherokee," recorded privately at a 1942 jam session at Minton's. "Cherokee" had been a Parker feature when he was with the McShann band. Parker had already developed some of the routines he was to use in 1945 when he recorded his masterpiece, a version of "Cherokee" he called "Koko." (This is no relation to Ellington's minor blues "Ko-Ko.") The bridge is the most challenging part of this chord progression because it modulates through several difficult keys, whereas the A section stays in concert Bb and Eb. Parker's idea in the first bridge is a repeated note followed by a swooping lick. In the second bridge, with which the private recording ends, he uses a simple arpeggio, played in a complicated rhythmic pattern. Both of these ideas show up again in the famous "Koko" of 1945. (See music example.)

a) Beginning of the first bridge in 1945. First bridge in 1942 is similar.

b) Beginning of the bridge of the second chorus in 1945. Second bridge in 1942 is similar.

Example 13–3. Charlie Parker, phrases used on the bridges of "Koko" (1945) that appear in similar form on the 1942 "Cherokee" and later versions of "Koko."

By December 1942, Parker was playing tenor saxophone with the Earl Hines orchestra that would also feature Dizzy Gillespie and other modernist musicians. Due to the recording ban, this group was never recorded, but we can hear Parker's imaginative tenor saxophone work on private jam session recordings from 1943, issued on Stash Records.

In the spring of 1944, Parker went with Billy Eckstine. "Mr. B's" orchestra was the ideal finishing school. The fact that many of the most inventive modern musicians were in Eckstine's band together certainly lessened the potential harm the ban did to the developing music: The key musicians were hearing each other nightly. When in September 1944, tired perhaps of playing charts, aware of his own unreliability, and angry at racial insults the band received on a tour of the South, Parker resigned to take a job on New York's 52nd street, the bop era can be said to have begun. Its leading practitioner was ready.

BEBOP RECORDINGS

One can hear just how ready he was by listening to his recordings, even those he made as a sideman. On September 15, 1944 he went into the studios at the bidding of guitarist Tiny Grimes, a Charlie Christian protégé best known for his work that year with the Art Tatum trio. The band made four numbers—two sagging vocals, and two instrumentals, "Tiny's Tempo" and "Red Cross." Everywhere he's audible, Parker sounds exciting: His solo on the master take of the mid-tempo blues, "Tiny's Tempo," begins explosively, and he later uses those grace note pickups at the beginnings of phrases that are part of his distinctive style, as is the slight rasp he gives some notes for expressive effect. Here and on the two takes of "Red Cross" he plays with an assurance that make his fastest lines sound direct. "Red Cross," based on "Rhythm" changes, was the first Parker original to be recorded. The opening phrases of each A section end on two thudding quarter notes in the manner of "Mop Mop," but the third phrase has some chromatic surprises.

If 1944 was Parker's coming-out, in some ways 1945 was his banner year, the year his recording career began in earnest, in which he made some of his most durable masterpieces, and in which Gillespie joined Parker's band at the Three Deuces. On May 11, 1945, he recorded several classics with Gillespie, as mentioned in Chapter 12. On November 26, 1945, an extraordinary recording session took place for Savoy Records. It culminated in "Koko," but could have been a disaster. Part of the problem was Parker's sometimes casual attitude towards recording. Often he showed up at a session with a few lines—his compositions—scribbled on a scrap of paper, lines which his musicians would have to sightread. (It made it somewhat easier that most of his lines were based on popular songs—"I Got Rhythm" was a perennial favorite—or on the blues.) He wanted to keep sidemen off guard, a practice which sometimes produced performances of unusual freshness.

This session began inauspiciously: Bud Powell was absent, and Parker, who had also contacted pianist Argonne Thornton (also known as Sadik Hakim), offered Dizzy Gillespie as a substitute. Parker himself was in good

Tiny Grimes, Beverly, Massachusetts, 1980's. (Photo by Michael Ullman)

shape, except that his reed was squeaking, and his horn may have been mal-functioning. His other sidemen—Miles Davis, bassist Curley Russell, and Max Roach—seemed equal to the job of playing two new Parker blues and pieces based on "I Got Rhythm" and "Cherokee." They began with three takes of the attractive blues theme "Billie's Bounce."

Dissatisfied with the results on "Billie's Bounce," and evidently unaware they were being recorded, Parker and the band started fooling around with the chords of "Cherokee" at a relaxed pace. On this number, his longtime show-piece, Parker pours out ideas. This incomplete performance was issued as "Warming Up a Riff." The band made takes four and five of "Billie's Bounce," and then four takes of Parker's "Now's the Time," a simpler, riffing blues that would become one of his most famous compositions. Then came, with Argonne Thornton now on piano, three takes of the "I Got Rhythm" number, marred by Thornton's stumbling introductions, which Parker called "Thriving from a Riff." Later, this complex theme would be dubbed "Anthropology." Parker also ex-plored the chords of "Embraceable You" in a number called "Meandering."

Parker then, accompanied by producer Teddy Reig, who told interviewer Bob Porter that he wouldn't leave Parker alone in Manhattan during the middle of a recording session, went out to get some new reeds. When Parker returned, Miles Davis had fallen asleep on the floor. The first try at "Koko" is brought to a screeching halt when the owner of Savoy Records heard the recognizable tune of "Cherokee" and feared that he might end up paying royalties. It was to have gone like this:

> Intro, accompanied only by drums, using brushes:
> Eight bars unison, eight bars improvised trumpet, eight bars improvised sax, eight bars unison.
> Theme: Cherokee (AABA, each section 16 bars)
> Solos

The second take, with the theme statement omitted, has the same introduction and then two AABA choruses by Parker. These choruses are followed by a Max Roach drum solo, and then 28 bars that duplicate the plan of the introduction, less 4 bars.

It was the playing, though, not just the unique scheme of the record, that proved so influential. The introduction, in which Parker and Gillespie are accompanied only by the drums, has the kind of impact of Armstrong's solo preceding "West End Blues." Its darting phrases are played unconscionably fast, but it is Parker's ability to create significant ideas at high speeds in his solo that proved impressive, not the speed in itself. On the issued "Koko"—this must have surprised listeners in the forties—the solos begin without the statement of a theme. Parker's solo on "Koko" is composed of harmonically intricate lines, some of which cross easily between A and B sections. On the bridges he uses both of the ideas shown earlier.

On December 10, 1945, Parker and Gillespie became pioneers of a sort when they opened at Billy Berg's, a club in Los Angeles. At first, they were well received, but attendance at the club gradually dropped off. (By the standards of the day, the engagement was a failure, but the band lasted at Billy Berg's until February 3.) Later, Gillespie would say, "California was a long way away, and they were behind in evolution." The trip turned out disastrously for Charlie Parker.

It didn't have to be that way. At the end of 1945, Parker was voted the "New Star" on alto in the then-prestigious *Esquire* poll, and in January 1946 he began—rockily—what turned into a fruitful relationship with producer Norman Granz when he appeared with Dizzy Gillespie in a January 28 concert in Los Angeles that was part of Granz's Jazz at the Philharmonic series. Parker, delayed by a search for drugs, almost didn't make the concert. Once there he soloed, as did Lester Young, on a celebrated version of "Oh, Lady Be Good." It is fascinating to hear Parker and Young in their only recordings together. By this time the two had developed in divergent ways. Young was playing in his forties mode, with a heavier tone and in a more romantic style. Parker is light, funny, and given to perky double-time runs. Parker is harmonically complex; Young is harmonically straightforward. Parker had been looking forward to playing with his idol. He is said to have been disappointed that Young's style was so different from the thirties.

After the relative failure of his group's West Coast debut, Dizzy left for New York, leaving Parker with an airline ticket which the saxophonist promptly sold. Parker found a job at the Finale Club with a quintet featuring Miles Davis and pianist Joe Albany. And he found a good source of heroin in a wheelchair-bound man nicknamed Moose the Mooche. The grateful Parker wrote a tune for this man, recording "Moose the Mooche" on his first session for Dial Records, an independent label run by Ross Russell.

In April of 1946 two related things happened: In a police crackdown, the Finale Club was closed and Moose the Mooche was arrested. Parker was stranded. He showed up at a July 29 session for Dial sick and distracted, in withdrawal. He struggled through a couple of numbers, including a tortured, halting version of the ballad "Lover Man" (issued as "Loverman") that some listeners profess to enjoy. He later called it his worst record, "a horrible thing that should never have been released" (*Down Beat*, June 19, 1951). That night he was arrested after setting fire to his hotel bed and wandering, disoriented, around the lobby. He was sent to Camarillo State Hospital for six months. By January 31, 1947, when Parker emerged, healthy and rested, from Camarillo, bebop was beginning to be popular. He resumed his recording career in February with, among other tunes, "Relaxin' at Camarillo," for Dial. He also began drinking heavily, a practice that became his way of functioning when he was not using heroin.

Parker returned to New York City in April 1947, spending his first night jamming all over the city. That month he also reformed his quintet to feature Miles Davis, pianist Duke Jordan, bassist Tommy Potter and Max Roach. They would stay together approximately 18 months. It was Parker's tightest working band, and with this quintet he would make many of his most celebrated recordings. Those include two virtuosic takes of the George Gershwin standard, "Embraceable You," recorded on Oct. 28, 1947. (See Appendix 1 for music examples.) Parker also showed again his mastery of the blues when he recorded on September 18, 1948, the famous "Parker's Mood" (SCCJ). The development of his solo can be traced over five extant takes. The final take sounds inevitable – it was made into a vocal by bop singers Eddie Jefferson and then King Pleasure – especially its opening phrases. But the differing earlier takes prove that even these memorable phrases were improvised. Some of the added lyrics are shown on the transcription. (See music example.)

Example 13–4.
Charlie Parker, "Parker's Mood" (1948), first solo chorus on the master take, after the introduction. Underneath are shown some words added to it by Eddie Jefferson (1949–1950) and by King Pleasure (1953).

From December 1948 on, Parker recorded for Norman Granz. His Verve recordings, as they are now known, are uneven, but some of them are among his greatest statements. Granz frankly wanted to introduce Parker to a wider audience, something to which Parker did not raise objections, and he thought the best way of doing so was to feature the saxophonist in as many different contexts as possible: He tried everything from a standard jazz big band to Machito's Afro-Cuban jazz ensemble, from sessions with strings and vocals to

Parker at the Three Deuces in 1948, with Tommy Potter on bass and Miles Davis on trumpet. Note the cup mute. (Courtesy Rutgers Institute of Jazz Studies)

jam sessions. He had Parker play an album of Cole Porter songs during his last studio sessions in 1954—that this failed was the result of Parker's health and not the material. The masterpieces of the Parker Verve years include the ballad with strings, "Just Friends"—in his flowing improvisation Parker seems to enjoy his sweetly romantic accompaniment—as well as his own "Now's the Time" and "Confirmation" with quartets, and his choruses on "Funky Blues," an all-star jam session.

THE 1950S

Parker rarely sounded commonplace, but he saved his most exploratory solos for live performances. Amateur recording engineers like Benedetti captured some of his most harmonically daring work, despite the often poor sound quality. Live, he used altissimo register squeaks, and playfully earthy honks. He took longer, sometimes more loosely structured solos, than he did in studios. Listening to the best of the live tapes—at times he was too sick to perform well— one hears him arriving at a new stage of his development in the fifties.

He seemed to be laying the groundwork for the next generation. On the sides recorded in 1950 and issued as *A Night at Birdland*—Fats Navarro's last recordings—he is even more virtuosic than in the forties. He uses a smoother sound and a more legato attack, and he uses the type of sequential patterns that

John Coltrane would later pick up on. A night in Harlem at the Rockland Palace from 1952 is one of his best live dates available: During the middle of his solo on "Lester Leaps In" he transposes the theme, moving into bitonality in a manner that is completely relaxed and at ease—despite the punishing tempo of about 360 beats per minute! (This recording is the soundtrack of the opening number in the film *Bird*.)

Also from the Rockland Palace are two versions of the Gerry Mulligan tune "The Rocker." On "Rocker No. 2" Parker begins his solo with a quotation from Gershwin's "An American in Paris," which he transposes to another key, creating a sense of bitonality. He begins the fourth chorus with a humorous quote, and on the second A he plays a wild pattern that was picked up by the modernist Eric Dolphy. On the bridge he begins another sequence. (See music example.)

Example 13–5.
Charlie Parker's fourth chorus on "Rocker No. 2" (1952).

At this point in his career, Parker's playing suggested various directions to come. The patterns and harmonic complexity suggest John Coltrane, the vocalisms, Ornette Coleman. Parker's caustic humor gives one a taste of Sonny

Rollins. Even earlier, in the 1947 Carnegie Hall "A Night in Tunisia" with Gillespie, one can hear something of Ornette Coleman in the uninhibited wailing quality of some of Parker's phrases, as in the last A section of Parker's first AABA chorus.

It's unclear where he might have gone with his music. Parker's admiration for Stravinsky, Hindemith and other 20th century composers was sincere. He is supposed to have approached experimentalist composer Edgard Varèse for lessons, and even to have written Arnold Schoenberg, then teaching at U.C.L.A., presumably for advice. He met with composer Stefan Wolpe, who taught several jazz composers such as Johnny Carisi, but Parker never followed up on this meeting. More promisingly, he asked a composer with a jazz background, George Russell, to write for him.

Parker was serious about making musical progress. He was also serious about his own compositions. His pieces, it has been said by Frank Tirro and others, are merely improvisations written down, but he deserves more credit than that. His themes have little of the virtuosity of his improvisations, and their motivic content is thoughtfully presented, as is heard in the rhythmic study he called "Cheryl" (a blues), and in the written counterpoint of "Chasin' the Bird" and "Ah-Leu-Cha." No one would confuse even his "Billie's Bounce" with his improvisational approach: The theme has a clearly patterned use of certain rhythmic ideas. In contrast, when Parker solos on it, he uses freer, non-repetitive rhythms and he double times.

The fifties started promisingly for Parker. He had had good luck in the summer of 1949, when he was a spectacular success, feted and adored, at the International Jazz Festival in Paris. That fall he toured with a quintet, first with Kenny Dorham on trumpet and then with the young Red Rodney, a Jewish musician who evidently talked him into playing a bar mitzvah. During the first half of 1950, Parker performed with his quintet, leading a band that included a small string section and oboe. He was inordinately proud of those strings, but they restricted his repertoire and didn't always please his fans. In July, Parker was booked into Birdland with the strings. A *Down Beat* review of August 25 commented with what now seems astounding irreverence: "Bird has allowed his playing to degenerate into a tasteless raucous hullabaloo."

In November 1950, Parker went for a week to Sweden, where he was lionized once again. Parker is glorious on the issued private recordings, and the Swedish musicians acquit themselves well. In February of 1952, Parker and Gillespie appeared on television, where after being introduced by host Earl Wilson, and presented with plaques celebrating their winnings in the 1951 *Down Beat* polls, Parker and Gillespie played "Hot House." This is the only existing footage of Parker with sound. He won that year's *Down Beat* poll as well, as he did every year between 1950 and 1954.

Still Parker's time was running out with extraordinary rapidity. In 1953 and 1954, he performed mainly with pickup groups. One such group that played in Toronto's Massey Hall on May 15, 1953 was spectacular enough. It had Gillespie, Parker, Bud Powell, bassist Charles Mingus and Max Roach. Taped by

Mingus and released on his Debut Records, the music was brilliant, but the concert was a flop for its sponsors. Only 35 percent of the tickets were sold.

Parker began 1954 playing as a single in Boston at the Hi Hat, and then in February he went on tour as a guest with Stan Kenton: He was featured on only two numbers, "Night and Day" and "My Funny Valentine." While he was in California, Parker's daughter Pree, whom he conceived with Chan Richardson, died on March 7. Parker sent off a series of increasingly poignant, and increasingly incoherent, telegrams to Chan, all in one night, and then returned to New York. After several weeks performing, he took his family to Brewster on Cape Cod to recuperate. In late August he was back in New York, playing with strings in Birdland. Within the first week he fired his strings, creating such a ruckus that he was banned from the club. He attempted suicide by drinking iodine and finally made the front pages in this country: A picture of Parker being loaded into the ambulance appeared in the now-defunct *New York Daily Mirror*. He was in Bellevue Hospital for the first 10 days of September.

On September 28, 1954, Parker committed himself to Bellevue again. He would be released on October 15. His health, always precarious, was broken. He suffered from ulcers and yet continued to drink as a way of killing his craving for heroin and numbing his pain. Death may have been on his mind. After the death of trumpeter Hot Lips Page in Boston, Parker visited the morgue to observe the body. During Christmas week, Ross Russell heard Parker, then virtually unable to play, at Le Club Downbeat. He was separated from Chan, living around Greenwich Village with friends. Writer Robert Reisner met him, homeless, sick, his horn in pawn, on January 1, 1955 at a jam session at the Open Door.

His last engagements were disastrous. Parker was booked in the beginning of March 1955 into Birdland with Powell and Mingus. Powell appeared incapacitated, and Parker refused to play. On March 9, he was to go to an engagement in Boston's Storyville. Instead, he ended up at the Baroness Nica de Koenigswater's apartment in the Hotel Stanhope. He was suffering from ulcers, from cirrhosis of the liver, and he was having trouble breathing. A doctor tried unsuccessfully to check him into a hospital. On March 12, 1955, before his 35th birthday, Charlie Parker died in the Baroness's apartment. The exact circumstances are still unclear, although it's usually said that he died while watching the Dorsey Brothers television show.

14 The Fifties, Cool, and Third Stream

In the fifties, the key musical problem for players of modern jazz was what to do with the legacy of Charlie Parker: how to develop what he left with them, how to create a personal statement without ignoring his contributions or without merely evading his influence.

Jazz styles coexisted and jazz stylists collaborated in this period. The decade which saw the deaths of Parker, Lester Young, Art Tatum, and Billie Holiday was also the period of Louis Armstrong's greatest recognition and of the renaissance of Duke Ellington. The fifties began in the height of the bebop revolution, saw what was called "the birth of the cool," and the aptly called "hard bop" and "soul jazz" of the mid-decade. The period ended with Miles Davis popularizing modal jazz—through his 1959 recording *Kind of Blue*—and with the advent of Cecil Taylor, Ornette Coleman, and free jazz, jazz free from the chord sequences that liberated Charlie Parker and seemed to burden many of his successors.

It is remarkable how fast the fascination of the first generation beboppers with chords and chord changes turned into something else: Instead of "making the changes," some musicians started to talk of "running the changes"—a subtle denigration of the bopper's technique—or even, as composer George Russell put it, of meeting the "deadline" of the chord change. Insightfully, Russell calls the history of jazz since the forties a prolonged "assault on the chord."

Bebop had its composers and arrangers—Russell, Tadd Dameron, Gil Fuller among them—but all too often performances followed the formula whereby a chorus of melody (played in unison) was followed by strings of solos and a reprise of the melody. John Lewis said he founded the Modern Jazz Quartet because he longed for more complex forms, and a more careful weaving of composition and improvisation. Some of the most ambitious—and impressive—compositions for jazz orchestras were written in the fifties by the likes of

234

Charles Mingus, Gunther Schuller, George Russell, Ellington of course, and J.J. Johnson.

Some thought that in bebop the gentler side of jazz was prematurely abandoned. Many innovative musicians of the fifties defined themselves by looking to the more lyrical masters of the swing era as sources, while retaining the lessons of bop they felt still applied. A whole school of saxophonists—they included Stan Getz, Zoot Sims, Warne Marsh and others—were entranced by the soft tone and gracious, long lines of Lester Young's playing. These players, with their varying styles, were often white. Most were later identified as part of the "West Coast school," which drew on the gentler side of Charlie Parker as well: Parker's "Yardbird Suite" was a favorite composition, and a model for a melodic kind of improvisation. (See music example.)

Example 14–1.
Charlie Parker, "Yardbird Suite," first two A sections.

Not everyone approved. Musicians, and their audiences, seemed split between those who wanted to emphasize melody and make rhythms subtler and those for whom jazz meant a powerful beat. In 1955, Art Blakey followed up on his contributions in the forties by forming the Jazz Messengers. He had already led a group by that name in 1947—this new edition caught on. The bluesy groups of pianist Horace Silver and the gospel-tinged singing of Ray Charles were widely admired in the late fifties. "Now they call it swing" Billie Holiday had sung in 1938 in a bemused complaint about the way the music was labelled: "First they called it ragtime . . . Now they call it swing." Critics and historians found new labels for the jazz of the fifties: More than ever before, the musicians were clustered in schools and movements.

Its promoters found new ways of presenting jazz, whether mainstream or progressive, to use another label for post-bop jazz. In the forties, college students, eager to hear the latest thing and to be in on what is still called the scene, scurried to seedy nightclubs to hear jazz. In the fifties, the music came to them. College concerts became popular and helped popularize certain groups, especially the Dave Brubeck Quartet. With some regularity, jazz was presented in the same way as classical music, and its fans could go to hear the music without buying drinks—and without lying about their ages. These concerts were often organized by the students themselves—music departments were, as of yet, uninterested in what they considered a popular music about which, it was argued, everyone who cared already knew enough. To some students, jazz, particularly its cooler styles, became a sort of cachet to sophistication: The *Esquire* man dressed well and acted cool, and read the magazine's annual jazz polls. Others loved the music for itself.

The concerts allowed some musicians to play their most challenging arrangements to sympathetic audiences. The jazz festival tended to provoke more raucous performances, but its effect has been more far-reaching, introducing countless thousands to players and styles, resurrecting the careers of great figures and creating a kind of carnival atmosphere around the music. This atmosphere was sometimes annoying to musicians, but proved welcoming to hordes of music lovers. As the number of nightclubs declined inexorably from the fifties until the eighties, the festivals have thrived—according to the *New Grove Dictionary of Jazz*, by the mid-eighties there were at least 700 annual jazz festivals worldwide.

Armstrong and Parker and Bechet played at European events—Armstrong at the Nice Jazz Festival in 1948, the first jazz festival, and Parker and Bechet at the Festival International de Jazz in 1949, which took place in Paris. The first American festival was the Newport Jazz Festival, which began in 1954, run by George Wein, then the operator of the Boston nightspot, Storyville. Supported by two members of a prominent Newport family, the Lorillards, the Newport Jazz Festival, important in other ways, suggested by their participation the growing respectability of the music it celebrated.

Ellington's success at the 1956 Newport Jazz Festival would have spread through the jazz grapevine, but it is unlikely that his performance would have changed the course of his career if it hadn't been released on a long-playing record. The so-called microgroove discs were introduced by Columbia in 1948, at about the time that magnetic tape was being marketed for the first time. The combination meant, quite obviously, that longer performances could be recorded than ever before, and that those performances could be issued as played. The impact in the fifties on jazz was enormous. For the first time, musicians found that they could stretch out on recordings. Immediately, recorded jazz became closer to what musicians were playing in clubs. Sometimes what was played in clubs was recorded: Magnetic tape meant that it was feasible to record live sets wherever the music was played.

Magnetic tape had other effects. Engineers could now edit recordings, cutting what they did not want on a record, covering up mistakes, and, at times, splicing together different takes of a single tune to make a composite. Almost immediately, some musicians—and engineers—used these capabilities creatively. *Louis Armstrong Plays W.C. Handy*, Armstrong's 1954 Columbia recording, was originally issued with composite takes that combined the best sections of several attempts at the songs Armstrong plays. And it also included an overdubbed version of "Atlanta Blues," which has Armstrong brilliantly accompanying his singing with his own trumpet. Lennie Tristano's 1955 Atlantic record employed overdubbing, allowing him to add to his own solo piano lines, and a slight speeding up of the tape to change the tone. Clearly some fans, and musicians, had reservations about the seeming intrusion of a new technology on the creative process. Tristano's follow-up record for Atlantic, *The New Tristano*, came with this prominently displayed sentence: "No use is made of multi-tracking, overdubbing or tape-speeding on any selection."

The music was, inevitably, changing. Charlie Parker liked to challenge his musicians, to see how far he could take them and his music. There was also an element of gamesmanship in his uptempo performances. A version of "Anthropology," broadcast in 1951 and featuring Dizzy Gillespie, is taken at 310 beats per minute. Probably no other trumpeter besides Gillespie could have created at that time as coherent a statement at this speed.

MILES DAVIS, GIL EVANS, AND THE BIRTH OF THE COOL

For Miles Davis, there was no point in trying to be Gillespie. Davis created his contained lyrical style while with Charlie Parker, partly out of self-defense. His early solo statements, sometimes halting, occasionally eloquent in a new way, showed him learning from Parker while defining himself in opposition to the older man's style. He didn't hear music that went as high as Gillespie's trumpet, Davis said, and he couldn't play comfortably with Gillespie's speed. He became famous while with Parker, but finally felt thwarted.

He left Parker in 1948 and fell in with a group of composers and instrumentalists who were hanging around the 55th Street apartment—down a flight of stairs, by a Chinese laundry, through the boiler room—that was rented by Gil Evans. Parker and Gillespie hung out there, and so did Miles Davis and several of his colleagues. Evans was the oldest of the group—he was born in 1912 in Toronto—and was the most experienced. He had led a band in California in the thirties. (The trumpeter Jimmy Maxwell was in that band, and he remembers that even then Evans was interested in unusual tonal colors, asking the reeds to double on oboes and flutes.) In the forties Evans worked for the innovative big band of Claude Thornhill, producing elegant arrangements whose richness of tone, subtlety of harmonic motion and gentle rhythms seemed wholly original. In 1947, he wrote moody counter-melodies to Thornhill's sparse piano on "Lover Man." He was concerned with tone at a time when most young jazz musicians were concentrating on speed. He scored ballads to fit Thornhill's taste for dreamy music—Evans said Thornhill's music "hung in a cloud." (When it didn't work, it seemed to dissolve in a mist.) The band's soft, low sound was enhanced by its unusual instrumentation—several of its saxophonists also played flutes, and the low brass included not only the usual trombones (two in this case) but also two French horns and a tuba which played not bass lines but harmony with the brass. Evans was to retain something like this instrumentation long after he left Thornhill.

Evans also showed himself adept at orchestrating uptempo bop tunes. He begins "Donna Lee" (November 1947; BBJ)—which though usually attributed to

Charlie Parker was actually written by Miles Davis—with a jolt, a dissonant out-of-tempo exchange between Thornhill's airy piano and the drummer. After the winds state a long, uptempo bop line, Thornhill plays a Basie-ish chorus which includes references to the old standard "Indiana" (in ABAC form) on whose chords "Donna Lee" is based. Only then does a small group within the band play Miles Davis's melody, which its composer had recorded with Charlie Parker a few months before.

Despite the confusion over its authorship, the line has Davis's stamp. Unlike Parker's more rhythmically irregular compositions, this melody is comprised of a continuous flow of eighth notes. After the melody is stated, the drummer, who has been playing high-hat all this time, switches to ride cymbal to back up half-chorus solos by trombone and tenor saxophone. Then the band plays a wild half-chorus variation on the theme. The rest of the piece includes a guitar solo, the small group within the band playing the last half of the theme, and a coda that is similar to the introduction. Evans treats the theme of "Donna Lee" freshly, sandwiching it between two dissonant, modern-sounding sections. One also notices his restrained use of the tonal resources of the band. They all play together only in the introduction, coda, and during the half-chorus variation on the theme.

Evans's arrangement of Parker's "Anthropology" survives in one complete and one incomplete studio take from September 1947, as well as on reissues of radio broadcasts. (Some of these have been issued under the alternate title, "Thrivin' on a Riff.") It features a solo by alto saxophonist Lee Konitz. Konitz seems to come from a different world than the other soloists. He plays a tart, sinuous few bars that show him already offering an alternative to Parker.

Konitz and four other Thornhill alumni would also take part in the Miles Davis "Birth of the Cool" sessions, which were preceded in 1948 by two weeks of work by Miles Davis's "tuba band," as some called it, at the Royal Roost. With a personnel and instrumentation that reflects the Thornhill band, for which Gerry Mulligan also arranged, this nonet may have been Gil Evans's idea: Its arrangers—Mulligan, Evans, Johnny Carisi and John Lewis—were all part of the 55th Street coterie. But it took Miles Davis to pull the group together. Mulligan has said, "He took the initiative and put the theories to work. He called the rehearsals, hired the halls, called the players, and generally cracked the whip." Davis was the leader, but he wanted the music to do more than merely feature himself. Interestingly, Gil Evans has said that he first wanted Parker as his soloist, but that Parker wasn't ready to "use himself as a voice, as part of an overall picture, instead of a straight soloist" (Chambers, *Milestones I*, p. 98). The band brought out Davis's tense lyricism, in arrangements that seemed, in their gravity and understated depth, to signal a new direction in jazz. The six winds were arranged in pairs, high and low—trumpet and trombone, French horn and tuba, alto and baritone saxophone. The remaining three members, the rhythm section, usually included the great bop drummer Max Roach, and John Lewis on piano.

The nonet's appearances at the Royal Roost, where the band was alternating sets with Count Basie, didn't thrill its audiences, and the band as a working unit no longer existed on January 21, 1949, when they made their first of three recording sessions. The others were in April 1949 and March 1950. All together, the band recorded a dozen arrangements, five by Mulligan, three by John Lewis, a single piece – the masterful blues "Israel" – by Johnny Carisi, two by Gil Evans, and Miles Davis's "Deception." (Miles Davis is given arranger's credit on this number, but it is likely that the work was done mostly by Evans. If not, this would be the one time Davis wrote a harmonized band arrangement.) Given the multiplicity of talented arrangers at work, it is remarkable how clearly the pieces belong together. There are distinctions to be made, of course: Mulligan's bouncing lines and Lewis's lightly swinging ensembles seem typical of these men, and the slow-moving "Moon Dreams" had to be by Gil Evans. The pieces don't uniformly underplay the rhythm – Max Roach is active on Mulligan's "Jeru" – or obscure the soloists. But their rich, sometimes thick textures sound a new note, as does the instrumentation. On "Godchild," Mulligan has the theme stated by his baritone sax and tuba.

Davis's "Deception" is a transformation of George Shearing's "Conception." (Davis was fond of clever titles like this. His version of Parker's "Confirmation" was called "Denial," and his version of Monk's "Well, You Needn't" was "I Didn't.") Best known for the soft smooth sound of his quintets, which we discuss later in this chapter, Shearing was admired by musicians for his sophisticated writing. Shearing's AABA "Conception" begins on an unstable chord, with the result that the beginning of each A section is initially unsettling tonally – the listener seems to grope for the key. The A sections are each twelve bars; the bridge is eight bars. (See music example.)

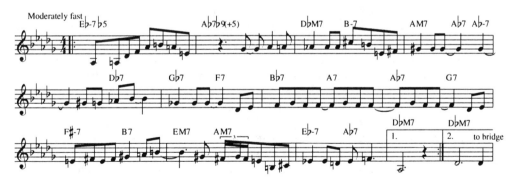

Example 14–2.
George Shearing, "Conception," A section.

As its title suggests, the plan of "Deception" is even more unusual. Davis's group plays it in the key of C instead of D♭ major. Although Evans and Davis maintain the heart of Shearing's chord progressions, they include many substitutions. They also subtly change the form. In "Deception" the A sections become fourteen bars each as bars 7 and 8 of Shearing's original are extended into four measures, with a pedal point beginning in measure 7. The bridge is a standard eight bars long, but it moves so subtly into the final A that it is difficult to hear without counting where the last A begins. Beginning with half of the revised A section, the arrangement in itself is deliberately tricky:

Introduction comprised of measures 7–14 of revised A

One full chorus of AABA (each A is fourteen bars, B is eight)

Davis solos over ABA (first A is not repeated, but an extra measure is inserted during the last A!)

J.J. Johnson solos over BA

Band plays A

Coda

Later recordings of "Conception" by Davis and by pianist Bill Evans use aspects of this nonet version.

Davis and Gil Evans also collaborated on "Boplicity" (SCCJ). Davis originally credited it to his mother, Cleo Henry, a peculiar choice given his strained relationship with her. With its chorus of theme statement and two subsequent choruses, the AABA piece is three choruses long. The Smithsonian Collection mistakenly says that there are only two choruses. They err as well in saying that the final A of the first chorus is extended to nine-and-a-half bars. It is not. The band plays the final eight bars of the first chorus and continues through the first one-and-a-half measures — two if you include the silent beats — of the second chorus. The beginning of the second chorus is clearly marked by a drum fill, by Mulligan's entrance over the band, and by the walking bass. Mulligan's baritone solo, less jaunty than in later years, takes over the first two A sections of the second chorus, successfully maintaining the restrained mood of the beginning. This time there's a rhythmically tricky ten bar B section in which Davis and Evans have expanded the first four bars of the original bridge into six with a continued downward moving phrase. Davis's solo trumpet enters for the final four bars of this ten bar bridge. The band finishes the last eight bars of the chorus, and continues into the first two measures of the third and final chorus.

A methodical sounding Miles Davis picks up where the band leaves off in this new chorus — on bar three — and solos during the rest of the first sixteen bars of the chorus slowly, melodically, in a spacious manner adapted to his surroundings. (There is some confusion in the Smithsonian notes here as well — by giving the band the first two bars of the first A section and Davis a full eight, they mistakenly create an A of ten bars.) Pianist John Lewis takes a short, bouncy solo on the bridge, and the band plays the A and ends — there is no coda. All the hallmarks of the Miles Davis-Gil Evans cool style are summarized in this short track—the dark sonorities, the clear melodies whose simplicity is masked by an intricate arrangement, and a smooth, easy-going rhythm section, in this case with Kenny Clarke on brushes.

In "Boplicity" and elsewhere, Evans uses elevenths and thirteenths, flatted and sharped. Other writers were doing the same. More distinctively, Evans employs the contemporary technique found in Debussy and Hindemith of having several of the winds move in parallel lines. When they are moving in parallel thirds, the result is simple harmony. But Evans might have the winds a fourth apart or a flatted fifth, or in thirds with a few strange accidentals thrown in to produce notes outside the basic key. Such passages are heard in "Moon Dreams."

The slow-moving "Moon Dreams" is both dreamy, as the title of this popular song by Chummy McGregor implies, and, in Gil Evans's arrangement, insistent. Its harmonies are thick, challenging, and they shift seamlessly like layers of clouds. Evans doesn't mean it to swing but to lope along: Bassist Al McKibbon plays on beats one and three. The most startling, and innovative, part of the arrangement is the coda, in which everything suddenly comes to a stop under the wry-sounding held note of Miles Davis. A contrapuntal passage ensues in which a little motive using a minor third is passed from the alto to Davis's trumpet to the French horn, played here by Gunther Schuller. There seems to be little forward motion, but the coda has considerable tension because of its dissonance and voicings. It's a remarkable ending.

The mood of these sessions, their particular sobriety and the sonorities of the various arrangements, had an important, if not always definable, effect on the jazz of the fifties. (The effect built more slowly than one might expect. Perhaps that is because the pieces were issued on 78's over the space of a year and a half. Eight of the Capitol recordings were finally assembled on a ten-inch long playing record in 1954. They've been in print almost constantly ever since.) These sessions widened the scope of jazz. Three of the four composers went on to greater prominence in the fifties. The exception, Johnny Carisi, recorded several tunes on a Gil Evans record, *Into the Hot*, in 1961 but unfortunately made little impact since, although he was still actively composing. Gil Evans, as we shall see, would collaborate on a series of sessions with Miles Davis.

GERRY MULLIGAN AND THE MJQ

Gerry Mulligan would lead some of the best loved small groups of the fifties, and one that usefully illustrates the interest of many of his contemporaries in lighter textures and a more democratic interaction among band members. Mulligan played with a light, singing tone. That and his easy facility of phrasing suggests his debt to Lester Young and, in his gruff romanticism, to Ben Webster. Serge Chaloff, a speedy player in Woody Herman's band, was his main rival on baritone before the emergence in the late fifties of Pepper Adams.

Mulligan was originally known as a composer and arranger—in 1946, Gene Krupa recorded his arrangement of "How High the Moon," and the following

Chet Baker, Boston, 1980's.
(Photo by Michael Ullman)

year, his composition "Disc Jockey Jump." In 1949, Mulligan was playing and writing for the Elliot Lawrence Orchestra, which recorded his "Elevation" (BBJ). Perhaps he was even then dreaming of leading his own big band, which he would first do in the mid-fifties. He became famous in 1952 with a piano-less quartet featuring trumpeter Chet Baker, bassist Bob Whitlock and drummer Chico Hamilton. The group was immediately labelled "cool." A *Time* review of February 2, 1953 drew the distinction between the Mulligan Quartet and bebop, a distinction that, whether one shares its values or not, helps explain the relative popularity of cool jazz: "In comparison with the frantic extremes," the anonymous writer said, "his [Mulligan's] jazz is rich and even orderly, is marked by an almost Bach-like counterpoint. As in Bach, each Mulligan man is busily looking for a pause, a hole in the music which he can fill with an answering phrase."

The piano-less quartet developed a curiously open, spacious sound. Its members played strings of solos, but would also improvise inspired commentary behind each other. Elsewhere the winds soloed together: In one session that included a third wind, Lee Konitz, the group sounded like a cool version of Dixieland. The Mulligan quartet suggested another change in the balance of jazz groups. Because of its general spareness, the quartet brought forward the bass player in a way bebop groups couldn't.

Its first hit was "My Funny Valentine" recorded on September 2, 1952. Here the counterpoint is not as important as the intense, confidential tones of Chet Baker, a strikingly handsome young man who by the end of the year was winning jazz polls on the basis of this solo. Because of his sparing vibrato, air of introspection, and limited range as a trumpeter, Baker was frequently criticized as a mere imitator of Miles Davis. He's something else: His controlled, halcyon tone was more open and relaxed than Davis's, though without Davis's inspiring intensity. (Baker's unassuming, even fragile lyricism, with its sudden flares of warmth, is closer to that of Bobby Hackett.) Baker seems to have been an intuitive player—pianist Don Friedman has commented that Baker didn't know the names of the chords on which he was improvising—but in the best of the Mulligan-Baker recordings we hear him nudging his way along, and we seem to share his discoveries. The result is surprisingly moving.

Mulligan used the success of his quartet's recordings to put together, also in 1953, a tentet date frankly based on the Miles Davis Nonet, that would record numbers such as the blithely bouncing "Walkin' Shoes." His relationship with Chet Baker foundered when Mulligan was incarcerated briefly as a result of drug use. He came back to find Baker a star and a restive one, ready to go out on his own. Later in the decade Mulligan would lead a swinging sextet with Zoot Sims. He recorded with his own big band in 1957, and led popular big bands in the early sixties and then again in 1982 and 1983.

Baker's story is more tragic—in the mid-fifties, admired for his trumpet playing and for his soft, high, fragile-sounding vocals, he was at the top of his profession, but unready for a success he barely thought he deserved. At a time when he was being considered a possible movie star, he picked up an addiction that he never shook. He was imprisoned in Italy in 1960, and nearly disappeared from view until his low-key comeback in the seventies. For several years, he played with intermittent brilliance. Then, gaunt and haunted, Baker died after a fall from a window in 1988. (He was the subject of Bruce Weber's documentary *Let's Get Lost*, named after one of his vocal performances with Russ Freeman.)

John Lewis, who arranged the bebop numbers "Move" (by Denzil Best) and "Budo" (by Bud Powell) for the Miles Davis Nonet, and who composed its "Rouge," was born in New Mexico in 1920 and educated at the University of New Mexico before World War II. He was a bebop pianist with a difference—he had and still has a delicate touch, and plays sparely. There's none of the headlong exhilaration of Bud Powell in Lewis's piano: Rather, he's given to clear melodic lines and carefully etched motives that are barely interrupted by sketchy left-hand chords. With what seems a deliberately limited technique, he manages to build powerful statements through his impeccable timing, and through the continuity and logic of his motives. As an accompanist, he plays carefully etched counter-melodies that suggest a polyphonic texture.

As soon would become evident, Lewis was one of the music's best composers, and he gathered around him a group for which his more deliberate piano style was perfect. His vehicle would be the Modern Jazz Quartet, which held together from 1952 until 1974 and then started up again in 1981. One of the most popular jazz groups of all time, the MJQ would be revered by fans and critics alike for its subtle interplay, for its vivid swing, and for the wit and intelligence of the compositions—mostly by Lewis, but including an occasional blues by vibraphonist Milt Jackson—that it performed in clubs, concert halls and colleges all over the world.

John Lewis at Harvard University in April 1980. Tom Everett, director of Harvard's bands, has his back to the camera. (Photo by Michael Ullman)

The Quartet played the blues and Bach, as one of their record titles suggests, and they had a way of making Bach sound bluesy and the blues sound baroque. From the beginning, their ballads were lush and romantic, and their uptempo pieces, propelled by Milt Jackson's exuberant virtuosity, took off. They exploited all the tonal variety available to such a limited instrumentation—vibes, piano, bass and drums—and their sound never got stale. (Connie Kay must be the only jazz drummer as well known for his bells as for his brushes.)

The group came together almost by accident. During the Second World War, John Lewis found himself in the same Special Services band as the great bebop drummer Kenny Clarke. He left the army in November of 1945, and a month later went to New York to attend the Manhattan School of Music. Prodded by Clarke, who was by then a member of the Dizzy Gillespie big band, Lewis submitted arrangements to Gillespie, including "Two Bass Hit," which he later renamed "La Ronde." Gillespie hired Lewis to join his rhythm section that included Clarke, Milt Jackson, and Ray Brown on bass, and he asked this quartet to spell the band by playing a few numbers in each set by themselves.

They discovered that they enjoyed playing with one another. Jackson, Lewis and Clarke recorded together in 1948 and in 1951, the latter with Ray Brown as well. They were known at that time as the Milt Jackson Quartet, after the obvious star of the group, but later they decided to become a cooperative. When on December 22, 1952, the first Prestige recordings were made, they were the Modern Jazz Quartet, and Percy Heath had replaced Brown on bass. Three years later, Kenny Clarke was replaced by Connie Kay in the quartet's last personnel change.

The MJQ's deportment is legendary; in the 1950's and 1960's the quartet, dressed in somber tuxedos, came on stage precisely on time, and Jackson and Lewis soberly introduced their carefully assembled programs. It was clear that the MJQ wanted to be treated with the same respect as a classical group, and they were remarkably successful in getting it. The critic Ralph Gleason wrote that when the MJQ made its debut at the Black Hawk club in San Francisco, the audience barely dared to breathe. By their insistently correct demeanor they helped to change the conditions in which jazz musicians play.

Their music must have reassured new listeners. Perhaps because they played graceful fugue-like passages in a chamber music atmosphere, or because they didn't have a saxophone or a trumpet making what might seem to be unmannerly noise, they became the favorite jazz group of people who didn't like jazz. They excited aficionados as well. Lewis's study of baroque music led him to write mini-fugues like "Vendome" and "Concorde." (A fugue is a baroque style of counterpoint which begins with the instruments or voices being added one at a time, each playing the theme in a different key.) The arrangements of popular songs were varied and often puckishly witty: The MJQ ended every chorus of "Rose of the Rio Grande" (1952) with a silly, scurrying phrase that begins with four sixteenth notes played in unison. "Delaunay's Dilemma" (1953), a jaunty original theme that seems to end with a hop, skip, and a jump, is dedicated to the French jazz scholar and promoter Charles Delaunay. It asks bassist Percy Heath to share the melody statement.

Lewis's most famous tribute, though, is a piece they first recorded in 1954: "Django," a memorial to Django Reinhardt. (A version recorded live in 1960 was issued on *European Concert* and is on the SCCJ.) It begins and ends with a graceful, suggestive lament played in a slow, loose rhythm. (See music example.)

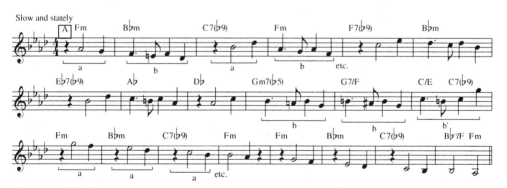

Example 14–4.
John Lewis, "Django," opening theme. Note two main motives, bracketed.

This section frames a bluesy set of chords on which they improvise in a rocking mid-tempo.

THE TRISTANO SCHOOL

"Cool" jazz was mostly a small band phenomenon—some would say it was mostly a media phenomenon. Many of its players concentrated on the melodic lines, and some used various kinds of counterpoint, whether written as with the MJQ or improvised as in the Mulligan-Baker quartet, to enliven those lines. That emphasis often, although not inevitably, meant toning down the rhythm section, with which some players had become frustrated: "I've come to feel increasingly inhibited and frustrated by the insistent pounding of the rhythm section," said composer and clarinetist Jimmy Giuffre. "With it, it's impossible for the listener or the soloist to hear the horn's true sound, I've come to believe, or fully concentrate on the solo line. An imbalance of advances has moved the rhythm section from a supporting to a competitive role." (From the notes to *Tangents in Jazz*, a 1955 record in which Giuffre wrote out much of what the bass and drum play, rather than allowing them to improvise freely.) Those solo lines were often played with a smooth, flowing sound derived from Lester Young, the hero of many of this group of progressive musicians.

A significant group of cool players gathered on the West Coast around the film soundtrack studios where many of them got work or at least looked for it. (Hence the other sobriquet for the cool school, "West Coast jazz.") The cool musicians were predominantly made up of white players, although even on the West Coast the groups were frequently integrated, including black musicians such as saxophonist Harold Land, the lyrical pianist Hampton Hawes and bassist Leroy Vinnegar.

Many of the most innovative players in the East—Lee Konitz, Warne Marsh, Billy Bauer—revolved around the blind pianist, Lennie Tristano. A native Chicagoan who was born in 1919 and died in New York in 1978, Tristano was a virtuoso pianist, a teacher and a kind of father figure of his own school, which had some things in common with cool such as the reverence for Lester Young. But he developed along his own lines: He had a smooth, fleet style, a subtle touch, and he was given to long lines and patterns filled with sophisticated syncopation and crossrhythms (that is, rhythms that momentarily suggest another meter). The rhythmic life in his playing is all the more remarkable because it doesn't come from strong accents. Rather, he would frequently turn the beat around by stopping and starting in unexpected places. Tristano began recording in 1945. By 1947 he was named *Metronome's* Musician of the Year, having caught the ear of critic Barry Ulanov, who paired him with Charlie Parker in several all-star groups.

Tristano started to teach in the forties. He concentrated on ear training, asking students to memorize his favorite solos: by Lester Young, Billie Holiday, and, in the seventies, by trumpeter Freddie Hubbard. He stressed the melodic line, tended to undervalue the rhythm section—although there are important exceptions, his drummers were frequently asked to swish away quietly with brushes—and he wrote contrapuntal lines, and sometimes devilishly difficult unison figures. As his part of the assault on the chord, he even experimented with completely free improvisation. As Tristano explained, "Free form means playing without a fixed chord progression; without a time signature; without a specified tempo. I had been working with my men in this context for several years so that the music which resulted was not haphazard." The music he was talking about was recorded on May 16, 1949, when, much to the dismay of Capitol Records, Tristano's sextet recorded the intriguing "Intuition" and "Digression." "Intuition" begins with Tristano playing what could have been a bebop line in the making—but it doesn't settle into chord changes and Lee Konitz then enters with an equally unsettled series of comments on what Tristano had been doing. As the other players enter, the improvisation becomes more dramatic, then ends in a sudden slowdown.

The sextet, which Tristano began leading in 1948, featured several of his students—Lee Konitz and tenor saxophonist Warne Marsh, guitarist Billy Bauer. Among the group's repertoire were some of Bach's "Inventions" for keyboard transcribed for winds. Tristano's own themes were usually based on standards, such as "How High the Moon." In his 1949 theme "Wow," Tristano transforms an Earl Hines piece, "You Can Depend on Me." "Wow" includes a stunning bridge passage for the saxophonists, who play a fast, boppish double-time line together with remarkable precision. "Crosscurrent," from the same date, is a lighthearted AA'BA piece with an original chord sequence. Its first A is close to

Lee Konitz in Boston, 1970's. (Photo by Michael Ullman)

that of "I Got Rhythm." The second is varied in that it introduces a descending chord sequence not found in the first statement. It leads in a complex way to the bridge. (See music example.)

Example 14–4.
Lennie Tristano, "Crosscurrent," first two A sections of theme (1949).

Konitz's solo stands out for its exquisitely shaped lines and its clever development. He negotiates the difficult opening chords of the bridge with ease. (See music example.)

Regrettably, Tristano rarely recorded, and what he did tape he often edited, sometimes fading numbers out rather than including the original ending. As we have noted, in the mid-fifties, he investigated the technique of overdubbing. Not everyone was ready for the results, which some critics took as something like poor sportsmanship rather than as an interesting experiment. Still, the results were fascinating. On "Turkish Mambo," Tristano overdubs twice, making three bass lines in all, each playing a repeated pattern in a different meter—with 7, 6, and 5 beats. Over these patterns one hears Tristano's right hand improvising soulfully.

The variety of his recordings show the limitations of the "cool" classification. "Requiem," a 1955 tribute to the recently deceased Charlie Parker, begins out of tempo, moves into a melodic line in the right hand and then, after a cadence (a restful pause), into bleak, startling chords. It's as if the pianist were too shocked to respond coherently. This his grief becomes organized: "Requiem" turns into an elemental blues, with Tristano's left hand outlining the most basic chords in jazz. "Requiem" is unaccompanied, except for a little overdubbing at the end. In 1962, Tristano recorded the astounding unaccompanied solo, "C Minor Complex," in which he plays a walking bass line in his left hand with great intensity while improvising dramatically virtuosic, motivically linked lines with his right.

Example 14–5.
Lee Konitz's improvised solo on "Crosscurrent" (1949).

In 1956, Tristano's protégé Lee Konitz recorded *Inside Hi-Fi*, on which he plays with musicians associated with Tristano. Konitz isn't merely cool here either, especially compared with Tristano's complicated, indirect-sounding repertoire. On *Inside Hi-Fi*, Konitz improvises an earthy blues, "Cork 'n' Bib," and then delves into the repertoire of Louis Armstrong, with openly melodic paraphrases of "All of Me" and "Indiana." For the notes to his *Very Cool* (1957) Konitz suggested to Nat Hentoff reasons for a change in his style, for a more careful attention to each note and a respectful treatment of written melodies: "One of my students brought me a record of Louis Armstrong playing 'Sleepy Time Down South.' Louis gets so deep into every single note. Every note is an expression of feeling. That's really playing." Over the years Konitz's style became less technical, more frugal in its choice of notes, warmer and more expressive in tone. In his later career, Konitz has continued to experiment—his *Duets* album (1967) has free improvisation—but he has continued to affirm his love of beautiful melodies elegantly stated. (He announced at a Carnegie Hall tribute to Fred Astaire that he'd like to play the way Astaire sang.)

In his early career, and then again for a time in the seventies, Konitz frequently recorded with another saxophonist from the Tristano circle, the distinctive tenor player Warne Marsh, who died in 1987 at the age of 60. Born in Los Angeles in 1927, Marsh worked with Tristano after 1948, when he moved to New York. Marsh, whose improvisations are always persuasive melodically, was not afraid of a vigorous rhythm section. In 1956, he recorded Cole Porter's "It's All Right With Me" with the powerful drummer Philly Joe Jones. It's a typical Marsh performance: After a respectful chorus of Porter's melody, Marsh plays a solo that uses his affecting tone—he always seems to have a catch in his throat—in choruses whose clarity of line and development complement the emotionalism of his sound.

ART PEPPER, STAN GETZ, AND DAVE BRUBECK

Perhaps the best musicians resist—though they do not absolutely defy—classification. Born in California in 1925, alto saxophonist and clarinetist Art Pepper served an apprenticeship in the big bands of Benny Carter and Stan Kenton—and on Los Angeles's Central Avenue, which he described as like what he imagined of "Harlem a long time ago." On Central Avenue this young white musician played and hung out with Dexter Gordon, Charles Mingus and others. Pepper was 17 in 1943 when he joined the great swing altoist Benny Carter. He performed in the band led by Lester Young's brother Lee at the Club Alabam and he idolized, but did not imitate, Lester. He joined Stan Kenton, recording with him in 1943, and then was drafted.

Pepper returned to Kenton after the war, soloing on the 1947 Kenton recording "Harlem Holiday" in short, tense flurries of notes, irregularly accented. In 1951, largely because of his playing with the hugely popular Kenton, Pepper placed second in the *Down Beat* poll. In that year he created a small masterpiece with the West Coast group of trumpeter Shorty Rogers. Influenced by the Miles Davis Nonet, Rogers's arrangement of "Over the Rainbow" immediately dispels the sentiment associated with this Judy Garland vehicle by assigning the melody to the rather sour sound of a French horn. Art Pepper opposes his bittersweet alto sound in the higher register to the lower brass sounds of the accompaniment in a solo that is alternately hesitant and eloquent, oblique and emotional. The arrangement is cool, but the intensity of Pepper's involvement and sound suggests passion equivalent to Parker's.

Intense and competitive, Art Pepper was not going to be cast simply as a cool player. His 1960 recording, *Gettin' Together*, was made with the Miles Davis rhythm section, a powerfully swinging trio. His goal was to become the world's greatest alto saxophonist. (In an interview he stated his disappointment when a friend described him only as *one* of the greatest alto saxophonists.) His heroin addiction interfered. Pepper spent much of the sixties and early seventies either in prison, ill, or in the San Francisco rehabilitation center Synanon. Unexpectedly, he returned to prominence in 1977. On methadone, he made a new series of recordings with an expanded set of stylistic devices. These included some squeals and squeaks he learned from John Coltrane. Pepper's best work was highly individual, impassioned, intense and yet controlled. His 1979 ballad performance, "Patricia," which he called his masterpiece, is both logical and deeply moving. Pepper died in 1982.

Art Pepper and Lee Konitz defined themselves stylistically by veering off from the Parker mold. Other alto players couldn't find a way to do that: Parker is responsible for making tenor saxophonists out of a lot of would-be altos. Even the skillful Sonny Stitt took up tenor as a way of establishing his own voice. Pepper and Konitz also looked backwards beyond the figure of Charlie Parker for models—Pepper to Benny Carter and Lester Young, Konitz to Young and, of course, to Lennie Tristano.

The Lester Young influence was decisive in the case of another "cool" player, destined to become one of the most famous saxophonists in jazz history. Stan Getz could hardly be called a West Coast player—he was born in 1927 in Philadelphia and moved early to New York. His first recording, in the band of trombonist Jack Teagarden, was made when he was 15. Getz played briefly with Stan Kenton and Benny Goodman but made his mark with Woody Herman's Second Herd, the bebop-oriented band that celebrated its reed section with "Four Brothers."

Getz used his lyric gifts, his light tone, and naturally song-like phrasing on Ralph Burns's "Early Autumn." Recorded in 1948 by the Herd, it was his first hit. The transcription illustrates the lovely melodies that Getz was creating even at this early stage, melodies which he plays with a technical and rhythmic mastery that keeps them accessible. (See music example.)

Example 14–6.
Stan Getz's first solo on "Early Autumn" by Ralph Burns with Woody Herman (1948). Getz plays freely, lagging behind the beat.

His recordings in the late forties show him very much in the cool mode, his fluid, even-tempered lines produced with a carefully controlled tone. "Four Brothers and Moore" from 1949 was made to celebrate the similarities amongst tenor saxophonists Getz, Al Cohn, Zoot Sims, Allen Eager and Brew Moore. Later they would diverge from the Lester Young model. Cohn developed a gruff, hard-edged tone and Sims a fluid, breathy sound. These two formed a successful two-tenor group. Getz in 1949 was a cool player dedicated, as one of his titles tells, to "Prezervation."

He also was observing what Parker and Tristano were doing. Guitarist Jimmy Raney's uptempo theme for a 1951 version of "Cherokee" entitled "Parker 51" has Getz and Raney working in improvised counterpoint, as Lennie Tristano and his guitarist Billy Bauer might have. The Getz solos on "Yesterdays" and "Everything Happens To Me," from the same Storyville club recordings, show the evolution of the tenor saxophonist's tone into the warmly expressive vehicle that made him such a celebrated ballad player. Getz had a light, carefully modulated vibrato—it can be a rapid quaver at the end of a phrase or broad and soft—and a breathy, relaxed, but still full sound. He played the whole range of his horn with a lyrical lilt, and he had considerable power. In repeated appearances at Carnegie Hall in the eighties, he asked that the microphones be turned off, and still managed to fill the hall and dominate the rhythm section. Getz was well known in the fifties, always at or near the top of the jazz polls, but the fame he received after his 1962 recording *Jazz Samba* was so startling that critics talked about his resurrection. (The Brazilian impact on jazz will be discussed in Chapter 20.) Getz died on June 6, 1991.

Stan Getz in the 1970's.
(Photo by Michael Ullman)

Cool or West Coast jazz is frequently talked about as a fleeting phenomenon, an early fifties fad. But the lasting public success of musicians like Getz suggests a different story. And "cool" sonorities and, more obviously, the emphasis by certain musicians on clearly stated melodies has had a lasting appeal. Two of the most popular jazz groups from the fifties were the George Shearing quintet and the Dave Brubeck quartet. Both leaders were pianists with at least one foot in the cool school. Born in London in 1919, Shearing recorded there as a Teddy Wilson-influenced pianist in 1939. He moved to New York after World War II, where in 1949 he formed his group with vibraphone, guitar, bass and drums. Shearing himself often played in what is called the "locked-hands" style popularized by Milt Buckner of Lionel Hampton's band. Shearing described it as consisting of "a four-note chord in the right hand with the left hand doubling the little finger melody played in the right hand, the whole structure occuring within one octave. In the quintet I added the guitar playing the melody in the lower register and the vibes playing the melody in the upper register." (See music example.)

Example 14–8.
An example of the locked hands style.

The quintet had a readily identifiable, commendably cool sound, and Shearing's boppish right hand lines—he said he was influenced by Detroiter Hank Jones as much as by Bud Powell—were often followed by the graceful vibraphone solos of Margie Hyams or, later, Cal Tjader. Shearing remained popular throughout the fifties and ever since.

But not as popular as Dave Brubeck, whose large, bony, animated face graced the cover of *Time* in 1954. Brubeck, a native Californian born in 1920, studied before and after World War II with French composer Darius Milhaud, then teaching at Mills College, whose 1923 "La Creation du Monde" was one of the first classical works to include jazz elements. Brubeck was, he admits, a mediocre reader of music, but he studied counterpoint, fugue and composition with Milhaud. He formed a group with fellow students in 1946—it preceded the Miles Davis Nonet—that first recorded in 1948 as the Dave Brubeck Octet. Those recordings show the group's interest in counterpoint, and a relatively complex interweaving of solo and written passages. Arrangements like Brubeck's of "The Way You Look Tonight" (1950) show that Brubeck was working in the same field as Davis and at the same time.

Dave Brubeck (facing camera) talking to Lionel
Hampton, at Newport, probably 1981. (Photo by
Michael Ullman)

Later he formed a trio and then added in 1951 the remarkable alto saxophonist Paul Desmond, who once compared his own undefinable, perfectly
distinctive tone to a dry martini. It has a wider appeal. His sound is light, and its
every inflection is perfectly controlled—remarkably the higher Desmond goes in
pitch, the more fetching his tone becomes. His louder notes can almost bark,
and at key points in a chorus his horn seems to develop a slight rasp. He's a cool
alto saxophonist, but he doesn't sound anything like either Lee Konitz or Art
Pepper.

Desmond's unrushed improvisations provide a striking contrast to Brubeck's heavy-handed piano playing—Brubeck's solos move inexorably towards
thumping final choruses. What isn't predictable about Brubeck is his harmonic
sense, which leads him into extraordinary dissonances. Brubeck may have been
proud of his advanced harmonies, but it's a good bet that he was prouder of his
experiments with time. As a soloist he frequently began with single note melodies, then settled into block chords and finally set one hand against the other,
playing in more and more complicated rhythmic schemes.

Brubeck also experimented with another aspect of time—meter—which led
to his most popular record, *Time Out*, recorded in 1959, on which the quartet
played pieces in various meters, including the 5/4 of Desmond's great hit, "Take
Five." It was assumed at the time that audiences were responding to the
experimental aspect of this set of recordings: It is just as likely that they were

caught up by the exquisite melody that Desmond wrote for "Take Five," or by the dramatic switch—it feels like a fall—from the 9/8 introduction of "Blue Rondo à la Turk" to the 4/4 blues on which Desmond improvises. The quartet that made this album—Brubeck, Desmond, bassist Gene Wright, and the remarkable drummer Joe Morello—stayed together until 1967. Desmond went on to reaffirm his grounding in the cool school in recordings with Gerry Mulligan in 1957 and 1962. He recorded repeatedly with the lyrical guitarist Jim Hall, made a reunion record with Brubeck and then died of lung cancer in 1977. Brubeck continues as a leader, with his sons and others, but has never found such a perfect foil and counterpart.

THE THIRD STREAM

The music of Brubeck's quartet, with its emphasis on improvisation, doesn't sound much like the Miles Davis Nonet, the archetypal "cool" group. As the fifties progressed, the term "cool"—always imprecise though originally useful—was stretched mercilessly. At first critics meant by cool jazz the music of the Davis nonet and of its offshoots, many of which were on the West Coast: the Shorty Rogers band, the Mulligan Tentette, John Graas's group. Cool jazz was jazz with a controlled sonority, possibly including "classical" instruments such as the flute, French horn or tuba. These groups emphasized writing for a group—not merely providing unison themes but intricate harmonies and countermelodies.

   Much of the preoccupation since the fifties of jazz composers with writing fugues, rondos, and extended jazz pieces came out of the cool movement. In some ways anticipated in the twenties and thirties by Gershwin, Milhaud and others, these composers took a step in the direction of so-called classical music. Classically oriented composers were intrigued by the rhythms and vitality of jazz, and as Igor Stravinsky demonstrated in his 1945 "Ebony Concerto," written for the Woody Herman band, some classical composers were also interested in the sonorities of the jazz band. Some were also interested in improvisation. When in the fifties more classical composers began to approach jazz, one of them, Gunther Schuller, coined a label, "Third Stream," to identify "a genre of music located about halfway between jazz and classical music." (He used the phrase in a lecture given around 1957, and then again in a 1961 article, "Third Stream," in the *Saturday Review*. This article has been reprinted in his collection, *Musings*.)

   The term remains useful. It helps describe the pieces commissioned by Brandeis University in 1957, pieces by Charles Mingus, George Russell, Schuller himself, and by Harold Shapero. Russell's "All About Rosie" is a powerful piece of three short movements based on a folk tune. It begins with a kind of fanfare for trumpets, and then seems to build layers of tension. The second movement is a lazy walk through the same theme that begins with a saxophone statement over an ambiguous, initially unformed harmonic background. The last movement is a kind of mini-concerto for improvising pianist Bill Evans, who enters after the complicated, but swinging ensemble statements.

Russell of course was writing in this mode before he heard that a "third stream" existed. His earlier masterpieces include "A Bird in Igor's Yard," recorded in 1949, and the 1956 "Concerto for Billy the Kid," another feature for Bill Evans. These pieces preceded Schuller's statements on the genre. As recorded in June 1957, Schuller's "Transformation" is perhaps the clearest early example of third stream music. Schuller's description makes "Transformation" sound something like a grab bag: In it, "a variety of musical concepts converge: twelve-tone technique, *Klangfarbenmelodie* [tone-color-melody, building a melody out of different tone colors], jazz improvisation [again Bill Evans is the soloist], and metric breaking up of the accent." It begins with a short passage of twelve-tone writing. This technique, introduced by Arnold Schoenberg, restricts a composer to a preset series of notes which are manipulated—in order—in various ways. It forces the composer to avoid tonality and its resultant "clichés."

The transformation from which the piece gets its title occurs as one instrument at a time begins to play what is recognizably jazz. Eventually we have a swinging rhythm section with classical elements gradually intruding until, and this is the second transformation, the piece returns to a "classical" mode. As Schuller says, and this seems true of many third stream pieces, "Transformation" presents jazz and classical elements "in succession—in peaceful coexistence—and later, in close, more competitive juxtaposition."

Other composers have followed Schuller's lead, presenting a hybrid of jazz and classical elements. We might mention J.J. Johnson's 1956 *Poem for Brass*, Bill Russo's *An Image of Man* (1958) and Jimmy Giuffre's *Mobiles* (1959) among many valuable examples. But composers such as Charles Mingus found other ways of extending forms and, thus, of escaping being mired in clichés. Mingus had been classically trained and in the early fifties was writing what we might call third stream pieces, but he eventually found this approach too inhibiting. For Mingus, the next movement in jazz—the reemphasis of the blues and rhythmic bases of the music in what has been called "hard bop" or "soul jazz"—was liberating.

15 Mainstream, Hard Bop, and Beyond

In an article published originally in *Down Beat*'s yearbook for 1958, "The Funky-Hard Bop Regression," critic Martin Williams said he observed since the mid-fifties "the gradual dominance of the Eastern and then national scene in jazz by the so-called 'hard bop' and 'funky' schools," a movement inspired by soul singer Ray Charles and gospel musician Mahalia Jackson and led by pianist Horace Silver and Art Blakey and Max Roach. That two of these leaders are drummers suggests something about new priorities in rhythm. By the mid-fifties, with the advent of the aggressively rhythmical, blues-oriented extension of bop called "hard bop," drummers were combining a boisterous—and sometimes dominant—beat with the aggressive accents popularized by early bop drummers.

As we have seen, "cool" jazz players frequently restricted their drummers to light, precise accompanying figures. One explanation of the hard bop movement is that other musicians, frequently black, were eager to "restore" the beat to jazz. This explanation doesn't make sense. Cool players never lost the beat, and hard bop players had not gone through a cool phase. Art Blakey didn't create his characteristic style when he became tired of cool jazz. He had been playing vigorously since the forties, and had nothing to prove.

The jazz messages of drummers Max Roach and Art Blakey and later, Philly Joe Jones, were complex, poly-rhythmic statements. The drummer in the fifties accompanied, but also commented on and completed, his soloists' statements. In so doing, he prompted a barrage of criticism from listeners who thought he was too loud, or even crude. After the founding in 1955 by Art Blakey and Horace Silver of the Jazz Messengers, and of Silver's own quintet the following year, some found in the coalescence of the hard bop style a steamy emotionalism that was especially welcome after what they saw as the tepid waters of cool jazz. Others heard, in its characteristic repertoire of down-home blues and gospel-oriented pieces, jazz marches and funky dance tunes, a retreat from the most stringent demands of Charlie Parker's sophisticated playing of popular songs.

Not everyone was in retreat. The fifties saw the resurgence of the careers of Miles Davis and Thelonious Monk, the emergence of their protégés, tenor saxophonists Sonny Rollins and John Coltrane, and the first, startling recordings of avant-garde musicians Sun Ra, Cecil Taylor, and Ornette Coleman. It also saw the most brilliant bebop band since the original Charlie Parker quintets. Max Roach, who shares with Kenny Clarke the credit for popularizing the practice of keeping a beat on the ride cymbal, was of course the innovative drummer in Parker's group, in which he played from 1947 to 1949 and again in the early fifties. His tight, dry cymbal sound, his crisp rhythms and precise attacks, his attentiveness to pitch and use of space and carefully developed motives in his solos, made him one of the most influential modern drummers. Roach was also a fine and knowledgeable composer, and a natural leader, and in 1954 co-founded, with a young disciple of Fats Navarro and Dizzy Gillespie, the Clifford Brown-Max Roach Quintet. The timing was perfect. Twenty-four years old, the trumpeter Clifford Brown had become one of the greatest jazz soloists. His playing, already celebrated for its fluency and imagination, took on a rhythmic grace, an added ease at whatever tempo he was confronted with, and a variety that made his phrases billow and float as naturally as silk in a gentle wind. A brilliant melodist with a big, singing tone, Brown was playing with warmth, forthrightness—there was little of Gillespie's quirkiness in him—and with a

Max Roach in Boston in the 1970's. (Photo by Michael Ullman)

headlong swing reminiscent of the young Louis Armstrong. Two years later he was dead, a victim of a car crash that also killed the pianist Richie Powell (Bud's brother) and Powell's wife.

At his death, Brown had played trumpet for only twelve years. When he was 15, in 1945, his father gave him his first trumpet. By 1951, Brown was praised by a touring Charlie Parker and hired by the leader of a rhythm-and-blues band called Chris Powell and His Blue Flames, with whom he made his first recordings in 1952. In June 1953, his own "Brownie Speaks," recorded at a session led by altoist Lou Donaldson, shows off his fat tone and his cleanly articulated lines with their long, shining runs. Only when these impressive solos are directly compared with later ones can they be faulted. Even in 1953, he could construct gorgeous melodic lines at mid-tempo, as in the opening bars of "All the Things You Are," recorded in September during a stop in Paris with the Lionel Hampton band. But at times he would seem almost driven at fast tempos; he might string together pairs of eighth notes in the first chorus, varying the pell-mell action only with an occasional triplet. A year later he sounded effortless and expansive on even the fastest numbers.

Perhaps he hadn't yet found his perfect drummer. In August of 1953 and February 1954, Brown recorded with the rough, bashing Art Blakey. He had already recorded with Kenny Clarke and the exciting newcomer Philly Joe Jones, as well as—with the Hampton orchestra—the superb Boston drummer Alan Dawson, who became one of the leading drum teachers in jazz. But in late March 1954 he began the collaboration with Max Roach that made Brown famous. What Roach offered Brown was firm support and a clear, ringing sound in a style sensitive to dynamics and to Brown's developing solos: Roach saved his busiest—and loudest—playing for Brown's hottest moments. Whereas we can hear Blakey pressing Brown on the Blue Note recordings made live at Birdland in February of 1954, Roach let Brown's own melodies unravel. Given his ready virtuosity and his love of uncluttered melody, Brown didn't need to be pushed. In July 1954, a month before the first recording session of the Clifford Brown-Max Roach Quintet (sometimes Roach's name is given first), he recorded such tunes as "Blueberry Hill" and "Gone With the Wind" and his own "Joy Spring" and "Daahoud" with a group of West Coast musicians. On "Blueberry Hill," which had been an easy-going hit for Glenn Miller in 1940 and would be a hit again as sung in 1956 by the blithely rocking Fats Domino, and on "Joy Spring," a gentle, bouncing number, Brown seems to be discovering the value of disengagement, of one step backward taken. Beneath the lilting surface of "Joy Spring" lies a harmonic challenge. "Joy Spring" does not quite have an AABA form, because, as in "All the Things You Are," its second A is in a different key from the first. The bridge modulates quickly through several keys as well. So the performer must be alert to keep up with this gentle number.

His poise and the incomparable appeal of his improvised melodies make Brown's playing with Roach so memorable. In the two years they had as a team, Brown and Roach went into the studios together 15 times, to make *Clifford Brown with Strings,* a favorite album of virtually every modern trumpeter, two albums of jam sessions, and several albums with the quintet. Brown also accompanied the singers Sarah Vaughan and Helen Merrill.

The quintet remade tunes that Brown had recorded earlier, such as "Daahoud," "Joy Spring" and "Cherokee," and Brown sounds even better, more richly inventive, on these versions. If he sputters a little on the "Cherokee" recorded with Blakey in 1953, his 1955 version is played with warmhearted panache. Like most players of the day, Brown made a study of "Cherokee." Philology has issued a fascinating private tape of Brown practicing "Cherokee" alone, from this time period. On *Live at the Beehive*, Columbia issued a live "Cherokee" from November 1955 on which Brown plays with wild abandon over Roach's ferocious drumming.

Brown's solo on the August 1954 version of "Joy Spring," with its tunefully witty phrases, holds together so well that it is difficult to present an excerpt as shown here. During the first A, Brown uses triplets—and space—to add rhythmic flexibility to his lines. Just as striking is the songfulness and logic of the long line that comprises the second A. (See music example.)

*Brown may have intended to slide up to Db.

Example 15–1.
Clifford Brown, beginning of his solo on "Joy Spring" (August 1954 version).

The bridge contains a surprise—Brown plays in double time, and begins with a little turn that is repeated sequentially a whole step down to fit the changing chords. The last A begins with a shout. Brown leads into the second chorus with a sly repetition of a blue note—A♭—and then a G. (The procedure is reminiscent of Lester Young, and of the way Navarro led into his second chorus on "The Squirrel.")

Like Miles Davis, Brown developed an uncanny ability to invent short, unexpected phrases that tell whole stories. At the beginning of his second chorus of the Sonny Rollins original "Pent-Up House," from his last studio recording on March 22, 1956 (private tapes have been issued of later live dates), he plays an almost childlike six-note melody, varies it in a repetition, and then gradually walks away from it in a nine-measure phrase. But the melody stays with you (SCCJ).

One of the dominant figures of modern saxophone playing, Sonny Rollins had replaced the underrated Harold Land, the group's first tenor saxophonist, in December 1955. Born in New York in 1930, Theodore Rollins was playing with classmates like altoist Jackie McLean and drummer Art Taylor while still in high school. Rollins was part of a new, hip generation of New York musicians, one that was introduced early to the most demanding standards of jazz playing, and also to the drugs that would doom or inhibit the careers of so many young musicians in the fifties. Having studied, metaphorically, at the feet of Charlie Parker, whom pianist Hampton Hawes called the nearest thing to God he ever encountered, the black musicians of this generation were more assertive, and they were maturing in a period when black people were demanding social justice and respect. It is easy to count off the musicians whose careers foundered during those years because of drugs, alcohol and neglect. It's crucial to remember those—among them Sonny Rollins and John Coltrane—who shook off drugs and made musical statements that demonstrated their social activism as well as their musical brilliance.

Like many black musicians of his generation, Sonny Rollins wanted, among other things, to use his music to make a political statement. He did so in the 1958 recording *Freedom Suite*, which he wanted to dedicate to the struggles of African-Americans. His notes explained his motivation: "America is deeply rooted in Negro culture: its colloquialisms, its humor, its music. How ironic that the Negro, who more than any other people can claim America's culture as his own, is being persecuted and repressed, that the Negro, who has exemplified the humanities in his very existence, is being rewarded with inhumanity."

The *Freedom Suite* suggests something of the difficulty of making music work in this way. Listening merely to Rollins's themes, including the sprightly walking number that appears after eight minutes, it is difficult to discern a political program. Perhaps the gesture of the title, and what would have appeared in Rollins's original notes to the album had he been allowed to publish them, were meant to make the point. It is also possible that Rollins's working on longer forms and freer improvisations was in itself an example of the kind of ambitious freedom he desired. In another mood, Rollins was to tell Art Taylor that he was one of the first players to talk about racial injustice in this way, and that that was an important step: "Yet in a way I think music should be judged on what it is. It should be very high and above everything else. It is a beautiful way of bringing people together, a little bit of an oasis in this messed-up world. If I look at it like that, then I have to reject the idea of trying to put politics in music" (Art Taylor, *Notes and Tones*, p. 172).

Partially because it includes lyrics, Max Roach's *We Insist—Freedom Now Suite* from the fall of 1960 is more politically persuasive. It should be seen as part of a series of Roach works, a series continuing to this day, that included pieces such as "Mendacity" and "Garvey's Ghost" from the 1961 *Percussion Bitter Sweet*. In his recordings from the late fifties, we see Roach recovering from the loss of Clifford Brown and, in a burst of creativity, becoming an important composer. As a soloist, Roach has always been extraordinarily orderly, even compact. His band with Clifford Brown took up where Charlie Parker's quintets left off: One difference is that Roach and Brown liked tighter, more complete arrangements, provided by Richie Powell, often adding effective introductions and codas to their basic bebop texts. In the late fifties, Roach was experimenting with longer forms. He was participating in what George Russell called the assault on the chords.

Freedom Now Suite features the brassy, rhythmically powerful vocals of Abbey Lincoln. It includes notably the nearly vicious-sounding "Driva' Man," where the remarkably adaptable Coleman Hawkins is featured, and a duet between Lincoln and Roach, "Prayer/Protest/Peace," in which Lincoln's wordless improvisations are set against Roach's commentary and steady beat: In the "Protest" section, Lincoln erupts in a series of shrieks and screams, while Roach flails wildly. Just as important as these occasional experiments in free-form improvisation is the conception of "All Africa" and "Tears for Johannesburg," both of which include Nigerian drummer Olatunji and both of which take as a model the open-ended music of Africa—once the rhythmic grooves are established, they could go on for hours. Roach's band for this recording consciously cut across the generations: Coleman Hawkins, tenor star since 1924, appears, as does a bright young trumpet player, Booker Little. Little would make some seminal recordings with alto saxophonist Eric Dolphy during 1961, only to die that October at the age of 23.

SONNY ROLLINS

From the first—he recorded with Bud Powell, J.J. Johnson and others in 1949—Sonny Rollins demonstrated a gruffly direct, unromantic tone that had much of Coleman Hawkins' depth without the older master's immediate warmth and broad vibrato. Rollins was working on something else. Originally an alto saxophonist, he formed his early style on Lester Young's and Charlie Parker's playing, and he, like John Coltrane, was influenced by the imposing way saxophonist Dexter Gordon had adapted bebop to the tenor. We can hear Rollins's roots in the early recordings with Bud Powell, where his solos on "Bouncing With Bud" and "52nd Street Theme" are composed of long, boppish lines. His timing—as we observe in the little delays at the beginnings of his phrases on "Wail," and in certain unexpectedly truncated phrases—will become one of Rollins's strengths.

Rollins's first recordings as a leader came two years later, when he was playing often with Miles Davis. In January 1951, after Davis's session left some spare studio time, Davis played the piano while Rollins soloed on "I Know." The

Sonny Rollins at the Jazz
Workshop, Boston, 1979.
(Photo by Michael Ullman)

title, probably by Davis, was a sly acknowledgement that the arrangement used Parker's chords from "Confirmation," adding a pedal point. The following December, Rollins recorded eight tunes, including his "Mambo Bounce," the first of a series of West Indian dances inspired by his Trinidad-born mother. The connection with Charlie Parker—and Rollins's deviations from the Parker model—were displayed at a 1953 Davis date in which the trumpeter had both Parker and Rollins playing tenors.

On June 29, 1954, Davis and Rollins recorded three Sonny Rollins tunes: "Airegin"—his slightly camouflaged tribute to the African nation "Nigeria"—"Oleo," and "Doxy." As a composer Rollins has a well-defined personality—he's direct and distinctively melodic. Several of his pieces, including the ones Davis recorded on June 29, have become jazz standards. In an extension of the swing riff style, his tunes usually take one motive and work off of it. (His improvising, while it often develops motives, never does so as simply as does his writing.) "Doxy" is in the swing style, and its familiar changes—very comfortable for the improviser—sound something like the 20's warhorse "How Come You Do Me Like You Do?" "Oleo" is based on "I Got Rhythm." Here the rhythm is tricky, since its idea is to take a three-note motive and turn it inside out and upside down. (See musical example.)

In 1955, Rollins took the first of three retirements, this time to practice and reportedly to cure himself of a drug addiction. At the end of the year, a much improved Rollins joined the Clifford Brown-Max Roach quintet, evolving within the next year into more than the latest hot tenor player. From 1956 until he temporarily retired again in August 1959, he proved himself one of the most individual, and most commanding, improvisers in jazz. In his best recordings,

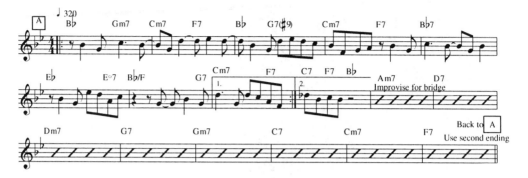

Example 15–2.
Sonny Rollins, "Oleo."

he seemed to wed much of the fluency of Charlie Parker with the puckish humor and dramatic timing of Thelonious Monk. He picked up the Monk influence directly: Rollins worked with Monk in 1954, and recorded with the pianist several times. There is urgency as well as wit in his playing. He introduced a highly personal repertoire—who else would play "I'm an Old Cowhand"? Rollins began in 1956 introducing a series of ecstatic calypsos, of which "St. Thomas" is his most famous: His playing on these pieces is joyously lyrical. Perhaps the West Indian influence may be responsible for Rollins's unique melodic and rhythmic style. He had other influences: He played boldly, using, when it counted, the honks and hollers of rhythm and blues.

In "Pent-Up House," made with Brown and Roach in March 1956 (SCCJ), Rollins follows Clifford Brown's urbanely melodic solo by picking up on the trumpeter's last three-note phrase, playing it slowly, humorously. After this beginning Rollins plays more broadly, and seems almost garrulous in the process. He ends the first chorus by quoting the theme. The Rollins choruses suggest an extraordinary, and unusual, orderliness in improvisation. (See music example.)

It was this orderliness that impressed Gunther Schuller when he wrote a perhaps overly persuasive article on a Rollins recording from 1956, "Blue Seven" (SCCJ) (*Jazz Review,* November 1958; reprinted in Schuller's *Musings*). This is a twelve-bar blues introduced by Doug Watkins's walking bass. Rollins enters quietly with a theme based on the emblem of bop—the flatted fifth. He proceeds to toy around with this interval for the rest of his solo, which Schuller praised for Rollins' repeated use of a motivic figure, suggesting that this figure generates the rest of the solo. (See music example.)

He is, it seems to us, and to Lawrence Gushee, who responded to Schuller in the *Jazz Review* (February 1960), only partially correct: Here as elsewhere in his playing, Rollins uses a repeated phrase as a kind of reference point, returning to it when it is convenient to him, to remind us of where he started, or because its rhythm is particularly persuasive to him, or, even perhaps, when inspiration

Example 15–3.
Sonny Rollins, "Pent-Up House," first two choruses of his solo preceded by the end of Clifford Brown's solo (1956).

Example 15–4.
Sonny Rollins, "Blue Seven," first two measures of saxophone solo, showing main motives and relationship to chords (1956).

flags. What is clear is that the contrast between a repeated figure and the more free-flowing, longer and more expansive phrases, is one of the appeals of this piece. His procedure is in fact quite similar to that of his drummer, Max Roach, some of whose most famous solos (such as the unaccompanied "Conversation," September 1958) keep returning to a clearly identifiable figure, which can be as simple as a few taps on a snare drum. The principle is that of conversation, as Roach's title implies—the figure doesn't generate the other voice it is conversing with, but its stubborn recurrence serves as a kind of resting place for the ear. Roach uses this principle in his April 1966 tribute to swing drummer Big Sid Catlett, which has a recurring theme in the rhythm of Catlett's showpiece, "Mop Mop." (See music example.)

It is perhaps ironic that Schuller praises Rollins for sticking to his subject on "Blue Seven": Elsewhere the tenor saxophonist is one of the great quoters in

a) "Mop Mop" or "Boff Boff") as played by Leonard Feather's All Stars in 1943 with Big Sid Catlett on drums.

b) Max Roach, "For Big Sid" (1966), beginning of drum solo.

Example 15–5.
"Mop Mop" theme and Max Roach's version of it.

jazz, making witty reference to a host of popular songs. And it's distressing that Schuller's analysis of "Blue Seven" seems to have intimidated Rollins himself. Later he said that one of his periods of withdrawal from jazz resulted from this bit of analysis, which seemed to force him to create in other pieces what he didn't actually do in "Blue Seven." In 1959, Rollins temporarily retired—it was said that he was dissatisfied with his playing, and felt that the new, chordless jazz of Ornette Coleman was a threat and a challenge. In 1962 he returned to recording and performing, playing at first with the sensitive guitarist Jim Hall. His tone was even richer, more centered, than before. His virtuosity was still evident, but he used it more sparingly—his every note seemed to have melodic importance. His melodies were daring harmonically, even to the point of suggesting bitonality. And yet his work of the sixties remained lyrical.

His April 1962 recording *What's New* focussed on Latin rhythms. After Hall's thoughtful choruses on "If Ever I Would Leave You," Rollins begins an absorbing solo that builds gradually towards more and more complex lines, lines that are harmonically extended. He reprises the theme broadly, even operatically, and then begins a relaxed coda in which he plays rhythms on one note and chattering phrases over the delightful Latin beat of the rhythm section.

For some months beginning in the summer of 1962, and again for a tour of Europe in 1963, Rollins hired two musicians associated with Coleman—trumpeter Don Cherry and drummer Billy Higgins—and in a pianoless group attempted to come to terms with Ornette Coleman's "free" jazz approach. He continued to play standards, but with a difference. In extended, enthusiastic solos, he might change tempo or key. He never abandoned the chords completely as Coleman did. In between the tours with Cherry and Higgins, Rollins's quartet featured pianist Paul Bley, an early collaborator with Coleman. Bley's effect on the group can be heard on the album *Sonny Meets Hawk* (July 1963), in which Rollins performs with Coleman Hawkins. On "All the Things You Are," Bley's introduction and solo have a delicate, otherworldly quality in strong contrast to the hard-swinging, harmonically funky phrases of Hawkins and the dancing exuberance of Rollins.

In July 1966, Rollins recorded for Impulse an album based on tunes he had written for the British film *Alfie*, which has Michael Caine playing the part of a sexually active ne'er-do-well. Rollins's strangely disjointed, yet engrossing, solo on the jaunty "Alfie's Theme" is a perfect example of his rethinking of improvisation. Hardly a straightforward discourse on the chords, the solo shows Rollins's obsession with the rhythms underlying a melody. The musical example shows the original theme, and then one of the arcane rhythmic variations to which he subjects this theme. The solo builds in a series of starts and stops, of mini-climaxes. (See music example.)

a) "Alfie's Theme," A section.

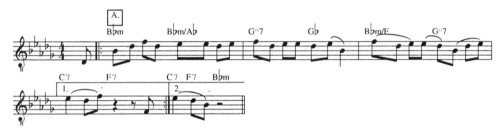

b) One of Rollins' improvised variations on the above, from the middle of his solo.

Example 15–6.
Sonny Rollins, "Alfie's Theme" and a sample of his improvisation.

ART BLAKEY AND HORACE SILVER

In 1948 and 1949, Max Roach's nearest rival as a drummer-leader, Art Blakey, visited Africa and studied its drumming. Blakey discouraged comparisons of his own music with African drumming, but he adopted several devices he may have heard there—including rapping on the side of his drum and using his elbow on the tom-tom to alter the pitch. (These techniques, whose ultimate derivation was African, had been used by previous African-American drummers, including Sid Catlett.) Several times in his career Blakey arranged sessions with multiple drummers. Still, he was best known as the leader—from 1955 until his death in 1990—of an enduring institution in small band jazz, the Jazz Messengers.

Born in Pittsburgh in 1919, Blakey drummed with Mary Lou Williams in 1942, with Fletcher Henderson in 1943 and 1944, and with the great Billy Eckstine band—the "cradle of bop"—from 1944 to 1947. By the 1950's his lusty, bashing style was in place. He's exceptionally accurate as well as powerful. Blakey's trademark as a drummer may be his forceful, quartz-steady closing of the hi-hat on every second and fourth beat, which became standard practice during the fifties. This beat is accompanied by strong attacks on the ride cymbal, and by frequent loud snare and bass drum accents in triplets or other cross-rhythms. He might chatter on the rim of a tom-tom for color, stutter in triplets on his snare, or dig his elbow into a tom-tom to change its pitch. He uses drum rolls that seem to explode. He rarely goes in for merely subtle effects: When he works over the tom-toms he sounds ready to swing a marching band.

His power forces his musicians to play hard, while in some ways limiting and controlling their improvisations. At the beginning of a wind solo, Blakey seems to let the rhythmic bottom fall out with a sudden hush. By the end of the second chorus, he's building inexorably, and the horn player must too. There's little room for romanticism in most of his bands: Typically, even his pianists develop a steely, extroverted sound. "Playing with Art Blakey," Horace Silver said, "you'd have to play a more propulsive, hard-driving beat . . . Art is native-like—it's like going into the jungle" (Ullman, *Jazz Lives*, p. 75). In 1947 Blakey introduced the rehearsal band he called the Seventeen Messengers, and then in December he recorded with eight members of that group for Blue Note. The Jazz Messengers as it is thought of today was started as a cooperative band by Blakey and pianist Horace Silver. In 1955, the quintet these men started—it also featured trumpeter Kenny Dorham, tenor saxophonist Hank Mobley and bassist Doug Watkins—recorded *Live at the Cafe Bohemia*, resulting eventually in three albums. In 1956, with Donald Byrd on trumpet, the Jazz Messengers recorded the album that helped give their music, and the music of countless followers, its name: *Hard Bop*.

In the tradition of bebop, Blakey's Messengers focus on soloing. Their arrangements are minimal: The horns play a theme, then solo at length and then repeat the theme. Nonetheless the Jazz Messengers developed a characteristic repertoire, because of Blakey's practice of encouraging his band members to write. On October 30, 1958, the edition of the Jazz Messengers that included the young trumpeter Lee Morgan, tenor saxophonist and composer Benny Golson, and pianist Bobby Timmons made what is in some ways the classic hard bop album: *Moanin'*. Timmons's title tune is a strutting blues that begins with a call-and-response pattern—the piano calls and the winds respond—that represents the essence of the new hip churchiness.

Morgan, just 20 at the time of the recording, takes a delightfully relaxed solo over the slapping shuffle beat, heavily accented on two and four, of Blakey.

Art Blakey around 1980.
(Photo by Michael Ullman)

Morgan was in the tradition of Clifford Brown in his early career, but even so he had a swagger and fat tone that was his own. His greatest success came in the sixties, discussed in Chapter 20.

Just as striking as "Moanin' " is the invigorating Benny Golson composition, "Blues March." "Blues March" has a delightful melody placed over a march beat rendered zestfully, even explosively, by Blakey, who behind the melody thumps along in 4/4 in deliberately plodding unison with the pianist. This march seems really to draw on marching bands, rather than the New Orleans bands, and it draws attention to the fact that many jazz players from World War II on got their basic musical training in high school bands and in the army. "Blues March" may be Benny Golson's biggest hit after his memorial to Clifford Brown, "I Remember Clifford" and his walking number, "Killer Joe," but while with the Messengers he wrote more subtle tunes that have become standards, including the purring "Whisper Not." A blustery, yet sophisticated saxophonist, Golson left Blakey in 1959 to form the Jazztet with trumpeter Art Farmer.

Blakey found a valuable replacement in tenor saxophonist and composer Wayne Shorter, who joined the band in 1959 bringing with him "Lester Left Town," a tribute to the recently deceased Lester Young with a suggestive, bouncy descending line as its main melody. Shorter stayed with Blakey while the personnel shifted around him until 1964. By 1961, he was part of the Jazz Messengers that brought trumpeter Freddie Hubbard, trombonist Curtis Fuller, and pianist Cedar Walton to prominence. Shorter, who would later help move Miles Davis away from his bop repertoire, wrote the band's most lasting charts.

Amidst the regular recordings of his working band, Blakey interspersed special projects. Recurrently, Blakey, who took the Muslim name Buhaina, got together with other drummers to reassert the connections among African, African-American, and African-Cuban drumming. Several dates included Latin players, such as his two-volume *Orgy in Rhythm* (1955) and his more ambitious *Holiday for Skins,* recorded in 1958 with drummers Art Taylor and Philly Joe Jones and a septet of Latin percussionists. Blakey reasserted the African connection with *The African Beat* in 1962.

The first pianist of the Jazz Messengers, Horace Silver, left the band in 1956 to try to make it as a leader. Silver was born in 1928 in Norwalk, Connecticut to a family that came originally from a one-time Portuguese colony, the Cape Verde islands off the coast of northern Africa. He proudly describes his family as "very racially mixed—we had white, black, Portuguese and Indian." The first music he remembers hearing were Cape Verdean tunes at house parties, simple, melodic pieces often, he says, in a minor key. He started playing saxophone and boogie-woogie piano, and listening to blues. His piano influences were, and this is more typical of his generation, Teddy Wilson and Art Tatum. Immediately he realized, however, that he couldn't copy Tatum—he hadn't the technique—and needed to develop a more circumscribed style. At first bebop sounded strange to him, but he learned to admire Bud Powell and Thelonious Monk.

By 1950, Silver was playing in a swing-oriented band around Connecticut. There Stan Getz heard and hired him, and used him and his catchy tunes on recordings. Silver moved to New York, where he accompanied Lester Young and in 1954 recorded with Miles Davis. When he was asked in 1956 by agent Jack Whittemore to put together his own band, he was surprised, but ready.

He had already produced a series of popular compositions, including the amusingly casual "Doodlin' " from 1954, and his gospel-like "The Preacher" from 1955. His 1956 recording *Six Pieces of Silver* proved to be an important "hard bop" session, introducing a swaggering Silver composition, "Sister Sadie."

Horace Silver at Sandy's in Beverly, Massachusetts, 1970's. (Photo by Michael Ullman)

Sophisticated though they are, these craftily arranged six pieces project an uncomplicated, joyous funkiness. His arrangements usually have, in the fashion of the bop bands, the horns playing the theme in the first chorus. Often, though, Silver adds written riffs and linking passages later that color and diversify the series of solos.

His "Señor Blues," a Latin-jazz hit from 1956, has a low-to-the-ground contained feeling that is sustained by Silver's crisp accompanying figures: Silver accompanies with a repeating rhythmic vamp. As a soloist, he's rarely expansive—he keeps his right hand arched over the keyboard, plays circular figures and closely voiced, stuttering chords, making ample use of the tremolos and crushed notes of the blues pianists. There are none of the widely sweeping runs of a Bud Powell in his playing. But what he does is distinctively melodic. There's humor in his blues, apparent from the title of one of his hits, the hip-waggling "Filthy McNasty," and from another piece, "Blowin' the Blues Away." There's lyricism as well. Perhaps the lyricism comes from his Cape Verdean background, to which Silver paid tribute in his popular "Song for My Father" from October 1964 and "The Cape Verdean Blues" of the following year.

CHARLES MINGUS AND ERIC DOLPHY

In Silver's wake there were plenty of less interesting, though ostensibly "soulful" records made in the late fifties and sixties by players eager to tap a popular market, but more serious musicians sought ways of integrating the churchy, bluesy strands of African-American experience with the innovations of modern jazz. We have mentioned one of these, the bassist and composer Charles Mingus. Mingus's first musical hero was Duke Ellington. Even after he was affected by bebop—he played with Charlie Parker—Mingus would spend much of the rest of his career trying to wed Ellington's sonorities with the passionate music of the black church.

Born in Arizona in 1922 and raised in Los Angeles, Mingus became a virtuoso bassist—with Ray Brown and Oscar Pettiford, the most influential of his generation—and a sterling composer of righteous blues, long-lined ballads, and complicated longer pieces. A turbulent man, a "tyrannical" leader, according to one of his band members, Mingus also led a series of exciting small bands in the late fifties and sixties. "Don't play that again," he is said to have warned a soloist after a particularly successful chorus—don't repeat yourself. But he hectored and bullied his players on stage, editing them as they went along, to try to make them fit his conception. Sometimes it worked splendidly: Some players, such as trombonist Jimmy Knepper, saxophonists Jackie McLean and, later, Bobby Jones, rarely sounded as good as when they were with Mingus. Others he wore down: His longtime pianist Jaki Byard, exhausted by the hassles of playing with Mingus, left Mingus in 1964 after two years. (He would play with him again briefly six years later.)

After studying with bassist Red Callender, Mingus started composing—his innovative "Chill of Death" from 1939 and "Half-mast Inhibition" from around 1940 were recorded finally on the albums *Pre-Bird* (1960) and *Let My Children Hear Music* (1971). He was also innovative as a bassist early on. He bragged that he had introduced pedal points—a repeated bass note, maintained despite changing chords—into jazz. As Brian Priestley noted in *Mingus: A Critical Biography* (p. 25), Mingus was telling the truth. He plays a pedal point in 1945 behind the first four bars of Illinois Jaquet's saxophone solo on "Jaquet Mood" (sometimes mistakenly issued under the name "Merle's Mood").

In the forties he played with Kid Ory, Louis Armstrong and Lionel Hampton. For Hampton he wrote a bass feature, part avant-garde jazz and part swing, called "Mingus Fingers." The piece, whose recording was proof of Hampton's open-mindedness, begins with impressionistic flute and clarinet runs based on the whole tone scale. Then Mingus enters, featuring himself on the theme as Ellington had featured Jimmy Blanton. Despite the interesting colors of the muted brass, flute and clarinet behind him—another hint of Ellingtonia—the theme seems headed towards a fairly straightforward AABA form until the end of the bridge, at which point the last A does not appear. Instead there is a complicated build-up by the whole band. This launches Mingus, who uses the bow during the break and then plucks his way through a fluent solo which involves some impressive dexterity at the end.

He even breaks up the rhythm at times behind Lionel Hampton's restrained vibraphone solo—one of the few solos in Hampton's long career that could be called restrained! Hampton is followed by a passage of dissonant chords, after which Mingus walks while the trombones state a theme for the first two A sections, and the trumpets engage in a wah-wah dialogue with the saxophones barking back in short attacks. This is downright Ellingtonian. Again we encounter the buildup, with woodwind lines racing through it, at the point where one would expect the final A section. A final whole tone run by Mingus brings on a coda with Hampton and the band. "Mingus Fingers" is one of a relatively few Mingus compositions for big band, the longest being the posthumously performed *Epitaph*. Mingus also arranged a spooky "Body and Soul" for Hampton—it appears uncredited on a recording of a 1948 broadcast.

Mingus became famous in 1950 as the one black member of the Red Norvo Trio. It was a remarkable chamber group. Bop guitarist Tal Farlow was known for his speed and lyrical sound. Veteran vibraphonist Red Norvo had played with Paul Whiteman in the twenties, led a band featuring singer Mildred Bailey in the thirties, accompanied Benny Goodman in 1944 and 1945, and recorded "Hallelujah" with Charlie Parker in 1945. Mingus provided the drive, the warm centered sound, that Norvo wanted, and in the trio's recordings, he proved as buoyant a soloist: He showed himself the heir to Jimmy Blanton.

He quit when the trio went on television, and Norvo gave in to pressure to exclude Mingus. Television wasn't ready for an integrated group, and his companions weren't ready to make a stand. Mingus settled in New York, and took part in the rehearsals and recordings of a loose confederation of composers and players called the Jazz Composer's Workshop. Teo Macero and Teddy Charles were the other mainstays of this workshop. For Mingus, the independence of such self-organized groups was desirable: He started his own record company, Debut, in 1952, and in 1960 helped organize a counter-festival to the Newport Jazz Festival. With such musicians, he recorded some early works which were played with a cool sonority he would later abandon. "Eclipse" from 1953 brings out Mingus's classical leanings more clearly than did "Mingus Fingers." "Eclipse" was originally written for Billie Holiday, although it is highly unlikely that she performed this exotic setting of a poem. As performed with singer Janet Thurlow, it begins out of tempo with Mingus and cellist Jackson Wiley bowing their instruments. After Thurlow's first vocal chorus, the out-of-tempo introduction returns, this time extended for several measures while Mingus brings in lines for flute and alto supported by low notes for trombone and baritone saxophone. Meanwhile drummer Kenny Clarke has been restricted to ominous rolls using mallets on his drums. The piece ends as Thurlow intones the last few lines of the poem. The powerful bass lines that underpin these arrangements make Mingus's music seem about to erupt.

It did by 1955. It is startling to go from Mingus's highly dissonant, experimental "Gregarian Chant" of 1954 to pieces such as his "Haitian Fight Song," recorded in 1955 and again in 1957. In the interim, Mingus decided that he would not write down what he wanted his musicians to play: He decided to teach them by ear instead. The results were liberating. Mingus went back to the blues and also to the sounds of the church: When they weren't playing one of his gorgeous ballads (such as the May 1959 "Self Portrait in Three Colors") his bands would wail, shriek and cry, and Mingus would prod them by yelling along with the horns. (In the sixties, his favorite ejaculation was, "I know what I know.") He didn't become a "soul" player—he was too difficult to categorize. When he talked about the blues, he sounded ambivalent. He made *Blues and Roots*, he said, at the urging of his record producer, who was responding to critics who said he didn't swing enough. His response was complicated: "I thought it over. I was born swinging and clapped my hands in church as a little boy, but I've grown up and I like to do things other than just swing. But blues can do more than just swing. So I agreed."

Blues and Roots (February 1959) is part of a legendary series of structurally fascinating, rowdy, and impassioned small band recordings by Mingus, usually featuring trombonist Jimmy Knepper and drummer Danny Richmond. Richmond's story gives a fascinating insight into Mingus's world. He started playing rhythm-and-blues saxophone and then began on the drums. Mingus heard him play drums, hired him in 1956, and remolded his style. He spoke of Richmond as if he had been at one time putty in his capacious hands.

Mingus said he could never play his "Haitian Fight Song" without thinking of racial hatred and strife. The 1957 version (SCCJ) begins with a powerful bass introduction. Mingus's big tone and agile technique are used ominously—listening to this solo is like waiting for a thunderstorm to break. The theme that follows consists entirely of a repeated note idea in the minor mode played stiffly with a kind of stuttering expectancy over a pedal point reiteration of the G tonic—as in the modal jazz to come, there is no chord sequence, just a tonic. (A melody played by the tenor saxophone in the 1955 version is not used here.) In both the beginning and ending statements of this theme, Mingus has the band build slowly and terrifyingly in a crescendo that climaxes with an eerie Mingus scream over the wild flailing of Knepper's trombone. For the solos, Mingus uses the chord progression of a 12-bar minor blues. After the first two choruses of the trombone and saxophone solos, Mingus suddenly doubles the tempo for two choruses. When he shifts back to the original tempo, he has the rhythm section play stop-time for a chorus. He also has the band play backgrounds to the solos, and, in the final ensemble, asks them to improvise collectively. The recording builds to Mingus's final ecstatic, hair-raising shout. Here was a sophisticated music that was every bit as openly emotional as gospel, and as drivingly powerful as rhythm and blues.

Mingus uses collective improvisation daringly, and for new expressive effects, drawing from his ensembles a raw group shout or, at times, a sarcastic collage of simulated street sounds. At the end of "Pithecanthropus Erectus," recorded in January 1956, his group's free moans, played over an accelerating rhythm section, simulate the story—presumably anguished—of that ancestor of modern man. At the same session, Mingus had his players create traffic sounds in the introduction to "A Foggy Day." "Reincarnation of a Lovebird," his 1957 tribute to Charlie Parker, begins with his players throwing out little snatches of Parker melodies in an apparently rehearsed, out-of-time, dialogue. His use of tempo changes within a single piece is almost unique in jazz, though standard practice in classical music.

Charles Mingus at the Jazz Workshop, Boston, 1970's. (Photo by Michael Ullman)

He liked to evoke earlier jazz figures. He paid tribute to Jelly Roll Morton with a rollicking, good-natured theme "My Jelly Roll Soul," to Lester Young with the cooly elegant blues "Goodbye Pork Pie Hat" and to Parker with the amusing "Bird Calls" and a piece called "Gunslinging Bird," which he later said should have been entitled – "If Charlie Parker Were a Gunslinger, There'd Be a Whole Lot of Dead Copycats." He liked to play games with titles. His 1960 version of "All the Things You Are" was entitled "All the Things You Could be by Now if Sigmund Freud's Wife Was Your Mother." In 1971, he took the title of a Morris West novel, *The Shoes of the Fisherman,* and made "The Shoes of the Fisherman's Wife are Some Jiveass Slippers."

In 1960, when "free jazz" was being introduced by Ornette Coleman and others, Mingus had a small group with alto saxophonist Eric Dolphy, with whom he had a special affinity. Like Mingus, Dolphy was brought up in Los Angeles, where he was born in 1928. Dolphy studied clarinet, then alto saxophone, flute and bass clarinet. He was a virtuoso on each instrument. His alto saxophone playing was particularly influential: Dolphy took the bebop style of Charlie Parker and made it more angular. Dolphy's flute playing was just as eloquent as his alto, though marginally more conventional: His tone is not as startling on that instrument. Dolphy also became the first jazz virtuoso on bass clarinet. He went further than Parker harmonically, and he developed his own, often almost awkward sounding rhythms which are very different from Parker's fluid lines. Typically he would begin a solo in a flurry from the outer limits of the harmony involved, and his alto had a sharp, voice-like quality. The titles of the first records under his own name – *Outward Bound* and *Out There* (both 1960) – seem perfectly appropriate.

Dolphy featured his bass clarinet on solo versions of Billie Holiday's "God Bless the Child," which appears on three of his recordings. In each recording, Dolphy introduces the piece with a technically difficult swirling figure that moves over much of the range of the clarinet, and then interposes Billie Holiday's melody in fragile segments. Behind the wall of technical devices, the melody sounds as innocent as a child peeking shyly around a fence. (See music example.)

In 1962 he performed at the Ojai Music Festival the solo flute work, "Density 21.5" by avant-garde classical composer Edgard Varèse. In 1962 and 1963, Dolphy performed a series of pieces by third stream composer Gunther Schuller, including his "Densities," on which he played clarinet, "Night Music" featuring his bass clarinet, and an alto saxophone feature that had been recorded with Ornette Coleman in 1960, "Abstraction" (all on *Vintage Dolphy,* GM Records). In doing so, Dolphy helped realize a relationship between avant-garde jazz and the cutting edge of twentieth century composition that continues to be important today.

His goal was to make his instruments speak "like a human voice," as he once said. Mingus took him literally. On October 20, 1960, on "What Love," Mingus and Dolphy vocalize freely on their instruments – just the two of them, Dolphy chattering volubly, cackling comically, Mingus barely enunciating in

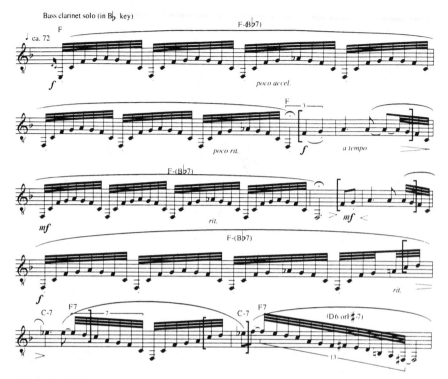

Example 15–7.
Eric Dolphy's bass clarinet solo version of "God Bless the Child," first A
section, from the Copenhagen recording, September 8, 1961. Brackets show the
notes of Billie Holiday's song. This example is in B♭ key, one whole step
higher than concert pitch.

mumbling bursts of excited commentary. This was avant-garde playing perhaps,
but when the two, in an earlier, live performance of Mingus's "What Love"
recorded at Antibes in 1960, engage in comparable conversations, an appreciative crowd eggs them on. Mingus asserted that Dolphy and he knew exactly
what each was saying to the other.

At the October 1960 session for Candid Records, Mingus also recorded a
celebrated number, "Fables of Faubus," a complicated piece involving several
tempo changes during each solo and including some street theater in its verbal
denunciations of Governor Orville Faubus of Arkansas, whose resistance to
desegregation made him notorious. The year before, Columbia Records had
objected to his outspoken chanting and singing and made him record "Fables"
as an instrumental. (See music example)

Mingus's groups with Dolphy were among his most electric. But Dolphy
was interested in exploring other opportunities as well. He toured Europe with
John Coltrane in the winter of 1961–1962, worked as a leader and freelanced with
Mingus in the next years, and returned to Mingus for a European tour in 1964.
To Mingus's dismay, at the end of the tour he elected to stay in Europe—but
died there of heart failure in June. He was 36.

Example 15–8.
Charles Mingus, "Fables of Faubus," beginning of theme and some of the words. In some recordings the intro continues under the A section.

Mingus's later career was varied and somewhat erratic. In September 1962, he recorded the trio pieces with Duke Ellington and Max Roach that were released as *Money Jungle.* In 1963, he recorded a moody solo piano album, and an extended piece for larger ensemble, the balletic *Black Saint and the Sinner Lady.* With almost the same ensemble, he recorded later that year one of the best versions of "Mood Indigo" outside of Ellington's own performances. Then he made no studio recordings for eight years and only a few live ones.

The fault was not entirely his own. The late sixties were hard for acoustic jazz in general and for Mingus's uncompromising work. (His personality, also uncompromising, did not ingratiate him with recording executives.) This bleak period is dramatized in Thomas Reichman's hour-long documentary *Mingus,* filmed in 1966 and released in 1968. This movie shows Mingus being evicted from his apartment, with sheets of his music scattered about and trampled on.

In 1971, he was asked by Columbia Records to make a big band album: *Let My Children Hear Music.* He assembled a collection of his extended pieces for large ensembles written over a thirty-year period. On "The Shoes of the Fisherman's Wife are Some Jiveass Slippers," orchestrated by Sy Johnson, he incorporates many of his typical devices—rapid shifts in mood and tempo, elegantly lengthy themes, sections of free blowing—in an arrangement whose wideranging sonorities are made to sound entirely natural. Throughout much of the seventies, Mingus travelled with a small, enthusiastic band, but seemed less interested than previously in shaping its sounds to his own vision. By 1977, he was feeling the first effects of amyotrophic lateral sclerosis—Lou Gehrig's disease. Still, with the help of Jack Walrath and Paul Jeffrey, he completed that year the extended works "Three Worlds of Drums," "Cuumbia and Jazz Fusion" and "Three or Four Shades of Blues." In January 1978, he finished another Parker tribute, "Something Like a Bird." All were recorded under his supervision, though he was no longer able to play. His last works, songs commissioned by singer Joni Mitchell, were completed in 1978 when Mingus was virtually paralyzed. He died on January 5, 1979. After his death, researcher Andrew Homzy discovered the unfinished and frayed score of a piece that had been partially performed and recorded in 1962: Mingus's eighteen-part, two-hour work entitled "Epitaph." Gunther Schuller was called in to complete this collection of well-known Mingus tunes and new material, all intended by the composer for a thirty-piece band. It was finally performed and recorded in 1989.

ERROLL GARNER, OSCAR PETERSON, AND BILLY TAYLOR

One of the most important developments of the mid-fifties was the return to public performance of Thelonious Monk, whose music was discussed in Chapter 12. At the beginning of the decade, he was a neglected figure. After a wrongful conviction on drug possession—he was arrested when driving a car in which another man was carrying drugs—he had lost his cabaret card, a card issued by the New York police that entertainers needed in order to perform in New York bars and clubs. Although he continued to record, he would rarely perform live. Things began to turn for Monk in 1955, when he began recording for Riverside Records, and the breakthrough came in 1957, when he was able to perform with a quartet—the first included John Coltrane—during a long engagement at the Five Spot in Manhattan. Monk became a star, a symbol of hipness.

Two of the other most popular jazz pianists since the fifties are Erroll Garner and Oscar Peterson. They are very different figures. Peterson was schooled in classical music, practiced feverishly as a youth—up to eighteen hours a day, he asserts—and developed a suave and forceful technique, if not the harmonic and rhythmic daring, that rivalled Art Tatum, his acknowledged master. Garner was a self-taught pianist who was said not to be able to read music: His grunting rhythmic vigor, his stuttering block chords in his left hand, his heavily accented, stiff-legged stride patterns were extensions of Earl Hines. But there was more to him than that: His impressionistic harmonies, especially on ballads, show an active mind well able to hear—and to imitate—much of what was happening in twentieth century music.

Garner (1921–1977) must have learned from Fats Waller as well—he had some of Waller's delight in dynamic contrast and other extravagant pianistic gestures, such as a heavy chord followed by exaggeratedly light repetitions. Like those of Hines, his improvised introductions—mini-compositions sometimes—were barely related to the tunes that followed, but they charmed and surprised audiences: They seemed sometimes to surprise Garner as well. There was no more effervescent instrumentalist in the late fifties, and yet Garner rarely said a word to his audiences. His uninhibited rhythms and short, easily grasped phrases made his warmth available to all. And it didn't hurt that he wrote at least one universally loved song: "Misty." Garner, who recorded with Parker in 1947, and soloed on 52nd Street, was a poll winner in the late fifties: His 5,910 votes in the 1958 Playboy poll, for instance, outdistanced Brubeck, who came in second with 5,897, and his 1955 recording, *Concert by the Sea*, was one of the best-selling jazz albums of the decade. Garner died in 1977.

Born in Montreal in 1925, Oscar Peterson had already recorded in Montreal (in 1944 and 1945) when he was introduced to American audiences by Norman Granz in 1949. Granz launched the pianist, who became virtually the house pianist of his various record labels, at a Carnegie Hall concert. Peterson, an extraordinarily fluid and adaptable artist, toured with Granz's Jazz at the Philharmonic troupes, and recorded for Granz with scores of musicians, notably Ben Webster, Lester Young, Dizzy Gillespie, and in the sixties and the seventies, with Clark Terry and Milt Jackson. (It is likely that Peterson has recorded more than any pianist in jazz.) By 1951, he had assembled, in imitation of Nat Cole, a trio of piano, bass and guitar: From 1953 to 1958, when Peterson decided to substitute a drummer for the guitar, this trio featured guitarist Herb Ellis and bassist Ray Brown. The trio with drummer Ed Thigpen and Brown, Peterson's most celebrated group, lasted from 1959 until 1965.

Peterson can make piano playing look easy. A large man with capacious hands, he is best known for his powerful swing on uptempo tunes—and on compositions such as John Lewis's "The Golden Striker," which he unexpectedly makes into an uptempo swinger. A Peterson performance might start with some gentle strumming and the careful etching of a ballad's theme: It tends to end, after a gradual crescendo, in thumping block chords decorated by showy glissandos. In between, Peterson might interject a chorus of stride, concentrate on left hand walking tenths, or dazzle his audience with Tatumesque runs. The outlines of his uptempo performances can be predictable, but he always plays with tremendous drive and great blues feeling.

On ballads, he concentrates on melody rather than on his exuberant technical accomplishments. Listeners should not overlook the touchingly modest recordings of Cole Porter tunes such as "Everytime We Say Goodbye" and "In the Still of the Night," found on *Oscar Peterson Plays the Cole Porter Song Book* (Verve, 1959). A supremely accomplished musician, whose unaccompanied solo playing in the eighties has developed increasing depth, Peterson has never been a revolutionary: He's not pushing any boundaries, except technical ones.

Another technically gifted pianist is Billy Taylor, born, like Garner, in 1921. Taylor got involved with the modernists early on, becoming a protégé of Tatum at the same time that he mastered the music of Parker and Gillespie. He went on to perform with both of them and with his own trios. He composed many fine bop compositions and eventually wrote for bands and orchestras. He is admired for his lyrical sense (displayed on his gorgeous 1954 recording of "Theodora") and for his ability to improvise counterpoint with both hands as equals. Taylor, who earned a Doctorate of Music Education in 1975, is known as one of the most eloquent spokespersons for jazz on television and radio, and in his books and many articles.

Marian McPartland, born in England in 1920, is a marvelous modern jazz pianist whose trio work in the 1950's predated some of the romantic stylings of Bill Evans. More recently, she has proven to be adept at totally spontaneous improvisation without any preset chords. On her unique radio program, "Piano Jazz," ongoing since 1979, she chats and performs with guest pianists. A regular highlight is her freely improvised portrait of her guest.

Billy Taylor at Tufts University, Medford, Massachusetts, 1980. (Photo by Michael Ullman)

Among other pianists, the remarkable Phineas Newborn, a Memphis native with a particularly fluent technique, took Art Tatum as his model, and in Los Angeles, Hampton Hawes brought a particular bluesiness and lyricism to what he learned from Bud Powell. All of these artists played a vital part in the resurgent jazz scene of the late fifties, a period of an almost confusing amalgam of styles, movements and directions. Several developments seemed inevitable to contemporary observers. Drummers would inevitably be, Martin Williams presciently suggested (*Down Beat*, 1958), moving toward playing more and more complex polyrhythms. George Russell observed the signs that musicians were moving away from the fast chord changes of bebop: "modal" jazz, which Miles Davis popularized, was one sign, and the beginnings of "free" jazz, as seen at least by a few in Cecil Taylor, was another. One astute observer, Gunther Schuller, felt confident enough in 1958 to predict the future: He believed that on the one hand, the structured improvising he had described in Sonny Rollins, with its thematic and motivic unity, was one answer to where jazz was going. Another was towards larger and more complex compositions. No one could have predicted the advent in 1959 of Ornette Coleman, whose virtually free quartet performances transformed part of the landscape of jazz. Nor could Schuller have predicted that in a year Sonny Rollins would have retired, albeit temporarily, and that John Coltrane would take his place as the tenor saxophonist of the future.

At the center of much of what happened in the fifties and sixties was trumpeter Miles Davis, who was, as already discussed, featured in the Charlie Parker quintet, and who was a key figure in the cool school. That was in the forties. By 1955, after a brief retirement of his own, Miles Davis was hot.

16 Miles Davis

> *"That's what I tell all my musicians;*
> *I tell them be ready to play what you know*
> *and play above what you know. Anything might happen*
> *above what you've been used to playing."*
> —Miles Davis

Few musicians brought as many new sounds and sights to the jazz world as Miles Davis. An intense, ambitious musician, he managed in an era of virtuoso instrumentalists to make a limited instrumental technique suggest infinite possibilities. Part of his success came from his remarkably pure sound: Muted or with open horn, a Miles Davis solo seems confidential, and yet piercingly straightforward. Davis said that he discovered his sound in lessons with the East St. Louis trumpet teacher Elwood Buchanan, who told him to stop using vibrato, because he would be shaking soon enough in life. He had something of Louis Armstrong's mastery of the dramatic opening: The beginnings of his solos startle and awaken. Through much of his career, those solos were developed with a clarity, an intentness, that his heros would have admired: "I learned about improvising from Bean [Coleman Hawkins], Monk, Don Byas, Lucky Thompson, and Bird" (*Miles: The Autobiography*, p. 78).

He must have learned about assembling a band from Ellington. One of the great leaders in jazz, Davis, like Ellington and Mingus, consistently put together groups stronger than their individual parts. In the forties, he fit into the Charlie Parker quintet, he realized, because "I gave Bird space." Later, he would hire musicians to fill up the space around his own playing without intruding on his own. He looked for contrast—Coltrane's effusive, multi-note solos with his own spare statements, or pianist Red Garland's delicate chording over drummer Philly Joe Jones's powerful cymbal work. Davis showed a preference for tough tenors (Sonny Rollins, Coltrane, Hank Mobley, George Coleman), light-fingered pianists (Garland, Bill Evans and Herbie Hancock) and, from the mid-fifties on, robust drummers who booted the band along.

In the fifties the trumpeter changed the manners in jazz performance when he turned his back on audiences and refused to announce his tunes. No Louis Armstrong stage tricks for him. (But when asked a leading question about

Armstrong, he praised the older man's playing: It was impossible, he asserted, for a trumpeter to play something Armstrong hadn't already done.) Later Davis helped improve working conditions for jazz players when he insisted on playing only three sets a night. Previously, musicians were frequently expected to perform for 40 minutes and take 20 off during as many as six hours. Davis's common sense on this issue was not universally appreciated. Some fans grumbled that modern jazz musicians no longer enjoyed playing the way the older ones had.

Davis's accomplishments were impressive. So was his gruff, withdrawn, and even lordly manner, even among his musicians. Bassist Miroslav Vitous said that Davis spoke to him only once in the many weeks that he played with him in the early seventies, and that was to ask his young sideman to rush another group off the stage so that the trumpeter could play and go home. Davis auditioned pianist Herbie Hancock by inviting him over to his house, and setting him up in the cellar with bassist Ron Carter and drummer Tony Williams. He told them to play and listened over the intercom. Hancock had to ask whether he made the band. Davis's laconic criticisms, his infrequent bits of advice, and occasional orders to band members, have become legendary. He told a succession of his pianists to play like his hero, Ahmad Jamal. He made an electric pianist out of Herbie Hancock by having the instrument set up when Hancock showed up for a recording session.

Miles Davis in Ypsilanti, Michigan, early 1970's.
(Photo by Michael Ullman)

Davis's development was as swift as it was public. Davis was born on May 26, 1926. He had a comfortable childhood in East St. Louis as the son of a tough, but doting, well-to-do father, and a less understanding mother. His early years were, inevitably, marred by racism. Davis remembers being the best trumpet player in his high school, at a time when he was imitating the flamboyant style of Benny Goodman trumpeter Harry James: White students got the first chair. When he was 15, Davis got a union card and a job with a jumping small band called Eddie Randall's (sometimes spelled Randle's) Blue Devils. That band brought him local recognition, including praise from one of his idols, trumpeter Clark Terry, whose equally clear, rounded tone and jubilant virtuosity earned him a stint with Count Basie, and in the fifties, with Duke Ellington. Davis's world opened up in the summer of 1944 when the Billy Eckstine big band came to St. Louis shy a trumpet player. Davis was asked to sit in. Later he said, "I couldn't read a thing from listening to Diz and Bird," who were both in the band.

He made his way in the fall of 1944 to New York City, ostensibly to study at the Juilliard School of Music. He found himself learning more from Gillespie, Coleman Hawkins and from Thelonious Monk. Davis's autobiography reveals Monk's far-reaching influence on him. That may be surprising, but it makes sense: Davis learned from Monk's rhythms, his dramatic use of space in solos, and from his insistence on melody. He also liked Monk's "manipulation of funny sounding chord progressions" (*Miles: The Autobiography*, p. 58). Davis became a student of chord progressions. His questions and observations inspired George Russell's theoretical studies which continue to today: In the forties Davis told Russell that he wanted to know every possible chord.

Sitting in with Coleman Hawkins and Eddie "Lockjaw" Davis on 52nd Street, Miles Davis found favor with older musicians. He first recorded behind vocalist "Rubberlegs" Williams on April 24, 1945. This was a session he later said he would rather forget, and on which he was mostly inaudible. He was featured at his second session, with Charlie Parker, on November 26, 1945. Nineteen years old and nervous, he seemed at first a somewhat bumbling, insecure stylist without the agility or panache of Dizzy Gillespie. Gillespie took over the trumpet chair at the session for the virtuoso performance of "Koko." Davis was reviewed brutally as someone trying to sound like Gillespie and failing.

But Davis's tentative phrases contained the germ of an original idea: a mellower sonority for modern jazz. Two years later, he would record four of his own tunes for Savoy, and this time Parker would be a sideman on tenor saxophone. A 21-year-old who could make a tenor player out of Charlie Parker knew what he was doing. He found the proper setting for his trumpet sound in compositions like "Milestones" and "Sippin' at Bells" which were darker in texture than comparable Parker arrangements. Davis's pieces were intellectual, intricate. His distinctive voice as a player began to emerge as well on ballads with Parker such as the 1947 "My Old Flame" and "Out of Nowhere," recorded for Dial.

Davis played with Charlie Parker relatively steadily between 1945 and 1949. By 1949, he was disturbed by what he perceived as Parker's irresponsibility to the band, and eager to try a different kind of music. "Bebop," he said, "didn't have the humanity of Duke Ellington." In the "Birth of the Cool" arrangements, discussed in Chapter 14, the trumpeter "wanted the instruments to sound like human voices, and they did" (*Miles: The Autobiography*, p. 118).

Dizzy Gillespie was wary of some members of the cool school: "Musically speaking, the cool period always reminded me of white people's music. There was no guts in that music, not much rhythm either" (*To Be or Not . . . to Bop*, p. 360). Still, he generously praised the gutsiness of Miles Davis because of his ability to play the blues. A series of appearances by Davis with the Tadd Dameron Quintet in Paris during May of 1949 show that Davis had also mastered the fast tempos of bebop. Perhaps because he was subbing for Fats Navarro, Davis played brightly flaring, uptempo lines on "Ornithology" and "Rifftide." French critic Henri Renaud, who was present, notes the audience's surprise: "On medium and fast tempos, people expected him to play *mezzo forte* and he played *forte*. Everybody thought he only felt at home in the medium register of his horn, only to discover that he could brilliantly court the high notes." His extroversion may also have been the result of his happiness at the way he was received in Paris: Miles Davis wasn't the first jazz musician to be overjoyed at the respect with which European audiences and musicians treated him. At any rate, the contented trumpeter announced the tunes for Tadd Dameron's set, and played joyfully. If later he did not choose to follow up on this style, it is because he had other goals.

Davis's developing style was something more than Gillespie played lower or slower. Soon, Davis could do some things Gillespie shied away from. By the 1950's, his blues had a rich, down-home quality. On cuts like the 1951 "Bluing," Davis sounds sophisticated while suggesting a chaste intimacy unparalleled in modern jazz. "Miles is deep," Gillespie has said—deeper into the blues than Gillespie himself. Dizzy was once criticized for his thin tone; from the beginning Davis's was vibrant. Gillespie is for many listeners an acquired taste, while Davis's music seems to arouse instant passion. (But not universal love: In 1989 and 1990, Whitney Balliett and Stanley Crouch wrote scathing indictments of Davis's entire output.) Gillespie's trumpet, one might say, dances before your eyes; Davis's breathed down your neck.

The years between 1951 and 1954 have often been described as a period in which Davis, plagued by a drug problem, uncharacteristically fumbled. He played less in New York and recorded less frequently. But 1951 was not totally disastrous. Davis was signed to a contract with Prestige and recorded his first date on January 17, 1951 with Sonny Rollins. The second Prestige date in March was under the leadership of Lee Konitz, and included George Russell's "Ezz-thetic," a daring transfiguration of Cole Porter's "Love for Sale." On his third Prestige session, in October, Davis came back into the studio with two young saxophonists, Jackie McLean and Sonny Rollins, and sounded in their nervy company like an old master. Rollins was already revered locally, according to Davis. It was a session devoted primarily to the blues—"Bluing"—and to Davis originals such as "Dig." The results were mixed—Rollins had a persistent squeak and McLean was edgy throughout—but Davis's playing showed his beautifully matured sound. And on "It's Only a Paper Moon," he laid out the melody with sublime bounciness and good cheer that belied his image as uniformly intense, even dour.

Soon Davis was in bad shape. Most of 1951 and early 1952 were for him a period of "deep fog." In 1952 and 1953, he wandered, playing inconsistently with a variety of personnel, popping up for occasional dates such as his recorded appearance in St. Louis with tenor saxophonist Jimmy Forrest and a local rhythm section. He was sick. Characteristically, he decided to cure his addiction himself by force of will. He went home to East St. Louis and locked himself in a room until he was, at least temporarily, cured. Then, not wanting to return immediately to the temptations of New York, he went to Detroit.

Tommy Flanagan remembers playing piano with Davis in a club called the Bluebird. Tenor saxophonist Billy Mitchell was the ostensible leader, but Davis, bearing the prestige of his records with Charlie Parker, more or less took over. "We just cooked," remembers Flanagan, adding: "Miles always knows exactly what he wants. That makes him easy to work with." Flanagan recorded with Davis in 1956, but didn't last with the Davis quintet. Davis instructed the pianist to play "block chords, not the way Milt Buckner did. In the style of Ahmad Jamal." Jamal was an unexpected interest of Davis's. A Pittsburgh-born pianist, Jamal formed in 1951 a trio called The Three Strings—like other trios led by Nat Cole and Tatum, it consisted of a guitar, bass and piano. He played chamber jazz—some called it cocktail jazz—with a light, clear tone and in an unhurried, sophisticated style. His most famous recording was the 1958 *Ahmad Jamal at the Pershing,* which he performed with bassist Israel Crosby and drummer Vernell Fournier. It contained "Poinciana" which he introduces with his subtle version of the block chord style, and "But Not For Me," whose melody he sketches way up in the treble and in dancing chords—in his solo he repeats a little six note phrase a dozen times. Jamal's repertoire, which included "Surrey with the Fringe on Top," "Green Dolphin Street" and his own "Ahmad's Blues" became a source for Davis, who recorded all these tunes and others that Jamal helped popularize.

During 1951 and 1952 Davis continued to record, for Blue Note with such cohorts as J.J. Johnson, and then for Prestige in January 1953, first with Parker on tenor in a troubled session that ended when Parker became intoxicated, and then more genially with Al Cohn and Zoot Sims, white tenor saxophonists influenced by Lester Young. The latter date seemed to suggest that he was returning to his earlier "cool" style.

Davis had a different idea, as he demonstrated in a celebrated session, recorded on April 29, 1954. Leaving others to exploit the innovations of his 1949 recordings, Davis assembled a group that included drummer Kenny Clarke and pianist Horace Silver and recorded "Blue 'n' Boogie" and "Walkin'." Of this session, Davis said: "Man, that album turned my whole life and career around." Characteristically, Davis knew exactly what he was doing: with "Walkin'," Davis said, "I wanted to take the music back to the fire and improvisations of bebop. . . . But also, I wanted to take the music forward into a more funky kind of blues" (*Miles: The Autobiography*, p. 177). "Blue 'n' Boogie" begins with a drum solo by Kenny Clarke whose vigor announces the Davis renaissance. The trumpeter's confident solo has a continuity and liveliness that shows him at a new level—taking full advantage of the relatively recent innovation of the long-playing record, Davis builds a solo over his series of choruses, creating gradual shifts in tension that keep his solo fresh today. He's even better, simpler and, as he said, funkier, on "Walkin'," the Richard Carpenter blues that became a staple of Davis's repertoire. Once the Davis record was released, it became a staple of everyone's repertoire.

Eight months later, on December 24, 1954, Davis led a session that surpassed even "Walkin'." Davis added Thelonious Monk to three quarters of the Modern Jazz Quartet of the time—vibraphonist Milt Jackson, bassist Percy Heath and drummer Kenny Clarke—and recorded six tracks. The standouts are the two takes of Milt Jackson's familiar, easy-going blues, "Bag's Groove," and two of "The Man I Love." By this time, Davis's placement of phrases was perfection itself, natural and yet surprisingly personal, and his tone was lustrous. He chose casual, walking tempos, and then in a move that created mild controversy, asked Monk to lay out behind his own solos.

Davis's explanation is succinct and reasonable: "Trumpets don't have that many notes, so you really have to push that rhythm section and that wasn't Monk's thing. A trumpet player needs the rhythm section to be hot even if he is playing a ballad. You got to have that kicking thing, and most of the time that wasn't Monk's bag. So I just told him to lay out when I was playing, because I wasn't comfortable with the way he voiced his changes, and I was the only horn on that date. I wanted to hear the rhythm section stroll without a piano sound. I wanted to hear space in the music. I was just starting to use the concept of space breathing through the music—composition and arrangements—that I had picked up from Ahmad Jamal, and we even cut a tune he used to play that I loved—'The Man I Love' " (*Miles: The Autobiography*, p. 187). A renewed sense of intimacy with the listener, appropriate to Davis's style, resulted. Monk may have been offended, but he contributed striking solos on "The Man I Love" and "Bag's Groove" (discussed and transcribed in Chapter 12).

Davis, like other musicians, feared that the new editing technology of tape would take away some of the spontaneity of jazz. Believing that even the mistakes are part of jazz, he practiced what he preached: Some issues of the first take of "The Man I Love" begin with a false start. Then one hears the musicians disagree over the introduction, and Davis's voice saying to the recording engineer, "Put this on the record—*all* of it."

After the dispute, both takes of "The Man I Love" demonstrate the richness of the trumpeter's matured sound. He creates an eloquent sketch of the melody, with some heartfelt lyrical additions. Both takes of the Milt Jackson blues, "Bag's Groove," are compelling as well, but the more famous first take is surely one of the greatest jazz recordings. Davis sounds buoyant and relaxed—even chipper—on the exquisite first take, where his strolling phrases have an internal logic that is particularly noticeable in this informal setting. Here and elsewhere in this period, Davis often begins a new chorus with a motive he can develop for the first eight measures—he may be following Lester Young in this practice. (See music example.)

Example 16–1.
Miles Davis, "Bag's Groove" (1954), last three choruses of opening solo.

Davis plays with an almost exaggerated triplet feel, habitually tonguing the second of every pair of eighth notes to produce a near staccato. He reserves his high notes for the dramatic last choruses. Davis is orderly, even on this session dedicated to a succession of solos by strong, carefully matched, personalities.

The remaining piece from the session, "Swing Spring," has been described as modal (*Milestones I*, pp. 194-195). Its scalar theme may have suggested modal jazz to some listeners, but underneath the solos one hears a variant of "I Got Rhythm" changes, not a modal lingering on one or two chords. Still, its quirky theme provokes a finely restrained Miles Davis solo and several exuberant choruses by Milt Jackson, whose bluesy depth and subtle use of dynamic accents helped to make him the premier influence on modern jazz vibraphone.

THE QUINTET WITH JOHN COLTRANE

By 1956, Davis was back at the top of his profession, having been rediscovered as a result of his new recordings and, perhaps, as a result of his appearance at the Newport Jazz Festival of 1955. He had assembled a quintet with customary care, beginning with drummer Philly Joe Jones. Jones, who had recorded with Davis in January 1953, was a brilliant technician with an explosive, polyrhythmic style and a bright airy cymbal sound that seemed to illuminate Davis's own playing. "Philly Joe was the fire," Davis said; "he *knew* everything I was going to play; he anticipated me, felt what I was thinking." Sometimes unnervingly so: "Sometimes I used to tell him not to do that lick of his with me, but *after* me. And so that thing that he used to do after I played something—that rim shot—became known as the 'Philly lick' " (*Miles: The Autobiography*, p. 199). (See music example.)

Example 16–2.
The "Philly lick" that Philly Joe Jones used to do with Miles Davis. This instance from "Dr. Jekyll" (also known as "Dr. Jackle"), a blues in F from the album *Milestones* (1958), near the end of Davis's solo.

Pianist Red Garland joined the band, and was instructed to play those light Ahmad Jamal block chords—his delicate solo style provided contrast as well. The bassist was the young, powerful Paul Chambers. Davis's tenor soloist was John Coltrane. Davis has written, "The group I had with Coltrane made me and him a legend" (*Miles: The Autobiography*, p. 197). But, as he also notes, the band was plagued by the drug problems of its members, particularly by those of Jones and Coltrane. The group nonetheless lasted from 1955 to April 1957, after which Davis began forming a new group, eventually a sextet, with alto saxophonist Julian Cannonball Adderley added. Coltrane, free of his habit, rejoined at the end of the year.

In October 1955, Davis, still under obligations to Prestige Records, began recording for Columbia Records as well. On an album entitled *Round About Midnight*, Davis plays Monk's " 'Round Midnight," in a Gil Evans arrangement recorded in September 1956, with a smoky intensity that made it a jukebox hit on 45 rpm. Davis never states the theme directly. Rather he improvises a spare version of it, leaving long and unexpected silences. It's a suggestive, introspective solo, and an orderly one. He begins the second A section with a high descending motive of two notes, which he repeats an octave lower. Then he returns to the notes of Monk's theme, but holds the last one, refusing to resolve it to the tonic. (See music example.)

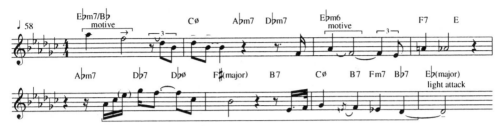

These notes are in Monk's theme, with different rhythms.

Example 16–3.
Miles Davis, "'Round Midnight" (1956), second A section of the improvisation, played with a mute.

He pushes across the structure of the chorus at the end of the bridge, where he begins a descending line that continues into the last A. These and other touches in this moody and illuminating solo make it one of Davis's most affecting.

Among the last tunes for Prestige, in October 1956, was Davis's recording of "My Funny Valentine." In an article on three Davis recordings of the Rodgers and Hart tune — recordings made in 1956, 1958, and 1964 — musicologist Howard Brofsky suggests that Davis may have recorded the first "My Funny Valentine" to counter Chet Baker's hit record of three years before: to show who was boss on trumpet. This theory would be more believable had Davis recorded it in an earlier session. Using an evolutionary model — inappropriately, we believe — Brofsky argues as well that "by 1964, Davis's 'My Funny Valentine' had evolved into a great solo," as if earlier versions were workshops for the later. Davis played "My Funny Valentine" on scores of occasions. Like other jazz musicians, he approached a familiar repertoire more and more freely, if only to avoid repeating himself.

But Brofsky is of course right that there are useful comparisons to be made between these three recordings, with their three separate rhythm sections. The first, with Garland, Chambers, and Jones, is the most intimate, as well as the sparest, most classical. Yet it has a thrust that makes it exciting. In the middle of the first A section he rises dramatically to a high note, a gesture that recurs in some form on each recording. By 1958, Davis had a more romantic pianist, with a fuller sound than Red Garland — Bill Evans. The "My Funny Valentine" of that year is the slowest of the three versions. It is also, paradoxically, the most extroverted. Surely the setting, a party thrown by Columbia Records at the Plaza Hotel, had something to do with the mood. Evans sets the initial tempo, and he offers a richer, more varied accompaniment, which, though played gently, is also busier and more suggestive than Garland's. Davis is busier as well, his lines longer, more florid, and darting. This time in the middle of the first A section he plays a dramatic scalar passage upwards—it seems an exhilarating rush—and then returns.

By 1964, Davis had been playing "My Funny Valentine" for almost a decade. The performance from Lincoln Center is a more stylized, even extravagant performance than either of the two earlier ones. Pianist Herbie Hancock begins, out of tempo, and Davis joins him eccentrically, after a moment of silence, with a low, almost sputtered sketch of the first phrase, its last note cut short. Davis plays the second phrase of the first A section with more conviction, including the sweeping scale upwards. The final A section of the first chorus has new sounds—Davis almost growls, he holds the valves down halfway to get a choked effect ("half-valved" notes), he clips a series of downward notes, and then, after this mincing phrase, he ascends to the climactic high note in full force. Davis has developed a speech-like style, exotic as well as intense, full of extravagant gestures and witty asides. Remarkably, behind Davis the rhythm section goes through slow time, medium swing, even a Brazilian beat. It is clear that this inventive young rhythm section has made Davis's new freedom possible.

Davis began experiencing a new freedom in his playing during the late fifties in his collaborations with Gil Evans—as in the 1959-1960 recordings contained in *Sketches of Spain,* whose centerpiece was a reworking of a classical concerto for guitar and orchestra, Rodrigo's "Concierto de Aranjuez." Davis plays a version of the guitar part over a lushly arranged wind orchestra, and on "Saeta," assumes the part of a solo singer approached by a marching band. (This was actually inspired by a field recording made in Spain that was available on a Columbia LP.) In a solo centering around a few pitches over a gradually complicating but harmonically static background, he "vocalizes" on trumpet with half-valved notes, stentorian exclamations, and some twisting self-involved phrases

Gil Evans at the Public Theater, Manhattan, 1980. (Photo by Michael Ullman)

that lead naturally to an ending in which the band seems to march away from him.

Flamenco music involves soloing on a scale rather than a series of rapidly moving chord changes. Gil Evans and Davis had been working in this area before *Sketches of Spain*. In 1958, Evans and Davis recorded their marvelous version of *Porgy and Bess*. In an influential interview with Nat Hentoff for *Jazz Review*, Davis commented: "When Gil wrote the arrangement of 'I Loves You, Porgy,' he only wrote a scale for me to play. No chords. And that other passage with just two chords gives you a lot more freedom and space to hear things. I've been listening to [classical composer Aram] Khachaturian carefully for six months now and the thing that intrigues me are all those different scales he uses. Bill Evans knows too what can be done with scales. All chords, after all, are relative to scales and certain chords make certain scales. I wrote a tune recently that's more a scale than a line. And I was going to write a ballad for Coltrane with just two chords."

The advantages of a piece written over scales or a limited number of chords are to Davis obvious: "When you go this way, you can go on forever. You don't have to worry about changes and you can do more with the line. It becomes a challenge to see how melodically inventive you are. When you're based on chords, you know at the end of thirty-two bars that the chords have run out and there's nothing to do but repeat what you've just done – with variations" And he concluded, "I think a movement in jazz is beginning away from the conventional string of chords, and a return to emphasis on melodic rather than harmonic variations" (*Jazz Review*, December 1958; reprinted in Martin Williams, ed., *Jazz Panorama*).

If the movement in jazz was away from the conventional series of chords, that movement received a crucial impetus from *Porgy and Bess* and from Davis's crucially influential record of 1959, *Kind of Blue*. *Porgy and Bess* is one of the most accomplished large jazz works yet created. The Gil Evans orchestration suggests an enlarged "Birth of the Cool" band. It's bottom heavy and weighted towards brass – there are four trumpets, four trombones, three French horns, and a tuba, to which are added two saxophones and two flutists, who perform on piccolo and alto flutes as well. Cannonball Adderley is present from Davis's then-current sextet, as is the rhythm section, but not Coltrane. Davis is featured throughout before the sober, but still quite jazzy and varied, backgrounds – backgrounds that include startlingly brassy explosions, as at the very beginning of "The Buzzard Song," and passages of gathering dissonance over pedal points, as in "I Loves You Porgy." On "Gone," the drums of Philly Joe Jones play the melody with the band, and then take over from it. (Elsewhere, Jimmy Cobb is the drummer.) Everywhere we hear intensely personal touches from Evans's orchestra, and yet his most daring devices serve to highlight Davis's voice. *Porgy and Bess* is as rhythmically lively as it is sonically fascinating. Davis's trumpet is frequently exposed, and it is always expressive: He recreates wrenchingly the cry of the Strawberry Woman, and with his pure, cleverly manipulated tone, he manages to suggest the anguish behind "Bess, Oh Where's My Bess."

Porgy and Bess was recorded in the summer of 1958. In March of the following year, Davis re-entered the studio, this time with his regular band members Coltrane, Adderley, bassist Paul Chambers, and drummer Jimmy Cobb. Bill Evans, who had left Davis in November 1958, returned to play piano on every number except "Freddie the Freeloader," which featured the sparkling work of the group's current pianist, Wynton Kelly. With Bill Evans's help, Davis had prepared a surprise that would keep the band from playing complacently. He presented the band with sketches of new tunes, primarily modal tunes over a bare minimum of chord changes. They were to play these sketches and improvise. The resulting record was *Kind of Blue*—remarkably, it is composed mostly of first takes. (The exception was "Flamenco Sketches," which required two takes. The alternate performance has since been issued on *Miles: The Columbia Years.*)

There was some rehearsal. The band went over the beginning of "Blue in Green" four times, establishing the chord changes and the mood. They played roughly from 23 seconds to almost 3 minutes each time, and then they produced the classic complete take. Something similar happened on most of the other pieces. "All Blues" may have been previously rehearsed—only the complete take was recorded.

The most influential piece has been "So What." In some ways it couldn't be simpler. Its moody introduction was written by Gil Evans, who orchestrated it for Davis's Carnegie Hall concert in 1961, also issued by Columbia. This introduction was rehearsed by pianist Bill Evans—no relation to Gil—and bassist Paul Chambers. They still sound momentarily unsteady at the introduction's end. After Paul Chambers pauses, he plays the theme of "So What." It is an AABA piece of thirty-two bars: Its innovative aspect is that the A section is based simply on a D Dorian scale—and a D minor chord—and the B section takes the same theme and merely transposes it up a half step, so that the improviser moves from D Dorian to E♭, and back again for the final A. (See music example.)

The theme would be memorable, even if it were not repeated obsessively. It consists of a simple, two-bar call by the bass, to which the piano and winds respond with what clearly sounds like the words "So What."

Then the band improvises. Davis's clear, concise solo is one of the most celebrated in jazz. It was set to words by Eddie Jefferson, transcribed and performed on a George Russell album called *So What* in 1986, and memorized by young players. Davis sets out in measures two and three a little motive that he returns to. He builds his A sections to some extent on this triadic motive. In the B sections, he uses a different approach, using crawling scalar lines that ascend or descend slowly to establish a striking tension. At the beginning of the second chorus of Davis's solo, Paul Chambers stops walking the scale and plays around a pedal point—a technique that was unusual in 1959, although later Ron Carter popularized it behind Davis. Bill Evans plays clusters of chords, and with Paul Chambers creates a nervous vamp. (They do the same at the start of Coltrane's second chorus.) Over this, Davis plays a spacious phrase, then repeats it an octave lower, reminiscent of the example already shown on " 'Round Midnight." (See music example.)

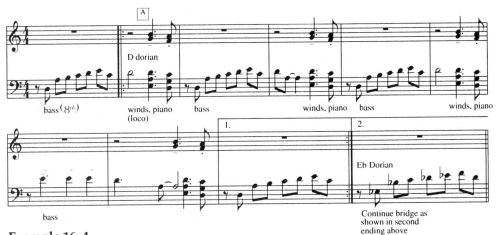

Example 16–4.
Miles Davis, "So What," beginning of theme.

Example 16–5.
Miles Davis's trumpet solo on "So What" (1959), first one-and-a-half choruses.

Interestingly, Davis, with his spare style, mostly chooses tones that fit the Dorian mode, as does Evans. Coltrane and Adderley play with greater freedom over the static background, Coltrane in an intense, purposeful investigation of the relevant scales, and Adderley, a bebopper to the last, in brilliant, but skittish passages that seem to yearn for the blues. The soloists may have been presented with a chord, or a scale, or both combined. Still, Davis does not seem to have asked them to restrict their solos to the notes of the relevant scales. Hence the problem some theorists have with calling this "modal jazz."

But the name stuck, as did the influence of this session. *Kind of Blue* signalled a new approach to jazz. It also marked the end of Davis's remarkable group. As noted above, by the time *Kind of Blue* was made, Bill Evans had already quit the sextet to form his own trio. Within the next year, Adderley and Coltrane left to form their own groups. Davis had to rebuild.

He did so under pressure. In 1958, he was the hottest thing in modern jazz, but the next year saw Ornette Coleman bring his free jazz to the Five Spot, where he became the center of a sometimes comical controversy, as critics, musicians and fans hailed his music as the wave of the future or denounced his music as anti-jazz. Miles Davis condemned the newcomer, and then found himself in the unusual position of assembling a band that was, for him, relatively conservative. He had trouble finding a tenor player, settling finally on Hank Mobley. He wasn't satisfied. When in 1961 he recorded *Some Day My Prince Will Come*, with its lovely version of the title song—it came from Walt Disney's animated film *Snow White*—Davis induced Coltrane to come back and play on several tunes, and Philly Joe Jones to play on one. Soon, as Davis has written, "the music was starting to bore me."

THE QUINTET WITH HERBIE HANCOCK

Davis's father died in 1962—a profound shock. That year he made his most disappointing session with Gil Evans, *Quiet Nights*, designed to capitalize on the bossa nova craze. (See Chapter 20.) The spirit seemed to be going out of his music. Step by step, he regrouped. He hired tenor player George Coleman, and then bassist Ron Carter, who was performing with trumpeter Art Farmer. Then he made a startling move, hiring a 17-year-old drummer from Boston, Tony Williams. When pianist Herbie Hancock was added in May 1963, Davis had the rhythm section he needed.

Tony Williams was its heart. Williams could play at the fastest of tempos with a buoyant and sometimes explosive style, full of surprising dynamic contrasts. He played on top, or even a little before the beat, and constantly introduced polyrhythms: The independence of his hands and feet is amazing. Williams's solos were frequently composed of percussive effects without meter. Hancock and Carter were equally free-spirited. In live performances, each member of the rhythm section was free to introduce new ideas, and the others—Williams in particular—would spontaneously pick up on each new tempo,

Ron Carter in the 1980's. (Photo by Michael Ullman)

rhythm, or motive. Eventually Davis would snap the band back into a groove with one of his dramatic solo entrances (See also Chapter 19).

Miles Davis was in some ways the most conservative member of his own quintet, which beginning in September 1964 included tenor saxophonist Wayne Shorter. Shorter, born in Newark in 1933, provided much of the new repertoire for Davis. Originally a Coltrane disciple, Shorter developed his own, peculiarly serene, saxophone style. In the sixties Shorter became what Davis called "the intellectual musical catalyst for the band," to which Tony Williams provided the fire (*Miles: The Autobiography*, p. 274). His compositions suggested a new way of playing. Shorter's lazy melodies with their unorthodox harmonic changes often lacked a second theme or bridge. They were often of unusual length, as for example, "E.S.P.," the 14-bar title number of a 1965 Miles Davis album. Its melody repeatedly goes up and down the interval of a fourth until its third and last phrase.

During his time with Davis, Shorter made his own records for Blue Note, introducing such originals as the waltz "Wild Flower" and the ballad "Infant Eyes," and in February 1966, his modified blues in 6/4, "Footprints". It appeared on Shorter's *Adam's Apple*, and then again on the Miles Davis album *Miles Smiles*. The Davis version was recorded in October, and it shows the impact Davis and his quintet could have on a piece. Shorter's own version sounds rather traditional: Davis's is dark and splashy, as the trumpeter stretches out his notes and phrases, while Ron Carter and Tony Williams impose other rhythms over the basic 6/4 meter.

The languorous sound and monolithic quality of certain Shorter pieces demanded new rhythmic energy in the drums. In the 1967 recording of Shorter's "Nefertiti" the horns merely repeat—for over ten minutes—the droning Shorter melody, while Williams solos underneath. Davis's own playing changed. As noted earlier, he was looser and used a broad repertoire of expressive effects. On some numbers—"E.S.P." is only one example—he began using a more chromatic style on fast numbers. Here Wayne Shorter takes the first solo, negotiating the odd chord changes in his fluent, unemphatic way. Miles begins in comparable fashion, but then, rather than outline the chords, he seems to noodle his way through them, erupting several times in bright upward runs. One can only speculate on his motives. Shorter has presented him with changes that might have seemed strange at first to someone of Davis's generation. He gets through them by avoiding a clear outlining of the chords. The method works, and manages to create a particularly modern effect. In fact, Hancock may be imitating Davis's wary attitude towards the changes when he offers a mostly one-handed, trumpet-like, solo on "E.S.P."

DAVIS AND FUSION

Musically, Davis seemed satisfied with this quintet. But towards the end of the sixties, jazz was being swamped commercially by rock. (See Chapter 21.) Some jazz musicians ignored the new pop. But Miles Davis was interested. Soon he was saying that he could, if he wanted, create the best rock and roll band in the business. He made the transition gradually, and with more complex motives than some give him credit for. Of course, he had one of the most flamboyant lifestyles in jazz, buying expensive sports cars only, it would seem, to crash them. He needed money. Davis was also used to being in the vanguard of music: But the vanguard was then thought to be related to the free jazz of Ornette Coleman, John Coltrane and Cecil Taylor. As Davis stated repeatedly, that music was unpalatable to him. Besides, Davis saw more than economic possibilities in soul music, rock and roll and in electronic sounds. He genuinely admired guitarist Jimi Hendrix, and soul singers James Brown and Sly Stone. And rock may have piqued his lifelong interest in salvaging the banal.

It happened gradually. On *Miles in the Sky* (1968), the quintet played Williams' churning and exploratory "Black Comedy," but Davis's "Stuff" had an unmistakable pop beat, and Hancock played electric piano on it. "Stuff" had an extremely long, dry theme composed of haunting little riffs and lots of space. Davis was finding a challenging and unique approach to what would be called fusion. Hancock, and on one cut his eventual successor, Chick Corea, also played electrically on the 1968 sessions for *Filles de Kilimanjaro*, which used the approach of "Stuff" throughout and was advertised as "Directions in Music," playing down the jazz label in hopes of improving sales. *In a Silent Way* (February 1969) featured both keyboardists plus a third, Josef Zawinul, who wrote the title track, and guitarist John McLaughlin, newly arrived from England. The record consisted of four evocative pieces by this dense sounding group, over a steady danceable beat, spliced together by Davis's longtime producer, himself a musician, Teo Macero. More and more, Davis's records seemed segmented, as with Macero's help he presented us with spliced sections taken from longer, looser performances. These recordings alarmed critics while delighting larger and younger audiences.

The double album *Bitches Brew* was the breakthrough—it quickly became his bestselling record. Recorded in three sessions in August 1969, *Bitches Brew* reflected changes in Davis's rhythm section over the past year: Chick Corea had finally replaced Hancock, Ron Carter left and was replaced by Dave Holland from England, and the brilliant Jack DeJohnette took the chair of Tony Williams, who started his own fusion group. This new rhythm section plus Shorter was the core of Shorter's "Sanctuary" on *Bitches Brew*. For the other cuts, Davis added at various times Benny Maupin on bass clarinet, Joe Zawinul and Larry Young on electric pianos, McLaughlin on guitar, Harvey Brooks on electric bass, and several percussionists.

The pieces were simple vamps over rock and soul-influenced rhythms. Yet *Bitches Brew* hardly condescended to an unsophisticated audience: It is composed of open-ended improvisations, not carefully engineered pop tunes, and these improvisations are spacious, free, and informal and are backed by chords that are often dissonant. Davis's own playing seems to take aspects of his style—darting runs, piercing single notes that bend and twist—and isolate them. With his increasing use of space, some of his solos seem a series of disjointed gestures, dramatic and striking in themselves. Not the patient constructions of his earlier years, these solos fit the context.

We can hear this new style in music Davis recorded in 1970 (according to Chambers) as a soundtrack for a documentary film about the pioneering black boxer Jack Johnson. The rhythm section vamps for a while in the key of E major. Then McLaughlin changes to the key of B♭, a better key for the trumpet, to introduce Davis's solo. The bass stays in E for the beginning of Davis's solo, creating quite a clash, and then moves to B♭ as well. Davis alternates little rhythmic repeated notes with dizzying chromatic runs. (See music example.)

Davis had a reasonable explanation for his style of playing with his fusion bands. The rhythm section of a fusion group is so busy, he said, that it is essential to leave spaces—a trumpet cannot compete with the rhythm or cover it up, so he must work his way around it. Davis remained sensitive to the sound of the ensemble.

In the fifties Davis was often criticized for stalking offstage after his solos, leaving his bands on their own. With his fusion groups all this changed. He was clearly in charge. On stage, he was a sight: Dressed extravagantly in leather, furs, and the latest sunglasses, he would stalk around wolfishly. He would call out rhythms to a variety of percussionists, a couple of guitarists, and occasionally to as many as three keyboard players, signalling this soloist or that as if their sounds were an extension of his own playing. More than ever before, the orchestra became his instrument—he even took up the organ so that he could better direct the group and in order to add a Gil Evans-like texture to the background. This was a difficult music to record, and not all of the heavily edited records that CBS released captured the admittedly intermittent excitement of the Miles Davis show. The 1970 album *Miles at the Fillmore* suggests what

a) Vamp before trumpet solo and during its first eight measures.

b) Davis's entrance over the vamp.

Example 16–6.
Miles Davis, "Right Off" (1970), vamp and beginning of trumpet solo.

the Davis band could accomplish live. On these sides, one hears, with only some connecting portions edited out, the wild freedom of the rock jams that Davis's groups could get into. Each set, named after the night on which it was played, is a casually strung together suite. "Friday Miles" begins with a free improvisation over a drum beat by Jack DeJohnette and a vamp by bassist Dave Holland. For about six minutes, saxophonist Steve Grossman and keyboardists Chick Corea and Keith Jarrett interact. Then the band goes into a rehearsed theme with a slow rock feel. After a percussion interlude, Davis re-enters with a free, out of tempo melody that jolts the band into another rehearsed piece, a slow, ominous funk groove that turns out to be the title cut of *Bitches Brew*. This introduces a free exchange between the two electronic keyboards, and then the theme of *Bitches Brew* recurs, and holds until the end of the set. Fascinating, original, this set in no ways condescends to a rock audience. Nonetheless, in 1975, amid speculation about his health, wealth, and possible dissatisfaction with his music, Davis withdrew at what seemed the height of his popularity.

He returned in 1981, more at peace with himself and with his audiences. While his live sets were still frequently more free, he recorded more thoroughly rehearsed, pop-style arrangements, returning to an occasional popular song. In 1982, he recorded *Star People,* and demonstrated on the title cut that he could still play an evocative blues. For a decade, older fans asked themselves and each other if he would ever again record something like "My Funny Valentine." They couldn't have foreseen that the popular tune he would perform most often in the

Miles Davis in 1989.
(Warner Brothers
promotional photo by
Richard Rothman. Courtesy
Rutgers Institute of Jazz
Studies)

eighties would be by Cyndi Lauper—her "Time After Time," which he recorded in 1985. He collaborated with Marcus Miller on a series of projects, including the 1986 *Tutu*, and he even became something of a sideman to this synthesizer player and keyboardist on *Siesta* (1987).

It's certainly wrong to say that Davis sold out to a new technology, preferring a clever engineer to a live band. When Davis assembled a band in the 1970's that included a British rock guitarist, an Indian tabla player, a couple of recalcitrant electric pianists, and a Fender bassist straight out of rhythm and blues, he was creating for himself and for his players new musical problems. That is what he always had done: Many of his solutions from the past sound as fresh and original as when they were first recorded. He said he never wanted to look back. He did so at least once: In Montreux, Switzerland on July 8, 1991, he played some of the Gil Evans arrangements he had made famous decades before with a jazz orchestra directed by Quincy Jones, recorded for eventual release. It was uncharacteristic for this forward looking soloist. It was also a fitting ending to a career that had been linked since 1948 with that of Gil Evans, who had died in 1988 at the age of 75. Davis shared Evans's interest in sonorities, in the passion of improvisation wedded to a cool, orderly progression of sounds. But it's difficult to sum up either musician—at the end of his life Gil Evans was leading what might be described as a rock and roll big band, whereas Miles Davis was trying to elicit Gil Evans textures out of electronic instruments. After a stroke, and after fighting an onslaught of ailments including pneumonia that finally put him into a coma, Miles Davis died in Santa Monica, California on September 28, 1991, at the age of 65.

17 John Coltrane

"I was closer to Coltrane than to anyone else, so I can speak with more authority on him than on others. He was perfectly aware of what he was doing and had almost supernatural control over what he was doing. Even though it gave an impression of freedom, it was basically a well thought out and highly disciplined piece of work."
—Elvin Jones, in Taylor, *Notes and Tones*, p. 228

"He kept trying to reach new levels of awareness, of peace, of spirituality. That's why I regard the music he played as spiritual music—John's way of getting closer and closer to the Creator."
—Albert Ayler, in Nat Hentoff's notes to *Albert Ayler Live in Greenwich Village*

Few musicians have had as wide—or as varied—an effect as John Coltrane, who in less than a decade moved from being a reasonably obscure, and not entirely popular, sideman in the Miles Davis Quintet to being, at the time of his death in 1967, the most influential modern jazzman. In the sixties, players talked about his personal authority, his control over his saxophones, his ability as a soloist to wed passion and discipline, and his continuing evolution as a musician. They also talked about his spirituality, his use of music in compositions such as *A Love Supreme* to suggest and evoke meditative states. A master blues player and balladeer, he was a father figure to the avant-garde. When in 1965, Coltrane, then a commercially successful recording artist, appeared at a concert under the rubric "New Black Music," he seemed to validate the most daring music of the time. Modest, serious, intense, and quietly self-possessed, Coltrane was, as free jazz scholar Ekkehard Jost called him, the "superego"—the conscience—of the movement.

No one was more serious about music. Miles Davis has said that "music and life are all about style" (*Miles: The Autobiography*, p. 398). To Coltrane, music was something more: Playing was his research, his intellectual challenge, his means of investigating as well as expressing spiritual moods. His titles, such as "Peace on Earth," "Vigil," "Pursuance," and "Expression," suggest what he was doing and what he was looking for. The spiritual element in his music made its mark on the style and repertory of countless jazz groups, few of which approached his power and discipline. A relentless self-critic, Coltrane practiced constantly—some would say obsessively—changed mouthpieces regularly, and, more importantly, continued to grow and develop.

Using an extremely open mouthpiece (one with a large opening, requiring lots of breath), Coltrane produced a bright, large, piercing sound on tenor. Up high, there's a tension in his tone, which wasn't universally popular—the conservative critic Philip Larkin referred to "the vinegary drizzle of his tone" (*All What Jazz,* p. 46). He used the whole range of the horn, honking ecstatically down low, rushing upwards in a swirl of arpeggios, sometimes emitting a wild shrieking up high or playing several notes at the same time in what saxophonists call "multiphonics."

Not all of his playing was wild or aggressive, as one can hear in a session he did in 1962 with Duke Ellington. The collaboration was the clever idea of producer Bob Thiele. For a long time Coltrane had insisted on rerecording take after take of his pieces. Thiele thought to bring the perfectionist Coltrane and the pragmatic Duke Ellington together in the studio, presumably so Ellington could teach the saxophonist how to make peace with his own music. Ellington did, telling Coltrane that there was no need for second takes, that the passion comes at the first. This session produced two sublime ballad performances by Coltrane—an "In a Sentimental Mood" that Johnny Hodges said was the best he had ever heard, and "My Little Brown Book." The latter is a Billy Strayhorn composition that Ellington recorded with a vocalist in the forties to little effect. Coltrane resurrects the piece as an instrumental in a straightforward, lyrical performance that is as gentle as it is tactful. Coltrane's approach to slow pieces, such as his own "Naima" and "Dear Lord," was characteristically serene, glowing, peaceful.

More typically, Coltrane challenged his audiences, which sometimes responded ecstatically and sometimes with dismay or satire. In the early sixties, he

John Coltrane, 1960's.
(Courtesy Rutgers Institute
of Jazz Studies)

went through a period when he would sometimes obsessively investigate a single mode or chord. Pianist Dave McKenna, who admired Coltrane, said he once heard Coltrane play two pieces, each an hour long. In his exaggerated account, he says: "The first was an F^7 chord; the second one was a G^7. I liked the F^7 better." Miles Davis once complained to Coltrane that his solos were too long. Coltrane said he didn't know how to stop, and Miles responded, "Take the horn out of your mouth." Some listeners criticized his aggressive style, and the length of his solos. Coltrane frequently agreed—at several times in his career, he pulled back, saying that he learned that he could say what he needed to say more economically.

As this self-criticism suggests, Coltrane was never merely self-indulgent; neither did he see himself as an entertainer. On stage he was investigating how far his music could take him, how much he could wring out of a chord or sequence. Often audiences were willing to follow him. When the newly formed John Coltrane Quartet finished the first night of its debut engagement in 1960 at New York's Jazz Gallery, his fans jumped to their feet, chanting "Coltrane, Coltrane." C.O. Simpkins reported that a man from the audience, dressed in a loin cloth, leapt onto the stage, dancing his approval. He was joined by Thelonious Monk, who twirled in tight circles, presumably in response to Coltrane's music. *The New York Daily News* urged its readers to hear John Coltrane, "a tenor saxophonist who has the future coming out of his horn."

He didn't let critics, or audiences, change his music unnecessarily. Considering the challenge his sometimes radical restructuring of the forms and sounds of jazz presented to listeners, Coltrane was remarkably popular: *A Love Supreme* was a worldwide hit. He recorded frequently, performed regularly, and travelled widely. He was a unique phenomenon, a serious explorer in music whose audiences continued to grow with him.

Born on September 23, 1926 in Hamlet, North Carolina, Coltrane was raised in High Point, by a family notable for its strength and pride. His grandfather was a preacher. Coltrane would always remain close to his mother, and to his cousin, for whom he later wrote the memorable "Cousin Mary." Those who knew him as a child remembered him as a quiet, likable boy.

He started on clarinet in a community band, and soon settled on the alto saxophone. In 1943, Coltrane's father died, and his mother moved to Philadelphia in search of work. Coltrane first finished high school, and then followed her. He started working in a sugar factory and enrolled in the Ornstein School of Music, where he met saxophonist Bill Barron (1927–1989). Soon he was friends with tenor player Benny Golson (b. 1929) as well. Golson remembers Coltrane's scholarly interest in theory at this time: "John used to sit in an overstuffed chair in our living room with one leg dangling over the arm and his alto resting on a cushion. I'd play some piano chords and he'd take right off. Then we'd switch and John would play piano. He must have picked up piano by himself. Even then, I could tell that he knew harmony, and knew it well" (J.C. Thomas, *Chasin' the Trane*, p. 29).

According to Golson, Coltrane and he first heard Charlie Parker live at a concert at the Academy of Music, where Parker played in Dizzy Gillespie's group. (Parker researcher Norman Saks places this concert in early June 1945.) Coltrane, Golson remembers, was immediately excited by Parker's music. At the end of 1945, Coltrane was drafted into the navy, and sent to Hawaii, where he played in a band. Lewis Porter and Phil Schaap have turned up recorded evidence of the impression Parker made on the younger saxophonist. Just before he was discharged in July 1946, Coltrane recorded eight tunes privately with white musicians from another navy band—the bands were still segregated. The nineteen-year-old altoist does a creditable, though not yet professional, job on then recent Parker originals such as "Koko" and "Now's the Time." He also plays a Tadd Dameron number that Parker had recorded, "Hot House."

Returning to Philadelphia in 1946, Coltrane resumed his studies, and found to his delight that bebop was blossoming in Philadelphia. Besides Golson, and Bill Barron, Coltrane befriended the Heath brothers—he would later call saxophonist Jimmy Heath influential on his development—pianist Ray Bryant, drummer Philly Joe Jones, and composer Cal Massey.

He worked with local rhythm and blues bands, walking the bar embarrassedly and honking his horn to please the crowds. Then, it is believed, in 1948, he got a job with a genuine star—alto saxophonist and blues singer Eddie "Cleanhead" Vinson. Vinson formed a sextet with Coltrane, pianist Red Garland, and trumpeter Johnny Coles. To get the job, Coltrane had to switch to tenor. He spoke of the switch later: "When I bought a tenor to go with Eddie Vinson's band, a wider area of listening opened up to me. I found I was able to be more varied in my musical interests. On alto Bird had been my whole influence but on tenor I found there was no one man whose ideas were so dominant as Charlie's on alto. Therefore, I drew from all the men I heard during this period . . . I picked up something from all of them, including several who haven't been recorded" ("Coltrane on Coltrane"). He became more interested in Coleman Hawkins, and his way with arpeggios. Hawkins supplemented what he learned from Lester Young: "Even though I dug Pres, as I grew musically, I appreciated Hawk more and more."

By 1948, Coltrane was using heroin. That wasn't all. When trying to kick his addiction, he frequently turned to alcohol instead, and when he wasn't drinking, he sometimes ate excessively. In the meantime, his musical education continued. In 1949, Dizzy Gillespie hired Coltrane, along with his friend Jimmy Heath, to play in his big band. He made his first professional recordings with the band on November 21, 1949, but played no solos on the date. However, he can be heard on several broadcasts with a Gillespie small group in 1951. He mentioned several key influences: "At that time, I was trying to play like Dexter Gordon and Wardell Gray . . . I heard in them lots of the ideas of Lester Young, who was my first influence. So when I made the switch to tenor, I was trying to play like them" (Gardner, "Jazzman of the Year"). But he soon found he liked Sonny Stitt (1924-1982) best of all. Stitt is often remembered as an alto saxophonist who sounded something like Parker. He was equally a tenorist, and the Parker resemblance came largely from the common influence of Young. Coltrane commented: "He sounded like something between Dexter and Wardell, an outgrowth of both of them. All the time, I thought I had been looking for something and then I heard Sonny and said, 'Damn! There it is! That's it!' (Gardner, "Jazzman of the Year").

Coltrane joined the jump band of alto saxophonist Earl Bostic in 1952. Bostic was popular with the rhythm and blues set, and he played florid versions of ballads as well—his big hit was "Flamingo" from 1951. But Coltrane discovered that Bostic was a fine technician: "He showed me a lot of things on my horn. He has fabulous technical facilities on his instrument and knows many a trick" ("Coltrane on Coltrane"). Then, in 1954, Coltrane joined the small band of the great Ellington alto saxophonist, Johnny Hodges. Hodges was as elegant as Bostic was rough. Coltrane praised him wholeheartedly: "We played honest music in this band. It was my education into the older generation. I really enjoyed that job. I liked every tune in the book. Nothing was superficial. It all had meaning and it swung. And the confidence with which Rabbit (Hodges's nickname) plays. I wish I could play with the confidence he does" ("Coltrane on Coltrane").

By 1954, then, Coltrane had played Ellington tunes with Johnny Hodges, bop with Gillespie, and blues with a score of groups, famous and obscure. (Blues shouter Big Maybelle pronounced him her favorite musician.) He had an intense, down-home bluesiness, technical brilliance and an increasing harmonic ingenuity. Late in 1955, he was playing in Philadelphia with organist Jimmy Smith. He was seeing a woman whose Muslim name, Naima, would become the title of his most famous composition. Then the drummer Philly Joe Jones contacted him to say that Miles Davis was forming a new band and that Coltrane should audition.

COLTRANE WITH MILES DAVIS

Davis had already played with Coltrane at a job at the Audubon Ballroom in New York City. That night Coltrane was replacing altoist Jackie McLean, and was paired with Davis's other tenor, Sonny Rollins. Davis remembered that Rollins blew Coltrane away. In fact, Coltrane was a late bloomer by jazz standards. By 1955, Coltrane had only one solo issued on records—a brief blues solo from 1951, recorded when he was with Gillespie. Davis was unenthusiastic about Philly Joe Jones's recommendation of Coltrane. That is, until the first rehearsal. Then he knew that the saxophonist had exactly what he needed. Coltrane first performed with the band at the end of September 1955 in Baltimore, where he married Naima Grubbs with the Davis band as witnesses. Davis was thrilled with the music from the first night.

For many, the legend began when the Davis quintet recorded Monk's " 'Round Midnight" for Columbia. Davis's solo on this 1956 recording was discussed in the previous chapter. After a rehearsed break by the band, Coltrane enters blithely, with a slurred, outgoing version of the melody. As the rhythm section suggests double time, Coltrane adds unusual ornaments to a melody that has already been beautifully implied by the trumpeter. But Coltrane's work at this time was inconsistent. On 1956 Prestige recordings with Davis, Coltrane is swaggering and confident at one moment, tentative the next.

As already noted, the Davis Quintet was in trouble because of the drug habits of Coltrane and Philly Joe Jones. According to Davis, Coltrane, who had by that time moved to New York, sometimes couldn't play and was unreliable. In April 1957, Davis fired Coltrane after a backstage incident in which Davis punched and slapped his star saxophonist. Thelonious Monk witnessed the assault, told Coltrane he shouldn't put up with that treatment and asked him to join his group. Coltrane recorded with Monk that month, and joined Monk's group later in the year. Another important phase in the saxophonist's career began.

His dismissal proved the shock that Coltrane needed to rid himself of drugs. Soon after Coltrane left Davis, bassist Reggie Workman confronted him about his addictions to drugs and alcohol. Coltrane considered his friend's words, and the direction his problems were taking him, and decided to reform. While his mother prayed for him in the next room, he went "cold turkey"—quit abruptly. He won the battle, and, rejuvenated, began to work harder than ever on his music. Coltrane, who had been studying religion and philosophy, felt that the experience had a religious aspect. In his 1964 notes to *A Love Supreme*, he wrote: "During the year 1957, I experienced, by the grace of God, a spiritual awakening which was to lead me to a richer, fuller, more productive life. At that time, in gratitude, I humbly asked to be given the means and privilege to make others happy through music. I feel this has been granted through His grace."

In May 1957, Coltrane made his first recordings as a leader, for Prestige. *Coltrane* included an authoritative ballad performance on "While My Lady Sleeps," to which Coltrane had added a pedal point. In June, he was back in the studio with Monk playing on an all-star session that also featured Coleman Hawkins. In the fall, he performed with Monk in an extended engagement at the Five Spot.

This extended encounter with the stubborn, brilliant pianist-composer whom Coltrane called, precisely, "a musical architect of the highest order" was important to Coltrane, as the saxophonist readily acknowledged: "I felt I learned from him in every way—through the senses, theoretically, technically. I would talk to Monk about musical problems, and he would sit at the piano and show me the answers by playing them" ("Coltrane on Coltrane").

Coltrane said that Monk gave him complete freedom. Part of the freedom resulted from Monk's habit of falling silent behind his horn soloist, as heard on the quartet's distinctive recording of "Nutty." (The recordings with Monk are undated but appear to be from July 1957.) Although Coltrane said that Monk taught him how to play more than one note concurrently on the saxophone, most of the pianist's lessons were more general. Sometimes he taught merely by the way he played or wrote. On "Nutty," Monk uses his melody in his own solo, as if demonstrating to Coltrane what to do with it. Coltrane really emerges on "Trinkle Tinkle," a Monk theme with a scurrying motive that challenges and inspires Coltrane. It is an AABA piece, in which the A sections have two extra beats tagged on at the end of each section. When the improvisation starts, the musicians ignore this eccentricity and stick to the straight 32-bar format. Coltrane launches into a restless, even furious solo, often producing a speedy succession of notes that arrive in a smear. He uses the highest register and occasionally honks as a kind of punctuation.

He was ready to go back to Miles Davis, who rehired him at the beginning of 1958. (Sonny Rollins, who had been filling in, now went off to form his own group.) It was a newly confident Coltrane that returned to the Davis band. He was playing sweeping solos with astonishing vigor. Coltrane seemed to have a compulsion to get to the bottom of things, to exhaust the possibilities of each musical situation. Listening to him at this period could be like observing a cubist painting: You get to see all sides of a subject almost simultaneously. Ira Gitler called his approach "sheets of sound," suggesting that the overall effect was more important than individual notes. What Gitler was hearing was Coltrane's way of superimposing or stacking up chords, of playing arpeggio on top of arpeggio. Miles Davis explained it this way: "What he does, for example, is to play five notes of a chord and then keep changing it around, trying to see how many different ways it can sound. It's like explaining something five different ways."

In order to fit in all these variations on chords, Coltrane played fast sixteenth note runs and arpeggios. Not simple arpeggios, though: The notes were grouped in irregular clusters of five or seven notes and, in another legacy from Monk, they included wide leaps of interval. On pieces with the Davis sextet such as "If I Were a Bell" (*Jazz at the Plaza*) and "Straight No Chaser" (*Milestones*), Coltrane solos rapidly and at great length. He needed that length, as he said at the time, "to get it all in." (See music example.)

Coltrane was pursuing two lines of musical investigation. He was exploring the complex harmonic ideas he had worked on throughout his career, a study which would culminate in one of his greatest recordings, "Giant Steps." Meanwhile, with Miles Davis, he would begin to experiment with modal playing. In 1960, he explained what Davis had been doing: "He was moving in the opposite direction [from bebop] to the use of fewer and fewer chord changes in songs. He used tunes with free-flowing lines and chordal direction. This approach allowed the soloist a choice of playing chordally (vertically) or melodically (horizontally) . . . I found it easy to apply the harmonic ideas that I had . . . But on the other hand, if I wanted to, I could play melodically" ("Coltrane on Coltrane").

In the spring of 1959, Coltrane made two crucial recordings, *Kind of Blue* with Miles Davis, illustrating the modal approach, and *Giant Steps* with his own quartet. Actually, Coltrane's fast-moving piece "Giant Steps," with its string of angular chords, was recorded twice, first on April 1 with Cedar Walton on

Example 17–1.
John Coltrane's solo on "Straight No Chaser" with Miles Davis on *Milestones* (1958); end of first chorus, and second chorus, showing rapid "sheets of sound."

piano, but that session wasn't released until years later. He remade the tune with pianist Tommy Flanagan on May 5, soon after *Kind of Blue* had been recorded. Like Walton before him, Flanagan was thrown by "Giant Steps": It's worth remembering that Coltrane's composition was an innovative challenge to even the best professionals. According to Flanagan, "Giant Steps" was a challenge because it "was a little irregular—like a song usually relates a minor seventh to a [dominant] seventh to a major. Well, Trane might have things going major-major-major. It made you think a little different, if you weren't ready for it. If the tempo was fast, you *couldn't* think of it" (Ullman, *Jazz Lives*, p. 120). It didn't help that Coltrane took the piece at a tempo of 290 beats per minute! (See music example.)

Coltrane had no trouble with the line or with his solo—effortlessly, he tosses off exuberant phrases, collecting notes in groups that seem to expand and contract. In many places he repeats little rhythmic patterns in order to get through the chord changes, an approach that has become standard on all instruments. (See music example.)

Still, "Giant Steps" can be seen as Coltrane's goodbye to bebop—he "runs" the chords at a punishing tempo before moving on to play the modal music of Miles Davis, which he does with even greater success. On "So What," Coltrane's

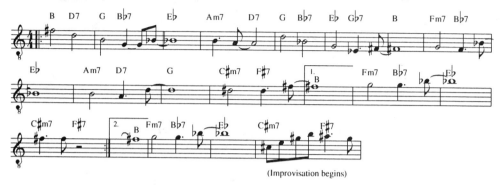

(Improvisation begins)

Example 17–2.
John Coltrane, "Giant Steps" (1959).

Example 17–3.
John Coltrane, "Giant Steps" (May 5, 1959), first two choruses of his improvisation.

solo combines a yearning spiritual intensity with inexorable logic. During the first sixteen measures of his solo, he works on a single short motive, while Bill Evans plays bold chords behind him. Liberated by the slow harmonic movement of Davis's modal music, Coltrane sounds ready for his own band.

COLTRANE FORMS HIS OWN QUARTET

He was slow to reach a decision to leave Miles Davis, but in 1960, after a spring tour of Europe with Davis, he struck out on his own. His group's personnel would change over the first months as Coltrane searched for his ideal group. He opened at the Jazz Gallery in May with Steve Kuhn on piano, Steve Davis on bass, and Pete LaRoca on drums. Kuhn is an imaginative player, but within two weeks, Coltrane replaced Kuhn with a rhythmically bolder, more percussive pianist, McCoy Tyner, who would remain with him for the next five years.

Tyner was a wise choice. Coltrane needed a counterweight, someone to converse with, and to enrich the sound. At times he needed to be left alone. Tyner played from the beginning with a big sound, and he could sound warm, even lush, while at the same time maintaining a powerful rhythmic flow. He also knew when to fall silent, as he explained: "A rhythm section is supposed to support and inspire a soloist, and it is a very sensitive thing . . . Sometimes when John is soloing I lay out completely. Something very important is involved here, I think. The pianist tends to play chords that the soloist knows are coming up anyway. Normally, all the pianist does is try to give him a little extra push in the accompaniment and possibly to suggest some new ideas. When the pianist isn't there, the soloist can concentrate purely on what he has in mind with fewer limitations or boundaries . . . So it is all a matter of giving the soloist more freedom to explore harmonically."

From his first recordings with Coltrane, Tyner contributed a bright, ringing sound that comes partly from his spread-out chord voicings. Over the next few years Tyner developed a particular type of voicing in intervals of a fourth that was to characterize his sound in the quartet, and that proved influential. A fourth is the interval taken up by four scale notes. For example, in the key of C, the major scale begins C-D-E-F, so C and F constitute a fourth. In the key of C, F is the fourth note in the scale. To extend the chord in fourths beyond C and F, one takes F as the root, and counts upwards to the fourth note in an F-major scale: B♭. If you play C-F-B♭, or G-C-F, for example, you will get an idea of the sound of Tyner's voicings. A good example of his approach occurs on his 1962 trio recording of his unusual 24-bar blues "Inception." (See music example.)

Tyner must have heard the appropriateness of fourths for Coltrane's increasingly modal music. Coltrane frequently played melodies with motives that took up the interval of a fourth. A favorite was the motive D-F-G, with which he started his "So What" solo. So chords in fourths matched perfectly. Besides, Tyner's open voicings sounded more unresolved than the more familiar triads, and perhaps he heard this abstraction as appropriate to Coltrane's spiritual music. Other aspects of Tyner's style—his speed, his thunderous tremolos, and

Example 17–4.
McCoy Tyner, "Inception" (1962), end of fifth improvised chorus and beginning of sixth, showing use of chords in fourths over a C dorian scale in the bass.

his habit of jumping his left hand down for a low ringing pedal note, added to the depth and drama of his sound.

Tyner was important to Coltrane's quartet. Drummer Elvin Jones, Coltrane's closest collaborator and musical kindred spirit, was its heartbeat. Elvin Jones, the brother of pianist Hank and trumpeter Thad Jones, replaced Pete LaRoca. Jones shared Coltrane's amazing physical stamina. More importantly, he shared the saxophonist's powerful interest in complex rhythms. "I especially like his ability to mix and juggle rhythms," Coltrane said of Jones. "He's always aware of everything else that's happening. I guess you could say he has the ability to be in three places at the same time." Jones implied the basic rhythm in a highly elliptical manner that swung ferociously. Jones's strength allowed him to accompany Coltrane for hours at a time—as the quartet developed, Coltrane would frequently enter into long duets with just the drummer, giving the same concentrated attention to rhythm that he had in an earlier time applied to chords.

Through 1962, Coltrane experimented with several bass players, including his friends Reggie Workman and Art Davis, sometimes using two at a time. Finally he settled on a relatively unspectacular, but completely solid, bassist, Jimmy Garrison. Garrison's simple patterns helped drive the rhythm section without cluttering its texture. Garrison, who liked to strum the bass like a guitar—he cited Scott LaFaro and Charlie Haden as influences—added a sound

McCoy Tyner at Newport, 1980's. (Photo by Michael Ullman)

that some critics compared to flamenco guitar. As a soloist, he was less virtuosic than some others Coltrane performed with: His depth of sound made up for it.

While assembling this "classic quartet," as this group has come to be called, Coltrane began experimenting with the soprano saxophone. Coltrane had for years been pushing the upper limits of his tenor, as if yearning for an extended range, and a thinner, more exotic, tone. He had heard the modernist Steve Lacy, who specialized in the soprano. He knew the older work of Sidney Bechet, and he found the soprano close to the sound of Middle Eastern and African reed instruments. Coltrane first recorded on soprano in an experimental session with Don Cherry and other members of Ornette Coleman's band. He was intrigued by what Coleman was doing, and wanted to get the feel of the alto saxophonist's music, but this session of July 1960 wasn't released until after Coltrane's death. Coltrane's first hit on soprano, recorded that October, was the Rodgers and Hammerstein waltz, "My Favorite Things," best known as sung by Julie Andrews and a crew of delightful children in the movie *The Sound of Music*. By playing "My Favorite Things," Coltrane wasn't indulging in a Miles Davis-like effort to absorb an unusual repertoire. The tune perfectly fit his purposes. At least it did once he rewrote it. The structure of this waltz tune is AAB. The A sections use the "raindrops and roses" tune: The text enumerates blissfully the singer's favorite things. The B part introduces the threats to this bliss: "when the dog bites," and so on. (The threats aren't serious—the song ends cheerfully.) Coltrane plays the two A's at the beginning, but saves the B section for the very end.

In between, he stretches out the song indefinitely. He has the rhythm section begin with a vamp in E minor, and he comes in when he's ready. After the first A section, as Coltrane plays a short solo, the rhythm switches to the more cheerful E major as a kind of informal interlude. Then it's back to E minor for the second A. At the end of this second A, the soloist—Coltrane or Tyner, or Eric Dolphy in live performances from the winter of 1961 to 1962—plays over the E minor vamp as long as he wants, and then gives a cue when he wants to solo on the E major vamp. The cue, as we can hear clearly in Tyner's solo, was a return to the theme. After all the solos, the long-awaited B section is performed, and the piece is brought to an end.

Coltrane's structuring of "My Favorite Things" allowed his band a new kind of freedom, to use a favorite word: The success of each performance depended on how it was used. To many it sounded Eastern and incantatory. That might have been Coltrane's point. Coltrane was fascinated with the music of other cultures. His notebooks contained pages of scales from different countries, from Indian, African and Middle Eastern cultures. He collected Ravi Shankar's records of classical North Indian music, and was inspired by Olatunji's African drumming. (His "Tunji" was written in honor of this master African percussionist.)

Coltrane frequently uses short motives which he then develops, as he does in the frenetic performance of "Impressions" recorded live at the Village Vanguard in November 1961. Coltrane has pianist Tyner sit out during most of this AABA modal piece, based on the same scales as Miles Davis's "So What." Later even the bass drops out and amidst the intense shrieking and hollering of his improvisatory duet with drummer Elvin Jones, one hears Coltrane worrying the

The John Coltrane Quartet in Milan, Italy, December 2, 1962: McCoy Tyner, piano, Jimmy Garrison, bass, and Elvin Jones, drums. (Photo by Riccardo Schwamenthal. Courtesy Mitsuo Johfu. Print provided by Yasuhiro Fujioka)

little motives that underly his solo. Using a technique that is more typical of Indian music than of jazz, he is orderly as well as committed.

The Indian music that Coltrane heard employed a constant drone played on a string instrument called the tamboura. Coltrane, who once dreamed of a beautiful drone, soon incorporated the drone in the bass, and to some extent, in the piano. He remained interested in Africa too. Coltrane's first recording for Impulse, the label that would record him from 1961 until his death in 1967, was *Africa/Brass*, with a large group of winds arranged by Eric Dolphy and an extra bassist. Dom Cerulli's liner notes described the way Coltrane prepared for these sessions: "He listened to many African records for rhythmic inspiration. One had a bass line like a chant, and the group used it, working it into different tunes. In Los Angeles, John hit on using African rhythms instead of [swing style] 4/4, and the work began to take shape." So Coltrane asked one of the bassists on "Africa" to maintain a drone, reflecting his interests in both African and Indian music.

Coltrane wasn't studying the music of other cultures as a kind of a musical tourist, looking for new colors or potential fads. His investigations reflected his deepening religious fervor, his spiritual beliefs. He looked to Indian culture, to its religions as well as sounds, as a possible source of spiritual strength. (That his interest coincided with, or perhaps helped spawn, a fad in the United States and elsewhere for Indian religiosity was hardly his fault.) Coltrane finally came to see his music as an extension of his probably uncategorizable religious beliefs. "My goal," he said, "is to live the truly religious life and express it through my music. If you live it, when you play there's no problem about the music because it's part of the whole thing. When you begin to see the possibilities of music, you desire to do something really good for people, to help humanity free itself from its hangups. I think music can make the world better and, if I'm qualified, I want to do it. I'd like to point out to people the divine in a musical language that transcends words. I want to speak to their souls." (*Newsweek*, July 31, 1967)

Coltrane spoke most directly to people's souls in his four-part devotional suite, *A Love Supreme*. Recorded on December 9, 1964, this piece became Coltrane's most popular album—500,000 copies were sold in its first year. Even listeners unaccustomed to jazz were drawn to its spirituality, to its remarkable combination of intensity and serenity, of broad, easily recognizable ballad-like lines and rhythmically powerful improvisations. In the mid-sixties, college students would demonstrate their hipness by roaming their campuses chanting "a love su-preme." A group of Californians went one step further, starting a church that builds its services around the playing of *A Love Supreme*. The idea, which Coltrane never approved, and which his widow has attempted to suppress, was that the saxophonist might be some kind of saint.

Coltrane did intend *A Love Supreme* to be a serious statement, and he took unusual care with it. He picked out a drawing of himself for the inside of the album and chose a pensive photo of himself for the front and back covers. He wrote the notes to the record, and composed a poem that states its prayerful message. The music has a carefully worked-out plan. The four sections of *A Love*

Supreme—Acknowledgement, Resolution, Pursuance, and Psalm—suggest a kind of pilgrim's progress, in which the pilgrim acknowledges the divine, resolves to pursue it, searches, and, eventually, celebrates what has been attained in song. On Impulse, the piece runs around 33 minutes. (A second version, recorded the next day, featured Archie Shepp, but has been unavailable.) A live performance from France in July 1965 is longer, about 48 minutes on CD; a comparison of the extant versions shows that Coltrane probably presented his group with a simple sketch for each part, and relied on the band to fill out the piece. We can tell this because only the basic themes are the same on both versions.

"Acknowledgement" begins with a fanfare, after which the first section is based on a repeating bass riff. (See music example.)

Example 17–5.
Bass part from "Acknowledgement," part one of John Coltrane's *A Love Supreme* (1964), showing the words that are chanted later.

Tyner and Jones enter with their own rhythms, while Coltrane improvises, using the bass riff as a motive or generating idea. With impressive discipline, he builds a coherent solo almost entirely out of this short, abstract, musical idea, building a musical world that is internally consistent and self-sufficient. Towards the end of "Acknowledgement," he begins to repeat the bass ostinato, moving it through all 12 keys, as if to suggest universality. Then he and Garrison chant the words "A Love Supreme" to the tune of the bass riff. In this way, Coltrane shows us the meaning of the first part. Everything that has been played so far has been based on a riff, whose spirit is withheld until we have worked through the piece. Coltrane suggests that supreme love is omnipresent, as was the riff, but is often unrecognized—that it can be apprehended, but only through a process of investigation and discipline. The chanting of the actual words indicates what has been achieved in the first part.

The second and third parts are based on regular chord progressions. "Resolution" has a rhythmically powerful eight-bar theme, which is repeated three times at each occurrence. Coltrane plays with his usual vigor, and Tyner takes an exciting solo that is virtually a duet with Elvin Jones. Coltrane returns in an adventurous solo that continues to investigate the descending lines of the original theme. The third part of *A Love Supreme*, "Pursuance," is a fast twelve-bar blues that begins with an Elvin Jones solo.

Coltrane wrote of "Psalm": "The fourth and last part is a narration of the theme, A Love Supreme, which is written in the context." What he meant was that his psalm-like improvisation over a bass drone and free rhythmic background is more than an impressionistic rendering of his poem, as has usually been thought. He is in fact "reciting" the poem, as a preacher would, one note for each syllable, but on a saxophone. He begins with four notes, "A Love Supreme," then continues "I will do all I can to be wor-thy of thee, O Lord." He uses a little melody for each occurrence of the phrase "Thank you God." At the very end, he plays "A-men" on the saxophone and the piece ends as a second unidentified saxophonist momentarily joins in. (See music example.)

A Love Supreme, like *Giant Steps* before it, was a watershed recording. Coltrane moved rapidly in the next months. Now famous and a commercial success, Coltrane had become something of a father figure to the avant-garde. He behaved responsibly. In 1964, Coltrane helped the younger saxophonist Archie Shepp land a contract with Impulse. In his live performances, sometimes over the protests of his regular quartet, he allowed young musicians to sit in. He was being generous, but he was also thinking about thicker textures in his music, both melodic and rhythmic. On June 28, 1965, he gathered 10 other musicians together to make one of his most awesome—and daunting—recordings, *Ascension*. (Both takes are on CD.) Besides his regular quartet, and bassist Art Davis, who had worked with him previously, Coltrane engaged trumpeters Freddie Hubbard and Dewey Johnson, alto saxophonists Marion Brown and John Tchicai, and tenor saxophonists Pharoah Sanders and Archie Shepp.

Probably influenced by Ornette Coleman's 1960 double quartet record, *Free Jazz*, which is discussed in Chapter 18, Coltrane created in *Ascension* a 40-minute piece that linked passages of group improvisation with scarcely less intense solos. All this is generated by a five-note theme, somewhat like that of *A Love Supreme*, which he states at the beginning and which is taken up again at various points in the piece. Although the textures change throughout the piece, often one hears a mighty jumble of improvising instruments. Coltrane was lending his considerable prestige to the idea of "free jazz," or jazz without preset harmonies or, in some cases, preset themes. However, Coltrane's own solos were as orderly as ever, intent on developing motivic ideas. His riveting solo on "Ascension" Edition II (Take 2) moves along the same lines as the one from "Impressions" back in 1961—but now there is no steady beat behind it.

By September 1965, saxophonist Pharoah Sanders had joined Coltrane's group—his harsh shrieks and wails of wavering pitch made him what Ekkehard Jost has called a "sound player." Coltrane's performances, as can be heard on *Live in Seattle* with Sanders in September 1965, were becoming wilder. Sanders in particular seemed to be making a whole language out of the sounds that Coltrane used for emphasis, or at climactic moments. He squawked and squealed almost obsessively—whereas Coltrane used such effects more sparingly, and after some preparation.

Partially because he wanted to hear different rhythms, and partially because Jones was unreliable, Coltrane hired a second drummer, Rashied Ali. (Jones had been incarcerated for drug abuse in the summer of 1963, during which time Coltrane used drummer Roy Haynes to replace him.) Elvin Jones, asserting that, with Ali on stage, he could no longer hear what was going on

Example 17–6.
The beginning of "Psalm," part four of John Coltrane's *A Love Supreme* (1964), showing how the words of Coltrane's poem are expressed in the saxophone solo.

rhythmically, at first tried to outplay the second drummer, who reciprocated. For a while, dismayed audiences heard a barrage of drumming that threatened to drown out the rest of the group. Even so, the band managed to record one remarkable album, the suite *Meditations*. Its opening theme is a rhythm played by the two horns, which unfolds over a thunderstorm of drumming.

Jones and McCoy Tyner, unhappy with the music, left John Coltrane by the end of 1965. Coltrane replaced Tyner with his wife, pianist and harpist Alice McLeod Coltrane. Immediately, the music changed. Ali's rhythmically free drumming implies many directions at once—Jones, like Coltrane, drove straight ahead. Alice Coltrane was a gentler, less emphatic pianist than Tyner: Her soloing on piano suggested the flowing harp she also played so well. (She has since proven to be a fine organist as well.) Sanders added a melodic counterpoint and an arresting array of tone colors to what was Coltrane's freest music— music without fixed beats, harmonies, or modes.

Coltrane was moving away from the music that had made him popular. Judging from contemporary accounts, and from the few recordings, the results were mixed. Listeners as intrepid as avant-garde saxophonist Anthony Braxton and violinist Leroy Jenkins were disturbed by what seemed to them a formless live appearance by this Coltrane group in Chicago. Yet Coltrane's own solos remained thoughtfully structured, as he continued to investigate the manipulation of short motivic phrases. He was pushing the limits of that kind of ap-

Alice Coltrane acknowledging the applause, Ann Arbor, Michigan, around 1970. (Photo by Michael Ullman)

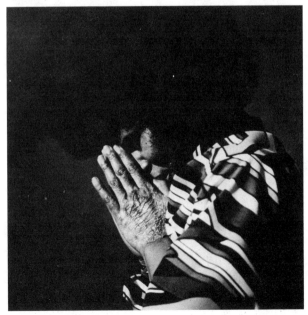

proach, but he wasn't abandoning himself to musical anarchy. He wasn't satisfied—he never had been satisfied with his own music. But he would see where the music would take him.

In July 1966, the Coltrane quintet travelled to Japan, where they were warmly received. Photographs of Coltrane taken during this tour show him holding his side. He was suffering the pangs of the as yet undiagnosed disease, liver cancer. In February and March 1967, Coltrane recorded an album of duets with Rashied Ali, and the imposing quartet album, *Expression.* These would be Coltrane's final recordings, and they have a new-found clarity in them, and a well-earned serenity. His tone is open, rich, and he's using more vibrato than before. These last works suggest that Coltrane, whose mastery of the tenor saxophone seems actually to reach a new level on "Expression," was moving towards a more controlled, and contained, music. On "To Be," he plays the flute for the first and last time on record. He never got to show where he would take jazz. He died of liver cancer on July 17, 1967, at the age of 40.

He left the new generation of jazz players bereft, if not completely rudderless. In the late sixties and early seventies, his example loomed over the more adventurous jazz players. Virtually every young tenor saxophonist mimicked his tone and learned his solos. Some disciples tried to emulate his spirituality, in albums such as Pharoah Sanders's *Kharma* (1969). But he was equally critical to the development of Michael Brecker's smooth fusion style. A disciplined man

Pharoah Sanders in Ann Arbor, early 1970's. (Photo by Michael Ullman)

whose music was, enigmatically, free and controlled, Coltrane extended the range and the sounds of the saxophone in ways we now take for granted. Coltrane showed the way. Coltrane revived interest in the now omnipresent soprano saxophone. He inspired a generation of musicians with the notion that music was not merely a way of life, but a way to a better life. Most importantly, he left behind recordings whose depth and intensity still inform and instruct the jazz world.

18 Ornette Coleman

In 1959, Ornette Coleman set the New York jazz world on its ear. He had been living in Los Angeles, and was brought East through the good services of MJQ members John Lewis and Percy Heath. After studying at the Lenox School of Jazz, a short-lived venture whose faculty included Lewis, Gunther Schuller, and other leading lights, the saxophonist opened with his quartet at the Five Spot opposite the hip young bebop band of Benny Golson and Art Farmer. His music was unprecedented, and so was the response. With an anguished tone, Coleman played on a white plastic alto sax what seemed like naively wandering solos to bouncy, childlike tunes he had written himself. His sideman Don Cherry, his cheeks ballooning, made thin, folklike utterances on a pocket trumpet (a small cornet), while the pianoless rhythm section—consisting of bassist Charlie Haden and drummer Billy Higgins—kept time. What especially disturbed listeners was that Coleman and Cherry did not follow chord progressions during their solos, but went melodically wherever their ears led.

The result was unsettling and yet at the same time airy, open, even unimposing. Coltrane's rhythms came right at a listener: Coleman's danced around blithely. Almost immediately, the quartet became the music's cause célèbre and a center of controversy, denounced by some, who thought Coleman was jiving, and praised by others, who found the new kinds of freedom in the music intriguing, even if a little scary. Leonard Bernstein pronounced Coleman a genius, which didn't help him in jazz circles, and Roy Eldridge called him a fraud, which didn't hurt him among young fans.

There was other adventurous music about, but nothing quite as unexpected. Coltrane had, after all, evolved publicly into a challenging player, and he was clearly an extension of mainstream jazz. Cecil Taylor was not yet known. Ornette Coleman might have sprung from the ear of Jove, and what he was playing was unclassifiable. Of course, dependent as it was on a close-knit ensemble, the music didn't really come out of nowhere. During years of obscure woodshedding in Los Angeles, the Ornette Coleman Quartet had reevaluated every aspect of jazz playing, rhythmic, harmonic, structural, and tonal, and put the pieces back together in a new way. Their self-educated leader, soft-spoken, thoughtful, and fascinated by every aspect of modern culture, ignored as best he could the hostility his music sometimes aroused, and spoke almost naively of the revelations that led to his "free jazz," as it would soon be called. The music, he insisted, came naturally to him.

At the beginning of his professional career, he had been playing blues and bebop. In other words, he had been following chord sequences in preset patterns. He saw the reason for doing so, but also felt that the practice had its drawbacks: "Using changes already laid out," he told A.B. Spellman, "gives you a place to start and lets the audience know what you're doing, I mean if they can whistle the song in your solo. But that means you're not playing all your own music, or all the music you're playing's not yours" (Notes to *Ornette on Tenor*, Atlantic Records). He asked himself, what would happen if, instead of running the chords, a musician played a tune's melody, and saw where that would lead him. Perhaps the player would be intrigued by the first phrase of a written melody, and might want to repeat it several times, inverting it, stretching it out, or decorating it, using it as a motive, or a contour. The soloist could play the same phrase in different keys, as Charlie Parker was known to do. He could toy with one part of his written melody for four or seven bars, and then take up another part. Or he might move on to investigate a phrase that he had just thought of in his solo. "The theme you play at the start of a number," he told Whitney Balliett in his frequently poetic speaking style, "is the territory, and what comes after, which may have very little to do with it, is the adventure."

His playing generally had, and has, a tonal center, but he changes that tonal center as he plays. Coleman might start off a solo roughly in B^b, as he does on the tune "Long Time No See," and then move to another tonal center, in this case D. (Ekkehard Jost has transcribed part of this 1970 solo.) Coleman felt that if he had freedom to do this sort of thing, he could play *himself* rather than the changes.

Of course, he could not do so with a conventional bebop rhythm section. In that case, a pianist would be laying down chords, following the structure of a chorus, and the bassist would be walking along the same path. The drummer would be playing the driving, charged patterns that modern jazz percussionists had perfected. Coleman made adjustments. After performing with several pianists, including Don Friedman and Paul Bley, and after recording with pianist Walter Norris, he decided to eliminate that instrument from his group. His bassist, left without a predictable sequence of chords, had to learn to follow the soloist, whether Coleman or Don Cherry, playing notes in his walking lines that were compatible or complementary or suggestive. The drummer had to maintain a rhythm that supported the musing, exploratory sounds of the rest of the group. When New Orleans drummer Ed Blackwell took over for Billy Higgins, he played melodic tom-tom patterns that seemed to gambol around the solo lines, rather than push them.

Ornette Coleman recording the album *Science Fiction* in 1971, with bassist Charlie Haden visible behind one of the low walls, or baffles, that are used to keep the sound of each instrument separate. (Courtesy Rutgers Institute of Jazz Studies)

The music fit Coleman's personality. A modest man, Coleman was uncomfortable with the process of dictating to a rhythm section. His method, he said in a 1978 interview, "has to do with using the melody, the harmony, and the rhythm, all equal." Although he essentially made each of the few musicians he had worked with relearn his approach to his instrument, whether drums, bass, or trumpet, Coleman still insisted he wanted to hear musicians play themselves within the context of his music. The rhythm section doesn't merely accompany: "Everyone is playing lead. Everyone's also playing what they think would be best if they had their own band."

Self-expression, always important to jazz, became the key factor in Coleman's groups. Nat Hentoff told an altogether characteristic story of Coleman, who confided to him that his favorite avocation was "taking long walks and seeing people do things they know how to do." He added: "I don't care what it is—sports or a craft—so long as a man is showing delight in a skill he's developed. It's relaxing to watch a man express himself." Coleman then told Hentoff of seeing a Hawaiian juggler at Radio City Music Hall balancing four full cocktail glasses on top of a slab of wood, which was held up by a sword balanced point to point on a dagger in his mouth. "It was the most beautiful piece of art I'd ever seen" (Hentoff, *The Jazz Life*, pp. 245–46).

As if his approach weren't innovative enough, Coleman plays with a hard, powerful tone, bends the pitches of some notes to the emotional demands of the moment, and sometimes honks in the manner he learned in rhythm and blues bands or climaxes a solo with a high-pitched squawk. He wants the sound of the human voice in his playing, and he adjusts his pitches accordingly: "There are some intervals that carry that *human* quality if you play them in the right pitch . . . You can always reach into the human sound of a voice on your horn if you're actually hearing and trying to express the warmth of a human voice" (quoted in Nat Hentoff's liner notes to *Something Else!*, 1958). He makes those human sounds in unique compositions that have been more readily accepted than his own playing: slow dirges with names like "Sadness" and "Lonely Woman", rubbery middle tempo tunes that bounce along unconcernedly ("Doughnuts") and humorously frantic uptempo numbers ("We Now Interrupt for a Commercial"). Even in 1959, at its first New York gig, his quartet sounded like none other. (Perhaps one should say *especially* in 1959: Coleman's virtuosity as a player increased rapidly during that year, and his intonation in later years became more conventional.)

Ornette Coleman was 29 in 1959, and he had been playing music since he was 14. He was born to a poor family in Fort Worth, Texas—he would never receive formal music lessons. He took up alto saxophone in high school when, unexpectedly, his mother was able to buy him one. He played with boyhood acquaintances, some of whom, such as drummer Charles Moffett, tenor saxophonist Dewey Redman, and trumpeter Bobby Bradford, would later record with Coleman. He heard black folk music ("guys playing kazoos and various kinds of odd instruments, combs for example," he said in Spellman, *Black Music*, p. 84) in his neighborhood, and he heard other indigenous musics as well. "I had my own band when I was 17. I learned the white repertory, the Mexican repertory, the black repertory. I copied things off the radio, off records. White people liked 'Star Dust,' black people liked 'Flying Home.' I would buy sheet music and teach songs to the band. We learned things like Pete Johnson's recording of '627 Stomp.' The alto solo on that [by Don Stovall] first made me want to play the saxophone" (Whitney Balliett, *American Musicians*, p. 403).

In his high school band, Coleman began to play tenor saxophone. He listened to soul blues stars, "guys like Roy Brown, Charles Brown, Lonnie Johnson, and Gatemouth Moore," and, in Fort Worth, he backed up Kansas City blues star Joe Turner. "That's the only kind of music I would play in public, for singers who were singing the blues" (Spellman, p. 95). He remembers making a lost recording in 1949 with the touring minstrel show, "Silas Green from New Orleans." But mostly he stuck to rhythm and blues, the driving-riff based, urban blues style just then developing. Rhythm and blues bands used jazz instrumentation—horns and piano, guitar, bass and drums—and they featured instrumental solos more frequently than did other blues bands, especially tenor saxophone solos derived from Lester Young's honk as extended by the likes of Illinois Jacquet, Arnett Cobb and Gene Ammons. The wildest of all was Big Jay McNeely, who would prance across a stage or a bar, lie on his back and kick his feet, while playing an ecstatic series of squeals.

Shy though he was, Ornette Coleman imitated McNeely: "I'd lie on the floor and play and do all those other gimmicks," he told Hentoff (*The Jazz Life*, p. 233). Even so, he was developing his own ideas of what his music might sound like. For the next few years, he was subject to a series of tragi-comic misadventures, as he tried to work out those ideas in the traditional rhythm and blues bands with which he was performing. He went as far south as Natchez, Mississippi with one band: there he was fired for teaching band members a bebop tune. He moved on to New Orleans where with a local band, he appeared in Baton Rouge. One night, he decided to try one of the solos that kept popping into his head. He was taken outside by some local toughs who, in the most primitive form of music criticism, beat him and destroyed his saxophone.

Back in Fort Worth in 1950, he joined the band of the popular blues singer Pee Wee Crayton. Crayton took him as far as Los Angeles before firing him. Coleman stuck it out in Los Angeles for two years before retreating to Fort Worth. Then, in 1954, he settled in L.A. working as, among other things, an elevator operator. He studied music theory in the elevator. He also attended jam sessions, where he was scorned by musicians as prominent as Dexter Gordon. But, his luck changed in one crucial respect. He found several musicians interested in what he was doing.

COLEMAN FORMS HIS OWN GROUP

Cornetist Don Cherry, born in Oklahoma City in 1936, was raised in L.A. He met Coleman in a record store on a hot day—he remembered later that the bearded Coleman was wearing a heavy overcoat in 90 degree weather. Charlie Haden was born in 1937 in Shenandoah, Iowa to a family of country singers: Haden's first professional engagements were his appearances on the Haden

Don Cherry at the Village Gate, Manhattan, early 1980's. (Photo by Michael Ullman)

family's radio show. (Their theme song was the Carter Family hit, "Keep on the Sunny Side of Life.") Drummer Billy Higgins, born in 1936, was a native of Los Angeles, where he too had played with rhythm and blues bands, as well as jazz groups.

These men, and others such as bassist Don Payne, began rehearsing with Coleman, who immediately presented them with the challenge, as he put it, of deciding what to play after you play the melody. As the woodshedding continued, they developed the group dynamics crucial to Ornette Coleman's music. Their break came when bassist Red Mitchell heard a Coleman composition he liked and he brought Coleman to producer Lester Koenig, the owner of Contemporary Records. Koenig decided to record him with a conventional rhythm section (on *Something Else: The Music of Ornette Coleman*, 1958) and with a pianoless group (on *Tomorrow is the Question!*). In the meantime, Coleman's group had been working with the pianist Paul Bley, who hired them to perform at the Hillcrest Club in the fall of 1958. Bley described the audience reaction: "Every set we'd go up and we'd play and the club would totally empty out . . . And as soon as the band stopped they would all come back in." The band played some jazz standards: Two bootleg recordings of them doing Parker's "Klactoveedsedstene" and other numbers have been issued. Nonetheless, they were fired.

Coleman's witty compositional style was evident on his first Contemporary albums. The compositions are often irregular in length: "Mind and Time" has ten bars, and "Giggin'," a blues, thirteen, yet, they still feel natural. Others, such as the seemingly straightforward blues "Turnaround" (on *Tomorrow is the Question!*), are deceptively simple. The first two phrases of this blues, so named, Coleman said, "because the blues is a change of feeling which goes from one thing to another," suggest a strong, folk-blues riff. The third phrase introduces the "turnaround," with an unexpected sequence of (implied) minor chords (C, C#, B, A, C minor, and finally G minor[7]). This last phrase turns us around — brings us back to the original riff — but, like so many of the last phrases of Coleman's compositions, it also seems to open outwards. (Coleman describes his "Endless," on the same album, as having "the quality of an endless cadence," which of course defeats the purpose of a cadence, which is meant to suggest closure.)

Coleman's solo on "Turnaround" begins, outrageously, with a quotation of the first eight bars of Richard Rodgers's "If I Loved You," from the musical *Carousel*. Coleman's quotations throughout this period rarely come from hip jazz solos — he prefers banal popular songs, and occasional classics: The beginning of Tchaikovsky's famous Piano Concerto in B^b Minor was a favorite. In "Turnaround," Coleman moves from Richard Rodgers to the gutbucket blues in C, playing bent long tones, and clarion high notes rendered with a strong vibrato. In his last chorus, he pointedly plays a phrase in B^b in an early example of his shifting of tonal centers. Still, "Turnaround" doesn't yet reflect all of Coleman's ideas about an ensemble: He recorded it with the highly skilled, but relatively traditional, rhythm section of bassist Red Mitchell and drummer Shelly Manne.

When he moved to Atlantic Records, he was able to perform with his own rhythm section. John Lewis helped Coleman obtain a contract with Atlantic Records that resulted in a half dozen albums in a couple of years. These early records contain some of Coleman's most admired compositions. Perhaps the most striking is "Lonely Woman," recorded on May 22, 1959 and issued on *The Shape of Jazz to Come.* It is introduced by bassist Haden who strums a slow, evocative pattern over Billy Higgins's cymbals. Higgins plays essentially in double time, creating a tension in the rhythm. The melody, stated by Coleman and Don Cherry, is slow, agonized, and insistent—at one point Coleman breaks away with a high, shrieking phrase, and then returns to the ragged duet. (See music example.)

Example 18–1.
Ornette Coleman, "Lonely Woman" (1959), beginning of theme.

While Coleman solos, Haden continues to play slowly rising lines, full of repeated notes, that underpin the whole piece. Coleman begins musingly, and then, locking into the beat, moves into a sample of his rhythm and blues style that brings an appreciative shout from one of the band members. After a restatement of the theme, Haden strums the piece to a close. It is as if the two horns strolled in with an anguished message, and then, just as casually, sauntered off. The piece has an attractive shape—it also is difficult to classify. It's an organized cry from the heart, bluesy and unprecedented.

Coleman's playing tends to be blues-inflected, although he frequently sidesteps the regularity and the reassurance of the twelve-bar blues form. One of his titles, "Blues Connotation," a ten-and-a-half bar blues, suggests accurately what he is about. He refers to other musics in a similarly disembodied way. He gives us something of the flavor of the Mexican music he heard in Fort Worth in his "Una Muy Bonita" on *Change of the Century.* Also on the same record is his "Ramblin'," a blues in D that manages, especially in Charlie Haden's solo, to suggest the country music Haden grew up with: It's like hearing echoes of the

Carter Family or the Delmore Brothers in a thoroughly modern blues. On the 1959 "Ramblin'"—a bootleg version with Bley from the previous year was also issued—Coleman's arrangement calls for bassist Haden to alternate sixteen bars of strumming with twelve bars of walking bass while, similarly, Billy Higgins alternates a vamping rhythm with twelve bars of swing drumming. Over this, Coleman plays a solo remarkable for its melodic logic and for its blues inflections: long, bent tones, growls and whole measures where he harps on the blue third (F natural). His last "chorus" is one of his most expressive. It includes a simple motive, an ascent from B to the tonic D, and then introduces one of his favorite blues riffs. He builds the next two phrases out of this riff, one in the same register, and the second an octave lower. Then, as he did earlier in the solo, he wails on long notes, and skillfully works those wails into a phrase by tagging them with shorter valued notes. (See music example.)

Example 18–2.
End of Ornette Coleman's solo on "Ramblin'" (1959).

Coleman didn't mean to repudiate bebop: He wanted to build on it. Repeatedly, in tunes such as the three-themed "The Legend of Bebop," Coleman refers to Charlie Parker. In his notes to "Bird Food," Coleman wrote: "'Bird Food' has echoes of the style of Charlie Parker. Bird would have understood us. He would have approved our aspiring to something beyond what we inherited. Oddly enough, the idolization of Bird, people wanting to play just like him, and not make their own soul-search, has finally come to be an impediment to progress in jazz." His admiration for Parker continues: In 1985 Coleman recorded "Word for Bird."

In his music for his quartet, Coleman tried to construct pieces that forced his musicians away from clichéd bop riffs. We can see the process at work in

"Congeniality," from the 1959 *The Shape of Jazz to Come*. Its first phrase (A) is a four-bar, offbeat line that begins with a descending arpeggio and ends on a held note. Then Coleman introduces a contrast, a thoughtful three-bar phrase (B). Finally there is a long phrase (A) whose last four bars turn out to be the four bars Coleman began with. (See music example.)

Example 18–3.
Ornette Coleman, "Congeniality" (1959), beginning of theme.

The rest of the theme alternates between A and B, with some variations. "Congeniality" is a delightful sequence of short events, each fresh-sounding, unexpected and yet in a logical order. The theme leads to one of Coleman's most inspiring early improvisations. Towards the end of his solo, Coleman includes his quotation from Tchaikovsky. (See music example.)

Example 18–4.
Ornette Coleman, excerpt from near the end of his solo on "Congeniality" (1959).

The eclectic Coleman even recorded the Gershwin ballad "Embraceable You." His unusual approach to this song is discussed in Appendix 1.

In December 1960, he assembled an octet that paired Coleman's regular group, which now included Cherry, Haden, and drummer Ed Blackwell, with another quartet of reedman Eric Dolphy, trumpeter Freddie Hubbard, bassist Scott LaFaro and drummer Billy Higgins. They recorded two takes of a revolutionary piece, "Free Jazz." Gunther Schuller called the original issue, take two, "undoubtedly the single most important influence on avant-garde jazz in the ensuing decade." (The shorter first take was issued only in 1971, on *Twins*.) With its provocative title, and its cover by the controversial artist Jackson Pollock, it was clearly meant to be a major statement. It's a daring one, and now, decades later, we can still be impressed by Coleman's ability, a year after he came on to the scene, to organize a recording session that included, besides himself, seven of the premiere young players in a totally new context.

"Free Jazz" (the long take) is a thirty-six minute piece built around minimal "themes." At its beginning, we hear a flurry of fast-paced playing which leads momentarily to a series of loosely played chords, and then to a solo by Eric Dolphy on bass clarinet. As he solos, the bassists and drummers are actively playing, trumpeter Don Cherry is adding commentary, and the other horns gradually assert themselves until all four are exchanging lines over a bouncing mid-tempo.

But Coleman has clearly set up some roles for them to play. The two quartets are separated in the stereo recording. On the right, drummer Blackwell and bassist Haden are dedicated to keeping the beat. Scott LaFaro, on the left channel, plays fast decorative lines: He and Higgins challenge the basic pulse by maintaining a double time feel throughout. (Coleman and Cherry are on the left: Dolphy and Hubbard on the right.) In essence, this is the kind of division Coleman would make in his later electric groups, creating a "funk" rhythm section on one side of the stage and a freer section on the other. When in 1987 he presented his acoustic and electric bands together for the first time under the auspices of Tufts University, he was commissioned to write a piece for the combined bands. He called it "DNA meets $E=mc^2$," and explained that those were the forces of the two bands, acoustic and electric, natural and atomic.

In *Free Jazz*, Coleman used written material as well, which he would bring in on cue to end a section or a solo. These might be another iteration of the aggressively held long note chords, or, about 20 minutes into the piece, a tuneful up-tempo melody that could have come out of one of his "bebop" compositions. This theme dominates the last part of the piece. For the rest, "Free Jazz" depends on the soloists' ability to make orderly statements, or fragments of statements, and to weave a logical way among the suggestions of the other performers. It's a lively, cacophonous piece, less intense than sprightly, and certainly less forbidding than most people imagine. It contains passages that are immediately intriguing, even amusing, as when the two basses duet, and exchange a silly sounding descending group of notes that finally suggests little to either of them.

Because of its many interwoven lines, and lack of obvious climaxes, "Free Jazz" sounded cacophonous and undramatic at first, even to Coleman's fans. It didn't lead immediately to Coleman's playing with a larger group. It didn't lead immediately to anything. By 1962, Coleman was working less, and then usually with a trio that contained the classically trained bassist David Izenzon and Coleman's friend from Fort Worth, drummer Charles Moffett. Izenzon fre-

Charlie Haden in Detroit,
about 1971. (Photo by
Michael Ullman)

quently bowed his accompaniments, producing a wailing sound that appealed
to Coleman, and Moffett played rhythm in a manner informed by bop, swing,
and rhythm and blues. This trio played a climactic concert on December 21, 1962
at Town Hall in New York City, a concert in which a string quartet played
Coleman's short piece, "Dedication to Poets and Writers." The Coleman band
was joined for one tune by "Nappy Allen's Rhythm and Blues Trio." Some of
this concert, but not the rhythm and blues piece, was issued on ESP Records.
The missing r & b tune turns out to have been the crucial music. In 1981,
Coleman told Quincy Troupe in *Musician* magazine: "In 1962, I hired a rhythm
and blues band, a string quartet, and my own trio, and performed an original
work at Town Hall. I started playing with them not thinking about fusion or
anything, but because I wanted to have more color to improvise from, to get
away from thinking about improvising. The more voices I had to inspire me, the
freer I felt I could be from improvising. I went from there to writing for string
quartets and symphonies."

He also went, in what would become a pattern in his career, into something like retirement. He was dissatisfied with the music business—he had
received precious little money from his recordings—with his groups of musicians, which included some unreliable drug addicts, and with his own playing.
Unable to support a large group, he was looking for a way of providing new
sounds, and colors, but he had temporarily run out of practical ideas.

He reemerged in 1965, having learned idiosyncratic ways of playing both
the violin and the trumpet. On violin, he produced almost a wall of sound, as he
sawed away in tense, upbeat rhythmic patterns. On trumpet, he generally paid
more attention to individual notes: But even on this instrument, he might play
casual lines for a while, and then some furious, smeared passages. Coleman

introduced these instruments, or, as he would put it, these colors, during a yearlong stay in Europe that began in July 1965. With Izenzon and Moffett, he made a stirring live recording at a concert in Croydon, England (August 29, 1965), with remarkable performances of "Doughnut" and "Sadness."

At Croydon, he also introduced another piece of chamber music, his "Sounds and Forms for Wind Quintet." His career as a self-taught composer for classically oriented groups would culminate in the 1971 symphony, "Skies of America," recorded by the London Symphony and introduced in New York at the Kool Jazz Festival of 1972. He was not betraying his interest in improvisation. Ideally, he has said, he would have his symphony musicians interpret his lines freely.

In America in the sixties, Coleman would perform, for a musician of his stature, infrequently. When he did appear, or record, his playing was as strong as ever. In 1966, he recorded *The Empty Foxhole* with bassist Haden and with his then 10-year-old son, Denardo Coleman, playing drums. The uninhibited drummer added a new kind of voice. (Then an inspired amateur, Denardo would in the next decade become a powerful percussionist, and a mainstay of Ornette's electric bands.) His father's "Good Old Days" from that date is a dramatic blues played over a beat so flexible it does not make sense to count it. The piece has three sections. The initial section consists of a riff given five times at the outset in the tonic D (in later occurrences, it is repeated a more symmetrical four times); the second section has a riff which goes, as do most blues, to the fourth degree in the scale and back to the tonic; and finally there is an extended phrase which suggests a series of tonalities. This outline is reminiscent of "Turnaround." As is so often the case in Coleman's compositions, the earlier phrases suggest a clear tonality and direction, and the last leads off in new directions. What's new is that Coleman is playing more often without a steady swing feeling.

In 1967, Coleman won a prestigious Guggenheim Fellowship for composition: He was the first jazz artist so honored. The award led to a flurry of performances, this time with a quartet that used as a second voice Coleman's old Texas friend, tenor saxophonist Dewey Redman. Haden remained with the group, and Coleman used as drummers Ed Blackwell, Elvin Jones, or his son Denardo. In the original Coleman Quartet, Coleman and Don Cherry had comparable voices: In bebop style, they introduced the pieces in rough unison, and their improvisations were similar. Coleman used Dewey Redman in a different way, frequently having him set bluesy riffs against which Coleman soloed. Coleman became the solo voice in what sometimes sounded like a futuristic rhythm and blues band.

That's exactly what Coleman was headed for. After recording *Skies of America*, Coleman made a second record for Columbia Records, *Science Fiction* (1971). It was an admirably varied collection of music, and it suggested new directions. "All My Life," another of Coleman's wistfully yearning slow numbers, is sung, rather gently, by vocalist Asha Puthli over the complex drumming of both Billy Higgins and Ed Blackwell. On "Law Years," one of Coleman's most attractive lines, Charlie Haden is the main soloist: He comes on after a coherent,

Drummer Ed Blackwell,
Woodstock, New York,
1979. (Photo by Michael
Ullman)

intent short solo by Coleman, a minor masterpiece that ends in a climactic high
note. "Rock My Clock," a humorous version of a rock song, best predicts where
Coleman would go next. It features his untamed violin and trumpet in frenetic
statements over a rock and roll beat.

COLEMAN AND FUSION

While Coleman was thinking of how to produce a more "popular" group sound,
he received an unlikely stimulus. In January 1973, he travelled to Morocco,
where he heard Moroccan bands with what sounds like a miscellaneous personnel: They might include three or more drummers, a string section, and a quartet
of flutes. Robert Palmer accompanied Coleman, and told Drew Franklin of the
Village Voice about the experience: "Ornette told me after we'd come back that all
his life, he'd played either dance music, which he felt restricted him a lot, or his
own music, which gave him the freedom to create but didn't always get that
visceral connection with an audience he'd felt growing up, playing rhythm and
blues." Rather optimistically, Palmer adds, "In Jajouka [a Moroccan village], he
saw that you could have both at once."

In the next years, Coleman assembled, step by step, an electric band called
Prime Time, which he unveiled in 1975. His idea was not merely to produce
dance music. He had been wishing for years for a group that could produce all
the complex lines of an orchestra, and he remembered the popular appeal of
rhythm and blues. He wanted a group that sounded bigger, that could suggest
more rhythms and tonalities to the soloist, but at the same time he wanted to
end his isolation as an "avant-garde" figure. He explained Prime Time, which

eventually had pairs of electric guitars, electric bassists, and drummers, and which played at volumes that brought out each instrument's overtones, to Quincy Troupe in *Musician:* "You see, I couldn't afford to have an orchestra, which is what I would prefer to have. The guitar is the most popular social instrument, especially to white people; it is what the tenor saxophone is for most black Americans. Anyway, the guitar takes up a lot of the string section. Having two of them usually means you use one for the rhythm and one for the melody. What I have done in my band is that to one of the bass players, I'll say I want him to play the rhythm equivalent to this line, then I'll want to play the harmony equivalent, and I'll give the guitar that number [the melody]." He goes on to say that the band does not have to reach a climax at a certain prearranged spot— "it can happen instantly and according to the way the mood and feeling of whatever we're playing dictates."

In essence, he's extended the principles behind his *Free Jazz*, while redesigning the group's sound around a danceable beat. He frequently has one drummer playing funky rhythms, while the second offers more tangential rhythms. On *Of Human Feelings* (1979), bassist Jamaaladeen Tacuma offers snapping bass lines strongly influenced by rhythm and blues, as does guitarist Charles Ellerbee. A second guitarist, Bern Nix, adds delicate, pointillistic lines that seem to come from outside the tune. Coleman's own horn dominates the group, which seemed constantly to form and reform itself around his solos. "What I'm trying to do with Prime Time," he told Robert Palmer, "is to develop a musical presentation that will make people feel as comfortable as if they were

Ornette Coleman at Carnegie Hall, probably his 1978 concert. (Photo by Michael Ullman)

listening to a song, but at the same time play music that's as free as anything they ever heard in their lives . . . People have started asking me if I'm really a rhythm-and-blues player, and I always say, why, sure. To me, rhythm is the oxygen that sits under the notes and moves them along, and blues is the coloring of those notes, how they're interpreted in an emotional way" (*New York Times*, June 24, 1981).

In Prime Time, Coleman has assembled a band that has the physical immediacy of rock and roll without betraying the intellectual content of his earlier music. To combine two of his titles, you could say he's making "Feet Music" that is "Dancing in Your Head." Coleman remains the band's major soloist. The others react, each in his own way, within their given roles, to what Coleman is playing. Sometimes this band sounds like inspired disorder, and, sometimes, when the band members are most attuned to one another, it seems like a balanced chamber group.

Coleman did not abandon acoustic music. In his stimulating 1987 recording, *In All Languages*, he recorded alternate versions of a half dozen tunes notable for their humor and variety. He recorded them first with his acoustic quartet and then with Prime Time. "Feet Music" is a danceable blues riff in the tradition of "Turnaround." Its second phrase is taken to the subdominant, as in a traditional blues, and the third leads towards, but does not establish, new keys. On the quartet version, Coleman plays a funky tenor saxophone solo. On the slower, more expansive Prime Time version, he sticks to alto, and somehow makes his riffs sound lyrical over the backbeat provided by Denardo, and over the jumble of lines by the two guitarists.

His Chaplinesque love of the unexpected, of disruptions and surprising juxtapositions in music, make Coleman a humorist as well as a revolutionary. His "Latin Genetics," performed twice on *In All Languages*, has a Mexican-style theme made up of descending arpeggios played in a sprightly rhythm in A♭ major. This theme founders against a bizarrely unrelated boppish theme (played in swing time on the acoustic version). It comes from a different world and a different key—this "bridge" is played first in G major and then in A♭ major. Coleman then returns to the Mexican theme (in A♭) as if the interruption never occurred. His "Space Church (Continuous Service)" in the Prime Time version begins with fast licks and then with a synthesized, churchy organ sound, and it has an "ethereal" theme that would be cloying, except that it is constantly threatened by a disco beat by one drummer, free drumming from the other channel, and by a series of portentous synthesized chords. His titles, such as "Macho Woman," make one laugh—and think.

In late 1985 and into 1986, Coleman toured and recorded with guitarist Pat Metheny, a popular fusion instrumentalist with a longstanding interest in Coleman's work. Metheny was prepared for this tour. With Coleman's colleagues Charlie Haden and Dewey Redman, he had recorded Coleman's "Turnaround" in 1980. With Haden and Billy Higgins, he recorded in 1983 three lesser known Coleman compositions, "Humpty Dumpty," "Rejoicing," and "Tears Inside." The critically acclaimed Coleman-Metheny tour introduced the saxophonist and his compositions to a new audience, while demonstrating Metheny's ability to create uninhibited free improvisations with a barrage of computerized equipment. Their work together is documented on the album *Song X*.

As the eighties ended, Coleman spoke of a projected work called "The Oldest Language," which would be played by American musicians and others from all around the world. In some ways he is hopelessly impractical and idealistic. Rather than be underpaid, for years Coleman did not work. As his onetime producer John Snyder has said, at a time when he didn't have an apartment, Coleman was looking to buy a building. He bought one, which he hoped to turn into a school and living quarters for artists. The idea, which never came to fruition, was a good one.

All of Coleman's ideas seem to be. His early music, with its space, whimsicality, and freedom, was crucial to the development of much of sixties and seventies jazz. To the avant-garde community, Coleman represented an alternative to the fervid, intense music of John Coltrane. He has survived three decades on the outskirts of the entertainment world, and has produced a large body of work that will always be intriguing and suggestive. He may never perform "The Oldest Language," which as he envisions it, would be a huge work. But it's foolish to bet against him.

Coleman tells the story of a young man he met on a trip to Japan. This Japanese saxophonist came up to Coleman before a concert to ask for a lesson. Coleman told him he couldn't talk about such a thing then. The student appealed to Coleman again as Coleman drove off after the show. Coleman sloughed him off. Later he knocked on Coleman's hotel door. Coleman told the young man not to be impractical, that the band was returning to New York. When, some weeks later, the youngster knocked on Coleman's door in Manhattan, Coleman started to give him lessons.

Coleman admires inventiveness, and persistence. He has spent a lifetime looking for a music that would allow each member of his band to fully express him or herself. Original to the point of idiosyncrasy, Coleman has made his ideas, and his personality, count. For all its daunting complexity, and sometimes equally daunting simplicity, his music is in the best jazz tradition: It comes from the heart, and, though deeply personal, it's meant to communicate. In his own words, and with his own spellings, Coleman has suggested a keynote of his career: "Their are endless ways to take but their is only one way to give and that is in person."

19 Bill Evans and Modern Jazz Piano

Rhythm sections quickly absorbed the lessons of the Miles Davis, John Coltrane, and Ornette Coleman bands. Drummers seemed to take another step forward in the sixties. Following the lead of percussionists such as Roy Haynes, whom some have called the father of avant-garde drumming, and of Elvin Jones and Philly Joe Jones, and finally of the young Tony Williams, many drummers played chattering or thunderous rhythms often remarkably independent of the basic beat. Bassists became more virtuosic than ever, until their high, guitar-like lines provoked rumbling criticisms from Charles Mingus, who wondered aloud why the youngsters played so much in the upper range of the instrument.

In doing so, they were of course imitating one aspect of Mingus's own prodigious technique. There was, briefly at the beginning of the sixties, another model, in the Bill Evans Trio that featured bassist Scott LaFaro and drummer Paul Motian. This trio became the most celebrated group of modern jazz's most influential pianist—his nearest rival in impact is McCoy Tyner, who was discussed in Chapter 17. Whereas Tyner is all steel-driving power, Evans was a warmly romantic master of touch and chords. He came along at the right time. When many jazz players were feeling jaded with the procedures of bebop—with its well-known licks and fast-changing chord sequences—Evans showed that with the proper harmonic sophistication and melodic skill, one could revivify the ballad. Evans, who died in 1980, was a master at reharmonization—his 1961 "My Foolish Heart" is a celebrated example. He also became a master, as we hear on his 1958 unaccompanied solo "Peace Piece," of modal playing, an interest Evans shared with McCoy Tyner. His voicings, especially his tendency to play chords with intervals of a perfect fourth, have been influential. He uses this technique in his accompaniment to Miles Davis on "So What," a recording whose impact was so wide that a recent text, *The Jazz Piano Book* by Mark Levine, has a chapter called "So What Chords." In solo pieces, Evans's rhythmic freedom, his absolutely natural use of rubato, is as illuminating as his lyricism. (We hear such playing throughout his 1968 *Bill Evans Alone.*) However mildly they start, in their middle choruses his solos seem to surge into an expanding universe. As Evans became more excited, he unfolded phrases of greater and greater length. In his trios, Evans sought to collaborate with his drummer and bassist, rather than dominate them.

Probably because of his lyricism in pieces such as the "Love Song from Spartacus" (1963) and "Danny Boy" (1962), Evans became a popular figure in jazz in the sixties and seventies. Popularity didn't help his personal life: In an unusually frank essay accompanying *The Complete Fantasy Recordings* of Bill Evans, his friend Gene Lees discusses the addictions that took Evans's life.

Speaking to Dan Morgenstern in *Down Beat*, Evans, who was born in New Jersey in 1929, said that he did not decide to become a musician until after he attended Southeastern Louisiana University and had served in the army. He had showed talent long before he made that decision: Unissued tapes that Evans made of his playing when he was a teenager show him developing from a Teddy Wilson imitator in the mid-forties to an austere Tristano-ish modern soloist and finally to the mature romantic as he's known. (These tapes also include excerpts of Evans playing Mozart, Shostakovich, and other classical composers.)

His first commercial recordings were made in 1954, with Jerry Wald's dance band. He recorded in 1955 with guitarist Dick Garcia. Sometime that year he met composer George Russell, when a friend brought Evans to the Russells's Manhattan apartment on "a quiet Sunday afternoon." Russell remembers him as pale, bespectacled, and so uncommunicative that these sophisticated urbanites finally suggested a trip on the Staten Island Ferry just to get out of the house.

Bill Evans, Boston, 1980. (Photo by Michael Ullman)

After the boat ride, Evans played for Russell, whose "mouth hung open when I heard what came out of the piano." Russell was offered an RCA contract the following year, and wrote "Concerto for Billy the Kid" for Evans. On this mini-concerto, recorded on October 17, 1956, Evans emerges as an aggressive player fond of long, intricate lines. (On the ballads from these sessions, he displayed his lush, chordal style.) In 1957, Russell recorded his "All About Rosie," a longer and even richer piece that also features Evans in a swinging mood. (This piece is discussed at the end of Chapter 14.) Evans recorded his first album as a leader in 1956. It didn't do well: Riverside producer Orrin Keepnews said that by the end of 1957, *New Jazz Conceptions* had sold only 800 copies.

Nonetheless, by 1958, Evans was the young pianist to watch. He was working with Miles Davis, and was recording again for Riverside as a leader. The cover of his 1958 album, *Everybody Digs Bill Evans*, was decorated with encomia by famous musicians: Miles Davis says on it, simply, "I sure learned a lot from Bill Evans. He plays the piano the way it should be played." Later, Evans's accompaniments on "So What" and "All Blues" (on *Kind of Blue*) became inseparable from the solos themselves.

The highlight of *Everybody Digs Bill Evans* is the unaccompanied "Peace Piece," on which Evans solos for eight minutes over a modal vamp. Orrin Keepnews tells us that Evans was working on an introduction to Leonard Bernstein's "Some Other Time" when he hit on this vamp, and decided to use it as the basis for an improvisation. Now that "Some Other Time," recorded later in the session but not on the original record, has been issued, the vamp can be heard in its original context as well. Evans begins "Flamenco Sketches" on *Kind of Blue* with the same vamp, which is a little like the repeating left hand of Chopin's "Berceuse," Opus 57, that Evans may have known.

"Peace Piece" and his recordings with George Russell—including the 1960 *Jazz in the Space Age*, on which he duets, free of chords, with pianist Paul Bley—demonstrate that Evans was, early in his career, open to experimental contexts. On "Peace Piece," Evans muses at first over his gently swaying left hand figure. Later he plays glassy dissonances, interests us in a rapidly descending figure by playing it at different volumes and with different intensities, and then pulls back gracefully. This early masterpiece, with its seeming references to composers such as Erik Satie, influenced later developments, such as the lengthy Keith Jarrett solos of the 1970's. (See music example.)

In November 1958, Bill Evans left Miles Davis, first to rest and practice at his brother's house in Baton Rouge, and then, back in New York in the spring, to form his own piano, bass and drums trio. In deciding on this instrumentation, he was following a recent trend. Now ubiquitous, the piano trio with bass and drums only arrived in the late fifties. Since the thirties, there had been piano trios, led by Clarence Profit, Art Tatum, or—the most popular of all—Nat Cole. But they featured piano, guitar, and bass, as did Oscar Peterson's first groups. The shift to drums presented several advantages in the fifties. In an age when modal playing was becoming common, and free playing possible, the presence of a guitarist strumming chords could be an impediment. Then again the sheer

a) Beginning

b) Excerpt from near the end.

Example 19–1.
Bill Evans, "Peace Piece" (1958), two excerpts.

success of Oscar Peterson's trio, which added a drummer in 1958, proved influential, as were the hit records of Miles Davis's favorite pianist, Ahmad Jamal. Jamal's "Poinciana," on one of the most popular records of 1958, helped popularize the piano trio with drummer. Three years earlier he had recorded it with guitar and bass, and no one noticed.

Evans hired drummer Paul Motian, an unusually sensitive and inventive accompanist, and Scott LaFaro, who had begun his career as a jazz bassist only three years earlier, with the Chet Baker band. LaFaro was 23 when he joined Evans. By the time he joined Evans, he had also worked with Sonny Rollins and Harold Land in Chicago, had been briefly one of the house bassists at the Lighthouse Cafe, and had toured with Benny Goodman. He recorded with Ornette Coleman in 1960 and 1961.

He blossomed in the Evans trio, and in doing so, helped create a new sound in jazz rhythm. Evans opened up the trio democratically to reduce, though not eliminate, the dominance of the piano. Evans's spacious, musing style allowed him to cede space to his bassist quite naturally, and LaFaro's sensitivity and aggressiveness allowed him to produce fast, high melodic lines, and then to recede gracefully as Evans finished ideas that his bassist started.

Evans enjoyed playing the Miles Davis repertoire. His meditative version of "Blue in Green," recorded on December 28, 1959, captures the gently mysterious mood of the Davis composition. And the performance shows Evans's habit of beginning modestly, and then gradually loosening up, to play longer, more relaxed and rhythmically exciting lines. (A version of "Blue in Green," recorded in Canada during an August 1974 concert, is the title tune of a Milestone release. At the same concert, Evans reprised another Davis composition, playing an expansive "So What.")

On the live version of "Solar," recorded at a marathon session at the Village Vanguard from June 25, 1961, Evans begins to state the Miles Davis theme, until, suddenly, LaFaro bursts in to finish what Evans started. It is usually clear who is playing lead in the Bill Evans trio, but it's never clear for how long he'll be doing it. (The title "Solar," referring to the sun, is another Davis joke, since it's based on "How High the Moon.") We can observe the unique interplay among the members of the trio in their recording of LaFaro's delicate "Jade Visions." As often with this trio, the piece begins modestly, first with LaFaro solo, and then with all three, as Evans plays the repeated notes of the theme so lightly that, in concert with Motian's cymbals, he sounds like he's playing wind chimes.

When it recorded these tunes, and others such as Evans's own "Waltz for Debby" (JP), the Bill Evans Trio was one of the most exciting small groups in jazz: adventurous, lyrical, and full of admittedly genteel surprises. (See music example.)

Two weeks later, LaFaro was killed in a car crash in his hometown of Geneva, New York. He was 25.

Evans was devastated. He spent much of the rest of his life trying to recreate the trio he had with LaFaro and Motian. In the next 19 years, he would work primarily with bassist Chuck Israels, whom he found in 1962 and who would stay with him, on and off, until 1966, with Eddie Gomez, who was with Evans from 1966 through the late seventies, and, at the last, with the young Marc Johnson. He continued to develop as a pianist. If his earliest recordings used standard, Bud Powell voicings, by the late fifties Evans had become more original, voicing in clusters of notes. His lovely touch brought out the ringing juxtapositions of the close notes in tightly voiced chords without sounding

Example 19–2.
Bill Evans, "Waltz For Debby," bridge of fourth chorus (1961 recording, original take; alternate was issued in 1984), showing interaction with Scott La Faro. Note that this section is not played as a waltz; the improvisation is in 4/4.

harsh. Evans's harmonies and voicings frequently sound soft-edged, almost elusive, suggestive and open rather than definitive. This effect would be particularly important to later pianists dealing with open forms.

Particularly in his recordings from the seventies, Evans had an active left hand. Often he would use his left to converse with the right, offering not simple comping, but a complex series of effects, as he moved between bass notes and chords, sometimes presenting little melodic lines that countered or mimicked those of his right hand. His right hand lines had a Tristano-esque rhythmic complexity—his use of triplets, and his willingness to stop and start lines in surprising places are influenced by Lennie Tristano, and, Evans said, by Tristano's onetime student, saxophonist Lee Konitz. By the end of his life, Evans was using a more percussive touch, and throwing in exuberant double time lines and fast runs.

He looked on jazz as conversation. Some of the highlights of his recordings from the sixties come during the exquisitely sensitive duets with an equally lyrical voice, that of guitarist Jim Hall, on *Intermodulation* (1966). Then there were Evans's innovative *Conversations with Myself* (1963), in which he overdubs his own piano to produce four- or six-hand performances. Miraculously, with this technique he manages to produce enlivening, witty performances of pieces such as " 'Round Midnight," and "Stella by Starlight."

He also played solo piano. On the grandly singing "I Loves You, Porgy" that he recorded at the Montreux Jazz Festival in 1968, Evans's lyricism is unabashed. (This Verve album won a Grammy.) In 1962, he recorded an eloquent version of "Danny Boy," a piece many hip players wouldn't touch with a 10-foot pole, although Tatum and Ahmad Jamal had recorded it. His ballad performances, "I Believe in You" (1962) or "Love Theme from Spartacus" (1963), were subtle, sometimes ethereal, but never fragile or brittle. Evans's warmth, his beautiful tone and exquisite and sometimes lilting manner of stating a melody, his subtle harmony and natural lyricism, ensured that his music would be heard.

PAUL BLEY, CHICK COREA, AND KEITH JARRETT

As an influence, Evans didn't entirely supplant Bud Powell and Thelonious Monk. Steve Kuhn and Don Friedman, two pianists who became known in the early 1960's, were often lumped together as Evans protégés, but both developed unique approaches that reflected the works of the bop pioneers as well as developments in classical music. Still, Evans's style, his harmonic explorations and voicings, were decisive in the careers of many younger pianists, including Herbie Hancock, Chick Corea, and Keith Jarrett, the most popular pianists of a younger generation.

Corea and Jarrett appear to have also been influenced by Evans's contemporary Paul Bley, who was born in Canada in 1932. Early in his career, Bley was intrigued by Dave Brubeck's forays into bitonality—the pianist would at some times venture into a different key than his rhythm section. Bley soon was himself taking a flexible approach to a tune's chord changes. After performing in New York in the early fifties, he moved in 1955 to Los Angeles. Between 1956 and 1958, he was leading a quintet that sometimes included Ornette Coleman and his cohorts. In the private recordings of the Bley-Coleman group, Bley sometimes interrupts the flow of chords on a piece to harp on a chord that temporarily intrigues him, or repeats a sequence instead of moving on as the tune's structure would seem to demand. He finishes without resolution, creating an open-ended effect similar to Coleman's free modulations.

As he matured, Bley's playing became frequently pithy and epigrammatic, though he was not averse to broad, spacious statements of tunes such as Carla Bley's "Ida Lupino." (Born Carla Borg, composer and bandleader Carla Bley was for a time married to Bley.) When Bley played with a trio, he showed himself interested in taking the type of group Bill Evans had pioneered and extending it. He showed how far he could go in his trio record, *Japan Suite,* made in 1976 with bassist Gary Peacock and drummer Barry Altschul. *Japan Suite* is totally improvised, full of shifting tempos, and intriguing interactions. Powerful though he can be, Bley takes care not to dominate: His spare comments behind Peacock's opening solo are suggestive rather than imposing. Bill Evans had also recorded with Peacock—in 1963. In fact Evans, Paul Bley, Keith Jarrett, and Ornette Coleman often hired the same sidemen. Longtime members of Ornette Coleman's groups, Dewey Redman and Charlie Haden formed half of a famous Keith Jarrett quartet from the late sixties through much of the seventies—the fourth member was Paul Motian, once Bill Evans's drummer. Evans recorded with drummer Jack DeJohnette, who also recorded two albums entitled *Standards* with Keith Jarrett and Gary Peacock. The interweaving personnel suggest their common interests and mutual influences.

Herbie Hancock has been well known since 1963, when the then 23-year-old pianist was hired by Miles Davis for what turned out to be a five-year tour. He seemed to have two styles: a light-fingered, impressionist approach, and a funky, gospel-tinged blues style, which he first demonstrated on Donald Byrd's "Pentecostal Feeling." He came by both styles honestly. Brought up in Chicago, he was a classical prodigy who played the first movement of Mozart's "Coronation" Concerto (K. 537) with the Chicago Symphony when he was 11. He became interested in jazz almost by chance. "When I was in high school, I heard a guy, Don James, who was in my class improvising in one of the variety shows that our school had." He grilled his classmate on what he was doing.

The answers were satisfactory. Before Hancock graduated to go on to Grinnell College, he was leading a student jazz band. He transcribed solos by Oscar Peterson and George Shearing, and learned harmony, he says, by studying the records of the Hi-Los, a sophisticated popular vocal group of the time. Trumpeter Donald Byrd hired Hancock during a Chicago snowstorm in 1960 when the regular pianist got stranded. Hancock played with Byrd from 1961 to 1963. In that period he also performed with Eric Dolphy. As he told Nat Hentoff for the notes to his 1964 *Inventions and Dimensions*, "In December 1962 and January 1963, I worked with Eric Dolphy. It was my first exposure—as a participant—to 'free' music. I mean to a way of playing that allowed for more spontaneity than anything I'd been involved in before. At the beginning, I thought I'd be afraid to play just anything I felt, but as I got used to it, the experience gassed

Herbie Hancock at a synthesizer, promotional photo, probably around 1980. (Courtesy Rutgers Institute of Jazz Studies)

me so much that I decided to plan for a record session in that vein. I've been further stimulated to think about it during my time with Miles Davis."

Hancock's experience with the Miles Davis band was crucial. His friend, drummer Tony Williams, kept him in touch with avant-garde jazz, and Davis taught him, Hancock says, how to get to the heart of a composition, and encouraged his spontaneity. Working at the breakneck speeds of Davis's up-tempo pieces, Hancock developed a spare, suggestive accompanying technique. He also worked on a free-and-easy approach to ballad playing, as we can hear in the delicate, cleverly stated introduction to "My Funny Valentine," recorded in Tokyo in July 1964.

He was working with the great new rhythm section of Ron Carter and Tony Williams. They were trying new things nightly. On the Davis recording of "Autumn Leaves" made in Berlin in September 1964, accompanying Wayne Shorter, they forsake the chord progression to pursue an increasingly intense vamp. During his solo on "Walkin' " Hancock slows the tempo down almost to a stop, and then gradually returns to the original, shockingly fast tempo. Carter and Williams go right along with him: No one misses a beat. (On the same tune, in July 1964, they followed the lead of saxophonist Sam Rivers, playing freely, without a beat, and then returned to the original tempo.) Hancock's plastic sense of rhythm reflects his years with Tony Williams as well as his listening to the Bill Evans trio. His fleet, single-note lines, lightly articulated, reflect his classical training as well as the approach of Lennie Tristano. He became a valued accompanist. When playing "So What" on the album *Four and More*, Miles Davis left large spaces for Hancock to fill. The pianist doesn't merely comp behind him: He invents intriguing ideas that create a continuity and support Davis needed. Though more spread out, Hancock's suggestive voicings are descended from Evans's.

During his years with Miles Davis, Hancock recorded under his own name for Blue Note. His first album, *Takin' Off* (1962) featured an all-star group that included veteran tenor Dexter Gordon and trumpeter Freddie Hubbard. It produced a hit in Hancock's soulful "Watermelon Man," which was rerecorded by, among others, conga drummer Mongo Santamaria. Hancock became known as an intriguing writer, whether for soul blues such as "Blindman, Blindman" (1963) or freer works such as the numbers on his album *Inventions and Dimensions* (1964). Even in the sixties, Hancock's range was notable and his technique striking as we see in his willingness to play freely over the beat, in his distinctively plastic rhythmic sense, and in his overt funkiness—always with a light touch—on the blues. He made overtly commercial records—he told Len Lyons that "Watermelon Man" "was written to help sell my first album." He also wrote intriguing pieces that became popular because of what they suggested to other musicians.

In 1965, Hancock recorded an album of his compositions, *Maiden Voyage*. Its influential title cut couldn't be simpler in outline—it's a modal piece in AABA form. It's an atmospheric piece, largely because of its distinctive soft Latin-rock feel, enhanced by the dramatic cymbal work of Tony Williams. This stripped down composition unfolds over a distinctive piano vamp, formed on what are called suspended chords, which have an elusive, unresolved quality. (The feeling of suspension comes from building a chord out of fourths or fifths rather than thirds—the musical example illustrates this voicing, one of Hancock's favorites.) Each chord in "Maiden Voyage" lasts for four bars. The A melody has few notes—its opening upward fourth gives the effect of a fanfare. The B section is a variation of the A—it has a similar melody that begins up a fourth from the A—but that melody relates differently to the underlying chord, and it continues in its own way. (See music example.)

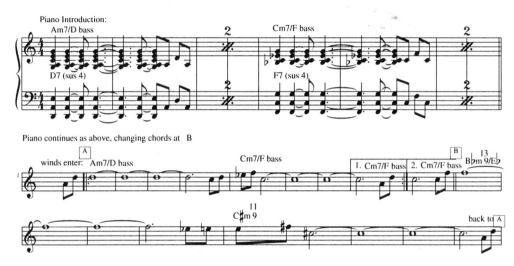

Example 19–3.
Herbie Hancock, "Maiden Voyage."

On this recording Freddie Hubbard creates a remarkable trumpet solo—richly expressive, totally personal—that is widely admired. In this composition Hancock was moving with the times, simplifying the chord sequences and even the melody, and creating a floating, casual sense of time.

In the early seventies, Hancock led his own experimental groups, featuring extended improvisations in a band that included saxophonist and bass clarinetist Benny Maupin, trumpeter Eddie Henderson and, on synthesizers, Patrick Gleason. Bassist Buster Williams and drummer Billy Hart filled out the rhythm section of a band that sometimes included trombonist Julian Priester. Although this band sometimes indulged in open-ended free jazz explorations, Hancock, stimulated perhaps by the success of Miles Davis's "rock" bands, soon reintroduced a funky beat. His fusion work is discussed in Chapter 21. Much of the rest of his career has been in fusion, but Hancock has never settled on funk—or jazz—exclusively. In the eighties he began playing and recording acoustic piano concerts again.

When Herbie Hancock left Miles Davis, he was replaced by Armando "Chick" Corea. Corea was born in Chelsea, Massachusetts in 1941. His father, who was his first teacher, led Latin bands around Boston. Corea listened early on to bebop, and was inspired by Bud Powell and then by Horace Silver, whose solos he transcribed. In the early sixties he played in the Afro-Cuban bands of Mongo Santamaria and Willie Bobo. The pianist in such a band plays what is called a *montuno*, a short rhythmic figure, often two bars long, that is repeated throughout the piece: One can hear Corea play such a figure on Santamaria's "Carmela" (on *Go, Mongo*, Riverside Records, recorded in 1962). These montunos are played with both hands, often in octaves or in tenths. Corea's jazz style frequently includes passages where his two hands are perfectly coordinated in this manner.

In 1964, Corea was working with the hard bop trumpeter Blue Mitchell, and, in 1965, he played with flutist Herbie Mann, whose Latin-tinged band scored a big hit at the Newport Jazz Festival. The recordings Corea made with Blue Mitchell sold fewer copies, but were probably more important to the young pianist, for Mitchell recorded several of Corea's early compositions. "Tones For Joan's Bones" is a typically complicated Corea piece, in ABCAD form and with several rhythms and moods. "Tones for Joan's Bones" became the title cut for Corea's first album as a leader, recorded in 1966 with trumpeter Woody Shaw. On this piece, Corea's sparkling improvised lines suggest the percussive clarity of McCoy Tyner as much as the sensitivity of Bill Evans. In the next two years, Corea would play with Stan Getz, who recorded his "Litha" and "Windows" in 1967.

Chick Corea at Baker's Keyboard Lounge, Detroit, 1972. (Photo by Michael Ullman)

In 1968, Corea was performing with Miles Davis. He had been recommended to Davis by fellow Bostonian Tony Williams. Davis featured Corea on the electric piano, as we hear on "Petits Machins," recorded on June 19. In 1968 he also recorded, with bassist Miroslav Vitous and drummer Roy Haynes, one of his most exciting records, *Now He Sings, Now He Sobs.* Corea's right-hand solos with Blue Mitchell demonstrated, sometimes baldly, the influence of Bud Powell. By the time of his first records as a leader, he was an original pianist who was reaching out harmonically and structurally towards free improvisation.

His trio was tougher, freer, and less romantic than the Bill Evans group. It depended on the quicksilver reflexes of Haynes and of Vitous, who had been trained in a Czechoslavakian conservatory since he was in his early teens. (Vitous would go on to be a charter member of a key fusion band, Weather Report.) Because Corea was interested both in developing his compositional sense, and in expanding the freedom of the group's interactions, the pieces on *Now He Sings, Now He Sobs* range from the complicated title cut to the ostensibly simple 12-bar blues, "Matrix" (JP). "Matrix," which seems to owe something to McCoy Tyner's "Reaching Fourth" (1962), has three phrases mostly stated by Corea in two-handed octaves—as in the Tyner piece, the first climbs, the second busily whirls, and the third descends. The theme of "Matrix" is played with rhythmic freedom, not in a clear 12 bars, but the the solos take place over a quick tempo. With his bright, percussive touch, his absolutely sure rhythm, Corea produces long, swirling lines, pentatonic and chromatic runs, and left-hand chords reminiscent of Tyner. It is virtuosic, and somehow innocently cheerful. (Corea's "Matrix" solo was later orchestrated and recorded by the Lee Konitz nonet.) (See music example.)

By 1970, Corea and bassist Dave Holland left Miles Davis to explore acoustic free improvisation and their own compositions. On *The Song of Singing,* they played, with drummer Barry Altschul, the gently dancing Dave Holland theme "Toy Room," and moved immediately into loose, free, and stirring group improvisation. They paid tribute to Ornette Coleman, playing a zestfully funky version of his "Blues Connotation." On this tune, Corea's spiky accents reflect another of his masters: Thelonious Monk. The clarity and force of his playing come out of the best of bop; the approach to the tune reflects Ornette Coleman. Corea's trio forged a brilliantly satisfying compromise between bop and free jazz.

To this group Corea added the Chicago-born reed player and composer Anthony Braxton. They called the group Circle, and their initial record, recorded live in Paris, was remarkable. They played several of Braxton's spiky pieces, Dave Holland's "Toy Room," and a long "There is No Greater Love," treating this standard with much of the freedom they used with their own compositions. A seemingly impromptu piece, "Duet," begins with a long, gracefully wandering introduction by Corea, after which he is joined by Braxton on alto saxophone. Braxton begins with some of his most lyrical playing on record, and then picks up on a hiccuping phrase with which Corea began. Braxton begins a

Example 19–4.
Chick Corea's first two improvised choruses after the theme of "Matrix" (1968).

kind of conversation with himself with this as his material, alternating rough, growling phrases with more traditionally sounded notes. Remarkably, Corea finds a way to accompany him. (Braxton is discussed in Chapter 22.)

Circle was an important group, but it was not to last. On a West Coast trip late in 1971, Corea abruptly broke up the band in order to find a music with wider appeal. Even before, on his two albums entitled *Piano Improvisations* (April 1971), his playing had something of a willed innocence, a calculated simplicity that suggested a musician who was putting unusual restraints on himself. Perhaps those restraints came from his adherence to the quasi-religious philosophy called Scientology, with its emphasis on self-realization with the goal of becoming what scientologists call "clear." In March 1972, Corea recorded again with Stan Getz in a quintet that included Tony Williams, bassist Stanley Clarke and the Brazilian percussionist Airto Moreira. Getz recorded five Corea compositions, including "La Fiesta," "Five Hundred Miles High" and "Captain Marvel."

To perform in these pieces and others, Corea, with Clarke and Moreira, had already formed his popular band, eventually to be called Return to Forever. (Many of his titles from now on would suggest childlike concerns.) Corea's keyboards were the only electronic instruments in this group, which was notable for its Brazilian influence: It featured Moreira and his wife, Brazilian singer Flora Purim. Corea's *Light as a Feather* (1973) included an infectious Corea composition, "Spain," which comes in three distinct sections, and begins with an introduction based on Rodrigo's "Concierto de Aranjuez." (See music example.)

to a variant of [A],
then back to [B],
then solos.

Example 19–5.
Chick Corea, first two themes of "Spain" (1972), after the introduction.

The soloists improvise over the chords of the third section, which is played in samba rhythm. Equally appealing is Corea's infectious "La Fiesta," from the album *Return to Forever*. The group Return to Forever garnered Corea the fame he wanted while still allowing him to grow as a composer. The second Return to

Forever, which he started in the mid-seventies, featured electric guitarist Bill Connors in 1973 and Al DiMeola starting in 1974, and is discussed in Chapter 21.

During most of 1969, Chick Corea's tenure with Miles Davis coincided with that of another keyboardist, Keith Jarrett, who was born in Allentown, Pennsylvania in 1945. Jarrett's presence there was surprising. Jarrett was dedicated to the acoustic piano, and Davis had him play first electric organ, and then electric piano. Presumably the Miles Davis aura compensated him for what he perceived as the indignity of playing an inappropriate instrument. Like Corea and Hancock, Jarrett was a child prodigy trained in classical music. While still a teenager, Jarrett gave in his hometown a solo concert of his own music. After high school—and after a brief tour with the sweet dance band, Fred Waring's Pennsylvanians—Jarrett moved to Boston to attend the Berklee School (now College) of Music. By 1965 he was trying to establish himself in New York City. He worked with Roland Kirk and clarinetist Tony Scott, but his break came when Art Blakey heard him in a jam session, and hired him. They recorded *Buttercorn Lady* in 1966 with trumpeter Chuck Mangione, now a famous fusion composer. With Blakey, Jarrett performed in a brisk style: His solo on "Secret Love," though dominated by single note lines, moves wittily in unexpected directions, both harmonically and rhythmically.

Jarrett blossomed in the Charles Lloyd Quartet, with which he played from 1966 to 1969. Lloyd was a phenomenon. In the late sixties his group was one of the most popular in jazz, both in America and abroad, and among rock as well as jazz fans. The saxophonist and flutist was born in Memphis in 1938, but lived from the fifties on in California. In 1961, he worked under drummer Chico Hamilton, and three years later he performed with Cannonball Adderley's sextet. In 1965 he led a group that featured Herbie Hancock and guitarist Gabor Szabo. Then, in 1966, Lloyd struck gold with Keith Jarrett, drummer Jack DeJohnette and bassist Cecil McBee.

The appeal of Lloyd's quartet was various. Lloyd played a modified— tamed, one might say—version of John Coltrane's style, and he doubled on the sweet-sounding flute. Many of his tunes, like "Island Blues," or "Sombrero Sam," were mellifluous, gentle, and readily comprehensible. The quartet seemed the perfect California band, designed for the Woodstock generation. They performed long, sometimes ecstatic versions of tunes with seductive titles such as "Dream Weaver," "Journey Within" and "Love Song to a Baby" in rock venues such as the Fillmore West. Lloyd's goal was "to transform things and make this a blissful place." His instinct for drama was sure: He prefaces his "Forest Flower '69" with a free, unaccompanied solo in which he uses many of the devices—squeaks, swirls, and half-articulated notes—that had been developed by avant-garde saxophonists. Lloyd uses them for near-comic effect. His transition into the pretty harmonies and Latin beginning of "Forest Flower" resolves whatever tension the solo set up. No wonder the quartet was popular.

Frequently Jarrett stole the show. His technique was if anything more eclectic than Lloyd's, drawing on the lyricism of Bill Evans and Paul Bley, on Bud Powell's right-hand lines, on classical music, gospel and on the techniques

The Charles Lloyd Quartet, probably 1967. Keith
Jarrett is in the foreground. In the back, from left:
Ron McLure, bass, Jack DeJohnette, drums, and
Lloyd. (Courtesy Rutgers Institute of Jazz Studies)

of free improvisation. He uses gospel chords and rocking left-hand vamps to
create space for his right-hand melodies. Much of the early Jarrett style can be
heard in his solo on "Forest Flower" recorded live in Monterey in 1966, and in
his accompaniment to the Lloyd solo that follows. (See music example.)

Unlike most post-bop players, Jarrett also loves simple harmonies. Over
repetitive vamps, he takes extended solos with broad, arching shapes, with
extended crescendos and repeated returns to simple, gospel-like figures and
melodies. The first, untitled, number of his celebrated concert at Koln on
January 24, 1975, has him inventing a 26 minute improvisation in G major based
largely on an alternation between two simple chords—A minor and G major. He
begins slowly, with spinning right-hand lines and hesitant chords, but by the
sixth minute of the piece he has settled into a groove. Over a loud rhythmic bass
made up of these two chords, he begins working on a simple melody—B down
to E, up to C; B down to D, back to B. Here, he is typically songful, working
patiently with the simplest materials.

He's fascinating to watch: He rises from his bench, bends over the piano,
twisting his thin frame like a piece of licorice while chanting in unison with his

Example 19–6.
Keith Jarrett, end of his first improvised chorus on "Forest Flower—Sunrise"
(1966) with the Charles Lloyd Quartet.

top notes, or tunelessly. His solos provoked ecstatic responses from audiences, and puzzled commentary from critics. Jarrett is known for his arrogance as well as for his virtuosity: He wrote in the notes to his *Solo Concerts* box that such an album "has never been done before unless you classify it as an opera or as a competitor of the 'Well Tempered Clavichord' " of Bach. His attitude has alienated some critics and musicians, but there is no question about his astounding musical gift.

Jarrett is a restless musician, and something of a prodigy—he regularly plays soprano sax as well as piano, and on his second album as a leader, the 1968 *Restoration Ruin*, he played nine instruments by overdubbing. He also sang. Jarrett is sometimes at his best embroidering simple material. We can hear him brilliantly transform Bob Dylan's "My Back Pages," in a lyrical masterpiece from *Somewhere Before*, made live in 1968 with bassist Charlie Haden—Ornette Coleman's bassist—and drummer Paul Motian. As noted above, this trio, with the addition of tenor saxophonist Dewey Redman—also known for his work with Coleman—gave the Jarrett quartet the feeling of an Ornette Coleman group more oriented to chord progressions, but it retained its own streak of romanticism. With this quartet, Jarrett composed intriguing vehicles and demonstrated a flexible approach to free playing. On "Rotation" from *Mysteries* (1976), one hears long lines that could be bop-derived but are played in a free context, and one notes the unusually active conversation between the pianist's hands: Jarrett plays lines as well as chords with his left hand. (That aspect of his technique may have come from Bach, whose music he has recorded.)

Jarrett's technique is eclectic: At a solo concert in Bremen recorded during the summer of 1973, he plays quiet, Bill Evans-inspired melodies, refers to Debussy, and introduces an ostinato bass line, which he transforms into a boogie-woogie pattern. Those sections come early in an hour-long improvisation. He worked on and off between 1974 and 1980 with Norwegian saxophonist Jan Garbarek in what was sometimes called his European quartet. He was also composing chamber music. In 1980 Jarrett recorded a three-movement work for piano and orchestra, *The Celestial Hawk*. He temporarily stopped playing solo jazz concerts in 1984 and began giving classical recitals. He has since 1987 returned to solo improvising, this time including shorter versions of jazz standards as well as free pieces. He has recorded several albums of standards with bassist Gary Peacock and drummer Jack DeJohnette.

PIANISTS IN THE TRADITION OF ELLINGTON AND MONK

In his solo concerts, Jarrett appears to show the influence of the South African pianist Abdullah Ibrahim (b. 1934). Ibrahim is one of a group of modern pianists who developed the percussive, harmonically intriguing styles of Duke Ellington and Thelonious Monk rather than follow the lead of Bud Powell. Monk—and Ellington—have helped reestablish an orchestral style of piano playing. Ibrahim's strengths are his indomitable rhythmic power and the lyrical lilt of his compositions, whose dancing quality derives from African traditional music and African pop.

Ibrahim was born Dollar Brand in Capetown in 1934. Since the mid-seventies, he has performed solo, and recorded with a small band he calls

Ekaya. One of the group's masterpieces is a work that Ibrahim wrote about home when in his chosen exile from South Africa. It's a slow, graceful, luminously nostalgic dance that he calls "Water from an Ancient Well," recorded in 1985. Ibrahim's is a unique acoustic fusion music, bringing an African lyricism and rhythmic life to modern jazz.

Although Randy Weston was born in Brooklyn in 1926, he considers that his musical roots are in Africa. Weston plays with a percussiveness that derives from Monk and Ellington, while his rhythms and orchestral approach derive from what he heard in Africa. Weston is also a remarkable composer. He has written simple, infectious blues lines ("Berkshire Blues"), graceful waltzes ("Little Niles"), richly harmonized tributes ("African Lady"), and whimsical lines such as the oft-recorded "Hi-Fly," which is based on a leap upwards of a fifth and a return to the original note, which repeats itself like a bouncing ball running out of steam.

Among pianists of Weston's generation, we can single out Mal Waldron, also born in New York in 1926. Also influenced by the percussive sounds of Ellington, Monk, and Bud Powell, Waldron's playing is percussive, economical and full of tart harmonies and effectively repeated phrases that seem to build tension in an orderly fashion. In the late fifties, Waldron became Billie Holiday's last accompanist. Soon, Waldron was also working with members of the avant-garde—his composition "Fire Waltz" appears on the 1961 *Eric Dolphy at the Five Spot*. In 1965, he emigrated to Europe, where, in the eighties, he teamed up with soprano saxophonist Steve Lacy in a series of performances and recordings.

Since the end of the sixties, pianists had a great range of styles to choose from, even without using electronic instruments. Jaki Byard, who has played with Mingus and Dolphy, introduces ragtime and a hyperactive strain of stride into his often comic performances. On numbers such as "Tea for Two," which he recorded live for Prestige Records in 1965, he introduces a frenetic imitation of a famous Art Tatum performance; he also plays in a free style.

The voicings of modern pianists have become more open, more suggestive. These voicings are used for different purposes. A pianist such as Joanne Brackeen draws on the powerful chordal style of McCoy Tyner as well as the driven right-hand lines of Bud Powell. Andrew Hill, best known for his Blue Note recordings from the sixties, has a dense, Monkish style, which he plays in free and modal contexts. One shouldn't discount the influence of the free playing of Cecil Taylor, with its shimmering, overlapping lines, played in irregular phrase lengths, its sudden poundings, and wavelike motions, dense or suddenly lyrical and understated. Don Pullen, another Mingus alumnus, has drawn on Taylor, producing with his relatively small hands darting lines punctuated by tonal clusters—he'll even use his fist at times. In the eighties, pianist Marilyn Crispell appeared in the Anthony Braxton quartet: Her spiky, fleet style in the eccentrically structured Braxton pieces, or in free jazz, has been consistently exciting. So has the more linear, swinging playing of Geri Allen. Her ability to move from structured improvisation into exciting Taylorish free playing and back seems to point the way for jazz piano. Its near future is in capable hands.

20 The Sixties: Big Band, Bossa Nova, and Soul

In the fifties, as previously discussed, musicians extended the bebop tradition in at least two directions, creating cool jazz and hard bop. In the turbulent sixties, the soloists who were emphasizing the roots of jazz continued to be influenced by rhythm and blues, by gospel, and by urban blues. Their music, seen by many as a reaffirmation of the basics of African-American culture, was frequently called soul jazz. A contrast to more cerebral styles of jazz, it was part of a movement among young African-Americans who, proud of their people's accomplishments and rich cultural tradition, took a newly enthusiastic look at black popular music. Like avant-garde jazz, the "soul" movement in jazz was related, albeit indirectly, to the political struggles of the sixties—to the civil rights movement, to the speeches and autobiography of Malcolm X, with his proud insistence that black is beautiful. And it was perhaps a healthy reaction to some jazz critics and fans who separated the music they loved from a more commercial music popular among black audiences. The distinctions among some types of African-American music—gospel, blues, jazz, rhythm and blues—were at least blurred in the sixties.

The effects of the political turmoil of the era on jazz were various, and complicated. The rage many musicians felt about racial injustice, epitomized in the sixties by the assassinations of Martin Luther King and Malcolm X and by inner city riots, was expressed more or less directly by some avant-garde players in screaming, inchoate solos amid a barrage of barely organized sounds from free ensembles. Some listeners felt that this music put them up against a wall of sound. A more traditional response to political agony might be illustrated by big band composer Oliver Nelson, who in the sixties wrote his tuneful "Afro-American Sketches," "Kennedy's Dream," "Black, Brown and Beautiful," and "Self Help is Needed," and by composer Gary McFarland, whose ironic six-part suite, *America the Beautiful*, was subtitled, "An Account of its Disappearance."

The counterculture of the late sixties and early seventies, and all the reasons the so-called establishment offered young people to drop out, led to Pharoah Sanders's broadly meditative "Karma" (1969), on which Leon Thomas chants "The creator has a master plan, Peace and happiness for every man," and to Sun Ra's assertion (in 1972) that "Space is the place," the place where men and women can live freely and happily. In the seventies, when political despair frequently replaced the more active ferment of the previous decade, John McLaughlin's Mahavishnu Orchestra, with its "Visions of the Emerald Beyond" (1975), became popular. Such musicians seemed to be urging us to withdraw into a presumably more pleasing meditative state, to acknowledge "The Smile of the Beyond."

There was nothing otherworldly about the varieties of rhythm and blues and soul music that influenced some jazz in the fifties and sixties. The gospel-tinged, dance-oriented musics of Wilson Pickett, Etta James, Otis Redding, Ray Charles, James Brown, and later Aretha Franklin had their predecessors in jazz. The screaming saxophone of King Curtis on "Memphis Soul Stew," of Hal Singer on "Cornbread"—even the titles suggest a new attitude towards black culture!—harked back to Illinois Jacquet's 1942 solo on "Flying Home" with the Lionel Hampton big band. According to *The Autobiography of Malcolm X*, in 1940 Lionel Hampton's was the favorite big band among Eastern black folk, who responded ecstatically to its insistent beat. In the book *Listen Up*, Quincy Jones called Lionel Hampton's "the first rock and roll band. There's no question about it—it's the first band I ever heard that was concerned with having a big funky beat and really seduced an audience with a passion" (p. 46). The pounding, honking Jacquet style on "Flying Home" had a wide-ranging influence, and some direct imitators. Honking saxophonist Mighty Joe Houston had a hit in the mid-fifties with his version of "Flying Home." In 1955, veteran Texas tenor Arnett Cobb pushed the piece towards absurdity in "Flying Home Mambo." (Even Ornette Coleman, as noted earlier, trained in this style of music.)

Blues singers had been a part of the big bands, which sometimes edged towards rhythm and blues. And after the big band period had waned, Louis Jordan scored big hits with little bands, singing humorous songs like "Ain't Nobody Here but Us Chickens" (1946) in a hip, confiding voice, and then wailing on alto sax. The small jump bands of Louis Jordan and of such figures as the West Coast singer-drummer Roy Milton were the immediate predecessors of rhythm and blues, and they kept the rollicking blues alive where jazz players would find them. If the blues in jazz led to rhythm and blues, soul, and rock and roll, the favor was returned in the sixties, when jazz players reemphasized their roots, and "soulfulness" became a standard by which jazz was often judged.

Hard bop and the blues helped give rise to soul jazz. Cool jazz had its stepchild in the sixties as well—the seductive, Brazilian variation on the samba called bossa nova. That both styles, hot and cool, were popular suggests that jazz fans had developed considerable range as listeners, and that jazz was able to reach fans of other kinds of popular music. Cannonball Adderley's version of "Mercy, Mercy, Mercy" (1966) amongst soul hits, for instance, and Stan Getz's

1963 version of "The Girl from Ipanema," reached a wider public than the hard-core jazz fans. They affected the music scene as a whole, making some modern jazz seem more accessible than ever before.

They did so in a period when jazz needed a commercial boost. Despite the popular successes of Dave Brubeck and Erroll Garner, Oscar Peterson, Ella Fitzgerald, and a few others, the future of jazz playing was becoming more murky as the decade wore on. The problem, simply put, was that all over the country many of the small clubs that had sustained the music were closing. Fewer people were going out at night—some preferred to stay home and watch their televisions, on which they saw evidence of increasing violence in the neigborhoods where many of the jazz clubs were found. Racial tensions in the jazz world may have scared some listeners off, especially white fans who heard the insistence of young musicians that jazz was a black music, and wondered where they fit in.

There seemed to be a shift in the way people wanted to listen to music. Such shifts had occurred earlier. Big time jazz in the twenties was presented at large clubs and theaters in which the bands were part of stage shows. In the swing era most people danced to the music in large dance halls, and a few heard it played in small clubs. Such clubs proliferated in the forties, until 52nd Street boasted over a dozen places simultaneously presenting jazz. Those clubs gradually succumbed to commercial pressures, rising rents and shifting tastes. Some of the best known jazz spots closed or changed their formats in the sixties and seventies. By the end of the sixties, Birdland in New York was operating under a new name and presenting rhythm and blues acts. Other well-known clubs alternated jazz bookings with comedians, female impersonators, or budding rock groups. Some clubs were torn down in the type of urban renewal project that raised rents astronomically in Manhattan and other major cities, and that made a small jazz club a grave economic risk.

The result has been that from the sixties to the present, jazz musicians have complained about the decreasing numbers of places where they can perform, and the number of working bands—groups that stick together and play long tours—have decreased to a handful. Jazz festivals, concerts, and college dates have supported well-known musicians, but it has become increasingly difficult for apprentice musicians to get the kind of experience in jam sessions and local clubs, sometimes with visiting greats, that earlier players could depend on.

BIG BANDS IN THE SIXTIES

Curiously, during this period some sounds of jazz were more and more widely heard. It's easy to forget the role of television and the movies in popularizing jazz in the late fifties and sixties. There were few serious presentations of the music at its most challenging on the air—"The Sound of Jazz" from 1957 is the most distinguished example—but jazz compositions were often used to provide theme music. Henry Mancini, a fan of Gil Evans and the Thornhill band, set the tone with his themes and background music for the *Peter Gunn* television series in 1958, and for the *Mr. Lucky* series from two years later. In the sixties, the big band of Maynard Ferguson could be heard providing background music for car chases, and movie directors who wanted a sophisticated atmosphere turned to jazz composers and West Coast jazz soloists for their scores. Quincy Jones scored the influential soundtrack to *The Pawnbroker* in 1964. J. J. Johnson and Benny Carter, among other distinguished big-band composers, worked steadily in West Coast studios for decades.

These musicians were successful because they were able and willing to adapt to the needs of the media, and to make their jazz-honed skills work—at least sometimes—in the marketplace. Drawing on bebop arranging styles to which they added a more modern funkiness, these composers helped keep the big band sound alive, at least in the studios. Oliver Nelson was both an arranger and a saxophonist who in his short life (1932–1975) performed in small band sessions, in the Louis Bellson and Ellington bands (briefly) and led a variety of ensembles. He is best known as a composer of albums such as his *Blues and the Abstract Truth* from 1961. On that small band date, he introduced his 16-bar C minor blues, "Stolen Moments," which has become a jazz standard. Just as interesting is his boppish tribute to country music, "Hoe Down." The album features Nelson's keening tone on tenor sax, contrasted with the driving, eccentric-sounding saxophones and flute of Eric Dolphy. Bill Evans and Freddie Hubbard are also featured.

Nelson became the regular arranger for a variety of musicians, including organist Jimmy Smith. A consummate professional, he produced brassy, bouncy arrangements that left plenty of space for his featured soloists. He could be commercial: In 1965, Nelson arranged the popular *Goin' Out of My Head* for Wes Montgomery, and thus figured in that guitarist's gradual move towards pop. But even there, on "Twisted Blues," one finds a swinging, hard driving chart in which the band is used to punctuate—to exclaim shoutingly at the ends of phrases, and to create bright climaxes. Montgomery's brilliant early albums such as *The Incredible Jazz Guitar* (1960) were eventually followed by more commercial efforts such as *California Dreamin'* (1966) and the song just mentioned. His last albums—he died in 1968—held little interest for jazz fans. But his impeccable melodic lines, his playing in octaves, and quickly moving chords would make Montgomery the most influential guitarist since Charlie Christian.

In the sixties and early seventies, Oliver Nelson also seemed to be split between concert jazz and commercial music. He had largely dropped his progressive saxophone playing, and never again hired as untraditional a soloist as Eric Dolphy. He started to write film scores, such as the score for *Death of a Gunfighter* (1969), a movie whose main interest now is the way Lena Horne is used as the love interest for Richard Widmark. In 1966 he wrote a dynamic concert piece, *Sound Piece for Jazz Orchestra*, but then composed the music for the television series *Ironside*, whose pilot was made in 1967. He composed a heartfelt tribute to John F. Kennedy in 1967, and in 1971 paid tribute to Ellington in *Black, Brown and Beautiful*. He had learned something from Ellington's use of woodwinds—Nelson used a clarinet trio and muted brass on "End of a Love Affair" with Wes Montgomery. But his arrangements are more typically punchy and hard driving.

So are those of Quincy Jones (b. 1933), who even before he paired up with Michael Jackson was the best modern example of a musician able to make it in both jazz and pop worlds. Quincy Delight Jones, whose story has been told in the documentary film and book *Listen Up! The Lives of Quincy Jones,* moved from Chicago to Seattle when he was 10 years old. Soon afterwards, he took up trumpet and started hanging around jazz musicians, including singer Ray Charles. Jones pestered the singer for advice on arranging, and a few years later confronted trumpeter Clark Terry, then with the Count Basie Orchestra, with similar questions. Jones's early friendships were longlasting: In the late fifties, he arranged *Basie: One More Time* and *Basie-Eckstine* for the band leader, and in 1959, *The Genius of Ray Charles* for the singer.

In 1951, Jones accepted a scholarship to a Boston conservatory, the Schillinger House. He left almost immediately to join the Lionel Hampton big band, a band that included Clifford Brown. Hampton recorded Jones's "Kingfish"—his first recorded composition. In 1953, Jones used the opportunity that being abroad with Hampton provided of recording Quincy Jones's Swedish American All-Stars. By the end of the fifties, he seemed ubiquitous, having arranged dozens of albums—for singers Helen Merrill, Dinah Washington, Sarah Vaughan and Jackie and Roy, for Dizzy Gillespie and Cannonball Adderley and James Moody, Milt Jackson and Billy Taylor. He could write hard-rocking arrangements, but as he demonstrated on the 1957 "Blues at Twilight," which he wrote for Milt Jackson's *Plenty Plenty Soul,* he could write a sweetly relaxed blues line as well. He had a commercial bent, and considerable intellectual curiosity as well: He took 18 months off to study composition in Paris with the famous classical teacher, Nadia Boulanger.

After a 1956 state department tour with Dizzy Gillespie, he assembled a band of the best young bebop musicians he could find and recorded *This is How I Feel About Jazz.* In 1959, he formed a band for the European tour of the show *Free and Easy* and when the show folded, he toured with the band. The tour was an economic disaster: He ended up selling off the rights to his compositions to buy tickets to get his players home. That may have been a crucial experience for Jones, who would never again ignore the business side of music so thoroughly— and who would never again take a big band on the road. His reticence is typical: Most of the big band composers from the sixties on would assemble recording groups, or bands for special occasions, but would rarely keep a band together for long tours.

This rare failure modified but did not impede Jones's career—in 1961, he took a job as a producer for Mercury Records. By 1964, he was a vice president. In 1961 he received his first Grammy nominations, for *The Great Wide World of Quincy Jones* and for his arrangement of "Let the Good Times Roll" for Ray Charles. He also recorded *The Quintessence* for Impulse, a brilliant album in which he tries to combine the punch of post-Kenton big-band writing with some of the subtlety of Basie's swing and Ellington's textures. He's ingenious: The mid-tempo rocker "Hard Sock Dance" begins quietly and builds to two solo trumpet breaks, one by Freddie Hubbard and one by Thad Jones, each of which is answered by the drums of Bill English. Behind the extended trumpet solos that follow, Quincy Jones writes riffs whose rich voicings, and use of the clarinet, remind us of Ellington. His main melody is suave, bouncy, and memorable. Jones brings out the exoticism of Bronislau Kaper's "Invitation" with a flute stating the first part of the melody and later some jagged brass riffs behind Oliver Nelson's alto. And he begins the beautifully crafted ballad "Quintessence" with a subdued brass fanfare—the brass includes a quartet of French horns, joined by tuba, trombones and muted trumpets. That piece becomes a showpiece for Phil Woods, whose brash virtuosity has made him one of the best loved mainstream musicians. The varied, dynamic, but rarely intrusive accompaniment to the alto saxophonist's first winsome, and then more typically upbeat solo, demonstrates why Quincy Jones is such a popular arranger among singers.

As the sixties ran by, and times got worse for jazz, Jones scored some commercial dates, making *Quincy Jones Plays the Hip Hits* and an oddly jumbled collection, *Quincy Plays for Pussycats*. In 1965, he took what seemed a surprising step at the time, producing an album for bubble gum rock-and-roller Leslie Gore. He spent the next few years on soundtracks, returning in 1969 to straight ahead jazz, this time with a quartet of women singers behind a big band, on *Walking in Space*. Then, in the seventies, his arrangements for the movie *The Wiz* led to a relationship with Michael Jackson, and the ultimate pop fame. He hadn't abandoned jazz—he doesn't seem to want to abandon any of the music he's touched. His *Back on the Block* (1989) weds bits of jazz with rap, gospel and the blues. His goal, he said, was "to make an album that incorporated the whole family of American black music. From gospel to jazz, everything that's part of my culture" (*Listen Up*, Foldout following p. 169).

Quincy Jones tried touring with a big band, and then gave it up, focusing instead, as did Oliver Nelson, on recording projects rather than struggling to keep an expensive band going on the road. Nonetheless, there were a handful of working big bands. The one led by trumpeter Don Ellis from the late sixties until his premature death in 1978 was unique. It recorded wild jazz-rock pieces in complicated meters such as 7/4 and 19/8, and developed a following.

As mentioned in Chapter 14, Gerry Mulligan also led a big band, first organized in 1960, which featured his light, tastefully orchestrated swing. Mulligan also commissioned arrangements from Gary McFarland, George Russell, and from valve trombonist Bob Brookmeyer, who would become a major arranger for the eighties. His band demonstrated its range in recordings, including its 1961 version of George Russell's challenging "All About Rosie," and the deftly swinging, light-footed "Blueport," a Mulligan piece recorded in 1960. Mulligan disbanded in the mid-sixties, but big bands remained close to his heart and he occasionally regrouped. With a more vigorous rhythm section than he

Thad Jones in Cambridge, Massachusetts, 1970's.
(Photo by Michael Ullman)

had previously used, he made *The Age of Steam in 1971,* and then, in 1980, the grandly swaggering *Walk on the Water.*

Two longlasting big bands took up where Mulligan left off in the sixties—the East Coast Thad Jones-Mel Lewis big band, and the band Toshiko Akiyoshi and Lew Tabackin started on the West Coast. In 1965, cornetist Thad Jones joined with the experienced big band drummer Mel Lewis to form an 18-piece rehearsal band, designed to feature Jones's writing. The brother of pianist Hank and drummer Elvin Jones, Thad was a virtuoso cornetist, whose advanced harmonic ideas were largely suppressed in his nine years (1954-1963) with the Count Basie band. But Basie did encourage Thad to write, recording such Jones numbers as "Mutt and Jeff," with its clever bass and flute unison line.

The Jones-Lewis band brought together some of the best musicians in the city, instrumentalists like baritone saxophonist Pepper Adams, trumpeter Snooky Young, and bassist Richard Davis, who were eager to play big-band jazz, no matter what the pay or circumstances. The band got its first break in February 1966, when it was booked for the first of many years of Monday night engagements at the Village Vanguard. The band's enthusiasm was notable from its first recordings, *Presenting Thad Jones-Mel Lewis and the Jazz Orchestra* (1966) and *Live at the Village Vanguard* (1966). From the very outset, Jones's arrangements became more and more challenging, featuring fast, intricate ensembles for the winds, or opening odd spaces for duets, such as the bass-piano chorus on "The Waltz You 'Swang' for Me." Jones and Lewis also encouraged the writing

Mel Lewis in Cambridge, 1970's. (Photo by Michael Ullman)

of Bob Brookmeyer, whose sweet and sour "Willow Weep for Me" was featured on their first album.

By the end of the sixties, the orchestra was travelling, and Jones was investigating new ideas. "Central Park North," from 1969, sounds at times like an updated "American in Paris." It's designed to evoke the modern city, and includes sections that sound like traffic jams, extended improvisations over a boogaloo beat, and a sweetly evocative solo by Thad Jones on fluegelhorn. The eclecticism of the arrangement is still surprising: The felt coherence of the piece is satisfying.

A year later, Jones-Lewis would record Thad's most popular ballad, the soberly celebratory "A Child is Born." The same album included "Us," a good example of Jones's ability to write directly appealing, in this case funky, music that nevertheless utilizes modern crunching dissonances. (See music example.)

In the seventies Jones's arrangements were being played by college bands across the country, and the band's personnel, although constantly changing, remained topnotch. But this fruitful partnership dissolved when Thad Jones left the band in 1979 to go to Europe. One of their last records together was perhaps ironically named *New Life*. Jones died in Copenhagen in 1986. Mel Lewis led the band until his death in 1990, and it continues today, still at the Village Vanguard.

Toshiko Akiyoshi was born in China to Japanese parents in 1929. She moved with her family to Japan in 1947, where she, already a talented pianist, heard jazz for the first time. She learned to play bebop, and play it well. In 1954, in a series of jam sessions recorded at the Mocambo Club in Yokohama, one can hear Akiyoshi solo on "Donna Lee" in a Bud Powell style. Later she impressed Oscar Peterson, who helped her get a scholarship at the Berklee School (now College) of Music. While at Berklee, from 1956 to 1959, Akiyoshi began playing with alto saxophonist Charlie Mariano, whom she married. They recorded in 1960 for Candid, and again Akiyoshi showed off her bright, percussive piano style, but also her original writing style.

Example 20–1.
**Thad Jones, excerpt from score of "Us" (1970). Ninths, elevenths and
thirteenths are indicated over the saxophone line.**

A still more important part of her career started in 1973, when she and
saxophonist Lew Tabackin, who became her second husband, started a rehearsal band in Los Angeles, where he was playing with the "Tonight Show"
orchestra. Designed to showcase Akiyoshi's writing exclusively, the band recorded *Kogun* in 1974. It was an immediate success, especially in Japan. In this
album and the ones that followed, Akiyoshi demonstrated her ability to use
aspects of Japanese traditional and classical music in a jazz setting. In doing so,
she introduced new sounds to jazz. The piece "Kogun" begins with the chanting
of a singer from the Japanese Noh theater, accompanied traditionally by woodblocks. The sliding, ominous quality of his voice is later imitated by the reeds
in a particularly suggestive, eclectic, and to Western ears, exotic, big-band
chart.

Akiyoshi has written more traditional jazz pieces, most of which feature
devilishly difficult ensemble passages, but her masterpieces are influenced by
her experiences in Japan. These include the 1976 suite, "Minamata," the name of
a village whose people were poisoned by mercury and other industrial wastes.
It begins with a child's song and moves to a trumpet solo over some eerily extended chords, which seem to hang motionlessly behind the bebopping horn. The tragedy to come is suggested by a tsuzumi drummer, and
by the stark singing of a Noh master. Akiyoshi was no more able than Thad
Jones or Oliver Nelson or Quincy Jones to bring back the big band permanently,
but she continues to suggest in a powerful way new directions for jazz writing.

THE BOSSA NOVA

The gently melodic bossa nova, which means something like "new flair," was introduced to American audiences through the thrilling retelling of the Orpheus myth called *Black Orpheus*, a Brazilian movie which won the Cannes Film Festival Grand Prize in 1959. Set in Rio de Janeiro at carnival time, *Black Orpheus* features a dynamic score by Antonio Carlos Jobim and Luiz Bonfa. *Black Orpheus* includes scenes of excited dancers wheeling and prancing over a large, rumbling drum choir that shows a powerful African element still present. Just as important, and more influential in the United States, were the songs: "Manha de Carnaval" and "Samba de Orfeu," by Bonfa, and "O Nosso Amor" and "Felicidade" by Jobim. The haunting "Manha de Carnaval" would in the ensuing decade be recorded by dozens of jazz players, and "Felicidade," with its constantly surprising melody and chords, proved almost as appealing.

At the heart of the bossa nova is an ostinato (repeated) pattern that derives from the samba. (See music example.)

a) Bossa nova (slow and medium tempos)

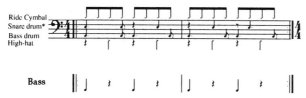

b) Samba (fast tempos)

* Use stick in clavé style.

Example 20–2.
Sample ostinato patterns. (Sambas are often written in 2/4, using halved note values, but one is given here in 4/4 for comparison.) More patterns are in *Creative Coordination for the Performing Drummer* by Keith Copeland (Carl Fischer, 1986).

Over this beat, and its variations, Jobim and Bonfa wrote beautifully crafted melodies, arranged in a manner that suggested the cool school of jazz. As Stan Getz told writer Gene Lees, "In the early 50s, Jobim and Gilberto listened to records of the progenitors of the cool school—which were Miles Davis and myself. And they took the traditional samba, which is hot music—street samba—and put in the harmonies that we used in cool jazz, and the languid approach we used, and out came the bossa nova." Jobim thinks that there was an indigenous cool school in Brazil unrelated to jazz: "I really think that the cool school was there because there was a reaction in Brazil at the time against the pompous: the tango singers, the bolero singers, that were very, you know, 'projecting' their beautiful voices."

Jobim wasn't the first to meld Brazilian popular music and jazz improvisation. As John Storm Roberts has suggested in his book *The Latin Tinge,* another guitarist, Laurindo Almeida, preceded him. Almeida was born in Sao Paulo, Brazil in 1917. From 1947 to 1949 he was with the Stan Kenton Orchestra. Brazilian music was one of its innovations: Kenton featured Almeida in 1947 on "Journey to Brazil." In 1954, Almeida recorded an album of Brazilian music with reedman Bud Shank, whom he had met in the Kenton orchestra, and with bassist Harry Babasin.

Laurindo Almeida Featuring Bud Shank is not a complete melding of the two traditions. Almeida holds strictly to the conventional rhythms of Brazilian music, while bassist Harry Babasin roams more freely. Shank uses more of the double-time figures and blue notes of bebop than would Stan Getz in his samba albums, but he's similarly cool in tone and conception. The sound of Shank's saxophone over Almeida's acoustic guitar on numbers such as "Blue Baiao" was influential. (A baiao is a dance.) Roy Harte, the drummer on the date, said the group intended to combine "the baiao beat with jazz . . . to achieve the light swing feeling of the baiao—combined with jazz blowing. In order to get this, I played brushes on a conga drum, not a snare drum . . . Actually I was trying to play with my right hand to Bud's jazz blowing, and with my left I was putting in the samba color with Laurindo's playing."

Almeida visited Brazil soon after this record was released, and played it for some of his musician friends, including Joao Gilberto, whom Almeida credits as the inventor of the bossa nova. The credit probably should be shared among a group of musicians. Singer Flora Purim has spoken of the Brazilian musical scene in the fifties: "At that time, what was popular was very conservative. The bossa nova was like an oasis . . . very mellow, full of harmonies and melodies, a lot of influence from progressive jazz. The real beginners were Joao Gilberto, Ton (Antonio Carlos) Jobim, and Joao Donato, and a bunch of avant-garde poets. They would write poetry for the musicians and the music was being written for the poets. It was like a renaissance" (John Storm Roberts, *The Latin Tinge,* p. 14).

Gilberto recorded Jobim's "Chega de Saudade" in 1958. That year Laurindo Almeido recorded another album, *Holiday in Brazil,* with Bud Shank. Then, in the spring of 1961, guitarist Charlie Byrd toured Brazil and brought bossa nova songs back with him to the United States. He introduced them to Stan Getz. In February 1962, Getz and Byrd recorded the album *Jazz Samba,* with versions of "Desafinado" and "Manha de Carnival." The short version of "Desafinado," in which Charlie Byrd's solo is edited out so that the piece would fit a 45 rpm single, became a juke box hit. *Jazz Samba* was on the Billboard charts for 70 weeks, and was for a time the best-selling album in the "pop" category.

Antonio Carlos Jobim, probably 1970's. (Courtesy
Rutgers Institute of Jazz Studies)

It's easy to see why. Although Byrd should be given credit for introducing
Getz to bossa nova, the tenor saxophonist dominates the recording by virtue of
his husky lyricism. Getz demonstrates in this album that he was one of the great
melodists in jazz, and he seems to have perfect tact. Getz was already a master
the early fifties, but he had problems with drugs, and at the end of the decade he
was living in Scandinavia. *Jazz Samba* reestablished him as the most popular jazz
tenor player. (Leonard Feather's 1963 *Down Beat* article on Getz was called "The
Resurgence of Stan Getz.")

Getz developed a new, more commanding lyric style in his samba recordings, with a broader tone and more relaxed phrasing. Using space effectively, he
seems to sing throughout the album with Byrd. The result definitively introduced a new kind of lyricism and a new beat into jazz. By the end of 1962 Getz
had also made *Big Band Bossa Nova* with "Chega de Saudade" and "Samba de
Uma Nota So (One Note Samba)." In February 1963, Getz recorded for the first
time with Luiz Bonfa and Jobim, playing with unusual force on "So Danco
Samba." Then, in March 1963, with Jobim on piano and with vocals by Joao
Gilberto and Astrud Gilberto, he recorded *Getz/Gilberto*. This was the first record
ever reviewed by *Life,* and it included the enduringly popular "Girl from
Ipanema." This song featured the charmingly naive singing of Astrud Gilberto,
as well as that of her husband, Joao Gilberto, who also played guitar on the date.
Evidently, Getz suggested, over the objections of her husband, that Astrud join
in. Astrud's small, piping voice, her shy delivery, and bell-like tone, make the
record, which started a career that has lasted into the nineties. (See music
example; note the 16-bar bridge of this otherwise regular AABA form.)

Example 20–3.
Antonio Carlos Jobim, "The Girl From Ipanema." (Getz's recording is in D♭ major.)

When, after her chorus, Getz enters, he sounds bearishly gruff. The contrast, accented by drummer Milton Banana who keeps the beat on swishing cymbals behind Getz, is delightful, as is the more explosive Getz solo on a new, faster version of "So Danco Samba." Already a popular hit, *Getz/Gilberto* would win a Grammy as record of the year.

Earlier, in May 1962, Dizzy Gillespie recorded "Desafinado" and "Chega de Saudade" with Argentinian pianist Lalo Schifrin. In the following October, Dizzy Gillespie received enthusiastic notices for his playing of bossa novas with his quintet in Philharmonic Hall, and a Carnegie Hall concert in November presented Jobim, Gilberto, and the Brazilian pianist Sergio Mendes as well as Getz, Byrd and Gillespie. The music spread rapidly, and widely: In the jazz world, Cannonball Adderley recorded with the Sergio Mendes group in December 1962. Mainstreamers Zoot Sims and Clark Terry appeared on bossa nova albums. In 1963 Sonny Rollins recorded *What's New* with several bossa nova arrangements of standards. The veteran Coleman Hawkins recorded a bossa nova album, *Desafinado*. Flutist Herbie Mann, who had already recorded Latin jazz with Caribbean musicians, travelled to Brazil in October 1962 to record with a variety of musicians, including Mendes, just before Mendes came north. (Mann scored his greatest success at a 1965 Newport Jazz Festival, playing "Comin' Home Baby" with a band that included Cuban-born hand drummer Patato Valdes and the young Chick Corea.)

With characteristic ingenuity, Ellington responded to the music with his album *Afro-Bossa* (1963), a personal mixture of Latin and jazz-based rhythms. Ellington intended to show that the bossa nova, descended indirectly from African rhythms, was not as new as it appeared. Prematurely suggesting the passing of a fad, in the notes to his 1965 bossa nova album, alto saxophonist Paul Desmond joked that the music should by now be called bossa antigua, substituting old for new. *Bossa Antigua*, which exploits Desmond's tart romanticism, also demonstrates the lasting appeal of the Brazilian rhythms.

Their influence went beyond jazz—Eydie Gorme had a pop hit with "Blame It on the Bossa Nova." And the influence lasted past the sixties, partially because jazz musicians continued to find Jobim's compositions—and Brazilian rhythms—valuable. In 1977 Sarah Vaughan recorded an album called *I Love Brazil*. Three years later, Ella Fitzgerald added a new songbook to her collections of tributes to American songwriters: *Ella Abraca Jobim*. The bossa nova has changed the landscape of jazz—ever since 1962, Latin American musicians have collaborated more frequently with their North American peers, who have in turn kept their ears tuned to the Latin music scene. *Getz/Gilberto* was the catalyst. Without it, *Native Dancer*, the incandescent collaboration between saxophonist Wayne Shorter and Brazilian singer-composer Milton Nascimento recorded in 1974, would have been unthinkable. This album, with its eerie falsetto singing by Nascimento that is so affecting on "Ponte de Areia," in turn encouraged the jazz sambas of Americans such as Pat Metheny, and Brazilians Ivan Lins and Djavan. In the nineties, "Latin" is no longer a tinge, as Jelly Roll Morton once dubbed it: It's a potential world of new music.

Jazz players were investigating the music of other cultures in the sixties, and, perhaps as a result, they were introducing new sounds and instruments. Saxophonist Yusef Lateef was intrigued by the sounds of the Middle East, as well as Africa, and he played the blues on oboe. He brought Eastern scales into jazz recordings. Other black musicians looked affectionately to Africa for inspiration, absorbing and trying to reproduce some aspects of African rhythm playing at a time when many African pop musicians were beginning to adapt African-American rhythm and blues. The complex, overlapping rhythms of African drumming became a model to some. (The lyrics of an Archie Shepp recording go, "African drums, we love you so well.")

The introduction of Brazilian sambas into jazz coincided with the African influence to produce a new interest in percussion instruments. The example of John Coltrane, who corresponded with Indian sitarist Ravi Shankar, encouraged some jazz players to also look at the music of India. Coltrane studied eastern religions—he owned the inspirational book *Autobiography of a Yogi*—and his *A Love Supreme* was followed by other musical tributes to spiritual enlightenment by Pharoah Sanders and others. Music in the sixties and seventies often had extra-musical associations, spiritual or political. A suite such as Alice Coltrane's *Journey in Satchidananda* (1970) was perceived as an offering to a greater spirit and as, potentially, a mystical experience. To some of these musicians, freedom in musical techniques—the freedom from pre-determined form, chord changes, the freedom to expand the sounds an instrument could make—was directly linked to political or racial freedom.

SOUL JAZZ

Other musicians were interested not so much in musical freedom as in directness and honesty. In an interview with Len Lyons, Horace Silver, whose compositions in the fifties helped launch the blues-oriented "soul jazz," makes an argument for his music's apparent simplicity: "I've found in composing that being simple and profound—having in-depthness in your music—is the most difficult thing to do. Anybody can write a whole lot of notes, which may or may not say something . . . But why make it complicated for the musicians to play? Why make it difficult for the listeners to hear?"

Silver's influential kind of funkiness, which he defines as a "down-home feel," was popularly successful in the sixties. In his compositions, Silver made simplicity work, partially because of his sprightly and varied rhythms. He spawned a school of imitators, some merely eager to cash in on his commercial success. That success made some uneasy. One strange legacy of bebop has been a body of jazz fans and critics who distrust music—any music—that is commercially successful. It was the popularity of "soul jazz," and its seeming rejection of the probing investigations of the avant-garde, that prompted Amiri Baraka (formerly Leroi Jones) to call soul jazz unsympathetically a "mood music for Negro colleges." The "soul" label was certainly overused: Even Coleman Hawkins produced an album called *Soul*, but it included a version of the English folk song "Greensleeves," an unlikely soul classic.

Still the impulses behind the music were frequently sincere. The interest in gospel and blues was part of the times: Whereas earlier a sophisticated jazz player might turn his or her back on country blues, or would acknowledge gospel music only in parodies, in 1960 John Lewis wrote one of his most emotional pieces for the Modern Jazz Quartet—"Pyramid"—after hearing gospel singer Mahalia Jackson in what he described as "one of the most moving concerts I have ever experienced." Soul music was tied in with a more general celebration of African-American culture. In the bebop era, jazz musicians were urban, even urbane, and their fans by and large shunned anything that looked or sounded country—even the blues. Things had changed by the late fifties, when Horace Silver wrote "Home Cookin'," one of the first of dozens of numbers by dozens of composers celebrating what Silver called "grits and greens and all that stuff." Charlie Parker played the blues, but it's doubtful he would have named a tune "Cornbread," or "Back at the Chicken Shack." His "Now's the Time" became, when slightly rewritten, a hit r & b dance, "The Hucklebuck." Still Parker never did what saxophonist Archie Shepp did in 1968, which was to create a kind of avant-garde funk on his own r & b numbers, "Stick 'Em Up" and "Abstract."

The gospel influence on modern jazz could be heard throughout the forties and fifties in the brassy blues and ballads of singer Dinah Washington, who is discussed in Chapter 23. But she wasn't a shouter. Gospel singing in all its intensity and virtuosity was translated into rhythm and blues and jazz later in the fifties. Singer and pianist Ray Charles made the style seem inevitable. Charles was born in Florida in 1930. In his sixth year, he became blind as a result of glaucoma. He took up the piano early—when he was 15 he had his own group. Still a teenager, he moved to Seattle—he says he was so unhappy in Florida, he asked a friend to find on a map the place that was furthest from home and still in the United States. In Seattle, Charles worked with a trio as a singer, basing his early singing and playing on the soft voice and sophisticated piano style of Nat King Cole and on the blues ballads of Charles Brown.

Soon he added a grit to his voice and started singing the blues. Charles was also a fan of gospel groups, of the Dixie Hummingbirds and the Swan Silver-tones. By the early fifties, he was singing secular music in a blues-tinged gospel style. Charles could be nakedly emotional, or coy and insinuating. His range

Ray Charles at a recording session in 1963. (Courtesy Rutgers Institute of Jazz Studies)

372 *The Sixties: Big Band, Bossa Nova, and Soul*

expanded: In his rocking numbers, he would soar into a vibrato-laden falsetto, growl some low notes and rise up again in an exaggerated wail. He punctuated his performances with dramatic whoops and yells, as in "Drown in My Own Tears" (1955), and by 1958 featured a trio of women, the Raelets, to provide the response to his calls. In 1955, Charles had a hit with a relatively glib-sounding gospel number in the tradition of Horace Silver's "The Preacher," "Hallelujah, I Love Her So." In 1958, he recorded bebop with Milt Jackson—Charles played alto sax as well as piano—and he was being touted by Atlantic Records as "the genius."

He was also coming into his own as a singer. His shouting 1959 gospel-blues hit "What'd I Say?" began with an electric piano solo—Charles was one of the first to use an electric keyboard regularly—and after a few choruses of stomping up-tempo blues, and a few seconds of simulated crowd noise at the break when a listener had to flip to the second side of the 45, Charles introduced a call and response pattern based on his wordless hums and moans, which are mimicked by the Raelets. The number ends wildly, with Charles shouting and the band shrieking, before the gospel-like final cadence. A few months later, Charles recorded one of his most accomplished albums, *The Genius of Ray Charles*, with arrangements by Quincy Jones. The success of that album led to others like it, including the 1960 *Genius Hits the Road*, in which Charles scored his biggest hit: "Georgia on My Mind."

What is most striking about Charles's early career is the range of things he tries—from teenybop rock and roll to bebop, gospel and urban blues. In 1961, he went one step further, recording the first of a series of country-western albums. He was widely adored. Jazz critics seemed as enthusiastic about Ray Charles as his black fans and the wide-eyed teenaged fans of early rock and roll. Charles's seemingly naked emotionalism struck a chord. More than Dinah Washington or even Sam Cooke, a gospel-turned-pop singer, Ray Charles set the stage for the popular careers of the likes of Aretha Franklin. To jazz, he added what he calls in his big-band version of "One Mint Julep" "just a little bit of soul, now." Two of his band members, saxophonists Hank Crawford and David "Fathead" Newman, recorded some of the best soul jazz instrumentals.

Much of soul jazz emerged naturally, as we have suggested, from the hard bop bands of the fifties. Hank Mobley, who had been with Miles Davis in the fifties, made his hard-swinging *Workout* in 1961: It had tunes such as "Smokin'" and "Greasin' Easy." Trumpeter Lee Morgan, a stalwart in the Art Blakey band, had a hit with his 1963 boogaloo blues, "The Sidewinder." (See music example.)

It also featured the bold tenor saxophone of Joe Henderson, whose charismatic playing on soulful tunes as well as on difficult bop themes made him an influence on the younger generation. Morgan would spend much of the rest of his career trying to recreate his big hit. Freddie Hubbard, another Blakey alumnus, would become one of jazz's most popular trumpet players: His biggest hit, recorded in 1970, was the funky "Red Clay." The innovative and hard-driving Chicago saxophonist Eddie Harris had several funky hits in the 1960's.

A couple of pianists had hits as well. Bobby Timmons, who was born in Philadelphia in 1935, wrote the gospel-tinged "Moanin'" which he recorded with Art Blakey's group in 1958, with Lee Morgan on trumpet. Its first phrase has a catchy piano line answered by a chorus of horns who might as well be saying "A-men." Then there's a stiff-necked, martial-sounding bridge and a return to the relative restraint of the theme. In 1959, Timmons left Blakey to join the Cannonball Adderley Quintet. The hit on one of Adderley's popular albums, *The Cannonball Adderley Quintet in San Francisco*, was Timmons's jazz waltz, "This Here." A witty and articulate man, Adderley introduces the piece to a live audience, calling it "simultaneously a shout and a chant," and saying that its title should rightfully be pronounced "DisHere." These pieces sent Timmons out on his own, where he tried to match their appeal with soul numbers such as "Dat Dere." Oscar Brown Jr. put lyrics to "Dat Dere": His version reached more people than Timmons's trio rendition. Only 39, Timmons died in 1974.

Example 20–4.
Lee Morgan, "The Sidewinder" (1963), beginning of theme.

Cannonball Adderley and his cornet-playing brother Nat went on to greater success, playing soul blues as well as bebop. In 1960, the brothers recorded Nat's "Work Song," with its percussive imitation of a chain gang hammer stroke, and Cannonball's "Sack o' Woe." Their greatest "soul" success came on a piece by their Austrian-born pianist, Joe Zawinul. Recorded live in 1966, "Mercy, Mercy, Mercy," with Adderley's introductory preaching and Zawinul's churchy electric piano solo, sums up the genre.

Rhythm and blues in the fifties and soul in the sixties proved a boon for some mainstream jazz saxophonists who had been pushed aside by bebop. Several odd matchups and a group of unexpected hits resulted. In 1951, Ben Webster found himself recording tunes such as "Oopy Doo" with rhythm and blues impresario Johnny Otis. Jimmy Forrest, who had previously played with Jay McShann and Andy Kirk, in 1951 took the central section out of a more complex 1946 Ellington composition named "Happy-Go-Lucky Local," and played a honking solo he called "Night Train." (When asked about the plagiarism, Ellington told Stanley Dance "it hurts and it's offensive.") Texas tenor Arnett Cobb always had a blues-based style—his "Smooth Sailing" (1950) was another juke box favorite. Clifford Scott's tenor solo was largely responsible for the popularity of organist Bill Doggett's "Honky Tonk" (1956), and by searching through personnel lists, one can find the names of many jazz players supporting rhythm and blues singers: The marvelous saxophonist Budd Johnson, former musical director for the Earl Hines band, was a mainstay at Savoy Records.

What these and other mainstream saxophonists discovered was that big tones and their ability to play catchy melodies and rocking mid-tempo blues – in short, dance numbers – could be commercial assets. Some of the most successful saxophonists from the fifties on have worked in this fuzzily-defined field of blues-based popular jazz. In the sixties, Arnett Cobb recorded his tough blues in small band sessions for Prestige, Ben Webster growled through a session with organist Richard "Groove" Holmes, and Gene Ammons, once a member of the Billy Eckstine band, started calling himself "the boss" and recorded with organ groups. Tenor saxophonist Stanley Turrentine worked with Ray Charles and with the rhythm and blues band of Earl Bostic, where he replaced John Coltrane. He played with Max Roach and Horace Silver, and became popular as a sideman with two Hammond organ players, Jimmy Smith and Shirley Scott. He went on to stardom in the seventies with tunes such as his "Sugar" (1970).

The organ was not new. The first electronic organ, in which electricity is used to simulate the sound of air passing through the pipes of a conventional organ, was manufactured by the Hammond company in 1935. Organist Glenn Hardman used this relatively primitive instrument in 1939 on his suggestively titled "Upright Organ Blues," featuring Lester Young. In the forties the instrument would be taken up by Wild Bill Davis and Milt Buckner, and it was used in gospel churches. By the mid-fifties the organ trio – usually an organ, tenor saxophone, and drums – was particularly popular in small bars in black neighborhoods. Such a trio was economical, and produced a loud, throbbing sound. No bass player was needed. While a drummer kept a rollicking beat, the organist would produce a bass line with his feet on the pedals, support a sax solo with two-handed chords and riffs, and solo with piano-like runs.

No one was more responsible than Jimmy Smith for bringing the Hammond organ out of the chicken shacks and backroom bars and into the mainstream of jazz. With the agility of a great drummer, Smith produces walking bass lines with the organ pedals, thunderous chords with both hands, and runs with his right hand that are astonishing for their speed and accuracy. He has the fastest trill in the business. Smith, who was born in Norristown, Pennsylvania in 1925, began as a pianist. He took up the Hammond organ in 1951, and began a series of Blue Note records in 1956, demonstrating at first his technical exuberance on bebop tunes – "Yardbird Suite" and "Billie's Bounce" – and then in the ensuing years his particular brand of funkiness in "The Sermon," "See See Rider," and in his 1963 version of the Ray Charles hit, "I Got a Woman." Smith favors a throbbing tone and breathless phrasing, with scalar passages that billow upward and down again without a break, to be followed by staccato chords, repeated patterns, and stuttering phrases that sound like hiccups. Many of his recordings after 1962, when he switched to Verve Records, featured the big band of Oliver Nelson, who provided the same kind of swaggering good time arrangements for Smith that Quincy Jones provided for Ray Charles. Nelson opens "Walk on the Wild Side" with bells ringing over a walking bass line. Then a clarinet trio states the beginning of the theme, the brass answers, and, in a sweeping phrase that opens the piece up, the saxophones take over. Bright, brash, and cheerful, as well as powerful, "Walk on the Wild Side" moves to one of the great entrances in jazz soloing. After the band finishes its statement, the bells return, accompanied only by a snare drum. This device, coming after an exultant big-band sound, builds the tension for Smith's entrance. He seems to pounce with a startling, intense four-note phrase. Regrettably, he can't maintain the excitement he created, and his solo devolves into notes rapidly repeated without much effect. Nelson also arranged the popular album that paired Smith with Wes Montgomery.

Smith helped sustain the idea that jazz could be good fun. His popularity helped the careers of a new generation of organists, who frequently appeared in tandem with blues-oriented tenor saxophonists. Charles Earland ("the Mighty Burner") teamed up with Texas saxophonist Houston Person, and Jack McDuff played with Jimmy Forrest and Gene Ammons and Willis Jackson. (George Benson was one of McDuff's guitarists before he moved off on his own.) Stanley Turrentine left the aegis, but not the aura, of Jimmy Smith, when he joined the quartet led by organist Shirley Scott.

Scott was born in Philadelphia in 1934. Like most organists, she began as a pianist. (She also played trumpet in high school.) She turned to organ at the behest of a Philadelphia club owner, who in the mid-fifties got her an instrument after Jimmy Smith had proven popular in the neighborhood. Scott soon developed an original style, less purely athletic than Smith's despite her technical skills. Scott uses full two-handed chords, and she's willing, as on "Blue Piano" from the 1963 album *For Members Only*, to be romantic. Where Smith would repeat a note restlessly, Scott patiently holds it, and then shies away in a quick diminuendo. She also can play with a biting, bluesy attack, and she's alert to the more subtle uses of volume. In the late fifties she performed with Eddie "Lockjaw" Davis. Scott then spent the sixties working with her husband Turrentine, writing tunes such as "The Funky Fox," with its call-and-response between tenor and organ. She's a subtle accompanist, and has proven, on *For Members Only* and elsewhere, that she can adapt the organ to a big-band setting. Don Patterson was another fine bop oriented organist, and recorded with Sonny Stitt. With their experience in bebop, Scott and Patterson sounded more adventurous than many jazz organists, whose styles were limited, perhaps by the expectations of the audiences in the small, smoky clubs they usually worked in. The limitations were perhaps too strict—no major new Hammond organ player has emerged since the sixties and the heyday of soul jazz.

One musician, Larry Young, tried to break the mold of the burning, blues-bashing Hammond organ player. Young was born in Newark in 1940. His father was an organist, but Young started out on piano. His early recordings beginning in 1960 demonstrated that Young could play both bebop and a funkier kind of blues. A little later, in the series of recordings for Blue Note under his own name that started in 1964, Young became more adventurous. Influenced, he said, by John Coltrane and Cecil Taylor, he made *Into Somethin'* and then *Unity* for Blue Note. On the latter, Coltrane's drummer Elvin Jones provides a loose, but dramatic rhythmic background for Young and his brilliant guests, saxophonist Joe Henderson and trumpeter Woody Shaw. Young demonstrated his light, deft style, sometimes pushing at the boundaries of the harmonies of tunes as varied as "Softly as a Morning Sunrise" and "Monk's Dream." Young proved that the organ was equal to Monk's craggy lines, and throughout his Blue Note records, he demonstrated that it could be part of a flowing rhythm section. The organ could accompany gracefully as well as dominate. On tunes such as "Of Love and Peace" Young used the organ's otherworldly sounds to create a new kind of jazz mood. In 1968 Young made an attempt to reach more people, recording the funky *Heaven on Earth* with the young guitarist George Benson. His later career was enterprising, but ultimately frustrating. In 1969, he recorded on the Miles Davis album *Bitches Brew*. Then for two years he worked with the seminal fusion group *Lifetime*, led by Davis's drummer Tony Williams. In the seventies, he searched futilely for a wider audience until his premature death in 1978.

Larry Young had worked both as an avant-garde player and in what was first called jazz-rock and then, later, fusion. Fusion was an inevitable development. The sixties saw the perfection of stereo LP's, the emergence of ever-more powerful FM radio stations, and the worldwide distribution of inexpensive 45 rpm records. Sales of popular music skyrocketed. The influence of black music was everywhere—in the talking blues of Bob Dylan, the shouting blues of the doomed Janis Joplin, in the rock and roll of the Rolling Stones. In the sixties and seventies, while the Beatles were dominating the pop charts and Motown was buoying black pride through a string of rhythm and blues hits, rock, not jazz, was the music of the times: Jimi Hendrix, not Wes Montgomery, was the guitar hero of the era. For young musicians who may have heard of Jerry Lee Lewis—or the Rolling Stones—long before they were aware of Bud Powell, the energy of rock was inspiriting, and its way of reaching a mass audience was seductive. While mainstream jazz went into an economic slump in the seventies, fusion groups managed to keep improvisation—improvisation over a soul beat—alive before a large public.

21 Fusion

Mainstream jazz musicians remember the seventies as a dreadful time—jazz clubs folded, colleges lost interest in presenting concerts, and record companies, inspired by the immense profitability of some rock groups, preeminently the Beatles, searched for superstars of their own. The Beatles, in fact, became something of an obsession, even among jazz players. When in 1966 drummer Art Taylor began interviewing his peers for his book, *Notes and Tones,* he asked Kenny Clarke and Erroll Garner and Carmen McRae and each of his other subjects what he or she thought about the Beatles. Today the question appears quaint. At the time, the immense success of the British rock groups, and of other rock and roll, appeared causally related to the woes of the jazz musicians. Hip college students once found jazz cool and mysterious and sophisticated. The Woodstock generation had little tolerance for that particular kind of sophistication. They went for the Beatles, or for Jimi Hendrix and politically oriented folk music instead. Threatened by rock, jazz players at first reacted scornfully to the naive sounds they were hearing everywhere. Eventually, younger jazz musicians, some of them following Miles Davis's lead, introduced electronic instruments—synthesizers, keyboards, guitars, and even electronic winds—into a music that had previously been proud to be "acoustic."

The reaction to this development was as mixed as the motives of those who "went electric." Twenty years later, fusion remains the most controversial, even divisive, subject among jazz musicians. Some, young and old, refuse to consider fusion seriously. Trumpeter Wynton Marsalis, a leader among young musicians, has repeatedly opined that a jazz musician who plays fusion is "selling out." And it must be faced that some musicians experimenting with a "rock" beat and electronic instruments were frankly, and even cynically, in search of commercial success. Most deliberately courted younger listeners who, raised on rock, found a steady beat and an electronic twang appealing. Freddie Hubbard expressly stated that his fusion records were not his best, but that he hoped the money he made from them and the new listeners he won would eventually enable him to return to a living playing more straight-ahead jazz. Many musicians shared this hope, and in a surprising number of cases it came true.

But then, some musicians were themselves raised on this popular music, as well as on electric blues, early rock, and rhythm and blues. In these cases, the return to an accessible, danceable music meant a return to their roots, and an acknowledgement of influences outside the jazz world. Herbie Hancock played for Miles Davis, but he admired the brilliance of Sly Stone and Stevie Wonder as well. So did Davis himself, who, as we have noted, required his pianists to play electronic instruments. Musicians with that kind of attitude found that fusion opened a world of possibilities, especially for the jazz composer.

Besides, jazz musicians were honestly intrigued by the new sounds and instruments: the hard-body electric guitars with their ability to sustain notes, bend them, and to provide feedback; the electric Fender bass which, first manufactured in the fifties, provided a dominating sound that forced bands to rethink the balance of their ensembles. Jazz players from all styles had experimented with electronic instruments even before pop musicians found them intriguing: Monk Montgomery started playing electric bass in 1953. Such disparate figures as Marian McPartland and Ray Charles played electric pianos in the fifties at the same time that Sun Ra was exploring a variety of electric keyboards. Electronic instruments were peripheral to the work of those musicians: They were central to fusion. The instruments themselves changed. Electronic instruments kept improving until, in the seventies, electronic keyboards were computerized: They could include synthesizers, tape loops, and sampling mechanisms which allow a single musician to create credible imitations of string choirs or vocal choruses, chunky bass lines, or eerie otherworld effects.

Jazz-rock was a misnomer. With few exceptions, fusion drew more on soul music—especially that of James Brown and, later, Sly Stone—than on rock. By the end of the sixties, rock bands typically used electric guitars and basses and drums; soul groups added horns to a rhythm section of organ (or other electric keyboards), electric guitar and bass, and drums. That instrumentation is closer to the typical jazz band than the rock groups were. Besides, most rock used folk and blues-based chords, simple I, IV, and V progressions, and within these progressions harped on the basic triads with an occasional seventh—but rarely a ninth or eleventh—added to the chords. Such limits were incompatible with the improvisational styles of modern jazz. Soul, on the other hand, uses repeating modal vamps similar to those found in Coltrane or Miles Davis, albeit over quite different rhythms. The chords in a James Brown performance are voiced in the jazz manner, including ninths, elevenths and thirteenths. Finally, most rock at the beginning of the seventies was still using a pounding rhythm with accents on 1 and 3, a rhythm usually played by the bass and drums together. Soul has the shift towards 2 and 4 characteristic of jazz swing, and also incorporates separate parts for the bass and guitar and drums. So instead of one beat performed redundantly, soul presents several interlocking beats. Modern jazz rhythm is provided by separate parts—walking bass, cymbal and hi-hat, snare drum accents, and comping piano. The difference is that the jazz rhythms are improvised and non-repetitive. In soul the parts are repeated over and over to establish a groove.

One can hear such a groove on James Brown's "Get It Together" (1967), which is split between two sides of the LP, *I Can't Stand Myself When You Touch Me*. On the first section, Brown sings over the interlocking, repetitive beat laid down by his band. (See music example.)

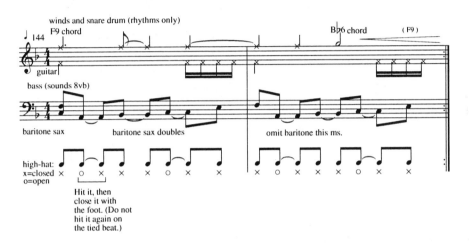

Example 21–1.
Rhythms and bass line of the vamp for the A section of "Get It Together"
(1966), by James Brown with Hobgood and Ellis.

In the manner of some gospel music, and in a manner that was picked up by rap singers, his vocal is rhythmic. More than traditional jazz, this music sounds African. In the second part of "Get It Together," Brown leads the band in a kind of jam session-rehearsal. He keeps the groove going in the drums and bass, asks for softer volume from the horns, then tells all but the rhythm section to lay out. He calls for the horns to give him one "hit"—a short accented chord—whenever he says "Hit me." Soon he is asking for two, then three and four "hits." As the piece continues, he asks the guitarist to make his comping busier, and he instructs the baritone sax to take up a vamp in counterpoint to the bass guitar. Then he asks the winds to play long wah-wah chords. This on-the-spot, exposed direction, this playing with the music, would become a feature of Miles Davis fusion bands. Brown leaves room for improvisation and spontaneity, while maintaining a steady beat. His musicians generally know what part they will play, but not how long they will play it.

In the early seventies, Brown recorded "Soul Power" (mislabeled as "Get Up, Get Into It, Get Involved" because it comes directly after that number without a pause) at the Apollo Theater. This piece, with its double-edged call for political action—or for a noisier crowd—is based, as was Miles Davis's "So What," on a vamp in the D Dorian mode. The rhythm is of course different. (See music example.)

Example 21–2.
James Brown, "Soul Power" (1971), excerpt from published score of the A section. (On the recording, rhythms are different, primarily in the bass part.)

The song has a structure typical in Brown—there are two parts, each built on repeated vamps. The A section goes on as long as one wishes—as in Coltrane's "My Favorite Things." The B section, which is in a different key, functions as a kind of bridge: It has a definite length, sixteen bars. The song moves between the sections repeatedly, Brown calling for the B section each time by yelling, again, "Hit me" or, more directly, "Take me to the bridge!" This is a modal piece with plenty of room for improvisation. The improviser here is Brown, whose vocal in his rhythmic rap, jazz scat style. His technique of providing a musical cue to move from a first section of indeterminate length to a structured bridge became common practice, as one can hear in fusion bands such as Weather Report.

Brown wasn't the only soul star influential among jazz musicians. Sly Stone was admired—and imitated—by Herbie Hancock, Miles Davis, and others for his jazzy instrumental writing, his lyrics, and perhaps even for the racial and sexual mix in his band. His line, "The beat is getting stronger, the music's getting longer," from "I Want to Take You Higher" could have been the motto of the fusion movement. There were other influences and parallel developments. Fusion artists admired Coltrane's modal vamps and solid melody playing, they listened to Kool and the Gang, a soul band whose winds were jazz-influenced, and many were bowled over by the English rock group Soft Machine, whose *Soft Machine Third* included a soul beat and some complicated writing for the winds using unusual meters. Hatfield and the North, and Gong, were other English rock groups that experimented with fusion just before 1970. Around the same time there were American groups that played real jazz-rock, as opposed to jazz-soul. They included Blood, Sweat and Tears, whose trumpeter Lew Soloff has gone on to a distinguished jazz career; Chicago; and Dreams, whose personnel around 1970 reads like a who's who of fusion stars-to-be: saxophonist Mike Brecker, trumpeter Randy Brecker, drummer Billy Cobham, bassist Will Lee, keyboardist Don Grolnick.

TONY WILLIAMS AND JOHN McLAUGHLIN

Still, the second godfather of fusion—after James Brown—was Miles Davis, through whose band many of the future fusion leaders passed. These included Tony Williams, Herbie Hancock, Chick Corea, Wayne Shorter, Joe Zawinul, John McLaughlin and Miroslav Vitous. Davis spearheaded and legitimized the movement with his watershed albums, *In a Silent Way* and *Bitches Brew*, recorded in 1969. There had been earlier signs of fusion. In 1967, vibraphonist Gary Burton, an innovative virtuoso, employed electric guitarist Larry Coryell who, before joining drummer Chico Hamilton and then Burton, had worked his way up through rock. Coryell brought the blues to Hamilton's group—he was featured on the downhome blues, "Larry of Arabia." He seemed to move Burton, a maverick with his own important repertoire of compositions, closer towards the blues and rock as well. In 1972, Coryell went on to form his own fusion band, Eleventh House. In 1969, another group, The Fourth Way, featuring electric pianist Mike Nock, began recording something like fusion—some have called them the first real fusion band, but the Fourth Way broke up before it had a major impact.

The Tony Williams band Lifetime didn't flourish either—formed in 1970, it broke up in the winter of 1971. But it did have an impact. Before Williams left Miles Davis in 1969, he had approached British guitarist John McLaughlin about forming a group, encouraging McLaughlin to come to the United States. McLaughlin, a self-taught guitarist who said he was influenced by Django Reinhardt and clearly listened to Hendrix as well, had been playing with British jazz and rock musicians, including bassist and singer Jack Bruce of the popular rock trio Cream. He came to the United States in 1969, and found himself with startling rapidity in recording sessions with Miles Davis. His rock-oriented, fluent style, his virtuosic, extroverted approach to blues and modal pieces, his use of extreme dissonance and electronic distortion, brought something new to Davis's music. In McLaughlin, Tony Williams felt he had found the perfect guitarist for his fusion group.

Lifetime also included organist Larry Young, as we have noted, and, eventually, Jack Bruce. Lifetime recorded *Emergency* in 1969, and *Turn It Over* the following year. "Emergency" moves between a fast bluesy section in which McLaughlin's Hendrix-like runs are accompanied by distorted chords from Young, and slow, spacey improvisations in which both guitar and organ seem to float above Williams' beat. The drummer is in control—he doesn't so much signal a change of tempo as demand it with a rapid accelerando. The piece is rhythmically alert, vibrant, and free. It isn't traditional jazz, but it is hardly rock either. That may have been Williams's problem. By the end of the year, he was complaining to *Down Beat* that "rock musicians don't really consider us rock. They think we're trying to play up to them, and we're not. And I'm not trying to get away from jazz because I want to make money . . . I've got all these things coming down on me." The band's free improvisations, and their sophisticated repertoire, proved too much for most rock fans, and jazz people were put off by the distortion of McLaughlin's guitar and Williams's heavy beats. The band broke up in 1971, but not before they had recorded Coltrane's "Big Nick," demonstrating that Coltrane could be a healthy influence on rock, and a surprisingly upbeat version of jazz composer Carla Bley's "Vashkar."

In 1970, McLaughlin went on to record the acoustic album *My Goal's Beyond*, which was influenced by his recent conversion to the wisdom of the Indian mystic Sri Chinmoy. With its use of Indian scales, its Indian percussionist supporting bassist Charlie Haden and drummer Billy Cobham, among others, *My Goal's Beyond* suggested a different kind of fusion. It included a dignified, lyrical version of Mingus's "Goodbye Pork Pie Hat." The next year, McLaughlin took two members of that band, Cobham and violinist Jerry Goodman, hired bass guitarist Rick Laird and keyboardist Jan Hammer, and formed the influential fusion group, the Mahavishnu Orchestra.

The Mahavishnu Orchestra used distorted guitar lines, ringing cymbal patterns, and an aggressively pounding beat. Its exotic sound was created by its leader's compositions and his long, fluid runs. "Birds of Fire" begins with crashes of a gong interrupting a silent background. Then McLaughlin enters with a rapid repeating pattern of 18 distorted-sounding eighth notes, high in the treble. While the keyboard continues this pattern, the bass and violin enter with the obsessive, threatening figure that underlies much of the piece, and then McLaughlin and the violinist project the wide-ranging theme, with its suggestions of the rapid runs of Indian music. (See music example.)

With its elaborately arranged compositions, its alternation of precise ensemble effects with passages of free-flowing improvisation, McLaughlin's "Birds of Fire" is typical of the band, and of fusion. On pieces such as "Hope" and "Dance of the Maya," McLaughlin gives each solo instrument—excepting the drummer—a rhythmically complicated, speechlike melody, often with the violin in unison with the guitar, while the rhythm churns away in unexpected meters with measures of seven, eleven, or eighteen beats. Surprisingly, "Dance of the Maya" enters into a chugging Robert Johnson feel, but in 6½-beat patterns, sounding for a few minutes like an otherworldly Chicago blues band. At its best, Mahavishnu produced exuberant numbers that fused a wide variety of elements. The band had range, as they demonstrated on the yearning, but still lighthearted acoustic country piece, "Open Country Joy." The disbanding in 1975 of the first Mahavishnu Orchestra helped mark the end of the first, most enterprising period of fusion music.

Example 21–3.
John McLaughlin, "Birds of Fire" (1973), beginning of theme after the
introduction.

FUSION BANDS OF HERBIE HANCOCK AND CHICK COREA

Two years earlier, Herbie Hancock had made jazz's first million-selling album,
Headhunters. He got to *Headhunters* circuitously. Like Davis and like most players
who came from mainstream jazz backgrounds, his music became more and more
experimental before he turned around and got involved in fusion. Hancock's
sextet in 1971 featured the Coltrane-influenced Benny Maupin on reeds, and
Patrick Gleeson on synthesizers. This group's early performances were particularly adventurous, featuring extended free improvisations and sometimes
funky vamps.

On the first records of this band, *Mwandishi* (1970) and *Crossings* (1971),
Hancock played electric piano and used overdubbing modestly. Gradually, he
began to indulge his interest in different kinds of keyboards and synthesizers.
As he told Len Lyons, his practice of Nichiren Shoshu Buddhism helped lead
him to fusion. While chanting one day, he came to a realization: "My mind
wandered to an old desire I had to be on one of Sly Stone's records. It was
actually a secret desire of mine for years—I wanted to know how he got that
funky sound. Then a completely new thought entered my mind: Why not Sly

Herbie Hancock with the group that recorded the
album *Thrust* in 1974. Mike Clark, drums, is on the
floor, and Hancock is on the chair. Bennie Maupin is
holding his bass clarinet. (Courtesy Rutgers Institute
of Jazz Studies)

Stone on one of my records? My immediate response was: 'Oh, no, I can't do
that.' So I asked myself why not. The answer came to me: pure jazz snobbism"
(Lyons, *The Great Jazz Pianists*, p. 276).

In the studio, Hancock gradually changed his approach: "Little by little,
things that happened in the studio became more prominent in the shaping of the
music." Through overdubbing, tape loops, added resonators, "the recording
process itself becomes part of the composition of the music." By 1973, his jazz
snobbism definitively put away, he had sufficiently mastered the new technology to make *Headhunters* with its explicit tribute to Sly Stone. He introduces
"Sly" with rapid staccato chords that are repeated and that alternate with a more
open and relaxed sounding bass line. This leads to a gentle theme stated
wistfully by soprano sax and synthesizer. After a return to the initial staccato
section, Hancock begins to solo over a bass line, while Patrick Gleeson adds
guitar-like comments. Maupin solos on soprano sax over a doubled beat with its
boiling rhythms provided by the rest of the band. As in a soul band, every player
except the soloist becomes a member of the rhythm section.

"Chameleon" is performed over a dancing two-bar bass line, played repeatedly by Paul Jackson. Over this phrase, the band plays counterlines and
eventually a modest theme, that is repeated with some of the same insistence
with which Jackson offers the bass riff. As in a soul piece, the bass riff substitutes

for the changing chords of a jazz standard—the soloist plays over this riff for however long he or she wants. But in "Chameleon" that is not all. In this case, the first soloist is synthesist Gleeson, who sounds like a metallic, electric guitar—that is, until he goes into simulated bird calls. Living up to its name, the piece changes midway, after a break, and a new, complex, but somewhat more relaxed rhythm enters. This time Hancock solos on Fender Rhodes electric piano, with gentle, spacious, musing lines that float upwards over synthesized string sounds. Finally, there is a return to the initial section, with Benny Maupin soloing on soprano. (He's heard elsewhere on bass clarinet and flute, and was originally known as a tenor saxophonist.)

Hancock followed *Headhunters*, whose success probably surprised even him, with the soundtrack to a particularly nasty movie, *Death Wish*. His darkly threatening music, funky, urban, and fragmented, fits the gritty style of this Charles Bronson vehicle about a relentless urban vigilante. Later albums, such as *Flood* (issued only in Japan), offered elaborate live versions of his funkier numbers. Hancock was impressed by the success of the "Chameleon" single, and by the tricks and techniques he learned in the studio. By 1974, he was giving solo concerts on electronic instruments, performing, for instance, in Tokyo on Fender Rhodes electric piano and five separate ARP synthesizers. Surrounded, and occasionally overwhelmed by equipment, he and Weather Report's Joe Zawinul ushered in a new era for jazz-fusion keyboardists. He had an electric String Ensemble that produced sustained notes that sounded something like a string section, a Hohner Clavinet for wah-wah rhythm sounds, and a couple of preset keyboards, which could reproduce the sound of any prerecorded instrument. These came with tape loops that allowed him to establish a rhythm pattern—or a melodic phrase or chord—that repeated itself as long as he desired. Live, Hancock was soon able to improvise with aplomb on these new instruments.

By 1980, to make *Mr. Hands*, he overdubbed a half dozen instruments, and used a voice synthesizer, a Vocoder, which, as he once announced in embarassed tones at a concert in Manhattan's Lincoln Center, allowed anyone to sing. His weirdly altered vocals thrilled few listeners. Most of the patterned numbers of *Mr. Hands* seemed designed for jukeboxes. In the seventies and eighties, Hancock has alternated between acoustic recordings—piano duets with Chick Corea, or with versions of the Miles Davis band with a substitute trumpeter—and increasingly mechanical recordings whose main interest comes from his minimalist writing and manipulation of the studio. This pattern of returning to an occasional "acoustic" jazz context is also typical for musicians of his background.

Chick Corea might have spoken for all fusion-band leaders when he stated in the notes to his 1977 album *Musicmagic* that his goals were to have "musical fun with no barriers of musical style or type of audience." The fusion bands of Chick Corea have always had the distinctive stamp of their leader, whose background in Latin and Spanish music as well as jazz remains influential. His melodies are always appealing, and his arrangements often elaborate. His orchestral writing has a grandiose streak, as if he were writing for bullfights. Corea came to fusion after breaking up the avant-garde group Circle in 1971. He dissolved that group suddenly in the middle of a California tour because, he felt, they weren't reaching enough people. He was training in Scientology, the philosophy of L. Ron Hubbard, with its emphasis on clearing the minds of its adherents of whatever was holding them back from communicating. Scientology taught him to look within for the problem, and Hubbard's optimism suggested that it would be easily solved.

Luckily, Corea had the Latin and Portuguese and Spanish musics of his youthful years to fall back on. Corea enthusiastically founded the Brazilian-influenced Return to Forever, whose exhilarating success ensured Corea's career. One facet of the first Return to Forever's success is the stunningly fast and dramatic playing of bassist Stanley Clarke. When that group disbanded, Corea and Clarke went on to form a more rock-oriented fusion band, first with guitarist Bill Connors, and then, in 1974 with electric guitarist Al DiMeola and drummer Lenny White. In DiMeola, and Clarke, this band had an electric guitarist and an electric bass guitarist whose rapid scales rivalled Django Reinhardt's. Live, the quartet would play a relatively simple riff, and fall into what sounded like a rock-blues jam. Corea, DiMeola and Clarke played dramatically off of each other's uptempo phrases before ecstatic audiences of young fusion fans. Their first album, *Where Have I Known You Before*, features compositions by Clarke and White, as well as Corea, and includes the title cut, an acoustic piano solo, as well as the relatively moody "Song to the Pharoah Kings." On the opening of this long number, Corea plays organ and a synthesizer that sounds something like Wayne Shorter's soprano sax. Then the band goes into a hearty theme meant to sound Middle Eastern—it is typical Corea, ebullient and somehow congenial.

Its textures suggested that Corea wanted a larger group. That's what he got by 1975, when he hired a horn section, including as soloist his former saxophonist Joe Farrell, and recorded and performed with groups including strings, a variety of percussionists and vocalist Gayle Moran, who is also Corea's wife. For these groups, Corea wrote extended suites on unexpected themes—such as *The Mad Hatter* (1978)—that proved Corea's range. He brought horns back into fusion, and he revived his Latin-influenced style. The band on the particularly exuberant live version of "The Musician" (1977) sounds like an expanded Return to Forever, with Gayle Moran taking Flora Purim's part. At its best, Chick Corea's music of the seventies and eighties had a musical sophistication wedded to a particularly attractive, innocent-sounding lyricism. Both the musical sophistication and innocence of attitude seemed ingrained parts of Corea's personality. Corea has formed what he calls his "Akoustic Trio" so that he can play the standards he still loves on occasion, and he has written ingratiating classical chamber works.

WEATHER REPORT

Back in 1969, both Corea and Hancock took part in the Miles Davis recording session that became *In a Silent Way*. The title cut was written by the third keyboardist at the session, the Austrian-born Joe Zawinul. He had written the piece as part of a suite, and he said it was meant to represent the Austrian hills which he remembered from his childhood. Zawinul recorded the piece a year later on his own album, *Concerto Retitled*. Born in 1932, Zawinul grew up in Vienna and studied at the city's famous conservatory. He played with Friedrich Gulda, a spectacular pianist with notable recordings in both classical and jazz, and emigrated to the United States in 1959. He worked briefly for Maynard Ferguson, then for two years with Dinah Washington. He became famous, as noted earlier, with Cannonball Adderley, with whom Zawinul played from 1961 to 1970. In that period, he wrote the soul-jazz hit "Mercy, Mercy, Mercy," and gradually developed a funky style based as much on Horace Silver as on his previous piano heroes, Tommy Flanagan and Hank Jones. But his was an electrified keyboard style: In the seventies Zawinul would become a master synthesizer player and electric pianist.

He would do so in the longest lasting, most influential fusion group. Weather Report was founded by Zawinul and saxophonist Wayne Shorter in 1970. They finally parted company in 1985: The back cover of their last record, *This is This*, has a picture of them shaking hands amicably. For the first version of their band, Shorter and Zawinul got together with Czech bassist Miroslav Vitous and percussionists Airto Moreira and Alphonse Mouzon. Their early performances were based on the Miles Davis model to which Shorter and Zawinul had contributed. They featured medleys of original tunes, sometimes loosely strung together, and they included plenty of room for improvising. Theirs were also moodier, more atmospheric than Davis's performances. With Weather Report, Shorter developed the wistful, elusive side of his playing: Over the years he began to sound less and less like the hard bop saxophonist who had performed with Art Blakey. He wrote tunes that managed, despite their tight

Weather Report around 1980. From left: Joe Zawinul, Wayne Shorter, Peter Erskine, Jaco Pastorius. (Courtesy Rutgers Institute of Jazz Studies)

structure, to sound open-ended, unassertive and yet memorable, and his playing took on the same qualities.

Zawinul not only played synthesizers—he learned to improvise convincingly on them, changing the mood and textures of Weather Report's pieces
seemingly at will. The group's first record, *Weather Report* (1971) featured a long
version of Zawinul's "Orange Lady." It's a piece that seems to undulate, as one
musician after another comes to the fore, improvises over a steady beat, or no
beat at all, and fades back into the ensemble. At a live recording in Tokyo the
next year, the group expanded that number and others, until it became a new
kind of free jazz. Starting in the mid-seventies, though their live performances
were much looser than their recorded arrangements, Zawinul made sure that
the contributions of the members of Weather Report were organized. There
were some crucial personnel changes. Looking for a funkier sound and tighter
performances, Zawinul and Shorter found drummers who could provide a
relentless disco-type beat to underpin each piece. They also replaced Miroslav
Vitous with electric bassist Alphonso Johnson, and then with Jaco Pastorius.

Pastorius helped define the sound of Weather Report's most popular
records. Born in 1951, Pastorius grew up in Ft. Lauderdale, where he died after a
barroom fight in 1987. He was a member of Weather Report from 1975 to 1980.
Pastorius played the fretless electric bass with the flamboyance and drama of a
rock star. Still, he was a solid, well-trained musician, whose ballads were as
effective as his uptempo funk. He played stunning uptempo jazz, as we hear in
his "Donna Lee" on his own album. His buoyant, resonant tone—he sounded
like a greatly enlarged acoustic bass—added a new range to Weather Report's
sound.

In 1976, they made *Heavy Weather*, Weather Report's most popular album.
It spawned a hit, "Birdland," which Zawinul named after the defunct nightclub
that had been dedicated to Charlie Parker. "Birdland," which would be recorded
by Maynard Ferguson, Manhattan Transfer (with lyrics added), and a host of
others, is hardly bebop: As played by Weather Report, it is an intricately
assembled, many sectioned short piece, an exhilarating fusion mini-concerto.
Like many of Zawinul's compositions, "Birdland" is built out of short motives
that are strung together tantalizingly in rhythmically unpredictable ways. Its
several short themes are presented in a dramatic sequence. It begins with a
simple rising lick based on a G major triad along with a passing tone, the C. This
lick is played by a synthesizer. After a surprising three iterations of this lick—not
the expected four—a countermelody is added by Jaco Pastorius's high, guitarlike
bass. He's using harmonics. This joyously bouncy countermelody is played four
times and then the full band comes in with the more staccatto, martial-sounding
theme that contrasts vividly with the blithe section that preceded it. After a bass
pedal note—a held G—we hear the third theme. This section creates a sense of
expectancy. At its end, the G is held again and Zawinul improvises funkily.
Then we are introduced to the grandest, and also most ingenious, section of the
piece, the fourth "Birdland" theme. A harder-swinging relative of the second
theme, it is mostly made up of different permutations of the G major triad, but it
is unforgettable. (See music example.)

Example 21–4.
Joe Zawinul, climactic theme of "Birdland" (1977). The saxophone and
keyboard play mostly triads, as shown in measure 1, while the bass provides
missing notes, such as the C♯ in measure 2, and fills during rests.

There is much more to come in the piece—Zawinul leaves space for some
free jamming over the pedal point, and concludes with a delightfully unexpected descending series of chords played as a wild fall. This leads us back to the
beginning. Zawinul has made his transitions as interesting as his themes.
(Composition, Beethoven said, is the art of making transitions. Zawinul, who is
not known for his modesty, told *Down Beat* that as a composer "I ain't afraid of
Beethoven.") In "Birdland" Zawinul has written a piece that allows his players to
express their musical identities, while creating a shapely, sprightly work. In this
respect, he's an electrified Ellington.

Not every arrangement was this controlled. Some pieces have a more
straightforward exuberance, such as "Night Passage," from the 1980 album with
the same name. Zawinul and Weather Report could do other things as well.
Zawinul's "Dream Clock" from the same album is a beautiful, almost reverent
ballad. After establishing a serene background with his synthesizers, Zawinul
gives the melody to Pastorius, and then to Shorter. Shorter's lyricism is well
known—Pastorius's sensitivity, his beautifully expressive phrasing of the melody, is a revelation. Still, in 1980 this version of Weather Report came to an end
when Pastorius founded his own group, Word of Mouth. He recorded two
impressive albums—the second with a big band—and then his career foundered
on his personal problems.

Under Zawinul's direction, Weather Report moved in the eighties towards
tighter arrangements and a still more popular sound. They never approached
real pop music, but the balance of the group, a balance of talents, and a balance
between writing and improvisation, was offset. Wayne Shorter seemed to be
fading from the group. In live performances, he would solo effectively, and at
some length. On record, his presence was barely felt. There was controversy:
After an overeager *Down Beat* reviewer panned their *Mr. Gone*, Zawinul wrote a

hostile letter to the editor that became a cause célèbre. Finally, in 1985, Shorter left to form a quartet, and Zawinul assembled a new band, The Zawinul Syndicate.

PAT METHENY AND OTHER FUSION ARTISTS

The first fusion groups were started by distinguished jazz players like Shorter and Zawinul. The next generation included young players who had not spent as much time in mainstream jazz groups—"paying their dues," as musicians like to say—but who proved to have superb jazz credentials when called for. Foremost among them were the Brecker Brothers, trumpeter Randy (b. 1945) and saxophonist Michael (b. 1949), who worked with the band Dreams mentioned earlier. Mike has become one of the most imitated saxophonists in jazz, admired for his sleek tone, uninhibited emotion, and sterling virtuosity. Alto saxophonist David Sanborn (b. 1945), who is well known for his work on dozens of pop recordings, earned jazz credentials playing and recording in the Gil Evans Orchestra during the 1970's.

But by the eighties fusion was being played by groups without jazz backgrounds. The lyricism and compositional skills that Weather Report brought to the music, the open-ended funk of Herbie Hancock, had given way to formulaic performances of an extroverted, showy music. There have been some bright spots, fusion players with greater musical curiosity than the rest. One of them is guitarist Pat Metheny. Metheny was born in 1954 in Lee's Summit, Missouri, a small town close to Kansas City. He grew up listening to country music, band music, and the Beatles. A country musician who lived near his family taught him to strum a G chord. Later he saw the Beatles's movie *A Hard Day's Night* 15 times; but by the time he reached high school, he wouldn't listen to anything but mainstream jazz. Metheny identifies with great melodists, and his best music has the immediate, folksy quality that he associates with home. It's difficult to categorize. Metheny calls it jazz: "If it's not jazz, and maybe it's not, then I don't know what to call it. My music is based on the principle of playing bebop: It's chord changes and improvisation on the changes."

Metheny learned from jazz players. In 1968, he won a scholarship to *Down Beat's* National Stage Band Camp. Soon he was learning the basic vocabulary of jazz in jam sessions with Kansas City musicians. By 1970, he was idolizing Jim Hall and listening to Gary Burton. When Burton asked Pat Metheny to sit in with his band at the 1973 Wichita Jazz Festival, Metheny knew most of Burton's repertoire. Burton convinced Metheny to move to Boston, offering him a teaching assistantship at the Berklee College of Music, where Burton was an instructor. He hired his young friend to play in his band as well.

Metheny made the first of three albums with Burton in 1974. The next year Metheny made his first album as a leader, *Bright Size Life*, with Jaco Pastorius and the vibrant, original drummer Bob Moses. On the title tune, Metheny shows himself able to exploit the sounds—woozy glissandos as well as bright, plucked

Gary Burton and bassist Steve Swallow at the Jazz
Workshop, Boston, 1970's. (Photo by Michael Ullman)

tones—native to the electric guitar while still improvising like a jazz guitarist.
The session has a contained quality, partly the result of Metheny's determination to establish his voice as a composer: It is surely Pastorius's most decorous
session. But it was a varied and promising debut, with its five-minute version of
two Ornette Coleman compositions ("Round Trip/ Broadway Blues"), its classi-
cal-sounding solo, "Unity Village," and the sprightly "Missouri Uncom-
promised," the first of many compositions referring to his home state.

After *Bright Size Life*, Metheny began alternating surprising small-group
and solo albums with albums by his fusion quartet, including in its first years the
Bill Evans-inspired pianist Lyle Mays, bassist Iark Egan and drummer Dan
Gottlieb. Their first record, *Watercolors* (1977), featured tight harmonies played
on keyboards and guitars, solid drum rhythms, careful dynamic shadings and,
frequently, ostinato bass figures over which Metheny and Mays solo. Gradually
the group became looser—especially after *American Garage*, which contains,
besides the wonderful, countryish "Heartland," a stiff, 13-minute composition
"The Epic." Metheny discovered from "The Epic" that he prefers more spontaneous playing, even from himself. "A good solo will always have more weight
than a hip composition."

Increasingly, Metheny began demonstrating his interest in synthesizers
and electronically altered sounds. And other sounds as well: "As Falls Wichita,
So Falls Wichita Falls" (1980) has a breezy, cheerful melody played by Metheny,
by Mays on piano and autoharp, and by percussionist Nana Vasconcelos on the
Brazilian berimbau. Brazilian music played a major role in Metheny's music by
the end of the 1980's.

Metheny is another artist who likes to make room for acoustic jazz in his
touring schedule, and he is brilliant in such contexts. He recorded *80/81* (1980)

with bassist Charlie Haden from the Ornette Coleman groups, with Jack De-Johnette, best known for his work with Miles Davis, and with saxophonists Dewey Redman and Mike Brecker. They play Coleman's blues "Turnaround," they improvise freely on "Open," and, best of all, they play two "Folk Songs," actually written by Metheny and Haden. (Haden grew up in a town 15 miles from Lee's Summit, and he has even deeper roots in country music than does Metheny.) In December 1985, Metheny recorded *Song X* with Ornette Coleman, Haden, DeJohnette and, as a second drummer, Coleman's son Denardo. They then engaged in the successful tour mentioned in Chapter 18 that helped bolster Metheny's jazz reputation while building a new audience for Coleman. Their sound was unusual, combining fusion with free jazz.

It was a sound that Ornette Coleman was pioneering with his electric group, Prime Time. Prime Time, which like other of Coleman's groups, has remained the taste of a minority of listeners, nonetheless helped spawn what might be called avant-garde fusion in bands led by his protégés guitarist James Ulmer, drummer Ronald Shannon Jackson, a bassist Jamaaladeen Tacuma, and others. By 1973, when he began to play and study with Coleman, James "Blood" Ulmer had played gospel music, worked with funk groups in Pittsburgh and Columbus, Ohio, and travelled with Art Blakey. After his experience with Coleman, he started a group that used the beat of soul bands and their open-ended compositions, the instrumentation of a rock band, and solos that could have come out of the avant-garde. Over this mix, Ulmer would sing gruffly the cynical lyrics he had written to tunes such as "Are You Glad to Be in America?" (1980). "Jazz is the teacher," one of his songs goes, and "funk is the preacher." Critics didn't know what to call this music: Gary Giddins tried "jazz-funk," which Robert Palmer expanded to "futuristic jazz-funk." C.J. Safane went all the way with "harmolodic diatonic funk." Ulmer's jagged, unexpected guitar licks were intriguing, as were the solos on his records by alto saxophonist Oliver Lake. Despite an appearance at the Kool Jazz Festival in New York, the band never took off, even when Ulmer recorded his own version of rock, *Black Rock* (1982).

Ronald Shannon Jackson was Ulmer's drummer—he had played previously with Cecil Taylor and Coleman. Between 1980 and 1985 Jackson made, with a group he called his Decoding Society, a series of records that mixed funk and jazz and that were full of the interlocking rhythms that Prime Time introduced. It was a larger and more light-hearted group than Ulmer's—one of its numbers was "Dancers of Joy." *Eye on You* (1980) presented short melodies played by the ensemble, followed usually by free improvising. It sounded for the most part like an Ornette Coleman group. Jackson didn't break through to a larger audience, but there is little evidence that he intended to. Surprisingly, his electric guitarist, Vernon Reid, did, with a band he calls Living Colour, a rock group that opened for the Rolling Stones on their 1989 Steel Wheels tour.

Jackson's group leaned towards what avant-garde jazz musicians have been doing: The band of Jamaaladeen Tacuma, once an electric bassist in Prime Time, tends towards funk. Tacuma is the most heralded electric bassist since

John Scofield in Boston, 1980's. (Photo by Michael Ullman)

Jaco Pastorius. His is a more electric, funky sound. Tacuma learned from Ornette Coleman, he said, "that as a musician, you have to try to go beyond the limits of style to play pure music." His records include chanted vocals over a soul groove, free soloing by the likes of Coleman and David Murray, and a sparkling dance beat that is often based on a synthesized drum sound. This mixture has been effectively captured on Tacuma's 1983 recording, *Renaissance Man*.

In the eighties and into the nineties, commercially successful fusion groups include bands like the Yellowjackets and Spyro Gyra whose interest in jazz seems minimal, and who have emphasized arrangements rather than improvisation. Few groups have maintained the balance between the two that seems central to jazz and that Weather Report sustained in its best years. The freshest musical ideas and many of the most interesting musicians in fusion have come out of the bands of two elder statesman of jazz—Miles Davis and Ornette Coleman. Both of those masters acknowledged the lessons of soul bands such as James Brown's Famous Flames and the later JB's: that one can solo freely and inventively over extended, intricate rhythm riffs. The future of fusion may still be in the hands of Davis's and Coleman's alumni—of the musicians we have mentioned, and guitarists such as John Scofield.

22 The Avant-Garde

"If something sounds good to you, then it has a structure. It's just a matter of going and figuring out what that structure is." —Roscoe Mitchell

"Anything not told, wasn't yet known."
—Carla Bley (Notes to *Escalator Over the Hill*)

In the early sixties, the music being pioneered by Ornette Coleman, John Coltrane, Sun Ra, and Cecil Taylor, was called the "New Thing" or "Free Jazz." Neither label is entirely appropriate: The music was new, but it wasn't a single "thing," nor was it necessarily totally "free." Ekkehard Jost begins his book *Free Jazz* with an anecdote about a musician at a concert of "free jazz" who played a popular song over and over again in defiance of what the other musicians were doing. This musician was asked to practice his particular form of freedom elsewhere.

As this anecdote suggests, the often fiercely distinctive members of the avant-garde developed, often over months or years of private rehearsals and public performances, their own shared conventions as well as individual musical habits. No one would confuse the ensembles of Sun Ra with those of Taylor, or of Coltrane with Ornette Coleman. Free jazz, the new thing, or avant-garde, was largely free from chord changes and sometimes of a steady beat. It also reflected the individual musical personalities of its creators—the intensity of Coltrane and of Pharoah Sanders, the exoticism of Don Cherry, the extravagance of sound and conception of Albert Ayler, the ripe tone and rhetorical flair of Archie Shepp, the intellectuality and sheer muscle of Cecil Taylor. In the sixties, the avant-garde in jazz also included the advanced harmonic thinking of Eric Dolphy, the rigorously extended modal compositions of George Russell—he called them "pan-modal"—the humor of the Art Ensemble of Chicago, the sardonic and sometimes goofy wit of Carla Bley, the order of Anthony Braxton and the chaos of quite a few others.

It was controversial, but not monochromatic. The music was never popular—indeed, as free jazz musicians challenged their listeners's expectations with shocking timbres, extended performances without regular chord changes, with surrealistic poetry, and political raps, it could hardly have been meant to be

394

popular. As with any experimental music, there were many failed performances, and a few amateurish performers as well. We have heard groups dedicated to total musical freedom who began performances without a theme or
plan. In happenings that unfolded like a boxing match between two counter-
punchers, each player awaited the first move of the others. Inevitably these
performances began with a few tentative sounds and ended in a cacophony of
group improvisation. More often groups in the avant-garde relied on composed
themes and preplanned strategies as well as free improvisation, and used
musical cues to move from one section or theme to another.

The jazz avant-garde drew on the jazz that had preceded it, and it extended jazz conventions already in place. As early as 1956, in pieces such as
"Pithecantropus Erectus," Charles Mingus had already introduced a wild kind
of collective improvisation into modern jazz, and Miles Davis had popularized
modal jazz in 1959. The new players would frequently call upon their groups to
improvise together in open-ended structures that might be modal, might follow
informally shifting tonalities, or might be largely atonal. Jazz rhythms had
already become looser and multilayered when played by Roy Haynes, or by
Elvin Jones. Drummers such as Sunny Murray, Milford Graves, Beaver Harris,
and Andrew Cyrille went even further than Jones, sometimes eliminating a
steady beat, providing instead a wash of surging rhythms and colors. The
melodies of the new music, derived from bebop or from twentieth century
classical music, could be either jaggedly complex, or disturbingly simple, as in
Grachan Moncur's "Space Spy," which involves a series of long tones played
impassively on the leader's trombone. (A live recording of Roscoe Mitchell's
"Nonaah" begins with a single saxophone phrase that is repeated dozens of
times. The interest is in the ways Mitchell varies the tone, and the emotional
content, of each iteration.) The sound of the players's instruments was frequently extravagant, but here again, the new jazz musicians found precedents in
earlier jazz—Archie Shepp in the tone of Ben Webster, and Albert Ayler in the
broad vibrato of Sidney Bechet.

For many African-American musicians living in the United States in the
sixties, musical freedom was connected with a protest against oppression, racial
discrimination, and against the white domination of the marketplace. Many
avant-garde musicians were dedicated to making an inclusive statement about
their lives through their music. From the late sixties on, avant-garde musicians
frequently produced their own concerts and put out their own records. In
Chicago and St. Louis and Los Angeles, musicians banded together into cooperative groups to exchange ideas and compositions and to present concerts. In the
seventies a few players opened up what were called lofts in previously abandoned warehouses or storefronts. Once again Ornette Coleman was in the
forefront when he began to give small concerts in his Prince Street domicile in
Manhattan—one concert, *Friends and Neighbors*, was recorded in 1970. One of the
most successful lofts was run by reedman Sam Rivers, who found a place in
Manhattan's Soho district, and presented music in what was also his living
space. At first, few listeners found their way to the Studio Rivbea's dimly lighted

door on Bond Street. But by 1976, when Douglas Records recorded a series of albums entitled *Wildflowers* at the Studio Rivbea, the place had been discovered, and lines formed outside the Rivers's home hours before a performance. (Ironically, the success of this and other such ventures in the neighborhood led to an increase in rents that was disastrous to the loft movement, as few musicians could afford to stay in the large spaces they had helped popularize.) These organizations and musician-run ventures were designed to present alternatives to the economic structure that seemed to stifle, or at least that inadequately rewarded, their kind of innovation. These musicians attempted to raise the political as well as aesthetic consciousness of their listeners and they saw that they needed to develop their own ways of presenting their music. Economic independence would ensure the progress of their art.

Isolated — sometimes intentionally — from popular culture, many black musicians made a conscious effort to integrate their music with the wider African-American culture. Cecil Taylor wrote poetry and the New York Art Quartet invited poet Amiri Baraka to read his "Black Dada Nihilismus" on their 1964 record. Archie Shepp was a playwright as well as a musician: In his 1969 notes to *Freedom and Unity* by cornetist and valve trombonist Clifford Thornton, he connects this music recorded in 1967 with the alienation of Bigger Thomas, the hero of Richard Wright's classic novel *Native Son,* and sees the position of the black avant-garde musician as related to the plight of Huey Newton, the then jailed Black Panther leader. Others, including saxophonist Noah Howard in 1972, appeared with dancers who improvised movements along with the music.

Richard Wright has written that he was able to conceive of Bigger only after moving north, where he "was able to come into possession of my own feelings." Coming into possession of their own feelings might be called the ultimate goal of the avant-garde musicians of the sixties. To do so, many felt they had to shuck off the conventions of bebop, and loosen the inhibitions imposed on them by racism. To many members of the avant-garde their music meant investigating themselves and probing the outside world, and many, heroically, kept searching despite long periods when they could not find work. Even major figures such as Cecil Taylor were frequently unemployed, and it's safe to say that every avant-garde musician we will be talking about, with the exception of Coltrane, has been underemployed for much of his or her career.

SUN RA AND CECIL TAYLOR

Eccentric though he is, a decided outsider even in the world of modern jazz, the man who calls himself Sun Ra set the tone for much of what happened in the avant-garde in the sixties. Every performance by the big band of Sun Ra was multidimensional, often featuring dance, song, and a variety of compositions. Sun Ra was born Herman Blount in Birmingham, Alabama in 1914. He has kept much of his early life a mystery, but it seems clear that he never felt at home in Birmingham: He prefers to say that he is a mystic from another planet. In 1946 and 1947 in Chicago, he was arranging and filling in on piano for a band led by the veteran Fletcher Henderson. Soon he began leading his own groups, which by the mid-fifties he was calling his Myth-Science Solar Arkestra. He began recording in 1954. Eventually his performances became theatrical. The band dressed up in dramatically bespangled, metallic robes that prefigured Star Trek, while Blount, now known as Sun Ra, stalked around the bandstand in a variety of sunny headresses. Looking out-of-this-world, the players frequently chanted Sun Ra's obscure poems or metaphysical advice.

The message seems to be the Dickensian one that the world is in a muddle, and that we need to get a new perspective on our lives in order to live humanely and preserve the planet. Sun Ra may have been one of the earliest ecologists. In his presentations, with chants like "Space is the Place," he dramatized his own alienation, disillusionment, and hopefulness. He's amusing—nothing provides a sprightlier introduction to avant-garde jazz than a live performance by Sun Ra—but he also pleads with his audiences to become more conscious and more compassionate. Remarkably, he assembled a fiercely loyal group of excellent musicians who have stuck with him for decades through some thin years. These musicians include the dynamic bop-to-free tenor player John Gilmore, altoist Marshall Allen, and baritone saxophonist Pat Patrick. Gilmore was particularly important—John Coltrane said he got the stop-and-start approach to improvisation that we hear on the 1961 Village Vanguard recordings partly from listening to Gilmore break up the beat with Sun Ra.

Their early records sound like hard bop arranged for a band with eccentric instrumentation—a pair of tympani added to the rhythm section on the 1956 "Call for All Demons," for instance. But by 1960, Sun Ra was also including

Sun Ra in costume at an electric keyboard, probably in the mid-1970's. (Courtesy Rutgers Institute of Jazz Studies)

extended jams over an enlarged, sometimes African-sounding rhythm section, and free improvisations such as "The Magic City." In the mid-sixties, he would record *The Heliocentric Worlds of Sun Ra* (1965) and *Nothing Is* (1966) for the important new music label ESP. (This New York based label recorded everything from a demonstration record in Esperanto, the proposed universal language, to selections from *Finnegan's Wake,* from the marginally obscene rock group The Fugs, to important albums by Ornette Coleman and other jazz-oriented avant-gardists. Their optimistic motto was "You Never Heard Such Sounds in Your Life," and they were frequently right.)

Sun Ra was a pioneer in another way too. Beginning in 1954 or 1955, early in the Arkestra's career, he began putting out his own records on his Saturn label. The records are rarely dated, and some of them have been issued without identifying numbers. Still, however haphazardly, they document the growth and development of a band that has held together for almost 40 years. Sun Ra has range: The Saturn records include free improvisations, but then Sun Ra performances in the eighties included furiously uptempo renditions of Fletcher Henderson arrangements from 50 years before. Sun Ra's theatricality, his spaciness, alienation, and dedication to what remains an obscure form of higher consciousness and to celebratory good fun, made him a prophet—though largely unsung—of the sixties. His use of silence in extended pieces, his emphasis on sounds, including those of a wide variety of instruments, represented an alternative to the intensity of the John Coltrane school. Sun Ra was in many ways the prime influence on the post-Coltrane avant-garde, that of Anthony Braxton, and the Art Ensemble of Chicago, especially its member Roscoe Mitchell.

Pianist Cecil Taylor presented another, though equally intense, alternative to John Coltrane. Born in 1929, Taylor grew up in a middle-class family on Long Island. His mother was a pianist, and he began taking lessons when he was five. In 1952, he entered the New England Conservatory at a time when it was unprepared to deal with black culture or popular music. Taylor was listening to jazz intensively at this point—he was influenced, he said, by the piano playing of Dave Brubeck, with its overlapping, rhythmic phrases, harmonic density, and strong accents. Ellington and Monk were equally important to him, as was Bud Powell—"Where are you, Bud?" Taylor asks in the notes to his 1966 album *Unit Structures.* All of these pianists were composers with strikingly percussive piano styles. Perhaps Taylor was also influenced by Dick Twardzik, a unique figure around Boston who died in 1955. Twardzik's one album as a leader includes "A Crutch for the Crab," with its unusual textures—chiming sounds made by rapidly alternating chords in both hands, repetitions of single notes—and harmonic intricacy. (Such devices may also be heard on a recently issued private recording of solo Twardzik, and on his 1955 date with Chet Baker which proved to be his last.) Taylor added to these influences an interest in twentieth century classical music. Some listeners attacked Taylor as too closely tied to Europe to be a jazz player.

He was a new kind of jazz player, one who talked of "rhythm-sound energy," who defined his own athletic improvisations as related to dance and

Cecil Taylor in Detroit around 1970. (Photo by
Michael Ullman)

those of his ensemble as a "group chain reaction." He claimed that music is
always larger than the instrument on which it is played, and he pushed the
piano to its limits. His sound is unmistakable: Other pianists, including Monk,
have clumped their elbows down on the keyboard, but no one has duplicated
Taylor's rapid-fire, chattering lines high in the treble. Pecked out sometimes
with two fingers, these make him sound like a typist possessed. He will alternate chords between his two hands in the Brubeck fashion, but so fast that he
sounds like a drummer as much as a pianist. He will work himself up to a
furious pitch, and then, suddenly and without warning, subside into a spare,
relaxed melody, still harmonically dry. (Even at his most romantic, Taylor's
closer to Debussy's astringency than to Ravel's lushness.) For all their overlapping density, his lines are cleanly articulated, and his sonorities are brilliant.

Taylor's first recording, *Jazz Advance*, was made in December 1955 for
Transition, a small company based in Cambridge, Massachusetts. With soprano
saxophonist Steve Lacy, who is still a major figure in new jazz, the classically-
trained bassist Buell Neidlinger, and the self-taught drummer from the Virgin
Islands, Dennis Charles, Taylor paid oblique tributes to some of his heroes. He
played Ellington's "Azure," and Cole Porter's "You'd Be So Nice to Come Home
To." He performed Monk's "Bemsha Swing." While the bass and drums maintain the chorus structure of each piece, Taylor solos over them with strangely
wandering right-hand lines, and occasionally both hands chording at once. In
July 1957, the Taylor quartet was introduced to a not entirely enthralled crowd at
the Newport Jazz Festival. As recorded on Verve, they began with "Johnny
Come Lately," which had Lacy stating the Billy Strayhorn theme impassively
while Taylor, ostensibly in the background, seemed to jump all over and around
him. Lacy was a good sideman for this stage of Taylor's career: In the sway of
Monk, he played shining solos using the chords of the tunes they were playing,
and he was inventive—and strong enough—to sustain his train of thought in
front of Taylor's increasingly vibrant, startling playing. Yet Taylor's solos still

have a semblance of the conventional left-hand comping and right-hand melody lines.

In his recordings of 1960 and 1961 for the Candid label, Taylor no longer refers to bebop piano conventions. (These recordings, *The World of Cecil Taylor* and *New York R&B,* have been reissued, with many enlightening alternate takes, by Mosaic Records.) Mostly Taylor focuses on his own spiky, irregular compositions. The melodies and sequences are sometimes difficult to perceive. His "Port of Call" is, as the invaluable notes in the Mosaic set by bassist Neidlinger tell us, an eighty-eight bar composition in E♭. Taylor improvises, however, on only eight bars. On the newly issued take, we can clearly hear his left hand playing the repetitive sequence of chords that fit those eight bars. In these sessions, Taylor plays a twelve-bar blues, "O.P.," dedicated by its composer Neidlinger to the great bop bassist Oscar Pettiford. When Neidlinger played the then unissued "O.P." for classical pianist Glenn Gould, Gould exclaimed, "This is perhaps the most formidable pianism these ears have heard; this is the Great Divide of American piano playing." What one hears on this blues as well is a new approach to rhythm: a surging and relaxation of tempo that corresponds to the greater and lesser tensions in the music.

For this kind of rhythm, a freer drummer was indicated. Taylor found this drummer in Sunny Murray, who was on some of the Candid material in 1960. More than anyone else, Murray was responsible for the development of the coloristic, unmetered style of free-jazz drumming in which the percussionist, rather than marking time, contributes to the collective improvisation by accentuating freely and exploring the timbres and pitches of the drum set. In Murray's case, this was often a stripped down drum set—he's been known to perform with a high-hat, snare, and bass drum alone. Although at first Murray kept a fairly conventional beat, he learned to create a kind of busy, multidirectional counterpoint behind Cecil Taylor. Three of their early pieces were released in 1961 under Gil Evans's name on *Into the Hot.* The three pieces are Taylor's "Pots," "Bulbs," inspired by the lights in Central Park, and "Mixed," a musical description of a love relationship with a "nascent section, recognition" and then "travail and descent." "Mixed" is perhaps the most ambitious piece. Its romance is rendered with sweet passages unprecedented in Cecil Taylor—the Mingus-like melody that is the first in-tempo theme must be "recognition." The dissolution leads the piece towards an unsettling disorder.

"Bulbs" is a masterpiece. Its swirling melody lines, performed with a jubilant roughnesss, lead into fast, swinging solos by Taylor and by alto saxophonist Jimmy Lyons. Lyons became a longstanding member of the Taylor ensembles. At first he played Charlie Parker-derived lines made distinctive by their new context. Gradually he developed his own fragmented, but persuasive style, until he was one of the most distinctive alto saxophonists in the new jazz. The bassist Henry Grimes rounded out this quartet, which was one of Taylor's finest groups.

But it was impossible, with the limited work that Taylor was getting, to keep this group together. Sunny Murray left to go out on his own, recording for

ESP in 1966, and then three records for the French BYG label in 1969. From 1965 to 1975, Cecil Taylor worked with drummer Andrew Cyrille, who pioneered what he calls "conversational rhythms," rhythms that approach speech-like patterns. His most impressive recordings from that period include *Unit Structures* and *Conquistador* for Blue Note. Both were recorded with enlarged groups in 1966, including two bassists who interact with each other freely. *Conquistador* appears to be more loosely organized. The title composition begins with a strikingly fast, clean, upwards-moving phrase on the piano, that is repeated and answered. This clear articulation of phrases is typical of the mature Taylor—he will lay out a phrase that is repeated, varied, expanded, or merely decorated, he will put that phrase in relation to an answering movement, and when he has worried that combination enough, he will move to a new, often preplanned phrase or section. In *Unit Structures,* which has Ken McIntyre on oboe and bass clarinet, Taylor demonstrates his typical working methods. The winds render his themes in a rhythmically free way, while the piano heavily ornaments and comments on their rendition. "Enter Evening" (SCCJ) begins as shown in the example. (See music example.)

Example 22–1.
Cecil Taylor, opening theme of "Enter Evening" (1966). Played freely, without barlines. Dotted lines show notes that occur together.

Later in the piece, when the winds drop out, Taylor takes an intense solo, more motivic than usual. As Henry Martin has noted, Taylor begins with small note patterns, mostly fourths and tritones and rising arpeggios. He builds to agitated waves of sound, and ends, after an interjection by the bowed bass, much like he began (*Enjoying Jazz*, p. 181). (See music example.)

In a sense, the piano solos continuously—only rarely, as behind the trumpet and bowed bass duet on "Conquistador," is Taylor willing to provide an unobtrusive accompaniment.

In concert, Taylor, with or without his ensemble, has been known to

a) **Beginning of exposed piano improvisation, without the winds.**

b) **End of exposed piano improvisation, after interjection by bowed bass.**

Example 22–2.
Cecil Taylor, beginning and end of his solo on "Enter Evening" (1966).

perform a single piece for nearly three hours without a break, in displays of stamina that have wrung audiences dry yet left the pianist, usually clad in a white sweat suit and sneakers, bouncing spryly on his toes like a cocky middleweight at the end of the second round. His solo performances, such as the masterful *Indent* from 1973, expand from identifiable kernels of melody and rhythm which are gradually swamped in Taylor's athletic pianism—his rapid-fire repeated notes, stuttering chords, flashy treble scales, and thunderous crashes for climaxes. A fan of ballet and modern dance, he has performed extended works with dancers. Sometimes he offers his own eccentric version of dance. In Boston in 1990, he darted onstage, freezing in angular positions that made him look like a minor Hindu deity, and chanted surrealistic poetry before sitting down at the piano. Although he will still play at great length, he has started to edit his solos, frequently offering gemlike pieces of a couple of minutes. In the nineties, he continues to perform with the quicksilver speed and power, with the structural intelligence and occasional Ellingtonian melodicism, that have characterized his music for decades.

ALBERT AYLER, DON CHERRY, AND ARCHIE SHEPP

In some ways the most surprising—and disturbing—music of the sixties came from saxophonist Albert Ayler. Ayler developed the most startling sound in jazz—an immensely loud, cavernously hollow tone which he rendered with a broad, sentimental vibrato that overwhelms the listener and dominates the other members of the band. Ayler used his hugely inflated Sidney Bechet-tone to play folk-like melodies—he's the only avant-garde player known to have improvised on "La Marseillaise"—and for obstreperous free improvisation in which he offers extended passages of unihibited high screaming. There's something outrageous about Ayler's music—he plays simple tunes with uncertain, wavering pitch, and he seems to wear his heart on his sleeve. Ayler expresses sheer emotion as openly as a gospel choir.

That may have been his intention. A religious man who titled pieces "Spiritual Unity" and "Love Cry," Ayler sought to play music that is "beyond this world." Coltrane saw Ayler as an extension of Coltrane's own work, playing the "higher frequencies" of the horn, and developing spiritual qualities in music that approached the ecstatic. Ayler could also play the blues. One of his early jobs was with Chicago blues harmonica player Little Walter—Ayler's tone might be inspired by the amplified wail, the overtones and bent pitches, of Walter's harmonica. Ayler had experience with older forms of jazz as well. The drummer Milford Graves told Valerie Wilmer: "I think one thing he proved was that he could traditionally blow his horn. He could really play honky-tonk, he knew all the gut things, and, not taking away from any other horn players, he was the kind of horn player with whom I could really play my axe. You could see Albert knew exactly what was happening" (*As Serious As Your Life,* p. 96). Ayler was interested in something other than instrumental virtuosity, however: As he once put it, "You have really to play your instrument to escape from notes to sound."

Ayler, whose younger brother Donald was a trumpet player with his band, was born in 1936 in Cleveland. His father, a violinist and tenor player, taught him the alto sax. Albert Ayler's earliest professional experience came with rhythm and blues bands and with Little Walter. In his twenties Ayler entered the army, and when he was discharged in 1962, he stayed in Europe where he had been stationed, evidently playing with Cecil Taylor in Copenhagen in the winter of 1962. After making several recordings, including the January 14, 1963 session with European musicians that produced the iconoclastic versions of standards on *My Name is Albert Ayler,* he moved to New York City.

There he was able to put together a trio with innovative bassist Gary Peacock, a disciple of Scott LaFaro, and with Sunny Murray. The next two years,

1964 and 1965, were Ayler's most productive. This group recorded *Spiritual Unity* and an expanded group—with trumpeter Don Cherry, altoist John Tchicai, and trombonist Roswell Rudd added—recorded *New York Eye and Ear Control,* intended as a film soundtrack. *New York Eye and Ear Control* (July 17, 1964) is a largely forgotten masterpiece, a successor to Coleman's Free Jazz and a predecessor of Coltrane's *Ascension.* It is a group improvisation among fascinating, well-balanced instrumentalists. John Tchicai's cool, motivic playing interjects new thematic material throughout, while with blustering self-assurance, Roswell Rudd demonstrates his background as a tailgating trombonist. Cherry opens the piece with a beautifully expressed, improvised melody, using a dark, more serene tone than he had with Ornette Coleman. Peacock's bowed bass becomes another, gruffer horn. There's wildness in *New York Eye and Ear Control* as well.

Unable to find much work around New York, the quartet of Ayler, Cherry, Peacock, and Murray travelled to Europe, and recorded the album *Vibrations* (originally entitled *Ghosts*) in Copenhagen on September 14, 1964. The opening notes of the long version of "Ghosts" on *Vibrations*—he recorded "Ghosts" repeatedly—have him expounding the Calypso-like melody with an alarming sense of urgency and force. He begins his solo by taking the catchy second phrase, shown in the example, and distorting it sarcastically, smudging and distorting its pitches. (See music example.)

He was rarely this thematic for long, and his playing soon grows more agitated, supported by the irregular pulse of Murray and Peacock. Ayler interjects high squeals and r & b honks.

Example 22–3.
Albert Ayler, part of theme and beginning of improvisation on "Ghosts"
(recording of September 14, 1964).

In 1965, Ayler, with his brother Donald now on trumpet, began to add marches to the avant-garde spirituals and folk-tunes of his repertoire, which included a version of "Motherless Child" he called "Mothers." He was writing down more of what he wanted his musicians to play. On "Bells," with alto saxophonist Charles Tyler added, a continuous medley of tunes is interspersed with brief solos and collectively improvised passages. The result is an odd mixture of cheerful, affirmative melody and free jazz excitement. By early 1966, Peacock and Murray were no longer working with Ayler: He never found the perfect replacements.

He did find, when he least expected it, a major label contract. At John Coltrane's urging, Impulse Records started recording Ayler towards the end of 1966. From 1966 to 1969, his Impulse albums—they would include *Albert Ayler in Greenwich Village, Love Cry, New Grass,* and *Music is the Healing Force of the Universe*—introduced a more eclectic, but in some ways simpler, Ayler. In a band whose personnel was becoming less stable, he introduced at various times a harpsichordist, vocalist Mary Maria, a cellist, and a violinist. (String players could of course play the wavering pitches of Ayler's saxophone style with relative ease.) He drew more obviously on mainstream jazz—his "New Ghosts" now sounds like a full-blown Sonny Rollins calypso, played in a tone that prefigured the sound Rollins would have in 1972. Other tunes are based wholly on bugle calls, or imitate the wobbly vibratos of lesser New Orleans marching bands. On "For John Coltrane" Ayler confines his improvisation in the middle, after a string passage, to a few repeated notes played at great length over a free rhythm. Ayler referred to r & b in *New Grass,* but his work, with its paradoxically simple melodies and hectic, free improvisations, with its parodies of marches, bugle calls, national anthems, and hymns, seems unsettled. Then, in 1970, his body was found floating in the East River. The exact circumstances of his death were never determined.

The exact nature of his influence is also hard to determine. He may in fact have affected Coltrane, who was an Ayler fan and sat in the audience during a 1966 Village Vanguard session. In February 1966, Coltrane and Ayler performed together at Philharmonic (now Avery Fisher) Hall in Lincoln Center, and Coltrane during his solo on *Ascension* uses the obsessive repetitions of a few notes which we identify with Ayler. As suggested above, he may have influenced, or been influenced by, Sonny Rollins's tone and repertoire. What is clear is that no one has played the saxophone quite like Ayler—although some avant-garde string players have approximated at times both his vibrato and slippery approaches to notes. Ayler played with some of the best avant-garde musicians of the sixties. The winds of *New York Eye and Ear Control*—trombonist Roswell Rudd, and saxophonist John Tchicai, and trumpeter Don Cherry—would, in varying combinations and with the substitution of Archie Shepp for Ayler, provide the basis of some of the most compelling recordings of the sixties.

Ayler's uninhibited emotion may have loosened up the style of trumpeter Don Cherry. Nonetheless, Coleman's quartet remained at first the model for groups in which Cherry appeared. These included the New York Contemporary

Five, which helped introduce tenor saxophonist Archie Shepp to a wider public. Their November 1963 recording, *Consequences,* opens with a fanfare on Cherry's "Sound Barrier," a piece that in the Coleman manner alternates this fanfare with a quick, irregular boppish line. Tchicai and Cherry take orderly solos. When Shepp enters, a different kind of voice is heard. Tchicai and Cherry's well-articulated phrases sound clear and direct. Shepp, with his dark, growling tone, with its buzzes and growls, and Ben Websterish huffing, sounds oblique, threatening. He enters noncommittally, and engages in some humor, with a truncated bugle call and a silly-sounding trill. Then, as he digs in, he works with motives—a growling phrase down low in the sax that he repeats. He sounds like a new kind of r & b player working over a riff. In his later playing, as will be seen, he becomes even more sensuous.

Tchicai went on to perform with Roswell Rudd in the New York Art Quartet, which in 1964 made a record for ESP and the next year made two, one for Fontana. On the latter, they have the gall to take a Charlie Parker tune, "Mohawk," and fragment it into an avant-garde piece, showing a new approach to tradition. Rudd's trombone playing is new, but it is based on even older tradition, on the Dixieland playing that he had grown up with. Like certain other avant-gardists, Rudd reached back behind bebop to an earlier style, which he updated. Whereas in the forties J.J. Johnson played bop solos that could have been rendered on a saxophone, Rudd plays in a way that only a trombone can, emphasizing the slide and the instrument's dark and slippery tones. Throughout the sixties, avant-garde players would take Ornette Coleman's advice, that a musician should listen to what his instrument wants to play. Rudd and Grachan Moncur would become the key trombonists of the avant-garde. (In the eighties, George Lewis and Ray Anderson took up where they left off.)

After leaving Ornette Coleman, Don Cherry had worked with Steve Lacy and briefly with Sonny Rollins. After playing with Ayler and the New York Contemporary Five, he moved to Europe in 1964, where he began performing with the Argentinian tenor saxophonist, Gato Barbieri, a player whose reliance on overblowing and wide vibrato links him with Ayler and Pharoah Sanders. Cherry made a celebrated series of recordings for Blue Note, including *Complete Communion* (1965), *Symphony for Improvisers* (1966), and *Where is Brooklyn?* (1966). Especially in the first two, he shucked off much of the Coleman influence and produced original, wholly satisfying music. His procedure was simple. He would write a series of attractively tuneful melodies and riffs, which he would play on his trumpet. After an introduction, the group would improvise, either in a series of solos or together, on the first melody, until Cherry signalled that it was time to move to the next. The result was a coherent work of several parts, a free jazz symphony. Sonny Rollins noted, "Don is a very individual musician. For a time I had the tendency to lump Don and Ornette together. But now I've discovered that Don is a musician in his own right."

Cherry's interests continued to broaden. In 1969, he would record a remarkable series of duets with Ed Blackwell issued on two albums as *Mu—Part One* and *Part Two.* He became more interested in folk music, and he studied the music of Africa, India, and even Turkey—one of his records, the 1969 *Live in Ankara,* was made with Turkish musicians and featured Turkish folk music as well as tunes by Ornette Coleman, Cherry, and Pharoah Sanders. In the seventies he began to play new instruments—a variety of flutes, an African xylophone, an African harp. He discovered surprising convergences in the music he studied, including a background riff played in Africa that was also the basis of a John Lee Hooker blues.

In 1979, Cherry joined with sitar player Colin Walcott and Brazilian percussionist Nana Vasconcelos to form Codona, a group which played everything from Stevie Wonder to Japanese folk songs in a spacious, meditative way. Previously Walcott had spent over a decade with the acoustic folk-jazz group Oregon. After three records, Codona came to an end in 1984 when Walcott was killed in a car crash. Don Cherry has continued to investigate folk traditions, and has recorded his own versions of black popular music. A Cherry performance might include a jazz rap or reggae, or what sounds like a fifties song by the Platters, except that its lyric is about a wayward butterfly ("Butterfly Friend"). His music is an intriguing mixture by one of the gentlest and most ingratiating figures in the avant-garde.

Don Cherry moved from Ornette Coleman's music to world music. Archie Shepp was from the beginning a more eclectic figure, performing in his own style with Cecil Taylor, with the Coleman-influenced New York Contemporary Five, and becoming a protégé of John Coltrane, who recommended him to Impulse Records. Born in Fort Lauderdale in 1937, Shepp grew up in Philadelphia and got a degree in drama and literature at Goddard College in Vermont. He then moved to New York, ostensibly to find work in theater. But, he was also an accomplished saxophonist. Bassist Buell Neidlinger introduced him to Cecil Taylor, and in 1960, as noted above, he recorded with Taylor for Candid. In 1962, he co-led a group with trumpeter Bill Dixon that recorded a single record for Savoy. Shepp's notes to this album promulgate his belief that music is a political and social force and that the music of the present must reflect the pressures of the time, just as the field hollers of farm workers reflected the pressures of their time and situation. On the Dixon-Shepp record, he used short riffs and tense little phrases to play a deeply felt version of Leonard Bernstein's "Somewhere" full of expressive slurs and caustic growls. The message of Stephen Sondheim's lyric from *West Side Story,* which is sung by the star-crossed lovers, is that there's a place for them somewhere—though definitely not here. Shepp says that "the song had a very special, personal meaning for me."

In 1964 he dedicated his first recording as a leader to John Coltrane. The cover of *Four for Trane* has a photograph of Shepp sitting on some stairs, looking unconcerned and professorial with his pipe held in his mouth. Coltrane stands behind him, his brow knitted, hovering over the younger man in avuncular fashion. Coltrane's concern, and Shepp's almost theatrical confidence, are typical of both men. The album contained four early Coltrane compositions—the four for Trane—and one for and by Shepp, his frightening "Rufus (Swung, his face at last to the wind, then his neck snapped)." Shepp was at this point under the sway of one aspect of Coltrane's style—he manipulates short, aggressively stated motives in a rhythmically alert manner. But he never shared the older man's at one time compulsive interest in harmony, which led to "Giant Steps." And unlike Coltrane, Shepp approaches ballads with a broadened, sensuous tone, lurching rhythms, and a dramatic flair. The beginning of his phrases can be almost inarticulate, as he seems not to tongue his reed. In mid-phrase he might push at his tone, creating an aggressive braying, and then pull back immediately in mock-delicacy. His model is one of the greatest of ballad players, Ben Webster, but even Webster does not approach "Prelude to a Kiss" with the leering sensuality of Shepp.

Shepp also has something of Mingus's ferocious humor. His compositions, such as "Rufus," include extreme tempo changes, great silences, and scurrying Ornette Coleman phrases. Like Ayler, he also writes pieces that sound like marches. Some of his performances are free and open-ended—in the early seventies at a place called the Strata West Gallery in Detroit, he once performed a two-hour set of free improvisations accompanied only by a pair of drummers. His *The Magic of Ju-Ju* (1967) has Shepp improvising over a chorus of percussionists. He also incorporates poetry and song into his writing. "Mamarose/A Poem for Malcolm," for instance, is a musical piece whose poem is shouted in distorted tones that make it sound like another saxophone solo.

Shepp became one of the most recorded, and most outspoken, avant-garde figures of the sixties and seventies. He was an important influence in one respect especially: From the beginning he talked and wrote about the importance of reevaluating the history of African-American music, of reviving its values and

Archie Shepp at the Ann Arbor Blues and Jazz Festival, probably 1972. (Photo by Michael Ullman)

demonstrating its relevance. In his notes to *Mama Too Tight* (1966), he wrote: "Our aim here is not to 'overthrow' the many valid musical references that are extant, but to include them wherever possible." The value of Ornette Coleman to him, Shepp goes on to say, is that Coleman revitalized the blues, restoring them to their "free, classical (African) unharmonized beginnings." When he plays the blues, Shepp suggests, he's thinking more of the likes of the Texas bluesman from the twenties, Blind Lemon Jefferson, than of bebop. (Jefferson's "Black Snake Moan" begins with a wildly exotic moan in indeterminate pitch that in another context might be considered avant-garde.) The title tune, "Mama Too Tight," is a joyously bouncy blues with a rhythm and blues beat. It's thirteen bars, Shepp tells for people "who bother wid dat." He sounds both proud of having written a thirteen-bar blues and diffident about revealing his pride.

He performed less often in the seventies and eighties. His skill at expressing his forceful ideas brought him teaching positions, first at the State University of New York in Buffalo, and then at the University of Massachusetts in Amherst. He continued to record, however, often returning to mainstream jazz pieces: He had written in his notes to *Mama Too Tight* that the music needs "to return to Bedford and Watts," to communicate with black youth. In 1977, Shepp recorded a series of duets with pianist Horace Parlan. Their repertoire consisted of astonishingly fresh, respectful versions of spirituals such as "Deep River" and "Steal Away to Jesus." In the next year, he recorded another masterful series of duets, this time with the South African pianist Abdullah Ibrahim (Dollar Brand). In 1976 and 1979, he recorded fiery duets with drummer Max Roach. Shepp could be exasperating: Arriving an hour-and-a-half late at a New York concert in the seventies, he declared—to the evident displeasure of his band of black musicians who had been on stage from the beginning—that he belonged to an African people with a different sense of time than his predominantly white audience. But he was always inspiring, an avant-garde musician who found new ways of expressing his highly developed lyricism and who paid a wholesome tribute to a wide range of African-American music.

MUSICIANS OUT OF CHICAGO

To some in the sixties, the spirit-filling, note-packed intensity of Coltrane's improvisations were a challenge. To others it meant a door was closed to them. The young Anthony Braxton, who grew up in Chicago, heard Coltrane and decided that he could go no further in the direction of intensity than Coltrane had already gone. He had to find another way. He was in the right place. After Sun Ra took his Arkestra out of Chicago in 1961, moving to New York and eventually settling in Philadelphia, there was a temporary vacuum in the Chicago avant-garde. It began to be filled by the pianist Richard Abrams. He assembled a rehearsal band that came to be known as the Experimental Band, which played Abrams's compositions and those of a cluster of young musicians who would become central to the development of avant-garde jazz, Roscoe Mitchell, Joseph Jarman, Anthony Braxton and Maurice McIntyre among them.

In 1965, Abrams founded the nonprofit Association for the Advancement of Creative Musicians (AACM). Their organization reflected "an emergent need to expose and showcase original Music which, under the existing establishment (promoters, agents, etc.), was not receiving its just due." The organization worked. It presented concerts, and workshops, offered new composers forums for hearing their own music and young players a chance to express themselves. The violinist Leroy Jenkins was one of its first members. There wasn't much call for a jazz violinist, so Jenkins felt lost until he met up with the AACM. He heard a concert by Roscoe Mitchell and joined up: He was accepted immediately by musicians who saw the possibility of saying something original in jazz on the violin: "They were excited by the possibilities of the violin. [As opposed to bebop, the music of the AACM] was more of a conversational thing. There was more inflection, more dynamics in their music. I started to bring out the full violinistic potential in the music. Now I'm playing double stops, chords, dis-chords, harmony, disharmony, everything." During his time in this stimulating environment, Jenkins wrote for all types of AACM bands, including a 22-piece orchestra.

The Chicago musicians's openness to the possibilities of the violin in jazz was not mere chance. The AACM developed an aesthetic that involved open-ness to a whole range of sounds and instruments. They rebelled against the restrictions of bebop instrumentation, which limited a front line to trumpet, saxophone, and perhaps a trombone. If the music is about sounds rather than swing, as they suggested, then the widest variety of sounds is desirable. Har-monicas, accordions, bassoons, fifes, Japanese kotos, gongs, harps and bells began appearing on the Chicago musicians's recordings. Everyone played, it seemed, a dozen instruments. Everyone was a percussionist—everyone was a kind of painter in sound. It was not important to become a virtuoso on each instrument—an impossible task—but merely to be able to evoke appropriately suggestive sounds from whatever instrument one was confronting, whether a contrabass clarinet or a self-made percussion instrument such as Henry Thread-gill's hubkaphone, a collection of hubcaps.

Perhaps the seminal recording of this movement is the Roscoe Mitchell Sextet's *Sound*, recorded in 1966. The first of a series of Delmark records docu-menting the AACM's music, it contains three pieces: "Ornette," Mitchell's tribute to Ornette Coleman; "Little Suite," which Mitchell calls "a suite of colors"; and "Sound." What one notices immediately about "Sound" is its sense of space, of sounds patiently spread out over a background of silence. It begins with a cymbal crash and roll, and a soft held note—an A—by trombonist Lester Lashley, and then introduces the main theme, expressed by the solo alto of Mitchell playing drawn-out tones sotto voce over the bass of Malachi Favors, occasionally tolling a low A, and the cymbal roll of Alvin Fielder. (See music example.)

Next the muted trumpet is added for harmony as the trombone and bass continue intermittently to play their low A's. The winds finish playing the main theme together. This presentation is punctuated by the occasional ringing of a

Example 22–4. Roscoe Mitchell, opening theme of "Sound" (1966).

small bell. The first improvisation that follows this extended theme is a quiet one by the band on a variety of small percussion instruments to which Mitchell adds a gentle phrase on recorder until he is supplanted by trumpeter Lester Bowie making a variety of smeared, suggestive sounds. Later, trombonist Lester Lashley enters, gradually becoming more agitated than any of the previous soloists, and demonstrating that this kind of music can move into something resembling the energetic style of improvising that Coltrane was still pioneering. In fact, that is one of the strengths of Mitchell's music: It can change shape and mood without losing its structural or conceptual rigor. This may be called free jazz, but it is an austere freedom within strict, self-imposed constraints—Mitchell thinks of them as strategies that assure that one's playing renews itself.

Mitchell has become best known as a member of the Art Ensemble of Chicago, one of the groups that spun off from Richard Abrams's large orchestra. Three members of this band—saxophonist Mitchell, trumpeter Lester Bowie, and bassist Malachi Favors—were on Mitchell's *Sound*. They were joined by a second saxophonist, one even more dedicated than Mitchell to experimenting with secondary instruments—Joseph Jarman. Jarman and Mitchell had been playing together since 1961 or 1962, when they met in college. These players appeared in Chicago in a variety of groups and on records, under the leadership of first one and then another of them, and sometimes with added personnel. Hoping to find more work, the band moved to Paris in 1969 where they became the Art Ensemble of Chicago. There, despite some hard times—the band lived together in campsites for a while—the Art Ensemble became a vibrant group that demonstrated that Coltrane's was not the only direction exploratory jazz groups could take. In 1969 they recorded a series of records for the Parisian label BYG.

These included the suggestively titled *Message to Our Folks*. On the cover are the four musicians, each dressed in a different way and implying a different role. Malachi Favors is pictured digging in a field with a shovel. Joseph Jarman, dressed in a Salvation Army uniform, clutches a Bible and looks down his nose in mock self-righteousness. Mitchell wears a slick sharkskin suit; he's brandishing a knife. The tuxedoed Bowie clutches both his trumpet and a revolver. With a certain amount of irony, they suggest roles black males have taken in our culture. The music does something comparable. They offer a comic version of "Old Time Religion," with Jarman preaching apocalyptically over the bowed bass of Favors and the responses of the band. Then they play a tight rendition of Charlie Parker's "Dexterity." After the clearly stated theme, one hears relatively free soloing, as each horn—using smears, wide skips, and, in the case of Bowie, half-valved sounds—seems to undermine the implications of the cleanly stated

Joseph Jarman and bassist Malachi Favors of the Art Ensemble of Chicago, Ann Arbor, 1972. (Photo by Michael Ullman)

theme. Finally, the first side ends with "Rock Out," a rock and roll tune played over Favor's Fender electric bass. The Art Ensemble seems simultaneously to be reaching out to "our folks," playing African-American music and evoking their past, and subverting that music while criticizing that past.

The Art Ensemble became a quintet in 1970 when they added the drummer Don Moye. The addition of a professional percussionist opened up new possibilities: The Ensemble could swing conventionally, as they do in "Charlie M.," their tribute to Charlie Mingus, they could present wildly improvised "energy" music, and they could convincingly play dance rhythms. Eventually the Art Ensemble garnered a major contract, and recorded for ECM such seemingly contradictory titles as *Nice Guys* (1979) and *Urban Bushmen* (1980). As they continued to work together, their live performances became tighter, and more fluid. In the eighties, some saw this fluidity as slickness, and longed for the more haphazard, and surprising, group of the late sixties. But their particular mixture of collective improvisation and composition, their humor, theatricality, and frequent power, continue to fascinate. Today, they gather together for tours and for recordings, while pursuing their individual projects, such as Lester Bowie's brass band, Brass Fantasy.

Paris drew other Chicago musicians in the late sixties and early seventies, including the three members of an AACM group called the Creative Construction Company: Trumpeter Leo Smith, violinist Leroy Jenkins and Anthony Braxton. Alto saxophonist Anthony Braxton, who was born in Chicago in 1945, began his teens admiring—idolizing, he says—two saxophonists, Paul Desmond from the Dave Brubeck group and John Coltrane. He tried leaning against

Anthony Braxton at the Jazz Workshop, Boston, 1975.
(Photo by Michael Ullman)

pianos and looking nonchalant in the Desmond manner, but found nonchalance incompatible with Coltrane's intensity. Later he would find a way to combine the cool intellectuality of Desmond's music with some of the extended saxophone techniques Coltrane was pioneering. In the end, he developed an important new approach to making music that is full of intensity.

In 1966, after a stint in the army, Braxton returned to his home city and joined the AACM. In 1967, he formed the Creative Construction Company. Then, in 1968 he recorded *For Alto*, an unprecedented double album of solo saxophone improvisations. It was a startling production, then considered eccentric despite the fact that Sonny Rollins had given solo saxophone concerts. (Since then, many Chicago-influenced wind players have recorded solo.) Like his peers in Chicago, Braxton was voracious intellectually. By 1968, he was listing his influences as Paul Desmond, Ornette Coleman, Eric Dolphy, Jackie McLean, the German composer Stockhausen, Miles Davis and James Brown. As a teen he was bowled over by Coltrane, and also by his first hearing of Schoenberg's short piano pieces, his Opus 11. But his music does not refer to these diverse influences in any obvious way.

No one was more eclectic, or more orderly. Like Roscoe Mitchell, Braxton decided that unplanned free improvisation would eventually result in a musician repeating him or herself. To avoid that he created categories of music for himself, series of compositions, each series exploiting a compositional ploy or a saxophone technique. In a solo performance, he might assign himself the task of playing with a certain rhythm, or with a specified sound—he's created whole solos around his growl. Braxton never used conventional titles for his pieces—he substitutes charts of his own which mystify his fans. Braxton explains the charts to his musicians, and occasionally in liner notes. In the example shown, the chart specifies performance details such as where the musicians are supposed to stand in relation to each other, and in what directions they are to face. (See music example.)

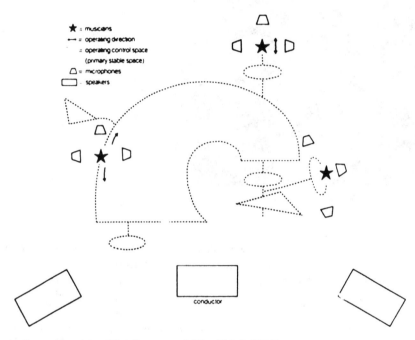

Anthony Braxton, title diagram of "For Trio" (1977)

The album also reproduces the score, which consists of a number of short notated phrases which the musicians combine in various ways.

Braxton is a serious, sensitive musician, and his music sounds remarkably fresh. Nonetheless the Creative Construction Company merely puzzled Parisian audiences, including those who had welcomed the Art Ensemble of Chicago. Braxton attributed the Construction Company's unpopularity to their lack of a rhythm section—even the Art Ensemble had a bass—and to the perceived intellectuality of their music. Called "cold," a criticism that has unfairly plagued Braxton, the trio returned to the United States. Braxton went to live at Ornette Coleman's Manhattan apartment. Soon he was heard by Chick Corea, and entered the group Circle. When Corea, desirous of a more popular music, broke up Circle in 1971, Braxton went out on his own.

In the seventies he made a series of definitive recordings of his music for Arista Records. His quartets, which often included Dave Holland on bass and

Barry Altschul or Jerome Cooper on drums, extended the legacy of Eric Dolphy while presenting a new voice. They are much more accessible than some critics have said. *New York, Fall 1974* begins with a fast, boppish piece that might have been by Dolphy, were it not for the way certain phrases of the melody are repeated in a manner that seems to stall forward progress. On this piece, the rhythm section burns in straight-ahead fashion, and the alto saxophone solo has, despite Braxton's complicated playing with rhythms, a fluidity that is entirely convincing. Braxton is also a humorist: At a live quartet performance in Boston's Jazz Workshop during the spring of 1976, the first date with trombonist George Lewis, Lewis played a phrase that hinted at a Sousa march. Braxton looked up, and then countered with an answering snippet. They trembled on the edge of parody, and then took the plunge, dragging drummer Altschul into an effectively raucous distillation of a Sousa march. Then on his big-band record for Arista, Braxton actually recreates a march—except that the performance stops on one chord somewhere in the middle, and includes a free improvisation. This new music march ends with Jon Faddis squeaking on a piccolo trumpet over a high-stepping ensemble.

Braxton shares the Art Ensemble's interest in new sounds—he plays a wide range of horns, from the contrabass clarinet, whose low notes sound like moving furniture, to the high sopranino saxophones. Inspired by marching bands, Charles Ives, and Stockhausen, he has written a large, wholly notated piece for four orchestras. In the eighties, he continued to play solo concerts and investigated new ensembles that could play every kind of music he could think of. He began performing with pianist Marilyn Crispell, precisely because "With Marilyn, I am free to introduce march music, totally notated pieces, no music or vertical harmony music—she can execute in every area." Braxton has consciously striven to create his own world of music, and he has succeeded admirably. That, he thinks, is in the best tradition of jazz: "I didn't want to play like Desmond or Coltrane or Dolphy, because the thing I admired most was the fact that they created their own universe." Braxton is currently a professor at Wesleyan University in Connecticut where he will surely open new doors for the next generation of musicians.

Leroy Jenkins had an even rockier time than Braxton when he moved to New York after the Creative Construction Company's stay in Paris. His greatest critical success came in the first half of the seventies when he was part of a cooperative trio in the Chicago tradition, the Revolutionary Ensemble. One revolutionary aspect of the group was its instrumentation—it featured Jenkins on violin with the bassist Sirone and drummer Jerome Cooper. The Revolutionary Ensemble was founded in 1970, and it recorded four times before breaking up. Air, another trio with an AACM background, seemed to take up in 1975 where the Revolutionary Ensemble left off. The members of Air were all Chicagoans, who began playing together in the early sixties. Saxophonist Henry Threadgill went to college with Roscoe Mitchell and Joseph Jarman, with whom he also performed in the early sixties. Steve McCall was a veteran drummer who had worked with a variety of great tenor saxophonists such as Gene Ammons and Lockjaw Davis, and had been a founding member of the AACM. Finally, the trio included bassist Fred Hopkins, who had begun playing bass while at Chicago's DuSable High School and worked with numerous members of the AACM. From the beginning the trio had a particular bluesiness and rhythmic power, which it could sustain even during long free improvisations.

One defining aspect of their repertoire came to them by chance. In 1971, the drama department at Columbia College in Chicago was mounting a play for which they wanted to use the music of Scott Joplin, but in updated renditions. They hired Threadgill to do the arrangements and Air to play the score. This experience helped formalize an interest of many avant-garde jazz players, who were then looking back into jazz traditions that preceded bebop. Air went on to record *Air Lore* in 1979, with versions of two Joplin rags, and of two Jelly Roll Morton compositions, the 12-bar "Buddy Bolden's Blues" and the more complex "King Porter Stomp." Their renditions have a charming, antiquated quality. McCall rapped away on his snare drums in march time while Threadgill played the Joplin or Morton melodies in comically stiff fashion. The combination of probing contemporary compositions and light-hearted arrangements of early jazz tunes distinguished Air's performances. In the eighties Threadgill carried those strengths into his popular sextet recordings, with their punning references to gospel music and the blues, and their challenging writing for an unusual instrumentation.

THE WORLD SAXOPHONE QUARTET

By opening up jazz to new instrumentation in bands that frequently lacked a piano and sometimes even a drummer, AACM musicians provided an alternative to what many more conventional players were doing in the sixties and seventies: imitating Charlie Parker or John Coltrane. One couldn't merely play Parker licks in a solo saxophone concert—how many such licks can one memorize? Playing without a rhythm section, one had to find new solutions to old problems: How does one sustain rhythmic interest? The new solutions were sometimes liberating, and some of the most stimulating music of the seventies and eighties was played by groups that hardly looked like conventional jazz bands. One of these was the World Saxophone Quartet. Composed of four experienced saxophonists—Oliver Lake, Julius Hemphill, David Murray, and Hamiet Bluiett—the World Saxophone Quartet can sound like an Ellington sax section. That is primarily because Bluiett has the heartiest baritone sound since Harry Carney, because tenor saxophonist David Murray founded his sound partly on Ben Webster—recently he's begun to look like Ben Webster—and because they recognize that Ellington created inventive sounds and arrangements for a saxophone section. (Arthur Blythe, who has subbed on alto with the group, has a vibrant tone that at times recalls Johnny Hodges.)

Three of the original members of the WSQ—Lake, Hemphill, and Bluiett—were part of the Black Artists Group, a cooperative organization begun in St.

Louis in the sixties. The musicians in the group, which originally contained trumpeter Lester Bowie, developed a relationship with members of the AACM, and they played in each other's concerts. Oliver Lake had already had a varied musical experience: He had heard black church music, and his first instrument was a bass drum, which he played in a drum and bugle corps. As a saxophonist he played bebop and standards. Writing for informal rehearsal bands, Lake soon became adept at creating compositions for unusual groups—you cannot write bebop tunes, Oliver Lake has said, if you're not sure you're going to have a drummer or a bass player. Baritone saxophonist Hamiet Bluiett has a deep, bluesy sound and a rhythmic drive that has enabled him to play solo blues that sound as richly authentic as anything coming out of New Orleans. Julius Hemphill is perhaps the premier writer of the group: With a rhythm and blues background—he performed with Ike Turner, Tina's husband, before moving to St. Louis—he too has a deep understanding of blues culture.

The WSQ was formed in 1976, after its fourth and youngest member, tenor David Murray, moved from California, where he was born in 1955. The group's solution to the problem of playing without a rhythm section is based on the powerful sound and rhythm of Bluiett. On numbers such as his "Hattie Wall," which the WSQ often used as a theme, Bluiett plays repeated rhythmic figures— ostinatos. Sometimes he is joined by a second saxophone, as the quartet splits in two, with the other half playing a composed melody or improvising. The roles can switch with other members taking over the rocking rhythms, while Bluiett solos. Or the rhythmic figure might be suspended, and all four saxophonists can enter into collective improvisation until one or another of them takes up the ostinato figure again, bringing the music back to its rhythmic core. Given its instrumentation, one might expect the WSQ to play abstract-sounding exercises: In reality they're much closer to an advanced kind of dance music, as "Steppin'" (SCCJ), one of their most popular pieces, suggests. On "Steppin'," they play alto flute, two soprano saxes, and bass clarinet, presenting a rhythmic bassline with a long-toned theme: As the piece develops, there is a long middle section which is mostly free improvisation. The band's music has swagger. So do its members, who frequently march onstage, dressed in tuxedos that would have made Ellington proud, and already playing "Hattie Wall" or another of their strutting themes.

LARGE GROUPS IN AMERICA AND EUROPE

Small groups, partially because of economic reasons, have dominated avant-garde jazz. That is not because the musicians have lost interest in larger textures; nor are they devoid of ideas about what to do with them. George Russell has continued to produce intriguing big band works. Special grants have allowed musicians such as Oliver Lake, Richard Abrams, David Murray, and Julius Hemphill to produce several large pieces for orchestra. But for the most part financial constraints have prevented contemporary musicians from being able to learn their trade by working over time with a big band.

The few exceptions since the sixties have demonstrated how much valuable music may have been lost as a result. The Jazz Composers Guild, a cooperative group founded by trumpeter-composer Bill Dixon in 1964, formed the Jazz Composers Guild Orchestra, which in 1966 became the Jazz Composers Orchestra Association (JCOA). It was led by two composers, Mike Mantler and Carla Bley. In 1968, this organization recorded a two-record set of Mantler's compositions, designed to provide a challenging setting for invited soloists Don Cherry, Cecil Taylor, Larry Coryell, Roswell Rudd and Pharoah Sanders. For the most part, Mantler has his orchestra play thick, threatening chords that set up a soloist and punctuate the solos. Simple though the approach may be, Mantler's sketches added body and substance to some of the best soloing by major avant-garde musicians.

As a writer, Carla Bley has a somewhat lighter, more whimsical approach than Mantler. Her accomplishments are remarkable. Born in Oakland in 1938, she learned piano from her father, and then moved as a teenager to New York. She studied with George Russell and began composing. She married pianist Paul Bley, who had considerable success playing her pieces—he still introduces her "Ida Lupino" as his one hit. Then she began working on larger pieces. She composed the ingenious "A Genuine Tong Funeral" for vibist Gary Burton in 1967, and the following year she wrote and orchestrated much of bassist Charlie Haden's *Liberation Music Orchestra* recording.

The Haden-Bley collaboration was particularly striking. It was conceived, Haden wrote, when the bassist first heard songs sung by the freedom fighters of the Spanish Civil War, the struggle against fascism that preceded the Second

Carla Bley in Boston, early 1980's. (Photo by Michael Ullman)

World War. He was particularly inspired by the brigades of foreign volunteers who formed the Abraham Lincoln brigade in the war against Franco's fascists. Haden and Carla Bley created a suite of these strongly melodic, martial songs that became the first side of *Liberation Music Orchestra*. To Haden, that doomed struggle had a contemporary analogy: The second side of the album has his "Song for Che" – Cuban revolutionist Che Guevara was killed in 1967; his "Circus '68 '69" was meant to reflect the chaos surrounding the Democratic Convention of 1968, with its riot by police and protesters. The album includes Ornette Coleman's compassionate "War Orphans," a new jazz version of "We Shall Overcome," which was the theme song of many civil rights marches, and a typically raucous Bley interjection, her "Drinking Song."

Besides its political content, *Liberation Music Orchestra* was important to jazz for its manner of mixing extravagantly, even sentimentally stated, melodies with the improvisational techniques of free jazz. Bley takes pieces such as the march "Song of the United Front," by the German composer Hanns Eisler (1898-1962) with words by Bertolt Brecht, and makes a sardonic, yet still committed, arrangement. The stomping march rhythms, the sarcasm and biting humor of much of the music, reflect the crucial influence on Carla Bley of the German (and later, American) composer Kurt Weill, who wrote the famous "Threepenny Opera," "Mahagonny," and "Happy End." The relevant Weill works were influenced by early jazz. In operas, often accompanied by what sounded like a thirties dance band, Weill found a way to exploit music-hall melodies, tubby brass band waltzes, march rhythms, and other trappings of popular culture, while writing in a mordant, politically aware style. Starting with "Drinking Song," Bley seems to have captured much of his sound.

She does so in the beginning of her most ambitious work, and the most ambitious work of the Jazz Composer's Orchestra, an operatic piece written by Bley with lyrics by Paul Haines called *Escalator Over the Hill*. Bley calls it a "chronotransduction": In German opera tradition, this mixture of song, spoken text, and orchestral music might have been called a *singspiel*. Recorded in several sessions between 1968 and 1971, *Escalator Over the Hill* enacts several scenes around a hotel lobby. The text by Haines ranges from political barbs to sublimely foolish comments on the supposed pointlessness of the modern world. It ends with the chanting in various voices of "Again," which becomes an endless hum as the last groove of the record is made to skip back into itself like a tape loop. (Bley plays games with recording technology: In one of her pieces for big bands, she wrote a section that sounds exactly like a scratched record skipping back over the same few measures. Many copies of the Bley record were actually returned for what listeners heard as a flaw.) Earlier, a doctor sings that people are raised like animals, like "chickens for legs." There's plenty of political cynicism: "Vote for something weak and to the point," the doctor continues. (See music example.)

One is most impressed by Bley's beautifully performed, tonally varied orchestrations, the ensembles from different styles of music, tango to country-western, the varied uses of voices, professional and unprofessional – Linda

Example 22–6.
Carla Bley, beginning of "Like Animals" from *Escalator Over the Hill* (1971), with words by Paul Haines.

Ronstadt and Sheila Jordan and Jeanne Lee sing on this piece, as does Charlie Haden and the Andy Warhol film star Viva—and the powerful solos. Those solos include several by Roswell Rudd, whose brash, braying, extroverted sound is perfect for Bley's work, as well as an exciting rock guitar side by John McLaughlin, and gentle trumpet playing by Don Cherry. The use of voices is also ingenious: Some characters chant, some improvise, and others read. The piece is a triumph of organization—it was a three year project done on a small budget by cooperative musicians. It also announced the readiness of a new generation of musicians to create brilliant ensemble work in a constantly evolving style.

Regrettably, the Jazz Composers Orchestra made only a few more records—dedicated to the writing of Roswell Rudd, Don Cherry, and Clifford Thornton—before dissolving under the weight of internal and economic problems. By that time they had demonstrated the applicability of avant-garde soloing techniques to music with a wide range of styles. Drawing on Weill and brass band music, Bley's writing was European as well as African-American, and it proved influential on European musicians who might have felt excluded from a blues-based improvisatory music.

These include the Dutch composer and saxophonist Willem Breuker, who leads the Willem Breuker Kollektief. A normal set by this ten- or eleven-piece band might include weirdly distorted marches or circus music, snatches of Ellingtonia and of Kurt Weill, blues, tangos, a smoothly swinging ballad in mid-thirties style, hints of Eric Dolphy, Klezmer, and of the movie music of Nino Rota, all interspersed with free solos. Breuker has recorded his own, very competent version of Gershwin's "American in Paris," songs from "Threepenny Opera" and "Mahagonny," and reverential versions of Ellington classics such as "Creole Love Call." Breuker's soloists often use the instrumental techniques—the squeals, hollers, frenetic runs and chordless meanderings—that were developed by avant-garde players in the sixties, when black innovators were associating free jazz with political liberation and racial pride and anger. A set by the Kollektief shows startlingly that those techniques can be used in more light-hearted ways. Breuker is a humorist, a parodist.

Breuker's radical approach to a wide range of material is typical of other large European ensembles, such as the Vienna Art Orchestra, led by Mathias Ruegg, and pianist Alexander von Schlippenbach's Globe Unity Orchestra. These are musicians trained in twentieth century classical music who are interested in improvisation as well as composition. The Vienna Art Orchestra has recorded a double album of tributes to the French composer Erik Satie, whom they remake into a modern minimalist: Their set is called *The Minimalism of Erik Satie.* "Reflections on Meditation" includes a wordless, widely skipping vocal by Lauren Hutton over an insistent rhythm played on a triangle. The Globe Unity Orchestra, an international group of leading European improvisers directed since 1966 by the German pianist Schlippenbach, has recorded versions of Thelonious Monk and Jelly Roll Morton, and the repertoire includes free group improvisation as well.

These are among the most distinctive, and suggestive, large ensembles in contemporary jazz: Their polish, their wide-ranging repertoire, and the frequent power of the soloists, is remarkable. Europe has been able to sustain such large groups, despite the counterculture politics and vision of Breuker and Ruegg, during a period when similar large orchestras have foundered in the United States. As a result, some of George Russell's large pieces, for instance, have been recorded by the Swedish Radio Orchestra rather than in America. Europe has also produced innovative smaller groups and soloists in the avant-garde: English guitarist Derek Bailey, who has recorded with Anthony Braxton; Dutch drummer Han Bennink; English saxophonist Evan Parker, among others.

Avant-garde jazz techniques have proven compatible with parallel developments in contemporary classical music, in which the Europeans are particularly well trained.

They are also compatible with more mainstream jazz. Today, it's quite likely that one will hear a Coltranish modal solo in a fusion concert—such as the ones saxophonist Joe Lovano plays with electric guitarist John Scofield. Pianists such as Geri Allen and Don Pullen play structured pieces that include choruses in which they move outside the chord structure in bursts of free improvisation. The rhythmic innovations, the multilayered approach to the beat that Elvin Jones and other drummers pioneered, can be heard in virtually any young jazz drummer. Sometimes scorned or summarily dismissed, the giants of the avant-garde—and many of their followers—have changed the sound of jazz irrevocably.

23 Jazz Singing Since the Thirties

In the swing era, every band had a vocalist, a "girl" or a "boy" singer. Prosperous bands had both. Those singers sat on stage with the band during the entire set; they were brought to the mike to sing a couple of ballads or a novelty number, which the women did in a bright, cheerful voice, all gaiety and sunshine, and the men rendered in a high, skybound tenor. Band leaders rarely took them seriously. One of the best band vocalists, Peggy Lee, joined Benny Goodman in 1941 and immediately wanted to quit—Goodman featured her in tunes designed for her predecessor Helen Forrest, and didn't think it necessary that they should rehearse. Lee had to adjust.

It helped if the girl or boy vocalist was attractive. In his book *The Golden Age of Jazz*, William Gottlieb reproduced his photograph from the mid-1940's of a star struck male fan, staring close-up and open-mouthed at June Christy, while his girlfriend gives her dumbfounded lover a wry stare that presages trouble later in the evening (p. 133). The life of band singers looked glamorous, but they were perhaps more frequently adored than respected.

Of course the vocalists had the last laugh. After World War II, when the big-bands were in trouble, the most famous band vocalists—Ella Fitzgerald, Sarah Vaughan, Frank Sinatra, Billy Eckstine, Peggy Lee, and Lena Horne among them—became more popular than the bands that spawned them. More people know Doris Day today than know the Les Brown band in which she got her start. The big-band experience of these singers proved important, teaching them to phrase with a jazz ensemble, to sing on pitch and project their voices to a sometimes indifferent audience. Only a handful of important jazz singers, Nat Cole among them, emerged in the forties without big-band experience.

ELLA FITZGERALD, SARAH VAUGHAN, AND DINAH WASHINGTON

There were hundreds of band vocalists; nonetheless, jazz singing came to be dominated by a handful of key figures. Among the black women, Billie Holiday, Ella Fitzgerald, Sarah Vaughan, and Dinah Washington were the most influential. Holiday's contributions are discussed in Chapter 11, and in Appendix 1. The drama that she enacted in each song helped define modern jazz singing. Holiday's voice turned bittersweet in the forties, and then went sour in the fifties, before her premature death in 1959. That bittersweet quality, the air of worldy knowledge, even cynicism, was passed on to singers such as Carmen McRae and Abbey Lincoln, Shirley Horn and Sheila Jordan.

Billie Holiday transcended and finally escaped the role of a big-band singer. Ella Fitzgerald perfected it. Born in 1918, she was raised in an orphanage in Yonkers, New York. She got her break in 1934, winning an amateur night contest at the Harlem Opera House. She went on to win the justly famous amateur night at the Apollo Theatre in Harlem. The audiences at these shows sometimes made stars out of local talents, but they were notoriously impatient with the second-rate. Ella Fitzgerald was so nervous before appearing, it is said, that she had to be pushed onto the stage. She had originally intended to dance – she sang instead, either because of the success of a previous dancing group or because she was too shaky to move her legs. (Her stories differ.) Given the circumstances and her age (16), her appearance was an astonishing success. Afterwards, she was introduced to Chick Webb, who with his wife eventually adopted her as well as hired her as his band's vocalist.

Ella Fitzgerald in the late 1950's. (Courtesy Rutgers Institute of Jazz Studies)

On June 12, 1935 she made her first recordings with Webb's powerful big band, beginning with "I'll Chase the Blues Away." It was a suggestive choice to launch one of the most illustrious careers in American music. She has spent a career chasing the blues away. (In fact, one of her least attractive albums is the misconceived *These are the Blues* from 1963.) She would become known for her ability to infuse joy into the most trivial lyrics, to sound uplifting where Holiday would be dramatic and intense. Holiday said she was influenced by Armstrong and Bessie Smith. Fitzgerald spoke of Armstrong as well, but among women she looked to the lively upbeat work of Connee Boswell and the Boswell Sisters, three white women from New Orleans who were recording in the early thirties.

Fitzgerald had a distinctive voice: flexible, shaded, bright but with a gritty edge. She brought to jazz singing the glowing bounce of her rhythm and the infectious good cheer of a voice that sounded buoyantly girlish in its natural range. Above that range she strained, but her agility and perfect pitch made the strain as expressive as a saxophonist's growl. She managed to sound endearing even when reaching for a low note, as in her version of "This Time the Dream's On Me" from the *Johnny Mercer Songbook* of 1964. With her ability to improvise, her uncanny swing, "rhythm and romance"—as one of her early recordings has it—have been the staples of her career.

But on "My Last Affair" from November, 1936, recorded with members of the Chick Webb band, she sounds unaffected by the supposed tragedy that she is narrating—she uses blues inflections as a device, which doesn't interfere with the general impression of a singer at odds with her material. That may be why her biggest hits with Webb were tunes like the lighthearted novelty "A-Tisket, A-Tasket," from 1938. Still a teenager, she sounds more comfortable with a song about a lost basket than with one about a lost lover. What is particularly remarkable about this performance is her blithely swinging approach to the last choruses, in which she trades phrases with the band, improvising with the ingratiating assurance of an old pro.

When Chick Webb died the next year, Fitzgerald began fronting the band, which foundered in the middle of the war. Fitzgerald found the rhythms of bebop uplifting. She started to scat, to improvise wordlessly, using her own invented language of nonsense syllables. One can hear the beginning of this development in numbers she made during the war, such as the remarkably poised "Cow Cow Boogie," a country-western boogie-woogie number she recorded in 1943 with the Ink Spots, a popular black vocal group. In her most cheerful manner, Fitzgerald scats briefly—she sounds like she's singing to herself—behind the recitation of Orville "Hoppy" Jones. Bebop brought scatting to the fore. Fitzgerald internalized some of the harmonic intricacies of bop and thrilled in its rhythms, as can be heard in her December 1947 "How High the Moon," recorded with the band she co-led with bassist Ray Brown. With its logical changes, based on the circle of fifths, "How High the Moon" became the foundation of hundreds of bop performances. Fitzgerald sings the first chorus almost straight—she can't resist one baroque decoration—and then begins to improvise with her own lyrics. On the third chorus, she's scatting with the accuracy and drive that distinguishes her work, singing hornlike lines that have led some critics to define jazz singing as any that sounds like a jazz instrumental. (In a sense, jazz singing does always sound instrumental: The instrument is the voice.)

On Gershwin's "Oh, Lady Be Good" from March 1947, her wit is abundant too. After the first chorus, where she sings the song basically as written—but fast—she begins her scat solo with a quotation from a march! (It's the "National Emblem March" by Bagley.) Her scat syllables are shown on the transcription. The second phrase takes a little idea and makes a sequence out of it, moving down each time. The second A section of this AABA chorus begins like Rossini's "William Tell Overture," then moves into more sequences and a bebop phrase ending. The bridge begins with hard riffing, and ends with the most complicated sequence of all, a three-note idea that she keeps changing harmonically. The chorus ends with a phrase that our transcriber, singer Alexandra Sweeton, remembers from the "Three Stooges." (See music example.)

Fitzgerald's career took off. Her style, which moved between bop and swing, meant that she could sing with almost anybody, and she improvised

Example 23–1.
Ella Fitzgerald's first scat chorus, after the theme chorus, on "Oh, Lady Be Good" (1947). In general, "i" is pronounced here like "ee."

with the best. She had been touring with Norman Granz's Jazz at the Philharmonic since 1948. In 1956, Granz signed her to his Verve label, and she is at her peak on a number of live recordings made over the next ten years, including a hair-raising up-tempo "Oh, Lady Be Good" from Los Angeles in 1957. She also began a celebrated series of recordings, the so-called "Songbooks," each dedicated to a single composer or lyricist. On these recordings, Fitzgerald proves herself a storyteller, beginning tunes such as Gershwin's "Oh, Lady Be Good" with the verse that tells a "tale of woe." On the *Gershwin Songbook* (1959), Fitzgerald sings this song convincingly as a ballad—her gentle plea for pity in the bridge is even touching. She infuses new life into "Over the Rainbow" and introduces to jazz fans many less well-known classics of American song. She's mostly respectful of the lyrics and melodies, but on the *Duke Ellington Song Book* (1957), where she was accompanied at times by the Ellington orchestra, she was able to let loose: She scats through "Rockin' in Rhythm" with the bubbling, joyous sound of her best live performances. The songbooks feature large orchestras, but occasionally Fitzgerald sang in more intimate contexts. For a now obscure movie, *Let No Man Write My Epitaph* (1960), she sang beautifully, accompanied only by pianist Paul Smith: She treats songs such as the blues "Black Coffee"— even "I Can't Give You Anything But Love"—as late-night meditations. Then there's the beautifully contained "In My Solitude" from the *Duke Ellington Song Book* in which she's accompanied only by guitarist Barney Kessel.

She must have liked that sound and feeling: Some of her best recordings of the seventies were made with guitarist Joe Pass for Pablo Records. These include the 1973 "You're Blasé" and the 1976 remake of "Solitude." But there were signs of trouble even on these recordings: the slight wobble in her vibrato in the verse of "You're Blasé." In the eighties, plagued by ill health, Fitzgerald lost most of the bloom of her voice, and yet she could still improvise with aplomb.

In the forties, Fitzgerald adapted to the bop era. Nurtured in the heart of modern jazz, Sarah Vaughan didn't have to. Her adventurous singing—lush, even extravagant—her harmonic daring and virtuosic extension of her range, all tie her to the heroic age of bop, even if she rarely scatted or imitated the up-tempo solos of the horn players who accompanied her. (She does scat at length on one number: "Shulie a Bop," which she used to introduce her musicians. She recorded it in 1954.) Vaughan—who was given the nickname "Sassy" because of her sharp tongue and "the Divine One" because of her talents—won the Apollo amateur contest eight years after Ella Fitzgerald had. She was born in 1924, and walked onto the stage of the Apollo to sing "Body and Soul" in October of 1942. By April she had been hired as vocalist—and second pianist—with the progressive Earl Hines band. It's doubtful that she got to play much piano there, but Sarah Vaughan is a singer, like Carmen McRae and Shirley Horn, with fine keyboard skills, and with the harmonic knowledge that those skills imply. She went from the Hines to the Eckstine band, where her vocals were featured as well as the leader's. In May 1945, she made "Mean to Me" in the studio with Charlie Parker and Dizzy Gillespie. After a brilliant introductory four bars by

Sarah Vaughan around 1960. (Courtesy Rutgers
Institute of Jazz Studies)

Charlie Parker, Vaughan enters with a lilt in her voice as she sticks relatively
close to the melody. She's more adventurous in her final half-chorus.

The mature Vaughan was a jazz singer like no other. She was gifted with a
huge range and astonishing control over phrasing and dynamics. She seemed to
have a group of voices. In midphrase she might sweep upwards from her deep,
chesty baritone range to mouth a few syllables in a barely audible whisper up
high. Her natural voice was big, rounded, and warm, but on occasion she would
affect a flat nasal quality, or, half-ironically, take on a winsome girlishness that
she would flash in front of an audience and then withdraw.

She could be positively extravagant in her use of technique, and yet,
especially early in her career, she sometimes reined in her voice tactfully. Her
"Lover Man" from 1945 is a sober rendition, notable for her thrilling use of
vibrato on syllables that she sustains unexpectedly—such as "sweet" in the last
chorus—and for her inventive, improvised descents towards primary notes. By
1950, when she recorded "Mean to Me" and "Nice Work If You Can Get It" with
a band that included Miles Davis, her voice had deepened, and her style
expanded. She begins "Nice Work" brightly, and then in the second eight bars,
imitates a girlish "sighing" sound as she sings "sigh after sigh." Later she sinks
to her chest voice, and to her rounded mid-range. She is experimenting with
tone as a kind of improvisatory device.

In 1950, she was *Down Beat's* top vocalist. She was still experimenting with
her sound, especially its vibrato. In 1954, she signed with Mercury Records, and

almost immediately started making some of her most celebrated records. "My Funny Valentine" was recorded, unpromisingly, with a large orchestra. Vaughan dominates it. She seems to slow down the first statement in a weighty, moving rendition. When she comes to the series of unflattering questions, "Is your figure less than Greek, is your mouth a little weak?," she suddenly sounds brassy and embittered. Then she drops downward, and sounds threatening when the lyrics are meant to be reassuring: "Don't change a hair for me." (Her 1973 version of "Valentine" is in SCCJ.) This is virtuosic singing, but with a difference that some listeners find troubling. Unlike Billie Holiday, Vaughan does not always present a coherent interpretation of a song's lyrics. She is more interested in the manipulation of her voice than in responding to a story. At times, when she assaults the most innocent melodies with a barrage of special effects, she seems to have her material surrounded.

Elsewhere those effects can be mesmerizing, as when, on "Embraceable You" (1957), she elongates the first syllable and then slides up to a delayed "brace me." "Lullaby of Birdland," recorded with Clifford Brown in 1954, begins with Vaughan singing wordlessly in unison with the horns. She begins "Polka Dots and Moonbeams" (1954) in an unexpected staccatto, and improvises a chorus of "Body and Soul" (1954) with a series of odd low notes over a double time rhythm. She's not infallible: Her version of "Summertime" (1957) begins lazily with a submerged, somnolent sound. When she gets to singing "and the cotton" she suddenly and for no apparent reason produces her most shallow tones. She sings "And your ma's" and then takes an unnecessary breath before finishing the phrase with "good looking." In these moments she draws attention to her technique. They might result from a desire to transform a too familiar song, and yet her use of pauses in another familiar tune, "Pennies from Heaven," is affecting and natural-sounding.

By the end of her years with Mercury—she left them in 1959—her producers must have been worried about the incursion of rock and roll. Thus one finds, in the midst of recordings of great material backed by top jazz musicians, versions of foolishly commercial songs like "Sweet Affection," in which Vaughan is accompanied by a quartet of male singers going "boom boom" and mouthing the title words repeatedly. They sound like they were all dressed in cardigans and loafers, and that their idol was Pat Boone. In mid-career Sarah Vaughan shouldn't have had to sing about going steady.

Perhaps that's why she moved on to other labels. Her career as a jazz singer was assured, whatever the vagaries of the pop market she and her producers aspired to. She remained active. As part of a series of records made for Mainstream, she scored a minor hit with a song about a sexually active elderly lion ("Frasier, the Sensuous Lion," 1974), she recorded shining tributes to Duke Ellington (1979), appeared with the Los Angeles Philharmonic in 1982, and wowed live audiences with an elaborately sentimental version of Stephen Sondheim's "Send in the Clowns," in which she used every vocal device she had developed over a long career to bathetic effect. Her taste was sometimes questionable, but Sarah Vaughan, who died in 1990 at the age of 66, took as many chances as any jazz musician, and sang with a suppleness, inventiveness, and range of effects that remain a benchmark.

Jazz, it is often said, is based on the blues. It is striking, therefore, that none of the three great singers just discussed — Holiday, Fitzgerald, and Vaughan — specialized in the blues. Despite the Kansas City blues and jazz tradition and despite the occasional cover of a blues or bluesy hit — Peggy Lee made a splash in 1942 with her relatively antiseptic version of blues singer Lil Green's "Why Don't You Do Right?" — many jazz singers since the swing era have, in fact, seemed eager to distinguish themselves from blues singers. That may be one key to the importance of Dinah Washington, who sustained in the forties and fifties a bluesy approach to jazz singing that tied her to earlier singers such as Bessie Smith, Mildred Bailey (an important white singer who made her name with Paul Whiteman in the early thirties) and Helen Humes of the Basie band. In her use of gospel inflections, she prefigured Ray Charles, Dakota Staton and Aretha Franklin.

Dinah Washington was born Ruth Jones in 1924. Growing up in Chicago, she learned piano and played in church with one of the founders of gospel music, the wonderful Sallie Martin. Later, after being given the stage name with which she became famous, Washington would bring something of the range and feeling of gospel music to jazz singing. Her use of the swoops and hollers of gospel added a rich emotionalism to her brassy singing, with its clipped enunciation and dramatic shifts in volume and intensity. Precise in her vocal effects, Washington excelled not only in blues, but in mid-tempo standards such as "All of Me," a song whose terse melody and monosyllabic lyrics fit her style perfectly. She liked to sing in bursts, pausing and then flinging the next phrase outwards with a dramatic gesture and with a broad, bleating vibrato. Her pauses are as dramatic as her sustained notes. For all the emotion in her singing, she seems tough and worldly: If she wore her heart on her sleeve, it wasn't for us to take advantage of. When she sings, "Is you is, or is you ain't my baby?," the lines sound accusatory. She jammed with the best — her "I've Got You Under My Skin" (1954) has Clifford Brown, Clark Terry and Maynard Ferguson on trumpets — and she could sound tender when properly moved, as she evidently was by Clifford Brown's death: Her version of Benny Golson's "I Remember Clifford" (1960), for all the prosiness of the lyrics, demonstrates the emotional range of her singing.

Early in her career she specialized in the blues. She was hired by Lionel Hampton and recorded four blues with his sextet in December 1943. The date was set up by critic and producer Leonard Feather, who wrote "Evil Gal Blues," which was Washington's first recording. (The song became popular — it was later recorded by both Etta Jones and Albinia Jones, the latter in April 1945 with a young Dizzy Gillespie behind her.) Washington's choruses follow Milt Buckner's "locked-hands" piano choruses. With her hard-sounding voice — it seems to glitter — she sounds distinctive even at age 19. At first, she would be typecast as a blues singer, but even in 1946 she recorded an "Embraceable You" that sounds bluesy without violating the mood of the song. Her first phrase sounds like Holiday, but the unique timbre of her voice, and her manner of soaring upwards to a dramatic high note and then suddenly subsiding, her bluesy phrasing, are distinctive. When she sings "I want my arms about you," she holds onto and twists the last words, turning a simple phrase ending into an extravagant blues-gospel gesture. She also takes Armstrong-like freedoms with the lyrics—she exhorts her recalcitrant lover not to be "a bring-down baby."

Washington reached near the top of her profession in the late fifties, after scoring a hit in 1959 with "What a Difference a Day Makes." Thereafter she was recorded with large string orchestras: As with Ray Charles, her earthy singing and manner stood out dramatically against the saccharine background that producers liked to provide successful popular singers. Despite her heavy drinking and her use of drugs, including diet pills, her death in 1963 was a shock: She was not yet 40, but her gospel-influenced, blues-drenched singing demonstrated to vocalists such as Ray Charles and Aretha Franklin the way blues, gospel, and jazz could profitably come together.

CARMEN McRAE AND OTHER FEMALE SINGERS

Carmen McRae has little of the virtuosic range and uses few of the extroverted effects of Sarah Vaughan or Dinah Washington, yet she's their equal. A skillful pianist, she's a dramatist in the Billie Holiday tradition, but one with her own sense of rhythm. Rather than imitate the Holiday lilt of the thirties, Carmen McRae introduces effectively organized rhythmic variations that illuminate her lyrics: With her transparent diction, and her clipped phrasing, she seems to be placing words like darts. Her voice isn't lush: She makes up for that with

Carmen McRae (left) and Betty Carter recording a live album in San Francisco in 1987. (Courtesy Rutgers Institute of Jazz Studies)

melodic and rhythmic improvisations that sound unforced because they accentuate the mood of the song and the meaning of its lyrics.

Her career developed late. Born in 1922, she too won the Apollo talent contest. In 1944, she sang with Benny Carter's orchestra, and then with Mercer Ellington's short-lived band. When that broke up in 1947, she stayed in New York, worked in various day jobs, and listened to bop. She recorded for the first time as a leader in 1954. (In 1955, *Down Beat* ran an article on her entitled "Carmen McRae Looks Back on her First Big Year.") Her recordings of that year included the "Just One of Those Things" she made for Decca. It is typical McRae: She articulates clearly in the first chorus, using a broad vibrato at the end of phrases, emphasizing the one possibly obscure word—"gossamer." In the up-tempo second chorus, she seems in fact to be slowing down—with consummate skill, she delays before "one—of—those things" in the first eight bars, and rearranges the rhythm of the chorus with both intelligence and charm.

She continued to record for Decca throughout the fifties, despite the occasionally bizarre ideas of her producers. These included an album dedicated to birds, which meant that she sang not only "Bye Bye Blackbird" and "Skylark," but "The Eagle and Me," and "Chicken Today, Feathers Tomorrow." She signed with Columbia in 1961, and, with a small jazz band, made a stirring tribute to Billie Holiday, offering her own tart versions of "Miss Brown to You" and "I Cried for You." McRae also sang one of Holiday's delicate tearjerkers, "Some Other Spring." Where Holiday was nostalgic, McRae sounds more seriously disillusioned. She dramatizes her tale, affecting at one point a speaking voice. Elsewhere she almost growls. McRae's stature has continued to grow, with recordings such as her 1972 album called *The Great American Song Book* or the 1976 club date at the Great American Music Hall in San Francisco. She's mesmerizing in 1972, singing and playing the piano alone on "As Time Goes By," recorded in a Japanese nightclub. She's just as convincing in 1980 with "A Ghost of a Chance," recorded with pianist George Shearing. McRae has her own kind of virtuosity: In 1988, she recorded an album of Thelonious Monk compositions. It includes a "Blue Monk" taken at a snail's pace. With her hardbitten voice and rhythmic thrust, McRae makes it work. In 1991, she recorded a disc of songs associated with her friend and peer, the late Sarah Vaughan.

A very different singer, Chris Connor, is also a mistress of the subtle manipulation of rhythms within standard songs. Connor emerged in the fifties from the Stan Kenton band. She followed in a distinguished line of white female singers that began with Anita O'Day, whose singing Connor's sometimes resembles. The Kenton band, with its crashing brass and its grandiose arrangements, might seem an unlikely source for vocalists, but Kenton must have had an ear for them. In 1944 he took Anita O'Day from another pressure cooker, the Gene Krupa band. O'Day, who was born in Kansas City in 1919, had become something of a star with Krupa, recording such geographical oddities as "Massachusetts" and "Just a Little Bit South of North Carolina" as well as "Skylark" and her biggest hit with Krupa, "Let Me Off Uptown." She shared the last with trumpeter Roy Eldridge. "Let Me Off Uptown" puts her, a white woman, in the anomalous position of explaining to Roy Eldridge the joys of Harlem. More importantly she swings the tune convincingly enough to set up Eldridge's shining trumpet. O'Day's sunny, sometimes husky, voice was strong enough to carry over the sounds of a big band, and her swing-based rhythm was sprightly and appealing.

When O'Day left Krupa for Kenton, she was joining what was for the time an advanced band. She had no trouble adapting. With her upbeat renditions of songs such as "Gotta Be Gettin'" (1944) she set the standard for a Kenton singer, and for many band singers to come. For many, O'Day's image as a consummately hip, elegant singer was fixed by her central performance of "Sweet Georgia Brown" in the 1958 film, *Jazz on a Summer's Day*. Filmed at the Newport Jazz Festival, she appears looking crisp and dignified in white gloves and hat, and she swings like mad. She can scat effectively, as for example, on the 1979 "Them There Eyes" she recorded for GNP.

O'Day was replaced in the Kenton band by June Christy, who maintained the O'Day style. When she was ready to leave Kenton, Christy recommended a more original singer: Chris Connor, who joined Kenton in 1953. She's most effective on slow ballads, such as in her fifties performances of "The Thrill is Gone" (1955) or "Lush Life" (1954) and the intriguing "Where Flamingos Fly," which she recorded in 1960. In this moody arrangement, Connor uses dynamics effectively, entering breathily, mysteriously, and gradually seeming to come forward. She picks up the rhythm in the narrative bridge—with its background material about why her lover is leaving for where the flamingos fly—and then stretches out the lament of the last section. She's telling a story in such an unaffected way that listeners overlook the skill of her rhythmic variations. She's equally effective, yearning and innocent, on her remarkable version of Ornette Coleman's "Lonely Woman." Her career flourished in the late fifties and early sixties, languished through the seventies, and then revived. She has always been supported by musicians, including pianist Ran Blake, who may have passed her influence on to a singer with whom he recorded, Jeanne Lee.

Helen Merrill has also been blessed by the support of jazz musicians. Her first recording, made in 1954, was arranged by Quincy Jones and featured Clifford Brown; she has recorded a series of duets with John Lewis and twice Gil Evans arranged whole albums for her. A white woman, she told Leslie Gourse that "Most of the important things that happened to me happened through black musicians." When Merrill insisted on appearing with black musicians in the fifties, she was kept off the television. In the forties, she sang briefly with Earl Hines and then hung around the bop musicians, performing on occasion with Charlie Parker. She has said that bebop sounded natural to her because when she was a child in Manhattan, her Yugoslavian mother sang folk music that sounded like Bartok.

There are few more charming singers. She has a small, breathy voice; she sings quietly and uses the breathiness as a device. Merrill's collaboration with

Gil Evans—simply called *Collaboration*—as rerecorded in 1987, revealed a Merrill with a lusher voice than previously. With Evans's rich, deep arrangements, this collaboration is one of the best sounding vocal albums ever made.

Vocalist and pianist Shirley Horn grew up on Billie Holiday. (She still remembers with anguish the day that her mother, cleaning house, threw out their Holiday 78's.) A Washington native, born in 1934, she sang around her home city, where she was heard by Miles Davis, who brought her to New York. Beginning in 1961, she recorded her first albums. They document one part of her sensibility—her light, expressive voice and her ability to render a song such as "Love for Sale" as if she were telling a story. But they did not feature her piano playing, and she is a singer who depends on her own choice of tempo, phrasing, and alternate chords. It wasn't until much later that Horn was recorded properly. On *A Lazy Afternoon* (1979), she sings "I'm Old-Fashioned" in short phrases, filling in with her piano—her own accompaniment allows her to be as short-breathed and flip as she wants. It also allows her on the second chorus to improvise, brightening the beat, holding notes, or shouting "I'm old-fashioned" and then waiting before adding, "That's the way I want to be." Horn was once, it was thought, doomed to be a favorite only among musicians, but in 1991, her album *You Won't Forget Me*, featuring her old friend Miles Davis, was for weeks the nation's best-selling jazz album.

One might call these singers mainstream. Others started with bebop and then influenced, and were influenced by, the avant-garde. Betty Carter has bebop roots. She was born Lillie Mae Jones in 1930, and grew up in Detroit. In the forties, she heard, and sat in with, Charlie Parker and Miles Davis. She learned to scat for practical reasons: "The field was open if you wanted to scat." Scatting—and bebop—offered her a way to find her own style. Between 1948 and 1951, Carter toured with the Lionel Hampton band. Hampton started to introduce her as Betty Bebop, a somewhat mocking version of the name of the cartoon character Betty Boop. Carter, who was then going by the stage name Lorraine Carter, didn't like it. Her style, as one can hear in her scatting of "Jaybird" on a 1948 broadcast with the Hampton band, and on "Cobb's Idea," a 1950 Hampton performance available on video, was true bop. She compromised with her nickname, taking the Betty from Betty Bebop and the Carter from Lorraine Carter.

But Betty Carter did not want to be thought of merely as a bebopping scat singer. She had her own message. In 1958 and 1960, Carter recorded twice with big bands. The albums include her imaginative readings of standards, and also some of her own fine compositions. "I Can't Help It" articulates a recurrent theme in Carter's work, her need to be herself: "Have you considered what it does to your soul? You sell it when you play some other's role." She began taking remarkable risks in her singing. With her neatly rounded, small, and high voice, she sings ballads in extraordinarily slow tempos, often ignoring their basic melodies. Her "Body and Soul" can sound like nothing you've ever heard before, as she sings, "My heart is sad," pauses dramatically, and then, skipping dramatically upwards, adds "and lonely." She'll twist a melody like toffee, skipping broadly, poking other notes out, or sagging dramatically, slurring a single syllable. She shifts tempos without warning—her accompanists have to be well-rehearsed to play Carter's intricate arrangements. Then there's her choice of notes—she will virtually rewrite every tune, creating an unparalleled tension with unresolved dissonance. Her "'Round Midnight" from 1975 becomes a study in different rhythms and new, remote-sounding melodies. For all her daring, Carter communicates with audiences: She half dances her improvisations, and everyone notes her committment and musicality. Her popularity soared in the seventies and eighties. She knew she deserved the success: One of her albums is called *Now It's My Turn* (1976).

Though she spent her early years in Johnstown, Pennsylvania, Sheila Jordan, whose daring singing is comparable in some ways to that of Betty Carter, was also a teenager in Detroit in the forties. There, though white, she had black friends who introduced her to Billie Holiday, Lester Young and eventually to bebop. When she was 16, she started singing professionally with two young friends who wrote words to Parker's tunes. She also sang as a soloist, rendering a chorus of "My Ideal" or "Where or When" straight, and then scatting in bop style. When Parker came to town, he asked her to sing along. Later she moved to New York, eventually marrying pianist Duke Jordan.

She was introduced to composer George Russell in 1960. That turned out to be her first break. Interested in her unique style, Russell asked her about her background: "So I took him to the town I came from. We took my grandmother to a private club where the miners hang out. There was an old miner down there who remembered me, and he asked me to sing 'You Are My Sunshine.'" Russell was intrigued that the favorite song of the local miners, who spent their bleak lives under the ground, should be about the sun. In 1962 he asked Jordan to record the song, which was written in 1940 by a man who would four years later become governor of Louisiana, Jimmie Davis. In Russell's striking arrangement the innocent-sounding theme is pitted against a bleak, bitter two-note figure and an aggressive bass line until it seems a voice crying out in the wilderness. After the introduction and several solos, the music stops, and Jordan enters, sounding totally exposed. She sings an eerie chorus, flattening and then embellishing the melody before the band returns with a series of dissonant counterstatements to the sweet, presumably hopeful, song.

Jordan has a small, flexible voice, with girlish highs and dramatic lows, and a uniquely personal technique. Jordan's fast, lyrical vibrato often appears dramatically in the middle of phrases, and in a single performance she might move from a sweet whisper to a metallic cry. Since the early 1980's she has performed more frequently, often in a duo with the agile bassist Harvie Swartz. For all her hornlike agility, Jordan conveys a radiant sincerity that makes us believe her when she sings, as she does in "The Crossing," that "it's the music that sets me free." Coming from another singer, the line would sound like a cliché.

Abbey Lincoln wants the music to set her free. A black woman, she has sung political songs in a bold, dramatic, sometimes even harsh, manner. She can sound like a militant Billie Holiday. Lincoln was born Gaby Wooldridge in

Chicago in 1930 and began recording in 1956. With a dark, brassy voice that seemed to change quality with every syllable, she emphasized the lyrics of even such well-known standards as "How High the Moon." She also acted, with great sensitivity, in such films as "Nothing But A Man" (1964), directed by the innovative Michael Roemer.

Lincoln often takes chances, and she's usually successful. Max Roach used her on *Freedom Now Suite:* She sings "Driva Man" with a pounding rhythm, and enacts, wordlessly, the imagined action of "Triptych: Prayer/ Protest/ Peace." She contributes some hair-raising screams to "Protest." Her choice of songs is always suggestive. She can convey tragedy, as in the remarkable unaccompanied solo, "Tender as a Rose," found on *That's Him.* And she can make an old song seem as current as a big city unemployment line, as she does with "Brother, Can You Spare a Dime?" (1991).

Lincoln's collaboration with Roach, like that of Sheila Jordan with George Russell or with Harvie Swartz, suggests ways that vocalists could, as Jordan has put it, become part of the band. A growing number of singers want their instruments, their voices, to fit in and mix it up with the musicians with whom they are performing. This isn't modesty: They want to be co-creators of the sound of whatever band they appear in, and they want the same freedom to improvise that the instrumentalists have. Jeanne Lee is an example. Born in 1939, she first recorded in 1961, in duet with the iconoclastic pianist Ran Blake. He has a terse, percussive style, full of thundering dissonances, dancing triplets, and dramatic shifts in texture: He'll follow a Kentonish explosion with the barest tinkle of a trill. His style seems to come from Thelonious Monk by way of Bartok.

Lee has a tone that shakes as little as mid-fifties Miles Davis, but she can interject a bluesy waver for effect. She approached lyrics with the utmost tact and intelligence. Then she went beyond them. With Sunny Murray in 1969, she sings wordlessly on "Suns of Africa." On her own album *Conspiracy,* recorded in 1974, she recites a short poem before scatting in pieces whose open forms allow her space to improvise freely, using words as well as a variety of expressive sounds: typical scat syllables, high-pitched moans, and delightfully floating long held notes. The trio recording *Companion* (1982), with her husband Gunter Hampel on vibes and reeds, and Thomas Keyserling on flute and alto saxophone, is typical of her dynamic free jazz. However far out she goes, behind Jeanne Lee's experiments are a background in blues and gospel that refreshes her and her work.

Not many jazz singers have followed her lead. Again, economics may play a part. There is little enough work for traditional performers, let alone avant-garde vocalists, however compelling. One other dramatic experimentalist is Urszula Dudziak. Dudziak was born in Poland in 1943. Inspired, she says, by Ella Fitzgerald, she took up jazz singing and in 1962 was heard by Krysztof Komeda, one of the prime movers of the surprisingly vital Polish jazz scene. She began working with violinist Michal Urbaniak, whom she married in 1967. In 1972, she made her most adventurous record, *Newborn Light.* The album consists of free, wordless duets with pianist Adam Makowicz (he also plays electronic instruments), including a tribute to Komeda. Dudziak has a beautiful soprano voice, with considerable range and accuracy. She brought new sounds into vocal improvisation, but she didn't often choose to follow up on this effort. When she and husband Michal Urbaniak settled in America, they were more likely to play fusion. Dudziak's accompanist on *Newborn Light*, Adam Makowicz, after a Polish career as an avant-garde player, came to America under John Hammond's wing and was hailed as a follower of Art Tatum.

Perhaps the most intriguing younger representative of the great tradition — or traditions — of female jazz singers is Cassandra Wilson, who is able to use her voice as another horn in free jazz in the manner of Sheila Jordan or Jeanne Lee, or sing standards such as "Blue Skies" (1988). Like Betty Carter, Sheila Jordan, and Jeanne Lee, Wilson aspires to be part of the family of instruments in group improvisation: She also shows the influence of great ballad singers, including Billie Holiday. She has a broad, warm voice, and the confidence to begin a number scatting casually, as she does at the beginning of "Shall We Dance," from the album *Blue Skies*. She often works in the band of saxophonist Steve Coleman. Carmen McRae has publicly worried about the future of jazz singing: Where will the younger singers come from? If Cassandra Wilson suggests an answer, they will come from jazz bands of which they are a vital part. They will no longer be either an added attraction, or the undisputed star of the show.

MALE SINGERS

There has always been considerable interchange among jazz singers of both sexes, and indeed, between white and black singers as well. Even if indirectly, every jazz singer learned, as Billie Holiday said she did, from Louis Armstrong and Bessie Smith. Many of the male singers learned as well from Bing Crosby, whose relaxed baritone — he worked hard to achieve that relaxation in his singing — opened up new possibilities for male jazz singers. (Crosby has had some unlikely fans: Evidently bluesman Robert Johnson cited him as his favorite singer.)

But in the swing era, for every Crosby-like baritone, there were a half-dozen boyish tenors, black and white, who sang in a manner that once seemed romantic, and now sounds dated. No wonder that many of the best male singers to emerge in the forties had a background in the blues. Even earlier, Jimmy Rushing from the Basie band seemed to fling his strained, cheerful voice at blues such as "Goin' to Chicago." Kansas City's Joe Turner was another — his powerful voice, captured on boogie-woogie numbers with Pete Johnson, provided the essential Kansas City blues sound. Listening to the live version of "Roll 'em Pete" recorded in 1947 in front of a screaming, ecstatic audience, one hears the first rock and roll singer as well. In the fifties, of course, Turner had a rhythm and blues hit with "Shake, Rattle and Roll."

The rounded baritone of Billy Eckstine (b. 1914), with its sensuous low range, was a kind of breakthrough for male jazz singers. The falsetto leaps, the high-pitched climaxes, of Eckstine's earliest ballads with the Hines band, such as the 1940 "My Heart Beats for You," betray the influence of Pha Terrell, but Eckstine soon became known for his ability to apply his smooth, rounded tones to the blues as well as ballads. But the Eckstine style as adopted by other singers could prove lugubrious. Some focused on tone rather than rhythm or the meaning of lyrics, as Earl Coleman did when he sang "Dark Shadows" with Charlie Parker. On the other hand, the lyrics as interpreted by Johnny Hartman are as unforgettable as his silken style on his classic 1963 recording with John Coltrane.

Of course not every male vocalist sang in the Eckstine manner. Pianist Nat King Cole (1917–1965) found in the forties that his light, urbane singing, with its hip mannerisms and pure tone, would make him more popular than his influential piano playing. He wrote sophisticated novelties such as his 1943 hit, "Straighten Up and Fly Right." Cole became extremely popular, hosting his own radio show in 1948 and 1949, and his own weekly television show during the 1956 to 1957 season, a unique achievement for an African-American. His ingratiating manner with novelty numbers worked with ballads as well: Eventually that manner was used to put across distressingly shallow songs such as "Those Lazy-Hazy-Crazy Days of Summer" (1963) and "Ramblin' Rose" (1962), and he left the jazz world behind.

Joe Williams (b. 1918) came from the same generation as Cole and Eckstine but did not become well known until he joined the Basie band in 1954. He is a remarkable artist. Williams's resonant, room-filling baritone is a marvel: For all his tonal richness, his lyrics come through with exquisite clarity. One of his trademarks is a use of bent notes to produce a half-spoken sound on the blues. He uses a broad vibrato to end his phrases. With Basie he sang blues such as "Every Day I Have the Blues" and managed to sound suave even when approaching Joe Turner's rollicking "Roll 'em Pete." Best known for his blues, he can also sing ballads: He's a storyteller on songs such as "She Doesn't Know (I Love Her)," in which he sacrifices a little of his gorgeous tone in favor of more speaking tones. He's at his best in "There's a Small Hotel" from 1961, improvising on the bridge, sounding inventive, rhythmically lively, and telling a story at the same time. Most of his talents can be heard in the 1966 "Night Time is the Right Time," recorded with the Thad Jones-Mel Lewis band: He begins with a cocky, half spoken message to a particular woman, and, using space with the patience of a master of time, gradually builds an intense, rollicking, and finally joyous performance. Since the fifties, he's been one of the most celebrated jazz singers.

Williams's contemporary Frank Sinatra is not always considered a jazz singer, despite his years with the Harry James and Tommy Dorsey bands. His exclusion is easy to understand: As a popular singer, he has rarely appeared with improvising musicians, and he doesn't scat. He rehearses meticulously and tends to repeat himself. Still, Sinatra has influenced other singers since the forties, and his best singing, such as the "Polka Dots and Moonbeams" he did with Tommy Dorsey, is built on jazz singing from Bing Crosby to Billie Holiday.

He has been, one might say, the cause of jazz singing in others, including Tony Bennett and Mel Tormé, both of whom seem more genuinely interested in jazz than does Sinatra. (Bennett named his son Danny after hearing Art Tatum play "Danny Boy.") Both of them have husky, earth-bound voices—Tormé's higher voice is called "the velvet fog"—and both bring to singing a musical intelligence that distinguishes them from a host of imitators and also-rans. Bennett—he was born Anthony Benedetto and first sang under the name Joe Bari—was touring with a Bob Hope show in 1950 when Columbia Records signed him. He ended up making a series of popular singles throughout the decade. He also sang with jazz musicians. In 1964, he recorded with Stan Getz, and then in 1976, with Bill Evans.

Mel Tormé is a little more dramatic. Tormé studied drums and piano, and began his prominent professional life in 1942 with Chico Marx of the Marx Brothers. He's had an especially productive relationship with arranger Marty Paich. In 1956, they recorded a "Lullaby of Birdland" that begins with Tormé singing cheerfully, with the delays and rhythmic displacements of jazz, over a bass alone and then over bass and drums. Later he scats over the band, using his full range, including a falsetto for high notes with a horn-like vibrato. It's not surprising to hear Tormé quote from the *Birth of the Cool* while scatting: Though more straightforward, Paich's arrangements are based on what Gerry Mulligan and Gil Evans had done for Miles Davis. The seventies and eighties saw Tormé settle into jazz. He appeared annually with musicians such as Gerry Mulligan and George Shearing at a series of concerts at the Kool (later JVC) Jazz Festival in New York, concerts that were dedicated to the American song.

Tormé uses bop and cool jazz in his work. The antecedents of bop singing go back to Louis Armstrong. Armstrong has been discussed in Chapter 6, but his influence pervades this chapter, as a singer of lyrics and of course as an early scat singer. In 1938, Leo Watson used nonsense syllables and jive lyrics to imitate the wind players he idolized. In turn Watson influenced the next generation, young boppers like Babs Gonzales, who made "Professor Bop" in 1949, and Eddie Jefferson. Jefferson was a pioneer at the bop method of setting words to recorded jazz solos. In jazz the singing of an instrumental line using lyrics (as opposed to scat singing) is called vocalese. "Parker's Mood" was set to words by Jefferson and King Pleasure, who copied, as literally as they could, Parker's notes and inflections. (See example in Chapter 13.) Jefferson's version, called "Bless My Soul," was recorded in 1949 or 1950, while Pleasure's more famous "Parker's Mood" was made in 1953. In a 1952 recording King Pleasure popularized Jefferson's setting of a 1949 James Moody tenor saxophone solo in "Moody's Mood for Love." Although Pleasure was the star, he gave credit to Jefferson for developing the vocalese approach: "I . . . developed Eddie's baby and delivered it to the public" (Pleasure's notes to a 1960 LP). The technique proved entertaining and musically valid, and a vocalese trio, Lambert, Hendricks and Ross (Annie Ross's early hit "Twisted" appears in Chapter 12) became one of the most exciting groups of the late fifties. Their first hit was an album of vocal renditions of classic Basie arrangements, which they recorded in 1957 using overdubbing. Jon

Eddie Jefferson in the 1970's. (Photo by Michael Ullman)

Hendricks of that group keeps the vocalese tradition alive into the nineties. His 1990 release, *Jon Hendricks and Friends*, teams him with Al Jarreau, Bobby McFerrin, George Benson (who is now as well known for his singing as for his guitar playing), and the Manhattan Transfer, a popular descendant of Lambert, Hendricks and Ross.

There have been a few male singers involved with the avant-garde. Joe Lee Wilson, who sounds something like a more extroverted Billy Eckstine, has appeared with adventurous groups. Singers have been brought in for special projects, as was gospel singer David Peaston, who sang with Lester Bowie's bands and in 1987 with Alice Coltrane before moving on to pop. Leon Thomas had more staying power. Thomas debuted with Basie in 1961. In 1970 he recorded with Oliver Nelson, and Johnny Hodges, but he made his biggest impact with Pharoah Sanders. It was Thomas who sang "The Creator has a Master Plan" in Sanders's 1969 recording *Karma*. He sang the words in his pleasant baritone, and then improvised, using a unique yodel—a kind of fluttering from the back of the throat—that he says he derived from the pygmies. (We have heard pygmy music without being able to trace the sound. The word yodel is of German origin, and yodelling is usually identified with Swiss music.) On modal tunes and in extended improvisations, Thomas scatted and yodelled in an attempt to sound not merely like a horn, but like a horn in the Coltrane tradition. Using idiosyncratic syllables and articulations as well as his yodelling, he created a unique style.

It didn't catch on, but the most popular jazz singers of the eighties, Bobby McFerrin and Al Jarreau, share something of Thomas's interest in performing like a virtuosic horn player. Jarreau creates some exotic percussive effects on his "Take Five," recorded live in 1977. McFerrin uses some of the techniques of bop singing—the rapid sequences of notes, the wide skips, and instrumental sounds—and improvises his own solos using scat syllables. On "Walkin'" from *Spontaneous Inventions*, he duets wordlessly with Wayne Shorter, imitating at times Shorter's nasal soprano sax, and then providing a spontaneous walking bass line. At times McFerrin imitates not merely a horn, but a whole band, interspersing bass notes that suggest a walking bass line with hornlike sounds rendered in a falsetto two octaves above. With his active, chattering style, McFerrin has been able to sustain whole performances as an unaccompanied solo vocalist. He leaps into falsetto for whole choruses, holds a microphone up to his throat to produce hollow bass sounds, pounds on his chest to add a rhythm track. At some point he decided that being a jazz singer was "limiting," but he has nonetheless picked up a series of Grammy awards as the best jazz vocalist. Despite its fatuous message, his "Don't Worry, Be Happy" made him a superstar. It was used in a Tom Cruise film in which every character had reason to worry; more importantly, it became a gold record, and led to his more frequent appearances on television—doing *Sesame Street*, late night shows and advertisements.

His success—and that of pianist-vocalist Harry Connick Jr., who has had an astonishing career imitating Frank Sinatra—must make him the envy of other, more stubbornly rooted jazz singers from Mel Tormé to Betty Carter. These others are not likely to change their styles as a result. What Betty Carter has said about learning her trade—that as a young singer, she "dared not imitate"—is true of the most distinctive jazz vocalists. Their lives may not always be comfortable, but they find other compensations. Betty Carter has spoken of the joy of confronting young audiences with her challenging art: "If I do something that I know is really musical and I get this wide-out smile from those young kids, it just lets you know how free I can be. Then with that feeling of freedom you can float through your music and they just come running to you. Because jazz is spontaneous. It's a beautiful feeling."

24 Conclusion

After surviving hard times in the 1970's, during which audience support was low and many jazz artists turned to fusion in order to stay afloat, jazz in the 1980's reached a new level of recognition. In the eighties jazz received what seems an extraordinary amount of media attention. It even received recognition from the American government. In 1987, the House of Representatives and then the Senate voted to support Joint Resolution 57 recognizing jazz as "a rare and valuable national American treasure to which we should devote our attention, support and resources to make certain it is preserved, understood, and promulgated." Many different factors seem to have brought about this improved attitude, including the success of fusion, the changing tastes of the baby boom generation as it matured, and a rising respectability for jazz that has made it once again fashionable.

The rocket-like ascension of trumpeter Wynton Marsalis to international fame, and to a series of Grammy awards, suggested to critics and historians that they were observing a jazz renaissance. It is a renaissance of a perplexing kind. Jazz was used to periodic upheavals—to young turks such as Armstrong, Parker, Coltrane unsettling with new ideas and new sounds. But here we have musicians—not merely the Marsalis brothers, Wynton and Branford, but such other fine musicians as trumpeters Roy Hargrove, Philip Harper and Terence Blanchard, saxophonists Donald Harrison and Antonio Hart, pianists Stephen Scott and Marcus Roberts—who are investigating the music of the past, preeminently bebop and the repertoire of the various Miles Davis groups, but also swing and Dixieland. It is a cliché of recent criticism that we have entered a period of musical conservatism in jazz—not a bad thing, necessarily, if what is being conserved and revitalized is good music in the first place—but a surprising development for a music that has always looked forward to the next revolution

Wynton Marsalis, 1980's. (Publicity photo by Mitchell Seidel.
Courtesy Rutgers Institute of Jazz Studies)

in style. It is common to find jazz fans and musicians asking each other, "What is new, what is really new?"

The 1980's witnessed the coexistence of many styles of jazz. The Preservation Hall Jazz Band of New Orleans, with some members in their 80s and younger artists filling up the ranks, was still touring and recording for Columbia Records. The big-band legacy was carried on by the Basie, Ellington, and Woody Herman bands even though their leaders had passed away, while innovative younger arrangers like Bill Kirchner and Bob Belden struggled to keep medium size bands alive. Occasionally an enterprising avant-gardist like saxophonist David Murray would assemble a big band.

Avant-garde jazz was developing a new audience from young people who were not necessarily fans of other types of jazz. But bop's great Dizzy Gillespie was still going strong, and Art Blakey continued to discover new talents such as the Marsalis brothers. McCoy Tyner and Sonny Rollins were playing powerfully in a basically acoustic idiom (Rollins had flirted with electronics during the 1970's), while Miles Davis and Ornette Coleman continued to experiment with two extremes of electronic music, Davis with the accessible pop side and Coleman with the experimental side. Fusion continued to be the best selling type of jazz, with new stars each year such as Najee and Kenny G., but there was barely any jazz content in their work. The fusion work of Joe Zawinul remained fascinating, along with that of Europeans such as Terje Rypdal and Palle Mikkelborg (who wrote a full-length orchestral piece for Miles Davis, *Aura,* in 1984). Many great players who are now primarily in fusion make it a point to tour as acoustic jazz musicians about once a year; they include Herbie Hancock, Chick

Members of David Murray Big Band at the Public Theater, Manhattan, 1980's. Julius Hemphill (left, with glasses) plays the straight soprano and next to him Murray plays tenor saxophone. (Photo by Michael Ullman)

Corea, and Pat Metheny. On the other hand, the iconoclastic pianist Keith Jarrett steadfastly eschews electronics.

Acoustic jazz found a powerful advocate in young trumpeter Wynton Marsalis, who first recorded with Art Blakey's group at the age of 18. Once he began recording as a leader in 1982, he quickly became one of the best known of all jazz artists with the help of a tremendous Columbia Records sales campaign. A phenomenal classical virtuoso as well as a fine jazz improvisor, Marsalis was the first artist ever to win Grammy awards in both categories. His jazz albums were initially modeled after the Miles Davis band of the 1960's, but by 1989, he was playing blues and Dixieland repertoire as well. Marsalis's older brother, saxophonist Branford, who toured and recorded with Wynton for several years, is also a superb jazz player with a respect for the jazz tradition, as witnessed by his 1989 LP and video with veteran bassist Milt Hinton. But Branford has also played in pop contexts, primarily as a regular member of Sting's band, along with the superb young pianist Kenny Kirkland who has worked regularly with the Marsalis brothers. On May 25, 1992, Branford began leading the Tonight Show's new band. There are still other Marsalises—younger brother Delfeayo is a trombonist and record producer, while Jason, the youngest, is an up-and-coming drummer.

Responding to the interest of young people all across the country, music departments in high schools and colleges are adding jazz programs. Institutionalized jazz education began in a few pioneering colleges and high schools in the late 1940's. Today many high schools have jazz ensembles, and colleges typically sponsor an ensemble, frequently a big band. And more and more schools are adding to their curricula jazz history courses, which train listeners as well as players—the audience of the future.

The best known jazz education program is that of Boston's Berklee College of Music. Founded 40 years ago, it attracts students from all over the world: Twenty percent of its students are international. The future of jazz lies partly in their hands. Certainly the music has become a kind of international language, popular in Japan, Europe, Africa and the Caribbean. When, in the late eighties, Dizzy Gillespie toured Cuba, he found himself playing bebop with local musicians who, he said, could teach him a thing or two about rhythms.

Today Japan is the leading jazz country outside of America. That country, with about half the population of the U.S., produces a disproportionate amount of fine jazz performers (primarily mainstream and fusion), jazz recordings, reissues (including hundreds of American albums no longer available in our country), discographies, and books of transcribed solos. The next largest jazz communities are in Western European countries such as France, England, Germany, and the Scandinavian countries.

Eastern Europe has produced its own jazz musicians since at least the thirties. They may have been relatively few in number, and in the swing era they may have tended toward straight dance music rather than jazz, but they have been celebrated in their own countries. Since the 1960's there have been outstanding contemporary artists who can hold their own in any context, but because of travel restrictions they have been little known in America. Perhaps the new freedoms in Eastern Europe since 1989 will allow Americans to hear more of them. Zbigniew Namyslowski is an outstanding alto saxophonist from Poland. The U.S.S.R., as it used to be called, produced many mainstream players—among them the trumpeter Valery Ponamerov who emigrated to New York and joined Art Blakey's band in 1977—and in the 1980's the Ganelin Trio became one of the best known avant-garde groups in the world, making a tour of the U.S. and even appearing on the "Today" television show.

There are many more women in jazz than ever before, and they are much more integrated into the jazz community. They play in all kinds of groups and have little need to form all-woman bands as they did from the 1930's right through the 1970's. Women are still overwhelmingly vocalists and pianists, and many are composers as well. Toshiko Akiyoshi and Marian McPartland are as active as ever, the latter regularly seeking opportunities to feature women on her innovative "Piano Jazz" radio program. Joanne Brackeen has been hailed as an outstanding pianist since she became recognized for her work with Stan Getz in the 1970's. Geri Allen and Rene Rosnes are among the leading acoustic jazz pianists of the early 1990's.

There is also a significant movement of classical musicians—even well established ones—to get involved in acoustic jazz. Historically, most of the activity has been in the other direction, with jazz players studying classical music. Wynton Marsalis is the rare exception who is truly at home equally in both fields. The more recent trend is for classical musicians, even some who have never played jazz, suddenly attempting it. Flutist Jean Pierre Rampal began the movement with the release in 1975 of fellow Frenchman Claude Bolling's *Suite for Jazz Flute and Piano* (actually the flute part required little improvisation), a light but enjoyable work featuring the composer's jazz piano. The tremendous success of this recording spurred numerous sequels pairing Bolling with classical artists. Some of these musicians, such as cellist Yo Yo Ma, eventually developed serious interests in jazz.

Independent of the Bolling association, the ever searching violinist Yehudi Menuhin and the younger virtuoso Itzhak Perlman have performed jazz live and on records. Richard Stoltzman, the best known clarinet soloist in classical circles today, has a longstanding interest in jazz, playing live and on records with small groups and with the entire Woody Herman Band. A young violinist from England, Nigel Kennedy, typically performs classical music as well as jazz in every recital. Because most of these artists came to jazz relatively late, and virtuosity is no substitute for experience, their jazz playing is rarely of the highest caliber. But their attempt to play jazz is one of the many indications of the new respect in which jazz is held. Another sign of this respect is that several classical pianists, among them Steven Mayer, Michael Campbell, and Orrin Grossman, are including written transcriptions of recorded solos by Tatum, Hines, Monk, and others in their recital programs.

This idea of recreating past recordings brings up the repertory movement in jazz today. The idea of a jazz repertory group that will recreate the great writing and even improvising of famous older groups began to develop in the late 1930's, as noted in Chapter 12. In the 1960's and 1970's there were small groups that specialized in the music of Monk or that got together for special tributes to Armstrong or Ellington. Among big bands, the repertory idea was found in educational settings. The big-band tradition is kept alive in thousands of high school and college bands which vastly outnumber professional bands. Many of the student bands concentrate on newly commissioned material, often

The Tufts University Jazz Ensemble around 1980. Director Lewis Porter has his back to the camera. (Collection of Lewis Porter)

by their own student composers or by their directors, but an increasing number make the effort to seek out notable scores of the past.

The National Jazz Ensemble, directed by bassist Chuck Israels and founded in 1973, and the New York Jazz Repertory Orchestra, an all-star group produced by George Wein beginning in 1974, were among the first professional big bands organized for the explicit purpose of preserving and extending, through new commissions, the repertory of masterpieces written for the jazz big band since the 1920's. Both broke up within a few years. Since then there have been a number of regional groups which have managed to survive, thanks to the dedication of their musicians, the availability of grants, and the building of their audiences. Columbus (Ohio), Toledo, Detroit, Cleveland and other cities have their own jazz repertory orchestras, all relying heavily on public funds for support.

In the eighties repertory groups proliferated. In 1986 the critic Gary Giddins organized the American Jazz Orchestra, which presents about six repertory concerts each year under the overall direction of John Lewis. Every August, beginning in 1988, Lincoln Center has offered a weeklong "Classical Jazz" festival built entirely around the repertory concept—one night for Benny Carter, one for Ellington, one for Jelly Roll Morton—as interpreted by Wynton Marsalis and critic Stanley Crouch. In 1991 Lincoln Center announced a yearlong commitment to jazz. The Smithsonian Institution founded a jazz repertory big band around the same time.

The repertory movement has its problems: Since jazz is dependent upon the momentary inspiration of the musicians, what exactly is the point of recreating past recordings in present concerts? Should the recreations be played strictly to the letter, including transcribed solos? Or somewhat interpreted, with new solos in the spirit of the originals? Or freely interpreted, with perhaps some changes in the writing and with new solos by the current soloists, allowing them free reign? The last would seem to be the solution most in keeping with the jazz spirit and tradition, but many repertory groups have not directly addressed these issues. Still, the repertory movement has produced many enjoyable concerts which are educational and appeal to a broad audience.

For all its acceptance, the jazz field is still in financial trouble. Jazz artists struggle to survive, and audiences are still small. There is limited help from the American government, despite the declaration in 1987 that jazz is a national treasure. Perhaps more disturbing, there is almost no mention of jazz in the American public school system, making it difficult to build young audiences. Yet, at the same time that musicians continue to suffer from a dearth of places—clubs, theaters and concert halls—in which to play, there are certainly signs of life in the jazz world. In 1989, Michael Ullman asked the young drummer Winard Harper about the state of the music. He refused to speculate on the future, but noted enthusiastically that young musicians with high hopes were still streaming into New York City—more than ever before, he felt.

The new generation of musicians is decidedly international, and each has his or her culture to draw upon. It's likely that the jazz of the future will continue

An all star gathering at the White House on April 29, 1969 in honor of Duke Ellington's seventieth birthday. From left: Dave Brubeck, Hank Jones, Jim Hall, Tom Whaley (Ellington's music copyist and longtime associate), Paul Desmond (in back), Earl Hines, Gerry Mulligan, Billy Taylor, singer Mary Mayo, Milt Hinton (in back), Willis Conover, (international jazz broadcaster and producer of this event), President Nixon, (hidden behind Nixon is Louis Bellson), Clark Terry (partly hidden), Ellington, Joe Williams, trombonist Urbie Green, J. J. Johnson, Bill Berry. (Courtesy Rutgers Institute of Jazz Studies)

to incorporate something of the rhythmic complexity of African-Cuban and other Latin musics, and that it will continue to draw on the work of European composers and improvisers. Perhaps it will acknowledge the melodies of Japan and be enlightened by the rhythmic bounce and lyricism of African popular music.

We have mentioned in Chapter 19 the South African pianist Abdullah Ibrahim (Dollar Brand), whose style was based on Monk and Ellington and yet whose playing is informed by the lilting, bittersweet music of his homeland. To Ibrahim, Africa and its traditions were like "water from an ancient well," a source of sustenance and spirit. Whatever happens to jazz in the future, its rich history, the music of King Oliver, Louis Armstrong, Duke Ellington, of Charlie Parker and Thelonious Monk, of Miles Davis, John Coltrane and Ornette Coleman, should continue to enrich the lives of listeners the world over. It's America's great art form, a life-giver with, as Sidney Bechet said, a long reach. It's still teaching people how they can feel and demonstrating what they can accomplish.

Appendix 1
Listening to Jazz

To the unaccustomed listener, a jazz solo, particularly a solo that strays far from an easily recognizable melody, can seem abstract, formless, linear. Yet most jazz performances take place over a repeated sequence of chords, the chords that underlie the piece that the group is performing. A composer might write an attractive song, as George Gershwin wrote "Embraceable You," and a jazz group will begin by playing a loose version of the 32-bar melody together. (Most songs that began in Broadway musicals have an introductory verse which jazz musicians rarely perform. Jazz musicians simply repeat the chorus over and over.) Then a soloist will create his or her own melody while the rhythm section essentially repeats an accompaniment to that 32-bar chorus. Experienced listeners will be able to "hear" the song, even when no one is playing the original melody, by following the chord progression. In fact, the procedure of most jazz is based on one main principle—that a nearly infinite number of melodies may fit any song's chord progression. The jazz musician's traditional task is spontaneously to compose new melodies that fit the chord progression, which is repeated over and over as each soloist is featured, for as many choruses as desired.

That spontaneous composition is called improvisation. Improvisation is not unique to jazz. All music must have been improvised originally, and was probably modified as it was passed from one person to another. Bach, Mozart, and many other great composers regularly improvised in public, reportedly with brilliant results. Improvisation within any medium requires a thorough and disciplined understanding of that idiom. It is not a question of "playing whatever you feel like." Ravi Shankar may in a sense play what he feels, but his music is not jazz; and a Freddie Hubbard trumpet solo would never be mistaken for Indian classical music. Both of these artists have years of experience within their particular idioms, and as a result have an ingrained sense of what is appropriate to their genre. It's also important to remember that standards vary as to what makes an improvisation. An early jazz player, as has been noted before, frequently worked out a solo on a new piece over time, and stuck to the basic outlines of that solo whenever he played that piece. The variations were frequently illuminating, but most of the solo, which was originally improvised, remained fixed. So, a listener should try to become familiar with the jazz traditions which inform a particular performance.

Jazz solos are frequently rendered especially distinctive by the characteristics of African-American music, the vocalistic growls, bends, slides and vibrato that have been found in African-American musics of all types. This vocal attitude is reinforced by the fact that each jazz musician is encouraged to develop a unique sound or tone, his or her own readily recognizable "voice." The result has been that even on a relatively intransigent instrument such as the piano, jazz musicians have developed original techniques to make their own sound: No one would confuse Monk with Art Tatum, or Cecil Taylor with McCoy Tyner.

One of the most important characteristics of jazz soloing is the sustained use of syncopation. In syncopation one sets up the expectation of one rhythm and pattern, and then introduces another. Essentially what one is doing is shifting accents to what are traditionally "weak" beats. Then in the places where one expects a strong beat, such as the first beat of a measure, one avoids that accent, either by holding a note through it, by introducing a rest, or by playing lightly. Syncopation is everywhere in jazz, and when different rhythms occur in different instruments playing simultaneously, an exhilarating surge of rhythmic complexity develops: The music swings. The musician soloing relates his or her particular syncopations, his or her subtle shifts of accent, to the underlying beat. The music swings when we feel a sensation of momentum, of a push and pull over the constant underlying beat. Swing is this sensation, not an intellectual realization, and it can be irresistible. It can be felt in its simplest sense through the following process: Count "1, 2, 3, 4" at a moderate tempo and have another person clap firmly on every "1" and "3." A third person claps loudly on "2" and "4." Now stop counting aloud, and one person will feel a pull towards the other, wanting to coincide. That tugging at the beat is crucial to swing.

Probably the single most useful skill for a jazz listener to work on is to be able to identify the underlying form of the improvisation one is hearing. Most pieces played by jazz musicians either have the form of popular songs with an easily identifiable structure or they are based on the blues. A song chorus with its chord progression most frequently occupies 32 measures in 4/4 meter. (Each measure in 4/4 time consists of four beats, so that if one counts to four along with the beat of the music, one will have covered one measure or bar. Count four beats 32 times, and one will have followed an entire chorus.) Most frequently, this song chorus is divided into four easily recognizable sections of equal lengths. The first section—which for convenience is called section A—is eight measures; that is followed by a repeat of section A (with new words, if sung); then comes a contrasting section, called section B, also eight bars. That contrasting section is called the "bridge" or "release" or "channel" by musicians. The bridge typically begins in a new key, and it leads back to another repetition of the eight bars of section A. (Thus its names: It forms a "bridge" between the second A and the final A, it "releases" tension, and in its last bars, it "channels" the music back to another repetition of the initial melody in the initial key.) This very common structure is referred to as an AABA form. "Body and Soul" is an excellent example: It has been recorded hundreds of times, including the recordings by Coleman Hawkins and Benny Goodman (both SCCJ). Note that in the first chorus of the Goodman, the clarinetist states the A sections, and allows the pianist to take over for the bridge. Later the two reverse the procedure. Other AABA songs include "Ain't Misbehavin'," and "Satin Doll." Other divisions are possible in 32-bar songs: "How High the Moon" is ABAB'. More rarely songwriters will extend the eight bar sections: Ray Noble's "Cherokee," and hence Charlie Parker's version of it called "KoKo," is an AABA song whose sections are each 16 bars. AABA tunes with music notation in this book include "Well, You Needn't" (Chapter 12), "Conception" and "Crosscurrent" (Chapter 14), "Oleo" (Chapter 15), "So What" (Chapter 16), "The Girl from Ipanema," with a 16-bar bridge (Chapter 20), among others. "Singin' the Blues" (Chapter 7) is an example of the ABAC form.

There is another form jazz musicians use regularly: It's a 12-bar form invented by African-Americans, and it's called the blues. Unlike AABA songs, in which songwriters invent their own chord progressions, blues have a fairly standardized sequence of chords. One 12-bar sequence, in which there is a chord for each measure, is shown in the example. (See music example.)

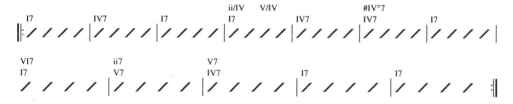

Example A–1.
Blues chord progression. Alternate chords are written above. The steady beat is represented by slashes underneath.

The Roman numerals are easily explained: If a blues is in the key of C, then C is the first note of its scale. A three-note chord (triad) built on C is a I chord. On the piano, play C, E, and G together four times and you have covered the first measure. Play four such measures. Then move to the fourth note in a C scale— F—and play a comparable chord, this time F, A, and C. Play that for two measures and return to chord I. Finally, in measure 9, you will move to the fifth note in the scale, play the chord G, B, and D, move down to the fourth, play F, A, C, and then return, as all blues do, to the home base, I. Of course, not too many blues stick to this bare outline: Typically, those basic chords are spiced up with an additional note, in the case of the I in C, a B♭, which makes that initial chord a I⁷ or dominant chord. And musicians will add other, more complex chord changes within the basic structure, a few of which are shown on the example.

Typically, a sung blues consists of three sentences, each with its accompaniment taking up four bars. Here's a lyric sung by Ma Rainey on her first recording in 1923: "Did you ever wake up, just at the break of day?" she asks. That question is repeated, as is typical in the blues: "Did you ever wake up just at the break of day?" The last line of this chorus of "Bad Luck Blues" answers or completes the idea stated in the previous lines: "With your arms around the pillow, where your daddy used to lay." (See music example.)

Example A–2.
Ma Rainey, second chorus of "Bad Luck Blues" (1923), showing trumpet fills by Tommy Ladnier. The chord sequence is a variation of the "standard" one. Main blue notes are circled.

To a jazz musician, the blues don't have to be sung: nor do they have to be sad, or even slow. In jazz, the word "blues" refers to the 12-bar chorus structure, not to the mood of the music.

The easiest place to start listening to the blues is with sung blues, preferably by classic blues singers—musicians like the famous Bessie Smith. (Her 12-bar "Lost Your Head Blues" is found on the SCCJ. Beware that her "St. Louis Blues" on SCCJ has a more complicated structure.) Or one can listen to Jelly Roll Morton's wonderfully simple "Mamie's Blues," a piece he said was the first blues he had ever heard. (He named it after the woman who played it for him.) When one has heard these sung blues repeatedly, it will be time to try instrumental blues. The SCCJ booklet, page 32, has a list of likely selections. Among the blues examples notated in this book are "Chimes Blues" and "Dippermouth Blues" (both Chapter 4), "Knockin' A Jug" (Chapter 7), "Twisted" and "Bag's Groove" (Chapter 12), "Hootie Blues" and "Parker's Mood" (Chapter 13), and "Matrix" (Chapter 19).

Blues can sound simple, basic, folksy. Often a jazz musician sounds especially relaxed and "soulful" playing the blues, which is exactly the point of returning to a well-known form with a tradition of expressing profound emotion. (In one recording session, Miles Davis growls a single word to his band, "Blues," and they take off. They don't have to prepare to play the blues.) The blues in jazz can be upbeat, even jarring, as in Ellington's "Ko-Ko" (SCCJ). Two powerful instrumental blues are Sidney Bechet's elegantly slow "Blue Horizon" and Meade Lux Lewis's boogie-woogie swinger, "Honky Tonk Train Blues" (both SCCJ). (The title of the latter refers to an interesting innovation by enterprising train companies, who became aware of the many African-American workers that had migrated to big Northern cities such as Chicago. They ran special trains back down south for workers going back to their original homes for vacation, and hired pianists to entertain. They turned a bar car into a honky-tonk, an informal club.) Both Bechet and Meade Lux Lewis mark the ends of their choruses. Each musician has a phrase with which, with minor variations, he ends each chorus. Listen for those phrases, count along, and eventually count off the choruses, and see how many 12-bar cycles are played in each case.

Musicians often talk about so-called "blue notes." These are "bent" notes, often below the expected pitch, that a singer or instrumentalist will typically place on the third note of the scale, to wring drama out of the alternation of major and minor third that one finds suggested in the blues chord progression. Musicians also blue fifths and blue sevenths, referring to those degrees of the scale. For example, the most prominent blue notes of Rainey's trumpeter are circled in the preceding example.

There has been considerable misunderstanding about blue notes among jazz listeners and writers. Certainly, the African-Americans who first created blues never needed to be aware of the theory of thirds, fifths, major and minor. They learned to hear the blues and to feel where blue notes fit in. Some writers have defined a blue note as a minor third, and speak of a blues scale that black singers supposedly use instead of a major scale. That unlikely scenario misses the point. The blue notes have their effect because of the alternation of major and minor thirds in the underlying chords—for example, in the key of C, the C^7 chord uses a major third, but the F^7 chord that comes next uses E^b, the minor third. Significantly, musicians who know theory always speak of the blues in C major, G major, and so on. They are thinking of the major scale, with the blue notes as essential colorations of that scale. A blue note is not simply a flatted third, anyway. It is a note whose pitch and sound are altered and bent for expressivity. That treatment of the note, as much as its lowered pitch, makes the note "blue."

People often contrast composition with improvisation. It makes more sense to talk of composers who improvise and composers who write their music down—remembering that many composers do both, and that the results are usually very different. Every jazz musician is a composer, because he or she composes music while improvising. As with any composer, once one has heard a lot of music by a certain person one is able to recognize the style. That is partly because one becomes familiar with that composer's favorite turns of phrase, what jazz musicians call "licks" and classical musicologists call "formulas." Every musician has a unique repertoire of licks, some original, some borrowed, as Charlie Parker borrowed a fragment of the famous clarinet solo from "High Society." Today, it's a rare jazz player who doesn't at one time or other play a Charlie Parker or John Coltrane lick.

It requires a lot of listening to recognize licks, because one not only has to become familiar with the style of the musician in question, but one has to know enough related music to be able to recognize quotations like "High Society" and to recognize which licks are used by other musicians as well. However, even beginning jazz listeners are able to identify motives. Often one hears a musician take a little idea and play around with it, repeat it higher or lower, faster or slower. That little idea is called a motive, and one of the joys of music listening is going along for the ride while the composer develops the possibilities within a motive. The famous first four notes of Beethoven's Fifth Symphony form a motive, because he plays around with those four notes in surprising ways for much of the symphony that follows. Thelonious Monk's "Blues Improvisation" (SCCJ) is an excellent introduction to the way an accomplished soloist can develop an extended solo by taking a series of motives and exploring each one before moving on to the next. (See music example, Chapter 12.) Note that the labelling of motives is arbitrary. One can use numbers, letters, whatever. But it is conventional to use a prime, as in a', to indicate a variation of the original motive, something that is not an exact repetition but clearly similar. Also bear in mind that Monk is an extremist—few soloists concentrate so exclusively on motives as he does.

The best way to study improvisation is to compare different versions of the same piece, by the same artist and by different ones, from the same era and from several eras. Let's do this now by looking at several versions of "Embraceable You," which George and Ira Gershwin wrote in 1930 for their Broadway show *Girl Crazy.* "Embraceable You" was chosen because of the variety of its recordings by jazz musicians: One could use any other ballad as a good starting place. The point is to familiarize oneself with the original song as written before one listens to its variations in jazz performances. Then one will be able to feel the direction of the chord sequences, and follow each section of the tune as it appears. For conciseness, only the beginning is used here. The music example shows the beginning of "Embraceable You" as written, with the chords indicated by symbols for those who can read them. The song is presented here in F major instead of the original G, because this will make it easier to compare with the jazz versions, most of which are in F. (See music example.)

The form of the whole chorus is best described as ABAC, but we will be studying just the first A section. Note that most of the song develops in four-bar phrases, with a sentence of lyric to each four bars. And note also the variations of the simple three-note motive with which the song opens. In the first measure, those notes begin on D; in the fifth measure, which takes up where measure

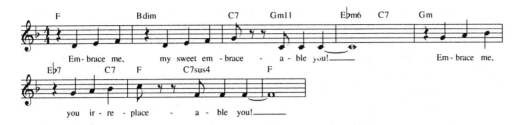

Example A–3.
Beginning of "Embraceable You," by George and Ira Gershwin.

three left off, they start on G. It is recommended that readers, while looking at the music and reading the lyrics, listen to a vocal version of "Embraceable You," such as Ella Fitzgerald's (which is part of her *Gershwin Songbook*), or the version by Nat "King" Cole included in the *Smithsonian Collection of American Popular Song*. Both singers take justifiable liberties with the rhythm, but reproduce closely the melody of the song. But now listen to the "Embraceable You" by Billie Holiday, thought by many to be the greatest jazz singer of them all, as recorded for Commodore in 1944. Her version of the first eight measures is given in the example, transposed to F major in this case from the key of C. (See music example.)

Example A–4.
Billie Holiday's interpretation of the beginning of "Embraceable You" (1944), master take 1.

Holiday hasn't been sufficiently praised for her acute sensitivity to lyrics, for her way of molding the melody, and her technique, to the meaning of the song. When she sings "embrace me" at the beginning of this "Embraceable You," she emphasizes the second syllable by raising the written note and accenting it. That makes sense musically, and in terms of the lyrics. Rather than following the sweep of the melody towards "me," which makes the singer sound as if she fears her imagined lover might be embracing someone else ("embrace *me*"), she seems to tell him exactly what she wants him to do ("em-*brace* me"). (She also changes the "you" in measure six to "my.") Holiday not only reshapes the melody by changing those first three notes, but she completely transforms the rhythm. Her rhythms sail loosely over the beat: They are not fully notatable, but the transcription will be helpful when read along with the recording. Notice, for example, that the melody that occupies measures two and three of the original are squeezed into measure 3 alone by Holiday. She begins measure five with the original three note motive—G, A, B♭, but adds a poignancy by falling away from the higher note. Holiday has been widely admired for the way she used the sound of her voice, and for her natural-sounding manipulation of rhythms that makes her artful singing sound so casual.

"Embraceable You" has been recorded by many jazz groups, including an informal aggregation of swing musicians put together by Eddie Condon and recorded by Commodore in 1938. After a relaxed introduction by trumpeter Bobby Hackett, tenor saxophonist Bud Freeman offers his highly embellished version of the melody, playing it as written at times, and paraphrasing or decorating Gershwin's lines at others. Freeman is followed by a graceful chorus of trombonist Jack Teagarden. Then comes the gem of the performance, a single chorus by Pee Wee Russell with a new melody so convincing it was reportedly transcribed and published as a new song. Russell's first eight bars are given in the example in their original key of F. (See music example.)

Example A–5.
Pee Wee Russell's clarinet improvisation over the beginning of "Embraceable You" (1938), with Eddie Condon and his Windy City Seven.

Russell's improvised melody has a logical internal balance, a poise found in only the great jazz solos. The first two measures descend, and are followed by the third ascending. Measures five and six are very much like a counter-argument to the first two, since they ascend and go into the same kind of triplet motive that distinguished measure two. Notice that measure five is the only one that quotes Gershwin's original: Russell is playing over the chords. The solo has an airy wistfulnesss that is partially the result of Russell's delicate, but almost sour tone, and partially due to his relaxed beat.

Before the early forties, jazz musicians tended to use fewer notes on a ballad such as this than they would on a faster tune, making it easier to follow their improvisations. It was often possible to hear in their solos the notes of the original melody. Later musicians tended to improvise more freely, employing more notes and a greater variety of rhythmic devices within a solo. Sometimes they would eliminate the opening paraphrase of the melody altogether, and simply launch directly into the chord-based improvisation. In other words, they would keep the chord sequences and structure of the original tune, but not the melody. That is what Charlie Parker does on his two takes in F major of "Embraceable You," recorded in 1947 (both SCCJ). Each strays far from Gershwin's melody in a different way, and the opportunity to compare two takes by a jazz soloist is always instructive. For one thing, one is able to tell how freely the artist improvises by seeing how different the takes are, as noted in the section on "Dippermouth Blues" in Chapter 4. Since Parker improvises very freely indeed, it helps at first to concentrate on the chords with which pianist Duke Jordan accompanies—they limn the outline of the tune. The first take is the more famous, for its extraordinary coherence despite a great variety of ideas. It begins with a little motive that is immediately developed several times, and which recurs later in various guises. Measure seven begins with something like Parker's own "Cool Blues" theme (recorded earlier that year) and continues with another motivic passage. (See music example.)

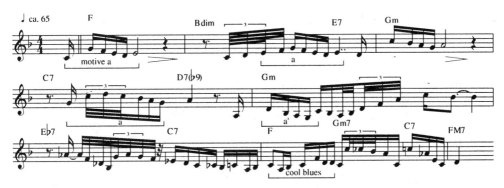

Example A–6.
Charlie Parker's first take improvisation over the beginning of "Embraceable You" (1947).

Other audibly motivic moments occur later (not shown in the example), in measures 11-12, 19-20, 23-24, and especially in 27-28, in which some listeners have heard a resemblance to the original motive. Parker's sole reference to Gershwin's theme is at the end of measure 21.

But Parker was not always so motivically oriented, and he proves that there are other ways of fashioning a powerful solo. The second take of "Embraceable You," is a free-flowing stream of melodic ideas, with occasional motivic relationships. In this version, Parker's melodies are full of unexpected pauses and rests, making it a fascinating study in rhythm and phrasing. (See music example.)

Since we will be talking about Ornette Coleman next, it is important to remember that Coleman has always said that he derived his style partly from

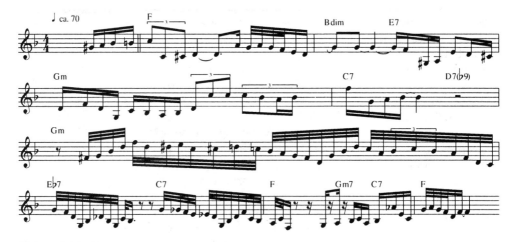

Example A–7.
Charlie Parker's second take improvisation over the beginning of "Embraceable You" (1947).

that of Parker. Many listeners have had trouble hearing this relationship but one can hear a precursor of Coleman's approach in such passages as measures 14-15 of this solo (not shown), as well as in many of Parker's live recordings.

Coleman usually plays his own compositions, but in 1960 he did record a version of "Embraceable You." After a deliberately brash, aggressively blaring introduction, he plays the melody as shown in the example, transposed from Coleman's key of E♭ major to F. (See music example.)

Example A–8.
Ornette Coleman's improvisation over "Embraceable You" (1960) at the beginning of the recording.

Coleman changes the rhythm of the melody, while retaining all of its basic pitches. His version seems much more abstract than Holiday's because he does not necessarily retain the four-bar phrase lengths, and because he separates the notes with rests, as in measure three of the transcription. He also injects a strong dose of the blues from his native Texas, beginning in measure five and leading into gospel-derived phrases later on.

After the theme statement, with some extra moments of free playing, Coleman brings the opening three notes of Gershwin's melody back in. The bass and drums accompany him now with "walking" jazz time while he improvises. This second "chorus" is freer than the first. Coleman makes up his own melodies and only refers to the chord changes rather than following them, while the bassist Charlie Haden keeps his ears on Coleman so that he may provide appropriate notes, sometimes following the implied chord change, and sometimes staying on one chord where that seems fitting. Coleman demonstrates his gift for remarkably concise motivic improvisation, wherein he develops a few ideas at great length. The little motive which he derives from Gershwin is repeated twice, then joined with another little motive (b). Then another motive appears at the end of measure three—it resembles motive b upside down—and it is expanded in the next few measures. In measure five he breaks out into what sounds like a compelling folksong. (See music example.)

Example A–9.
Ornette Coleman's improvisation over "Embraceable You" (1960) at the beginning of the second "chorus," when the bass starts walking.

Coleman was thoroughly aware, despite what some have said, of the danger that free jazz might degenerate into chaos. In order to compensate for the absence of harmonic progression, he relied more heavily on motivic thinking for unity in his music than do most jazz players. It works brilliantly.

Ornette Coleman's performance is absorbing for its daring and uniquely personal character. It deviates far from what Gershwin wrote, but that's not what makes it valuable in itself: Trumpeter Clifford Brown's "Embraceable You," found on his album recorded with strings, paraphrases Gershwin closely, but, with its radiant warmth and rhythmic liveliness, Brown's is still one of the greatest jazz versions. Jazz solos are judged by their emotional appeal, their felt cohesiveness, inventiveness, and personality. The greatest jazz musicians, as tenor saxophonist Lester Young used to say, "tell a story," a story that is both a surprise and a confirmation.

Appendix 2
Symbols Used
in the Music Examples

Note is accented and held less than full value.

Barely audible, "ghosted" note.

Note has pronounced vibrato. Symbol is placed approximately where vibrato occurs.

Indefinite sound due to slip of fingers.

Pitch is arrived at from below by adjustment of embouchure (slide). Sometimes, this is combined with a fingered grace note.

Note ends in a downward glissando (falloff).

Note ends in an upward glissando (doit).

Notes connected by glissando. Due to speed of glissando, individual notes cannot be transcribed. A straight line may also be used.

Note is flat by less than one half step.

Note is sharp by less than one half step.

Note is delayed by less than one sixteenth note.

Note is anticipated by less than one sixteenth note.

"Scoop." The pitch of the note dips down and up, almost simulating a "wah-wah" sound.

Double bar indicates beginning of a chorus or section

C^7, G^7, etc.   Dominant seventh chord, such as C-E-G-B^b.

Glossary

Accelerando. A speeding up, acceleration. (Italian)

Arrangement. A new version of a previously written piece. Jazz arrangements often include new chords for the piece as well as new material to be played during and between solos, and so on.

Arranger. Simply, one who creates an arrangement (q.v.). Jazz arrangers usually create so much new material for their arrangements that there is really no difference between arranging and composing. However, the word arranger is often used to refer to somebody who *only* reworks previously written pieces, while composer is used to refer to one who creates pieces from scratch.

Baiao. A Brazilian dance.

Bebop. Virtuosic jazz style with irregularly accented, long phrases and sophisticated harmonies. Most prominent between 1944 and 1950. Also called "rebop," or "bop."

Block chords. A series of big chords played with the hands moving in parallel (c.f. locked hands).

Blues. Frequently used song form in jazz. Also a separate tradition of African-American music. Usually a 12-bar form. Blues songs have a fairly standardized chord progression.

Bombs. Irregular accents played on the bass drum. A feature of bebop drumming, generally first attributed to Kenny Clarke.

Boogie woogie. A piano blues style based on a driving repeated left-hand part, often moving in eighth notes. First recorded in the late 1920's, became very popular from late 1930's on.

Bossa nova. A fusion of the harmonies and languid approach of cool jazz with several ostinato patterns derived from the Brazilian samba. Originated around 1960, soon became hugely popular.

Break. A momentary pause in the rhythm section, usually just one or two measures, which a band member will "fill," usually with an improvised phrase.

Bridge. The B section of an AABA form, generally eight bars long. Also called "channel" or "release."

Chord progression. A sequence of chords that underlies a composition, often 12 or 32 bars in length. The progression is repeated over and over during improvised solos.

Chorus. The form of a song, often 12 or 32 bars in length. In jazz the chord progression (q.v.) of the chorus, but not its melody, is repeated over and over during improvisations.

Coda. An ending to a piece that is not part of the repeated chorus but added on.

Cool jazz. A jazz style using a mellow tonal quality and smooth, flowing melodic lines partly inspired by Lester Young. Often classical instruments and techniques were used. Most prominent throughout the 1950's. Sometimes called "West Coast jazz."

Dorian mode. A favorite in modal jazz pieces. In comparison with the major mode, the Dorian has a lowered third and seventh degree. For example, to play a C dorian scale use the notes E♭ and B♭, or play the white notes from D to D for D Dorian.

Double time playing. Playing twice as fast as the other members of the band. It also refers to the whole band going into a tempo twice as fast as what preceded it.

Flatted fifth. The fifth note of a major scale lowered a half step. This was a favorite interval among bebop players.

Forte. Loud.

Fortissimo. Very loud.

Free jazz. A name often used throughout the 1960's for jazz performances that do not follow a repeating chord progression, and in some cases do not have a steady beat. Also, the name of an influential album by Ornette Coleman.

Fusion. A combination or "fusing" of jazz with other types of music, especially soul music and rock. Amplified and electronic instruments are used. Prominent since around 1970.

Hard bop. An aggressive, exuberant style that grew naturally out of bebop. Prominent beginning in the early 1950's.

Higher intervals. Notes occuring above the basic notes of a triad, so called because we count upwards from the tonic. These notes are used in jazz to create intriguing tensions over chords. The higher intervals of chords are a defining feature of modern jazz melodies. Also called "extended intervals" or "extensions."

Improvisation. The spontaneous creating of an original piece of music. It requires a great deal of practice and an intimate knowledge of the style of music in which one desires to create.

Jam sessions. Informal performances where musicians improvise at their leisure, often without an audience but just for the benefit of the musicians themselves.

Jazz-rock fusion. See *fusion.*

Lay out. Not play. For instance, when the piano player or drummer is asked to lay out, that means he or she does not play for the specified part of the piece.

Lick. A little melodic idea that a musician uses frequently. Jazz players can be identified by their characteristic licks. In classical analysis licks are called "formulas."

Locked hands. A specific type of block chord playing (q.v.), in which the right hand plays chords in close position and the left hand doubles the top note of the right, an octave lower. As the hands change chords they appear to be "locked" together in tandem.

Major triad. The chord formed by playing together the first, third, and fifth notes of any major scale.

Mezzo forte. Medium loud, not very loud and not very soft.

Modal jazz. A repertoire of jazz pieces, as opposed to a particular style of improvising. Modal pieces stay on each mode (and thus each scale and chord as well) for a long time, usually at least four bars per mode, in contrast with standard repertory which changes chords at least once per measure. Modal pieces often employ modes other than the familiar major and minor, such as the dorian (q.v.). Prominent since the late 1950's.

Mode. A type of scale (q.v.), defined by its particular sequence of intervals. The most common modes in jazz and Western popular music are major and minor.

Moldy fig. Derisive term used in the 1940's to refer to someone who only liked Dixieland and other old styles.

Montuno. A short rhythmic figure, often two bars long, repeated by the piano throughout the improvisations in a Latin music piece.

Motive. A short musical idea that the musician develops by creating some variations of it. A typical jazz solo will have several short stretches during which the artist becomes interested in developing a particular motive.

Pedal point. A long note, usually a low one, that is sustained even though the chords of the piece are changing and creating some dissonance in the process. Derives from the foot pedals of the organ, which can sustain notes.

Phrase. In music, as in speech, a complete thought which is usually marked off by a slight pause at either end. Also as in speech, a phrase is only part of the whole piece. Four bars is the most common phrase length.

Piano roll. A roll of paper with holes cut into it while a pianist plays. When played back on a specially designed player piano, the original performance can be reproduced. Most prominent in the early 1900's.

Ragtime. An African-American music with a lilting beat and, like a march, with several themes in each piece. Best known today as a piano music but also for voice and for bands. Most prominent in the early 1900's.

Rhythm and blues. A driving, riff-based, urban blues style relying on jazz instrumentation, especially tenor saxophone. Also called "r & b" for short. Most prominent during the middle 1940's through the 1950's.

Rhythm section. The drums, bass, and chord instruments (keyboards, guitars, and banjos). Unlike the winds, they play throughout a jazz performance, supporting all the soloists.

Riff. A little melodic idea that is repeated over and over again even though the chords are changing underneath, creating a great deal of rhythmic momentum. The riff must be compatible with the underlying chords, or else one or two notes of the riff may be changed to accomodate the chords as they change.

Rim shot. A sharp sound created by angling the drumstick so it hits the rim of the snare drum at the same time as the drum head.

Ring shout. An African-American dance and music, originally described in religious settings during the 1800's, in which dancers move in a circle, making short shuffling steps. Music accompanying the dance consisted of short repeated melodies.

Ritardando. A slowing down. Abbreviated "rit."

Scale. A series of pitches (notes) on which a particular piece is based. A scale is defined by its starting note and its mode (q.v.), as in "C major scale," "G minor scale."

Sequence. A short musical idea, or even a complete phrase, methodically repeated in different keys, usually going down. For example, if one repeats a short melody in the keys of E major, then D, then C, one has created a sequence.

Sideman. A musician who is not the leader of a band or recording session. Also called "sideperson."

Solo. A featured improvisation in a jazz piece. Also a verb, to solo. In jazz it is not truly "solo" because the rhythm section usually continues to provide accompaniment.

Sotto voce. Softly. Literally, in Italian, "under the voice."

Soul jazz. Jazz based on the style and rhythms of African-American popular music of the late 1950's and early 1960's.

Stock arrangements. Published orchestrations of popular material, meant to be played by groups of varying skills and instrumentation. Many rags were also published in stock arrangements, as were Sousa's marches.

Stride. A style of piano playing named for its left-hand figures, with a characteristic "oom-pah" sound, made by striking a single note low in the bass on the first and third beats of a measure, and filling in with a chord in midrange on beats two and four. Differs from ragtime in the swing feeling and the right-hand improvisation.

Swing. A sensation of pull and momentum found in jazz. It appears to result partly from the push and pull between layers of syncopated rhythms and the constant underlying beat.

Third Stream. A repertoire of music consciously combining jazz and classical music in various degrees. The composers are usually, but not always, from jazz backgrounds. The term was coined by Gunther Schuller in 1957.

Tonic. The first note of a scale and thus the strongest note in a piece based on that scale. Tonal pieces, including most jazz, usually end on the tonic note and tonic chord.

Twelve tone music. Music in which a composer restricts oneself to a preset series of notes which are manipulated in various ways. Introduced by composer Arnold Schoenberg. Also called "serial music," after the series of notes used. The series is also called a "row" of notes or a "tone row."

Vamp. A short pattern that is played over and over by the rhythm section. A vamp is often used as an introduction to a piece until the featured soloist is ready to begin.

Voicing. The way the notes of a chord are played, either on the keyboard or by several wind instruments. For example, the chord C-E-G could also be played E-G-C, the C could be played very low and the G very high, and so on.

West Coast jazz. See *cool jazz.*

Bibliography

GENERAL REFERENCE SOURCES

Bruyninckx, Walter. *70 Years of Recorded Jazz, 1917–1987.* Mechelen, Belgium: Bruyninckx, 1978–(ongoing). Massive and comprehensive discography. Sold by subscription only, with regular updates. The above title appears on the January 1992 update.

Chilton, John. *Who's Who of Jazz: Storyville to Swing Street.* London: Bloomsbury, 1972; fourth ed., New York: Da Capo, 1985.

Kernfeld, Barry, ed. *The New Grove Dictionary of Jazz.* London: Macmillan, 1988. (Two volumes.)

MAIN WORKS CITED

Allen, Walter. *Hendersonia: The Music of Fletcher Henderson and His Musicians.* Highland Park, New Jersey: Walter C. Allen, 1973.

Armstrong, Louis. *Satchmo: My Life in New Orleans.* New York: Prentice-Hall, 1954; Da Capo, 1986.

Balliett, Whitney. *Jelly Roll, Jabbo, and Fats: 19 Portraits in Jazz.* New York: Oxford University Press, 1983. Contents reprinted in Balliett, *American Musicians.*

Balliett, Whitney. *American Musicians: Fifty-Six Portraits in Jazz.* New York: Oxford University Press, 1986.

Basie, Count, as told to Albert Murray. *Good Morning Blues: The Autobiography of Count Basie.* New York: Random House, 1985.

Bechet, Sidney. *Treat It Gentle: An Autobiography.* New York: Hill and Wang, 1960; Da Capo, 1978.

Bennett, Lerone, Jr. *Before the Mayflower: A History of the Negro in America, 1619–1962.* Chicago: Johnson Publishing Company, 1962.

Bethell, Tom. *George Lewis: A Jazzman from New Orleans.* Berkeley: University of California Press, 1977.

Bigard, Barney, ed. by Barry Martyn. *With Louis and the Duke: The Autobiography of a Clarinetist.* London: Macmillan, 1985; New York: Oxford, 1986.

Brofsky, Howard. "Miles Davis and 'My Funny Valentine': The Evolution of a Solo," in *Black Music Research Journal*, 1983, pp. 23–45.

Brown, Scott and Robert Hilbert. *A Case of Mistaken Identity: The Life and Music of James P. Johnson*. Metuchen, New Jersey: Scarecrow Press, 1986.

Büchmann-Møller, Frank. "The Last Years of Lester Young," in Lewis Porter, ed., *A Lester Young Reader* (q.v.), pp. 122–126.

Carr, Ian. *Miles Davis: A Biography*. New York: William Morrow, 1982.

Chambers, Jack. *Milestones 1: The Music and Times of Miles Davis to 1960*. New York: William Morrow, 1983.

Chambers, Jack. *Milestones 2: The Music and Times of Miles Davis since 1960*. New York: William Morrow, 1985.

Charters, Samuel and Leonard Kunstadt. *Jazz: A History of the New York Scene*. Garden City, New York: Doubleday, 1962; Da Capo, 1981.

Chilton, John. Notes to *Roy Eldridge: The Early Years*. Columbia Records C2-38033. (1982)

Chilton, John. *Sidney Bechet: The Wizard of Jazz*. New York: Oxford University Press, 1987.

Collier, James Lincoln. *Louis Armstrong: An American Genius*. New York: Oxford University Press, 1983.

Collier, James Lincoln. *Duke Ellington*. New York: Oxford University Press, 1987.

Coltrane, John, with Don DeMichael. "Coltrane on Coltrane," in *Down Beat*, September 29, 1960, pp. 26–27; reprinted in *Down Beat*, July 12, 1979, pp. 17, 53.

Coltrane, John. Notes to *A Love Supreme*, Impulse Records A–77. (1964)

Corea, Chick. Notes on inner sleeve to *Musicmagic*, Columbia Records PC–34682. (1977)

Coryell, Julie. *Jazz Rock Fusion: The People, the Music*. New York: Dell, 1978.

Dance, Stanley. *The World of Swing*. New York: Scribner's Sons, 1974; Da Capo, 1979.

Dance, Stanley. *The World of Earl Hines*. New York: Scribner's Sons, 1977; Da Capo, 1979.

Davin, Tom. "Conversations with James P. Johnson," in *Jazz Review*, June through September 1959 (four installments). Partially reprinted in Martin Williams, ed., *Jazz Panorama* (q.v.), pp. 44–61.

Davis, Miles, with Quincy Troupe. *Miles: The Autobiography*. New York: Simon and Schuster, 1989.

De Toledano, Ralph, ed. *Frontiers of Jazz*. New York: Durrell, 1947; second ed., Ungar, 1962.

DeVeaux, Scott. "Bebop and the Recording Industry: The 1942 AFM Recording Ban Reconsidered," in *Journal of the American Musicological Society*, XLI/1 (1988), pp. 126–165.

Ellington, Duke. *Music Is My Mistress*. Garden City, New York: Doubleday, 1973.

Ellington, Mercer, with Stanley Dance. *Duke Ellington In Person: An Intimate Memoir*. Boston: Houghton Mifflin, 1978; New York: Da Capo, 1979.

Foster, Pops, as told to Tom Stoddard. *Pops Foster: The Autobiography of a New Orleans Jazzman*. Berkeley: University of California Press, 1971.

Franklin, Drew. "Ornette in Jajouka: Playing in the Register of Light," in *Village Voice*, June 23, 1987, Jazz Section, pp. 24–26.

Friedwald, Will. *Jazz Singing*. New York: Scribner's Sons, 1990.

Gardner, Barbara. "Jazzman of the Year: John Coltrane," in *Music 1962* (*Down Beat* yearbook). Chicago: Maher Publications, 1961, pp. 66–69.

Gillespie, Dizzy, with Al Fraser. *To Be or Not . . . to Bop. Memoirs.* Garden City, New York: Doubleday, 1979; New York: Da Capo, 1985.

Gitler, Ira. *Swing to Bop: An Oral History of the Transition in Jazz in the 1940s.* New York: Oxford University Press, 1985.

Goddard, Chris. *Jazz Away from Home.* London: Paddington Press, 1979.

Goodman, Benny and Irving Kolodin. *The Kingdom of Swing.* New York: Stackpole, 1939; Ungar, 1961.

Gottlieb, William. *The Golden Age of Jazz.* New York: Simon and Schuster, 1979.

Gushee, Lawrence (Larry). "Sonny Rollins," originally in *Jazz Review*, February 1960, pp. 33–34. Reprinted in Martin Williams, ed., *Jazz Panorama* (q.v.), pp. 253–257.

Gushee, Lawrence. Notes to *Steppin' on the Gas: Rags to Jazz, 1913–27.* New World Records 269. (1977)

Hammond, John, with Irving Townsend. *John Hammond on Record: An Autobiography.* New York: Ridge Press/ Summit, 1977.

Handy, W. C. *Father of the Blues: An Autobiography.* Arna Bontemps, ed. New York: Macmillan, 1941; Collier 1970.

Haskins, Jim. *The Cotton Club: A Pictorial and Social History of the Most Famous Symbol of the Jazz Era.* New York: Random House, 1977.

Hasse, John Edward, ed. *Ragtime: Its History, Composers, and Music.* New York: Schirmer, 1985.

Henderson, Fletcher. "He Made the Band Swing," *in Record Changer*, July-August 1950, pp. 15–16.

Hentoff, Nat. "An Afternoon with Miles Davis," in *Jazz Review*, December 1958, pp. 9–12. Reprinted in Martin Williams, ed., *Jazz Panorama* (q.v.), pp. 161–168.

Hentoff, Nat. "Garvin Bushell and New York Jazz in the 1920's," in *Jazz Review*, January, February and April 1959 (three installments). Reprinted in Martin Williams, ed., *Jazz Panorama* (q.v.), pp. 71–90.

Hinton, Milt and David Berger. *Bass Line: The Stories and Photos of Milt Hinton.* Philadelphia: Temple University Press, 1988.

Hodeir, André. *Jazz: Its Evolution and Essence.* New York: Grove, 1956; Da Capo, 1975.

Hodeir, André. *Toward Jazz.* New York: Grove, 1962; Da Capo, 1976.

Holbrook, Dick. "Our Word Jazz," in *Storyville*, No. 50, December 1973–January 1974, pp. 46–58.

Howlett, Felicity. *An Introduction to Art Tatum's Performance Approaches: Composition, Improvisation, and Melodic Variation.* Dissertation, Cornell University, 1983.

Hyman, Dick. "Keyboard Journal: The Art Tatum Tribute at Town Hall," in *Contemporary Keyboard*, October 1981, p. 62.

Jackson, Joy. *New Orleans in the Gilded Age: Politics and Urban Progress, 1880–1896.* Baton Rouge: Louisiana State University Press, 1969.

Jost, Ekkehard. *Free Jazz.* Graz: Universal Edition, 1974; New York: Da Capo, 1981.

Kaplan, Justin. *Walt Whitman: A Life.* New York: Simon and Schuster, 1986.

Kirk, Andy, as told to Amy Lee. *Twenty Years on Wheels.* Ann Arbor: University of Michigan Press, 1989.

Kmen, Henry. "The Roots of Jazz and Dance in Place Congo: A Reappraisal," in *Yearbook for Inter-American Musical Research*, Volume 8 (1972) pp. 5–16.

Larkin, Philip. *All What Jazz: A Record Diary, 1961–1968.* New York: St. Martin's, 1970.

Levine, Lawrence. *Black Culture and Black Consciousness: Afro-American Thought from Slavery to Freedom.* New York: Oxford University Press, 1977.

Levine, Mark. *The Jazz Piano Book.* Petaluma: Sher Music, 1989.

Lock, Graham. *Forces in Motion: Anthony Braxton and the Metareality of Creative Music.* London: Quartet, 1988; New York: Da Capo, 1989.

Lomax, Alan. *Mister Jelly Roll: The Fortunes of Jelly Roll Morton, New Orleans Creole and 'Inventor' of Jazz.* New York: Duell, Sloan, and Pearce, 1950; Berkeley: University of California Press, 1973.

Lyons, Len. *The Great Jazz Pianists: Speaking of Their Lives and Music.* New York: William Morrow, 1983; Da Capo, 1989.

Marquis, Donald M. *In Search of Buddy Bolden, First Man of Jazz.* Baton Rouge: Louisiana State University Press, 1978.

Martin, Henry. *Enjoying Jazz.* New York: Schirmer, 1986.

Mezzrow, Mezz and Bernard Wolfe. *Really the Blues.* New York: Random House, 1946; Garden City, New York: Doubleday, 1972.

Oliver, Paul. *Savannah Syncopators: African Retentions in the Blues.* New York: Stein and Day, 1970.

Palmer, Robert. "Coleman's Jazz-Rock: Pacesetter for the 80s," in *New York Times,* June 24, 1981.

Panassié, Hughes. *Louis Armstrong.* New York: Scribner's Sons, 1971; Da Capo, 1979.

Porter, Lewis. Notes to *Louis Armstrong and Sidney Bechet in New York, 1923–1925,* Smithsonian Recordings R026. (1981)

Porter, Lewis. "She Wiped All the Men Out: A Re-Evaluation of Women Instrumentalists and Composers in Jazz," in *Music Educators Journal,* September 1984, pp. 42–52, and October 1984, pp. 42–51.

Porter, Lewis. *Lester Young.* Boston: Twayne, 1985.

Porter, Lewis. "John Coltrane's 'A Love Supreme': Jazz Improvisation as Composition," in *Journal of the American Musicological Society,* 38/3 (Fall 1985), pp. 593–621.

Porter, Lewis. "Jazz in American Education," in *College Music Symposium,* 29 (1989), pp. 134–139. Reprinted in *Crescendo International* (London), August and September 1989.

Porter, Lewis, ed. *A Lester Young Reader.* Washington, D.C.: Smithsonian Institution Press, 1991.

Ramsey, Frederick, Jr. and Charles Edward Smith, eds. *Jazzmen.* New York: Harcourt Brace Jovanovich, 1939; reprinted 1977.

Reisner, Robert, ed. *Bird: The Legend of Charlie Parker.* New York: Citadel Press, 1962; Da Capo, 1973.

Roberts, John Storm. *The Latin Tinge.* New York: Oxford University Press, 1979.

Rose, Al. *Eubie Blake.* New York: Schirmer, 1979.

Russell, Ross. "Bebop," originally several articles in *Record Changer* (1948–1949). Reprinted in Williams, ed., *The Art of Jazz* (q.v.), pp. 187–213.

Russell, Ross. *Jazz Style in Kansas City and the Southwest.* Berkeley: University of California, 1971.

Russell, Ross. *Bird Lives: The High Life and Hard Times of Charlie (Yardbird) Parker.* New York: Charterhouse, 1973; Quartet, 1988.

Schafer, William and Richard B. Allen. *Brass Bands and New Orleans Jazz.* Baton Rouge: Louisiana State University Press, 1977.

Schuller, Gunther. "Sonny Rollins and the Challenge of Thematic Improvisation," in *Jazz Review,* November 1958, pp. 6–11. Reprinted in Martin Williams, ed., *Jazz Panorama* (q.v.), pp. 239–252, and also in Schuller, *Musings* (q.v.), pp. 86–97.

Schuller, Gunther. *Early Jazz*. New York: Oxford University Press, 1968.

Schuller, Gunther. *Musings: The Musical Worlds of Gunther Schuller*. New York: Oxford University Press, 1986.

Schuller, Gunther. *The Swing Era*. New York: Oxford University Press, 1989.

Shapiro, Nat and Nat Hentoff. *Hear Me Talkin' to Ya: The Story of Jazz by the Men Who Made It*. New York: Rinehart, 1955; Dover, 1966.

Shaw, Artie. *The Trouble with Cinderella (An Outline of Identity)*. New York: Farrar, Straus, and Young, 1952; Da Capo, 1979.

Simon, George. *The Big Bands*. New York: Schirmer, 1967; fourth ed. 1981.

Smith, Willie The Lion. *Music on My Mind: The Memoirs of an American Pianist*. New York: Doubleday, 1964; Da Capo, 1978.

Souchon, Edmond. "King Oliver: A Very Personal Memoir," in *Jazz Review*, May 1960, pp. 6–11. Reprinted in Martin Williams, ed., *Jazz Panorama* (q.v.), pp. 21–30.

Southern, Eileen. *The Music of Black Americans: A History*. New York: Norton, 1971; second ed. 1983.

Southern, Eileen, ed. *Readings in Black American Music*. New York: Norton, 1971; second ed. 1983.

Spellman, A. B. *Four Lives in the Bebop Business*. New York: Pantheon, 1966; Limelight, 1985. (Also published as *Black Music/Four Lives*.)

Stewart, Rex. *Jazz Masters of the Thirties*. New York: Macmillan, 1972; Da Capo, 1980.

Sudhalter, Richard and Philip Evans. *Bix: Man and Legend*. New Rochelle, New York: Arlington House, 1974; New York: Schirmer, 1975.

Tamony, Peter. "Bop. The Word," in *Jazz: A Quarterly*, 3 (Spring 1959), pp. 114–119.

Taylor, Art. *Notes and Tones: Musician-To-Musician Interviews*. Liege: Taylor, 1977; New York: Perigee, 1982.

Thomas, J. C. *Chasin' the Trane: The Music and Mystique of John Coltrane*. Garden City, New York: Doubleday, 1975; New York: Da Capo, 1976.

Troupe, Quincy. "Ornette Coleman, Going Beyond Outside," in *Musician: Player and Listener* (now simply called *Musician*), November 1981, pp. 72–80.

Tucker, Mark. *Ellington: The Early Years*. Champaign, Illinois: University of Illinois Press, 1991.

Ullman, Michael. *Jazz Lives: Portraits in Words and Pictures*. Washington, D.C.: New Republic Books, 1980.

Ullman, Michael. "Hank Jones: A Profile," in *Alternative Review*, September 1981.

Williams, Martin. "The Funky-Hard Bop Regression," originally in *Music 1958* (*Down Beat* yearbook). Reprinted in revised form in Williams, ed. *The Art of Jazz* (q.v.), pp. 233–237.

Williams, Martin, ed., *The Art of Jazz: Essays on the Nature and Development of Jazz*. New York: Oxford University Press, 1959; Da Capo, 1979.

Williams, Martin, ed. *Jazz Panorama: From the Pages of Jazz Review*. New York: Crowell-Collier, 1962; Da Capo, 1979.

Williams, Martin. *Jazz Masters of New Orleans*. New York: Macmillan, 1967; Da Capo, 1979.

Wilmer, Valerie. *As Serious as Your Life*. London: Quartet, 1977.

Discography

In this listing CD's are given whenever possible. Some LP's are listed that are not yet available on CD, and an asterisk (*) is placed after those that are certainly out of print. LP's may still be found in used record shops. However, the reader should check with CD stores as well because many jazz records are being reissued every week on CD's. In particular, two French companies, Classics and Masters of Jazz (the latter is more complete since it includes alternate takes) are reissuing hundreds of recordings from about 1920 through 1940 on CD's in series such as the complete Ellington, complete Basie, complete Armstrong, and so on. Please note that these complete sets and most sets listed below are available on separate CD's.

The prefix letters before the CD numbers are sometimes different in catalogs from the letters that appear on the CD's themselves. Also, the reissued Original Jazz Classics CD's produced by Fantasy are listed here simply as Fantasy/OJC, but the reader should be aware that the CD's show the name of the original company—Riverside, Contemporary, and so on. (In this listing we have not repeated information given in the text for titles available on the various Smithsonian collections. Their abbreviations—SCCJ, BBJ, and JP—are explained in the Preface.)

CHAPTER 4. THE EARLY RECORDINGS

James Reese Europe, "Castle House Rag"; Six Brown Brothers, "Down Home Rag"; Johnny Dunn, "Bugle Blues" and "Sergeant Dunn's Bugle Call Blues"; Kid Ory (Spikes' Seven Pods), "Ory's Creole Trombone" and "Society Blues"; all on *Steppin' on the Gas: Rags to Jazz 1913–27*, New World Records NW 269. Original Dixieland Jazz Band, "Livery Stable Blues," "Dixie[land] Jass Band One Step," "Tiger Rag," on *Original Dixieland Jazz Band: The 75th Anniversary,* BMG 61098-2. Louisiana Five, "Church

Street Sobbin' Blues," on *ODJB and Louisiana Five*, Fountain FJ101. Mamie Smith, "Crazy Blues," on *Mamie Smith, Volume One*, Document DLP 551. Freddie Keppard, "Messin' Around," and "Salty Dog," on *Freddie Keppard: The Legendary New Orleans Cornet*, Smithsonian R020.

Jelly Roll Morton, all works by Red Hot Peppers on *Jelly Roll Morton: His Complete Victor Recordings*, RCA 2361-2-RB. His 1923 and 1924 recordings are available on Milestone MCD 47018-2, and on Classics 584. "Mamie's Blues" on *New Orleans Memories Plus Two*, Commodore XFL 14942. New Orleans Rhythm Kings with Jelly Roll Morton on Milestone MCD-47020-2.

King Oliver, all titles on *Louis Armstrong* Volume 1 and 2, Masters of Jazz MJCD 1 and MJCD 2.

CHAPTER 5. SIDNEY BECHET

Bechet with Clarence Williams on *Sidney Bechet Volume 1, 1923*, Masters of Jazz MJCD 5. Blue Note recordings on *The Complete Blue Note Sidney Bechet*, Mosaic MR6-110. Victor recordings on *The Legendary Sidney Bechet, 1932-41*, RCA Bluebird 6590-2-RB.

CHAPTER 6. LOUIS ARMSTRONG

Bessie Smith recordings forthcoming on CD by Columbia Records. Ma Rainey on Milestone MCD-47201-2. The Armstrong Hot Fives and Hot Sevens complete on a series of Columbia CD's and on the Classics series. "Laughin' Louis" is the title cut of Bluebird 9579-2-RB, which does not mention that only the alternate take is included. *Louis Armstrong Meets Oscar Peterson*, Verve 825713-2. *Louis Armstrong Plays W.C. Handy*, Columbia CK 40242. This CD uses some different takes than the LP.

CHAPTER 7. JAZZIN' IN THE TWENTIES

Bix Beiderbecke on *The Complete Bix Beiderbecke in Chronological Order*, R-Records Bix 1-9, and on Masters of Jazz CD series. Beiderbecke with Wolverines also available on *Bix Beiderbecke and the Chicago Cornets*, Milestone MCD-47019-2.

Red Nichols, "Boneyard Shuffle," on *Red Nichols, Volume One*, Classic Jazz Masters CJM 24. Peck Kelley on *The Complete Commodore Recordings, Volume Three*, Mosaic. Also on *Peck Kelley Jam*, Commodore XF2 17017.

Jack Teagarden, "Knockin' a Jug," on Louis Armstrong, *Louis in New York*, Columbia CK 46148. Charleston Chasers, "Basin Street Blues," on Jack Teagarden, *I Gotta Right to Sing the Blues*, ASV Living Era AJA 5059. Louisiana Rhythm Kings, "Basin Street Blues," on *Jack Teagarden*, Time-Life JO8.* Lang and Venuti, "Farewell Blues," on *Big Band Bounce and Boogie Woogie: Trombone "T" From Texas—Jack Teagarden*, Affinity AFS 1015. "After You've Gone" and "Farewell Blues" also on *B.G. and Big Tea in NYC*, GRP Decca GRD 609.

James P. Johnson piano rolls, including "Carolina Shout," on Biograph BCD-105. Johnson recordings on *From Ragtime to Jazz: The Complete Piano Solos 1921-1939*, Columbia 85387. Johnson's classical works on *The Symphonic Jazz of James P. Johnson*, Musicmasters MMD 6066A. 1944 recordings on GRP Decca GRD 604, *Snowy Morning Blues*.

Eubie Blake piano rolls on *Eubie Blake: Blues and Ragtime, Volume One*, Biograph 1011 and on *Eubie Blake: Blues and Spirituals, Volume Two*, Biograph 1012. Fats Waller on *The Complete Fats Waller*, an RCA Bluebird series. *The Joint is Jumpin'*, Bluebird 6288-2-RB, has piano solos "Ain't Misbehavin'," "Numb Fumblin'," and "Handful of Keys."

Earl Hines with Deppe's Serenaders and some early solos on Milestone MSP 2012.* "Deep Forest" on Chiaroscuro 120.* Four early Hines solos on the Smithsonian's *Jazz Piano* collection. Earl Hines's big band, as well as his solos, reissued in the Classics series. Most of Hines's solo tributes to Duke Ellington, originally recorded by Master Jazz, in *Earl Hines Plays Duke Ellington*, New World Records 361/362-2. Many other superb Hines solo sets from the 1970's are on CD.

CHAPTER 8. DUKE ELLINGTON

Works from 1924 through the thirties on Classics and on Masters of Jazz (the latter with alternate takes). The recordings made between 1940 and 1942 on *The Blanton-Webster Band*, RCA 5659-2-RB. Fargo, North Dakota recordings of 1940 on Vintage Jazz Classics VJC 1019/20-2. Newport Jazz Festival 1956, "Diminuendo in Blue and Crescendo in Blue," on *Ellington at Newport*, Columbia CK40587. "The Queen's Suite," on *The Ellington Suites*, Fantasy/OJC CD-446-2. "Suite Thursday," on *Three Suites*, Columbia CK45825. *The Second Sacred Concert*, Prestige PCD-24045-2. Ellington, Mingus, Roach trio on *Money Jungle*, Blue Note CDP-7-46398. "Far East Suite," Bluebird 7640-2-RB. "And His Mother Called Him Bill," Bluebird 6287-2-RB.

CHAPTER 9. RIDIN' IN RHYTHM: THE THIRTIES AND SWING

All master recordings of Fletcher Henderson, Benny Carter, Don Redman, Chick Webb, Jimmy Lunceford, Andy Kirk, Benny Moten are complete on the Classics series. Lunceford, Moten (under the name of Count Basie), and others are on Masters of Jazz as well, with alternate takes added.

Benny Goodman's Bluebird recordings on RCA series. The 1938 Carnegie Hall concert on Columbia Jazz Masterpieces G2K-40244. The 1958 "World Is Waiting for the Sunrise" on Columbia P 13502. "Moonglow" and "Vibraphone Blues," on *After You've Gone, Volume 1*, RCA 5631-2-RB. The Goodman recordings with Charlie Christian on *The Benny Goodman Sextet*, Columbia CK 45144, and on *Charlie Christian: The Genius of the Electric Guitar*, Columbia CK 40846. "Ad-Lib Blues" was on Jazz Archives 42.* "Clarinet a la King" is the title piece of Columbia 40834. Goodman bop recordings on *Benny Goodman/Charlie Barnet: Bebop Spoken Here*, Capitol 052-80854.

Roy Eldridge recordings with Gene Krupa on *Uptown*, Columbia CK 45448. Tommy Dorsey with Frank Sinatra on RCA CD's. Artie Shaw's Bluebird recordings complete from 1938 through 1945 on RCA Bluebird cassettes.

CHAPTER 10. COUNT BASIE

All Moten recordings on Classics series and Masters of Jazz series (the latter with alternate takes). All Basie recordings 1936 through 1940 on four Classics CD's. *April in Paris*, Verve 825575-2. *Atomic Basie*, with "Lil' Darlin'," on Vogue VG-600008. Later sessions with Oscar Peterson, Zoot Sims, available on Pablo CD's.

CHAPTER 11. THE SMALL BANDS AND VIRTUOSO SOLOISTS OF THE THIRTIES

Chocolate Dandies recordings with Benny Carter and Coleman Hawkins, including "Bugle Call Rag" and "Dee Blues," on *Benny Carter and His Orchestra, 1929-1933*, Classics 522.

The Billy Banks recordings on Classics series of Henry "Red" Allen. Eddie Condon, "Pretty Doll" with Fats Waller on Jazz Archives JA-1.* Fats Waller on *The Complete Fats Waller*, an RCA Bluebird series.

Joe Turner with Art Tatum on *I've Been to Kansas City*, Decca/MCA MCAD-42351. Art Tatum, private recordings from 1955, on *20th-Century Piano Genius*, Emarcy 826129-1. Early recordings including "Tiger Rag" on Classics 507 and 560. *Art Tatum: The Complete Pablo Solo Masterpieces*, Pablo 7PACD-4404-2. *Art Tatum: The Complete Pablo Group Masterpieces*, Pablo 6PACD-4401-1 (as with most sets, also available on separate CD's).

Roy Eldridge, "After You've Gone," 1937 on *After You've Gone*, GRP Decca GRD-605. "I Surrender Dear" with Eldridge and Hawkins on *Complete Commodore Jazz Recordings*, Mosaic, and on the Hawkins series on Classics. Reinhardt recordings on seven volumes of *Djangologie/USA*, Swing label. "Tiger Rag," on *Django Reinhardt: First Recordings*, Prestige P-7614. Coleman Hawkins, *Body and Soul*, RCA 5717-2-RB. Hawkins complete from 1929 through 1940 on four Classics CD's.

Lester Young 1936 performances on Count Basie series, Classics 503. "After Theatre Jump," on *The Complete Lester Young on Keynote*, Mercury 830920-2. "D.B. Blues" and "These Foolish Things," on *The Aladdin Sessions*, Blue Note LA456-H2.* Recordings with Teddy Wilson 1956 on *Pres and Teddy*, Verve 831270-2.

Billie Holiday recordings of 1930s on *The Quintessential Billie Holiday*, a series of Columbia CD's. "Strange Fruit," on *Lady Day 1939–1944: The Sixteen Original Commodore Interpretations*, Commodore CCD 7001.

CHAPTER 12. THE SCENE CHANGES: THE FORTIES AND BEBOP

Pee Wee Russell's Commodore recordings on *The Complete Commodore Jazz Recordings*, Mosaic.

Coleman Hawkins, "Disorder at the Border" and "Woody 'n' You" and Gillespie titles cited with Calloway, Millinder, Raeburn, and others on *Dizzy Gillespie: The Development of an American Artist, 1940–1946*, Smithsonian P213455.

Charlie Christian at Minton's Playhouse, with "Stompin' at the Savoy," on Jazz Anthology 550012.

Billy Eckstine with Earl Hines on the Classics series of Hines, CC 567. The Eckstine Orchestra's recordings on *Mister B. and the Band*, Savoy SJL 2214 (partially issued on CD, Savoy ZDS 4401) and *Billy Eckstine Sings*, Savoy SJL 1127.

Mary Lou Williams, "Zodiac Suite," Folkways 32844. Chamber orchestra version on Vintage Jazz Classics VJC-1035.

Cootie Williams band with Bud Powell on Phoenix LP-1.* Bud Powell, "Cherokee," and others on *Jazz Giant*, Verve 829937-2. "Un Poco Loco" and others, including Navarro and Rollins, on *The Amazing Bud Powell*, Volumes One and Two, Blue Note CDP-7-81503 and 81504. Dexter Gordon with Bud Powell, *Our Man in Paris*, Blue Note CDP-7-46394.

Thelonious Monk's Blue Note recordings on *Thelonious Monk: The Genius of Modern Music*, Volumes One and Two, Blue Note CDP-7-81510 and 81511. *The Complete Riverside Recordings* of Monk on Riverside RCD 022-2, and many available separately. Monk's Prestige recordings on Fantasy/OJC CD-010-2 and 016-2. *Underground* is Columbia CK-40785.

Dizzy Gillespie with Parker on "Shaw 'Nuff," "Hot House," "Salt Peanuts," "Lover Man" with Vaughan, also the Gillespie big band on *Shaw 'Nuff*, Musicraft MVSCD-53. "Manteca," "Good Bait," "Cubano Be, Cubano Bop," on *Dizziest*, RCA Bluebird 5785-1-RB.

Woody Herman, "Down Under," on *Golden Favorites*, MCAD-31277. "Four Brothers," on *The Thundering Herds 1945-7*, Columbia CK 44108. Stan Kenton, *The Complete Capitol Recordings of the Holman and Russo Charts*, Mosaic Records 136. Bob Graettinger's "City of Glass" on Creative World ST 1006. "Malaguena" and "Dark Eyes," on Creative World ST 1041; "Elegy for Alto," "Monotony," and "This is My Theme," on Creative World ST 1037.

Wardell Gray, "Easy Living" and "Twisted" on *The Wardell Gray Memorial*, Volume One, Fantasy/OJC 050. Gray with Dexter Gordon on *The Hunt*, Savoy SJL-2222. "The Chase" with Gray and Gordon on *Dexter: The Dial Sessions*, Storyville SLP 814. Annie Ross's "Twisted" on Fantasy/OJC CD-217-2.

Fats Navarro with Dameron, Powell, Rollins, and others on *The Fabulous Fats Navarro*, Volumes One and Two, Blue Note CDP-7-81531 and 81532. Tadd Dameron, "Dameron Stomp," on *Harlan Leonard and His Rockets*, RCA LPV-531.* "Fontainebleau" is the title piece of Fantasy/OJC 055.

"Hot House" featuring John LaPorta with Parker and Gillespie was on *Charlie Parker, Lullaby in Rhythm*, Spotlite 107. Some J.J. Johnson early recordings on *Mad Bebop*, Savoy Jazz 2232. "Moritat" ("Mack the Knife") by André Previn with J.J. Johnson on Columbia CS-8541.*

Chapter 13. Charlie Parker

Parker with the Jay McShann band is on cassette MCA 1338, and will be on CD as well. Wichita transcriptions and the 1942 "Cherokee" on *Charlie Parker: First Recordings!*, Onyx 221.* "Cheryl," on *Charlie Parker and the Stars of Modern Jazz at Carnegie Hall, Christmas, 1949*, Jass J-CD-16, along with Tristano, Bud Powell and others. The live version of "Dance of the Infidels" is the title cut of Blue Parrot AR 701. "Lover Man" with Sarah Vaughan is on Gillespie *Shaw 'Nuff* cited above. *Charlie Parker, The Complete Savoy Studio Ses-*sions on Savoy ZDS 5500. *The Legendary Dial Masters*, Stash ST-CD-23 and Stash ST-CD-25. *The Complete Charlie Parker on Verve*, Verve 837142-2. *The Complete Benedetti Charlie Parker*, Mosaic 129. Rockland Palace recordings, including "Lester Leaps In" and "The Rocker," on *Bop City*, Audiofidelity AFE-3-7. The 1950 sessions from Birdland on *One Night in Birdland*, Columbia JG 34808.* The 1953 Massey Hall concert on Fantasy/OJC CD-044-2. For vocal versions of "Parker's Mood," see Chapter 23.

Chapter 14. The Fifties: Cool and Third Stream

Gerry Mulligan Quartet with Chet Baker, including "My Funny Valentine," on *The Best of the Gerry Mulligan Quartet with Chet Baker*, Pacific Jazz C27-95481-2, and on *The Complete Pacific Jazz and Capitol Recordings of the Original Gerry Mulligan Quartet and Tentette with Chet Baker*, Mosaic MR 5-102. Mulligan's early arrangements, including "Disc Jockey Jump" for Gene Krupa, on *Gerry Mulligan: The Arranger*, Columbia JC 34803.*

Claude Thornhill's recordings of Gil Evans arrangements on *Claude Thornhill: Tapestries*, Affinity AFSD 1040.

Miles Davis: Birth of the Cool, Blue Note CDP7-9286-2.

Modern Jazz Quartet early recordings on *Concorde*, Fantasy/OJC 002, and *Django*, Fantasy/OJC 057-2, and *The Modern Jazz Quartet*, Prestige 24005. "It Don't Mean a Thing," on *Pyramid*, Atlantic 1325-2.

Lennie Tristano's Capitol records, including "Crosscurrent," "Intuition," and "Digression," on *Crosscurrents*, Capitol Records M-11060.* "Requiem," "Turkish Mambo," "C Minor Complex," on *Requiem*, Atlantic 2SDX-7003. Lee Konitz's *Inside Hi-Fi* is Atlantic 90669-2 and *The Lee Konitz Duets* is Fantasy/OJC CD-466-2.

Art Pepper with Kenton on "Harlem Holiday," Creative World ST1078. Pepper with Shorty Rogers on "Over the Rainbow" on *The Complete Atlantic and EMI Jazz Recordings of Shorty Rogers,* Mosaic 125. *Art Pepper with Warne Marsh* is Contemporary VDJ-1577. "Patricia," on *Today,* Fantasy/OJC CD-474-2.

"Early Autumn" on *Woody Herman: Keeper of the Flame,* Capitol CAP-98453, "Parker 51" and others on *Stan Getz at Storyville,* Volumes 1 and 2, Roulette CDP-7-94507. Dave Brubeck octet on Fantasy/OJC CD-101-2. *Time Out* is Columbia CK 40585. Paul Desmond with Gerry Mulligan on *Two of a Mind,* RCA 9654-2-RB. *The Complete Recordings of the Paul Desmond Quartet with Jim Hall,* Mosaic 120. The 1975 recordings of Brubeck and Desmond are *The Duets,* A&M CD3290.

George Russell's "Concerto for Billy the Kid," Gunther Schuller's "Transformations," and Mingus's "Eclipse" on *Mirage: Avant-Garde and Third-Stream Jazz,* New World Records 216. "Concerto for Billy the Kid" also on *The George Russell Smalltet,* RCA 6467-2-RB. Mingus's "Revelations," Harold Shapero's "On Green Mountain," Russell's "All About Rosie," and J.J. Johnson's "Poem for Brass" on *Jazz Compositions,* Columbia PC 37012.*

CHAPTER 15. MAINSTREAM, HARD BOP, AND BEYOND

Clifford Brown-Max Roach on *The Complete EmArcy Recordings of Clifford Brown,* EmArcy 83806-2. Brown's West Coast session with Zoot Sims is *The Immortal Clifford Brown,* Pacific Jazz CDP-7-46850. His Blue Note recordings on *Memorial Album,* Blue Note CDP-7-81526. *The Complete Blue Note and Pacific Jazz Recordings of Clifford Brown* also on Mosaic M5-104. The Paris recordings on Fantasy/OJC 017-2, OJC 357-2, OJC 358-2 and OJC-359-2.

Sonny Rollins's *Freedom Suite* is Fantasy/OJC-067. His earliest Prestige sessions are on *Vintage Sessions,* Prestige 24096. "I'm an Old Cowhand" on *Way Out West,* Fantasy/OJC 337-2 (also on Contemporary with alternate takes added). "Pent-Up House" with Brown and Roach on *Sonny Rollins Plus Four,* OJC 243-2. "Blue Seven" and "St. Thomas" on *Saxophone Colossus,* OJC 291-2. *What's New* was RCA Victor LSP-2572*; four of its six numbers have been reissued on *The Quartets Featuring Jim Hall,* Bluebird 5634-2, as well as titles from *The Bridge.* The session with Coleman Hawkins is now *All the Things You Are,* Bluebird 2179-2. The group with Don Cherry, *On the Outside,* Bluebird 2496-2. *Alfie* is MCA/Impulse MCAD-39107.

Max Roach's *Deeds Not Words* with "Conversation" is Fantasy/OJC 304-2. *We Insist! Freedom Now Suite* on Candid CCD-79002. *Percussion Bitter Sweet* was Impulse AS-8.*

Art Blakey's *Hard Bop* on Odyssey PC-36809. *Moanin'* is Blue Note CDP-7-46516. A version of "Lester Left Town" on *Africaine,* Blue Note LT-1088. The band with Clifford Brown on the two volumes of *A Night at Birdland,* Blue Note 46519 and 46520. *Orgy in Rhythm* was Blue Note 1554*; *Holiday for Skins* was Blue Note 40048*; *The African Beat* was Blue Note 4097.*

Horace Silver's "Doodlin'" on *Horace Silver and the Jazz Messengers,* Blue Note 46140. *Six Pieces of Silver,* Blue Note 81539, has "Senor Blues." *Blowin' the Blues Away,* with the title cut and "Sister Sadie," Blue Note 46526. *Song for My Father* is Blue Note B2-84185. "Filthy McNasty" on *Doin' the Thing,* Blue Note B2-84076. *Serenade to a Soul Sister* on Blue Note B2-84277. *Cape Verdean Blues* is Blue Note 84220.

Charles Mingus's "Gregarian Chant" on *Jazz Workshop,* Savoy SJL 1113. "Mingus Fingers" is on *Mirage,* cited above. *Let My Children Hear Music* is Columbia CK 48910. "Pithecanthropus

Erectus" is the title cut of Atlantic 8809-2. *The Complete Candid Recordings of Charles Mingus,* with Dolphy, on Mosaic MR4–111. *The Black Saint and the Sinner Lady* on MCA/Impulse 5649. *Three or Four Shades of Blue* is Atlantic 1700-2. *Epitaph* conducted by Gunther Schuller on Columbia C2K 4528. Dolphy's "God Bless the Child" on *In Europe, Vol. 1,* Fantasy/OJC CD-413-2.

Erroll Garner's *Concert By the Sea* is Columbia CK 40589. *Oscar Peterson Plays the Cole Porter Song Book* is Verve 82197-2. "Theodora," on *The Billy Taylor Trio at Town Hall,* Prestige 194*. A superb album recorded in 1988 and 1989, *Ramsey Lewis and Billy Taylor: We Meet Again,* is CBS MK-44941.

CHAPTER 16. MILES DAVIS

The Paris session with Tadd Dameron was on *The Miles Davis/Tadd Dameron Quintet in Paris Festival International de Jazz,* Columbia 34804.* All of the Miles Davis Prestige material is on *Chronicle,* Prestige PCD-012-2. Davis's Columbia recordings are on CD. For example, "My Funny Valentine" from 1958 is on *'58 Miles,* Columbia CK 47835. The 1964 "Valentine" is on *My Funny Valentine,* Columbia PCT 09106, and on *The Complete Concert 1964,* Columbia/Legacy C2K 48821. Davis with Gil Evans on *Miles Ahead,* Columbia CK 40784; *Sketches of Spain,* Columbia CK 40578; and *Porgy and Bess,* Columbia CK 40647. *Kind of Blue* is Columbia CK 40579. *Someday My Prince Will Come* is Columbia CK 46863. *ESP* is Columbia CK 46863. *Nefertiti* is Columbia CK 46113. *Miles Smiles* is Columbia CK PCT 09401. *Miles in the Sky* is Columbia PCT 09628. *In a Silent Way* is Columbia CK 40580. *Bitches Brew* is Columbia CK 40577. *Star People* is Columbia C 38657. *Siesta* is Warner Brothers 25655-2.

CHAPTER 17. JOHN COLTRANE

For John Coltrane with Miles Davis see the Davis listings above. The other

Prestige recordings on *John Coltrane: The Prestige Recordings,* Prestige 16PCD-4405-2. Coltrane with Monk on Fantasy/OJC CD-039-2. Coltrane with Ellington on Impulse MCAD-39103. *Blue Train* is Blue Note CDP7-46095-2. *Giant Steps* is Atlantic 1311-2. *The Avant Garde,* Atlantic 7 90041-2. *My Favorite Things,* Atlantic 1361-2. *Impressions,* MCA/Impulse MCAD-5887. *Africa/Brass,* MCA/Impulse MCAD-42001. *A Love Supreme,* MCA/Impulse MCAD 5660. Both takes of "Ascension" on *The Major Works of John Coltrane,* Impulse GRD 2-113. *Live in Seattle,* Impulse AS 9202-2. *Meditations,* MCA/Impulse MCAD 39139. *Interstellar Space,* Impulse GRD-110. *Expression* was Impulse A-9120.*

McCoy Tyner's "Inception" is the title tune of MCA/Impulse MCAD-42000 and is also on MCAC-42233.

Pharoah Sanders's *Karma* is MCA/Impulse MCAD-39122.

CHAPTER 18. ORNETTE COLEMAN

Something Else!, Fantasy/OJC CD-163-2. *Tomorrow is the Question: The New Music of Ornette Coleman,* Fantasy/OJC CD-342-2. "Lonely Woman" and "Congeniality" on *The Shape of Jazz to Come,* Atlantic 1317-2. "Una Muy Bonita" and "Ramblin'," on *Change of the Century,* Atlantic 81341-2. *Free Jazz* is Atlantic 81341-2. *Ornette on Tenor* is Atlantic 1394-4. *The Art of the Improvisers* is Atlantic 90978-2. The trio with David Izenson and Charles Moffett on Blue Note BN 84224 and 84225. "We Now Interrupt for a Commercial," on *New York is Now,* Blue Note B2-84287. *The Empty Foxhole* was Blue Note BLP 84246.* The 1962 Town Hall concert was on ESP 1006* and will be out on CD. *Friends and Neighbors* was Flying Dutchman FDS-123.* *Skies of America* was Columbia KC31562. *Science Fiction* was Columbia KC31061. *Of Human Feelings* is Antilles ANCD 2001. "Latin Genetics" is on *In All Languages,* Caravan of Dreams CDP85008.

CHAPTER 19. BILL EVANS AND
MODERN JAZZ PIANO

Wes Montgomery, *The Incredible Jazz Guitar*, Fantasy/OJC CD–036–2.

Bill Evans, *The Complete Riverside Recordings*, Riverside RCD 018–2. Evans, *The Complete Fantasy Recordings* (from 1973 through 1979), Fantasy 9FCD–1012–2. Separately, *New Jazz Conceptions* is Fantasy/OJC CD–025–2; *Everybody Digs Bill Evans*, with "Peace Piece," is Fantasy/OJC CD–210–2; *Sunday at the Village Vanguard*, with "Solar" and "Jade Visions," is Fantasy/OJC CD–140–2. "Waltz for Debby" is the title track of Fantasy/OJC CD–210–2. Evans's duets with Jim Hall are on *Intermodulation*, Verve 833771–2. *Conversations with Myself* is Verve 821 984–2; *Bill Evans at the Montreux Jazz Festival* is Verve 827844–2. The anthology Bill Evans Verve 831 366–2 has "Love Theme from Spartacus," "My Foolish Heart" and "I Loves You, Porgy." (For George Russell, see Chapter 14 above.)

Paul Bley plays Ornette Coleman on *The Fabulous Paul Bley Quintet*, America 30AM6120*, and *Coleman Classics Volume One*, IAI 37–38–60.* Bley's *Japan Suite* is Improvising Artists AI 37–38–49. "Ida Lupino" is on *Open, To Love*, ECM 1023.

Herbie Hancock playing "Pentacostal Feeling" on Donald Byrd's *Free Form*, Blue Note B2–84118. Hancock's "Watermelon Man" on *Takin' Off*, Blue Note CDP–7–46506–2. "Blindman, Blindman," on *My Point of View*, Blue Note B2–84126. *Inventions and Dimensions* is Blue Note B2–84147. *Maiden Voyage* is Blue Note B2–46339. Hancock with Miles Davis on "My Funny Valentine" on *Miles in Tokyo*, CBS Sony CSCS 5146. "Autumn Leaves," on *Miles in Berlin*, CBS Sony CSCS 5147. "So What," on Davis's *Four and More*, CBS Sony CSCS 5145. Wayne Shorter's *Etcetera* was Blue Note LT 1056.*

Chick Corea is heard with Mongo Santamaria on "Go Mongo" on *Skins*, MCD 47038–2. First version of "Tones for Joan's Bones" on Blue Mitchell's *Boss Horn*, Blue Note 84257; later version on Corea's *Inner Space*, Atlantic 305–2. Herbie Mann's *Standing Ovation at Newport* was Atlantic 1445.* Corea's *Now He Sings, Now He Sobs* is Blue Note B2–90055. *Song of Singing* is Blue Note B2–84353. *Piano Improvisations* are ECM 811979–2 and ECM 829190–2. Corea with Circle on *Paris Concert*, ECM 1018/19 843163–2.

Keith Jarrett on Art Blakey's *Buttercorn Lady*, EmArcy 822471–2. "Forest Flower" was the title cut of Charles Lloyd's album Atlantic SD 1473*, and the later version was on *Soundtrack*, Atlantic SD 1519.* "My Back Pages" on Jarrett's *Somewhere Before*, Atlantic 8808–2. The Bremen concert is on *Solo Concerts*, ECM 827747–2. Most of *Koln Concert* on ECM 1064–2. *Mysteries* is MCA/Impulse 33113.

Abdullah Ibrahim, then known as Dollar Brand, was heard with Elvin Jones on *Midnight Walk*, Atlantic SD 1485. His "Soweto is Where It's At" is on Tintiyana 1975, Kaz CD 103. *Water From an Ancient Well* was Blackhawk BKH 50207–1.

CHAPTER 20. THE SIXTIES: BIG
BANDS, BOSSA NOVA, AND SOUL

Oliver Nelson's *Black, Brown and Beautiful* is RCA Bluebird 6993–2–RB. "Stolen Moments," on *Blues and the Abstract Truth*, MCA/Impulse MCAD–5659. Wes Montgomery's *Goin' Out of My Head*, Verve 825676–2. Gary McFarland's *America the Beautiful: An Account of its Disappearance* is DCC Jazz DJZ–615.

King Curtis's "Memphis Soul Stew" and Arnett Cobb's "Flying Home Mambo" on *Atlantic Honkers*, Atlantic 7–81666. Hal Singer's "Cornbread" and Paul Williams's "The Hucklebuck" on *The*

Roots of Rock 'n Roll, Savoy SJL 2221. "Ain't Nobody Here But Us Chickens" on *The Best of Louis Jordan*, MCA 4079-2.

Quincy Jones's *The Quintessence* is MCA/Impulse 5728. *The Great Wide World of Quincy Jones* is Mercury 822613-2. *This is How I Feel About Jazz* was ABC 149.* *Quincy Plays for Pussycats* was Mercury SR 61050.* *The Genius of Ray Charles*, Atlantic 1312-2. *Walking in Space* is A&M CD 0801. *Back on the Block* is Warner Brothers 9 26020-2. *Listen Up: The Lives of Quincy Jones* is QWest/Reprise 9-26322-2.

Presenting Thad Jones/Mel Lewis and The Jazz Orchestra was Solid State 18003*. *Live at the Village Vanguard* was Solid State 18016*. "Central Park North" was on Solid State 18058*. *Consummation*, with "A Child is Born," was Blue Note BST 84346*. *Suite for Pops* was A&M Horizon SP-701*. *New Life* has been reissued as A&M 75021.

Toshiko Akiyoshi-Lew Tabackin Big Band's *Kogun* was RCA AF1-6246*. "Minimata" was part of *Insights*, RCA AFL1-2678*. A selection is on Novus 3106-2-N.

Laurindo Almeida's *Brazilliance, Volume 1*, featuring Bud Shank, is World Pacific Jazz CDP-7-96339. Stan Getz, *The Bossa Nova Years*, Verve 4-823611-2, contains all his best known works in that idiom. Separately, Getz's *Jazz Samba* is Verve 810061-2; *Big Band Bossa Nova* is Verve 825771-2; *Getz/Gilberto* is Verve 810048-2.

Dizzy Gillespie recorded "Desafinado" on Philips PHM200-048. Cannonball Adderley's *Cannonball's Bossa Nova* is Landmark LCD-1302-2. Coleman Hawkins's "Desafinado" is on MCA/Impulse MCAD-33118. Ellington's *Afro-Bossa* is now Discovery 871. Paul Desmond's bossa nova recordings including *Bossa Antigua* are in *The Complete Recordings of The Paul Desmond Quartet with Jim Hall*, Mosaic 120.

Sarah Vaughan's *I Love Brazil* is Pablo 2312-101. Ella Fitzgerald's *Ella Abraca Jobim* is Pablo PACD 2630-201-2. Wayne Shorter's *Native Dancer* is Columbia CK 46159.

Much of Ray Charles's blues and r & b is on *Ray Charles: The Birth of Soul*, Atlantic 7 82310-2. Hank Mobley's *Workout* is Blue Note B2-84080. Lee Morgan's *The Sidewinder* is Blue Note CDP-7-84157. Freddie Hubbard's *Red Clay* is Columbia ZK 40809. Art Blakey's *Moanin'* is Blue Note B2-46516.

Cannonball Adderley's "This Here" is on *Live in San Francisco*, Fantasy/OJC CD-035-2. "Work Song" is on *Them Dirty Blues*, Landmark LCD 1301-2. "Sack o' Woe" is on *Quintet at the Lighthouse*, LCD 1305-2. *Mercy, Mercy, Mercy* is Capitol 4N-16153.

Bobby Timmons's *This Here* is Fantasy/OJC 104; his *In Person* is Fantasy/OJC 364. Ray Bryant's "Little Susie" was Columbia JCS 8244*. Ben Webster with Johnny Otis, including "Oopy Doo," is on *The Complete Ben Webster on EmArcy*, EmArcy 824836-1. Jimmy Forrest's *Night Train* is Delmark DD 435.

Many of the Jimmy Smith items mentioned are collected on *Jimmy Smith*, Verve 831374-2. *The Sermon* is Blue Note CDP 7-46097-2. *Back at the Chicken Shack* is Blue Note CDP 7-46402-2. Shirley Scott's *For Members Only* is MCA/Impulse MCAD-33115.

Larry Young is heard with Jimmy Forrest on *Forrest Fire!*, Fantasy/OJC 199. *The Complete Blue Note Recordings of Larry Young* are in Mosaic 137.

Chapter 21. Fusion

Many of the James Brown items mentioned are collected on *Star Time*, Polydor 849109-2.

"Larry of Arabia," on Chico Hamilton's *The Dealer*, MCA/Impulse MCAD-

39137. Tony Williams's *Emergency* is Polygram 849068-2; an anthology of Lifetime's recordings was *Once in a Lifetime*, Verve 2-2541. John McLaughlin's *My Goal's Beyond* is Rykodisc RCD 10051; *Birds of Fire* is Columbia PCT 31996; *The Inner Mounting Flame* is Columbia CK 31067.

Herbie Hancock's *Mwandishi* was Warner Brothers WS-1898*; *Headhunters* is Columbia CK 32731. His score to *Death Wish* was Columbia PC 33199*. *Mr. Hands* is Columbia PCT 36578, and *Thrust* is Columbia PCT 32965.

Chick Corea's *Return to Forever* is ECM 811978-2; *Where Have I Known You Before* is Polydor 825206-2; *The Mad Hatter* was Polydor 0798*.

"Orange Lady" was on *Weather Report*, Columbia C 30661*. "Birdland" is on *Heavy Weather*, Columbia CK 47481. *Night Passage* is Columbia CK 36793.

Pat Metheny is on Gary Burton's *Dreams So Real*, ECM 833329-2. Metheny with Paul Bley and Jaco Pastorious was on IAI 373846*. Metheny's *Bright Size Life* is ECM 827133-2. *Watercolors* is ECM 827409-2. *American Garage* is ECM 827134-2. *80/81* is ECM 843169-2. *Song X* is Geffen 24096-2.

James "Blood" Ulmer's *Are You Glad to Be in America?* was Artists House 13*. *Black Rock* was Columbia ARC 38285. Ronald Shannon Jackson's *Eye on You* is About Time AT-1003. Jamaaladeen Tacuma's *Renaissance Man* is Gramavision R21K-79438.

CHAPTER 22. THE AVANT-GARDE.

Grachan Moncur's "Space Spy" was on New Africa BYG 529321*. Roscoe Mitchell's *Nonaah* is Nessa 9/10. The New York Art Quartet's record with Amiri Baraka was ESP-1004* and will be on CD. Clifford Thornton's *Freedom and Unity* was Third World LP 9636*.

Sun Ra's *Supersonic Jazz* has been reissued on Evidence ECD 22015-2. His *Sound of Joy* is Delmark DS-413. *The Futuristic Sounds of Sun Ra* was reissued as BYG 529111. The ESP recordings include *The Heliocentric Worlds of Sun Ra*, ESP 1014, and *Nothing Is*, ESP 1045, both due out on CD. *Cosmic Tones for Mental Therapy* was Saturn 408. *The Magic City* was reissued as Impulse AS 9243*. "Watusi, Egyptian March" is on *It's After the End of the World*, BASF 20748.

Cecil Taylor's *Jazz Advance* is Blue Note CDP7-84462-2. His Newport performance was on *Masters of the Modern Piano*, Verve VE 2-2514*. The complete Candid recordings are Mosaic 127. Under Gil Evans's name, *Into the Hot* is now Impulse MCAD 39104. Taylor's *Unit Structures* is Blue Note 84237-2 and *Conquistador* is Blue Note 84260-2. *Indent* was Unit Core 3055.

My Name is Albert Ayler was Debut 140. *Spiritual Unity* was ESP 1002 and *New York Eye and Ear Control* was ESP 1016, both due out on CD. *Love Cry* has been reissued as GRP/Impulse 108 and *Live in Greenwich Village* as GRP/Impulse 39123. *Vibrations*, originally on Debut, was Arista AL1001.

The New York Contemporary Quintet's *Consequences* was Fontana 881013. Don Cherry's *Complete Communion* was Blue Note 84226*, his *Symphony for Improvisers* was Blue Note 84247*, and *Where is Brooklyn?* was Blue Note 84311*. The two parts of *Mu* were BYG 529301* and 529331*. Codona's three records were ECM 829371, 833332, and 827400.

The Archie Shepp-Bill Dixon Quartet was Savoy MG 12178*. Shepp's *Fire Music* is MCA/Impulse MCAD-39121. *Four for Trane* was Impulse A-71*. *The Magic of Ju-Ju* was Impulse A-9154*. *Mama Too Tight* was Impulse A-9134*. The duets with Horace Parlan are *Goin' Home*, Steeplechase SCCD-31079. *Duet: Archie Shepp and Dollar Brand*, Nippon Columbia YX-7532.

Joseph Jarman's *As If It Were the Seasons* is Delmark DS-417. Roscoe Mitchell's *Sound* is Delmark DS-408. "Cards," on *The Roscoe Mitchell Quartet*, Sackville 2009. The Art Ensemble of Chicago's *Numbers* was Nessa 1*, their "Tutankhamen" was on Nessa 2*. *Message to Our Folks* was BYG 529328*. *People in Sorrow* is Nessa 3*. The Art Ensemble's *Nice Guys* is ECM 827876-2. *Full Force*, with "Charlie M.," is ECM 829197. *Urban Bushmen* is ECM 2-1211.

Anthony Braxton's *For Alto* is Delmark DS-420/1. *Three Compositions of New Jazz*, Delmark DS-415. *Creative Orchestra Music*, Bluebird 6579-2. *New York, 1974* was Arista 4032*. Live performances with Marilyn Crispell are on *Duets*, Music and Arts CD 611. *For Trio* was Arista AB-4181*.

Richard Abrams's *Young at Heart, Wise in Time* is Delmark DS-423. *Air Lore* with Air is now Bluebird 6578-2. The World Saxophone Quartet's "Hattie Wall" is heard on *Live in Zurich*, Black Saint 0077. *Steppin'* is Black Saint 0027.

The Jazz Composers Orchestra's *Communications* has been reissued as ECM 841124-2. Carla Bley's *Escalator Over the Hill* is ECM/Watt 839310-2. Gary Burton's *A Genuine Tong Funeral: Dark Opera Without Words* was RCA Victor LSP-3988*. Charlie Haden's *Liberation Music Orchestra* is MCA/Impulse MCAD-39125.

The Willem Breuker Kollektief's "American in Paris" is on BVHAAST CD 8802. *Bob's Gallery* is BVHAAST 070. BNHAAST 050 has "Creole Love Call" and "Benares" from *Mahagonny*. The Vienna Art Orchestra's *The Minimalism of Erik Satie* is Hat ART 2005.

Chapter 23. Jazz Singing Since the Thirties.

The complete Ella Fitzgerald with Chick Webb is on five discs in the Classics series, but these may be withdrawn for contractual reasons. A selection of her early work with Webb, including some sides with Benny Goodman, and the Mills Brothers, is *Ella Fitzgerald, ASV Living Era* AJD 055R. Her work with the Jazz at the Philharmonic is found on *JATP/Ella Fitzgerald*, Verve 815147-1, and on *Lady Be Good*, Verve 825098-1. A selection of Fitzgerald's Songbooks is found on *The Songbooks*, Verve 823445-2. Separately, *The Gershwin Songbook* is Verve 821024-2. *Ella Fitzgerald Sings the Duke Ellington Songbook* is Verve 837035-2. *Let No Man Write My Epitaph* was Verve MGV 4043*. The duets with Joe Pass include *Take Love Easy*, Pablo 2310-702, *Fitzgerald and Pass Again*, Pablo 2310-772, and *Easy Living*, Pablo 2310-938.

Musicraft's early Sarah Vaughan recordings include *The Divine Sarah*, MVS 504, *The Man I Love*, MVS 2002, and *Lover Man*, MVS 2006. *The Divine Sarah Vaughan: The Columbia Years 1949-53*, Columbia C2K 44165 has "Mean to Me" and other recordings with Miles Davis. *The Complete Sarah Vaughan on Mercury* is a series of boxed sets. *Live in Japan, Volume One* is Mainstream 701 and *Volume Two* is Mainstream 702. "Frasier" was on Mainstream 404, *Sarah Vaughan and the Jimmy Rowles Quintet*.

"Why Don't You Do Right?" on *Peggy Lee: Collector's Series*, Capitol CDP 7-93195-2.

Dinah Washington's complete works for Mercury Records includes four sets of three CD's each. Some of the Roulette recordings are on *The Best of Dinah Washington*, Roulette 59031.

Carmen McRae's "Just One of Those Things" on *Here to Stay*, Decca GRD 610. *The Finest of Carmen McRae*, Bethlehem BCP 6004. *Carmen McRae Sings Lover Man and Other Billie Holiday Classics* was Columbia Records CS 8530* and is due out on CD. *The Great American Songbook* is Atlantic SD 2-904. *At the Great American Music Hall* is Blue Note 709-H2.

Anita O'Day is heard on Roy Eldridge with Gene Krupa, *Uptown,* Columbia CK 45448. Her *Cool Heat* was reissued as Polygram UNV 2679. Among her late recordings is *Mello'day,* GNP 2126. Chris Connor's singing of Russo arrangements with Kenton is on Mosaic 136. She sings "Lonely Woman" on *Free Spirits,* Atlantic 8061* and "Where Flamingos Fly" on Atlantic 8046*, *A Portrait of Chris. The Complete Helen Merrill on Mercury* is on Mercury 4–826340-2. Merrill's rerecording with Gil Evans is *Collaboration,* EmArcy 834205-1. Helen Merrill/John Lewis Mercury SRM-1-1150.

Shirley Horn's *Loads of Love* and *Horn with Horns* have been reissued on Mercury 843454-2. *A Lazy Afternoon* is Steeplechase SCCD 31111. *You Won't Forget Me* is Verve 847482-2.

Betty Carter on *Lionel Hampton and His Orchestra,* Alamac QSR 2419. Betty Carter's "I Can't Help It" was on *What a Little Moonlight Can Do,* ABC Impulse ASD 9321*. *Finally* is Roulette CDP-7-95333. One of her versions of "Body and Soul" on *Betty Carter,* Bet-Car MK1001. "'Round Midnight" is the title cut of Atlantic 80453-2. Her duets with Ray Charles are DCC Compact Classics DZS-039.

Sheila Jordan's "You Are My Sunshine," on George Russell, *Outer Thoughts,* Milestone M–47027. *Portrait of Sheila* is Blue Note CDP-7-89002. *Sheila* is Steeplechase SCS-1081. *The Crossing,* Blackhawk BKH-50501-1.

Abbey Lincoln's *That's Him* is now Fantasy/OJC CD-085-2. *People in Me* was Inner City 6040. *Abbey Sings Billie,* Enja R2 79633.

Jeanne Lee with Ran Blake, *The Legendary Duets,* Bluebird 6461-2. Sunny Murray's *Homage to Africa* was BYG 529303*, and Archie Shepp's *Blasé* was BYG 529318. Lee's *Conspiracy* was on Earthforms Records, unnumbered. *Companion,* by the Jeanne Lee, Gunter

Hampel and Thomas Keyserling Trio, was Birth Records 0036.

Ursala Dudziak's *Newborn Light* was Columbia CK 32902*. Cassandra Wilson sang on *New Air,* Black Saint BSR 0099. Her *Blue Skies* is JMT 834419-2 and *Days Aweigh* is JMT 834412-2.

Jimmy Rushing is heard on Count Basie, Classics 513. Joe Turner's "Shake, Rattle and Roll" is the title cut of New World Records 249. Pha Terrell with the Andy Kirk band on Classics 573. Earl Coleman's "Dark Shadows" is reissued as part of the Charlie Parker Dial masters listed above.

Count Basie Swings, Joe Williams Sings was reissued as Verve 825770, and some of its numbers are on *Count Basie and Joe Williams,* Verve 835329-2. Williams sang "She Doesn't Know I Love Her" on *Jump for Joy,* RCA Victor LSP-2713*. Some of his RCA recordings have been collected on *The Overwhelming Joe Williams,* Bluebird 6464-2-RB. A performance of "Goin' to Chicago" and "Roll 'em Pete" is on *A Swingin' Night at Birdland,* Roulette CDP 7-95335-2. *Presenting Joe Williams and Thad Jones/Mel Lewis* was Solid State 18008.

John Coltrane and Johnny Hartman is MCA/Impulse MCAD-5656. Some of Nat Cole's ballads on *The Very Thought of You,* Capitol C21Y-97769. His "Straighten Up and Fly Right" is on *Hit That Jive, Jack,* Decca Jazz MCAD-42350. The Dorsey/Sinatra Sessions on Bluebird 2 CPK-4434, 4435, and 4436.

Forty Years: The Artistry of Tony Bennett is Columbia/Legacy C4K 46843. *Tony Bennett/Jazz,* featuring Stan Getz, Basie, and others, is Columbia CGK-4-40424. The *Tony Bennett/Bill Evans Album* is Fantasy/OJC CD-439-2. *Together Again,* the second Evans-Bennett collection, was Improv 7117.

Mel Tormé's "Lullaby of Birdland" was on *The Tormé Touch,* Bethlehem BCP 6042. A different version is on *Sunday in New York and Other Songs About New*

York, Atlantic 80078-2. *Mel Tormé Swings Shubert Alley* is Verve 825158-1.

Eddie Jefferson's "Bless My Soul" on *Cool Whalin',* Spotlite SPJ-135. Jefferson also on *There I Go Again,* Prestige P-24095. King Pleasure's early works and Annie Ross's "Twisted" on Fantasy/OJC CD-217-2. *Jon Hendricks and Friends,* Denon 81757-6302-2.

Leon Thomas in Berlin was Flying Dutchman FD-10142*. Pharoah Sanders's *Karma* is MCA/Impulse MCAD-39122. Mark Murphy's *Bop for Kerouac* is Muse MR-5253. Al Jarreau's "Take Five" is on *Look to the Rainbow,* Warner Brothers 3052-2. Bobby McFerrin's *Spontaneous Inventions* is Blue Note B11E-85110.

CHAPTER 24. CONCLUSION

Wynton and Branford Marsalis, Terence Blanchard, and Donald Harrison all record for Columbia Records, the Harper Brothers for Verve. The Preservation Hall Jazz Band has four CD's on Columbia entitled *New Orleans,* Volumes 1 through 4. Branford Marsalis with Milt Hinton is *Trio Jeepy,* Columbia CK 44199, and there is a video as well. Miles Davis, *Aura,* is Columbia CK 45332. Claude Bolling's *Suite for Jazz Flute and Piano* is Columbia MK 33233. The American Jazz Orchestra performs Ellington on East-West 91423-2, and they perform with Benny Carter on MusicMasters 5030-2-C.

APPENDIX 1. LISTENING TO JAZZ

Ma Rainey, "Bad Luck Blues," on Biograph 12032. Morton's "Mamie's Blues" on *New Orleans Memories Plus Two,* Commodore XFL 14942. This and the Pee Wee Russell recording also on *The Complete Commodore Jazz Recordings,* Mosaic. Holiday's "Embraceable You" available separately on *Lady Day 1939-1944: The Sixteen Original Commodore Interpretations,* Commodore CCD 7001. Ornette Coleman's "Embraceable You" on *This Is Our Music,* Atlantic SD-1353.

Index

Music Credits

Examples 4–2, 4–3, 7–2, 7–3, 12–6, 12–8, 23–1, and A–2 transcribed by A. Sweeton. Example 12–8 © Prestige Music. Used by permission. Courtesy of Fantasy, Inc.

Examples 4–4, 5–4, and 13–5 transcribed by T. Varner.

Examples 7–1, 7–6, 11–1, and 12–7 transcribed by I. Monson.

Example 7–7 transcribed by Riccardo Scivales for his book *Harlem Stride Piano Solos* (Ekay Music, 1990). © 1926, 1989 by MCA Music Publishing, A Division of MCA Inc. All Rights Reserved. Used By Permission.

Example 8–1 Copyright © 1927 (Copyright Renewed) Mills Music, Inc. All Rights Reserved. Used By Permission.

Example 8–2 Copyright © 1931 by Mills Music, Inc. Copyright Renewed 1959. All Rights Reserved. Used By Permission.

Example 8–4 © 1986 by Tempo Music, Inc. All Rights Reserved. Used By Permission.

Examples 9–3, 9–4, 9–5, 9–6, and 9–7 transcribed by J. O'Gallagher.

Example 12–2 © 1944, 1978 by MCA Music Publishing, A Division of MCA Inc. All Rights Reserved. Used By Permission.

Example 12–3 © The Mary Lou Williams Foundation, Inc. d/b/a Cecilia Music Publishing Co. Used By Permission.

Example 12–4 transcribed by L. Porter and Steve Ash.

Example 19–2 TRO-© Copyright 1964 (renewed) and 1965 Folkways Music Publishers, Inc., New York, N.Y. Used By Permission. Different version transcribed in *Bill Evans 4;* that and *Bill Evans Piano Solos* distributed by TRO Songways Service, Inc., 170 N.E. 33rd Street, Ft. Lauderdale, FL 33334.

Example 19–3 © 1965 Herbie Hancock Music. Used By Permission.

Example 19–4 transcribed by Bill Dobbins and reprinted with his permission. © Litha Music, Inc. Used By Permission.

Example 19–5 © Litha Music, Inc. Used By Permission.

Example 19–6 transcribed by Bill Dobbins and reprinted with his permission.

Example 20–1 © 1969 D'Accord Music. Used By Permission. This version from Ray Wright, *Inside The Score* (Kendor Music, Inc., 1982), pp. 105–6.

Example 20–3 © Duchess Music. Inc. Used By Permission.

Example 20–4 © 1964 Windswept Pacific Entertainment Co. d/b/a Longitude Music Co. All Rights Reserved. Used By Permission.

Example 21–2 Copyright © 1971 and 1973 by Crited Music, Inc. Unichappell Music, Inc., agent for the United States. Used By Permission.

Example 21–3 © 1973 Warner-Tamerlane Publishing Corp. & Basque Music Inc. All Rights Reserved. Used By Permission.

Example 21–4 © 1977 by Mulatto Music. Used By Permission. International Copyright Secured. All Rights Reserved.

Example 22–1 © Unit Core Music. Administered by Mayflower Music Corporation. Used By Permission. Based on a transcription by Ekkehard Jost, with his permission.

Example 22–2 transcribed by Henry Martin for his book *Enjoying Jazz* and reprinted with his permission. © Unit Core Music. Administered by Mayflower Music Corporation. Used by Permission.

Example 22–3 © Syndicore Music, A Division of ESP-Disk Ltd. Used By Permission.

Example 22–5 © Anthony Braxton; Synthesis Music. Used By Permission.

Example 22–6 © Alrac Music. Used By Permission.

Example A–3 © 1930 WB Music Corp. (Renewed) All Rights Reserved. Used By Permission.